ADAM TO DANIEL

AN ILLUSTRATED GUIDE
TO THE OLD TESTAMENT
AND ITS BACKGROUND

EDITED BY GAALYAHU CORNFELD, ASSISTED BY BIBLE
SCHOLARS, HISTORIANS AND ARCHAEOLOGISTS IN ISRAEL

New York 1961

THE MACMILLAN COMPANY

© Hamikra Baolam Publishing House Ltd. 1961

First Printing

The Macmillan Company, New York
Brett-Macmillan Ltd., Galt, Ontario

PRINTED IN ISRAEL

ACKNOWLEDGEMENTS

The Chief Editor wishes to acknowledge the considerable help, criticism and advice offered by the following scholars:

Professor Ch. Rabin and Dr. H. Tadmor of the Hebrew University, Jerusalem, as well as Dr. M. Haran of the Hebrew University and Raphael Giveon, Mishmar Ha-emek. Dr. M. Naor, P. Lander, A. Agmon and P. Dagan, Tel Aviv, who collaborated in the composition and editing of "Hamikra Ledorenu", an extensive Hebrew commentary and evaluation of the Old Testament in the context of ancient history (in preparation), from which source material has been drawn for "Adam to Daniel". The criticism of Prof. Paul W. Lapp of the American University, Washington, is also gratefully acknowledged.

We acknowledge with appreciation the courtesy and help we have received from the following institutions and scholars who gave us the opportunity of going through their photographic files as well as their kind advice: R. D. Barnett, Keeper of Western Asiatic Antiquities and D. J. Wiseman, Assistant Keeper, the British Museum, London; The Louvre, the Archives Photographiques, Photographie Giraudon, Roger-Viollet, Réalités Paris; The Metropolitan Museum of Art, New York; The Department of Ancient Art, Brooklyn Museum; The Oriental Institute of the University of Chicago; The University Museum, University of Pennsylvania; Professor G. E. Wright, Harvard Divinity School, Cambridge, Mass.; The American Schools of Oriental Research; The Staatliche Museum, Berlin; Ny Carlsberg Glyptotek, Copenhagen; Beno Rotenberg, Tel Aviv; Prof. Y. Yadin, the James A. de Rothschild Expedition at Hazor; The Hebrew University, Jerusalem. Thanks are due to the photographic services of the museums, universities, individual excavators, institutions, and to our friends B.V. Berry, Ames, Iowa, and Ruth Michaelson, Tel Aviv, for providing photographs and reproduction rights. Acknowledgements have been registered on the last page.

We are grateful for the courtesy extended to us by the National Council of Churches of Christ in the U.S.A. in permitting us to quote the Revised Standard Version of the Bible, and to Princeton University Press for permission to quote from "Ancient Near Eastern Texts".

We are most grateful to Valerie Wheatley Mindlin, Sonia L. Senslive, Olga Lynford Hesky and Mr. E. Gerstein for loyal and unstinted help in reading copy, styling and correcting proofs, to Lilian Barki who typed the manuscript; and finally to Lilian Cornfeld, who retained her good humour throughout the whole intensive and concentrated effort of the Editor in meeting datelines.

FOREWORD

THE BIBLE AND ISRAEL

If justification is needed for another "book about" the Bible, it can be found in the fact that this new approach to Old Testament literature sets it against its background as understood in Israel.

Living in the land of the Bible and speaking the Bible's own language, scholars in Israel gain a closer understanding of the meaning of the words and patterns of the text. Also, because of their intimate knowledge of the indigenous cultural setting, they are apt to have a clearer insight into the ways of thinking of the ancient Hebrews and the forms of their social organization.

Secondly, this study makes use of all the resources of archaeology, ancient languages and modern biblical research. Discoveries unearthed in Palestine, Phoenicia, Egypt, Syria, Mesopotamia and the whole surrounding area, have provided the facts and literature that make up a complete picture of the civilizations of the ancient world. A complete understanding of the Old Testament is, we believe, only possible when it is seen as a part of this background of contemporary life.

Immediately the Bible stories are compared with contemporary literature, many correspondences become apparent. In the very first stories of the Creation, the Tower of Babel and the Flood, there are close similarities with Babylonian and Assyrian literature. Parallel records from Mesopotamia reflect to what extent the Patriarchal institutions are those of actual life. Ugaritic (Early Phoenician) parallels offer one of the sources for the epic style of the biblical narrative. Egyptian wisdom writings provide background to the Proverbs and biblical Wisdom literature.

The publication of "Ancient Near Eastern Texts relating to the Old Testament", contributed by eminent American scholars and edited by J.B. Pritchard, has made this ancient literature available to all in English translation. For the Bible itself, the "Revised Standard Version" (1952) gives what is considered to be a more correct translation of the Hebrew original. Quotations cited in the text are from this source.

Above all, archaeological exploration has given us a key to the everyday material life of man in the ancient world. It has solved many complex historical problems. For example the story of the conquest of Canaan and events of the period of the monarchy. The achievements in exploration have been crowned by the synthesis of biblical archaeology in particular by W.F. Albright, followed by G.E. Wright and, in the field of biblical history, by J. Bright, whose work parallels that of eminent European scholars such as M. Noth, A. Lods, J. Pedersen, H.H. Rowley. All have thrown new light on the stages of development of the religion of Israel and the road which our cultural ancestors followed.

Israeli students tend to regard the biblical text as an unusually accurate and reliable account of the events of ancient history and as the integral foundation of constructive criticism based upon the psychological and social patterns of the Bible, guided by relevant modern research. As throughout the whole of the Middle East, the archaeologist in Israel has delved deep into the past of Palestine. Especially notable were the Tel Qasile excavation by B. Mazar (1949–50) and the epoch-making excavations of Hazor, the largest city of Canaan, by Y. Yadin and an outstanding team of co-archaeologists. At the same time, Hebrew scholars have been making notable advances in the field of biblical interpretation. Significant among these is Yehezkel Kaufman whose most profound revision of the "documentary theory" since Wellhausen is based on an original evaluation of biblical sources. This constitutes the foundation of his monumental history of the religion of Israel, an important contribution to the insights of modern biblical research. N. H. Tur Sinai, M.H. Segal and U. Cassuto have made major contributions to our knowledge and understanding of the Old Testament and its language.

The reader will note that there are frequent references in this book to the views of many eminent scholars. But we gladly give recognition to tens of other authors whose ideas are reflected indirectly or who have contributed to our thinking. We have avoided the use of footnotes which would be confusing in a book made up, as it is, of such a variety of elements.

To reach a proper understanding of the biblical text as an integral part of near Eastern antiquity, it is necessary to make a correct assessment of the significance of the ancient popularity of storytelling by song, legend and ritual recitation. From this wealth of folklore, we gain a new idea of the history and beliefs of the Hebrews and of the attitude of those who experienced them. Hebrew lore mirrors the eternal, religious meaning which was attached to external events. Thus legend and saga are the most important clues to the atmosphere of ancient life and thought. Even the mythological and legendary parts of the Bible are now regarded as reliable reflections of ancient concepts, grounded in beliefs which were sincerely held and, in the context of their own environment, quite logical. We believe that to understand biblical traditions fully, the reader must not only approach the stories sympathetically, but with an informed historical imagination.

To the Hebrews any personal or political event was a medium through which God's presence and purpose was disclosed. From the point of view of the Hebrew narrator, the revelation of God became known through the affairs and crises of human life, which represented the working out of the divine purpose. The Old Testament does not purport to be simply a book of secular history or of the Hebrews. To those for whom it was written it was sacred history, because it gave a meaning to their present and past life, as interpreted by their faith.

The main problem of the modern reader is to discover the fundamental spiritual, social, economic and political forces from the religious terminology of the biblical documents, which tend to regard all historical experiences as manifestations of divine intervention. But we must never lose sight of the fact that the text is an exposition of Israel's beliefs. The story of the Hebrews and their faith is a phenomenon in the history of religion. As such, it is relevant both to the fields of theological interpretation of the Bible and also to the history of religion, and of Israel. Many traditions of the Old Testament are not so much historical traditions as theological interpretations of the past. Therefore the accuracy of biblical history and the "truth" of the interpretation must not be confused.

THE BIBLE AND MODERN MAN

The Bible has moved out of the isolation which it enjoyed for centuries as "sacred", into the main stream of the literature of world history. It is no longer the only source of our knowledge of ancient Israelite history. Instead, it is now possible to regard the ancient book, together with the entire field of Near Eastern antiquity, from the new perspective of modern scholarship. This approach in no way detracts from the intrinsic value of the book nor its sanctity.

However, there remains an *intellectual crisis over the Bible*. Many people still hold the specious idea that they can accept *either* the Bible heritage, lock stock and barrel, *or* the modern sceptical outlook in respect of the book. But our present understanding of biblical and ancient literature does not impose a choice between these alternatives. We can take both heritage *and* the modern outlook in our stride by understanding the narrator's point of view.

The Bible does not make for itself the assumption — and we cannot be asked to assume — that it should be exempt from all intelligent enquires. Indeed, we cannot take the Bible for granted, without asking ourselves how the highest form of religion and ethics came to be joined in this one book. The interesting intellectual exercises involved in answering this question cannot be set aside or rejected, except at the cost of lasting spiritual impoverishment. Moreover, the Bible, a product of the ancient Near East, remains a living force in the modern west. Is it not worth evaluating the reasons for this?

A CONDENSED BIBLE LIBRARY

This book has been planned to provide the reader with a condensed, well documented and illustrated picture of the Bible and the Bible world. With this one volume, the reader need not refer constantly to the many books, commentaries and guides that constitute a student's library of biblical subjects. We have also wanted to avoid sending him on frequent searches for biblical references given in the text. Instead, we quote the passages in question. Thus commentary and text can be read together and the reader can judge the conclusions of the most competent authorities side by side with relevant sources.

To this we add over 425 pictures, (many in colour) and maps which correlate text and background and immerse the reader in the atmosphere of antiquity as it is understood by competent people. This does not alter the fact that the best road to an understanding of the Bible is to read and re-read it until the text becomes familiar. But it must be read with understanding and historical insight as is suggested in this work.

The order in which we present the material gives the books in what informed and wise criticism suggests is the chronological order. It helps to place the books *in their environment*.

The Pentateuch: Emphasis is given (with quotations) to the narrative parts of the first five books (Pentateuch), and their contents are analysed in the light of our knowledge of the social and psychological patterns of the ancient world, drawn from all the available extra-biblical sources. Generally we do not resort to the "documentary" hypothesis of much modern commentary. This is not to be taken as a refutation of this discipline. Instead, we believe that the most fruitful road to an understanding of biblical traditions is to place them firmly in their setting and interpret the narrative as an integral part of the whole biblical concept. This cannot be done by literary criticism alone. It tends to splinter the different books as though they were derived from unrelated documents, although literary analysis of the Pentateuch (and some later books) has helped to establish a clear picture of passages where different stories are woven into what seems on the surface to be a uniform narrative. But we do not consider that this discipline is essential to understanding the original text for the purpose of our exposition

The historical books (*Joshua, Samuel, Kings, Chronicles*)*:* In addition to the text we pay particular attention to the background and factual events on which recent archaeological investigation has contributed much new evidence to supplement the biblical account. For instance, excavations in Israel have thrown considerable light on abstruse problems such as the Conquest of Canaan. In the same way, events in the time of the monarchy and prophets are illuminated by the evidence of Mesopotamian and Phoenician sources.

The influence of these and similar archaeological discoveries has been to show that Hebrew literary origins go back further than had been supposed. We believe that there is no reason to insist upon a late date for the development of Old Testament religion, but that much of it belongs to the early Mosaic period. Thus the documents making up the Pentateuch were not *ad hoc* writings but included material much older than the dates at which it was finally written down and edited. This approach is also important in determining the origins of Psalms which date from David, Solomon and thereafter. (The evidence does not support the theory that the bulk of the Psalms or Ruth were created after the return of the Jews from Exile). In dealing with this portion of the material, we have worked on the principle that if such writings have a remote origin, we should start with the most remote. Thus the theme of Psalms is introduced along with David's time because his personality acts, as it were, as the inspiration for the sacred songs of Israel—a view in which we follow W.F. Albright. The later portions of Psalms are dealt with in the appropriate chapters.

Prophecy: When we come to the literature of the 8th century, the prophetic writings of Amos, Hosea, Isaiah, Jeremiah and the other prophets are read both for their spiritual significance and in the context of the political and social history of their time. For example, Isaiah 30 would be meaningless without a grasp of the political problem which Judah faced at the time the prophet spoke. There are endless examples of this kind and the prophetic literature is accordingly dealt with alongside the historical books, without separating the two by the formal divisions which exist in the Bible.

Archaeology has of course provided a wealth of supporting evidence for the substantial reliability of the Bible narrative. But it also goes further. The affinities between ancient monuments and inscriptions and the Old Testament narrative often confirm or add to the Bible stories and occasionally correct them. These archaeological data do not displace the Bible narrative, but rather they offer a supplement which makes possible an objective study of the history of the Jewish people and sheds light on obscure passages.

The *last section of the Bible*, known as "*Writings*" in the Hebrew Canon, is not treated in its present order. Instead, we have related these writings — mainly Job, Proverbs, Ecclesiastes — to the Wisdom literature of Near Eastern antiquity and again to recent research in Egyptian, Mesopotamian and Phoenician literature. These indicate first their very remote origin and, secondly, their relative independence from prophetic writings or priestly literature concerned with cultic or religious matters.

Daniel — the latest book of the Old Testament and the conclusion of our presentation, is an example of the apocalyptic literature which emerged in the period between the Old and New Testaments.

We have attempted to weave a coherent narrative out of the varied elements of the Bible and to explain their meaning in terms which can be understood by the layman, of whatever religion. We lay no claim to be innovators in biblical interpretation. What we have done is to try to combine under one cover all the different areas of biblical science: the text, archaeology, historical and textual interpretation, documentary pictures and an abbreviated atlas It is hoped that many different readers will find the book useful, those whose interest in the Bible is purely a personal desire for better acquaintance with one of the source books of modern western civilization, as well as study groups in synagogues and churches and undergraduate students of the Bible and the history of Israel.

CONTENTS

Cherubim and symbolic trees on a ceremonial panel of the palace of Mari. See p. 19.

CHAPTER I

GENESIS

THROUGH THE EYES OF THE ANCIENTS

The very fact that we have been familiar with the Creation story from childhood can be a positive hindrance to our understanding of it now, when, in this age of many discoveries, new lights have been thrown upon it. We are too easily inclined to relegate it to the sphere of the remote and legendary, as a religious myth. But through a long series of amazing archaeological discoveries, this cluster of legends has now been moulded into a most interesting picture of ancient Hebrew civilization. Most of them remain valid as gems in a setting of Near Eastern antiquity.

In narrative form the biblical stories explain how, according to the ancient Hebrews, the cosmos and man first came into being. In the past these stories were a key to early Jewish and Christian scholars, relating the history of the ancient East, and the chief source was the Old Testament, which gave a clear and concise statement. Later, when science demonstrated the age of the world and of life on earth, there were apologists by the thousand who tried to "prove" the literal truth of the Bible, and to some extent the Scriptures suffered more "from well-intentioned friends than from honest foes". For naturally the ancient conceptions differed materially from modern scientific fact.

The present-day reader of the Bible must first consider what it was that the narrators wanted to express. He will not then stumble over the fact that these testimonies sometimes present a picture of the world which does not tally in some material aspects with that which the sciences have revealed to him today.

Our concern, therefore, is to evaluate and understand this record of beliefs and civilization in the context of their times. To do this we must turn back to Mesopotamian culture.

LITERARY FORMS IN THE BOOK OF GENESIS

The book of Genesis, in its present setting, may be divided into two parts, of which the first, chapters 1–11 presents a Hebrew view of the early history of mankind. This comprises the Flood; the rise of separate nations, and the genealogy of the sons of Shem (Semites); more particularly how the ancestors of the Hebrews were related to other nations, and how they emerged gradually into a separate and distinct existence beside them. Following this but related to the foregoing, the second part of Genesis (12-50) comprises in particular the history of the Patriarchs, the immediate ancestors of Israel.

As pointed out in our general introduction, the book of Genesis and other books of the Pentateuch are not all of a piece, as regards their underlying tales of pre-literary material. They reflect on the one hand patterns of ancient Near Eastern literature but on the other hand, they have a thematic arrangement which is specifically Hebrew.

The narratives of Genesis are probably the earliest examples of popular traditions among the Hebrews. They were not continuous narrations, but individual and separate, stories and legends which had existed independently in recitation and song or epic form before they were written down. They are examples of the story-teller's art from a time when literature was in its unwritten stage. But their connected thematic arrangement has a special significance.

The tales of the creation of the world and of Adam, are followed by that of Noah, survivor of the Flood, as described in Gen. 6–9. A genealogy in Gen. 5 links Adam to Noah through *ten* generations, described in the following chapter. Later comes the genealogical table of Gen. 11:10 – 26. Likewise of ten generations, it opens with Shem, son of Noah, and closes with Terah, the father of Abraham, the first Hebrew patriarch. This table links Noah to Abraham through a similar fixed pattern of ten generations. This placed in dramatic relief God's choice of Israel, from all the people of the earth. With this link the writer followed a conventional literary structure of fixed pattern, with a rhythmic structure and the repetitious formula of the succeeding ten generations: they form a systematic table giving precise ages: The first ancestor lived so many years and begat the second, and all the days of the first ancestor were so many years, and he died. (We shall deal later with the question of their extraordinary longevity.) This suggests that genealogical tables are a literary genre of antiquity reflecting the ancient view of the record of mankind. When the authors created these lists, they merely used the literary forms common to their environment and one must not search in them for a literally historical record of early man.

But another set of genealogical tables appears within the first eleven chapters of Genesis, one list in Gen. 4, the other in Gen. 10, and a comparison of these with those we have described, reveals notable differences of style and form. The repeated systematic formulae of precise ages does not appear. Instead the lists are folkloric and informal, and narrate fragmentary traditions and tales about the ancestors. These observations lead scholars to point to some implications about the literary structure of Genesis and its underlying background:

(a) The use of two sets of genealogical tables would indicate different traditions, each cast in a certain form and style. Into each of these forms are interwoven tales, most of them belonging to the cultural background of Mesopotamia.

(b) Therefore the contents of the tales of Genesis cannot be studied in isolation. They must be considered in the context of the literature of the ancient Near East, wherever the Hebrew motifs suggest points of similarity with Mesopotamian culture.

(c) One must make a distinction between the content of the chapters (traditions, tales) and the form in which the biblical authors cast them in order to teach religious truths, or to indicate their views on the generations of early man.

THE STORY OF CREATION

The keynote of the Hebrew exposition of the phenomenon of creation is given in the opening verses of the Bible in passages of marvellous sonority, expressive of the symmetry and magnitude of the creative acts of God. The survey is rendered in a form expressing a highly abstract conception of God the creator and embodying, probably, the sacerdotal thinking on the problem of cosmogony:

> "In the beginning God created the heavens and the earth (the alternate version is: "When God began to create heaven and earth"). The earth was without form and void, and darkness was upon the face of the deep (tehom) and the Spirit (or wind) of God was moving over the face of the waters. And God said, 'Let there be light'; and there was light. And God saw that the light was good; and God separated the light from the darkness. God called the light Day, and the darkness he called Night. And there was evening and there was morning, one day". (1:1–5)

(All Bible quotations — from the Revised Standard Version, (1952).

LIGHT AND ORDER IN A WORLD OF DARKNESS

Having created heaven and earth, God naturally introduced light into a world of darkness. A governing idea is expressed in the statement that God used merely his creating word: God said... and creation came into existence. Contrary to other ancient myths about the origin of the world, as we shall see, there is no wrestling with the primeval abyss, no struggle against other divine beings. Furthermore, since God is all-powerful, all that He creates is well made. This conception of the sublime freedom of the Creator evinces an abstraction of God and of cosmogonic order far in advance of Babylonian or Egyptian cosmogonies, even of a later day. But the text does not go further; it does not deal, for example, with the philosophical question of whether anything existed before God began to create. Minds more philosophic than the early Hebrews 'and later commentators' put there more than was implied and described this concept as a "creation out of nothing", but this is not intimated by the writers who conceived this opening chapter.

Thus, day by day, proceeds the theme of creation. It was creation by fiat for the first three days. From the fourth to the sixth day God's acts are described as works:

"And God made the two great lights, the greater light to rule the day, and the lesser light to rule the night; he made the stars also". (1:16)

The next stage was the separating of the seas from the land. Out of the seas the Creator then raised the dry land, which was ringed about by waters like an island. The first drawing below represents the Hebrew conception of the Universe.

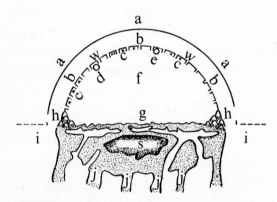

The Hebrew conception of the Universe. The Hebrews assumed that the universe consisted of a flat earth supported over a watery abyss. The solid arched firmament held back the waters above the earth and the heavenly bodies were attached to it. A circular range of mountains supported the firmament at the outermost limits of the earth. (a) Heaven, the dwelling place of God. (b) the waters above the firmament. (w) Windows. (c) Stars. (d) Sun. (e) Moon. (f) Arched firmament of heaven. (g) Earth. (h) Mountains and pillars of the firmament. (i) Tehom — watery abyss. (s) Sheol. (j) Pillars of the earth. (After S. H. Hooke)

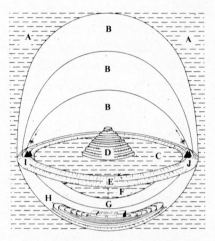

A Babylonian picture of the Universe. (a) Heavenly ocean. (b) the Heavens. (c) Terrestrial sea surrounding the earth. (d) Earth, pictured as a "world mountain". (e) Embankment or the confines of the sea. (f) Bottom of the ocean. (g) Nether world. (h) Palace of the nether world and its seven walls. (i) Mountains of the rising sun. (j) Mountain of the setting sun. (After Meissner)

The Hebrews did not think of the earth as a "world mountain" or speak of seven heavens, but their word for heavens was "shamayim" in the plural.

The second drawing above shows the Mesopotamian conception. It differs little from the Hebrew picture, with two sets of water and the dry island, earth, in the lower waters. To the Babylonians the earth was a "world mountain". Above and around it stretched the seven storeys of heaven. Below was the nether world palace with its seven storeys and walls. The Hebrews, on the other hand, conceived instead of the underworld as the dark cave She'ol "the pit", where the dead descended and lived with the "shades" of those who had gone before.

By special dispensation eight acts of creation were compressed into six days and the main phenomena of nature and the launching of life upon earth were called into being through the specific commands and works of God:

"And God said, 'Let there be lights in the firmament of the heavens to separate the day from the night; and let them be for signs and for seasons and for days and years, and let them be lights in the firmament of the heavens to give light upon the earth'. And it was so. And God made the two great lights, the greater light to rule the day and the lesser light to rule the night: he made the stars also. And God set them in the firmament of the heavens to give light upon the earth, to rule over the day and over the night, and to separate the light from the darkness. And God saw that it was good". (1:14–18)

It will be noted that light already existed before the heavenly bodies, the sun, moon and stars in the heavens. They do not merely give light as such. This is a familiar feature of other ancient cosmogonies, whereby these bodies existed mainly to govern the festivals and seasons. Their significance lies in the fixing of the calendar. The Babylonians named the signs of the zodiac after them. In the arrangement of his creative work, God established the world's first week; He made the heavenly bodies as signs of the seasons; in the symbolic language of the ancients, He made the world's time, which is the framework of history, for He is the Lord of history.

Finally, as the crowning accomplishment of creation comes *man*. He is privileged to be made in God's image, and he is to enjoy creation like no other creature; God gave him dominion over the rest of creation. Unlike Babylonian beliefs which saw man's condition as servile to the gods, man is here conceived as a superior being, in the likeness of God.

The Egyptian conception of the Universe. The sky-goddess Nut arched as the heavens over the earth, supported by the air-god. At his feet the earth-god, his left arm stretching along the ground. Watching are several gods. From a papyrus of the 'Book of the Dead', 10th century B.C.E.

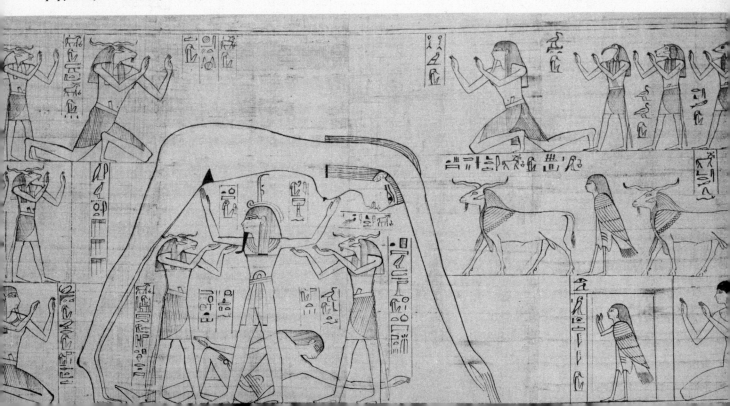

"Then God said, 'Let us make man in our image, after our likeness; and let them have dominion over the fish of the sea, and over the birds of the air, and over the cattle, and over all the earth, and over every creeping thing that creeps upon the earth'. So God created man in his own image, in the image of God he created him; male and female he created them. And God blessed them, and God said to them 'Be fruitful and multiply, and fill the earth and subdue it; and have dominion over the fish of the sea and over the birds of the air and over every living thing that moves upon the earth'...". (1:26-28)

To the biblical author the original connotation of "Let us make" was lost. The polytheistic import of the plural "us", (which the author used without sensing it) had reference to a divine cortege: the King of the world addressing other gods or attendants. This is in the spirit of a parallel Sumerian and Babylonian story of creation described below. The six-day divine work-week culminated in a day of celestial rest. This pre-literary tradition seems a distant echo of the Assyrian-Babylonian "shabbatum", the 15th day of the lunar month. This ancient concept was accommodated by the later editors of the story of creation to the holy conception of the Sabbath observance. The idea that all men must rest on the seventh day in imitation of God's rest is an essentially biblical idea, based on social customs which took root over many centuries. Its underlying mythic sources seem to precede in time the obligation of the actual Sabbath worship; but its historic cultic observance in biblical times gave the story substance, and it developed as a Sabbath within the context of the life and culture of the Hebrews.

The six-day frame of the creative work of God is patently modelled on a Jewish work-week with the Sabbath rest. Many scholars believe that the teaching takes its literary form from the Jewish calendar and the accepted cosmology of post-Exilic and Ptolemaic days. In content and spirit Gen. 1 mentions a credo that all elements in the tale of creation are shorn of any mythical content. This had a more profound effect than appears at first glance: Under the impact of Jewish tradition this observance assumed such importance later that it was perpetuated as *the* social institution of rest in our civilization. As we look for the origin of this, we discover that the number 7 permeated the thought of the ancients. Those who knew the seven-day week handed down also the seven-year Sabbatical cycle and the Jubilee year which follows seven sabbatical cycles. Finally, the motif and symbol 7 recur many times in significant biblical themes, as we shall see. The belief in 7 as a lucky number stems from this ancient origin.

THE SEVEN TABLETS OF THE BABYLONIAN CREATION EPIC

The idea that the Creation stories are unique has fallen into discard, although not without bitter controversy. Since the discovery of a complete version of the Creation Epic current among the Babylonians and Assyrians, which has survived in its cuneiform original on a series of Seven Tablets, now in the British Museum, a new viewpoint has gained ground.

Knowing that the first Hebrews came from Mesopotamia and were imbued with its civilization, it would be natural to find in their intellectual background concepts figuring in Mesopotamian myth and legend. A large proportion of the material in the first eleven chapters of Genesis can now be seen to have had its origin in factors common to Mesopotamia and to remote ancestors of the Hebrews in pre-patriarchal days. Actually the creation stories of the Bible and Babylonian myths about the origin of the world show at the same time similarities and also certain basic differences.

Two of the tablets of "Enuma Elish", or the Babylonian story of creation.

The third tablet of the Assyrian series relating the story of Creation. It is a copy bearing a text similar to older Babylonian versions. They may be traced in part to Sumerian originals dating from the 3rd millenium B.C.E.

GOD AND THE GODS

The deepest difference lies of course, in their concepts of divinity. The first chapter of Genesis begins with God existing as a transcendent deity outside of the world, to create it. He was when nothing else existed. Babylonian speculation, as revealed in the Seven Tablets of Enuma Elish, describes the creation of gods and does not distinguish between spirit and matter, considering both eternal.

A characteristic feature of ancient cosmogonies, i.e. surmises about the origin and structure of the world, is that the elements themselves represent original matter containing everything from which the world was made: what we mean when we speak today of "nature" or the "powers of nature". The elements had names and were the agents and in a sense parts of this "nature". The heavenly bodies — the sun, moon, stars and planets, and manifestations such as air, etc., were personified. The mythological stories woven about the careers of the gods, and the ritual at the temple shrines, form the ideological and emotional pattern of ancient belief and worship. Their cosmogonies may be naive to us, but they remain meaningful in their own setting. Ancient thought and knowledge could not reach, for instance, behind the primordial, static chaos which it conceived as the dark, primeval ocean, from which the seas and fresh waters on earth come. The Babylonians called the seas Tiamat. A monster goddess bearing this name personified the deep and is presented as the source and origin of everything. The Hebrew word "tehom" for the deep is borrowed from the Babylonian Tiamat. Its occurrence in Gen. 1 would suggest some common motif related to like traditions of creation. The interesting Babylonian Creation Epic presents certain points of contact as well as patent dissimilarities with Genesis.

CONFLICT AND CREATION

In the beginning, says the poem, there was nothing save a great waste of waters, personified by two deities, one, male, Apsu, the sweet water ocean, "the begetter of the great gods", and one, female, Tiamat, the salt water ocean, and Mommu representing probably the mist, while "their waters communicated as a single body". The heavens and earth did not exist, there were no plants or food. Creation began by carnal procreation on the part of the pair of gods. The couple had a numerous progeny of gods, but Apsu found before long that they were too independent and made too much noise. He resolved to destroy his descendants, but was himself slain. Tiamat determined to revenge this by a well planned attack on the newly created gods, (representing order and system). She spawned forth in her defence a host of hideous monsters with poisoned fangs.

Faced with this threat the gods elected as their leader one of their own number, the young god *Marduk*. The Babylonian myth regarded *Marduk* as the creator in the sense that it was he, with the assistance of the newly created gods like Ea, who overthrew the rule of the older deities. He is also the champion of good and justice. Thus the conflict between Tiamat and Marduk gets under way:

"The lord spread out his net to enfold her,
The Evil Wind, which followed behind, he let loose in her face.

When Tiamat opened her mouth to consume him,
He drove in the Evil Wind that she close not her lips.
As the fierce winds charged her belly,
Her body was distended and her mouth was wide open.
He released the arrow, it tore her belly,
It cut through her insides, splitting the heart.

Having thus subdued her, he extinguished her life.
He cast down her carcass to stand upon it.
After he had slain Tiamat, the leader,
Her band was shattered, her troupe broken up;
....
He made them captives and he smashed their weapons
Thrown into the net, they found themselves ensnared;

The poem proceeds:

Then the lord paused to view her dead body.
That he might divide the monster and do artful works.
He split her like a shellfish into two parts:
Half of her he set up and called it as sky,
....
The Great Abode, its likeness, he fixed as Esharra,
The Great Abode, Esharra, which he made as the firmament.
Anu, Enlil, and Ea he made occupy their places.
He constructed stations for the great gods,
....
Fixing their astral likeness as constellations.
He determined the year by designating the zones:
He set up three constellations for each of the twelve months".

Translation according to Ancient Near Eastern Texts; J. B. Pritchard (Ed.)

The god Ningirsu, (or perhaps a king by this name) holds a net containing his captives. This is recounted above in the Creation Epic "Enuma Elish".

Thus did Marduk divide the waters into those above and those below the firmament, and having formed heaven and earth, Marduk next set the stars in the heavens.

The three chief gods: Anu, Enlil, and Ea, "he made occupy their places". These are the three great gods of the Babylonian pantheon. They presided over the sky, the earth, and the world of underground waters.

It will be noted that Marduk created stars to mark the passing of time, and the moon not only to shine by night, but also to fix the monthly cycle and to regulate the reckoning of the days. The Epic implies that the luminaries preceded the creation of plant and animal life.

Symbols of the gods inscribed on a boundary-stone (Kudurru) in Mesopotamia, 12th century. Each symbol was connected with a deity, the crescent with Sinn; the 8-pointed star with Ishtar; the sun-disc with Shamash, etc.

A cylinder seal from Mesopotamia describing the seven-headed dragon of chaos being slain by two gods. Three of the heads of the dragon are alive and fighting; four heads hang limp.

Themes of this nature are very numerous in Near Eastern records and pictures. We will confine ourselves to a few of those which have a direct bearing on the Bible:

THE MYTH OF MAN'S CREATION

The Babylonian Creation Epic and Genesis both describe the creation of man through divine consultation as the climax of creation. Marduk and Ea's conference has a remote counterpart in the archaic biblical "let us make man", quoted above. But the similarity does not go any further, for the Babylonian description of man's origin is dismal indeed. **Marduk declared to Ea the plan he had conceived:**

> "Blood I will mass and cause bones to be.
> I will establish a savage, 'man' shall be his name.
> Verily, savage-man I will create.
> He shall be charged with the service of the gods that they might be at ease…

The wise Ea suggested that one of the gods be handed over as material for the creation of man. They seek out the most guilty among the forces of Tiamat: Kingu (also called Tiamat's spouse):

> "It was Kingu who contrived the uprising, and made Tiamat rebel, and joined battle.
> They bound him, holding him before Ea.
> They imposed on him his guilt and severed his blood vessels.
> Out of his blood they fashioned mankind.
> He imposed the service of gods upon them and set free the gods-".

(Translation according to Ancient Near Eastern Texts; J. B. Pritchard (Ed.)

Man is given over to the service of the gods, the underlying idea being that mankind was created to perform menial tasks, provide food and drink, to make life agreeable to the gods and practice religion for their benefit; but not, be it noted, for his own benefit.

Grateful for this last feat of creation, the gods then assembled, and resolved to build a sanctuary for Marduk. This is the Temple of Esagila, the Temple of Marduk in Babylon, their last labour, before men took over the work.

A detailed comparison of this Mesopotamian story of creation of the world with Genesis is most instructive. Whatever their difference is in spirit and in content, the strongest link connecting the Mesopotamian with the Hebrew epic is *the order of events* shared by both:

BABYLONIAN	GENESIS
1. The primordial water chaos of Tiamat and Apsu.	1. Existence of unformed earth and the deep (tehom).
2. Birth of Marduk, "Sun of the heavens".	2. Creation of light.
3. Fashioning of the sky from half of the body of Tiamat.	3. Creation of the firmament, the sky.
4. Squaring of Apsu's abode (the earth?).	4. Gathering the water together to form the earth.
5. Setting up of the stars, moon and sun.	5. Creation of luminaries in the firmament.
6. Forming man from the blood of a slain god mixed with earth's clay or dust, made for the service and worship of the gods.	6. Creation of man to have dominion over animals, fish and fowl.
7. The divine banquet and hymn to exalt Marduk as head of the Babylonian pantheon.	7. Resting of God on the seventh day.

(Following the late Prof. A. Heidel – The Babylonian Genesis and J. B. Pritchard – Archaeology and the Old Testament).

THE DIFFERENCE BETWEEN GENESIS AND THE EPIC OF CONFLICT AND CREATION

One of the differences is that corresponding events in each epic contain elements not shared by the other, such as the creation of animals, fish and fowl in Genesis, and the account of the building of Esagila in the Babylonian story: This was foremost among shrines in Babylon, the "chief of cities".

Both Genesis and the Babylonian myth express in their own symbols a fundamental notion of the world: The victory of cosmos over chaos, and creation seen as the reducing to order of a primal disorder. But Babylonian cosmogony, as explained, is not really a "creation story" as in Genesis, but a story of the growth of the cosmos through procreation of gods and struggles between their generations, while the gods themselves personify nature and its elements. But in the Bible God is an independent and self-existing source, or the creator of nature and cosmos. It has been pointed out that in the Bible there were scattered references (in Job 9:13, Psalm 89:11 and Isaiah 51:9) to a primeval conflict between Yahweh and mythological rebellious figures bearing the names of Rahab, Leviathan, the dragon, and the serpent. But the dogma in Gen. 1 shears off this mythological content. Any such tale would be a figment to be scrupulously avoided by the writers of the account of Creation. While Hebrew lore must originally have used myth or anthropomorphic concepts, it eventually de-mythed its concepts of a very ancient polytheist version of the primordial world.

The relationship between the accounts in Genesis and that of the Enuma Elish, the Babylonian poem, reaching back as it does into the early part of the second and into the third milleniums B.C.E., is still not clear. While some original factors may be common to both, and similarities between them are numerous they can have evolved directly from the Babylonian source. The best explanation is that both versions go back to common primary factors.

The origins of Mesopotamian literature have been set back another thousand years by the discovery of the literature of a people who preceded the Semites of the Old Babylonian period in Mesopotamia. They were the Sumerians, a remarkably creative people, responsible as far as we know at present, for the invention of writing. Their culture prevailed in lower Mesopotamia throughout the third millenium B.C.E.

Allusions to Creation are also found in the earlier Sumerian mythology, in a fragmentary version of the creation epic. It appears that they did not have one complete myth about the genesis of the world and they handed down no literary creation which would serve as a source for Enuma Elish. The Sumerian tales picture the beginning as a primordial period when both heaven and earth were united in a cosmic mountain. By the action of the air god, Enlil, a separation was made between the two elements, and man was created. It is therefore not impossible that the Assyrian and Babylonian tablets reproduced above may go back in part to Sumerian originals.

THE STORY OF EDEN

From the broad considerations of creation, cast in measured dignity, the narrative, from the 4th verse of Genesis 2 takes up, in more folkloric and informal vein, primeval stories of the creation of man from the dust in his traditional birthplace, Eden. It continues with his fall, the murder of Cain and the origins of nomadic society, listing their generations in a similar informal way. The imagery, figurative language and the antiquarian elements of the tale are cast in more archaic form than Gen. 1. They also represent the deity in the realistic physical and psychic likeness of man (termed anthropomorphism). These stories are attributed

The lands in which the people of Genesis moved occupied only a small area of the world.

by many scholars to the "Yahwist" tradition which they assume to be the oldest written literary strain of the Old Testament. In this older reference to the theme of creation, the narrators have skimmed over elaborate cosmological considerations and plunged into man's primeval legends. In the opinion of other scholars, this casual reference to the cosmic theme of creation, does not actually represent another account of creation, but is the narrators' view of the world, introducing the theme of Eden.

Chaos pervades this cosmic pattern, but it is a waterless wasteland:

"when no plant of the field was yet in the earth, and no herb of the field had yet sprang up – for the Lord God had not caused it to rain upon the earth, and there was no man to till the ground; but a mist went up from the earth and watered the whole face of the ground, then the Lord God formed man of dust from the ground and breathed into his nostrils the breath of life; and man became a living being, and the Lord God planted a garden in Eden, in the east". (2:5-8)

Somewhere in southern Mesopotamia lies the legendary land of Eden. The name, which is derived perhaps from the Sumerian "edin" meaning the plain or the steppe, is translated in the Greek Septuagint, "paradeisos" (i.e. garden), in English, Paradise, which conveys far more to our minds than is implied in the original text. The tradition that lies at the back of the story of Eden is rather specific and develops a sort of small world map of its own, which we give below.

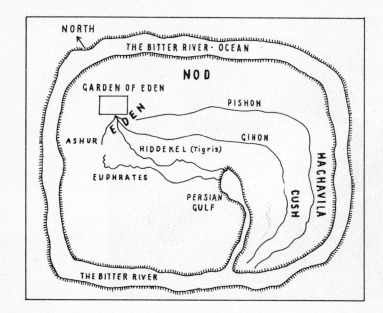

The four rivers flowing out of Eden. The interest in regions to the east and south is noteworthy. There is complete silence here about the west.

"A river flowed out of Eden to water the garden, and there it divided and became four rivers. The name of the first is Pishon; it is the one which flows around the whole land of Havilah where there is gold; and the gold of that land is good; bdellium and onyx stone are there. The name of the second river is Gihon; it is the one which flows around the whole land of Cush. And the name of the third river is Hiddekel, which flows east of Assyria. And the fourth river is the Euphrates". (2:10-14)

The ancient interest in the rivers and precious metals indicates composite traditions. The general geographical contour corresponds roughly to the little world highlighted in the map above, but its elements are half real, half legendary. Two of the rivers, the Euphrates and the Hiddekel (Tigris) are called by established names. The other two belong apparently to a different body of tradition connected with the legend of Eden.

The existence of the first ancestor is personalized in the story of Adam, which means "Man" in Hebrew. In a profound way the story portrays the character of human existence, its interdependence with God, with the soil, with woman and with animal life: For instance: "Adam" – man, is shaped directly from the soil, (in Hebrew "adamah"), which is a play on the word "adam". Both stem from the root "red". It also means a "groundling". He becomes a "living being", a body and spirit unity (not a "living soul" as other versions had it). The earth is the stage on which his life is played, for he becomes a tiller of the soil at the end of the story. We come across another interesting parallel in the long and beautiful Babylonian Epic of Gilgamesh. This hero was the legendary rash ruler of Uruk (the Biblical Erech) a very ancient town of the Sumerians. The goddess Aruru, the creatress of Gilgamesh, is called upon to make his double to be a match for him. Thereupon, she washes her hands, pinches off clay and creates the second principal character of the Epic, the valiant Enkidu, who became the hero's bosom friend. From which it may be implied that the forming of man from the dust or from clay was a current motif in the myth and epic literature of Mesopotamia.

THE TREE OF KNOWLEDGE

"The Lord God took the man and put him in the garden of Eden to till it and keep it. And the Lord God commanded the man, saying 'you may freely eat of every tree of the garden; but of the tree of the knowledge of good and evil you shall not eat, for in the day that you eat of it you shall die' " (2:15–17)

Primarily, according to the thematic Hebrew construction, man exists in relation to God and is dependent upon Him. God gives Adam a task "to till and keep it" (the ground). This detail has been overlooked by many interpreters who assumed that work is a part of the curse for man's sin. The curse is actually in the niggardliness of the soil or the fruitlessness of his labour.

This ground, states the old biblical tradition, is man's background and his freedom. The ancient popular tradition of Eden is imbued with these home truths, the language and expression of which also bear the marks of its pre-literary origins, of a naive legendary mythology. For example: God's personal relation with man is related in the speech of a father to a son. Notice the vivid portrayal of "the sound of the Lord God walking in the garden in the cool of the day" (3:8). It is implicit in the legend that God and man were alike in form, but unlike in their knowledge and power. This likeness, and its dimly veiled mythical origin, is duly attested in the language: "behold the man has become like one of us" (3:22), meaning God and His cortege. Man has become not only like God, but perhaps "like the gods"; we can trace here a remnant of Mesopotamian mythology embedded in the story. This, the portrayal of human existence and men's interdependence, is one of the central and ancient motifs of the story of Eden. It is woven into the other motifs which follow.

In the last resort the likeness of man and God was not complete, for God had withheld the "knowledge of good and evil" and enjoined man, under threat of death, not to eat from the magic fruit of the tree of knowledge. The idiomatic pair, "good and evil" in archaic Hebrew, or in Egyptian, does not refer to the traditional ethical apposition of good and evil as such, or as separate and opposed entities. They meant "everything", or worldly knowledge of everything useful. This gift, the knowledge of everything, had been a monopoly of divinity. The divinity in this legend is a jealous divinity. It emphasizes its superiority through possession of the magic secret of the Tree of Knowledge. As the story unfolds, the central motif is one of rivalry between deity and man.

MAN AND WOMAN

"But for the man there was not found a helper fit for him. So the Lord God caused a deep sleep to fall upon the man, and while he slept took one of his ribs and closed up its place with flesh, and the rib which the Lord God had taken from the man he made into a woman and brought her to the man. Then the man said, 'This at last is bone of my bones and flesh of my flesh; She shall be called Woman (Ishah) because she was taken out of man (Ish)'. Therefore a man leaves his father and his mother and cleaves to his wife, and they become one flesh. And the man and his wife were both naked and were not ashamed". (2:20–25)

The union of male and female is epitomized in the beautiful etiological explanation of woman's creation from man's rib. Why man's rib? An explanation may be sought in a Sumerian legend mentioned below.

Sumerian texts recently published by Professor Samuel N. Kramer provide earlier parallels to the story of Eden than were hitherto known. One describes the original "organization of the earth and its cultural processes" whereby Enti, the god of water, of wisdom and earthly productivity, established law and order and an inventory of knowledge, setting bounds for the sea and winds, and giving directions for building, husbandry and crafts in general.

The Greek-Babylonian historian Berossus preserved in his account the same myth of Oannes, the god who taught the newly created citizens of Babylonia the knowledge of writing, numbers and arts, agriculture, the naming of animals (husbandry), architecture, and all that was necessary for civilized life for man living in "edin" (probably the origin of Hebrew Eden). In the early biblical tradition the fact that Adam named the animals would be an affirmation of his intelligence, since for the Hebrew the name stood for the thing.

Another Sumerian text describes the paradise at "Dilmun", located by some scholars in Bahrein in the Persian Gulf and by others in South-West Persia: Paradise is "pure, clean and bright... where the lion kills not, the wolf snatches not the lamb". The god of the sun irrigated it with fresh water from the ground (as in Gen. 2:6). There, in Dilmun, birth was without pain or travail, until Enki was smitten with a deadly curse after eating eight plants which had been created by Ninhursag, the great Sumerian mother-goddess.

Another text describes the special creation of woman, called Nin-ti, a Sumerian expression which can be equally translated by a play on words as "the lady who makes live" and "the lady of the rib". In Prof. Kramer's opinion this recalls Eve "the mother of all living" fashioned from Adam's rib. Eve's name "Havah" in Hebrew, resembles "chay" or "living" (3:20).

THE TEMPTATION

"Now the serpent was more subtle than any other wild creature that the Lord God had made. He said to the woman, 'Did God say, "You shall not eat of any tree of the garden?" And the woman said to the serpent, 'We may eat of the fruit of the trees of the garden; but God said, "You shall not eat of the fruit of the tree which is in the midst of the garden, neither shall you touch it, lest you die" '. (3:1–3)

This serpent is not an ordinary snake, as we shall see. It is doubtful that it symbolizes sex, as primitive man did not sublimate his instinct with such symbols. But in the beliefs of antiquity, the serpent is one of the mythological demons which we have already met in the Babylonian myth of conflict and creation. This demon is a dangerous tempter of man and an enemy of the divinity, as witness the penetrating psychological process of temptation through his agency. He creates doubt in the woman's mind, then her senses are appealed to: "the woman saw that the tree was good for food". So she ate of it in defiance of the ruling.

The tempter does not heed that the divinity enjoined on Adam, under the threat of death, not to eat from the Tree of Knowledge: Man, says he, will not die when he eats the magic fruit, but will become more like the gods, knowing "good and evil": namely, he will possess their hidden knowledge. The rivalry stands out clearly here.

This is an answer to the question of why human beings, unlike animals, were ashamed of nudity; obviously because of man's new knowledge of decency, about which animals and primitive man, in blissful ignorance, knew nothing.

Two figures, a sacred palm tree and an erect serpent. Such symbols occur in the earliest texts and engravings. There may, however, be a pure coincidence of symbolism with elements in Gen. 3.

Serpent dragon of Mesopotamian myths. The dragon beast of Marduk, which adorned the Ishtar gate of ancient Babylon in the days of Nebuchadrezzar, is an illustration of the serpent who walked and not the crawling serpent.

"Then the Lord God said, 'Behold, the man has become like one of us, knowing good and evil; and now, lest he put forth his hand and take also of the tree of life, and eat, and live forever' – therefore the Lord God sent him forth from the garden of Eden, to till the ground from which he was taken. He drove out the man; and at the east of the garden of Eden he placed the cherubim, and a flaming sword which turned every way, to guard the way to the tree of life". (3:22–24)

This then is the legendary reason why mankind does not live forever in Eden and must toil over the face of the earth. Original man was expelled from Eden because the divinity saw him as a dangerous rival, trying to rise halfway to divinity. The element of disobedience in the text is only circumstantial. It is not the main consideration in the story. Man, indeed, does not die, as threatened. Instead God is threatened with man's immortality.

This would make man quite divine, which would be contrary to the order of nature and the cosmos. So God placed the "Cherubim" to bar the approaches to the Tree of Life. After this man can appreciate his true condition: that the good earth is the place where his life will be played out. He understands that he can never dream of immortality. But he will return to the ground in death, for from the ground he was made.

THE THEME OF THE TREE OF LIFE AND THE CHERUBIM IN ANTIQUITY

A Mesopotamian picture comes to mind in relation to the theme of the four rivers of Eden and the Tree of Life. It is not an illustration of the Garden of Eden, but we find in it elements which it would be difficult to consider as mere "coincidence".

Another common Mesopotamian theme is the Flowing Vase and the God with streams: A divine person, male or female, holds against its body a vase from which overflow streams of water. In order to indicate that these streams generate life, the drawing shows either fish in the undulating water, or some plant that juts out of the vase. The Mari panel portrays both fish and plants along the streams. The idea of the water of life goes back apparently to ancient themes of Babylonian iconography (holy statuary).

Cherubim. The representation of Cherubim placed "at the east of the garden" is abundantly illustrated by ancient Near Eastern and Israelite iconography as a winged lion with human head, or sphynx. These legendary figures were unlike the "angels" of medieval Christendom.

Winged beings kneeling beside sacred tree; from palace at Nimrud, Assyria.

This picture panel from Mari describes, in the centre of its lower register, two goddesses holding vases from which flow four free streams of water filled with fish to indicate life. At both sides of the panel appear two trees, one stylized, the other a realistic palm tree. Three superimposed mythical beasts advance towards the stylized tree. Their identification leaves no doubt as to their being three "Cherubim" posted there as vigilant guards. Below — central scene of the panel: the flowing vase, and the trees flanking the gate. First part of the 2nd millenium B.C.E.

THE LOST CHANCE OF IMMORTALITY IN THE MYTHS OF ANTIQUITY

The idea that man may obtain immortality by eating of the Tree of Life, or the bread and water of life, is common to both the Bible and Babylonian mythology. Such a character in the Babylonian myth is Adapa. He had been created by Ea, patron god of Eridu, one of the most ancient cities of the world, as recorded in cuneiform fragments of clay tablets; "To him, Adapa", the tablet reads, "he had given wisdom; eternal life he had not given him". Adapa's occupation was to provide bread and fish for Ea's sanctuary. He was out fishing on the Persian Gulf when the "South wind" upset his boat and plunged him into the sea. He avenged himself by breaking "the wing of the South wind", pictured as some sort of birdlike creature. Thus crippled, this wind was unable to blow refreshing breezes for a week. This annoyed Anu, the great god of heaven, who summoned Adapa to the ethereal regions for his action.

Ea, his divine father, instructed Adapa not to eat the food of death, or drink the water of death, which would be offered him by the god. The audience before Anu turned out to be as Ea described it, but with one important exception: the proffered food and drink were not the bread and water of death, but of eternal life. But he ate and drank of none. By heeding the advice of Ea, Adapa had missed his chance to gain, in addition to wisdom, which he had been given, the other prerogative of the gods, which is immortality. The theme of this myth, "man's squandered opportunity for gaining immortality", brings to mind verse 3:22 of Genesis, quoted above. The "food of eternal life" corresponds to the "fruit" of the "tree of life". In general, the two accounts agree in the thought that eternal life could be obtained by eating a certain kind of food or fruit. Whatever the relationship of the two stories, they make clear the pattern of ancient Near Eastern thought, which they knew and used.

Both in Adapa's story and in Genesis, appears the idea that man's possession of wisdom and immortality would constitute equality with the deity. In both, man gets the first, but misses the second. In each narrative, man is called by a supernatural voice to act in a way which is obviously contrary to his interest; the speech of the serpent in the one, that of Ea in the other.

The Babylonian epic of Gilgamesh contains both the elements of a magic plant that ensures immortality, and the classic tragedy of man's futile quest for immortality. In his struggle against the fate of all mortals, the hero seeks out the sole survivor of the Great Flood, in order to learn from him the magic secret. This is Utnapishtim, the Babylonian Noah, who related his story to Gilgamesh (See the Babylonian story of the Flood). Before Gilgamesh parts from Utnapishtim, the latter reveals to him the existence of a thorny plant at the bottom

Goddess with overflowing vase.

of the sea. If grasped, it will assure immortal life. Gilgamesh obtains the plant and calls it: "man becomes young in old age". Unluckily for him, he stops at a cool pool of water on his homeward journey. A serpent sniffs the fragrance of the plant and carries it off. The serpent sheds his skin immediately – a popular proof of the magic plant, which Gilgamesh once grasped and had now lost. The solution of his futile quest for personal immortality is also hinted at in his epic. Though he is destined to die, he is compensated with immortal fame. He is told to give up the chase for divinity and content himself with the comforts and realities of wife and children in his native town of Uruk. The epic stresses a message from his friend Enkidu (now in the underworld) to the effect that a man's welfare after death is in direct proportion to the sons he has left after him on earth.

The Gilgamesh motif of a mighty hunter between two lions carved on a pre-dynastic Egyptian ivory handle of a ceremonial flint-knife (according to H. Frankfort).

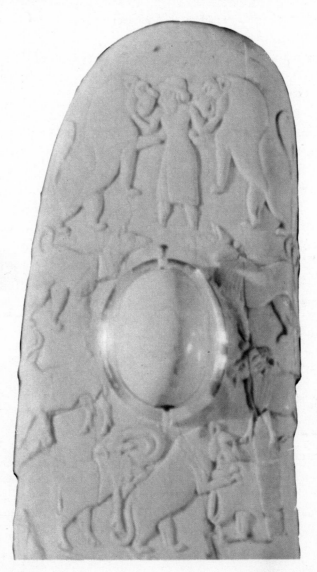

Offerings of the flocks, of the hunt and fishing. From right to left: Man leads a bull as his companion is guiding it by the horns. Three goats and an attendant, followed by man with four fish and group of three men with a bull. Man with a ram and another carrying a gazelle. Portrayal on a mosaic panel of Ur, in lower Mesopotamia, from the middle of the 3rd millenium B.C.E.

CHAPTER II

THE TWENTY GENERATIONS FROM ADAM TO ABRAHAM

AGRICULTURAL AND URBAN LIFE IN THE ANCIENT NEAR EAST

The genealogical tables of Genesis 5 & 11 (paralleled by Gen. 4 and 10) indicate twenty generations from Adam to Terah, father of Abraham. These patterns in Genesis assert that families and nations that sprang from Adam and Eve can be traced through their "toldot" or genealogies, and list actual people or eponyms, from whom descended groups and nations, or special classes of society. The fragments of genealogies appear in the form of a fixed systematic pattern in the Tables of Genesis 5 & 11, while their style is informal and folkloric in 4 & 10. This latter group interweaves and connects very remote traditions, which reflect at times complete stories, at others mere fragments or even folkloric oral traditions from prehistoric times. Both antediluvial legends allude to man's rebellion against the deities, resulting in the flood and the story of the tower of Babel.

The first children of Adam and Eve were Cain and Abel:

"Now Abel was a keeper of sheep, and Cain a tiller of the ground. In the course of time Cain brought to the Lord an offering of the fruit of the ground, and Abel brought of the firstlings of his flock and of their fat portions. And the Lord had regard for Abel and his offering, but for Cain and his offering he had no regard. So Cain was very angry and his countenance fell. The Lord said to Cain, 'Why are you angry and why has your countenance fallen? If you do well, will you not be accepted? And if you do not well, sin is crouching at the door, its desire is for you but you must master it' ". (4:2–7)

The probable meaning of the very difficult verse 7 is that Cain murdered a rival because of resentment and envy. Probably soil cultivation and cattle raising developed side by side; but God's preference for Abel's offering of the "firstlings" of his flock and of their "fat portions" reflects a semitic standard of values which regards the austere nomadic life as the good life.

The genealogy of Cain is connected with the establishment of the earliest city and with the development of the arts and crafts.

"Then Cain went away from the presence of the Lord, and dwelt in the land of Nod, east of Eden. Cain knew his wife, and she conceived and bore Enoch; and he built a city, and called the name of the city after the name of his son, Enoch". (4:16–17)

We sense in Cain's story a disconnection. Endless generations of critical readers have felt this confusion, and asked: Where did Cain get his wife, if Abel and Cain were Adam and Eve's only children? It is clear that the Cain and Abel story belonged to a different tradition which assumed the presence of other people in the world besides the family of Adam. The kind of rational and critical interest which characterizes our age was remote from the ancient narrators, particularly when it came to tracing ancestral genealogies.

Later, the generations take us to Lemech, his two wives, Adah and Zillah, and their children.

"And Lemech took two wives; the name of the one was Adah, and the name of the other Zillah. Adah bore Jabal; he was the father of those who dwell in tents and have cattle. His brother's name was Jubal; he was the father of all those who play the lyre and pipe. Zillah bore Tubal-Cain; he was the forger of all instruments of bronze and iron. The sister of Tubal-Cain was Na'amah". (4:19–22)

When we read these lines in the Hebrew text we meet an interesting play on words in which the ancient Hebrews delighted. The name of Jabal sounds like the verb "yabal" meaning to lead (flocks); the name Jubal resembles the "yobel" which means trumpet.

Jabal is connected with the development of pastoral and nomadic life; his brother instituted the art of music, both on the harp and pipes. Zillah's children are of a lower scale in the social order: Tubal-Cain is a wandering smith; he founded the art of forging metals, which played such an important part in the cultural advance of the late 3rd millenium and 2nd millenium B.C.E. Among nomadic Beduins smiths have an inferior status to those who own herds and soil. Na'amah, Zillah's daughter, seems to be the prototype of singing girls, associated in some way with wandering smiths, like oriental gypsies, the "nawar".

That different genealogies and traditions attach to Cain and his descendants is borne out by biblical traditions of a later time. There is ground for believing that the name of the Kenites, metal-craftsmen, tribesmen of southern Palestine and kindred of the Hebrews, is derived from "qain" meaning "smith".

Whether the Cainite civilization referred to in Genesis 4 originated in Anatolia, in Kurdistan or further east of Eden, or how it spread, is uncertain. The Biblical representation of the progress of the arts and crafts is well borne out by archaeology. The potter's wheel, the use of donkeys, primitive wheeled vehicles, bricks and cylinder seals are among man's discoveries in these earliest prehistoric sites.

There is no connection between this pre-biblical representation of the first arts of civilization, attributed to Lemech's children, and the epic fragment, with its grim insistence on relentless blood revenge, which follows the story of Cain.

"Lemech said to his wives: 'Adah and Zillah, hear my voice; you wives of Lemech, hearken to what I say: I have slain a man for wounding me a young man for striking me. If Cain is avenged sevenfold, truly Lemech seventy-sevenfold". (4:23–24)

The Song of Lemech or in fact a fragment of the original, is one of the oldest examples of epic style in the Old Testament. Other very ancient epic fragments, artistically moulded, will

Two harpists playing horizontal arched harps. From a fragment of a vase from Bismaya, lower Mesopotamia, early 3rd millenium B.C.E.

Lyrist and woman with black hair, perhaps a singer, reminiscent of Jubal and Na'amah.

Wooden model of man ploughing; from 3rd millenium in Egypt. Similar ploughs are portrayed on early Babylonian seals.

be found elsewhere and may easily be distinguished by their style and spirit as different from the literary material in which they are embedded.

ANTEDILUVIAN PATRIARCHS AND GIANTS ON THE EARTH

The long period from the time of the creation to the Flood is briefly traced in the Bible. But the thread of narrative links genealogically the descendants of Adam through Seth – another son of Eve, who is a replacement for their son Abel. With him and his son Enosh ("man" in Hebrew) begins the line of the antediluvian patriarchs.

Another set of genealogies from Adam to Noah follows in Chap. 5, naming the heroes of before the Flood. Enoch appears once again here, in a parallel tradition which relates that "he walked with God and he was not, for God had taken him" (5:24). This is the first recorded intimation that someone had been taken above instead of dying.

The genealogy is noted for the phenomenally long life-spans of its characters. Methuselah lived 969 years, which was only a little longer than some of his fellows, and because of this his name is a byword for longevity. But all are much younger than their Babylonian colleagues, the ten antediluvian kings who are listed on a Mesopotamian clay prism; Babylonian tradition ascribes to them life-spans of thousands of years. In comparison biblical longevity appears quite brief. This suggests that the recorded life-spans of Genesis cannot be considered in isolation, but are related to Mesopotamian traditions. One of these has been handed down in a later version by Berossus, a Babylonian historian of the Hellenic period, who names ten kings who ruled before the Flood, whose aggregate life-spans total 432,000 years!

One of the strangest items embedded in the antediluvian tale is verse 6:4:

"The Nephilim were on the earth in those days, and also afterward, when the sons of God came in to the daughters of men, and they bore to them. These were the mighty men that were of old, the men of renown". (6:4)

We may perhaps link the Nephilim of Genesis with the "mighty men that were of old", these semi-legendary heroes of prehistory whose memory and deeds are recorded in the ancient annals of Mesopotamia, Egypt and other lands of antiquity. These were the founders of the first dynasties, lawgivers and the like. The word Nephilim (in Arabic—nabil) means princes. So the Nephilim need not be interpreted as a race of "giants", but "great men". In this Hebrew tradition the crisis described was held as proof that these semi-divine and arrogant Nephilim were more bent on evil than good:

"The Lord saw that the wickedness of man was great in the earth, and that every imagination of the thoughts of his heart was only evil continually. And the Lord was sorry that he had made man on the earth, and it grieved him to his heart". (6:5–6)

In the opinion of G. Ernest Wright the tradition of the early "giants on the earth" may coincide with the beginning of the Dynastic Ages from 3000 B.C.E. (the Early Bronze Age) and the succession of kings who established the first great empires. Great personalities who stood head and shoulders above their fellow men began to emerge. Illustrations of the time may help to explain the fame of such "giants".

The Sumerian King List, naming the ten kings who ruled before the Flood. It gives ages between 21,600 and 10,800 years. A clean break in the Sumerian clay fragment is marked by a line drawn to divide the text from that describing events after the Flood.

THE STORY OF THE FLOOD IN THE BIBLE AND IN MESOPOTAMIAN TRADITION

There is an architectural unity in the spirit of the traditions related to the ten generations preceding Noah. The writers sketch the gradual deterioriation of man and an increase in sin and violence which parallel his increase in knowledge and skill. As he gains in power, man turns against his Creator and corrupts the earth through violence. There is an implied warning against the insidious dangers of man following his own designs without heeding his responsibility before God, to whom he is answerable. God is described as experiencing human feelings of grief that he had ever created man, and he decided to punish the world. Some steps were taken to curb this upsurge of man to semi-divinity, such as the reduction of man's hitherto phenomenally long life-span to "one hundred and twenty years".

As violence did not abate, drastic punishment was called for. This is obviously an etiological tale meant to explain the proverbial span which one Jew still wishes another.

Supposed figure of Gilgamesh, hero of a famous epic narrating, among other episodes, the Babylonian story of the flood. From the palace of Sargon II at Khorsabad (8th century).

Stela of Sargon who established the First Empire of Accad in Mesopotamia, towards the end of the 3rd millenium B.C.E.

Naram-Sin, Sargon`s grandchild of the dynasty of Accad, stands before a stylized mountain crushing his enemies by treading upon them. He does not affect to be merely a regal hero. His horned crown, such as adorns the gods, gives the impression that he claims divinity. Many inscriptions of Naram-Sin associated his royal name with the word for god (ilu) which precedes it. Moreover, Naram-Sin was considered to be the "God of Accad"—that is Accad's protecting spirit and personal god.

"Now the earth was corrupt in God's sight, and the earth was filled with violence. And God saw the earth, and behold, it was corrupt; for all flesh had corrupted their way upon the earth. And God said to Noah 'I have determined to make an end of all flesh, for the earth is filled with violence through them; behold, I will destroy them with the earth' ". (6:11–13)

Presumably the authors of the biblical story skilfully used the ancient tradition of the Flood as a vehicle of Hebrew faith, namely God's judgement in the affairs of history. From this verdict only Noah, a sole pious man, and his household, were excepted, for: "Noah was a righteous man, blameless in his generation" (6:9). Emphasis is centred on the motif that God's verdict was motivated by man's violence. The Mesopotamian version regards the sparing of one man as necessary for provisioning the gods after the slaughter of mankind. So God instructed Noah to build an ark according to exact specifications. He was told to take his family, and pairs of all the animals of creation, as well as supplies. The story which is well known to everyone is given in Genesis 6:9 to 9:13 and only its highlights and its morals need to be pointed out. The genre of Genesis 6 to 9 is didactic rather than historic. The tradition is common to biblical and Mesopotamian sources, and the inspired Hebrew storytellers of a later age used it to teach man a moral lesson. The point of the story was the horror of violence in God's sight. It seems that there are two trends in the biblical story. Into the earlier source is interwoven the more ritualistic Hebrew one which specifies that seven pairs of clean animals and two pairs of unclean animals were taken into the ark. The rain that lasted for forty days receded in two or three seven-day periods. The small variations in the tales are of particular interest to specialists, when comparing parallel stories of the flood with older Sumerian and more recent Babylonian texts which will be quoted in part.

THE MESOPOTAMIAN STORIES

One of the most spectacular finds of biblical archaeology was the discovery and deciphering by George Smith in 1872 of a large clay tablet which originated from the library of the Assyrian king Ashurbanipal. On it was described the Assyrian version of the Flood story; it was similar in essence to an older Sumerian legend discovered many years later, where the hero of the Flood was named Ziusudra. (This version was described on a clay tablet found in Nippur, in central Babylonia). The legendary hero appears in the Assyrian-Babylonian version, where his name is Utnapishtim "the day of life".

The episode of the Flood represents only one scene in the immortal Epic of Gilgamesh. The hero seeks the last survivor of the great Flood to learn from him the secret of immortality. After crossing difficult mountains and sailing across the Waters of Death, Gilgamesh at last meets Utnapishtim. The latter tells him of his salvation from the Flood through his obedience to the god Ea, the god of wisdom, who granted him a deathless state. And this is the story of Utnapishtim:

The gods in assembly had decided on the flood and destruction of mankind. The god Ea wanted to warn Utnapishtim, but it was apparently forbidden to divulge the proceedings of the assembly. So a stratagem was resorted to: Utnapishtim hid behind the wall of a reed and Ea spoke to the wall behind him:

The eleventh clay tablet from the epic of Gilgamesh from Ashurbanipal's library of tablets in Nineveh, giving the Babylonian and Assyrian version of the Flood in cuneiform writing.

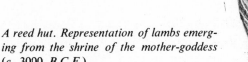

A reed hut. Representation of lambs emerging from the shrine of the mother-goddess (c. 3000 B.C.E.).

"Reed-hut, reed-hut! Wall, Wall!
Reed-hut, hearken! Wall, reflect!
Man of Shuruppak, son of Ubar-tuth,
Tear down this house, build a ship
Give up possessions, seek thou life,
Despise property and keep the soul alive
Aboard the ship take thou the seed of all living things".

Utnapishtim did as he was told, then the poet describes the approaching storm:

"With the first glow of dawn as a black cloud rose up from the horizon,
The gods lifted up their torches, setting them ablaze with their glare".
....
"The gods were frightened by the deluge,
And shrinking back they ascended to the heavens of Anu,
The gods crouched like dogs".

Ishtar, the sweet-voiced mistress of the gods, specially bewailed her part in the destruction of mankind by the flood:

"The olden days are alas turned to clay,
Because I spoke evil in the assembly of the gods
Ordering battle for the destruction of my people
When it is myself who gave birth to my people
Like the spawn of the fishes they fill the sea".

At the dreadful destruction which had been wrought all the gods mourned:

"The gods, all humbled, sit and weep,
Their lips grown tight, one and all".

The storm was brief but decimating. It lasted six days and six nights:

"When the seventh day arrived,
The flood-carrying south-storm subsided in the battle,
Which has formed like an army.
The sea grew quiet, the tempest was stilled, the flood ceased".

Utnapishtim surveyed the melancholy scene:

"I looked at the weather: a stillness had set in,
And all mankind had turned to clay".

At last Utnapishtim discerned a stretch of earth as the ship struck ground on the mountain. At Mount Nisir, one of the mountains of "Urartu", (rendered Ararat, north of the Babylonian plain) the ship held fast. He sent out a dove on the seventh day. This was followed by a swallow and a raven. The first two came back, but the raven did not return. Then he let out all "to the four winds and offered a sacrifice". The gods responded in a most undignified way to the sacrifice so gratefully offered by Utnapishtim:

"I poured out a libation on the top of the mountain.
Seven and seven cult-vessels I set up,
Upon their pot-stands I heaped cane, cedar-wood, and myrtle.
The gods smelled the savour,
The gods smelled the sweet savour,
The gods crowded like flies about the sacrificer".

After a council of the gods, Enlil went aboard the ship, touched the foreheads of Utnapishtim and his wife, and blessed them thus:

"Hitherto Utnapishtim has been but human.
Henceforth Utnapishtim and his wife shall be like unto us gods".

(Translation according to J. B. Pritchard (Ed). Ancient Near Eastern Texts).

This concludes the Babylonian account of the flood according to the Epic of Gilgamesh. The biblical account concludes as follows:

"Then Noah built an altar to the Lord, and took of every clean animal, and of every clean bird, and offered burnt offerings on the altar. And when the Lord smelt the pleasing odour, the Lord said in His heart, 'I will never again curse the ground because of man, for the imagination of man's heart is evil from his youth; neither will I ever again destroy living creatures as I have done, while the earth remains, seedtime and harvest, cold and heat, summer and winter, day and night, shall not cease". (8:20–22)

The sweet savour that rose was so pleasing, quoth an old saying with naive anthropomorphic touch, that God would not curse the ground with severe judgement. It would appear from the biblical text above that the behaviour of mankind was no better after the Flood than before it. But as the Hebrew version concludes, God became reconciled to the fact that the "imagination of man's heart is evil from his youth" or as we would say today, it derives from his natural instincts. He decided never again to resort to such forms of punishment and to implant a feeling of security in a world run according to His wishes.

The parallels between the biblical account and the Babylonian version are fairly obvious and at times remarkable for their resemblance, though the major part of the Epic of Gilgamesh is far different. Its polytheist spirit is in contrast with the basic purpose of the Hebrew narrative. In form the latter is impersonal and it purports to account for God's actions, his motives and his judgement by the depravity of humanity. The story told by Utnapishtim is in the form of an illustrative tale, in which he tries to convince his listeners that immortality was granted to him under unique circumstances, never again to be achieved by a mortal. It contains no judgement on the concern of the gods or on the moral conduct of man.

An older version of the Babylonian Flood story—the Atrahasis Epic—gives a very significant cause of the Flood:

"The land became wide, the people became numerous, the land hummed like a lyre (or: bellowed like wild oxen).
The god (Enlil) was disturbed by the uproar.
Entil heard their clamour.
And said to the great gods:
'Oppressive has become the clamour of mankind, by their clamour they prevent sleep' ".

Prof. J. J. Finkelstein calls attention to the Accadian term "hubbum" for uproar, which means a constant din or clamour of argument. The same epic uses another term, "immasu", corresponding to the biblical "hammas", or violence. Perhaps, then, behind one of the Babylonian versions was a concept similar to the biblical "the earth was filled with violence" (6:13), and this may have given rise to the Hebrew epic.

Although the Babylonian accounts are much older than the Hebrew, their exact relationship is still not known, though the theory that the biblical account may have been borrowed from them is unacceptable despite seeming affinities. What seems most likely is that a set of such themes spread over northern, southern and western Mesopotamia, and, stemming from the literature of the Sumerians and Babylonians, reached the remote ancestors of the Hebrews.

THE LAND OF THE FLOOD

As we pass from the realm of myth to that of legend, or popular tradition, we realize that the story of the flood goes back to some actual historic event. That the flood was not universal is self-evident, for according to excavations, no one flood affected the whole of the

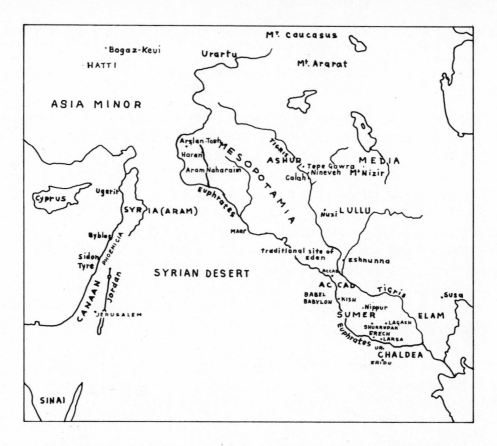

Map of Mesopotamia, cradle of civilization, the birthplace of writing. This map includes the traditional site of the Garden of Eden. Ancient Sumer, Accad, and Babylon are in evidence, as well as dozens of ancient cities and ruins.

Mesopotamian valley, and Near Eastern cultures show no radical break in their continuity, as would have happened in the case of the total destruction of humanity implied in the story. Professors Woolley and Langdon point out that, by digging under the land of ancient towns such as Ur, Kish, Shuruppak, Uruk, Lagash, Nineveh, they found virgin stratas of clean water-laid clay or silt deposits left by the flood, between 2.70 to 3.50 metres thick (8 to 11 feet). These could have been caused by an inundation, or several inundations. The flood deposits appear to belong to different dates. Beneath these stratas they found again traces of primitive settlements antedating even the days of the Sumerians, namely the antediluvian period. Over this clay remains of a later age were found. The existence of these layers is evidence enough of particularly severe floodings of the rivers Euphrates and Tigris at different times and places. Such violent inundations in flat country, coupled with terrific rains (which happen occasionally) would easily wash away primitive settlements and lowlands. In

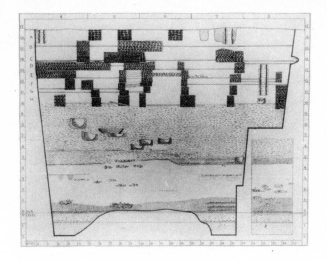

Sumer, or lower Babylonia, occasional torrential rains, and the floods of rivers, descending from the great mountains of the north, must often have created dire peril for the inhabitants, be they of Kish, Shuruppak, or Ur. In the biblical Flood story it is not stated where Noah lived, and the extent and times of these floods remain unknown. The Hebrew story: "All the foundations of the great deep burst forth, and the windows of the heavens were opened", indicates the terror in those times when men had not yet learned how to harness and diffuse the impact of these waters through canalization.

THE ARK: How should we picture the Ark? The Babylonians used to construct their river boats in various ways. They made *floaters* of closely packed and bound reeds, which they navigated by means of round "couffas" in the shape of enormous baskets, whose sides and bottoms were sealed with clay and asphalt. Examples may still be seen to this day on the Euphrates (see illustration below); Ancient clay cylinders often portray the "belem" with its

Boat made of clay; 3rd millenium B.C.E.

Air view of the Euphrates. When in flood it spreads over the plain.

Flooded desert plain in Western Mesopotamia after a rain-fall lasting several hours.

"Kelek" (raft) of a type also used by the Assyrians.

Ancient "couffa", skin-covered boat, transporting a heavy load of materials.

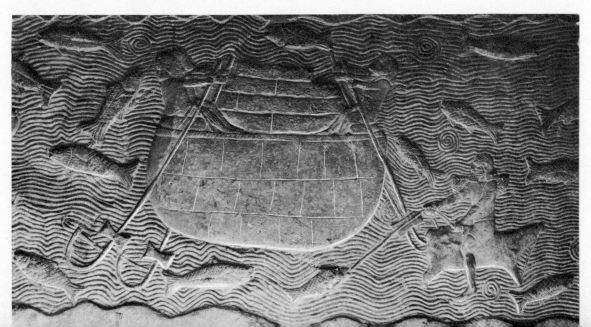

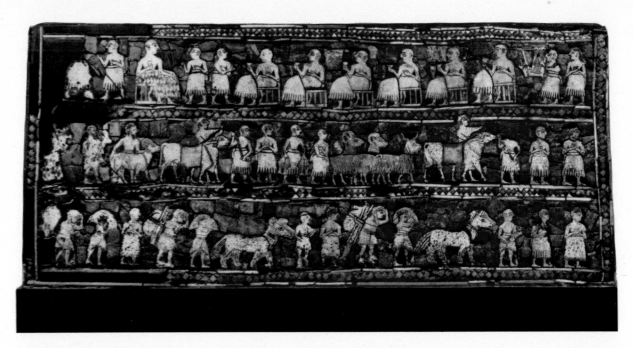

The right side of the upper register of this panel from Ur represents a lyrist and a woman with black hair, perhaps a singer. This mosaic panel in shell, lapis lazuli and limestone (25th cent. B.C.E.) depicts the celebration of a victory with music and feasting.

A primitive chariot driven by four asses. A faithful example of Mesopotamian art from the early third millenium B.C.E. Copper statuette found in Shara temple east of the river Tigris.

flat bottom, its prow and its stern standing up high. The Ark was of enormous proportions for ancient navigation: some hundred and fifty metres long; but the characteristics indicated in the Hebrew version give it cubic proportions, unlike a long-boat, and it is more able to float than to be navigated.

BIBLICAL GENEALOGIES AND NEAR EASTERN PREHISTORY

"The sons of Noah who went forth from the Ark were Shem, Ham and Japhet. Ham was the sire of Canaan. These three were the sons of Noah; and from these the whole earth was peopled". (9:18-19)

Genesis does not say where Noah and his family lived after the Flood, but only that the earth was repopulated by the descendants of Noah's three sons, Shem, Ham and Japhet. The chronicler regards Noah as the main link in the generations reaching to Abraham, and carefully notes that Ham, father of Canaan, is not of the same stock as Shem, the father of the Hebrews. This removes the Canaanites from the Semitic family in which they probably belong, and classifies them as Hamites. The contempt and superciliousness of the chronicler for the Canaanites is pointedly illustrated in a very old story about Noah and Ham:

"Noah was the first tiller of the soil. He planted a vineyard; and he drank of the wine, and became drunk, and lay uncovered in his tent. And Ham the father of Canaan, saw the nakedness of his father, and told his two brothers outside. Then Shem and Japhet took a garment, laid it upon both their shoulders, and walked backward and covered the nakedness of their father; their faces were turned away, and they did not see their father's nakedness. When Noah awoke from his wine and knew what his youngest son had done to him, he said:
'Cursed be Canaan;
  a slave of slaves shall he be to his brothers'.
He also said:
" 'Blessed by the Lord my God be Shem
and let Canaan be his slave' ". (9:20-26)

The point of the story of Noah the vinegrower is not his drunkenness, but his nakedness in an unguarded moment. The offence was only that Ham, the "father of Canaan", beheld his father naked, which was a sin; and that he dishonoured him by going and informing his brothers. They walked backwards and covered their father. The father blessed his other two sons and cursed Ham, and even more so his son Canaan. There is a propagandist purpose in this narrative: it justifies both Canaan's servitude to his brethren, and Israel's hatred of the Canaanites. The latter probably really arose from a period of hostilities between Hebrews and Canaanites after the conquest of the twelfth century B.C.E.

As we continue to read the genealogies, we note that the focus grows more and more narrow. The emphasis at the conclusion is on Shem, the ancestor of the Semites (see Gen. 10: 21–30), which include "all the sons of Eber" who embraced the Hebrews. (The final narrowing of the generations of Eber would come in the next chapter; read 11: 16–26).

Table of Nations: We turn now to Gen. 10, a great document, which with considerable historicity attempts to place all the nations known to the Hebrews into an organic framework, and to show their inter-relationship. A surprising number of names in this Table of Nations have been reliably identified, thanks partly to classical sources outside the Bible, and partly to the ancient descriptions which tell us so much about the world in which Israel lived.

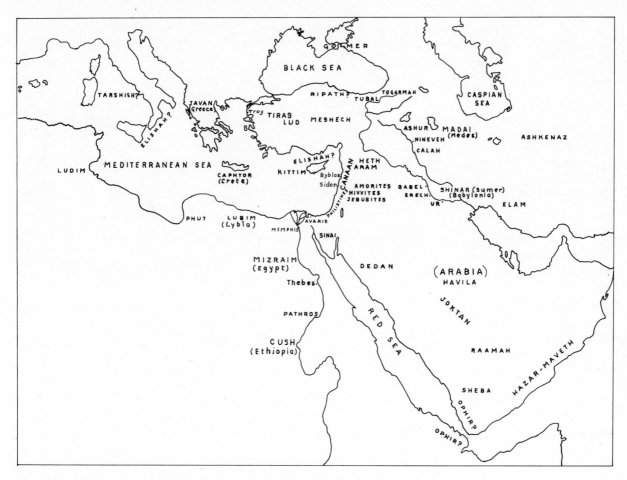

The Hebrew Table of Nations; from Gen. 10 *and related extra-biblical sources.*

W. F. Albright comments that "it shows such a remarkably 'modern' understanding of the linguistic situation in the ancient world.... that stands absolutely alone in ancient literature, without even a remote parallel even among the Greeks, where we find the closest approach to a distribution of the peoples in genealogical framework. But among the Greeks the framework is mythological and the people are all Greeks or Aegean tribes".

This Table is not the basis of the division of the races of mankind into the Aryan, Semitic and dark-skinned races. It knows nothing of the Far East and the Pacific and Atlantic races or of dark Africa south of Egypt. But it contains data about the geographical distribution of the ancient Near East, from the confines of Iran and Edom down to Arabia, of commercial and linguistic ties, and far-scattered tribes, "nations", countries and towns.

The Table claims ethnic predominance for the Semite and Japhetic peoples over the Hamitic peoples, for reasons explained above (though present-day anthropology sees this in a different light). Above all, this chapter, like the story of creation and the ten-generation

A Mesopotamian seal of the 24th century B.C.E. representing the liberation of the (rising) Sun god — Shamash or Marduk — from between two mountains. The deity with the bow is supposed to be the Warrior god — Ninurta. On the right of the Sun god is the Water god — Ea. On the left is the goddess of Fertility — Ishtar.

genealogy (Gen. 5) from Adam to Noah, has a broad conception of the cosmos under one God. It sees all men beneath the aegis of Israel's Lord, and points out that he has settled Israel's linear descent from creation for his own special purpose.

Nimrod: There is a most interesting story, that of Nimrod the mighty hunter and conqueror, in the Table. The record says:

> "The beginning of his kingdom was Babel, Erech, and Accad, all of them in the land of Shinnar. From that land he went into Assyria" (alternative version of the Hebrew: "went Ashur into Assyria") "and built Nineveh, Rechoboth, Ir, Calah and Resen, between Nineveh and Calah; that is the great city". (10:10–11)

According to this story, in the beginning Nimrod's kingdom was in Babylon, and from there he went to Assyria. This may not be historically true, but it accurately reflects the historic background pertaining to the early Babylonian and Assyrian kingdoms. The names of cities connected with him are well attested by archaeological research. The name Nimrod is preserved in that of the present-day Arab village Nimrud, where ancient Calah was excavated. The modern name Nimrud may possibly contain an echo of that used in antiquity for its chief protector, Ninurta, god of war and the chase. The biblical name Nimrod, according to E. A. Speiser, does not echo a god but the reign of the vigorous Tukutli-Ninurta I (1243–1207), who built Calah, Assyria's second capital, and conquered Babylon. The description of Nimrod as a builder and "mighty hunter before the Lord" well typifies characteristics of Assyria's early kings, as featured in illustrations of hunting scenes carved on rock.

Blue-glazed bricks from the shrine on the topmost stage of the ziggurat in Babylon, rebuilt in the 6th century.

Chaplet of gold beech leaves and beads of carnelian and lapis lazuli. Choker of gold and lapis lazuli beads. These belonged to ladies in waiting of queen Shubad of Ur.

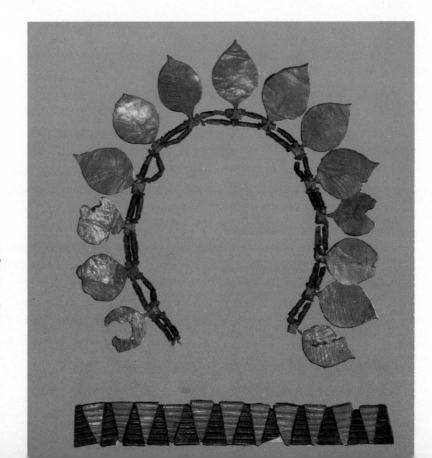

In lower Mesopotamia, the region at the head of the Persian Gulf, the dominant ethnic, political and cultural group in the 3rd millenium B.C.E. called its land Sumer (biblical Shinar). This phase is featured in material and written illustrations from Ur, Uruk (biblical Erech), Lagash, and Eshnunna, among others. Following this long phase of Sumerian ascendancy came the historic period of the first Empire under the Semitic dynasty founded by Sargon of Accad. Sumerian and Semite co-existed and contended with each other for political leadership until the end of the millenium, but the prevailing culture was very much of a joint effort. Though Accad was the main city and capital of this first empire in Mesopotamia, it has not yet been identified.

As the civilization of Mesopotamia expanded, it separated into different channels. In the south of Mesopotamia were the Babylonians, whose city Babylon (biblical Babel) became the capital of the great kingdom. Its peak of power and glory was reached in the 18th and 17th centuries under Hammurabi, one of the great rulers of Babylonia's first dynasty. The Semite inhabitants of western Mesopotamia were known as Amorites.

In the north a city on the river Tigris was rising slowly to ever-increasing prominence. Its name was Ashur, as was also that of its chief god. The state the city came to control was Assyria. The political tide swung for the first time decisively in favour of Ashur during the reign of the vigorous Tukutli Ninurta I.

The expansion of Ashur northward brought with it successive transfers of the capital of Assyria from Ashur to Calah and Nineveh. But Ashur remained the old tribal and religious capital in which the kings were buried, and Calah was the military capital of ancient Assyria until it was transferred to Nineveh. Thus Ashur, Calah and Nineveh were Assyria's successive capital cities, well known in history and through archaeological discoveries.

PREHISTORY IN THE BIBLE

Traditions handed down by the Hebrews tell nothing of the rise and fall of empires that took place between the time when civilization began in Mesopotamia and the time of the migration of the first Hebrew tribesmen to Canaan. It must be noted in this connection: (a) that the first specific Hebrew tribe of Abraham—in its genesis—is partly of Mesopotamian stock and civilization. (b) the tribe evolved its own character gradually, following a migration of Amorite tribes from Mesopotamia to the west and south, including Canaan. (c) in the period of their migrations, semi-nomadic peoples are too much engaged in their struggle for existence and too insignificant in number (even after they have settled on their own soil and in their common environment), to keep a record of remote backgrounds.

So it was in the case of the Hebrews, for apparently no record was set down in writing until many centuries later. Nevertheless, the Hebrews retained their own oral tradition. Later, when the interest of religious teachers or historians into the dim past, or into the background of the original tribe had awakened, they may have resorted both to the ancient oral tradition or to others stemming from Mesopotamia. We find signs and passing flashes of factual material of this kind in historic names in chapters 10 and 11.

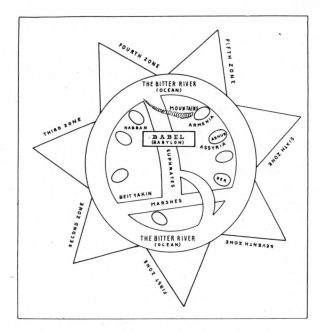

Babylonian world-map and its reconstruction.

The god Ashur, a deity of the Assyrians.

A king-list of the dynasty of Larsa, from the beginning of the 2nd millenium. It is written in wedge-shaped cuneiform script.

The site of Nineveh (Quyundjik)

THE TOWER OF BABEL

The very charming story of the original building of the mighty tower of Babel is etiological: It was an explanation by later generations to account for the fact that mankind—which stems from one family of Noah—developed so many mutually unintelligible languages. The story is well known (11: 1–9) and need not be repeated. It is an echo, incidentally, of one of the first migrations of human history in the prehistory of Iran and Mesopotamia. The scene is laid in this area, where once nomads, wandering and "spread abroad on the earth" had increased north and east of Mesopotamia, travelled down to the lowlands in Shinar, and settled there. They may have been the original Sumerians or their forerunners, the first to discover brick-making. The clay available in that alluvial soil led to the extensive use of sunbaked or burnt bricks and made possible heretofore unimagined developments in build-

King Ur Nammu who rebuilt the ziggurat of Ur in the 21st century B.C.E. is seen before deities at different platforms. On the third he is shown carrying a basket and surveying instruments. These suggest that the subject was the building of a ziggurat.

The ziggurat of Ur viewed from the north-west.

Restoration of the terraced temple tower or ziggurat of Ur, from the 21st century B.C.E. It was probably a similar construction to that known as the tower of Babel. Stairways leading to the top of the ziggurat can be seen. The terraces were of different colours — black, red, blue; the temple at the top was covered with silver. The terraces were also covered with bitumen and decorated with trees. This gave rise to the idea of the "hanging gardens of Babylon".

ing. In any case the newcomers decided to establish a settled way of life, namely to "build ourselves a city and a tower", which might be an idiom of those days for a permanent urban settlement, and security in the city-states of Mesopotamia. In the biblical epic, and genealogy, where the tower of Babel appears, it is used as evidence of the recurring theme of self-assertion, which prompted man to revolt against the Lord, for "nothing that they proposed to do will now be impossible for them". The inference is that they intended to invade the celestial territory. So the Lord thwarted their plan by intervening "and there confuse their language." He visited the town with his judgement and brought the building project to an end. By means of a Hebrew pun, the word Babel is identified with the verb "Balal", which means "to confuse". Thus it came about that men no longer spoke the same language. They dispersed in various language groups. Taken by itself the story would be pessimistic. But the biblical author appropriates it, nonetheless, and in spite of its inconsistency with the known diversity of races in early mankind. He is prepared to set forth the theological perspective of the primeval history of mankind; in other words, he interprets it as a prologue to what is to follow: The call of Abraham and the Chosen People.

The storyteller's explanation of the origin of the name of Babel as due to "confusion" is another example of popular Hebrew etymology. This name is actually a popular etymology based on two Babylonian words "Bab-Ilu", i.e., "the gate of God".

The tower of Babel story is not based on history. But it is a clear reference to the numerous "Ziggurat" or stage-towers built throughout the width and length of the valleys of the Euphrates and Tigris from the 3rd millenium B.C.E. onwards. They became a characteristic feature of temple architecture, as the church-spire was of the European. The original ziggurat of Ur consisted of baked clay bricks banded with bitumen mortar, forming three terraces, built in step-like stages. The ziggurat with its seven stages, gave rise to the legend of the tower of Babel. The identification of the tower of Babel with the ziggurat of Babylon, or with the vitrified remains of the ziggurat of Borsippa, namely Birs Nimrud seven miles south-west of Babylon, remains questionable. As cities in northern as well as in southern Mesopotamia possessed ziggurat, their existence and history would have been known to the remote ancestors of the Hebrews. The best preserved remains of ziggurat are those which were rebuilt later, with seven stages, those of Ur by Nabonidus in 550 and of Babylon and Borsippa by Nebuchadrezzar II (605—561 B.C.E.).

The first ziggurat of Babylon itself was called in Sumerian E-temen-an-ki, "Building of the Foundation of Heaven and Earth", and the temple in which it stood was called "E-sag-ila", meaning "House that Lifts up the Head" (compare this concept with the biblical quotation "a tower with its top in the heavens"). The E-sag-ila, it will be remembered, is mentioned in the Sumerian legend of creation "Enuma Elish", which was consecrated to the god Marduk. The base of the tower was 90 metres on each side and it rose 90 metres in height. A sanctuary to the gods was built at the top.

The sense of piety and pride attached to the building and restoration of the ziggurat is attested by old illustrations of the Sumerians and Babylonians.

An account of fields, crops and commodities from Kish (3100 B.C.E.). Clay tablet inscribed in early Sumerian linear characters immediately derived from pictographs.

A gold dagger with its hilt of lapis lazuli, studded with gold; from the same period.

This lyre from Ur is an example of the art and culture which flourished there a few centuries before the time of Abraham.

The intricate headdress of queen Shubad of Ur, with ornaments of gold leaf, lapis lazuli and carnelian, shown on reconstructed model head (c. 2500 B.C.E.)

Pictorial mosaic panel depicting a war expedition of the Sumerians (c. 2500 B.C.E.). On the left panel the upper register shows the prince (the large figure), the royal family, chariot and prisoners. Soldiers and prisoners are depicted on the middle register, and chariotry on the lower register.

Gold helmet from a tomb at Ur.

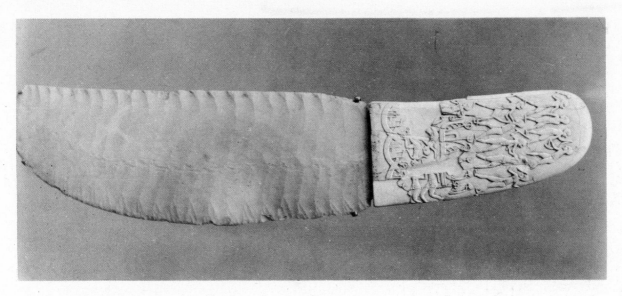

Ceremonial flint knife used for circumcision.

CHAPTER III

ABRAHAM

THE FIRST HEBREW MIGRATION FROM MESOPOTAMIA

Genesis 12 to 50 is in a different category from the preceding chapters. Firstly, the patriarchal stories are thematically clearer than the foregoing primeval history. The biblical narrators discern the destiny of the "people of the promise", Israel, in their modest inception, and the narrative bears out, through the vehicle of the patriarchal tales, Israel's struggle to realize her relation with God. The enduring facet of these narratives is, of course, to express the divine purpose for human life, as envisaged throughout the Bible. We must also note the sharp juxtaposition of the non-Israelite traditions up to this point with the call and promise of Abraham.

Abraham is called to create a community in which the sin and rebelliousness of mankind can be overcome. We must constantly bear in mind that the central themes of Israel's inner history in the patriarchal narratives are played out against the background of Israel's historic beginnings: these beginnings, and their historic context of antiquity, constitute their *outer history;* and the inner and outer histories are always intertwined in their narrative. Our knowledge of the world of Abraham, if not of Abraham himself, is considerable. The outline of the patriarchal age is clear. We shall start first with this general historic back-drop.

This second part of the book of Genesis, at the close of chapter 11 narrows its genealogies down, in order to place the descendants of Eber down to Nahor, who begat Terah:

"When Terah had lived seventy years, he became the father of Abram, Nahor, and Haran. Now these are the descendants of Terah. Terah was the father of Abram, Nahor, and Haran; and Haran was the father of Lot. Haran died before his father Terah in the land of his birth, in Ur of the Chaldeans". (11:26-28)

"Terah took Abram his son and Lot the son of Haran, his grandson, and Sarai his daughter-in-law, his son Abram's wife, and they went forth together from Ur of the Chaldeans to go into the land of Canaan; and when they came to Haran, they settled there". (11:31)

After the genealogy of the sons of Shem has mentioned Terah's sons, Abraham, Nahor and Haran, it passes into narrative. Where the migration account begins (verses 28-31), we find Terah in the territory of Ur of the Chaldeans (a later designation of this ancient metropolis of the Sumerians), of which most important new knowledge has been gained from excavations, including its tower, dedicated to the moon-god Sinn. Ur was one of the largest and wealthiest cities of lower Mesopotamia, near the Persian Gulf. It was destroyed by the invasion of the Amorites about 1900 B.C.E., but it is not known whether it may not still have been standing at the end of the patriarchal period.

The form of narration through genealogies in the Bible actually reflects the personification of tribal history. In speaking of the people, the Hebrew storyteller often used the name of the historic patriarchal father of the group for the people itself. This form may have helped those who were heir to Israel's oral tradition to bridge the time between the lives of great personalities, epochs, and significant events, and to provide a system of chronology (with which we shall deal in turn). This puts a different aspect on the dry genealogical tables (the "begats" of the classic versions of the Bible) or the stories opening with the titles "These are the generations of...".

A house of the early patriarchal period excavated at Ur. The single entrance leads from the narrow street into a paved courtyard surrounded on three sides by rooms. Private dwellings had a similar layout throughout the biblical period. On the right, artist's reconstruction of the house at Ur with balcony overlooking the courtyard. The balcony gave access to the rooms and to a flat roof.

Hebrew tradition does not ascribe a written record to Abraham but to Moses (we use the term tradition in the sense of "what was handed down"). It is fairly certain that the patriarchal narratives, for the most part, derive from oral traditions, many of which were written after the time of Moses. But such oral traditions of pre-literary times are not to be spurned. The reliability of transmission was assured by the incredible memories of the Orientals. Hermann Gunkel remarks that these traditions in Genesis break up into separate tales, each unit characterized by a few participants and the affairs of a few families, simple descriptions, laconic speech, all welded into big bold strokes of narration with artful use of suspense. This colourful and memorable mode of narration is a vehicle for family and tribal tradition especially suited to oral transmission. The extraordinary feature is that Hebrew memory had preserved such pre-literary traditions for more than a thousand years and set them down in writing so faithfully.

Since all the family names of the genealogy point to a Mesopotamian background, we may imagine the Terah clan as semi-nomads with ties both with Ur and Harran, though it seems that they were sojourners in the Ur vicinity, being more closely connected with Harran. The story may reflect a tribal migration from lower Mesopotamia. Some scholars try to identify this as a migration from the serious disturbances which beset the Near East shortly after the nineteenth century B.C.E. The general location of Harran has never been lost and a town by this name still exists on the Balikh, a tributary of the Euphrates. This was the chief city of the area which was later designated Padan-Aram "the Field of Aram" or Aram of the Two Rivers, with which the Hebrews associated the ancestral home of their people. The Israelites always acknowledged their kinship with their remote ancestors of this valley.

"'Your fathers lived of old beyond the Euphrates, Terah, the father of Abraham and of Nahor; and they served other gods'". (Joshua 24:2)

Towns in the neighbourhood of Harran and beyond the Euphrates which flourished at that period bear names of the families which occupied them, such as Tal-Turakhi, Sarugi, (Serug), Nakhur (Nahor). They are the names of the "brothers" as well as the ancestors of Abraham.

Hebrew tradition considered Abraham's kinsmen in Mesopotamia as nomadic Arameans. That is how they are called in the subsequent stories of Genesis and in Deut. 26:5... "a wandering Aramean was my father".

THE COMING OF THE AMORITES

In the latter part of the millenium a new Semitic wave began pouring into Mesopotamia from the wilderness to the west. These invaders took strongest root in Mesopotamia and northern Syria, where the Sumerians and Babylonians called them Amurru — "westerners", a name preserved in the Bible as Amorites. It is this wave that particularly interests us. In it must have been several closely related groups, one of these perhaps early Arameans. From shortly after 1900 B.C.E. we hear of states headed by Amorite dynasties in that part of the Fertile Crescent. It seems probable that these western Semites also pushed into Palestine and populated it at the beginning of the 2nd millenium. These various principalities included northern Canaan (Ugarit) and as far as the southern coast of Syria.

This famous Egyptian relief from the early 19th century depicts a party of western Asiatics, and may represent Amorite nomad metal workers. The men wear short skirts and sandals, the women long dresses fastened by a single shoulder-clasp, and shoes. One donkey carries two children and a bellows, and on another is tied a throwstick or mace, a spear and a bellows. These and the bows were the weapons used in the period. One man carries an 8-stringed lyre and a skin water-container on his back.

The Near East in the patriarchal period; Invaders in the Fertile Crescent in the first half of the 2nd millenium.

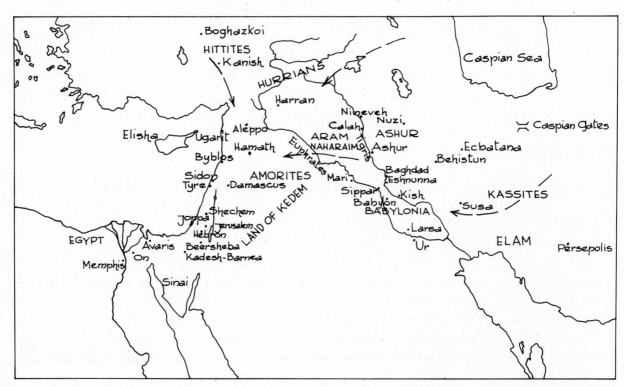

Fragment of a mural painting from Mari, showing men leading a bull to a sacrificial ritual; 17th century B.C.E.

MARI

A vivid picture of the time was provided by the recent discovery of about twenty thousand tablets at Mari, dating from the latter half of the 18th century B.C.E. Many of these documents represent diplomatic correspondence between the King of Mari and officials in surrounding Amorite states, some of them with Hammurabi himself. The Mari people had adopted the Accadian culture and spoke a language akin to that of Israel's ancestors. The Mari tablets illuminate the cultural background of the early partriarchal period. They are of extraordinary interest to the reader of the Bible, for they contain certain biblical customs, manners, and west-Semitic names. These are not identical with the biblical names, but they certainly point to a common western Semitic background, and are reminiscent of Hebrew names. The ancient records of the area mention names like Abraham (in the form Abam-ram) and Jacob (in the form Ya'aqub-ilu) as do other earlier documents in the kingdoms of Syria and Mesopotamia.

The Mari records and those of other places in Mesopotamia mention another troublesome group — the Apiru or Habiru — a term that in the judgement of many scholars is almost equivalent to Hebrews, as we shall see below.

But not only the Amorite invasion or conquest took place in the early part of the 2nd millenium B.C.E; other ethnic groups came into the picture. There were Hittites of Asia Minor who exerted influence on Syria and Mesopotamia, and the partially Semitic Hyksos, who had conquered Egypt in 1720. Most baffling of all are the Hurrians.

THE HURRIANS

The Hurrians, or biblical Horites, infiltrated in a steady stream into the Fertile Crescent, and into the political vacuum created by the downfall of the Sumerian dynasty of Ur, during the first half of the 2nd millenium B.C.E. They probably came from inner Asia. Until 1925 nothing was known of the Hurrians. But the discovery of thousands of clay tablets written in the Accadian language, at the Hurrian city of Nuzu (near the oil town of Kirkuk in present-day Iraq), has thrown a great deal of light on the patriarchal period. Many Hurrian customs, attested to by these tablets, contribute to our understanding of social practices in the patriarchal period. The Hurrians started coming down in ever increasing numbers from the northern Caucasian and Armenian mountains into the valleys of the Tigris and Euphrates. Their infiltration, which was not warlike, brought them first as settlers into northern Mesopotamia around Mari, Harran and Nuzu, until by the end of the 15th century, they were to be found in every part of western Asia, including Syria and Palestine. The Hurrians attained their greatest prominence in the new kingdom called Mitanni (1470—1350 B.C.E.), which extended from east of the upper Tigris valley to the coast of northern Syria. The Mitannian gods and kings often bear names which prove that some Indo-Europeans settled in Mitanni and even formed the core of Mitannian princes and knights. They were also present in Palestine in large numbers, and the Egyptians from the time of the 18th dynasty referred to the whole area as Hurru, namely Hurrian country. It is thought that they are the Horites referred to in the Bible.

By the middle of the second millenium B.C.E. these exceptionally active groups had made their presence felt throughout the Near East, leaving substantial traces of their influence and culture. Most of what they contributed was merely new versions of old traditions, which the Amorites and Hurrians had acquired from the Sumerians and Accadians in the third millenium.

The 14th chapter of Genesis which echoes an obscure story of invasions, and figures Abraham himself as a Hebrew military chieftain, mentions both Horites (Hurrians) and Amorites:

"And the Horites in their Mount Seir as far as El-paran on the border of the wilderness". (14:6)

"Then one who had escaped came, and told Abram the Hebrew, who was living by the oaks of Mamre the Amorite, brother of Eshcol and of Aner; these were allies of Abram". (14:13)

THE HITTITES

By 2000 B.C.E. Asia Minor had been invaded by various groups speaking Indo-European dialects, who infiltrated among the native inhabitants. They were organized into a system of city states. The most influential of these people called themselves Hatti (Hittite). By the 17th century, the foundations of a strong Hittite kingdom had been laid, which pressed southward into Syria. In 1530 Aleppo fell to Mursilis who thrust across Hurrian lands, raided northern Mesopotamia and sacked Babylon. To this period probably belongs the infiltration of Hittites into the highlands of Canaan. Beleaguered by Hurrian pressure and inner political difficulties, the Hittite kingdom finally retreated into Asia Minor.

Hittite stela: Teshub, the weather god, armed; from Tel Barsip.

Hittite stela: the god of war; 9th century.

Hittite documents were written in cuneiform, which they must have borrowed from Mesopotamia. These are our earliest record in a language related to Sanscrit, Greek and other languages of the west. The significance of the Hittites is that geographically they formed a land-bridge between the Semitic world and the Greeks.

They are particularly interesting on account of the insistence of Bible traditions in situating the sons of Heth (Hittites) in a prominent position in Hebron and the hills of Jerusalem in patriarchal times. Their early ethnological connection with Canaan is also attested by Ezekiel who describes Jerusalem as "thy father is the Amorite, and thy mother Hittite" (Ez. 16:3). Their military and economic interests carried their influence into Palestine which was referred to by the Assyrians as the Hattu land. Some scholars believe that the Jebusites of Jerusalem were related to the Hittites.

Seal of the Hittite king Hattusil over an agreement with the king of Ugarit (northern Syria), whereby the former undertook to return to the latter any persons taking refuge in the territory of the Habiru under Hittite jurisdiction.

THE KHAPIRU AND THE HEBREWS

There are many interesting references in the Mari and Nuzu tablets, and also in early Babylonian and Hittite documents from the beginning of the second millenium B.C.E., to a scattered and "troublesome" people. The Egyptians called them the Apiru, and the Accadians Khapiru. They appeared all over Anatolia, Mesopotamia, Syria, Canaan and northern Egypt. These Khapiru or Habiru are mentioned in texts over a time-span roughly coincident with the appearance of "Hebrews" in Genesis, and have therefore been equated with the first Hebrews from whom those of the Bible finally emerged. They were not an ethnic group, but rather a stratum of the society in which they lived. They wandered about as semi-nomads, "wanderers" or "outsiders" from one area to another, sometimes with their flocks and families and sometimes as skilled craftsmen, smiths, musicians and the like; sometimes they formed themselves into guerilla bands, raiding caravans and outlying communities; or they hired themselves out for specific clients, as mercenaries or as private or Government slaves on public projects when they were not forced to slave labour as captives. Some of them rose to the ranks of Government employees, or even positions of leadership in established nations.

But the Habiru in the whole area may not necessarily refer to the first Hebrews related to Terah and Abraham. They appear also at other places, such as at Hurrian Nuzu. It is probable that the biblical Hebrews belonged to this larger floating class of semi-nomads, and as the patriarchs moved away from Mesopotamia, they were part of the movement of these groups. Many scholars have remarked that *not all Habiru were Hebrews, but the Hebrews may have belonged to the Habiru.* The Bible suggests also that "Hebrew" is a much wider term than the later "Israelite".

It is also interesting that the term Habiru ceased to occur in ancient documents at about the same time that the term Hebrew ceased to be used in the Bible, namely after patriarchal times. Habiru had become absorbed in the various settled territories where they found themselves. The Hebrews came to identify themselves more closely with Canaan, where they settled permanently. Then the name Hebrews gave way to Bnei Yisrael, i.e. Children of Israel. In line with archaeological evidence (according to M. Greenberg), the placing of the Habiru in a wider context is no reason why the patriarchal movement may not have been part of a more inclusive one of the Habiru. The Bible describes Eber as the ancestor of all Hebrews (11:16 ff), namely of Abraham and his descendants Isaac and Jacob.

This background helps in understanding the picture of Abraham's wanderings, as a "sojourner" ("ger" in Hebrew), in the midst of the established people of Canaan, of Gerar and of Egypt. This description of Abraham is more correct than the romantic picture of him as a Beduin sheikh. The latter would have a different social and economic background from that of the early Hebrews.

The city of Hazor in Galilee played a prominent part in the events which took place in the middle of the Canaanite and Hyksos period, from the 18th to the 15th century B.C.E.

THE HYKSOS PERIOD IN PATRIARCHAL TIMES

In the wake of the Amorite invasion and the Hurrian and Hittite surge into the Fertile Crescent, and other political disturbances, came another tidal wave known in history as the Hyksos movement. The Hyksos were a motley horde bent on conquest. Many of them seem to have been Semites, but some probably were Hurrian and Hittite warriors. With these Indo-Europeans the horse entered the Near East and, effectively used for pulling the war-chariot, revolutionized the art of warfare. Aided by this new weapon, the Hyksos invaded Egypt about 1700 B.C.E. and dominated it for a century and a half. It is possible that they ruled not only Egypt but also Palestine and southern Syria. Their capital was Zoan (Avaris) or Tanis in the Delta of northern Egypt. They were finally driven out of Egypt by the Pharaohs of the 18th Dynasty, about 1570 B.C.E., and chased by them into Palestine. Indeed, several Palestinian cities were destroyed during the 16th century, and excavations furnish evidence of the intensity of the Egyptian campaigns. This heralded the "New Kingdom" in Egypt, as well as the "Amarna Age" in Palestine, characterized by the conflicts and troubled relations with the Palestinian and Syrian vassals of Egypt.

Abraham's migration and that of his clan was probably part of the tribal migrations of Amorites between western Mesopotamia and the eastern coast of the Mediterranean. The majority of scholars today place Abraham in the period known as the middle and late middle Bronze Age, roughly between 1750 to 1550 B.C.E. W.F. Albright and De Vaux place him between 1900 and 1700; H. H. Rowley in the 18th or 17th centuries, and C. Gordon as late as the 14th century B.C.E. (Amarna Age). The uncertainty is due in part to the uncertainty of the precise date of Hammurabi, the principal Amorite ruler of Babylon. In any case Hammurabi and Abraham are now considered contemporaries. Furthermore, this dating of Abraham is supported by the view that the Exodus from Egypt occurred in the 13th century B.C.E.

The age was one of great cultural and economic attainment, and the different parts of the Near East were aware of one another, and in frequent military, commercial and diplomatic contact. Abraham and his clan appear therefore in a populated, prosperous and self-assured age in western Asia.

THE TRADITION IN THE LIGHT OF THE EVIDENCE

Biblical scholars during the last century have discussed at great length the historicity of stories concerning Abraham and the patriarchs. Today archaeology demands a more general respect for the historical quality of the patriarchal stories. The historic kernel, in any case, is no more to be doubted than that of the Trojan wars in the Iliad. So whether we read Abraham's narrative as that of an individual, or as a personification of his clan, he represents a major movement and experiences without which it is not possible to understand the subsequent career of the Children of Israel. One of these is the intimate experience conceived in the "Berith" or Covenant between Abraham and God, and the evolution of monotheism which apparently originated in the time of Abraham and the patriarchs. The importance of the biblical concept of Covenant is that it gave rise to concepts and institutions which have become part of subsequent culture.

Archaeological research has uncovered a large number of inscriptions which have an important bearing on the laws of society in the patriarchal age. The material has not necessarily proved the accuracy of the narratives, nor have references to the patriarchs themselves been found, which provide a chronology for the events. But it has furnished a great deal of indirect evidence, which shows that these stories fit into the background of the age; and also evidence confirming customs and concepts which appear in the biblical stories. Professor W. F. Albright maintains that "as a whole the picture of Genesis is historical, and there is no reason to doubt the details and sketches of personality which make the patriarchs come alive with a vividness unknown to a single extra-biblical character in the whole vast literature of the ancient Near East".

THE BIBLICAL TRADITION OF THE WANDERINGS OF ABRAHAM

After narrowing down man's genealogy to the first Hebrews, the biblical narrator introduced Abraham, described as a "chastened" man, and a man of faith, who is called forth by the Lord to lead his clan and settle in a new country. The categoric promise is given that he will become a great people, and found a nation in which all the nations of the earth shall be blessed (12:2–3). This calling of Abraham and the Hebrews appears to foreshadow the thematic biblical view of the general human situation according to which they are called into existence to live as a people responsive to God's will.

Abraham, tradition says, migrated in nomadic fashion to Canaan. God promised that he would possess the land:

"Abram passed through the land to the place at Shechem, to the oak of Moreh. At that time the Canaanites were in the land. Then the Lord appeared to Abram and said, 'To your descendants I will give this land'. So he built there an altar to the Lord, who had appeared to him. Thence he removed to the mountain on the east of Bethel, and pitched his tent, with Bethel on the west and Ai on the east; and there he built an altar to the Lord, and called on the name of the Lord". (12:6–8)

Abraham did not settle in the fortified Canaanite towns. It seems that he entered Canaan from the east of Jordan, and proceeded to central Palestine, for his itinerary southward does not mention such an important large city as Hazor in Galilee. But he had contact with Shechem, an important city in the hills of central Palestine, in particular with the holy "place" of Shechem. This is a holy spot at which stood "the Oak of Moreh" the soothsayer or oracle, a traditional place of worship for the natives. But a more southerly neighbourhood and its holy "place" in Bethel claims attention. The biblical storytellers faithfully preserve the tradition which explains how Abraham built altars in the "places" of both Shechem and Bethel. The patriarch, the story notes, did not enter the Canaanite city of Bethel. He tented between it and Ai (where ruins of an ancient Canaanite sanctuary have been excavated). The narrators relate that the Lord appeared here to Abraham, connecting the "place" of Shechem with the solemn declaration that he will become a great nation. They thus confirm that the wanderer from afar had now reached the destination to which he had been called.

In the view of A. Alt the patriarchs were the founders of originally separate cults in which

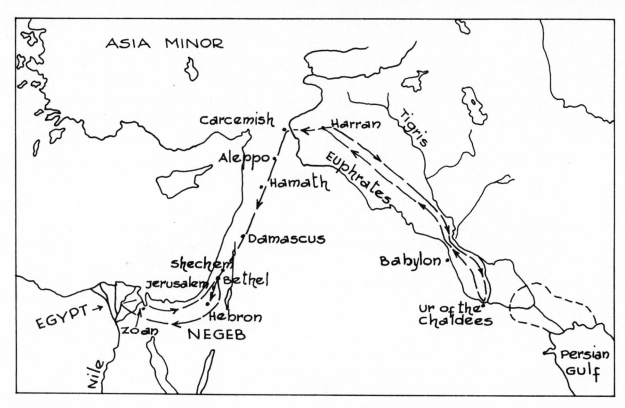

The wanderings of Abraham. "And Abraham journeyed on, still going towards Negeb". (12:9)

House wall of the early Hyksos period, dated about 1700 B.C.E. abuts on the city wall of Bethel, (present-day Beitin), which stood on the mountain road leading from Shechem to Jerusalem, some kilometres north of the latter.

the deity was given distinctive names compounded with the personal name of the founder: Shield of Abraham (15:1); Fear of Isaac (31:42, 53); Strong One of Jacob (49:24). Later these patriarchal deities were fused and equated with Yahweh. This correlates with the theory that Abraham, Isaac and Jacob were the leaders of distinct clans which eventually merged to form the Hebrews. This is based on the assumption that the patriarchs did not represent three generations in direct linear descent. It is known that the ancients often contracted generations, dropping out the unimportant individuals between significant ancestors. Opinions are of course divided on such theories.

The patriarch was also reported in the Negev, the extreme southern district where Beersheba lies. This was very much in the political and economic sphere of Egypt, and the kinglets of Canaan owed allegiance to the pharaohs. "Now there was a famine in the land," which obliged Abraham (and the same thing happened to his descendants, the sons of Jacob) to "sojourn there". He came back to Canaan when conditions were improved. The constant intercourse with Egypt in the Hebrew traditions is remarkably consistent with the extra-biblical evidence from Egypt and Palestine. By and large there is close similarity between the background provided by archaeology and that presupposed in Genesis. The semi-nomadic patriarchs played exactly the same role as local chieftains who lived in the hill country between thinly scattered fortified towns, who moved northward and southward according to the season and covenanted with their neighbours to ensure their safety and well–being.

The story of Abraham is not uniform in its character or pattern. He is mostly described as a lonely wanderer, but sometimes as a chieftain and warrior. An enigmatic episode is connected with a martial stage of Abraham's career as related in Genesis 14. He is defined there as "Abram the Hebrew". The implication has been explained in the previous section (the Habiru and the Hebrews). Abraham is there called a military leader, on the margin of a coalition between city-kings of southern Canaan who rebelled against alleged rulers and invaders from distant Mesopotamia. The allied kings from the north followed the "Kings' highway" east of the Jordan. They crushed the Canaanite coalition and made off with Lot, a blood-brother of Abraham. Abraham, advised of this, together with a band of three hundred and eighteen armed followers held his own in reputable fashion in pursuit of Lot's foreign captors.

AN EARLY INVASION OF PALESTINE

Abraham and his band of "hanikhim" (followers) corresponds almost exactly to the chieftains of the early part of the second millenium, with their "hanaku" or "hnku". We know from cuneiform texts in Mari, Ugarit, Alalah (a state north of Ugarit), and Boghazkoi (the Hittite kingdom), that city-states and tribes were linked by treaties or "covenants".

Although the opponents of Abraham cannot be identified with certainty, the personal names Tudhalia (Tidal in Hebrew), Ariukka (Arioch) and place-names which have been identified, fit well into the contemporary picture of the 18th-17th centuries. One of the Dead Sea Scrolls, now at the Hebrew University, has a passage elaborating on the events, and containing many new geographical names east of the Jordan, around the Dead sea and Canaan proper. This material gives Genesis 14 a new timeliness for the modern reader. Few stories in Genesis have had so much written about them. The antiquity of this story, and the accuracy of the names referred to in it are being constantly corroborated as new background material becomes available.

On his return from the campaign, Abraham met Melchizedek, a Canaanite priest of El Elyon (God Most High):

"And Melchizedek king of Salem brought out bread and wine; he was priest of God Most High.
And he blessed him and said.
'Blessed be Abram by God Most High,
   maker of heaven and earth:
And blessed be God Most High,
   who has delivered your enemies into your hand!'
And Abram gave him a tenth of everything". (14:18-20)

Abraham and subsequent Hebrew tradition identified El Elyon with Yahweh.

THE RELIGIOUS BELIEFS OF THE EARLY HEBREWS

It is hard to tell just what the religion of the Patriarchs was, as recorded in Genesis,

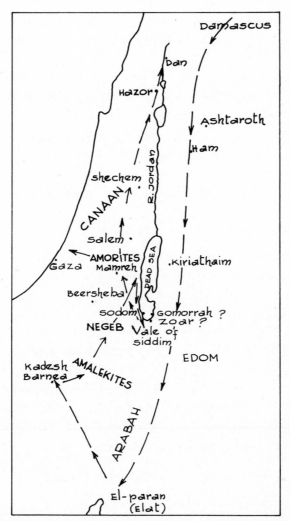

An early invasion of Palestine in the days of Abraham the Hebrew. (Gen. 14)

because by the time the earliest oral traditions were written they were somewhat overlaid with extraneous detail or interpretative remarks which pertained to a later, more monotheistic state of mind. The earlier traditions were revised in the light of concepts found in the later story of the Exodus from Egypt, and the experience of the Sinai Covenant. This was a far more solemn covenant than that of the Patriarchs. This national covenant between God and Israel represented an adaptation of the patriarchal form of covenant.

Many narratives and statements attributed to the patriarchs, when considered in the setting of the culture of the ancient Near East, help us to understand the probable character of the religious beliefs among the early Hebrews, before Moses and the Exodus. It will be remembered that when the clan of Abraham left Mesopotamia, they took with them a religion which in many respects was like the nature religion of the ancient Near East. Much later than the Exodus, in the time of Joshua, the Hebrews were reminded that their fathers had served "other gods" when they dwelt in Mesopotamia (Josh: 24, 2), and Joshua exhorted them to put away the remnant of their ancestral polytheism.

The name of the patriarchal deity of the early Hebrews is referred to in Genesis as "El-Shaddai" (i.e. "Almighty": 17: 1); it was apparently a mountain deity, or a storm deity, according to an etymology based on the Accadian "Shadu-el", mountain.

According to Alt's hypothesis this early religion had a strong resemblance to the El religion of their neighbours, the Canaanites, as illustrated in Abraham's encounter with Melchizedek (14:18–19). El was the head of both the "Amorite" and the later Canaanite pantheon of deities. Examining the patriarchal narratives for traces of the tribal religion, clues were found in the distinctive epithets applied to the "God of the fathers", such as "God of Abraham", the "Fear of Isaac" and the "Mighty One of Jacob". There is a large number of illustrations from antiquity of this type of family deity whom a patriarch would choose as his personal god and with whom he would enter into a special covenantal relationship.

Knowing how little the patriarchal clans differed ethnically from their neighbours, there does not seem to be any valid reason why they should have differed religiously from them in any radical way. The only clue that there was a certain uniqueness is in the Moses narratives, which place emphasis on the fact that the God of Moses is also the God of the fathers. A very revealing source, considered by many the oldest, identifies the deity by the name also known in the patriarchal age:

"'I appeared to Abraham, to Isaac, and to Jacob, as El-Shaddai, but by my name "the Lord" (Yahweh) I did not make myself known to them'". (Exodus 6:3)

In addition, the name of the divinity appears under other titles in these stories: "EL ELYON (El Most High; Gen. 14: 18); "EL OLAM" (El of Eternity, 21: 33); EL BETHEL (35: 7); EL-ROI (16: 13-14). Scholars believe that these names were associated with specific holy places and allude to a pre-Mosaic stage of religion of Canaan. While the picture is still far from clear, newer biblical and archaeological knowledge indicates that the patriarchs practised a religion which, while not monotheistic in our sense of the term, was not polytheistic either, even though it resembled in its ritual many of the practices of their neighbours.

It was the tribal practice to enter into a personal relationship, namely a covenant or agreement, with the deity, so that God would devote himself to the covenanters, in return for their exclusive agreement with him. This was not an agreement between equals, but as between a great ruler and those who promise to be his loyal subjects. So the divine protector was known to Abraham as "Your Shield". (15:1), whereby Abraham was to recognize and worship no other deity and God was to protect and seek the welfare of Abraham and his family exclusively. The deity took special care of the clan, and successive generations would choose and enter into the relationship anew. This form of covenant between a suzerain and his subjects, or between a god and a special tribe or family is attested to repeatedly in Near Eastern literature of the 2nd millenium B.C.E., including the Homeric Iliad. The divine protector was close at hand whenever needed, and was freely questioned, gave answers, and promises, and granted demands. This closeness of man to God was a social phenomenon which will be illustrated shortly in the dialogue between God and Abraham over the fate of Sodom (see Gen. 18). It is important to notice that in Israel's tradition of the divine covenant, the role of the patriarchs was two-fold: (a) They stood in a covenantal relation to the Lord (Yahweh); (b) They lived by faith on the one hand and experienced the faithfulness of God on the other. One point of the patriarchal narratives and their arrangement is to teach what the Bible meant by faith; an illustration is the description of Abraham as the "father of faith". This will make clear a most significant statement explaining Abraham's attitude:

"And he believed the Lord; and he reckoned it to him as righteousness". (15:6)

This implies that God required just that man should choose Him to be his God. Biblical Hebrew, be it noted, has no word for "religion". The true religion is designated as the "fear of God" (or Yahweh).

"But Abram said, 'O Lord God, what wilt thou give me, for I continue childless, and the heir of my house is Eliezer of Damascus?' And Abram said, 'Behold, thou hast given me no offspring; and a slave born in my house will be my heir'. And behold, the word of the Lord came to him, 'This man shall not be your heir; your own son shall be your heir'". (15:2–4) Another version of verse 4: "'he that shall come forth out of thy bowels and shall be thine heir'".

In the language of verse 4, the biological process of birth is graphically outlined as a child coming forth from the father's as well as the mother's "bowels." So God promised Abraham progeny. A close parallel of this language of divine promise—which is not peculiar to the Hebrews alone—is found in Keret's legend, one of the religious epics from the end of the patriarchal period, recorded in the Ugarit clay tablets in a language closely resembling archaic Hebrew. King Keret had lost all his brothers and remained childless.

"At his departure the family would disappear
And someone from his surroundings would 'inherit' ".

The legend of Keret, king of Sidon in Phoenicia.

The god El appeared to him in a dream and promised him a bride, Hurria, from a distant land Udum, who would give him new progeny.

> "El hath granted me her in a dream,
> The father of man – in a vision
> That a scion be born to Keret,
> A child to the servant of El".

This progeny was granted to King Keret by divine annunciation and blessing. The princess became his wife and the prophecy was fulfilled. Tradition seems to have had it that the biological process, familiarly referred to above, had to be supplemented with religious rites, and direct divine revelation to the prospective father as to the necessary sacrifice.

THE COVENANT OF CIRCUMCISION

Hebrew narrators were wont to link ancient customs into stories attributed to the patriarchs. We are familiar with the chroniclers' device of tracing to before Moses' time the "perpetual" laws of God. They placed circumcision into the context of patriarchal days. Thus Abraham was circumcised at the age of 99, Abraham's eldest son, Ishmael, at the age of 13. Circumcision is known to Jews as "Abraham's covenant" because of the tradition attributed to Abraham's time, of a far more solemn and binding covenant:

" 'This is my covenant, which you shall keep, between me and you and your descendants after you: Every male among you shall be circumcised. You shall be circumcised in the flesh of your foreskins, and it shall be a sign of the covenant between me and you. He that is eight days old among you shall be circumcised; every male throughout your generations, whether born in your house, or bought with your money from any foreigner who is not of your offspring, both he that is born in your house, and he that is bought with your money, shall be circumcised. So shall my covenant be in your flesh an everlasting covenant. Any uncircumcised male who is not circumcised in the flesh of his foreskin shall be cut off from his people; he has broken my covenant' ". (17:10–14)

This then was another great covenant, symbolized and hallowed by circumcision. It stipulated that He agreed to be the God of Abraham and his descendants, and Abraham and his descendants agreed to be God's own people. Whereupon the land of Canaan would be forever associated with this people and this God. In token of this, the family of Abraham would for all time practise the rite of circumcision. As further commemoration of this covenant, Abraham's name, hitherto spelt Abram, was changed to Abraham, and that of his wife Sarai, to Sarah. Their meaning is not quite certain, nor the reason why they were spelt consistently by the shorter name until Gen. 17.

Later ordinances imposed the act of circumcision upon Jewish children at the age of 8 days (since it was related that their ancestor Isaac was circumcised when a baby). Before Moses, circumcision was certainly practised at a later age, as in the case of Ishmael. Since Abraham is recognized as the father of Arabs (Ishmaelites), they also practise circumcision at about this age in great festivity. It is in any case an ancient rite known to the Egyptians and many peoples of the ancient Near East, with the exception of the Philistines, the traditional "Uncircumcised", an appellation of opprobrium to the Jews. The Philistines did not circumcise because they were of Aegean origin.

The later biblical tradition, which injected a deeper sense of religion into the writings of the Bible, plainly states that any male who has not kept "the covenant of the flesh" is to be excluded from the Israelite community. This means in Jewish tradition that by failing to be circumcised, a man breaks the covenant and has no claim upon the divine blessing.

PATRIARCHAL BELIEFS AND THEIR BACKGROUND

It is evident by now that the sequence of chapters in many parts of the Bible does not always follow events chronologically. We can distinguish such a pattern in Abraham's epic. The epic of his lifetime embraces a variety of events and institutions, and certain phases of the story do not fit into the others. But this is unimportant to the modern reader; what matters is the background of living conditions in which the traditions are placed.

A remarkable link between the patriarchal narratives and the social milieu of the middle Bronze Age has been provided by the discovery of close parallels between some of the customs of the patriarchs and those of the Hurrian city of Nuzu of the 15th century B.C.E., near the region of Harran from which Abraham's ancestors had come.

The evidence of Nuzu customs makes it quite clear that childless folk frequently adopted a freeborn person or a slave to look after them during their lifetime as a son would; and when they grew old, to provide for their burial and its attendant rites and inherit their estates. This is how Eliezer came to be called "heir of my house" i.e. the heir presumptive (see above 15:2–4). But the divine word intervenes: "This man shall not be your heir". How could it set aside the right of a legally adopted heir as long as he had fulfilled his filial duties? The Nuzu tablets give the answer: it provides that if the adopter shall afterwards beget a son of his own, the adopted son must yield to him the place of chief heir. There is, therefore, no longer any doubt in interpreting this passage.

The parallel with Nuzu customs is accentuated even further in the marriage laws of Abraham's household: Inasmuch as Sarah bore him no children for ten years after he had been in Canaan, she gave him Hagar, her Egyptian handmaiden, as a concubine for the express purpose of producing an heir:

"...and Sarai said to Abram, 'Behold now, the Lord has prevented me from bearing children; go in to my maid; it may be that I shall obtain children by her'. And Abram hearkened to the voice of Sarai". (16:2)

This is not an isolated instance of unusual feminine generosity. The marriage regulations of the time stipulate that if a wife is barren, she must furnish her husband with a slave wife. One Nuzu contract states that:

"If Giliminu (the bride) does not bear children, she shall take a Lullu woman (a slave) as a wife for Shennima" (the bridegroom).

The story goes on with the difficulties raised by Sarah and by the annunciation that Hagar is to bear a child, Ishmael:

"And the angel of the Lord said to her, 'Behold, you are with child, and shall bear a son; you shall call his name Ishmael; because the Lord has given heed to your affliction. He shall be a wild ass of a man, his hand against every man and every man's hand against him; and he shall dwell over against all his kinsmen'". (16:11–12)

Lest the 12th verse be misunderstood, it should be explained that the term "a wild ass of a man", is not an insulting one. The wild ass, noble, free and untrammeled, was then

Hunting the wild ass, as depicted by a mural painting of Doura-Europos; 2nd century A.D.

the aristocrat of animal life in the desert, and it was the choicest beast of the hunt. This description befits the proud and free Ishmaelite huntsmen.

But real difficulties arose when Sarah bore Isaac. Fearing that the primogeniture of Ishmael would dissociate him from the patriarchal descent, she demanded that Hagar, the Egyptian slave, be sent away with her child. The prescribed practices of the time protected the rights of the handmaid. Abraham would have been breaking a social custom if he drove Hagar out. But Sarah was adamant that Ishmael should not inherit along with Isaac. So Hagar was driven out and wandered about "in the wilderness of Beersheba" until she was exhausted. The well of water, which she discovered when the visitation of God caused her to open her eyes, saved her life and that of Ishmael.

The Nuzu clay tablets have made many contributions to our understanding of the legal customs and practices of the patriarchal period, thanks to the research of Prof. E. A. Speiser and C. H. Gordon. We shall deal with others later. The analogies are so numerous and striking that it is becoming generally agreed that the patriarchal narratives in Genesis portray a genuine social picture; and it appears that some of the reputedly legendary features are correct historically.

UNDER THE OAKS OF MAMRE

The oak of Mamre, high up in the hills near Hebron, was a sacred place, where Abraham made his encampment and met with the neighbouring Amorite clans. The site, though not its name, has associations with the very origins of Israel and it attained great significance for the Israelites in later times. In the saga of Mamre is an important—and independent—local tradition which explains its holiness.

The Lord's promise that Abraham would have a great progeny and that he, through his family, would inherit the land, was sealed with the Covenant. Yet it was incredible that the promise could be fulfilled, for Sarah, the chief wife, was barren, and the descendants of Hagar by Abraham were destined to be the sons of Ishmael, not Israel. The sequel is the tale of the three mysterious visitors who visited Abraham at Mamre to confirm the promise:

> "And the Lord appeared to him by the oaks of Mamre, as he sat at the door of his tent in the heat of the day. He lifted up his eyes and looked, and behold, three men stood in front of him. When he saw them, he ran from the tent door to meet them, and bowed himself to the earth, and said, 'My lord, if I have found favor in your sight, do not pass by your servant. Let a little water be brought, and wash your feet, and rest yourselves under the tree, while I fetch a morsel of bread, that you may refresh yourselves, and after that you may pass on -- since you have come to your servant'. So they said, 'Do as you have said' ". (18:1–5)

There the Lord, in the guise of an angel, appeared to him and announced that a son would be born to his wife. Sarah, who was eavesdropping on the conversation, is reported to have laughed heartily to herself, knowing that she had reached the age when this was physically impossible. Certainly this intimacy of men with gods and the reaction of God to Sarah's and Abraham's laughter, would be unthinkable among later generations who had a different attitude towards divine manifestations. But comparative evidence from Canaanite literature tends to justify and explain the meaning of this ancient story in its true context.

The direct mingling of men and gods in this story compares with Ugarit epic stories about Danael and his wife Dnto. An ancient king, Danael, had no son. He propitiated the gods with sacrifices. The god Baal responded by bearing Danael's petition to his father, the god El. Baal described the spiritual and material benefits which would come to Danael from a son; He prayed:

> "Will thou not bless him, O Bull El, my father,
> Beautify him, O Creator of Creatures,
> So there shall be a son in his house,
> A scion in the midst of his palace".

God was not conceived as impersonal in patriarchal times, and if we are to understand properly the biblical texts, we must develop a feeling for a social phenomenon of the times, the closeness of men to gods, and of the Hebrews to God. In our society a man who claims ·to have divine visitors is regarded as queer. That is why it is not easy for every modern reader, who is not familiar with the ancient background and literatures, to understand that aspect of Hebrew society. For the ancient Hebrews, the human and divine intermingled freely. The early direct relationship between men and gods is common to all the epics: Ugarit, Mesopotamian, Greek and proto-patriarchal. This simple personal contact between men and God was gradually eliminated.

THE DESTRUCTION OF SODOM AND GOMORRAH

A charming tradition illustrates how Abraham, on intimate terms with the Lord, dared to intercede with him, in the famous dialogue over the problem of the wicked people of Sodom and its few, hypothetical righteous men:

"Then he said, 'Oh let not the Lord be angry, and I will speak again but this once. Suppose ten are found there'. He answered, 'For the sake of ten I will not destroy it'. And the Lord went his way, when he had finished speaking to Abraham; and Abraham returned to his place". (18:32–33)

The wicked behaviour of Sodom and Gomorrah is metaphorically described as an "outcry"; "for we are about to destroy this place, because the outcry against its people has become great before the Lord, and the Lord has sent us to destroy it". (19:13). We find an echo here of a similar expression in the second Babylonian version of the Flood (The Atrahasis Epic) describing their "hubbum" or clamour, and "immasu" or violence, which disturbed Enlil's repose. In the present legend the noise and clamour of Sodom and Gomorrah having reached an intolerable pitch, God was impelled to destroy them:

"Then the Lord rained on Sodom and Gomorrah brimstone and fire from the Lord out of Heaven; and he over-threw those cities, and all the valley, and all the inhabitants of the cities, and what grew on the ground. But Lot's wife behind him looked back, and she became a pillar of salt. And Abraham went early in the morning to the place where he had stood before the Lord; and he looked down towards Sodom and Gomorrah and toward all the land of the valley, and beheld, and lo, the smoke of the land went up like the smoke of a furnace". (19:24–28)

Lot and his family were given a chance to escape, but through their folly the sons-in-law perished. Lot's wife turned into a pillar of salt because she lingered and looked back. Popular tradition connects her folly with, and likens her to, one of the many pillars of salt standing starkly against the skyline atop Mount Sodom. This is a great salt mass of a hill, some eight kilometers long, stretching along the southwestern end of the Dead Sea, as seen in the illustration below. (See also map of the invading kings to identify the names of the Cities of the Plain).

The narrative retails such a catastrophe remarkably briefly. The agency of destruction, "brimstone and fire from the Lord out of heaven" suggests volcanic phenomena accompanying an earthquake. But geologists tell us that the most recent volcanic activity in that area took place ages before Abraham's or Lot's time. Those who favour the theory of cataclysm to explain the story believe that the brief description sounds as though there was a tremendous earthquake at the southern end of the Dead Sea, within the deepest rift valley in the world, which lies 1290 feet below sea-level. It is suggested that the free sulphur, asphalt and salts in this area may have been mingled by an earthquake and resulted in explosion and fire. The whole story, some think, may be mythical; or it may refer to some very remote prehistoric event.

Earthquakes or some other destructive agents seem to have wiped out a civilization that had existed near the Dead Sea and east of the Jordan from the Stone Age (4000 B.C.E.) down to the Bronze Age (around the 20th century). This is the area which included the "five Cities of the Plain", or "the circle of the vale of Siddim". They were Sodom, Gomorrah, Admah, Zeboiim and Zoar. It is thought, by those who favour the geological theory, that these cities were situated south and east of the Dead Sea, most of them being now covered by the water.

We know also that nomadic peoples settled down in villages and towns before the 20th century B.C.E., just at the time when the dark age was settling over Palestine, due, apparently to Amorite invasions, and that these sites were abandoned about the 20th century B.C.E., as were the other towns and villages in southern Transjordan for some mysterious reason, the people returning to nomadic pursuits.

What follows the story bears no connection on the subject, but for the relation that Lot and his two daughters were the only survivors of that family. To forestall its disappearance the two daughters of Lot got their father drunk on successive nights and he unwittingly impregnated them with his seed. The elder of the two gave birth to the ancestor of Moab, and the younger to the ancestor of Ammon. The story may be from a cycle told in Moab of the destruction of the "Cities of the Plain" after which the surviving women took heroic action to preserve their tribe.

IN THE NEGEV

Abraham's sojourn in the Negev and the fact that he dug wells indicates that he possessed grazing and perhaps territorial rights. Disputes about wells would be inevitable in a land where water was so precious and nomads needed it for their flocks. We learn that Abimelech, King of Gerar, visited Abraham in the locality. He was anxious to conclude a treaty of mutual protection that would safeguard his descendants from Hebrew encroachments:

Mt. Sodom seen from the Dead Sea. Pillars of salt and gypsum are left standing on top after rains eroded the surrounding minerals.

"'. . . now therefore swear to me here by God that you will not deal falsely with me or with my offspring or with my posterity, but as I have dealt loyally with you, you will deal with me and with the land where you have sojourned'. and Abraham said, 'I will swear'. When Abraham complained to Abimelech about a well of water which Abimelech's servants had seized, Abimelech said, 'I do not know who has done this thing; you did not tell me, and I have not heard of it until today'. So Abraham took sheep and oxen and gave them to Abimelech, and the two men made a covenant". (21: 23–27)

The storyteller accompanies the covenant of Beersheba with a typical example of popular etymology, explaining "wherefore he called the place Beersheba; because there both of them swore an oath". According to this it derived the name because Beersheba in Hebrew may mean "well", or "b'eer", of the oath, "sheba". An alternative explanation given is: "well of the seven" (sheba is also seven in Hebrew), at which the seven lambs of the sacrificial covenant ceremony may hint. Both explanations seem to be incorrect, as the town and its name, in the opinion of scholars, already existed long before Abraham's sojourn there. In fact the original Beersheba is located a few miles east of the present town, on a hill. This hill, Tel-Sheba, has preserved the ancient name of the patriarch's town. It has not yet been excavated and may hold interesting facts in store. The name "sheba" may be derived from an old aboriginal clan.

The social and economic status of Abraham and the first Hebrews in Canaan and in other neighbouring lands where they wandered was that of "gerim" (sojourners). They were neither sedentary nor fully nomadic. They had perforce to normalize and protect their position among such tribes and city-kings of Canaan.

The dealings of Abraham and Isaac with Gerar afford several points of interest. According to an early account, king Abimelech had Sarah made lady of his harem. The story is much like that of her experience with Pharaoh in Gen. 12:10 ff. When Abraham was driven by famine to Egypt to save his life, he ingratiated himself with the king by an act of deceit involving his wife Sarah.

When Abraham had stated that Sarah was his sister, and Abimelech had discovered that she was in reality his wife, Abraham justified himself by asserting that she was in fact his wife but also his half-sister: the daughter of his father, Terah, but not of his mother. Regardless of the veracity of Abraham's claim, the incident demonstrates that in patriarchal society it was permissible for children of the same father though of different mothers to

Amorite worshipper praying to the divinity in a gesture of humility. Grains of incense are placed in the little container at his feet. A statuette from Larsa of the early 2nd millenium.

The bull was the symbol of the god of fertility, and this example of Sumerian art from Lagash conveys the feeling of life and power. The tiara that decorated the heads of divinities derived from a similar theme. The bull theme may be found in all civilizations of the eastern Mediterranean, and more particularly in Crete.

marry. The storyteller did not recast the ancient account handed down by patriarchal tradition, to make it conform to later mosaic legislation. Moreover the veracity of the background is upheld by the fact that people seeking favours would normally offer women as presents to local potentates. (See Illustration Chap. IV).

We must be on our guard against deducing actual "historical" information from such narratives as the parallel Abraham and Sarah stories. "Legend", points out H. Gunkel, "weaves a poetic web around historical memories and hides the circumstances of time and place". As in all ancient folk-literature, the story-cycles of Abraham, Jacob or Joseph consisted of kernels of historical fact in enveloping layers of legend.

Inconsistencies we find in the stories may be best explained by admitting the existence of different oral traditions which were compressed by the chroniclers into one without adjustment of details. The inconsistencies did not bother the compiler; and this is a phenomenon which occurs throughout the Pentateuch and in later historical books as well. The medieval Arab chroniclers have the same literary habits. They repeat traditions and feel no need to harmonize them.

The king of Gerar in the Abimelech story is called a Philistine. This designation is generally regarded as anachronistic because the name Philistine was applied to a Western people (Peoples of the Sea) which had migrated from Crete and the Aegean coastlands and isles around 1200 B.C.E., and settled in the coastal regions of southern Palestine. C. H. Gordon and I. Grinz consider that these "early" Philistines of Gerar came from a previous migration of sea people from the Aegean and Minoan sphere, including Crete, which is called Caphtor in the Bible and Ugarit tablets, and Caphtorian is the Canaanite name for Minoan. Their original home was that other great cultural centre of antiquity, the Aegean, which flourished throughout the 2nd millenium B.C.E., and is considered a major cradle of East Mediterranean, Near Eastern and European civilization. It has a close connection with the Hittite civilization, which stems also from an Indo-European migration into this sphere. This civilization spread by trade, navigation and migration to Asia Minor, North Canaan (Ugarit, etc.), South Canaan (Gerar). The early Philistines who came into contact with the early Hebrews, and the Mycenaeans of proto-historic Greece, to whom the most prominent Homeric heroes belonged, were different sections of this Minoan (Caphtorian) world. By the time of the Amarna Age, or late patriarchal age, these immigrants formed an important segment of the coastal dwellers of Canaan. Vestiges of Aegeo-Minoan art, pottery and tools abound in archaeological finds of this period. The art is remarkable for its vivacity and it injected a notable degree of liveliness into the art of the Near East, including Egypt. The most important role of Caphtor was its impact on both the classic Greeks of a later period and the early Canaanites, so that the earliest Greek, Canaanite (Ugarit) and Hebrew literatures have a common denominator in the Minoan or Caphtorian factor. We shall see that the early histories of the Hebrew and pre-Hellenic settlements, and migrations on the shores of the Eastern Mediterranean, were originally interrelated in certain ways and that the classic traditions of Greece and the treasures of the Near East will illumine each other. C. H. Gordon maintains that "the epic traditions of Israel starting with the patriarchal narratives are set in Palestine after the penetrations of the Indo-European Philistines from the west and the Indo-European Hittites from the north. When the Bible portrays Abraham as dealing with Hittites and Philistines, we have a correct tradition insofar as Hebrew history dawned in a partially Indo-Europeanized Palestine. This is reflected in Hebraic literature and institutions from the start".

This early Caphtorian migration was one of a long series that had established various Caphtorian folk on the shores of Canaan long before 1500 B.C.E. They had become Canaanitized, and apparently spoke the same language as Abraham and Isaac. They generally behaved peacefully, unlike the warlike Philistines of a later day, who fought and molested the Israelites. They were recognized in Canaan as the masters of arts and crafts, including metallurgy.

THE "SACRIFICE" OF ISAAC

Of all the stories that come down from ancient ritual that of the sacrifice of Isaac is one which has stirred humanity most. This is due more to the terrific test of faith to which Abraham

Men of Keftiu, from the Aegean Islands.

was put than to the sudden intervention before the drama turned into tragedy. That Isaac was not actually sacrificed is the moral of the story, which rejects child-sacrifice:

> "He said, 'Take your son, your only son Isaac, whom you love, and go to the land of Moriah, and offer him there as a burnt offering upon one of the mountains which I shall tell you'. So Abraham rose early in the morning, saddled his ass, and took two of his young men with him, and his son Isaac; and he cut the wood for the burnt offering, and arose and went to the place of which God had told him. On the third day Abraham lifted up his eyes and saw the place afar off". (22:2-4)

It is possible that the original form of Gen. 22 may have been a shrine recital to account for Israelite departure from Canaanite practice, although it appears rather as a test of Abraham's devoutness. The earliest ritual law (Exodus 34:20) provides that where the sacrifice of the firstborn would be "appropriate", he is redeemed and an animal substitute is found. (A symbolic remnant still lingering on is the Jewish religious custom, whereby the parents of the firstborn redeem him back from God: in Hebrew: "Pidyon-haben").

THE CAVE OF MACHPELAH - THE PATRIARCHAL BURIAL CHAMBER

According to the biblical tradition Sarah died at the age of 127 when Abraham in his declining years was living in Mamre. Burial customarily took place on the day of death, but Abraham had no land of his own there, not being a native. Therefore he had to make arrangements quickly, and to buy a parcel of land in the vicinity of Mamre. The lot, which included the Cave of Machpelah, belonged to a Hittite named Ephron. Abraham asked the leading citizens of the town whom he found assembled in the gateway—as was the custom—to sell him a certain cave at the edge of a field as a tomb.

Abraham's predicament was recognized, and human consideration for it was expressed in high courtesy. However, the negotiation was complicated by Ephron's insistence on selling him the whole field:

> " 'No, my lord, hear me; I give you the field, and I give you the cave that is in it; in the presence of the sons of my people I give it to you; bury your dead'. Then Abraham bowed down before the people of the land. And he said to Ephron in the hearing of the people of the land, 'But if you will, hear me; I will give you the price of the field; accept it from me, that I may bury my dead there'. Ephron answered Abraham, 'My lord, listen to me; a piece of land worth four hundred shekels of silver, what is that between you and me? Bury your dead'. Abraham agreed with Ephron, and Abraham weighed out for Ephron the silver which he had named in the hearing of the Hittites, four hundred shekels of silver, according to the weights current among the merchants". (23:11–16)

The 400 shekels of silver paid are equivalent to 4650 grams of silver at the rate then "current" with the merchants; a considerable sum at the time.

Ephron was not merely a shrewd manoeuverer as thought before. It seems that he was relying on his own Hittite code of laws. These specified that if a buyer purchased all

A tradition such as the sacrifice of Isaac was pre-Israelite and had a different meaning in its original context. The theme of the presentation of a child hostage and ram occurs, for instance, on this painting on an Egyptian tomb of the 16th century B.C.E.

Two small statues in the British Museum, dating from c. 2500 B.C.E., depicting a goat standing upright beside a thicket. These were found in the Great Death Pit at Ur, where at the king's burial, his family and household were buried alive. It has been customary to authenticate Isaac's story by calling these objects erroneously "the ram caught in a thicket".

of the seller's property, the latter was also free of feudal levies which he had to bear as long as he held on to any part of the land. But Abraham was trying to buy only a corner of the field, to side-step such obligations. Ephron refused to divide his property, and Abraham was forced to become responsible for the entire estate. The concluding words recording the sale read almost like a legal deed seeking to leave no loopholes. Consistent with Hittite and with traditional Palestinian Arab real-estate deals, even the exact number of trees is listed.

In the cave thus obtained Abraham buried Sarah. Later he himself was laid to rest there. In time the cave situated "over against" or near Mamre became the patriarchal burial chamber. The story was repeated from generation to generation and written in such detail in order to prove that Israel's ancestor bought the burial place of the patriarchs from the earlier population, the Hittites; and that his descendants, therefore, had a title to it, and it could not be taken away should the land come under foreign domination. Naturally the

Rings or bracelets, after the Egyptian manner, in gold and silver, which preceded coinage. They were cut in convenient forms and weights, so that by the use of balances satisfactory exchange could be effected. One silver shekel weighed about 12 grams and was worth about two-thirds of a dollar.

plot where all the patriarchs were thought to be buried was immensely important to the Jews. It was again sanctified as a shrine by King Herod and changed into a church in the days of the Crusades, and into a mosque by the Arabs in the 12th century A.D. This cave was eventually sealed by the Moslems in the Middle Ages; they built an enclosure and a mosque over and around it. They worship Abraham as a common patriarch and maintain independent traditions about him whom they call "the friend" (El-Khalil in Arabic). Since the days of the Crusades very few non-Moslems have come close to the alleged vault where according to Jewish, Christian and Moslem tradition, the remains of the Patriarchs were

Abraham's transactions with Abimelech (Gen. 20 and 21) mingled barter (the exchange of different commodities) with the exchange of silver. Egyptian scenes depicting barter in the 3rd millenium B.C.E.

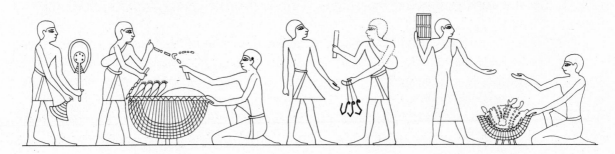

buried under the present buildings. It is shown to visitors on the rarest occasions, such as the visit of the Prince of Wales (Edward VII) and that of Dean Stanley in 1862.

ISAAC IS FARMING

Beside the story of Isaac's marriage to Rebekah, whom Abraham had fetched from his ancestral homeland — Aram-Naharaim — little more is said about Isaac. He seems to be little more than a replica of his father, particularly as a chieftain and a man of considerable wealth in the Negev, around Beersheba and Gerar. The most important thing about him is his position as an heir, and his story is interwoven with that of Abraham. The many promises Abraham received are related directly or indirectly to Isaac and his seed.

A famine sent Isaac to the fertile land of Gerar, near the present coast of Gaza. He is described as living in the city of Gerar itself. He tried his hand successfully at a season of farming and his yield was "a hundredfold", a statement worth recording because nomads are poor farmers as a rule. Isaac's experiment is an interesting example of a nomad beginning to settle down to semi-nomadism. A recurring pattern in the Near East is that nomads are attracted to sown acres, where they plant their crops, thus supplementing the living they get from their flocks. So they become agriculturists; they turn into villagers, usually still grazing their flocks, for that is a noble tradition, in keeping with their origin. Isaac's career apparently marks this transition to that intermediate stage.

A tomb in Jericho, from about the 17th century B.C.E. This is an example of family burial caves made familiar through excavations. This tomb shows the remains of a wooden table (left), bier (right), bowl, baskets and pottery. The dead were buried with objects used by them in life and with pottery vessels containing food for use by their shades.

In the patriarchal narrative, Shechem is seen as the focal point of the nomadic movements in the area. It was the foremost city of central Palestine in the 17th and 16th centuries B.C.E. and had control of the highways converging on the pass under its walls. A Northwest and East Gate, both flanked by towers and guard-rooms, were part of the double wall system of the city's defences.

Above: The East Gate of Shechem in the days of the Patriarchs, as shown by recent excavations.

Small Canaanite earthenware pitcher in natural size, from the time of the Patriarchs (15th century).

Shechem as Abraham and Jacob may have seen it. The ancient city lay at the opening of the valley between Mount Gerizim (left) and Mount Ebal (right). Within the valley proper is present-day Nablus.

CHAPTER IV

THE SAGA OF JACOB

To the biblical storyteller Jacob represents Israel, Esau is Edom and Laban, Harran. Their lives are related as personalized histories, although not every element in their stories can be explained on this basis. Sometimes the personal history is in the foreground, sometimes the tribal or national theme. Jacob's story-cycle covers too many episodes, spread wide geographically and chronologically, to fit into one single tradition and pattern. In fact the substratum of national history, rich with Near Eastern lore, is mirrored in two main phases of Jacob's life: first, his strife with Esau who is Edom; secondly, the cycle of stories of his career in distant Harran and their aftermath. Let us examine them first from the point of view of the biblical story.

First, how is the basic idea dealt with: that Esau (Edom), was outstripped by Jacob (Israel), though as the elder he should have had the more glorious history?

Rebekah, like Sarah, was barren, and would not have presented Isaac with sons but for the Lord's intervention, thus renewing the ancient promise of descendants. But a new complication arose: Rebekah conceived twins, Esau and Jacob. Esau came into the world first, and therefore had the right to be the heir. Jacob came at his heels: (in Hebrew eqeb: heel); hence the popular explanation of his name. But a name like Ya'aqub-ilu or Yaakob-il is found in Mesopotamia from the 18th century, and Ya'kob-har occurs among names of

Hyksos rulers around 1600 B.C.E. Jacob's name is taken to be an eponym of a distinct clan.

Already in their mother's womb, Jacob and Esau were struggling together as the kin nations, Edom and Israel, did in real life. Esau had won the first round. It is said that Esau was "admoni", ruddy, at birth. This story was prompted by a purpose, namely his connection with the nation of Edom. To accent the symbolism, men in Cretan or Egyptian art were coloured reddish brown. (Yellow was used for women.) In the Ugarit epic of the hero Keret, he is bidden by El to redden himself to become ceremonially fit. Such must have been the colour the males assumed for formal occasions or heroic purposes, for Esau was a skilled hunter and a man of the open spaces. The custom of colouring was widespread geographically, as we learn from the law of other tribes, ancient and otherwise.

One tradition contends, therefore, that God willed it that Jacob should supplant his twin brother when they were born; but other explanations are offered why Edom did not attain the position of firstborn and heir. Jacob was craftier than Esau and shrewdly tricked his twin brother. Esau sold him his birthright and this made it final in a strict sense and in consonance with the usage of the times:

> "Once when Jacob was boiling pottage, Esau came in from the field and he was famished. And Esau said to Jacob, 'Let me eat some of that red pottage, for I am famished'. (Therefore his name was called Edom). Jacob said, 'First sell me your birthright'. Esau said, 'I am about to die; of what use is a birthright to me?' Jacob said, 'Swear to me first'. So he swore to him, and sold his birthright to Jacob. Then Jacob gave Esau bread and pottage of lentils, and he ate and drank, and rose and went his way. Thus Esau despised his birthright". (25:29–34)

It is significant, however, that the compact between the two names Edom and "adom" (red) springs from real life experience of the time.

The purchase of title to the position of firstborn is not an incident without parallel. Patrimony or inheritance prospects in the Nuzu clay tablets were negotiated between brothers. A man in Nuzu in need of food sold his inheritance portion of an orchard to his brother in exchange for three sheep. This is comparable to some extent to the way the hungry Esau sold his birthright to Jacob for a mess of lentils: it was an uneven bargain in both cases.

AN ORAL BLESSING OF ISAAC

Furthermore Jacob tricked his twin brother out of their father's blessing. Before Isaac died it was his wish to confer a blessing, or death-bed will, on his favourite elder son Esau. He sent him out to hunt for game and prepare him savoury food. Through deception and the complicity of his mother, Jacob presented himself instead, pretending to be Esau:

> "So Jacob went near to Isaac his father, who felt him, and said, 'The voice is Jacob's voice, but the hands are the hands of Esau'. And he did not recognize him because his hands were hairy like his brother Esau's hands; so he blessed him. He said 'Are you really my son Esau?' He answered 'I am'. Then he said 'Bring it to me, that I may eat of my son's game and bless you'. So he brought it to him, and he ate; and he brought him wine, and he drank. Then his father Isaac said to him, 'Come near and kiss me, my son'. So he came near and kissed him; and he smelled the smell of his garments, and blessed him, and said,
> 'See, the smell of my son is as the smell of a field which the Lord has blessed!
> May God give you of the dew of heaven,
> and of the fatness of the earth,
> and plenty of grain and wine.
> Let peoples serve you, and nations bow down to you.

Be lord over your brothers,
and may your mother's sons bow down to you.
Cursed be everyone who curses you,
and blessed be everyone who blesses you!' ". (27:22–29)

Ancient belief held that words spoken in blessing, or in curse on solemn occasions, were efficacious and had the power, as though by magic, to produce the intended result. The blessing of the father was binding, and when Isaac discovered the deceit he held his blessing to be effective, even though it had been granted under false pretences:

"Then Isaac trembled violently, and said: 'Who was it then that hunted game and brought it to me, and I ate it all before you came, and I have blessed him? — yes, and he shall be blessed' ". (27:33)

Esau's bitterness burst out like a flame:

"Esau said, 'Is he not rightly named Jacob? For he has supplanted me these two times. He took away my birthright; and behold, now he has taken away my blessing'. Then he said, 'Have you not reserved a blessing for me?' Isaac answered Esau, 'Behold, I have made him your lord, and all his brothers I have given to him for servants, and with grain and wine I have sustained him. What then can I do for you, my son?' Esau said to his father, 'Have you but one blessing, my father? Bless me, even me also, O my father'. And Esau lifted up his voice and wept". (27:36–38)

In patriarchal society the effectiveness of this blessing was well understood. In Nuzu a man repeated in court the blessing his father had given him on his death-bed, willing him a wife. The terms of such a blessing were upheld by the Court. The Nuzu tablets recognized oral blessings and death-bed wills.

So Jacob, having received the history-moulding blessing from his dying father under the aegis of El-Shaddai, was destined to gain pre-eminence over Esau (Edom) as Israel did later (especially in the time of David).

The situation reflected the historic enmity between Edom and Israel. But the national background is scarcely emphasized, the family and personal history of the two brothers being the predominant theme.

Tradition holds that Rebekah, the mother, fearing Esau's revenge, and the bloodbath that might ensue within the tribe, commanded her favourite son Jacob to flee to her distant kinsman in Harran:

" 'until your brother's anger turns away, and he forgets what you have done to him; then I will send, and fetch you from there. Why should I be bereft of you both in one day?' " (27:45)

This is not a rhetorical question. By the laws of blood revenge, if Esau killed Jacob, the clan in turn would kill him. We have a parallel in the tragedy of the woman of Tekoa (2 Sam. 14:5–7).

THE SACRED PILLAR OF BETHEL

"And he came to a certain place, and stayed there that night, because the sun had set. Taking one of the stones of the place, he put it under his head and lay down in that place to sleep. And he dreamed that there was a ladder set up on the earth, and the top of it reached to heaven; and behold, the angels of God were ascending and descending on it"! (28:11–12)

This is the initial story in an old cycle relating Jacob's adventures in the territory of Laban, between eastern Syria and Harran, in north-western Mesopotamia. (In the subsequent narrative about Laban and Jacob, we will find that their herds ranged all the way from Harran to Gilead, east of Jordan).

The Lord appeared to Jacob in a theophany at the time of his despair. In a dream he experienced the vision of a ladder, or rather a stairway to heaven. God renewed the three-fold covenant given to Abraham: that he would give the land to Israel; that he would make Israel a great and numerous people; and that through Israel all the families of the earth would be blessed. On waking Jacob was filled with awe, but in no way mystified by the experience.

Jacob concluded that there, on that spot, was the gate of heaven. Some see in this a reminiscence of the steps or approach up a Babylonian ziggurat, called "Bab-Ilu", or the Gate of the Gods, as in the story of the Tower of Babel. Jacob raised up the low pillar on which he had slept and dreamt, and anointed it with oil to consecrate it. He vowed that if God would guard him, clothe and feed him and ensure his safe return, he would keep him as a God, and this place will become God's house (Beth-el in Hebrew); and he named the pillar Bethel. Jacob further vowed that he would pay the Lord tithes (a tenth) on all he would receive from him. In this attitude, effecting a bargain between man and God, Jacob confirmed the covenant, and established a regular sanctuary and cult at Bethel, where visiting worshippers paid tithes. A sacred pillar stood there many centuries later, focussing the worship of countless generations. This is probably the site of the altar which had been hallowed by Abraham (Gen. 12:8; 13:4).

The story of Jacob's dream at Bethel has all the earmarks of real cultic tradition. It has moreover undertones of mythological lore. It is widely held that it was originally an oral pre-Israelite tradition of a Canaanite cult legend, which had a completely different meaning. This independent unit of narrative material was not borrowed by the Hebrews. Rather it was appropriated by Israel who made this theophany her own, by baptising it into the faith of Yahweh, regarding the pillar at Bethel as in a special sense God's dwelling place, and associating with it the special sanctity of the "place".

The custom of the sacred pillar ("matzeba") is one of the central foundations of the patriarchal beliefs, and many of them have been discovered. They are usually small rectangles, flat and thin, more like small and humble grave-stones of today. They appear to have been erected chiefly to commemorate a theophany, a vow or sacred covenant rite, or even an ancestor or important official. The recent excavations at Hazor and other ancient sites have produced sacred slabs of this sort.

JACOB IN ARAM-NAHARAIM

THE JACOB-LABAN CYCLE

And so, assured that the Lord was going with him and would bring him back to the promised land, Jacob journeyed towards his kinsmen in "the land of the people of the east" (the sons of Kedem, in Hebrew). This was the region east of Syria and Transjordan and the territory bordering on Harran, in northwestern Mesopotamia, a vast stretch of pasture land for sheep and goatherders. In subsequent stories about Jacob and Laban, Harran is mentioned as the pivot of the clan's life and its problems; although the background of the events and dealings between the herders involved centre around stories of sheep and goatbreeding. The stories built around Jacob and Laban's personalities may or may not have had a substratum of tribal history, but their background may be linked with tribal migrations of Aram-Naharaim clans of northwestern Mesopotamia (Harran) or from the "land of the people of the east, namely eastern Syria, to Canaan, as personified by Jacob's migration. This cycle has been described by G. von Rad as a body of traditions which rest "like a bridge, on two pillars". On one side the span is secured to the story of Jacob's theophany at Bethel; on the other it is embedded in the story of Jacob's return to the promised land, where he met with the angel at the river Jabbok (32:22–32), then settled with his clan from Harran in Shechem.

ANALOGY WITH CONTEMPORARY CUSTOMS

The Nuzu tablets frequently illustrate customs found in the patriarchal narratives. But in the story of the relationship of Jacob and Laban (in Gen. 29–31), these are interwoven in the narrative in a way which does not occur later in the Bible; but specific Nuzu parallels exist from *the same place and the same time*. They are related specifically to the legal and social "situation in life" (Sitz im Leben) reflected in the Mesopotamian documents. The story would be hard to understand in the light of biblical customs prevailing later than the time of Moses. According to Prof. H. H. Rowley "their accurate reflection of social conditions in the patriarchal age, and in some parts of Mesopotamia, from which the patriarchs are said to have come, is striking".

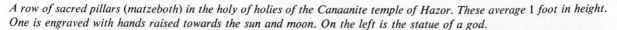

A row of sacred pillars (matzeboth) in the holy of holies of the Canaanite temple of Hazor. These average 1 foot in height. One is engraved with hands raised towards the sun and moon. On the left is the statue of a god.

Camels near the river Habur in Aram-Naharaim, Rachel's homeland.

It would be difficult to find an adequate explanation of the origin of these stories as their background at the time when they were woven by the genius of the people, as hero tales, or extensive legends, was very different from the conditions obtaining a few centuries later when they were composed in writing. It is hardly probable that those who wrote them could have invented so many details which now prove to be authentic. This points towards the conclusion that the oral tradition preserved these elements correctly throughout many centuries, and these were recorded, even though not properly understood, by the chroniclers. At any rate what we have learned from Nuzu and Ugarit correlates acceptably with the general picture of Genesis. This vindication has forced scholars to treat the patriarchal traditions with more respect than used to be the case a few decades ago.

Syrian shepherd; statuette from the early 2nd millenium B.C.E.

A clay tablet from Nuzu.

RACHEL THE SHEPHERDESS

When Jacob reached the "land of the people of the east", another famous and much-loved biblical romance was enacted, a favourite story-theme for the ancient Hebrews:

"As he looked, he saw a well in the field, and lo, three flocks of sheep lying beside it; for out of the well the flocks were watered. The stone on the well's mouth was large, and when all the flocks were gathered there, the shepherds would roll the stone from the mouth of the well, and water the sheep, and put the stone back in its place upon the mouth of the well. Jacob said to them, 'My brothers, where do you come from?' They said 'We are from Harran'". (29:2–4)

In the story the stone was so heavy that it took a number of men to move it. As Jacob was enquiring about Laban his daughter Rachel appeared in the role of shepherdess. Love lent Jacob great strength:

"Now when Jacob saw Rachel the daughter of Laban his mother's brother, and the sheep of Laban his mother's brother, Jacob went up and rolled the stone from the well's mouth, and watered the flock of Laban his mother's brother. Then Jacob kissed Rachel, and wept aloud. And Jacob told Rachel that he was her father's kinsman, and that he was Rebekah's son; and she ran and told her father". (29:10–12)

Jacob, unlike Abraham's servant, had brought no presents or bride-price. He entered his father-in-law's family on the terms dictated by customary law. When his uncle Laban asked Jacob what would be his terms for serving him as a member of his household, Jacob agreed to serve for seven years as a price for the hand of Rachel. Entering into a contract whereby a man pays in labour for his wife, is duly attested in the Nuzu tablets:

"The adoption tablet of Nashwi son of Arshenni. He adopted Wullu son of Puhishenni. As long as Nashwi lives, Wullu shall give (him) food and clothing. When Nashwi dies, Wullu shall be the heir. Should Nashwi beget a son, (the latter) shall divide equally with Wullu but (only) Nashwi's son shall take Nashwi's gods. But if there is no son of Nashwi's, then Wullu shall take Nashwi's gods. And (Nashwi) has given his daughter Nubuya as wife to Wullu. And if Wullu takes another wife, he forfeits Nashwi's land and buildings. Whoever breaks the contract shall pay one mina of silver and one mina of gold".

C. H. Gordon suggests: "To bring out more clearly the bearing of this text on the Hebrew episode we summarize the tablet, substituting 'Laban' for Nashwi, and 'Jacob' for Wullu; 'Laban', who had no son of his own, adopted 'Jacob' and made him his heir. If 'Laban' should beget a son in the future, that son and 'Jacob' were to share the inheritance, but only the begotten son was to take 'Laban's' gods. As a condition, 'Jacob' was to marry 'Laban's' daughter. 'Jacob' was forbidden to marry any other women under the penalty of forfeiting 'Laban's' property".

To what extent does the biblical account coincide with the tablets cited? Although the element of adoption in the Nuzu documents is absent in Jacob's story, there is much more to the background of the latter than appears at first sight. No sons of Laban are mentioned and Jacob entered into this bargain for the purpose (or in the hope) of being heir to the household, not only as the son-in-law of Laban but as the adopted son. When the seven years had been completed Laban deceived Jacob and foisted Leah on to him instead of Rachel:

> "And in the morning, behold it was Leah; and Jacob said to Laban, 'What is this you have done to me? Did I not serve with you for Rachel? Why, then, have you deceived me?' Laban said, 'It is not so done in our country, to give the younger before the firstborn' ". (29: 25–26)

In those days, getting the better of the other man was a sign of cleverness and the Nuzu contracts also reflect this attitude. Jacob came under Laban's jurisdiction, and on condition that he would work for Laban a further seven years, he could finally marry his beloved Rachel. Then he agreed to work another seven years to acquire flocks of his own. He managed by skill to acquire the best portion of Laban's flock of sheep and goats. Black sheep, or goats other than black or brown, were rarities, and those Jacob was to have. According to the story he employed an ingenious breeding device to use maternal impression on the unborn of the flocks. He set peeled rods in the watering-troughs, where the flocks came to breed, to impress the mothers of the "stronger of the flocks". Thus he managed to breed an ample supply of the new varieties:

> "and so the flocks brought forth striped, speckled and spotted... but for the feebler of the flock he did not lay them there; so the feebler were Laban's and the stronger Jacob's". (30: 39–42)

Jacob came besides into possession of great wealth: two wives, two handmaids brought in by his wives as marriage gifts, in accordance with Mesopotamian custom (they were also his concubines who gave him children) and a large retinue of servants and followers, and also children, of whom he had eleven.

But after twenty years of hard work Jacob's hopes were dashed. Laban had had sons born to him after their contract had been made; sons who, according to local usage, would become Laban's chief heirs rather than the adopted son. They were younger men who resented the position he had attained. The whole picture presented is of crafty tribesmen, each partly in the right, seeking loopholes in the laws. And Laban insisted on one item in the original contract: that Jacob would not be permitted to take another wife in addition to the two daughters of Laban.

The narrator of the story makes it clear that Jacob could only extricate himself from Laban's control by flight in the spring; and the two wives sided with their husband, agreeing that home was no longer the place for them.

Then Rachel did an extraordinary thing without Jacob's knowledge. She stole the "teraphim", Laban's family gods, or household idols. The custom was that Laban's true son would share inheritance, and receive the teraphim, symbol of his rights. Only if there were no son would Jacob possess them. Rachel's act was therefore designed to secure an advantage for her husband and children.

It is not likely in this case that the teraphim conveyed ownership of valuable property as Rachel was leaving the territory of her father. They may have betokened clan-leadership in the "land of the people of the east", or spiritual power, so that possessing them was of paramount importance.

THE COVENANT IN GILEAD

Laban pursued Jacob for seven days and caught up with him in the highlands of Gilead, east of Jordan. What troubled him more than the loss of his daughters, their husband and livestock, was the loss of the teraphim. He demanded indignantly: "but why did you steal my gods?"

> "Jacob answered Laban, 'Because I was afraid, for I thought that you would take your daughters from me by force. Any one with whom you find your gods shall not live. In the presence of our kinsmen point out what I have that is yours, and take it'. Now Jacob did not know that Rachel had stolen them. So Laban went into Jacob's tent, and into Leah's tent, and into the tent of the two maidservants, but he did not find them. And he went out of Leah's tent, and entered Rachel's. Now Rachel had taken the household gods and put them in the camel's saddle, and sat upon them. Laban felt all about the tent, but did not find them". (31:31-34)

As Rachel was unwell, religious custom prevented her father from forcing her off the saddle and the theft remained unexposed.

Laban and Jacob apparently agreed to maintain an amicable relationship on the basis of a new covenant. They exchanged blessings, made the covenant and set up a cairn and pillar ("matzeba") as a witness to their sincerity; the inanimate object was naively thought to "oversee" the covenant. They swore that neither would transgress the boundary to harm the other:

> "'This heap is a witness, and the pillar is a witness, that I will not pass over this heap to you, and you will not pass over this heap and this pillar to me, for harm. The God of Abraham and the God of Nahor, the God of their fathers, judge between us'. So Jacob swore by the fear of his father Isaac, and Jacob offered a sacrifice on the mountain and called his kinsmen to eat bread; and they ate bread and tarried all night on the mountain". (31:52-54)

This patriarchal clan covenant seems to reflect either a remote separation of the clans, or the story may serve to justify territorial status of later times, when the Israelite and Aramean peoples upheld a treaty of amity and marked the boundary between them. (The biblical author refers to "Aramean", when he means a nation which came into existence only long after the patriarchal period). They invoked their respective ancestral gods to judge between them: "The God of Abraham" and "The God of Nahor". Jacob also swore by a special epithet of God: the "Fear of his father Isaac" (meaning, according to the interpretation, the "Kinsman of Isaac"). This devotion to the God of one's father is one of the features of patriarchal religion that stemmed from the pre-Hebraic Semitic past. Jacob declared to his kinsman Laban:

> " 'If the God of my father, the God of Abraham and Fear of Isaac, had not been by my side, surely now you would have sent me away empty-handed. God saw my affliction and the labour of my hands, and rebuked you last night' ". (31:42)

An especially impressive conclusion of the compact was the animal sacrifice offered, and a meal at which the solemn covenant act was confirmed; to "cut a covenant" (the rite of sacrifice) and to "eat bread" remained a familiar idiom of Israelite religious symbols.

In eating and drinking, life is perfectly symbolized, and gains profound religious connotation. This is the root of the Jewish and Christian practice of grace before meals, for eating is the epitome of man's dependence upon God and other men. The central ceremonies of Judaism, such as the Passover, and the Eucharist of Christianity are reminiscent of such very ancient Hebrew cultic practices. The covenant between Jacob and Laban was of course a parity treaty made between equals, unlike the covenants between God as Lord and the Patriarchs, His servants.

THE NOCTURNAL ENCOUNTER

After Jacob and Laban parted, each going with his followers to his native land, Jacob prepared to win over Esau by a lavish display of gifts. He was afraid when he heard of Esau's approach "and four hundred with him". He strategically divided his retinue and possessions into two detachments, and led them to the river valley of Jabbok. After instructing his family and herds to go to the other side of the stream, he spent the night alone. There he had a nocturnal encounter with a supernatural visitor and opponent, described as an angel. With this angel Jacob wrestled until daybreak, but he finally received the blessing of the angel who declared that Israel would be the second name of Jacob:

> "Then he said, 'Your name shall no more be called Jacob, but Israel, for you have striven with God and with men, and have prevailed' ". (32:28)

Jacob's thigh was hurt, and he went away limping from the wound in his sciatic nerve. To commemorate this legend, Jewish tradition ordains that this nerve must be removed from the thigh of every animal slaughtered for food. In this text there is a superimposition on the later traditions of most ancient pre-Hebraic themes, some of which may be legendary. In the most ancient form of the story, the angel of Jacob may perhaps have reflected a folk tale about a night river-demon who must disappear with the morning light. When Israel made this legend its own, it transformed the demon into an angel, a messenger of God.

Traditions, such as the sacrifice of Isaac, the vision of Bethel, or the encounter at Jabbok, are pre-Israelite, (either Canaanite, or native cult legends that had a completely different meaning in their original version), but the biblical storytellers did not borrow them wholesale.

The Jabbok river valley.

They appropriated them and re-shaped their inner meaning in the light of faith in the Lord. In the process they retained nevertheless primitive elements that seem curiously inconsistent, such as this folk tale of Jacob's struggle with a night-demon: it was written later to accommodate, for instance, the change of Jacob's name to Israel.

This is the closing stage of the themes and tales of the Jacob-Laban cycle. Extensive legends created by the collective genius of the people were woven around Jacob; or around certain historical memories since forgotten. The people and later the chroniclers collected these into a saga of which Jacob was the key figure. In this scheme Jacob was twice visited by God: when his career was at its lowest ebb at Bethel, when he left Canaan, and then in the form of a nocturnal visitor, at a prosperous though critical stage of his life. This recurring theme is summed up in Jacob's words:

"'I am not worthy of the least of all the steadfast love and faithfulness which thou hast shown to thy servant, for with only my staff I crossed the Jordan; and now I have become two companies'". (32: 10)

Jacob's humble prayer in a crisis of his life, his own comparison of his former status with the present, harmonizes the inner religious theme of the story with the other theme of his experience. This man who understood the consequences of his actions (flight from his father's house, danger of dependence, trouble with his children), is still a man whom the grace of God had found. So tradition dwells on his many trials of faith, while describing him as a man to whom the election of God came without full merit on his part.

He had next to penetrate into Canaan, first winning Esau's favour. When they met at

In tablet 286 from the Tel-el-Amarna Letters, Abdi-Heba, governor of Jerusalem, writes to the king of Egypt: "This sayeth Abdi-Heba, thy servant. 'At the two feet of my lord, the king, seven times I fall down...' "

The crossing of Jabbok.

the edge of the Jordan valley, Jacob appeared at the head of his family and detachments:

"He himself went on before them, bowing himself to the ground seven times, until he came near to his brother". (33:3)

The sevenfold prostration is a widespread custom attested also in the Amarna letters and those of Ugarit, as shown in the illustration above.

Esau graciously pardoned his brother. The two and their clans effected a reconciliation.

Back in Palestine proper, other traditions tell, Isaac had been living all this time at Mamre, in Kiriat-Arba (Hebron), and Esau with him:

"And Jacob came to his father Isaac at Mamre, or Kiriat-arba (that is Hebron), where Abraham and Isaac sojourned. Now the days of Isaac were a hundred and eighty years. And Isaac breathed his last; and he died and was gathered to his people, old and full of days; and his sons Esau and Jacob buried him". (35: 27–29)

This wording implies no strained relations between Jacob and Esau, who co-operated peacefully. It makes no mention of Jacob's long absence. Many scholars believe that the tradition which embodies the Jacob-Laban cycle is an older one, and that which describes the meeting of Jacob and Esau at Isaac's funeral is a younger and fuller tradition. Hence the divergence between the two.

JACOB AT SHECHEM

The migration objective of Jacob was Shechem in the hills of central Palestine, just as it had been that of Abraham (12:6). It is as though this were to be his definite abode. He encamped before the city in the Shechem pass (see illustration in Abraham's story), and bought some land from Benei-Hamor (the sons of Hamor), the tribe that dwelt there. Presumably their tribal deity was Baal-berith (Lord of the Covenant) and this is how they are known to us in the story of the conquest of central Palestine by Joshua. This purchase is in a certain sense parallel to Abraham's purchase of the field and cave at Mamre. It is as though Israel's right to a certain piece of ground in the area had to be established; but Jacob's tribe also established a bond with the sacred pillars at Shechem through close tribal alliance with the natives. Jacob, we are told, "erected an altar and called it El-Elohei-Israel". This is the third pillar attributed to him, besides those erected at Bethel and Mitzpah in Gilead, but probably the sacred pillar at Shechem was much older than the biblical tradition knows, and was dedicated to the deity (El) of the ancient city. El, to the Hebrews, became short for Elohim or God. The Hebrews in patriarchal days, as represented by Jacob in this story, endowed the sacred pillar with a confessional name: El. Yahweh, the God of Israel, was identified with this ancient name. This identification of one ancient god with another is a mode of cultural absorption and conquest very common in the religious process of antiquity. It is another outstanding feature of religion in patriarchal times and later.

The outstanding feature of the prolonged sojourn of Jacob's clan in Shechem is the dramatic episode about the treachery of Simeon and Levi. The episode is set in typical purposeful and personalized form, and it is reflected in the tribal blessing attributed to Jacob on his death-bed (49: 5-7). Its background is perhaps connected with a dimly remembered period of Hebrew settlement in the highlands of central Palestine. This very ancient poem, considered one of the oldest oral traditions, reveals knowledge of an unlocalized tribal tale somewhat like it:

> "Now Dinah the daughter of Leah, whom she had borne to Jacob, went out to visit the women of the land; and when Shechem, the son of Hamor the Hivite, the prince of the land, saw her, he seized her and lay with her and humbled her. And his soul was drawn to Dinah the daughter of Jacob; he loved the maiden and spoke tenderly to her. So Shechem spoke to his father Hamor, saying, 'Get me this maiden for my wife'" (34: 1–4).

The seduction of Jacob's daughter by a young chief of Shechem and his father's attempts to settle the incident by gifts and marriage, provided a tense situation, where Simeon and Levi, members of the Hebrew clan, thought they could dictate terms to the natives:

> "They said to them, 'We cannot do this thing, to give our sister to one who is uncircumcised, for that would be a disgrace to us. Only on this condition will we consent to you: that you will become as we are and every male of you circumcised. Then we will give our daughters to you, and we will take your daughters to ourselves, and we will dwell with you and become one people'". (34: 14–16)

Intermarriage was apparently indicated in the adjusting of relationships between the semi-nomadic Hebrews and the natives; but now the Hebrew clansmen were bent on revenge. The terms imposed on the Shechemites involved circumcision. Contrary to the impression given here, however, circumcision is known to have been practised by the Canaanites. Simeon and Levi, treacherously taking advantage of the post-operative incapacity of the men of Shechem, attacked the unsuspecting city with the sword, killing the males, carrying off women, children and spoils. This displeased Jacob, the more so since he had few supporters and he was a "sojourner" who could ill afford enemies. Translated into tribal terms, this tradition seems to tell us that a Hebrew clan by the name of Dinah had entered into a compact, including intermarriage, with the city of Shechem (seat of the Baal-berith mentioned in Judges 9: 4). The tribe of Simeon and Levi resented the arrangement and raided Shechem, but the Shechemites retaliated so effectively that the two clans were almost exterminated. Some scholars think that the story reflects the capture of Shechem referred to in Judges 9 and has been secondarily connected with Simeon and Levi to explain their failure to achieve prosperity among the other tribes of Israel. Still another story about the Israelite capture of Shechem is reflected in later words of Jacob, in bequeathing this locality to Joseph:

> "'Moreover I have given to you rather than to your brothers one mountain slope which I took from the hand of the Amorites with my sword and with my bow'". (48: 22)

In both of these stories we have old echoes of the fall of this city, which made covenants with Hebrew invaders at different times. It is possible that Jacob was a more important figure than the simple patriarchal story would lead one to suppose. The remark above about his capture of Shechem points in that direction. Moreover, this stray hint could be a reminiscence of the events which, according to the Amarna Letters, led to the surrender of Shechem to the Habiru. Roving bands of Habiru infested the country and menaced the settled communities, adding to the general insecurity at the time when Egyptian rule in Palestine was on the wane. The rival city-states of Canaan and their kinglets engaged in international intrigues with

Members of a party of Asiatic nomads.
Egyptian painting of the 19th century B.C.E.

Bearer of gifts. From tomb of Ken-
Amun, Chief Steward of the King and
Overseer of the Cattle of Amun, a
title reminiscent of the Joseph story.
c. 1430 B.C.E.

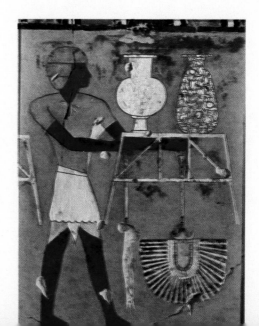

Egypt and the Hittites and fought petty local wars. The indications in the Bible may imply that the patriarchs were not ordinary nomads, whom an older school of Orientalists liked to compare with the present-day Arab nomads. Even though the latter live exotically in tents and move about, they are quite unsophisticated and detached from the current history of their time. They stand in sharp contrast to the Hebrew patriarchs, who had dealings with Amorites, Canaanites, Philistines (early Caphtorians), Egyptians and, of course, king-lets from all over the Near East. The patriarchs' careers seem to lie on the hub of the highly cosmopolitan Amarna Age, or very close to it.

Among the Amarna clay tablets is a letter written by Lab'ayu, ruler of Shechem, to the Egyptian king protesting his innocence, and saying among other things:

> "Further the king wrote concerning my son. I did not know that my son associated with the 'Apiru, and I have verily delivered him into the hands of Addaya. Further, if the king should write for my wife, how could I withhold her? If the king should write to me, 'Plunge a bronze dagger into thy heart and die!', how could I refuse to carry out the command of the king?"

Whatever its background in history may be, it is evident that the proto-Aramean strain, represented in the saga of Jacob, is the nomadic element referred to later in the Deuteronomic phrase "a wandering Aramean was my father" and that from this stock of Hebrew and "Aramean" origin sprang the clans who formed the beginning of a Hebrew settlement in Canaan, at Shechem and Bethel, long before the sojourn in Egypt and the Exodus out of Egypt. G. E. Wright maintains that "it has long been realized that Gen. 34 has behind it a tradition of a Hebrew relationship with Shechem which relates to early events not necessarily

Canaanite and Syrian figurines. 15th and 14th centuries B.C.E.

altered by the sojourn and exodus. Even during the Sojourn the city must have been under Israelite control; that is, a mixed Canaanite-Hebrew group of clans may have been united by covenant, worshipping a deity called "Baal-berith (Lord of the Covenant)". We shall deal with this view in the story of Joshua and Judges.

THE PILGRIMAGE TO BETHEL

After sojourning for some time in the Shechem area, Jacob received a divine command to go to Bethel and fulfil there the vows he had made to build an altar. Thereupon Jacob and his Aramean kinsmen journeyed to Bethel and there he built an altar and called the place El-Bethel, another confessional formulation like El-Elohei Israel, a name connected with the place before (cf. 33:20).

This clearly shows that foreign idols, probably clay figurines portraying deities, were still to be found among the people. This tradition, and the fact that Jacob had settled at Shechem with "Aramean" wives, his household and "all who were with him"—presumably other elements which had attached themselves to his group, suggests that the early proto-Aramean or Syrian element brought its ancestral gods into Canaan, and that such idols were in the midst of the people.

Thereupon Jacob and his household buried their idols under "the Oak" which was near Shechem: Jacob realized that his allegiance was not to these gods but to Yahweh. The contractual nature of the relation between God and his people stemming from the patriarchal period, remains a cornerstone of biblical religion throughout the Old and New Testaments.

The narrative of the pilgrimage to Bethel is more than just an incident in the private life of Jacob and his family. We shall see that Joshua (24:15–28) will repeat a similar request to the Hebrew tribes and their allied Canaanite kinsmen, and that a commemoration of this act existed in the time of King Jeroboam. The pilgrimage had always existed and these traditions must have originated at the Bethel cultic centre from earliest times. This was a national shrine which persisted until the days of the monarchy.

There were reminiscences of Jacob, however, at other places in that region, and the only way of getting them into the narrative was apparently to have the patriarch journey there. Rachel is a figure of great importance in the saga, as Jacob's beloved wife and as the mother of Joseph and Benjamin, who were to constitute the very core of the Israelite state. And so the narrative in Chap. 35 continues with the death of Rachel and the birth of Benjamin, for she died in childbirth. Tradition hails a copula-topped structure on the road from Jerusalem to Bethlehem as the "tomb of Rachel". It was actually erected in the 15th century A.D. over a monolith which marks an ancient grave. It is mentioned by the 7th century pilgrim Arculf. This shrine was frequented by Jewish pilgrims in Palestine until 1948 when the Arab-Israel War of Liberation broke out.

Another local story, attached to a place called Migdal Eder, is connected with the oldest roots of the Jacob traditions. It concerns Reuben, Jacob's eldest son, and an affair with his father's concubine Bilhah. It is of such a scandalous nature that it is reported with characteristic Hebrew conciseness. The biblical storyteller, while not suppressing scandal and "frauengeschichten" does not lavish time and words on sex and gossip, in line with the Bible's rigid and ascetic social code. This incident, a mere fragment of the vast Jacob saga, is necessary to the biblical storyteller for an understanding of Jacob's last blessing to his sons, and his paternal curse on Reuben, in Gen. 49: 4. But according to the oldest Jewish commentators, Reuben was not motivated by lust, but acted to protect his mother Leah and defend her interests. Commentators assume that Jacob made Bilhah his favourite after Rachel's death, whereupon Reuben seduced her and alienated the patriarch's affection from her. There is more to this than appears in a few short sentences. This motif is part of the epic repertoire of the East Mediterranean and comes up in the Iliad (9: 447–57), where Phoenix (like Reuben) received a paternal curse and no blessing for seducing his father's concubine. He also, like Reuben, was not motivated by lust. This goes to prove that the more we study the Bible, the more we have to respect the importance of the mere details which help to piece together and interpret biblical stories.

THE JUDAH AND TAMAR EPISODES

We hear little in the narratives preceding the Joseph cycle about the various sons of Jacob, the eponyms of the tribes which may have originated in later patriarchal times. That little, however, is most revealing. We learn about the clans of Simeon and Levi and the conquest of Shechem; then an episode about Reuben and Bilhah. Judah is mentioned among his brothers in the first installment of the Joseph stories which begins with Gen. 37. But the chroniclers had another tradition about Judah and Tamar (Gen. 38) which related to the ancestors of the tribe of Judah. This is an indication that this tribe had an early history independent of the other, northern, tribes of Israel.

Tomb of Rachel.

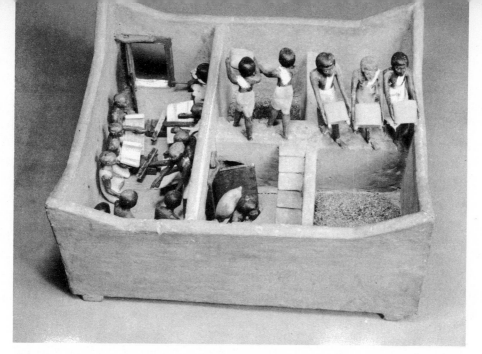

Wooden model of a large Egyptian granary being filled. Scribes are registering the intake.

CHAPTER V

THE JOSEPH STORY-CYCLE AND ITS SETTING

The Joseph story-cycle has a dominant Egyptian background, with Egyptian names appearing in the biblical record for the first time. These traditions may have once circulated independently in Egypt and have been unrelated to those of Abraham, Isaac and Jacob; but the Bible historians incorporated them into the continuous epic of Israel. Later traditions of Israel were anchored in the belief that Israel had come up out of the land of the Nile. This played the major role in the evolution of the Jewish religion. But another set of traditions, recorded in Genesis, held that Israel's ancestors (namely all the clans descended from the patriarchs), had previously gone down from Canaan to Egypt, and had increased there in the course of time and become a people. So the Joseph cycle was made to serve as the conclusion of the history of the patriarchs, and the prelude to the Exodus from Egypt, which is the dominating event in Israelite history and faith.

The personal fortunes of Joseph, who bears the name of the ancestor of the early Hebrew tribe of central Palestine (Joseph), were thus of great interest. The saga has become one of the most appealing narratives in world literature. It blends motifs of Egypt and Israel, and it has a strong emotional effect. Spun out of ancient Egyptian and Hebrew lore, it blended them in a single plot, in which scene follows scene with artistic development.

JOSEPH IS REJECTED BY HIS BRETHREN

Joseph was the spoiled young son of Jacob. The theme, common alike in folklore and in history, opens with the story of the younger, and apparently more gifted member of the family, kept down by the envy of the older members. Joseph, moreover, had the gift of interpreting dreams, and this faculty set him apart as a person of strange propensities among his half-brothers. He was sent by his father to Shechem, to find out how they and their flock fared. But they had wandered further north, to Dothan. The adventurous youth followed them there on the caravan route from east of the Jordan to the land of Egypt. Joseph's half-brothers hated him because he was the favourite, and even more because of the conceit of "this dreamer".

He had two dreams. In one he saw the family binding sheaves in the field, and each one's sheaf got into a circle around his, and bowed to it. In the second dream, the sun, moon and stars bowed down to him. This dream, a duplicate of the first, featured a characteristic trait of ancient tales of the Near East. The actual meaning is obvious, and requires no interpretation, and this is typical of the Hebrews' attitude to dreams. Indeed this dream drew Joseph's father's rebuke in rhetorical form:

> " 'What is this dream that you have dreamed? Shall I and your mother and your brothers indeed come to bow ourselves to the ground before you?' And his brothers were jealous of him, but his father kept the saying in mind". (37:10–11).

But the offended brothers reacted more drastically. They decided to be quit of him and his dreams, and plotted to kill him. From this point on, double strands of a story appear in the narrative of the treachery of the brothers and of how Joseph was sold into captivity. One account tells that Judah dissuaded the brothers from destroying Joseph and induced them to sell him to a caravan of Ishmaelites, who in turn sold him to an Egyptian notability. Another tradition avers that Reuben took the lead and had them cast Joseph into a pit; Midianite traders passing by drew him up, while his brothers were eating; they sold him in Egypt as a slave, to Potiphar, the "captain of the guard". The name of the Egyptian city is not mentioned. But the main point in the development of the dramatic theme is that Joseph was reduced to the lowest status, that of a slave, and the story ends with his triumph over his brethren.

JOSEPH IN EGYPT

In the telling there are a great many correct local and antiquarian details; many bits of Egyptian colouring which have been fully illustrated by Egyptian discoveries which would be inexplicable by later interpolations. The Egyptian colouring must have been given to the story by those who knew Egypt well.

Joseph rose high in the household of his master, who made him "overseer over his house" (39:4). This title is a direct translation of an office in the house of the great Egyptian nobles and officials, as was "he who is over the house" (41:40). The writer employs the correct title, exactly as it was used in the period. He simply adopted the Egyptian term and translated it into Hebrew.

The migration of Asiatic nomadic groups to Egypt has already been illustrated on the

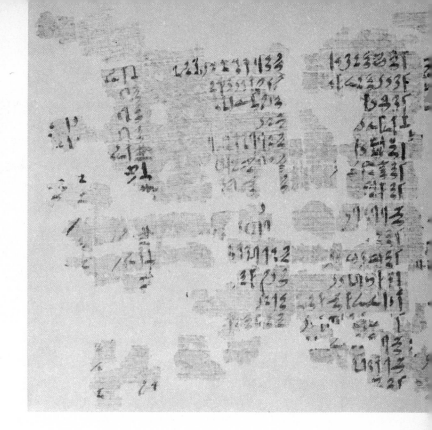

A striking illustration of Joseph's early life is found in the Brooklyn papyrus, dating from about 1800 B.C.E. Out of a list of 77 servants in an Egyptian household, 45 are Asiatics, men, women, children, probably sold in Egypt as slaves, like Joseph. Some adults bear Hebrew names such as Shifra and Menachem, and some have adopted Egyptian names. They are described as "chief over the house", house servants, brewer, cooks, storekeepers. The children bear Egyptian names.

Egyptian wall painting of the Clan of Abisha, 37 in number (reproduced in Ch. III). The painting dates from the early part of the second millennium, but it reflects a similar background to that of Hebrews coming to Goshen, although the picture represents wandering musicians and tinsmiths. But it is generally used to illustrate the descent of a Hebrew group as in the story of Joseph and his brethren migrating to Egypt.

In this Egyptian house Joseph fell from grace because of the machinations of Potiphar's wife, and was sent to the king's jail:

> "But one day, when he went into the house to do his work and none of the men of the house was there in the house, she caught him by his garment, saying, 'Lie with me'. But he left his garment in her hand, and fled and got out of the house. And when she saw that he had left his garment in her hand, and fled out of the house, she called to the men of her household and said to them, 'See, he has brought among us a Hebrew to insult us; he came in to lie with me, and I cried out with a loud voice; and when he heard that I lifted up my voice and cried, he left his garment with me, and fled and got out of the house' ". (39:11–15)

In the incident of Potiphar's wife's attempt to seduce Joseph, the circumstances are similar in plot to the Egyptian Tale of the Two Brothers, a folk tale from a 13th century papyrus about a virtuous young man, Bitis, who lived in harmony with his older brother, Anubis and his wife. One day, as the two brothers were ploughing in the field, Anubis sent his younger brother to the house for more grain. There his brother's wife was combing her hair and she attempted to seduce Bitis. She failed and became frightened. Then she set out to malign him. In the end her husband learned the truth. He killed his wife and "threw her out to the dogs" as befell Jezebel, a reputedly wicked queen of Israel (2 Kings, 9:33, 36).

This story is of interest not only because of this parallel, but because it documents with a specific story the proverbial Egyptian saying which warns young men of the wiles of an evil woman. The same motif occurs in the story of Bellerophon in the Iliad. This indicates

Representation of the "Mistress of Jubilations", the goddess Hathor, embracing the adolescent Pharaoh.

that such stories spread over Egypt, Israel and the Aegean and are common to East Mediterranean epics.

While in prison, Joseph rose in station. When the king's cupbearer, the "chief butler" and the "chief baker" fell out of favour they were also sent to prison, and it was Joseph who was commissioned to look after them. Egyptian inscriptions confirm the titles "chief of butlers" and "chief of bakers".

The cupbearer had a dream in which he saw a vine with three branches and grapes growing from it. He squeezed the grapes into a cup which he put into Pharaoh's hands. He was troubled by this dream and Joseph interpreted it for him thus: "The three branches are three days; within three days Pharaoh will lift up your head, forgive you and restore you to your office". As a reward, Joseph asked the chief butler to recommend him to Pharaoh and thus rescue him from prison.

Egyptian gardener drawing water in Apuy's house. A painting of the XIXth dynasty, reminiscent of Joseph's early background in Egypt.

The baker dreamed that there were three baskets on his head; in the topmost there was food for Pharaoh, namely roasted meats, but birds of prey descended and ate it. Encouraged by the favourable interpretation of the cupbearer's dream, the baker turned to Joseph who gave him a gloomy prediction: "Within three days Pharaoh will lift up your head from you, and hang you on a tree; and the birds will eat the flesh from you" (40:19). Egyptian inscriptions show the importance of the magician and the interpreter of royal dreams. Thus we know that dreams and omens were indeed regarded by Egyptians as extremely significant. Priests and magicians devoted a great deal of study to their meaning.

It is known from Egyptian inscriptions that the birthday of Pharaoh was an occasion for feasting, and sometimes amnesties were given to prisoners; which recalls the feast Pharaoh made for his servants on his birthday. Joseph's interpretations came true; the chief butler and the chief baker were released from prison, the one to life and the other to death. But the lucky chief butler forgot to help Joseph. The latter had to wait two years for Pharaoh to have dreams that it required his acumen to explain, so raising him from the status of a prisoner and slave to the highest position under the king. This is the famous dream of the seven fat cows and the seven thin cows, which is too familiar to be repeated here:

"Then Pharaoh sent and called Joseph, and they brought him hastily out of the dungeon; and when he had shaved himself and changed his clothes, he came in before Pharaoh". (41:14)

As Joseph realized, the dreams portended seven years of plenty followed by seven years of famine. The motif of seven-year cycles of plenty and famine runs through ancient Near Eastern myth and lore, and periods of drought are known to have lasted for several years. It must be noted, however, that Pharaoh's dreams seem too obvious to require interpretation. "The Nile," says J. A. Wilson, "might fall short of its full bounty for years of famine, but it never ceased altogether, and ultimately it always came back with full prodigality". The biblical Hebrews did not require interpreters to explain their dreams, but individual Hebrews, like Joseph, or Daniel in another age, interpreted dreams for foreigners. Some scholars believe that the religious genius of the Hebrews inclined them to a greater exercise of psychic qualities than other ancients.

The 3rd Chester Beaty papyrus (from the New Kingdom, or the latter half of the 2nd millennium B.C.E.) records a key to the interpretation of dreams. It contains several sections, each intended for worshippers of either Horus, Seth or other gods. Interpretations are derived from analogies: A good dream means profit, a bad dream — trouble; hot brew means losses; nails torn off means deprivation of the use of one's hands; being plunged in the Nile portends that one will be washed clean of one's ailments. A powerful person could therefore forestall trouble portended in his dreams. Every one of the great Egyptian temples possessed a "house of life" where ancient traditions and tracts of learning were preserved.

The biblical tradition about Joseph reflects familiarity with Egyptian court manners. It relates exactly how he prepared for his first royal audience; he shaved his head. Semites did not shave themselves clean, but Egyptians did.

Pharaoh characteristically had his dreams in duplicate, to convey that the events were imminent, and Joseph explained that this was meant to show that God was determined to fulfil the message and would shortly bring it to pass. Joseph advised that a competent director, "discreet and wise", be put in charge of a country-wide scheme, assisted by overseers, to collect "the fifth part of the produce of the land of Egypt", so that the granaries would be sufficiently filled during the "seven plenteous years" before the bad years began.

Gesture of placing the cup in the hands of the king. From a ceremonial picture showing the manner in which Pharaoh placed the cup in the hands of a god.

Bakery and Brewery. This was the province of Pharaoh's chief baker. Wooden model c. 2000 B.C.E.

THE SUPERINTENDENT OF THE GRANARIES

The stability of the country's economy largely depended on the grain harvest. Detailed records of the grain supplies were kept by scribes, as illustrated below. The office of "Superintendent of the Granaries" was especially important at all periods in Egypt, and it was a great day in the kingdom when this official, in solemn audience, presented to the king the "account of the harvests". If there had been "a better harvest than for thirty years" the Superintendent would be given special honours and decked with valuable necklaces:

Agricultural scene from the New Kingdom, during years of prosperity. Wall painting from tomb of Neb-Amun, Captain of Police on the west of Thebes, reminiscent of Potiphar, an officer of the guard of Pharaoh, who bought Joseph.

Painting of Egyptian scribes recording the harvest.

"So Pharaoh said to Joseph, 'Since God has shown you all this, there is none so discreet and wise as you are; you shall be over my house, and all my people shall order themselves as you command; only as regards the throne will I be greater than you'. And Pharaoh said to Joseph, 'Behold, I have set you over all the land of Egypt'. Then Pharaoh took his signet ring from his hand and put it on Joseph's hand, and arrayed him in garments of fine linen, and put a gold chain about his neck; and he made him to ride in his second chariot, and they cried before him, 'Bow the knee!' Thus he set him over all the land of Egypt". (41: 39-43)

The title "over my house" seems to be a direct translation of the highest post in the administration of the realm, namely that of major-domo of the palace and food administrator of all the land, which corresponds to the office of Vizier of Egypt or chief administrator in the country, second in power to the Pharaoh himself. Joseph may have exercised also the office of Superintendent of the Granaries, in view of the approaching famine, in addition to

Harvesting scene in Egypt.

his duties as Vizier. A study of Egyptian official records reveals that it was not an unusual occurrence for an Asiatic to rise to such authority. After 1570 B.C.E. slaves of the New Kingdom became favourites of kings. Under Merneptah, a certain Ben-Azen, native of a country east of the Lake of Galilee could rise, like Joseph, to a high position. The court scene of the induction of Joseph into office ended with the handing of Pharaoh's signet ring to Joseph; his elevation in rank, together with gifts of robes and other honours, is characteristically Egyptian. A Theban painting shows Hug, viceroy of Ethiopia, receiving such a ring. A relief from the period of El Amarna, portrays the investiture of Meri-re' by Ikhnaton with a golden chain for "he had filled the storehouses with spelt and barley". The original tradition from which this story stems thus contains genuine Egyptian titles and proper names, even though they may have been written long after the events related. It is told that, as Joseph rode in the second chariot of Pharaoh, the people cried before him "abrekh-venaton" which was

Scribes recording evidence of non-payment of taxes. This is reflected in the story of Joseph's administration. Relief from Sakkarah.

translated "bow the knee," but may be an Egyptian expression handed down in Hebrew transliteration, as shown below.

The biblical account here conforms closely to Egyptian texts and documentary illustration. It is related that when Rameses II appointed Nebounnef to the high post of first prophet to the god Amon, "His Majesty gave him his two golden rings and his golden staff... a herald was sent to proclaim over all the land that he was set over the house of Amon". Moreover, beautiful garments of linen had by then become fashionable among the upper class.

We read also in 50:26 about Joseph's reported life-span of 110 years, which was the traditional length of a happy and prosperous life in the Egyptian tradition.

Other striking instances of authentic local colour in the story are numerous. There is evidence of long famines in Egypt. Two inscriptions by officials, on the walls of their tombs,

Pharaoh bestowing collars and jewelry on a grateful official. Dating from the 19th dynasty.

Chariot of Tutankhamen, similar to the one Joseph rode in after his induction into office.

Rahotep and wife. Typical manner in which officials were represented in Egyptian paintings. From a tomb monument c. 2600 B.C.E.

give a laudatory synopsis of their good deeds, and claim, that they dispensed food to the needy "in each year of want". One official, Baba, records: "When famine arose lasting many years, I issued corn to the city in each year of famine". One inscription actually tells of a seven-year famine attributed to the days of Pharaoh Djoser (about 2700 B.C.E. and possibly later). He appealed to the god Khnum after a serious famine had lasted seven years. The god appeared in a dream and promised him that the Nile would rise, and flood the fields with sufficient water:

> " 'I was in distress on the Great Throne, and those who are in the palace were in Heart's Affliction from a very great evil, since the Nile had not come in my time for a space of seven years. Grain was scanty, fruits were dried up, and everything which they eat was short... The infant was wailing, the youth was waiting; the heart of the old man was in sorrow... The courtiers were in need. The temples were shut up. Everything was found Empty' ".
>
> (Translation according to J. B. Pritchard. Ancient Neer Eastern Texts.)

As daily life in ancient Egypt can be profusely illustrated from tomb paintings, inscriptions on stelae and monuments and papyri and other objects, Joseph's story may be understood against the Egyptian background. The evidence of Egyptian records serves to illuminate the present story-cycle, as in the epic of Moses in the following Book of Exodus. Perhaps a hint as to the locale in which Joseph lived and officiated is afforded by the reference to his marriage to the daughter of a priest of "On".

'On' was in Lower (northern) Egypt, on the eastern side of the Nile, a little north of the capital Memphis. Asenath bore Joseph a firstborn Manasseh, and Ephraim, a younger son.

> "And Pharaoh called Joseph's name Zaphenath-paneah; and he gave him in marriage Asenath, the daughter of Potiphera priest of On. So Joseph went out over the land of Egypt". (41:45)

The god Re, symbolized by the sun-disc, was worshipped at On, which the Greeks later called Heliopolis (City of the Sun). It was in keeping with Joseph's elevation to high rank, that Pharaoh gave him an Egyptian name and a family. This name, as recorded in the Bible Zaphenath-paneah, would be in Egyptian, Djepa-ntr-fnkh (God says he should live).

JOSEPH'S BRETHREN IN EGYPT

> "When all the land of Egypt was famished, the people cried to Pharaoh for bread; and Pharaoh said to the Egyptians, 'Go to Joseph; what he says to you, do'. So when the famine had spread over all the land, Joseph opened all the storehouses, and sold to the Egyptians, for the famine was severe in the land of Egypt. Moreover, all the earth came to Egypt to Joseph to buy grain, because the famine was severe over all the earth". (41:55–57)

The severe famine in Western Asia forced Joseph's brothers down to Egypt for food. Semites, coming in years of famine from Canaan and surrounding Near Eastern countries were familiar enough throughout Egyptian history. Egypt could always count on the revivifying Nile, while the region east of it (Canaan, Transjordan, the Negev), depended on precarious rain. This also indicates apparently a flow of great resources to the coffers of the Pharaohs, or the temples, which controlled great domains.

From here on the story of his brothers ties up with Joseph's career in the intricate but charming interlocking of scenes which the reader will find in Chapters 42 to 45. They proceed

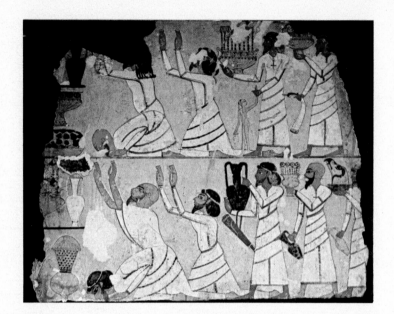

Scene representing the presentation of tribute by Semitic envoys from Syria. From the tomb of Sebekhetep at Thebes. About 1420 B.C.E.

with characteristic suspense towards a happy end. In the biblical scheme, the story serves to tie up the patriarchal age with the climactic point of the national epic, the deliverance of Israel from the mighty Egyptian nation, and the birth of a nation after the Exodus.

While rendering an old Egyptian folk tale, which may be embedded in Joseph's success story, the biblical writer's story conveys primarily a religious and moral lesson. And the Joseph story, in its dramatic context, seems to hint that the promise made to Abraham was moving towards its fulfillment: namely that the descendants of the sojourners in Egypt would inherit Canaan.

When the brothers came to Egypt, Joseph recognized them, but they did not recognize him, for he had become Egyptianized and he had grown older. He entertained them to a banquet and "so they drank and were merry with him". (43:34)

Joseph chose to tantalize his brothers by testing and frightening them, by putting his silver cup into one of their sacks, and then accusing them of having stolen it. In spite of this, surreptitiously he supplied the needs of their families. This part of the tale bears resemblance to a classic Egyptian story called the Eloquent Peasant, and his spirited argument with the chief steward who, though testing the peasant, saw to it that his family was looked after.

Silver cup, such as Joseph put in his brothers' sack of corn. Dating from the reign of Rameses II.

The Bible indicates that, as a result of the mission carried out by his sons, Jacob—whose name was now Israel (32:29)—and his clan, moved to Egypt, together with their belongings, as the relatives of the famous Joseph and at Pharaoh's request. They were a clan of seventy. This number (seven times ten) is also in keeping with the ancient epic tradition. The name Israel now replaced the designation Hebrews, and was already known in Canaan. It is also recorded as the name of one of the chariot warriors (or "mariannu") in a tablet in Ugarit, and of course on the famous stelae of Merneptah to be discussed later. The clan settled in Goshen, in the area east and south of the present-day Suez Canal, on the western edge of the Nile Delta. This district was the ideal place for shepherds to stay with their flocks. Joseph instructed his brothers to make it plain to Pharaoh that they were shepherds, so that he might assign them to this territory, apparently in keeping with precedent. This is also the area which the Hyksos conquerors of Egypt (1720–1570 B.C.E.) built up around their new capital Avaris, (later Tanis, or, Hebrew, Zoan). Joseph's brothers appeared before Pharaoh in Goshen, where they settled. The Pharaoh of the time treated Israel and his clan well.

The Bible fails to give the name of the Pharaoh who welcomed the clan, or his place of residence. But it sums up in a few sentences the manner of their entry to Goshen and thus reveals an important clue. Jacob sent his son Judah ahead to represent him before the court:

"He sent Judah before him to Joseph, to appear before him in Goshen; and they came into the land of Goshen. Then Joseph made ready his chariot, and went up to meet Israel his father in Goshen; and he presented himself to him, and fell on his neck, and wept on his neck a good while". (46:28–29)

Festival scene from the tomb of Nebamen, a "scribe who keeps account of the corn of Amen" at Thebes. The master and his guests do not sit around a table, but on chairs in a group, waited on by nude slaves.

When the Hebrews entered Goshen, Joseph rode his chariot and went to meet his father. On his return he reported to Pharaoh:

"So Joseph went in and told Pharaoh, 'My father and my brothers, with their flocks and herds and all that they possess, have come from the land of Canaan; they are now in the land of Goshen' ". (47:1)

The great Egyptologist, Maspero, remarked that chariots were not used for very long journeys. This lends weight to the theory that to achieve his plan, Joseph who must have lived in or near the king's capital, could make his return journey in a short space of time. The implication is that the residence of Pharaoh was situated close to the land of Goshen, or at Avaris or Rameses.

See map of the Eastern Delta of the Nile and the Land of Goshen (Wadi Tumilat) in Chap. VII.

We know from the Egyptians themselves that they were accustomed to admit nomadic peoples in need of food and pasturage into the area of the Delta, or near it. An Egyptian inscription from the 14th century B.C.E. indicates that it was customary for frontier officials to allow people from Palestine and Sinai to enter this section of Egypt, whenever a drought and famine desolated their land. The officials sent word to Pharaoh that such a group of nomads "who knew not how they should live, have come begging a home in the domain of Pharaoh... after the manner of your (the Pharaoh's) father's fathers since the beginning".

The Anastasi Papyrus contains a communication from a frontier official of Merneptah to his superior dated about 1220 B.C.E., informing him that certain Edomite nomad tribes had been allowed, according to precedent, to pass the fortress in the district of Thuku (the Hebrew Succoth) to pasture their cattle near Pithom "to keep them alive and to keep their cattle alive... in the domain of Pharaoh". It is indicated that the border officer conducted these nomads to the marshlands of Pithom "in the great Ka of Pharaoh" (Wadi Tumilat). We note with interest in the Egyptian papyri mention of Succoth and Pithom, towns in Goshen mentioned in Exodus, where the Hebrews had settled.

EGYPT DURING THE SECOND MILLENNIUM B.C.E.

Before attempting to correlate biblical events with their Egyptian setting, it is pertinent to bear in mind Egyptian trends during the eventful millennium. Egypt began to enjoy a position of political and economic supremacy in Syria and Palestine during its "Middle Kingdom", coinciding approximately with the beginning of the second millennium. Its kings were strong and wily enough to dominate the local Egyptian princes and to gain their loyalty. The maintenance of the ancient feudal system of land ownership and privileges was therefore a foregone conclusion, but local sensibilities and local initiative were not crushed by the central authority. They moved the southern capital of Thebes nearer to Memphis in Middle Egypt, where control could be kept over the northern and southern parts of the land, known respectively as Lower and Upper Egypt. Native authority underwent an eclipse when the country was subjected to Hyksos rule between 1720 and 1570 B.C.E. With the end of this interlude, native Egyptian dynasties recovered the old hegemony under the 18th and 19th dynasties called the "New Kingdom", which coincided approximately with the second half of the second millennium.

This may have immediately preceded the coming of Israel to Egypt (the 15th or 14th century B.C.E.). Egyptian domination abroad was passing through a new crisis during the Empire days of the 18th dynasty; while the small kingdoms of Syria and Palestine took advantage of this to increase their independence. They were in a more or less permanent state of war among themselves. No one of them succeeded in maintaining a position of predominance.

By that time, feudalism within Egypt proper had gone, and an age of absolute dictatorship and ownership of the land prevailed, such as is depicted in Genesis 47:19-20, where the system is attributed to Joseph's planning. We learn from Egyptian sources that the kings required efficient and resourceful prime ministers and able civil servants to administer the land and its resources. This gave talented common people an opportunity to rise to high positions. Accordingly the rise of Joseph fits in with this picture of Egypt.

WHEN WAS JOSEPH IN EGYPT? A HISTORICAL EVALUATION

Is it possible to say just when Joseph was in Egypt? Stray ideas occur as we strip the events of the current story from the folkloric romance. These hints, in the Bible text, have led scholars to suggest various theories and chronologies.

The record relates that Israel and his family were settled in the land of Goshen. Another version speaks, instead, of the "land of Rameses":

"Then Joseph placed his father and his brothers, and gave them a possession in the land of Egypt, in the best of the land, in the land of Rameses, as Pharaoh had commanded". (47:11)

It is true that the "land of Rameses" is artificially differentiated from the city of Raamses, one of the store cities the Israelites built in the later days of their bondage. Or it may be the name by which Egypt is called after the great Pharaohs of the 19th dynasty who were named Rameses (beginning 1305 B.C.E.); or it may have been called this in retrospect by the biblical writers much after the events related, and may be an anachronism. But if the mention of the land of Rameses is not an anachronism, it would lend some weight to one theory; that this reference fits in perfectly with the New Kingdom and dates the historic migration of the Israelites to Egypt in the early part of the 19th dynasty, which came after the Age of Ikhnaton (18th dynasty in the 14th century). The Pharaohs of the 19th dynasty established their capital at Avaris (Zoan), near the land of Goshen, after 1300 B.C.E.

However, a common theory dates Joseph in an earlier time, namely the days of the Hyksos ("Middle Kingdom"). A post-biblical Jewish historian, Josephus, had already linked the entry of Jacob's clan to the time of the Hyksos, who built their capital at Avaris (in the "plain of Tanis" or Goshen) about 1720—1700 B.C.E. The biblical chronology maintains that the Hebrews stayed 430 or 400 years in Egypt. This would also fit their entry during the Hyksos period and their exit in the 13th century. The Hyksos included many Semites, and conditions were right for the sympathetic welcome of Jacob's clan and for Joseph's rise to power. Moreover, Hebrew names like Yakub and Hur appear in the Hyksos lists of nobles. Thus the political change and the beginning of the bondage mentioned in Exodus 1:8: "there rose up a new king over Egypt, who knew not Joseph", would refer to Ah-Mose (Amasis I), who drove out the Hyksos from Egypt (1570 B.C.E.), destroyed their

Painting of Ikhnaton (Amenophis IV — XVIII Dynasty), beneath the rays of the sun, symbolizing the new religion of Aton.

Queen Nefert-ity, of graceful beauty. She remained faithful to her husband's faith in the living "Aton" symbolized by the sun, and stayed at Tel-el-Amarna after Ikhnaton's revolutionary reform had been stamped out.

capital, Avaris, and made Thebes his southern capital.

Such a theory may explain the mention of the Hebrews being "an abomination unto the Egyptians" (43:32; 46:34). However, since the biblical account depicts a peaceful migration to Egypt, the Hebrew settlement could not have been a part of the Hyksos movement itself, which was a conquest. Moreover, there was still feudalism during the Hyksos period, and the national economy was not based on royal ownership of the lands as in the days of Joseph.

That is why some scholars argue in favour of another theory identifying Joseph's Pharaoh with a period two centuries later than the invasion of the Hyksos, or the first half of the 14th century, namely the "New Kingdom" that of Ikhnaton (Amenhotep IV), one of the most remarkable men of ancient history. This sensitive idealist suppressed the worship of the god Amon and of all other gods associated with him, and declared that there was a universal god, Re of Heliopolis, symbolized by the sun-disc. He changed the divinity's name to Aton. He was "sole god, like whom there is no other". He changed his own name from Amenophis (Amenhotep) to Ikhnaton, and moved his capital and called it Akhetaton. This is the Tel Amarna of today, where the clay tablets, or the records of the Egyptian Foreign Office were discovered. This capital is many days travel from Goshen where the Hebrews had settled. It has been suggested that the record of Gen. 41-43 telling of Joseph's rise to power, seems to repeat Egyptian words which may instead mean "abrekhenaton", or "the friend of Ikhnaton". This would lend weight to the theory dating Joseph to the time of that famous king.

In his day many officials of Semitic and Asiatic origin rose also in the hierarchy of the royal court and served the king. One of them was Yanhamu, the king's Vizier in charge of Canaan. Some see a certain parallelism between him and Joseph. According to this theory, the "new king who knew not Joseph" would refer to Haremheb (1342—1303), actual founder of the 19th dynasty, who wiped out Atonism and anything connected with it and might have enslaved the Hebrews who had been favoured by the reformer king.

The Ani papyrus describes the judgement scene after death. The heart is weighed in the presence of the god Osiris. Ani himself was a scribe and governor of the granaries.

Rolls of inscribed papyrus were commonly buried with the dead. They included prayers and hymns to help the dead pass through the under-world and arrive at the "fields of peace".

Letter from a south Palestinian king to Yanhamu, vizier of Ikhnaton. Among the archives of Tel-el-Amarna.

Representation of a Syrian (or Palestinian) by Egyptians of the 15th and 14th centuries B.C.E. Bound Syrian captive at the head of a ceremonial walking stick of Tutankhamen.

Letters from Canaanite and Phoenician kings to the court of Ikhnaton. Found at Tel-el-Amarna. On the left, a letter from Rib-Addi of Byblos; on the right, a letter from Yahtiri of Gaza or Joppa (?). Below a letter from the king of Gobba, an unknown town.

There are other hints which point to the time when Joseph lived. The biblical account tells us how, through Joseph's planning, the silver, the livestock and the very persons and the land of the people were step by step converted into royal property:

> " 'and as for the people, he made slaves of them from one end of Egypt to the other. Only the land of the priests he did not buy; for the priests had a fixed allowance from Pharaoh, and lived on the allowance which Pharaoh gave them; therefore they did not sell their land". (47:21–22)

The New Kingdom (as the Empire period is also called) was to be an age of royal ownership of the land, and the people were nearly all serfs who were to cultivate the king's land and pay one fifth of all the crops to the royal granary. The biblical tradition does not comment on any social implications ascribed to Joseph's system of national economy. He used his new powers wisely, and served his sovereign brilliantly, and the story describes in simple terms the social and economic conditions of the time:

> "So Joseph made it a statute concerning the land of Egypt, and it stands to this day, that Pharaoh should have the fifth; the land of the priests alone did not become Pharaoh's". (47:26)

The tax of 20% is normal for the period. This was paid in grain delivered to the royal granaries in each provincial capital. A later chronicler remarks that the priesthood of Egypt was free from the heavy taxation imposed by the Pharaoh's absolute dictatorship. The temples had always derived their maintenance from the king's treasury and from their own very extensive properties, which archaeologists estimate to have been between 15—30% of the arable acreage of the land. On the present evidence of a large scroll dealing with tax assessments (The Wilbour Papyrus), it seems that the privileges of the temples under this new system were confined to an immunity which burdened the rest of Egypt. This new economic and social regime followed the former system of the "Middle Kingdom" which had been an age of feudalism, when Egyptian land was largely owned by powerful nobles. This ended with the expulsion of the Hyksos (1570 B.C.E.). In fact the landed nobility had disappeared and their place was taken by the bureaucracy of the government officials. Some scholars therefore place Joseph's tradition after the feudal days of Egypt.

In view of the complexity of the picture, it is not surprising that historians differ in assessing the evidence presented in the biblical account, and in comparing it with various Egyptian records of times when similar customs prevailed. None of the hints advanced by any theory gives certainty. A similar problem arises again in connection with the date of the Exodus, which, it is generally agreed, took place under the 19th dynasty.

THE PASSING OF THE PATRIARCHAL AGE

In the last three chapters of Genesis the narrative reverts from Joseph's story to the patriarchal pattern. Jacob in his illness expressed a wish to be buried in Canaan. The aged patriarch called for Joseph and the latter's two sons, Manasseh the elder and Ephraim the younger. He adopted and blessed them. Joseph properly stationed Manasseh at Jacob's right and the younger, Ephraim, at his left. But Jacob crossed his hands so that the right hand

Heren, a boat used to carry the soul of Pharaoh on his last journey. The guardian slaves are aboard and the "eye" painted on the side is to guide the boat in an unknown world. Funerary beliefs were dominated by magic and spells designed to assure the comfort and well-being of the deceased in that ageless world of blessed immortality "until that day cometh when one reacheth port in the land that loveth silence".

touched the younger, and the left the elder. This circumstance in Jacob's blessing provides the reader with an important etiological explanation of why the younger, Ephraim, or his tribe, became more important than that of the elder son, Manasseh. Once again we find the classical theme of a younger son eclipsing the older. This is familiar to Canaanite sagas in both the story of the Bible and Ugarit. The two brothers are, of course, personifications of the tribes that replaced the earlier clan of Joseph, about whom dim tribal memory relates:

Women mourners of ancient Egypt. They shrilled and they shrieked in unison, bared their breasts, raised their arms and clapped their hands over their heads. They cut off locks of hair from the root, covered their faces with dust and hung ropes over their shoulders. Egyptian tomb painting of the 14th century B.C.E.

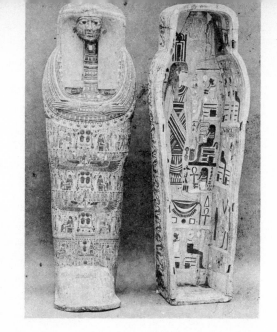

The mummy of Ta-ahuti (right) lay under wings of gold cloisonne.
This golden shell was the innermost of three coffins. The bodies
of Egyptian kings, nobles and other illustrious (and even ordinary)
people were embalmed by removing the organs easily susceptible
to decay and steeping the body in salt and spices of natron for 40
or 70 days, then swathing it in linen bandages hundreds of yards
long. The poorer people were swathed in bandages impregnated
in pitch. The Egyptians believed that the preservation of the body
for the soul's use after death was a prime religious duty and the
epitome of respectability. The picture at the centre is the outer
coffin of Ahmes; wood covered with stucco (early 18th dynasty).
Below, mummy of Ukh-hotep with mask (12th dynasty).

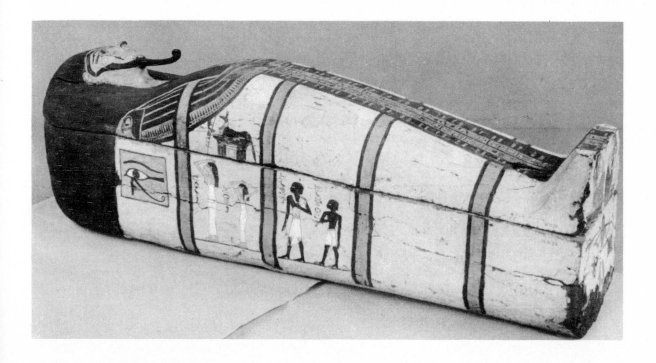

"Then Israel said to Joseph, 'Behold, I am about to die, but God will be with you, and will bring you again to the land of your fathers. Moreover I have given to you rather than to your brothers one mountain slope which I took from the Amorites with my sword and with my bow' ". (48:21–22)

We will never know the time spent by the Israelites in Goshen, between the deaths of Jacob and Joseph. But we can discern a tradition in the last chapter of Gen. (50) that keeps alive a memory dating back to Israel's stay in Egypt, describing the embalming of Jacob and Joseph. This is an obvious vestige of the Egyptianization of the Israelites in their land of adoption. A parallel tradition reports Joseph's request to Pharaoh, mediated by courtiers, for a leave of absence to bury his father in Palestine. The tradition is indefinite about the location of Jacob's burial. It is possible that this has some connection with the background of Egyptian crown interests in Palestine. Hebrew historians, at the time the story was composed, knew nothing of how the 18th or 19th dynasty Pharaohs controlled the land, but only that Jacob's funeral cortege, honoured by Pharaoh's court, had been an important event.

The book closes with Joseph's request that his remains be moved to Canaan. But a tradition of another origin, in this chapter, relates that he was embalmed (mummified) and placed in a sarcophagus in Egypt. This indication may suggest that the political climate at the time of his death was not the same as at the beginning of his glorious career. Otherwise his clansmen would have granted his wish to be buried in Canaan as was the case with Jacob.

JACOB'S BLESSING

Before his death, Jacob is reported to have pronounced a blessing over the tribes, in which the twelve actual sons, including Joseph, were singled out as the ancestors of the future tribes. Their characteristics, symbols and destinies are worded in poetic meter and prophetic cast. The graphic representation of the symbols of the tribes based on this blessing, have been retained by Jewish tradition. The rich and beautiful stanzas of Jacob's blessing (Chapter 49) must be read to be appreciated. They belong, in fact, to the oldest parts we know of the Bible and are among the most important sources for the earliest history of the tribes and will provide tantalizing problems for many generations to come. It is only conjecture to guess when this wealth of folk poetry was composed in writing. By then it had been assembled into one complete poem, combining dim and half-forgotten traditions, and the glory and emergence of the House of David. It is assumed that the composition of the poem in its present form dates to the period of the first Kings of Israel.

Not all sons, or tribes, shared alike in Jacob's blessing. Three of the sons, who came to grief as tradition has it, were not blessed at all. Reuben, destined for a history of trouble, had his misfortunes attributed to his misbehaviour with Jacob's concubine. Simeon and Levi were reproached with the treacherous attack on Shechem. They would also come to grief, and the Levites who would descend from Levi would not settle on the land, but be scattered throughout the tribal territories of Canaan as a sacerdotal class. Traditionally, all Jews named Levi, down to the present day, are direct descendants of the ancient tribesmen. Judah was not an eldest son, but he was destined as a leader over his brothers. This reflects, of course, the emergence of this tribe under the name of the House of David, and Yehuda (Judah) is singular for Yehudim (Jews).

CHAPTER VI

THE SOJOURN IN EGYPT. EXODUS AND REDEMPTION

BONDAGE AND THE BIRTH OF A NATION

"These are the names of the sons of Israel who came to Egypt with Jacob, each with his household; Reuben, Simeon, Levi, and Judah, Issachar, Zebulun, and Benjamin, Dan and Naphtali, Gad and Asher. All the offspring of Jacob were seventy persons; Joseph was already in Egypt. Then Joseph died, and all his brothers, and all that generation. But the descendants of Israel were fruitful and increased greatly; they multiplied and grew exceedingly strong; so that the land was filled with them". (Exodus 1:1–7)

The first problem we encounter in the Book of Exodus is the reiteration of seventy as the number of Jacob's descendants who migrated to Egypt. Many scholars regard it as a literary form which crops up in the style of legends, for instance the seventy sons of Ashera in the Ugarit myth and other genealogies of the chieftains in the Book of Judges and II Kings. It has been suggested that the traditions of Exodus, particularly Chaps. 1–15, form an organic literary unit or cultic recital, stemming from a memorial of Passover rites.

Though poor in historic detail, the recital shows that the existence of Hebrew shepherds in Goshen, on the eastern border of the Nile Delta, apparently aroused little interest, and the succession of generations is largely passed over in silence. The interval between Joseph's death and the Pharaoh of the bondage is summed up in the Book of Exodus in the single verse (the 7th as above), which stresses the numerical increase of the Israelites.

Then, a change of dynasty as well as of policy towards these people is reported in two terse sentences which are too obscure to serve as documentary history and leave almost no circumstantial clues in the drama that was unfolded:

> "Now there arose a new king over Egypt, who did not know Joseph. And he said to his people, 'Behold, the people of Israel are too many and too mighty for us. Come, let us deal shrewdly with them, lest they multiply, and, if war befall us, they join our enemies and fight against us and escape from the land.' Therefore they set taskmasters over them to afflict them with heavy burdens; and they built for Pharaoh store cities, Pithom and Raamses".
>
> (Ex 1: 8–11)

In the customary manner of epics, background is ignored, while the recital plunges straight into the scenes of the drama. The only causal relation is of a political change which occurred at an unknown stage. This is all one can go by starting from a historical vacuum which lasted many generations, up to the advent of the king who introduced the bondage. One must not regard these introductory remarks as a historical report, but as a short preface to a recital of the major theme, the drama of Bondage and Exodus, the epic which Jews have embodied in a memorial of rites chanted on Passover. One most striking feature of these introductory verses, for instance, is the glaring omission of the name of the "Pharaoh who knew not Joseph", or the Pharaoh of the Exodus later on in the epic.

The Hebrews were reduced to the status of slaves, burdened with the onerous corvee of building the "store cities" or the "treasure cities" in the Delta of Lower Egypt. This fact provides the only definite evidence by which we may attempt to determine the date of the Exodus and of related problems, such as the duration of the stay of Israel in Egypt. The answer to these complex questions must take many factors into consideration. One of these is the time when the Hebrews came to Egypt, and the probable date of Joseph's period. The duration of the Bondage of Israel in Egypt has long been a matter over which scholars differ considerably. This set of problems in general should be studied by (a) a proper evaluation of the nature of biblical evidence, and (b) in relation to the contemporary Egyptian background.

A) THE EPIC OF EXODUS: THE NATURE OF BIBLICAL EVIDENCE.

The nature of biblical narration and its order in Genesis and Exodus becomes clearer when it is critically read and interpreted as a literary form known nowadays as a *tradition-history* of the beginnings of Israel. It starts with Abraham's migration from Ur of the Chaldees and culminates with the conquest of Canaan. The motivation of this tradition-history is Yahweh's promise to the fathers and his covenant with them; in this sense the epic of Exodus is seen as the fulfillment of the promise he made to Abraham :

> " 'Know of a surety that your descendants will be sojourners in a land that is not theirs, and will be slaves there, and they will be oppressed for four hundred years; but I will bring judgement on the nation which they serve, and afterward they shall come out with great possessions' " (Gen. 15 : 13–14)

These verses are of course an insertion into the Abraham tradition, made after the Exodus. The tradition of Exodus must perforce be seen as the kernel and essence of this global tradition, because in the spirit of Hebrew history-writing the deity revealed itself under the hallowed and new historic name of Yahweh only on the occasion of the redemption of Israel from bondage. In the past he was known to the fathers only as El Shaddai:

> "And God said to Moses 'I am Yahweh (the Lord). I appeared to Abraham, to Isaac, and to Jacob as El-Shaddai, but by my name Yahweh I did not make myself known to them'". (Ex 6:2–3)

This indicates clearly that the Exodus represents the formation of Israel's historic faith and the foundation event from which its national history sprang. The record may not be regarded as a historical report in the usual sense. But the events begot a memorial of rites.

According to the Scandinavian school, the narrative of Exodus was interpreted as liturgical recitation, accompanied by dramatic presentations of the historical events commemorated in the Passover festival. This gives the cultic "situation in life" or actual background, from which sprang the oral narrative. This memorial of rites lives on, into this day, more than three thousand years after the event, in Israel's greatest feast, the Seder or memorial rite of Passover.

In line with the findings of "form-criticism" the Book of Exodus has grown in its present form out of the recitations of the Passover rite. It may be divided into two main parts: (1) The Exodus from Egypt and journey to Sinai under the leadership of Moses (Chap. 1–18). (2) Israel at Sinai (Chap. 19–40), comprising the inauguration of the Covenant (19–24), the construction of the Tabernacle (25–40), including the episode of the Golden Calf (32–34). In other words the book describes rites and laws as well as events. We find there the code and cult of early Israel. The same is true of the other books of the Pentateuch. As is the case with Genesis, the book contains no clue as to the names of its authors, except the traditional belief which attributes its authorship to Moses; many strata of tradition may likewise be observed in its composition.

The theme that resounds throughout the Old Testament is first sounded here. The national literature would not let the people forget that Yahweh entered history and proved himself mightier than the armies of Pharaoh, than the gods of Egypt. This basic belief has remained, in the hearts of the people, and in the heart of the Pentateuch (the first five books of the Bible), and in the eloquent little liturgy in Deuteronomy, a confession of faith recited when presenting the first fruits of the harvest at the sanctuary.

> "And you shall make response before the Lord your God, 'A wandering Aramean was my father; and he went down into Egypt and sojourned there, few in number; and there he became a nation, great, mighty, and populous. And the Egyptians treated us harshly, and afflicted us, and laid upon us hard bondage. Then we cried to the Lord the God of our fathers, and the Lord heard our voice, and saw our affliction, our toil, and our oppression; and the Lord brought us out of Egypt with a mighty hand and an outstreched arm, with great terror, with signs and wonders'"; (Deut. 26:5–8)

The stress laid by the ancient authors on Exodus as the most important initial epoch in the career of Israel stems from the decisive factor of the Egyptian experience in the development of Israel as a people, and in the identification of the tribes with a universal deity.

B) THE NARRATIVE AND ITS HISTORICAL BACKGROUND

The historic kernel of the Exodus itself cannot be questioned and it fits into the general framework of Egypto-Canaanite relations. It may have been just one exodus among others. It is known that famine and other drastic conditions impelled Semites to seek bread or pasture-land in the Nile Valley, and the natural sequel might have been the occasion of an Exodus from Egypt. The historian's problem, therefore, is to place, with the help of collateral information from other sources of the ancient world, the epic of Exodus in an historic context. We must appreciate that it is the end product of the cumulative oral memory of countless generations. Changes, accretions or deletions may have occurred in the course of transmission.

EGYPTIAN BONDAGE IN THE LIGHT OF EVIDENCE

a) ISRAEL IN EGYPT

Although there is no direct evidence in Egyptian records of Israel's bondage in Egypt, there can be little doubt that the ancestors of Israel had been slaves there and eventually escaped. The biblical tradition cannot be questioned, for it is unlikely that Israel would invent such an unheroic and shameful past. Accumulating discoveries about the biblical environment (though not of the actual events related) makes it worth mentioning some background material which gives objective support to the story.

Egyptian names were prevalent in early Israel. In particular members of Moses' clan, that of Levi, had Egyptian names, such as Pinehas, Hophni, Merari, Putiel. This indicates a connection with Egypt and that this branch was egyptianized. But unlike other foreigners in Egypt, who cast in their lot with the sophisticated people of the country, became thoroughly egyptianized and accepted as normal members of the Egyptian community, these Israelites were still linked with Hebrew traditions.

BRICKS WITHOUT STRAW

We are told that the first encounter of Moses and Pharaoh served only to anger the king and stiffen his attitude to Israel. This phase in the epic augured the stubborn resistance that was to unfold dramatically in the story of the contest with Pharaoh (in Ex. 5 to 15).

"The same day Pharaoh commanded the taskmasters of the people and their foremen, 'You shall no longer give the people straw to make bricks, as heretofore; let them go and gather straw for themselves. But the numbers of the bricks which they made heretofore you shall lay upon them, you shall by no means lessen it; for they are idle; therefore they cry, "Let us go and offer sacrifice to our God"'". (Ex. 5:6–8)

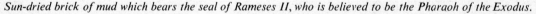

Sun-dried brick of mud which bears the seal of Rameses II, who is believed to be the Pharaoh of the Exodus.

A wooden model of brickmakers at work, found in a tomb. The central figure is digging mud to fill the basket once held by the kneeling man. The man on the left is pressing mud into a frame for forming the bricks, three rows of which are before him.

In ancient Egypt mud-brick was the almost universal building material, like the adobe houses constructed by the American Indians. For stronger bricks, it is necessary to mix the black mud with a considerable amount of chopped straw, or "teben". It was such a straw or grass that had been delivered to the brickmakers in the biblical account, previous to Pharaoh's anger, the story states.

> "The taskmasters were urgent saying, 'Complete your work, your daily task, as when there was straw.' And the foremen of the people of Israel, whom Pharaoh's taskmasters had set over them, were beaten and were asked, 'Why have you not done all your task of making bricks today, as hitherto?' Then the foremen of the people of Israel came and cried to Pharaoh, 'Why do you deal thus with your servants? No straw is given to your servants, yet they say to us, "Make bricks!" And behold, your servants are beaten; but the fault is in your own people'".
> (Ex. 5:13–16)

In spite of popular conceptions to the contrary, there is no scriptural evidence that the Hebrews made bricks without straw. The story states that the straw from the threshing floors

Brick-making scene in Egypt. Mud, generally mixed with chaff or chopped straw, is being worked with a hoe, carried away in a bucket and dumped on a pile. Bricks are shaped in rectangular moulds by pressing the soil into them, then drying them in the sun. Lying on the ground (upper right) are three bricks, from the last of which a wooden mould is being lifted. Taskmasters or foremen, carrying sticks, keep the men hard at work. The diagram below shows the complete process. From a wall painting in the tomb of Rekh-mi-Re, vizier of Upper Egypt about 1450 B.C.E.

was no longer delivered to the Hebrews, and that they had to gather such rubble as they could find to take its place, while the quota of bricks to be delivered remained the same. Thus the oft repeated phrase, to "make bricks without straw" does not represent the actual situation, but rests on a misunderstanding of the text and ignorance of the actual practice.

The execution of these public works is described clearly: The men were organized in groups under "foremen" recruited among the Israelites; these were answerable in turn to Egyptian "taskmasters" set over them, who would beat them if the quota was not met. Getting any work done without beating was rare in Egypt. It was less a matter of brutality than the normal relationship between men of unequal status in their daily work. The Hebrew foremen protested to Pharaoh. The stage was set for a contest between Pharaoh and Yahweh.

b) THE DATE OF THE BONDAGE AND THE EXODUS

In dating this period, scholars who ascribe the settlement of the Hebrews in Goshen to the time of the Hyksos, believe that the Exodus took place at the beginning of the 18th Egyptian dynasty, when Ahmose I expelled the Hyksos, and purged the Semites and Hebrews who had remained in the Delta region where the invading kings had been entrenched. It must be noted, however, that Ahmose, whose capital was Thebes in Southern Egypt, destroyed Avaris, their capital. That period, in the opinion of many historians, would be too early for the Exodus. In any case, this theory does not seem to fit the narrative from Ex. 1:9 and following verses, which assumes that the court of Pharaoh was not far from Goshen. There we find once again that the king's court was in the Delta area, as evidenced by the contact he maintained with the two Hebrew midwives who were supposed to cooperate with him in eliminating all male children; and more particularly by the story of the Egyptian princess who went down to the river to bathe and found herself near the Hebrew settlement where Moses was born: See map of the delta of the Nile and the Land of Goshen at the end of this Chapter.

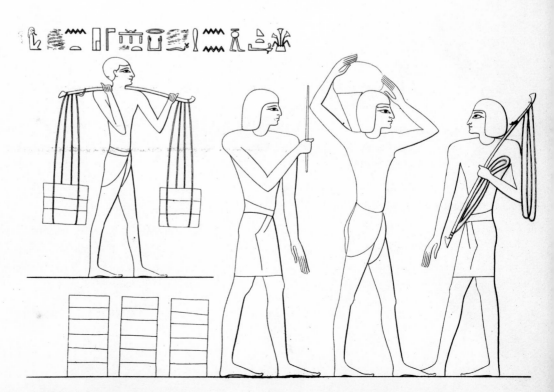

The dried bricks are carried off in a yoked carrier. A foreman is standing by.

This account presupposes the period of the 19th Egyptian dynasty (about 1305–1200 B.C.E.). The exodus would then have been between 1290 to 1230 B.C.E., though other dates have been suggested. At that time strong kings again re-established Egyptian authority in western Asia. Stelae of Seti I found at Beth-Shean in Israel bear tribute to his control of the country. He began the reconstruction of the old Hyksos capital, Avaris, and the project was continued by his son Rameses II (1290–1244), who built a city on the Delta site bearing his name, "The House of Rameses". The name of the city fits with that of the second city which the Hebrew slaves built, (Raamses). Pithom was older, but the finest structure there was the temple of the great builder. No royal building of an earlier Pharaoh has been found there; so if the Israelites worked on royal projects at Pithom, it must have been in the time of Rameses. His victories had provided him with prisoners. He not only rebuilt a new capital, but apparently set about the reclamation of this neglected border province. There was urgent need for protective walls and grain stores built of sun-baked bricks. He preferred to use available man-power living there rather than exploit Egyptians. Moreover the Hebrews who had been allowed to live there by the grace of a former king, had increased considerably. It was expeditious to exploit them "lest they multiply, and, if war befall us, they join our enemies and fight against us and escape from the land". (Ex. 1:10)

Egyptian records indicate that a city named Ne-Rameses was attached to the capital. It was situated along a canal and it corresponds to what the biblical account calls a store-city of Pharaoh.

According to an Egyptian document, Rameses II was one of the Pharaohs who used "Apiru" in his public projects. Some of them are represented as engaged in digging up stone for temples built by him. As a result of the conquests of Amenhotep II in Syria and Palestine, large numbers of Semitic and non-Semitic captives of war, including 3600 Hapiru, were brought to Egypt as state slaves. The military campaigns of other Egyptian kings from the 14th to the 12th centuries, produced similar results.

The city of Raamses was not just a "store city" as the later Hebrew tradition has it, but the royal capital, which is referred to in an Egyptian poem as the city which "none resembles in its likeness to Thebes". Poems in praise of the city have been preserved in Egyptian papyri. This Pharaoh, who was engaged in fighting great wars with the Hittites, his rivals for the possession of Syria, felt that a capital near the border was needed, both for the storage of grain for his army and for trade. From there he marched his army and chariots into Palestine to fight the great battle with the Hittites at Kadesh, illustrated on the walls of the Rames-seum at Thebes. It was difficult to keep a firm hand on Asiatic possessions (and markets) from places far up the Nile, like Thebes and Memphis. (The Egyptian Rameses is rendered Raamses in Hebrew).

We remember from Gen. 47:11 that when Jacob as an old man went to Egypt, it was called the "land of Rameses". The country could only be called so in the Rameside Age, which began late in the 14th century B.C.E. c.1311. These reasons incline most scholars to regard Seti I, Rameses I and Rameses II as the Pharaohs of the oppression. Those who favour an earlier date consider the biblical reference to the land or the city of Rameses an anachronism.

A Canaanite porter carrying a double-handled jar.
It is in the style of Egyptian representations of Canaanites and Syrians of the last quarter of the 15th century B.C.E. From a wooden handle for an ointment
spoon.

Seti I (1302–1290) at the battle of Kadesh in Syria,
"the Land of the Amurru" (Amorites). From an engra-
ving of the Temple of Karnak at Luxor.

The mummy of Seti I.

Shackled Syrian prisoners, heavily bearded, being led away by a bowman. From the rock-temple of Rameses II at Beit-ei-Wali.

Prisoners of the Egyptians from neighbouring lands. Bound with ropes, they are held by gods in the register above, who are presenting them to the king. A relief in the temple of Sahu-Re

Archaeological and historical considerations give strong reasons for believing that the Hebrew tribes finally entered the Promised Land, after the Exodus from Egypt, about the middle of the 13th century B.C.E., or during the third quarter. Now that the site of Raamses has been located at Tanis, and on the archaeological evidence, G. E. Wright — and many others are of his opinion — maintains: "We now know that if there is any historical value at all to the store-city tradition in Exodus (and there is no reason to doubt its reliability) then the Israelites must have been in Egypt at least during the early part of the reign of Rameses II." After much digging at Tanis by P. Montet, not a single object of the 18th dynasty has been found there. Moreover, after the 11th century, the place was not called Rameses, but Tanis, so that the use of the name Raamses for this town would not be an anachronism. This supports the dating of Ex. 1:2 in the reign of Rameses II.

This epic of Exodus mentions only one change of reign during the long period of bondage. According to P. Montet this important indication suggests that the former ruler, before Moses had come on the scene as a deliverer, had reigned a few decades. We know from Egyptian history that Rameses II reigned 67 years until the age of 90. If Moses was born in the early days of his reign and escaped from the wrath of this wilful Pharaoh — he had to bide his time in the wilderness. He also might not yet have attained the spiritual powers that would enable him to cope with the situation. In fact the biblical record indicates that

Herdsmen in Egypt.

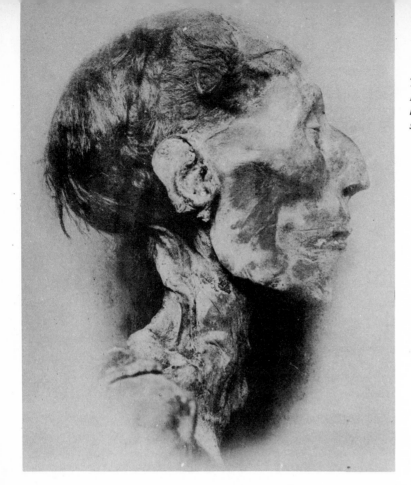

The mummy of Rameses II who reigned 67 years; he had many wives, 110 sons and 51 daughters.

"Moses was eighty years old, and Aaron eighty-three years old, when they spoke to Pharaoh". (7:7) Even if this ripe age is not taken literally, it may suggest that Moses started his career as a leader late in the time of Rameses II, or during the reign of his son Merneptah

c) WHAT WAS THE DURATION OF ISRAEL'S STAY IN EGYPT?

There is another problem to be considered in assessing the date of the Exodus. It is customary to compute the time the Hebrews lived in the Delta area (Goshen) as the conventional 400 years, according to the Hebrew record:

"The time that the people of Israel dwelt in Egypt was four hundred and thirty years. And at the end of four hundred and thirty years, on that very day, all the hosts of the Lord went out from the land of Egypt". (Ex. 12:40–41)

However this verse can be interpreted as referring only to the years of oppression as in Gen. 15:13-14. It must be noted that the Septuagint (first Greek translation of the Old Testament) complicates the matter by saying in Exodus 12:40 that the Israelites lived in Egypt *and in the land of Canaan* 430 years. In other words, that would cover the whole period from the call of Abraham to the Exodus. It has been observed by many that none of the figures in the Bible can be taken as exact, but must be weighed against archaeological and other evidence.

We have observed that the year reckonings and the genealogies in the Bible are not compatible, and cannot both be correct. Indeed the biblical genealogy (and other data) stand the test of critical evaluation better than the year reckonings. When Jacob came to Egypt, Joseph was a high official, and presumably not young. Moses, according to the biblical genealogy, was the great-grandson of Levi, the older brother of Joseph. Joseph lived to the ripe old age of 110 and he lived to see his great-grandchildren (Gen. 50:23), who in the natural order of things would be younger than Moses. Moses may have been born before or shortly after Joseph's death. In other words, it need not disturb us that the reckoning on the basis of genealogy, which is more compatible with the historical background, does not leave much time for Israel's Bondage in Egypt. This was terminated under Moses, as we observed, about the third quarter of the 13th century B.C.E. The gap between the coming of Israel to Egypt and the birth of Moses, could perhaps be spanned in a single lifetime.

MOSES

The figure of Moses towers above his people during the last stage of bondage and dominates the events of exodus and the wanderings. All we know about him is contained in the biblical narrative which we have no means of testing as a whole, save some details which may be considered in the light of background material.

No matter how sympathetically we view the biblical interpretation of the events of Moses' career, we must still, with our attitude to history, raise certain questions: who was Moses? where was the mountain of revelation? whence came his God, and what was the faith that emerged with him? what was the momentous and mysterious stirring from which came the great epic that tells us all we know about him?

Attempts to find answers to these unsolved riddles range far and wide. Martin Noth's opinion is that the Pentateuch in its present form is the work of later compilers or school of chroniclers; and that the figure of Moses is enlarged through the need to tie all the events of Exodus, Sinai, and all law to him; and that this is the root of the complexity of the Pentateuch. As the systematic appearance of Moses in all these themes cannot have occurred at their origin—because they are more sophisticated than the times of Exodus and Sinai and are the results of a later arrangement—this scholar is hard put to answer where Moses should be placed historically. He does deny the importance of Sinai, and minimizes Moses' all-embracing role as indicated throughout the Pentateuch.

Modern scholarship is aware of the need to approach this enigma in a critical spirit. H. Gressman tried to illumine the character of the narratives about Moses, scattered through the books of Exodus and Numbers. Assuming that the stories had been taken into later composition from the current tales preserved by the people, Gressman identified the individual units of narrative by diversities of type and sought to distinguish between those that were primitive and those that had received more or less elaboration. He found that the original popular traditions, which had not been obliterated by later redactors, had the literary form of "poetic" creations of the people. Genuine historical memories regarding the figure of Moses had been overlaid with elements of the supernatural or marvellous, so that in their final form these stories had the epic character of popular wonder tales. They were part of Israel's literary heritage; but they may not be regarded as historical data.

This approximates the view of most modern scholars, among them Prof. Martin Buber, who seeks answers to the riddle of Moses in the great epic of Exodus, which is built around him. Though it remains a problem whether he was the first and only founder of Israel's faith, it is undeniable that the events of Exodus and Sinai required a great personality behind them. As regards his historicity, it must be observed that if we disregard the tremendous influence and dynamic thrust of the enlarged figure of Moses, yet we would have to assume the existence of another religious personality, and by the logic of things, it would be someone of the same type (a man of his age and background).

THE FIGURE OF MOSES

Emerging from the Epic of Exodus and other biblical traditions is a figure of heroic stature. The focus is not so much on his personality as on his relation to God who prepared and summoned him to be the agent in the accomplishment of a purpose. But one may attempt to relate this personality to the known background.

a) HIS BIRTH AND LIFE EPISODES

"And when she could hide him no longer she took for him a basket made of bulrushes, and daubed it with bitumen and pitch; and she put the child in it and placed it among the reeds at the river's brink". (Ex. 2: 3)

As a baby Moses was exposed in a little vessel or basket which is explicitly described as having been constructed of reeds. This account is followed by that of his discovery by the Egyptian princess who went down to the river to bathe and found him among the flags of papyrus.

Egyptologists are perhaps justified in pointing out that a princess did not have to expose herself thus, when she could bathe in some secluded spot in the royal domain. But the sequel of the story required that "she saw the basket".

The tale has features typical of a number of stories about the birth and career of men who were destined for greatness. Being the favourite of a deity is a frequent motif in the biographies of ancient characters. King Sargon, the first king of the Accadian Empire in Mesopotamia was born, according to legendary tradition, of obscure parents who exposed him as a baby in a basket which they set afloat on a stream, until he was found.

"And the child grew, and she brought him to Pharaoh's daughter, and he became her son; and she named him Moses, for she said, 'Because I drew him out of the water' ". (Ex. 2:10)

The interpretation of the name, through a peculiar coincidence of the sound and a circumstance of the story, connects it with the Hebrew word "masha", to "draw out", because he was drawn out of the water. The play on words is a typical example of the popular ex-

Flags of papyrus on the Nile. It was amongst such that Moses' mother hid "an ark of bulrushes....and laid it in the flags by the river's brink". (Ex. 2 : 3)

Girls swimming. An ivory cosmetic spoon.

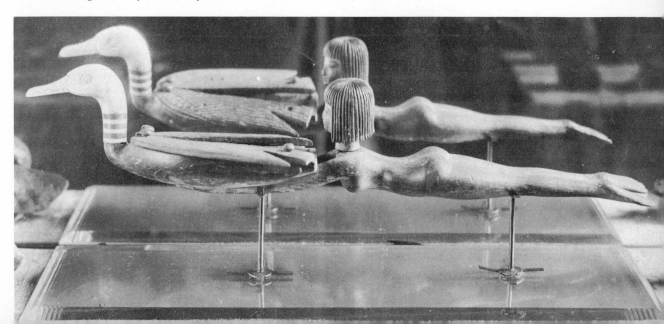

planation of names on such a basis. Like many derivations given in the Old Testament, it should not be taken too seriously, and the historical origin should rather be sought. The name itself is apparently nothing more than the Egyptian "mesu" (pronounced "moshe" by the Hebrews and "mosis" in the Greek form) connected with the Egyptian word for child. This word is preserved in Egyptian composites like Ah-Mose (child of Ah, god of light), Thuthmose, child of the god Thuth), or Rameses, as illustrated below. In the opinion of P. Montet these names incorporate that of the god on whose anniversary the child was born. It is in fact quite possible that the princess did not give a special name to the unknown infant, and contented herself simply with calling him "child". The name of Moses is apparently an indication of his Egyptian nurture, which, after all, is one of the main points of the story. The storyteller made a point that God was preparing the emergence of a deliverer, and even an Egyptian princess became contributory to God's plan.

The epic proceeds by chaining together a number of episodes which by their mere sequence, with a minimum of commentary, communicate the growing tension. Moses was brought up as the son of the Egyptian princess, but not ignorant of his origin and felt himself strongly drawn toward his Hebrew brethren, as is vividly shown by his impulsive action on seeing an Egyptian taskmaster beating a Hebrew workingman.

"One day, when Moses had grown up, he went out to his people and looked on their burdens; and he saw an Egyptian beating a Hebrew, one of his people. He looked this way and that, and seeing no one he killed the Egyptian and hid him in the sand. When he went out the next day, behold, two Hebrews were struggling together; and he said to the man that did the wrong, 'Why do you srike your fellow?' He answered, 'Who made you a prince and a judge over us? Do you mean to kill me as you killed the Egyptian?' Then Moses was afraid, and thought 'Surely the thing is known'". (Ex. 2:11–14)

Fearing for his life, he fled to the desert for asylum. He married into, and lived for some years with, a nomadic tribe of Midianites or Kenites whose priest was Jethro, Moses'

This group illustrates the composition of the name of Rameses, which is a composite of Ra, the moon -disc over the child's head, and Mesu, the plant he holds in his hand. Found at ancient Tanis or Avaris. The falcon Houroun (Horus) holds the child protectively.

Rameses II (left) and the god Ptah.

father-in-law. His status there was that of "ger" (resident) and he called his son Gershom "for I am a ger in a foreign land" (2:16). This episode, which seems authentic, indicates that Moses and his clan had connections with kindred people in the wilderness east of Goshen.

Years passed, the former Pharaoh died, and the unfortunate incidents of Moses' youth were forgotten. He was now a mature person ripe for greater experiences that would prepare him for deeper knowledge and responsibility. What has been related till now seems a prologue to the main episode at Horeb.

THE BURNING BUSH

The dramatic revelation at the burning bush, in the view of M. Buber, forms the central theme of the spiritual biography of Moses and the drama of revelation in a sequence of impressive scenes.

"Now Moses was keeping the flock of his father-in-law, Jethro, the priest of Midian; and he led his flock to the west side of the wilderness, and came to Horeb, the mountain of God. And the angel of the Lord appeared to him in a flame of fire out of the midst of a bush; and he looked, and lo, the bush was burning, yet it was not consumed. And Moses said, 'I will turn aside and see this great sight, why the bush is not burnt'. When the Lord saw that he turned aside to see, God called to him out of the bush, 'Moses, Moses! 'And he said, 'Here am I.' Then he said, Do not come near; put off your shoes from your feet, for the place on which you are standing is holy ground.' And he said, 'I am the God of your father, the God of Abraham, the God of Isaac, and the God of Jacob.' And Moses hid his face, for he was afraid to look at God' ". (Ex. 3:1–6)

Moses came accidentally, as it were, to the place where the deity dwells, and received the revelation from "him that dwelt in the bush" (Deut. 33:16). The description communicates a meaning that cannot be compressed into the limits of precise prose. One should read it with imagination and empathy to do justice to a sublime theme, as one would read a great poem.

In the Bible fire is frequently a symbol for manifestations of God. What Moses saw was a sign of the divine presence, and he understood that he was standing on holy ground at the foot of a sacred mountain. It would be futile to try to rationalize the burning bush. At first Moses was left wondering how it could burn without being consumed. But the focus of the narrative quickly shifted to the divinity which spoke in the accents of history, dealing directly with the problem that lay heavily on Moses' heart. Moses reflected and reached a fateful decision. It may perhaps be gathered from descriptions of the theophany that this encounter with God sharpened Moses' sense of responsibility, and made him more acutely conscious of the demands of the situation. He hardly expected that his ignorant kinsmen would realize who the God of their fathers really was. In any event they had not sought God during their long stay in Egypt. But it is the spirit of the tradition to show that the people were not abandoned by Yahweh while they were still oppressed. So he recalled the covenant with the Patriarchs and ordered Moses to go back to Egypt to save his brethren from their distress. He made known his purpose, his demands of Moses, and his promise to his people. Moses was to represent his people before God, and God before his people, and was designated a prophet (nabi).

With profound religious insight, the narrative lays stress on Moses' instinctive resistance to the charge laid upon him and the protests he offered in an attempt comfortably to remain a witness rather than to become prime mover in the unfolding drama. He contended that if he were to go to Israel in Egypt and tell them about his revelation, he would have to make God's name known to them. In Hebrew thought the name of the divinity is filled with mysterious power and significance as shown in the story of Jacob's encounter with the angel at Yabbok, and other instances. The Old Testament is imbued with the conviction that God is not merely an idea, far removed from earthly concerns, but is concerned with the world. He is a living entity with a name, who speaks and is addressed.

THE NAME OF 'YAHWEH'

"He said, 'But I will be with you; and this shall be the sign for you, that I have sent you: when you have brought forth the people out of Egypt, you shall serve God upon the mountain' ". (Ex. 3:12)

"Then Moses said to God, 'If I come to the people of Israel and say to them, "The God of your fathers has sent me to you," and they ask me, "What is his name?" what shall I say to them?' God said to Moses, 'I am who I am. And he said, 'Say this to the people of Israel, "I am has sent me to you"'. God also said to Moses, 'Say this to the people of Israel, "The Lord, the God of your fathers, the God of Abraham, the God of Isaac, and the God of

Jacob, has sent me to you": this is my name for ever, and thus I am to be remembered throughout all generations. Go and gather the elders of Israel together, and say to them, "The Lord, the God of your fathers, the God of Abraham, of Isaac and of Jacob, has appeared to me, saying, 'I have observed you and what has been done to you in Egypt'"; (Ex. 3:13–15)

The name of Israel's God is Yahweh — YHWH — the Lord, but the exact meaning of the name is uncertain. Scholars have reached no agreement either about its etymology, nor what the compact symbolism may imply on higher levels. The mass of discussion on this subject has no place here.

When asked his name God said: "I am Who I am" (Ehyeh Asher Ehyeh), but this also means "I will be what I will Be". There might be a self-interpretation in the centre of this dialogue. The divine name YHWH in any case seems to be derived from the verb "hayah" — "to be", so that the statement in the obscure verse 14 could mean "He who is always present".

W. F. Albright regards "to be" in the causative form, and thus the statement might be an abbreviation of a formula — in the third person — "Yahweh Asher Yihweh" — or "He Cause to Be What Comes into Existence": in other words, Yahweh is the creator of all and thes motivating power in all. Some scholars hold that defining the verb "to be" in the more active, phenomenological sense, expresses Hebrew dynamism, so that the statement implies: "He Who Executes His Promise". God enjoined Moses to say to the sceptical sons of Israel "Ehyeh (I Am) has sent me to you." This would mean that Moses could fulfil his mission because God was present with him and with his people. This seems to point to verse 3:12 "But I will be with you ...."

The etymologies suggested are at best rationalisations. We cannot get a clear notion of the religious understanding of Moses from the name alone.

There is also a presupposition in this passage, in which Moses asks for the name of the God of the fathers, that the name had not been introduced before that time. According to this statement, the name Yahweh was introduced into Israel tradition only during the time of Moses; and this seems truer to the actual situation. Cumulative evidence suggests that the name was introduced at the time of the Exodus. The significance of this revelation is again illustrated in Ex. 6:2–3, as explained at the beginning of this chapter (The Epic of Exodus):

THE CONTEST WITH PHARAOH

MAGIC AND SUPERSTITION

Exodus 5–15 must be read as the drama which it is; but the reader must make a distinction between the various elements which go to the composition of it. There is the historical nucleus that is at the heart of the tradition; the "miracles", signs and wonders; the folk-elements interwoven into the elaborate narrative; and the inconsistencies in the story itself, which is primarily an artistic and imaginative expression of the conviction that Yahweh was active in history, delivering his people and calling them to his service.

We have already considered the historical nucleus. A belief so ancient and entrenched admits of no explanation save that the Israelites did actually escape from Egypt. We may also be sure that a sizeable group of Hebrews and other western Asiatic clans engaged in construction work could not emigrate from Egypt without negotiations between their leaders and Egyptian officials.

We need not labour over the historic authenticity of the folkloric and legendary material.

The epic itself builds up intensive dramatic suspense: The sequence of events accompanying the end of slavery were so stupendous that they have impressed themselves forever on the memory of Israel. The epic of Exodus 1–15 moulds history into the actions of God.

The drama focussed upon the great individual antagonists, Moses and Pharaoh, whose stories balance each other. Whatever their relationship may have been, the oral tradition has preserved the story of a clash between them; but all the episodes are subordinated to the real conflict—that between Yahweh and Pharaoh.

Every visit of Moses and Aaron to the Pharaoh accentuated the crisis, and every plague increased the gravity of the situation. Then came the breaking-point. The narrator's purpose was to tell the story of the contest so as to glorify the God of Israel, and to show that he was so sovereign that the mighty Pharaoh and all his magic were mere puppets in his hands.

Pharaoh was himself considered a god. He had manoeuvred his political power in the Delta so as better to control his Asiatic empire; his grand building programme, exploiting thousands of despised slaves, was a part of his political ambition. With him, on one side of the contest stood his crafty magicians. On the other side was the "groaning of the people of Israel whom the Egyptians held in bondage" (6:5) to whom Moses tried to bring the message of a delivering God.

> "Moses spoke thus to the people of Israel; but they did not listen to Moses, because of their broken spirit and their cruel bondage. And the Lord said to Moses, 'Go in, tell Pharaoh King of Egypt, to let the people of Israel go out of his land.' But Moses said to the Lord, 'Behold, the people of Israel have not listened to me, how then will Pharaoh listen to me, who am a man of uncircumcised lips?' But the Lord spoke to Moses and Aaron, and gave them a charge to the people of Israel and Pharoah..." (6: 9-13).

Moses' brother Aaron, a Levite and a person well regarded among his brethren was designated as spokesman to the people and Pharaoh.

Four foreign chieftains. From a tomb wall-painting.

An Egyptian courtier presenting himself before Pharaoh.

"'See I make you as God to Pharaoh; and Aaron your brother shall be your prophet'". (7:1)

Moses was only metaphorically a god and the language expresses an indefinable feeling that Moses, while not god, was now something more than man, because the presence of God as prime mover had become evident through him; and his brother was to be his spokesman.

At the beginning of the conflict, Aaron and the Egyptian priests vied in magical stunts. No sooner had Aaron changed his rod into a snake, than Pharaoh summoned his wise men and magicians to do likewise with the aid of their occult knowledge; so Aaron's rod swallowed their rods. Though this mastery over serpents was meaningful to the Egyptians it was only a prelude.

THE PASCAL RITES AND RECITATIONS

The basic facts were that Pharaoh's heart hardened in the conflict between master and foreign slaves and that he opposed the Hebrew clans' deep urge to maintain their ancient cultic practices. In answer to Moses' inexorably repeated demand, "Let my people go that they may serve me", (namely offer sacrifice in the wilderness of Sinai), Pharaoh answered:

"'Go, sacrifice to your God within the land.' But Moses said, 'It would not be right to do so; for we shall sacrifice to the Lord our God offerings abominable to the Egyptians. If we sacrifice offerings abominable to the Egyptians before their eyes, will they not stone us? We must go three days' journey into the wilderness and sacrifice to the Lord our God as he will command us'". (8:25-27)

On the left: An Egyptian magician casting down his rod, which rears into a serpent behind him... "they cast down every man his rod, and they became serpents". (7:11–12) The central picture is from a scarab found in Tanis, and shows a snake-charmer performing before three gods. The drawing on the right shows either a man or a god leading three calves and carrying either a stick with a snake's head or a stick which has been changed into a snake. It appears in a bas-relief in an Egyptian temple.

Biblical tradition points out the close relation of the Hebrew clans to the southern Negev situated a distance away to the east of the Nile Delta and Goshen (which itself bears a Semitic name). In the southern Negev stood a holy mountain which was hallowed through the ceaseless migrations of clans from the Negev to Goshen or Egypt, and from there to the Negev. One tradition names it Mount Horeb, the other Mount Sinai. This is the site of the clans' ancient cult, and this is the holy mountain which the enslaved Hebrews yearned to reach. Before they were enslaved—says the tradition—their ancestors would go there from time to time, not only to Mt. Sinai, but even further, to Kadesh-Barnea in the Negev. This real tradition may have its 'Sitz im Leben' (situation in life) in the Negev or Sinai. It may be the place from which the original oral traditions sprang. The continuity of the old ritual tradition might explain how the rites of lamb sacrifices in the spring and the festival of unleavened bread, which are normal features among semi-nomads, were brought by the clans with them to Egypt. It is held by many scholars that Passover stems from a nomadic festival that antedated Moses. Originally the nomadic Hebrews did not keep up a constant, regular or elaborate ritual, but the springtime offering of lambs became linked with that of Exodus and so evolved into the Passover rite; with it is joined the rite of unleavened bread, also associated with the tradition of the flight from Egypt.

The oldest description of the Passover in the Biblical tradition indicates this ritual form:

" 'Select lambs for yourselves according to your families, and kill the passover lamb. Take a bunch of hyssop and dip it in the blood which is in the basin, and touch the lintel and the doorposts with the blood which is in the basin; and none of you shall go out of the door of this house until the morning' ". (12:21-22)

Whatever its original meaning, it acquired a radically new one as a result of Moses' interpretation.

It is held by many that the motif of protection and wonder is strongly in the forefront of later tradition which associates the old ritual with the theme of the sparing of the Israelites' firstborn; still its ritual kernel is significant:

" 'They shall eat the flesh that night, roasted; with unleavened bread and bitter herbs they shall eat it' ". (12:8)

" 'In this manner you shall eat it: your loins girded, your sandals on your feet, and your staff in your hands; and you shall eat it in haste. It is the Lord's passover' ". (12:11)

THE PLAGUES

As the conflict grew, Moses threatened Pharaoh, and predicted the advent of the plagues to punish Egypt, and they came about. Tradition attributes to him the powers of great magic familiar in Egyptian folklore; these enabled him to go further than the Egyptian sorcerers could, for they had always been charged with fighting natural scourges, troublesome individuals and communities in Egypt, and magic was their stock in trade. It has been argued that the ten plagues were common phenomena in Moses' day, as they were later. When taken by themselves they may indeed have been natural "plagues" which happened to occur at the same time and with special severity; and to have appeared significant to Pharaoh, as also to Moses, as evidence of the wrath of Yahweh.

Where the Exodus happened. See also map of the route of the Exodus and the Conquest in Chapter VII. P—Pithom (in Goshen). R—Raamses (in Goshen). S—Succoth. Me—Memphis. Tel el A—Tel-el-Amarra. Th—Thebes (modern Luxor). Je—Jericho. J—Jerusalem. K—Kadesh-Barnea. E-G—Etzion-Gaber.

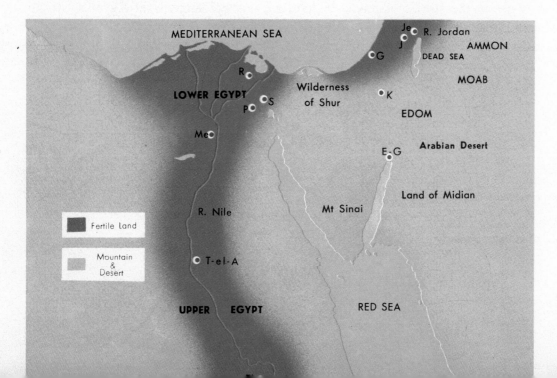

To us a "miracle" is a disruption of natural law. To the ancients it was an expression of supernatural activity. The phenomena of the overflow of the Nile in mid-summer (which coloured the water red) and other climatic vagaries such as "khamsin" dust-storms, which obscured the sky for days together, were considered as omens. So were the plagues of frogs and locusts, because the Egyptians believed that gods dwelt in animals. The Nile, which flows reddish in September, was worshipped by the Egyptians. So were deities symbolized by the fishes, frogs and locusts mentioned in the biblical account of the plagues. The plagues affected the god of earth (Seb), the god of heaven (Nut) and the sun god (Re, or Horus), which were blotted out by the summer dust storm. The final plague seems to have been an epidemic, but it was directed, in the account, against the person of the "divine king" (Pharaoh). The climatic moment in this series was the death of the firstborn of the Egyptians.

The Israelites who had a sense of God's presence in their midst believed that any event, ordinary or extraordinary, might be a sign of his will and activity, and to them these phenomena were an indication of God's purposeful activity. The account of the plagues is of course interpretive and gives one side of the picture, namely that of the Hebrew narrator. The point of the story is that Moses predicted the advent of the plagues and they came about. The account seems to point to the way Moses' predictions became significant to the Egyptians. The Egyptians as all the ancients, had always believed that disasters were due to a malevolent god and that a magician with sufficient sorcery could reproduce them at will. The disasters which were supposed to affect the Egyptians, might well have been regarded by them as being directed by a powerful magician, such as Moses (who attributed his powers to God), or as being directed against the various gods the Egyptians worshipped; for Moses predicted that God would visit his anger "On all the gods of Egypt I will execute judgement: I am the Lord". (12:12)

It matters little that Moses is considered in the Exodus epic as a sorcerer. The global tradition of the epic subordinated and absorbed Hebrew oral traditions of Egyptian origin into the comprehensive conflict between Yahweh and Egypt. It is not surprising that the superiority of Yahweh over other gods also found its expression on a primitive level.

It is not easy to separate the central elements in the tradition from Egyptian folklore. One may see in the stories of magic in Exodus, remote elements of Egyptian origin, or an artistic and imaginative expression of the conviction of the Hebrews that Yahweh was present and ready to deliver his people from servitude. Their faith in him was based on the experience

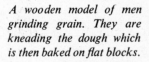

A wooden model of men grinding grain. They are kneading the dough which is then baked on flat blocks.

of the actual events which facilitated the escape of slaves from Egypt, for they perceived in them the work of God. They perceived it also in the Egyptian Crisis so vividly portrayed in Ex. 7 to 12. This was at the centre of Israel's confession of faith from the beginning, as is witnessed in the Song of Moses, one of the most ancient poems of the Bible (15:1–18).

The breaking point was reached when the firstborn were slain, and Moses' magic seemed to have prevailed over the Egyptians. Pharaoh was ready to give in. He summoned Moses and Aaron in the middle of the night and ordered them:

> "'Rise up, go forth among my people, both you and the people of Israel; and go, serve the Lord, as you have said. Take your flocks and your herds, as you have said, and be gone; and bless me also'". (12:31–32)

The people set out in haste. The record is correct in stating that the clans that had escaped from the Egyptian corvee were a "mixed multitude" called in one passage "erebrab" in the other "asafsuf", both derogatory terms. It is assumed that some of the groups that joined in this Mosaic movement were entire clans, each with its own patriarchal tradition. It is historically inaccurate to speak of them as clans at this stage, although the narrative repeatedly uses the term. They were not yet forged into the community of Israel.

But the statement that "their whole number was six hundred and three thousand" (Num. 1:46) men eligible for military service, in addition to women and children, is either an exaggeration or an idiomatic expression. In biblical typology a troop consisted of six hundred men and a "thousand" such troops would be a way of expressing a very large number of people.

A smaller figure would square more with the evidence of Ex. 1:15–22 that two midwives served the needs of all the clans of Israel during their stay in Egypt. The Goshen rural area could not have accommodated five times that number, nor could the wilderness of Sinai and the Negev have supported hundreds of thousands. The entire population of all the Beduin tribes of the Negev who had settled and multiplied there for many centuries before the advent of the new State of Israel in 1948, did not exceed 70,000! When a tribe numbering, say, 5,000 families migrated with their flocks, it formed a wide column stretching over a front of 12 miles and 3 miles deep. The wider the line, the more pasture the flocks would find. The deeper the line, the less pasture for the flocks in the rear. It is obvious that the fewer one imagines the Hebrews to have been, the more feasible would have been their migration through the arid wastes of Sinai, even if they started out in the autumn, when rain pools could be found in the wadis and depressions (though the old source assumes that the exodus started at Passover).

THE EXODUS

There was an end of opposition, for when Israel had escaped, Pharaoh went in pursuit with his chariotry to bring the people back. .

> "So he made ready his chariot and took his army with him, and took six hundred picked chariots and all the other chariots of Egypt with officers over all of them". (14: 6-7).

This was not an expeditionary army, but a large police force, even though the epic spoke of "all Pharaoh's horses and chariots and his horsemen and his army." Egyptian

Egyptian charioteers.

Wooden models of foot-soldiers, found in an Egyptian tomb

annals do not record this affray; and it is unlikely that this represented a serious Egyptian reverse. Moreover at the eastern frontier was a string of fortresses guarding the entry from the main trade routes to Palestine and Sinai. The narrative of the crossing of this desolate, but well protected frontier, suggests the problem facing Israel, to pass safely through the forts and natural barriers.

We can add little to what the biblical narrative tells about the well known events: The Hebrews attempted to escape across the frontier towards the Red Sea, as it was improperly translated. In Hebrew it is "Yam Suf" more properly the Reed Sea (Marsh Sea), for the Red Sea has no reeds. This cannot be very far from Goshen and Raamses and it is probable that the crossing took place at some point in the marshy lake district of the Isthmus of Suez which lies roughly in the present day area of the Suez Canal, between the Gulf of Suez and the Mediterranean. But it did not happen at the tip of the Red Sea (Gulf of Suez). Another very attractive theory has been advanced to explain in natural terms the miracle of the crossing of the Sea: A northern seashore escape route passes Pihahiroth, Migdol (fortress) and Baal-zephon (a Canaanite god). The route skirts the outside of Lake Bardawil, a lagoon north-east of el-Kantara. It is separated from the sea by a narrow spit of land. The shallow lagoon is an enormous salt-encrusted clay pan. If the pursuers took a short cut through this clay pan, navigable to chariots, they may have been caught in a break-through of waters caused by an easterly gale and high seas on the coast of Sinai, just beyond the narrow spit. East winds nowadays cause the waves to break through several times every year, at a half a dozen places, and in a short time they flood the Bardawil salt pan to a depth of 5–6 feet. Such a northern route however leads into the "way of the land of the Philistines" which the Hebrews were warned to avoid. But that admonition may signify that the Hebrews were aware of the danger and tried to avoid it. Their real destination was Sinai.

At some point along these natural frontiers of Egypt, the Hebrews were penned in between a body of water (the Reed Sea) with the Egyptians at their heels. Suddenly a way through the waters was opened for the Israelites. The "cloudy pillar" that led them suddenly shifted and stood behind them; darkness separated the two armies, delaying the Egyptians. With the shield of the "cloudy pillar" came a "strong east wind" that blew back the water through the night. God is represented, in anthropomorphic terms, as he:

"looked down upon the host of the Egyptians, and discomfited the host of the Egyptians, clogging their chariot wheels, so that they drove heavily". (14: 24-25)

A wind drove the water back, allowing the Hebrews to pass safely to dry ground and into the desert. The Egyptians were caught by the resurging flood, thrown into panic, and submerged.

We will never know the historical means of deliverance, but it would not alter the feelings of the people who lived through such a stupendous experience.

The original account has been considerably magnified in the folk tradition and embellishments blended together with it: as for example the division of the waters by the miraculous power of Moses' rod: (14:22–27). These show how the story was re-worked by later generations as this miraculous event, the most important news of the time, was re-told and rehearsed, especially during the celebration of the Passover.

Israel saw in the miracle a sign of the active presence and power in its midst, of Yahweh, who summoned the wind to serve his purpose. Though this cryptic phenomenon may be interpreted as the result of a violent storm, to the Hebrews the miracle was that it happened at that particular time and with that particular effect. To rationalize would be to eliminate the heart of the story, the power of Yahweh. The event was celebrated in Miriam's ecstatic hymn of praise—an oral recitation that is one of the oldest couplets of poetry in Hebrew literature, and may well have originated during the event it celebrates. With all the Israelite women following her with music and dancing Miriam, the sister of Moses and Aaron, took a tambourine and sang a spontaneous refrain never to be forgotten by the Hebrews:

"Sing to Yahweh, for he has triumphed gloriously; the horse and the rider he has thrown into the sea!" (15:21)

The Song of Moses (15:1–18) preceding this ancient couplet which must be read to be appreciated, is an elaboration of the same theme. Its reference to later situations proves that it arose in Canaan, probably in the period of Joshua or Judges. An insight into the nature of the faith of Israel at that time, is implied by verse 11, "who is like unto Thee, O Lord, among the gods?" God, regarded as supreme and beyond compare, was not the only deity, although he tolerated no rival.

Foreign peoples as represented by the Egyptians. A picture on a tomb of subject nations of Egypt, each one appearing as a prototype and identified by a name ring. c.1430 B.C.E.

Jebel Musa (traditional Mt. Sinai) toward the southern tip of the Sinai peninsula, and the plain of er-Rahah, where the Israelites supposedly encamped while Moses went up the mountain.

CHAPTER VII

THE WILDERNESS AND THE COVENANT OF SINAI

It would be difficult to reconstruct the details of Israel's wanderings in the desert, much as it appeals to our imagination. The itinerary is understandably obscure, but we are now gaining more knowledge about the area of the Nile Delta, the present Suez Canal, as well as Sinai, and have a starting point in Rameses or Avaris, which has been located by Pierre Montet.

Sinai is a triangular peninsula between the ancient eastern frontier of Egypt (present-day Suez Canal) and the Negev of south Palestine. It is some 150 miles wide in the north and about 260 long. The northern sandy coast of the Mediterranean, broken by the clay pan and lagoon of Bardawil, is about fifteen miles deep. Through it ran the shorter route, "the way of the land of the Philistines", to the coast. South of this belt lies the high limestone and gravel steppe, stretching about 150 miles. Two trades routes ran through it, one the way of "the wilderness of Shur" leading to southern Canaan through Kadesh-barnea and Beersheba (the Negev); the other to Arabia through Midian and the Head of the Gulf of Akaba (Ezion Gaber).[See the map in Chap. VI.] Below the plateau is the apex of the Sinai peninsula, an arid mass of granite mountains and gravel valleys, rising some 7500–8500 feet (2250–2700 m.). Here is the traditional Mt. Sinai, or at least where an early Church tradition thought it ought to be.

The Hebrews would have avoided the ancient northern military and commercial road between Egypt and Palestine, "the way of the land of the Philistines"; this was well guarded by desert forts near all water points. Their route would have been that of fugitives, of which there are indications in Egyptian stories of flight. They headed towards Succoth by way of the eastern edge of the Delta and lakes, which are now crossed by the Suez Canal, where they could not be so easily followed.

"Then the Lord said to Moses, 'Tell the people of Israel to turn back and encamp in front of Pi-ha-hi'roth, between Migdol and the sea, in front of Ba'al-zephon; you shall encamp over against it by the sea' ". (Ex. 14:1–2)

According to this older tradition in Exodus, the route led "onward from the Reed Sea, and they went into the wilderness of Shur; they went three days in the wilderness and found no water" (15:22). The passage suggests that Israel moved directly from Egypt to some spot between Migdol and Baal-Zephon where they crossed the "Reed Sea", and from there southeast ward to Kadesh-barnea.This is corroborated by Judges 11:16: "but when they came up from Egypt, Israel went through the wilderness to the Reed Sea and came to Kadesh".

FROM THE CROSSING TO SINAI

The distance from Goshen to Kadesh-barnea and Mt. Sinai seems to have been a three days' journey, as Moses claimed, through the wilderness of Shur. But then the slow moving column did not come to the waters of Kadesh but struggled on, finally arriving at Sinai. From here on we are faced with two accounts. These have been combined in the tradition of a route taken by a Hebrew group, possibly that referred to in the earliest Exodus account. It has also

The gravel steppe of Sinai at the edge of the wadi which serves as a path leading southward between Suez and Abu Zenim, an Egyptian settlement active in the 15th century B.C.E. A road led from there to the turquoise mines of Serabit-el-Khadem.

The alleged "Springs of Moses" (12 kms. south of Suez) into which he is reputed to have thrown a piece of wood thereby making them potable.

been suggested that the Bible combined the traditions of various groups fleeing from Egypt, some of which did not move directly to Kadesh. Important details have been omitted from each account; and confusion is increased when we look at the map of Sinai. Archaeology and historical geography cannot identify oases and temporary camp-sites named in each account, and it is impossible to compute their precise geographical location. Many theories of the route have been advanced and scholars are as far from agreement as ever.

All that one can go by in this labyrinth is a few place-names surviving in medieval traditions, and the general geographical configurations suggested by the biblical compilation. Moreover one must be guided by the most certain facts, namely the tradition of a prolonged sojourn of this group at Kadesh, and the subsequent roundabout wanderings and journeys towards eastern Palestine.

Israel's oldest poems treasure the memory of Mt. Sinai, or Mt. Horeb, which has been bound up since time immemorial with the presence of the deity, Yahweh. His appearance is described in all its splendour, in terms of awesome manifestations and the imagery of stormy winds, lightning, fire and quake. From this hidden and mysterious seat He issued forth to guide His chosen people to the promised land.

Ein Hawarah el Amara, 93 kms. south of Suez identified by local tradition with the spring of Mara, south of the "springs of Moses".

The routes of the Exodus and the Conquest, 13th century B.C.E. Three routes cut across the Peninsula. Another penetrates the southern tip.

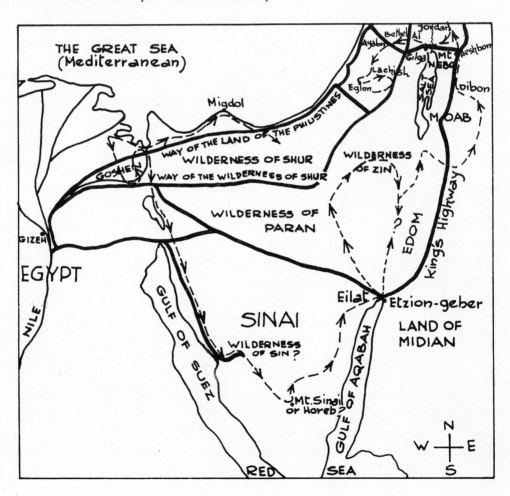

LOCATION OF MT. SINAI

There is an unbroken tradition reaching back to the fifth century A.D., and possibly much further, maintained by early Christian pilgrims and monks. This equates Mt. Sinai with the imposing granite mass of Jebel Musa (Arabic for Mountain of Moses) in southern Sinai. No debate was permitted about this and the stops en route to the mountain have been identified with springs, oases, and old Egyptian mining camps along the way. They are so identified by Arab traditions which take their origin from this source. Illustrations of certain localities are given below with the medieval and Arab traditional names, but without further evidence than the assumption that Mt. Sinai is Jebel Musa, or ought to be; though we must admit that we cannot be certain that this is so.

SINAI'S CONNECTION WITH KADESH

Modern research advances many reasons for locating the holy mountain in the general vicinity of Kadesh-Barnea or further east in Edom or Midian, which is at the head of the Gulf of Akaba, facing Arabia. It would be closer to both localities than Jebel Musa where the southern granite wilderness could not provide Israelite columns of any size with sufficient water and food for their cattle.

Several of the most ancient epics of Israel (which retain the oral recitations) picture Yahweh as moving from the holy desert mountain into the promised land to fight for His people or to bring them rain. They identify the desert cradle of Israel's religion with either Paran (south of Kadesh) or Seir "Edom", lying athwart and east of the Arabah, a valley leading from the Gulf of Akaba to the Dead Sea. In his blessing before his death Moses declared:

" 'The Lord came from Sinai, and dawned from Seir upon us;
he shone forth from Mount Paran' ". (Deut. 33:2)

" 'Lord, when thou didst go forth from Seir,
when thou didst march from the region of Edom,
the earth trembled and the heavens dropped,
yea, the clouds dropped water.
The mountains quaked before the Lord,
yon Sinai before the Lord, the God of Israel' ". (Judg. 5:4–5)

THE SINAI EVENTS

It is generally agreed that the Sinai tradition is quite as old as that of the Exodus and there is little doubt that the two were linked from the beginning. The revelation at Sinai, the giving of the Law and making of the Covenant are inseparably related in the oldest oral tradition. The deliverance from Egypt and its sequel, the guidance through the desert, are preparations for the events at Sinai. The ancient poem of Ex. 15:1–18 has Israel led from the Exodus to the holy abode and encampment by God's gracious act (hesed).

" 'Thou hast led in thy steadfast love the people whom thou hast redeemed,
thou hast guided them by thy strength to the holy abode' ". (Ex. 15:13)

Ex. 19 begins with the statement that finally the Israelites arrived at Sinai. There is no reason to doubt that the same group which escaped from Egypt with Moses then moved to Mt. Sinai, where it entered into covenant with Yahweh, to be His people.

> "On the third new moon after the people of Israel had gone forth out of the land of Egypt, on that day they came into the wilderness of Sinai. And when they set out from Rephidim and came into the wilderness of Sinai, they encamped in the wilderness; and there Israel encamped before the mountain. And Moses went up to God, and the Lord called him out of the mountain, saying, 'Thus you shall say to the house of Jacob, and tell the people of Israel'". (Ex. 19:1–3)

According to Deut. 1:2 the journey from Kadesh to Mt. Horeb (Sinai) took eleven days. This note may originate from a later tradition, for that is the time needed for slow-moving clans to traverse the old pilgrimage route in the Negev to Sinai. But it is as certain as anything can be that Sinai is a starting point of the tradition of the Covenant, which made Israel a people, and that the beginning of her faith lay there.

THE MAKING OF THE COVENANT

It is explicit that Yahweh carried Israel to that spot for a particular purpose. The solemn words, with which Yahweh summoned Israel to the mount express an obligation not to be "choice" and superior to other nations, but to be "chosen". This, Moses announced to the people, was the nature of the Covenant that Yahweh proposed:

> "'You have seen what I did to the Egyptians, and how I bore you on eagles' wings and brought you to myself. Now therefore, if you will obey my voice and keep my covenant, you shall be my own possession among all peoples, for all the earth is mine'". (Ex. 19:4–5)

It is true that the notions of "election" and "covenant" were not given formal statement by early Israel in the days of wandering. But both were fundamental from the beginning to her understanding of herself and her God. She believed that Yahweh, by His mighty acts, had rescued her from Egypt and in covenant had made her His people. This very early theme of cultic creeds, frequently alluded to in the most ancient poems, represents a people secure in the continuing protection of God's mighty acts (Judges 5:11). The notion of election was a very primitive one; it is not due to any merit on the part of Israel, but only to the immortal favour of God. The concept of the Sinaitic covenant is even less sophisticated.

The narrative goes on to describe the divine appearance on Sinai, which was accompanied by the giving of the laws that were to be binding upon the people:

> "On the morning of the third day there were thunders and lightnings, and a thick cloud upon the mountain, and a very loud trumpet blast, so that all the people who were in the camp trembled. Then Moses brought the people out of the camp to meet God; and they took their stand at the foot of the mountain. And Mount Sinai was wrapped in smoke, because the Lord descended upon it in fire; and the smoke of it went up like the smoke of a kiln, and the whole mountain quaked greatly. And as the sound of the trumpet grew louder and louder, Moses spoke, and God answered him in thunder". (Ex. 19:16–19)

There has been much speculation about the violent thunderstorm at Sinai and an unsubstantiated theory of a volcanic eruption has been advanced. But the traditional imagery of quake, wind and fire need not be taken literally.

Jebel Musa, in the granite mountains at the southern tip of the Sinai Peninsula. There is a savage beauty about the rugged, bare landscape, heightened by the mystery of the ancient land. Many scholars dispute its identity with Mt. Sinai.

The narrator probably draws upon such awesome phenomena in an attempt to describe the holiness of God and the majesty of His appearance. The same imagery was used in this same sense by Isaiah and in the Psalms.

THE COVENANT CEREMONY

"Moses came and told the people all the words of the Lord and all the ordinances; and all the people answered with one voice, and said, 'All the words which the Lord has spoken we will do'. And Moses wrote all the words of the Lord. And he rose early in the morning, and built an altar at the foot of the mountain, and twelve pillars, according to the twelve tribes of Israel. And he sent young men of the people of Israel, who offered burnt offerings and sacrificed peace offerings of oxen to the Lord. And Moses took half of the blood and put it in basins, and half of the blood he threw against the altar. Then he took the book of the covenant, and read it in the hearing of the people; and they said, 'All that the Lord has spoken we will do, and we will be obedient'. And Moses took the blood and threw it upon the people, and said, 'Behold the blood of the covenant which the Lord has made with you in accordance with all these words!'" (Ex. 24:3–8)

The ceremony of the making of the covenant (berit), though it blends elements from different sources, still preserves the forms of the ancient rite to which the Hebrews referred in their entreaties to the Pharaoh. There is a distinctly archaic form in verse 5 when "the young men of Israel" were ordered to conduct the sacrifice; this indicates that there were no priests at the time. The dashing against the altar of half the blood of the sacrificed animals is probably a symbol of Yahweh's participation in the rite. The other half was put in basins and Moses dashed it over the people when they pledged themselves, saying "behold the blood of the covenant...". This is the ancient belief that sacrificial blood has the power to bind two parties in covenant. Another more archaic belief in this efficacy of blood is found in the Amorite Mari tablets which describe how a treaty or covenant alliance was consummated in the rite of "killing the ass" (a sacrifice considered holy by the Amorites). This brings to mind Abraham's sacrifice in Gen. 15: 7–12.

The traditions of Ex. 20:22 to 23:33 are called the Covenant Code, because their ordinances were sanctified by the blood of the Covenant ceremony and Moses "wrote all the words of the Law".

THE COVENANT FORM OF THE DECALOGUE

The Decalogue starts significantly with a preamble giving the name and title of God, who spoke in a direct address and a prologue, in which He reminded His chosen people of His benevolent acts, which obliged them to perpetual gratitude. This Sinaitic covenant, based upon an accomplished act of grace, was issued in stringent terms. This is different from the patriarchal Covenant, for the patriarchs had only to trust in it, and it gave only unconditional promises for the future.

> " 'I am the Lord your God, who brought you out of the land of Egypt, out of the house of bondage.
> You shall have no other gods before me' ". (Ex. 20:2–3)

Then follows the Ten Commandments (20: 1-17). Several of the commandments are expressed in no more than two or three words: in Hebrew the Decalogue is called the "Ten Words", and the Covenant was made on the basis of the "words of Yahweh". The other commandments, much longer than originally framed, have undoubtedly been expanded in the course of time. It is probable that originally all the commandments were terse absolute demands.

In its present form the Book of the Covenant seems to refer to the whole body of law in Ex. 20 to 23: that is to say it includes the Ten Commandments as well as the Covenant Code (20:22 to 23:33). But the latter, the earliest body of Hebrew case law (civil law, etc), appears to have been adopted by Israel soon after the occupation of Canaan — the beginning of the sedentary life. It also includes laws of later times, reflecting the changing circumstances of Israel's history, which were added to the original Covenant. The case laws of this Book of the Covenant are again supplemented, with particular accent on their moral aspect, in Deut. 12 to 26. The nature and form of the Covenant is dealt with more fully in Chap. IX (The Faith and Laws of Israel).

THE SINAI NARRATIVES

THE OVER-RIDING UNITY OF THE PENTATEUCH

In dealing with the second part of Exodus and much of the Pentateuch, it is necessary to abandon chronological order, so as to understand the course of the narrative and of the Sinai tradition, for the compilers have introduced great blocks of legal proscriptions and ritual practices. For instance: The Israelites arrived at Sinai in Ex. 19:1. The Book of Numbers begins just one month after the erection of the Tabernacle, twenty days before the Israelites broke camp and left Sinai (Num. 10:11). All the intervening material has Sinai and Kadesh-Barnea as its locale. It would be 38 years before they would arrive at the Jordan, as related in Deuteronomy 1:3 and Num. 33:38. Their experiences throughout these years would be localized in Kadesh. Except for a few words at the end of Numbers 33, the period in the wilderness is not described. Nevertheless, these short episodes provide connecting links in the story of the redemption of the Hebrew people from their situation as a collection of clans to the formation of their life as a community, bound by the Covenant. In other words, the last half of the Book of Exodus, all the book of Leviticus, and the first ten chapters of the book of Numbers set forth incidents and laws related by tradition to the Sinai period.

But when the complex and uncertain legal corpora are removed from the Pentateuch, the Moses traditions assume much more manageable proportions. They are found in Exodus and Numbers alone, as Leviticus is entirely priestly law and Deuteronomy is largely a repetition of the law corpora of Exodus; their placing in the narrative offers little not already found in earlier books (except for Deut. 34, which describes Moses' death).

Therefore this material ties together in two main streams in the Sinai tradition. There is a unity in the traditions from the Exodus up to the settlement in Canaan which permits us to link the narrative of the book of Exodus with the scattered details of the book of Numbers and other parts of the Pentateuch.

The material in its present form in the Pentateuch clusters around the revelation and Covenant at Sinai and the reason for this explains many of the complexities and difficulties of the Pentateuch.

It must be emphatically stressed that the complexity of the Pentateuch is largely due to the habit of the compilers of attributing all laws to Moses; and also to a consequent unwillingness, or disinterest, on their part to organizing the legal material consistently. This perpetual need to tie later developments to the Mosaic age has given rise to differing interpretations of the meaning of Israel's birth and purpose. The crux of it all is the expanding significance of Moses.

Though the legal codes of all other ancient Near East people are presented as promulgated by kings, no law is ever so presented in the Old Testament. Laws are promulgated as the righteous will of Yahweh who is upholder of the Law (cf. Ex. 22:22–24). Although it is agreed by modern research that all laws in the Pentateuch, in their present form, are not unequivocably derivable from Moses, and are the result of later composition, it is nevertheless significant that the resolute linking of Israel's way of life to the days of wandering should revolve around the figure of Moses. Hence it has rightly been stressed by modern scholars

Wadi Feiran, approaching Jebel Musa from the north. The "shitta" is one of the rare trees in the desert and served to make the tabernacle. A group of Beduins graze their meagre cattle nearby.

that the astounding persistence of later Israel in regarding Moses as a lawgiver strongly urges some element of truth in the tradition.

THE LONG SOJOURN AT THE SPRINGS OF KADESH-BARNEA

Though the location of Mt. Sinai remains uncertain, Kadesh was the focal point to which the Israelites directed themselves upon leaving Sinai, and there they stayed for a long time before entering Palestine through Transjordan.

The Israelites arrived at Sinai in Ex. 19:1, and broke camp according to Num. 10:11. All the intervening material deals with laws for the people of the Covenant.

Many of the traditions about the sojourn in the wilderness had their original setting at Kadesh-Barnea. These are so unanimous and ancient that we must give due weight to them when they persist in identifying it with Sinai, and appreciate also the importance which this period in the wilderness had for the Israelites, who spent there perhaps 38 out of their 40 years of wandering. Indeed the part played by this district is probably greater than the narrative in its present form suggests.

Within a few hours travel of one another are two springs: one was Ein-Kudeirat, which is far more copious than the other, Ein-Kades, which still keeps its ancient name. Together these could have supported several thousand people for the period that tradition stipulates. This large group of oases is some fifty miles south-west of Beersheba.

The large oasis of Ein-Kudeirat (Kadesh Barnea). Remains of an Israelite fortress on the mound near the spring, dating from the early monarchy.

The stone wall fencing holy ground at Kadesh.

"'Then the Amorites who lived in that hill country came out against you and chased you as bees do and beat you down in Se'ir far as Hormah. And you returned and wept before the Lord; but the Lord did not hearken to your voice or give ear to you. So you remained at Kadesh many days, the days that you remained there'" (Deut. 1: 44-46)

Shortly after the Covenant of Sinai, chastened by an abortive attempt to enter Palestine from the south, the Hebrew clans retired to their base at Kadesh. From this point onward we face the greatest difficulty in tracing a single route of wanderings.

A RECENT SURVEY OF SINAI

A survey of the Sinai Peninsula was conducted by the Hebrew University, under Professor B. Mazar, during the few days after the Sinai Campaign (1956), and the Israel archaeologist Y. Aharoni made a close field survey of the Kadesh area. In line with Nelson Glueck's survey in the Negev, this authenticated the historical localities, though it does not help to solve the riddle of the location of Mt. Sinai, nor the itineraries of the wanderings. Y. Aharoni suggests that these cannot have followed a unified or planned route, but may have resulted from the splitting up of tribes, following the first abortive attempt at conquest. Some may even have wandered as far south as the granite mass of the Sinai Peninsula, while others stayed on at Kadesh, or wandered south of the Dead Sea. The sporadic narrative of Numbers

The spring of Ein-Kadesh in the desert of wanderings.

11–20, bearing the marks of both antiquity and authenticity, may perhaps reflect this.

The location of events of the wanderings near Kadesh may also gain support from the tradition that Israel fought Amalek in that neighbourhood (Ex. 17:8–16). The Amalekites lived south of Palestine, but not in southern Sinai, as is evident from the older version of the story of the water from the rock (Ex. 17:2, 7 and Num. 20:7–11). Close by was the wilderness of Zin, leading to the valley of the Arabah, south of the Dead Sea. As far as can be identified from the various names quoted in Numbers and Deuteronomy, this wilderness would have been one of the final stages of the wanderings before the Hebrews left Kadesh.

But they are elsewhere (in Num. 14) connected with the Negev south of Beersheba, and with the desert of Shur, west of Kadesh, an area closely associated with Rephidim.

Massa, Meribah and Rephidim, in the neighbourhood of Kadesh, lay in the El-Arish-Rephia-Quseimah triangle which, indeed, is the only district in the whole Sinai area in which a group of some size could have existed for any length of time.

As far back as 1914 T. E. Lawrence (Lawrence of Arabia) discovered an Israelite fortress, dating from the early monarchy, over the spring of Kadesh-Barnea (Ein-Kudeirat). The outstanding results of surveys by Nelson Glueck up to 1959, and by teams of Israel archaeologists during the Sinai Campaign and after, have been the discovery of two Israelite fortresses, one in that area and another at the southern spring of Ein-Kadis, which date from the 9th or 10th centuries B.C.E. They also found several sites in that locality which had been settled in the times of the patriarchs (the Canaanite period), during the Amorite migrations, (Middle Bronze Age) and earlier still.

These correspond with the broken pattern of the permanently or semi-permanently occupied civilized settlements in that part of the Negev. Another interesting discovery at Kadesh was a wall of unknown age enclosing a wide area. Archaeologists believe that it protected a holy site, such as a tribal centre of worship, or graves. A series of stone-built villages or caravanserai dating from similar periods was also found recently along the "King's Highway", which led from Kadesh, through the Wadi Murrah (Nahal Zin) to the southern end of the Dead Sea. This may have been the route the Israelites took on their first attempt to occupy southern Palestine, when they were beaten at Hormah, east of Beersheba. It seems that the area of Kadesh-Barnea was unoccupied at the time of the Exodus, when the Hebrew tribes moved into the district.

DISCONTENT AND MURMURINGS

In Numbers 11 to 20 there is a renewal of the Exodus theme: that in spite of the grace of Yahweh, the people continued to murmur and sometimes to rebel against the leadership of Moses.

The desert fare of manna was certainly not as good or nutritious as the abundant fare of Egypt:

"Now the rabble that was among them had a strong craving; and the people of Israel also wept again, and said, 'O that we had meat to eat! we remember the fish we ate in Egypt for nothing, the cucumbers, the melons, the leeks, the onions, and the garlic; but now our strength is dried up, and there is nothing at all but this manna to look at'". (Numb. 11:4–6)

The worship of a golden calf in Sinai may have represented the god Apis, the bull (or calf) of Memphis.

It is apparent that the "rabble", a collective name under which was lumped the "people of Israel", consisted of heterogeneous Semitic kindred clans that had joined the fugitives from the Egyptian corvee. Neither they nor the Hebrews were united overnight under the common Covenant allegiance, and they were incapable of sharing the leader's faith. Factors other than hunger and thirst caused dissent from his leadership: clan rivalry, vestiges of Egyptian cult, struggles for leadership; and there was sharp conflict with Moses at Kadesh. Dissensions over his leadership broke out in Moses' own tribe, the revolt being instigated by his brother and sister, Aaron and Miriam (Num. 12).

This was renewed on a larger scale by Korah who stirred up strife among the Levites; and by Dathan and Abiram who aroused other clans and important leaders against Moses (Num. 16).

The incident of the golden calf (Ex. 32) may perhaps also reflect the craving of the "rabble" for the cultic practices they had brought from Egypt. Where the book of Exodus takes up again the tale of the meanderings, the narrative is obscure and it is hard to explain how Aaron became associated with the "rabble" in worshipping a golden calf. The rest of the story emphasizes the anger of Moses who, on coming down from the holy mountain, broke the tables of the Law and called for the Levites to intervene to uphold him. Many scholars attribute this section to a later tradition, called the Priestly Codex of the Pentateuch (See Ch. IX).

Fowling scene.

Sun-dried fish. c. 1250 B.C.E.

*"We remember the fish we ate in Egypt". Fishermen
and fish from a wall painting c. 1485 B.C.E.*

Plain called "the encampment of the Israelites", before Jebel Musa and the alleged rock under which the Golden Calf is buried. In the background is a spot from which the block of stone was detached. This tradition is based on the theory that Mt. Sinai is in southern Sinai while many scholars locate it near Kadesh and the Negev in the south of Palestine.

THE ABORTIVE ATTACK ON SOUTHERN CANAAN

Eventually desert hardships and lack of living space, even at Kadesh, compelled the Israelites to look for an "inheritance of fields and vineyards" such as Moses had promised them. So a group of spies was sent out from Kadesh to survey the hill country north of Beersheba. This reconnaissance brought back the report:

"'We came to the land to which you sent us; it flows with milk and honey, and this is its fruit. Yet the people who dwell in the land are strong, and the cities are fortified and very large; and besides, we saw the descendants of Anak there'". (Num. 13:27-28)

Opinions differed as to whether the Israelites should enter the land or not, but the intrepid Caleb was in favour of attacking in spite of the odds against them. The rest, discouraged looked for a leader to guide them back to Egypt. Finally they decided to make the attempt:

"But they presumed to go up to the heights of the hill country, although neither the ark of the covenant of the Lord, nor Moses, departed out of the camp. Then the Amalekites and the Canaanites who dwelt in that hill country came down, and defeated them and pursued them, even to Hormah". (Num. 14:44-45)

So the Israelites fell back south of Beersheba, and away from the Amalekites, with whom they had more than one encounter.

In punishment for their faint-heartedness the generation saved from Egypt had to remain in the wilderness and waste there many unhappy years; but they were years in which they could live, multiply and build a stock of stout-hearted fighters.

They had no camels and could not go far from water.

We are told in Num. 10:29-32 that Hobab, son of Yethro, came to the holy mountain from Midian to meet Moses and was asked to accompany Israel as a scout in the promised land. "Come thou with us and we will do thee good". A theory held by many biblical scholars is that Yahweh, who appeared to Moses in the burning bush, was originally the tribal god of the Kenites or Midianites, from whom Moses learned the name. Ex. 18 relates that the priest of Midian, Yethro, Moses' father-in-law, greeted Moses and officiated over the sacrifice and common meal. Many have interpreted this as clear evidence that Moses derived the name and cultic and judicial features of his religion from the kindred Midianites.

There was a very close connection between Moses and Yethro from the very outset of Moses' career, which began near the Midianite holy places at the sacred mountain (Sinai-Horeb) and at the sacred springs.

It will be remembered that Moses married into the family of the Midianite priest. In any case he found inspiration and guidance among people who were closely related to the Hebrews. These were the Kenites. The name means "smith" and it is assumed that some of the Midianites were coppersmiths in the country round the Gulf of Akaba (present day Eilat), which is known to abound in copper ore, and in the Arabah, the valley leading north from the Gulf of Akaba to the Dead Sea.

According to one theory, this might mean that Yethro was already at that time a worshipper of Yahweh.

The traditions which speak of worshipping Yahweh three days' journey in the wilderness, reflect patterns of worship known to the Israelites. They had been supplemented by the contact with Midian. However, we know very little about the life of the nomadic Midianites and Kenites at that time.

THE DESERT SHRINE

After Sinai the most important feature of Israel's cult in the desert, the focus of attention in the encampments, was the portable Tent or Tabernacle (mishkan), wherein was placed the Ark of the Covenant. This desert shrine was the place of assembly of the clans, where petitions were offered. Here, it was thought, was God's dwelling place.

> "Now Moses used to take the tent and pitch it outside the camp, far off from the camp; and he called it the tent of meeting. And every one who sought the Lord would go out to the tent of meeting, which was outside the camp. Whenever Moses went out to the tent, all the people rose up, and every man stood at his tent door and looked after Moses, until he had gone into the tent". (Ex. 33:7-8)

The Ark was a portable chest made of acacia wood, (the only wood available in Sinai and the Negev) and was kept inside the shrine. According to tradition it contained the two stones on which were inscribed the Ten Commandments. Originally the Ark seems to have been a portable throne on which, Israel believed, Yahweh was invisibly enthroned. In times of wandering or of battle, He went before them as their leader. A short poem addressed to the Ark evokes something of the aura of holy power enshrining it:

A portable tent-shrine. From a bas-relief of the Temple of Bel (Roman period) at Palmyra in the Syrian Desert.

"And whenever the ark set out Moses said, 'Arise, O Lord, and let thy enemies be scattered; and let them that hate thee flee before thee'. And when it rested, he said, 'Return, O Lord, to the ten thousand thousands of Israel'". (Num. 10: 35–36)

This rite is commemorated by Jews in synagogues to this day when the Scroll of the Law is taken out of the holy chest.

The goat's hair for the tent cloth, and the ram skins, and lamb skins used in the construction of the Tabernacle, point to nomadic ways and reflect authentic tradition. This desert sanctuary may have been like the red leather tents known among ancient Semites. We know that the early Arabians, before their conversion by Mohammed, had portable tents similar to the Tabernacle. Some of these are still in existence today, and certain Arab tribes had a portable object which was, like the Ark, the visible focus of the seat where Allah abides.

The detailed description of the shrine (in Ex. 25 to 31; and 35 to 40) comes from later priestly authors. It is probably an idealized backward projection of the later Temple, or of David's tent-shrine (II Sam. 6:17).

These chapters of Exodus stress the organization of ritual under the Levites. It is assumed, therefore, that this passage represents the opening section of the literary sources, called the Priestly Codex, which was later incorporated and canonized into its present form in the Pentateuch. The Priestly Codex is continued in Leviticus, of which it is a major portion.

The priestly descriptions tell us that they had charge of the tent and Ark and at least some sacrificial rites. They also supervised the sacred lots known as Urim and Thummim, by which Yahweh's will was consulted (Ex. 28:30, Lev. 8:8), another symbol of the early cult in the desert. These were the symbols of the Kingship of Yahweh. The earliest poems hail Him as King; the Ark was Yahweh's throne, the sacred lots His tablets of destiny and the rod of Moses was His sceptre.

EVENTS OF THE WANDERINGS

Many interesting details of the stories of wanderings in the wilderness have been illustrated by exploration of the Sinai peninsula and first-hand knowledge of the locale.

The Quail – The hungry Israelites are said to have fed on flocks of quail which came up from the sea and covered the camp. In fact large numbers of quail now cross the Eastern Mediterranean from Europe during their winter migration to Arabia and Africa. They land on the northern shore of Sinai completely exhausted and are easily caught in nets placed there by Arabs in September and October. Strung bunches are sold in cafes and food shops in Egyptian towns. So it may be assumed that the Israelites did not wander into southern Sinai, but were near the Mediterranean; this is another factor which favours the theory of a northern crossing of the Sea of Reeds, and of situating Sinai near Kadesh rather than in the southern granite end of the Sinai peninsula.

Manna – The manna of Sinai on which the Hebrews fed, seems to be a familiar phenomenon of the area. Manna, called "mun" by the Arabs ("man" in Hebrew), is a honey-like sticky substance produced by two species of scale insects that suck large quantities of sap from plants in the tamarisk thickets of the valleys of central Sinai. The nitrogen they do not need they give off in the form of a honey dew excretion. It falls to the ground and is eaten by ants during the day; but during the night it accumulates and can be gathered for food. Rapid evaporation quickly changes it into sticky solids, in size from pinhead to pea, which are gathered by Arabs, who eat it as a relish on bread. One man can collect more than a kilogram a day at the peak of the season in June. Such quantities could hardly have formed the basic food of the Israelites who justly complained of the lack of meat and vegetables to which they were accustomed in Egypt.

The Water from the Rock –

"And Moses lifted up his hand and struck the rock with his rod twice; and water came forth abundantly, and the congregation drank, and their cattle". (Num. 20:11)

In the area of Horeb, Kadesh and Rephidim, Moses obtained water from the rock by striking it with his rod. Such an incident could have happened in this limestone region (which covers porous rock) but not in the granite mass of south Sinai. A former Governor of Sinai, Major G. S. Jarvis, describes how an Egyptian soldier by accident struck water from a limestone rock in that area. The smooth face of the rock crumbled exposing porous rock, whence came clear water. Desert people often look for underground water below the gravel or in the rocky sides of valleys, where traces of moisture indicate it. Moses may well have learned from experience the peculiarities of the rock in these areas.

Light-coloured formations on the branch of a tamarisk bush in Sinai. Plant lice excrete the drops of sweet Manna which will fall off and turn brownish.

Air view of the river and the lower Jordan Valley, looking north from Jericho.

CHAPTER VIII

CONQUEST AND SETTLEMENT

Biblical tradition insists that the Israelites conquered the promised land from the east of Jordan, and not directly from the south as they left Kadesh. But analysis distinguishes two strands of tradition describing the conquest. One strand pictures it as a conquest by unceasing war, and another as a peaceful and gradual infiltration.

CONDITIONS FAVOURING HEBREW INVASION OF CANAAN

Hebrew penetration east of Jordan and into Canaan required a favourable international situation: a balance of power in the corridor of Canaan and Syria, which Egypt and the Hittites tried to dominate through their Amorite and Canaanite vassals. The Hebrews could, and did, enter Canaan when there were no settled and strong empires that could keep them out. Perhaps at another time and under other circumstances the invasion under Moses, Joshua and other Israelite tribal leaders would have been no more successful than had been the earlier attempt to storm Canaan from the southern base of Kadesh-barnea. Israel had to bide its time and await its opportunities, convinced that "Yahweh your God is with you wherever you go" (Josh 1:9).

The political changes happened in a period when small states had a chance to come into being and evolve their new way of life though the narrator views the matter differently.

CONQUESTS EAST OF JORDAN

Num. 20 tells us that Moses asked the King of Edom for permission to pass through his land:

> "'Now let us pass through your land. We will not pass through field or vineyard, neither will we drink water from a well; we will go along the King's Highway, we will not turn aside to the right hand or to the left, until we have passed through your territory'. But Edom said to him, 'You shall not pass through lest I come out with the sword against you' ". (Num. 20:17–18)

There is a reference in Gen. 14 to the old highway east of Jordan, used by the four invading kings in their raid upon the Cities of the Plain in Abraham's time. It runs along western Edom all the way from Sinai, through the central Negeb, into Transjordan and Syria. It seems that the Israelites travelled along the Arabah, south of the Dead Sea, to Ezion-Gaberon the Gulf of Akaba, circumvented Edom from the east, then crossed eastward at the northern border, near the river Zered which runs into the Dead Sea (See Map of the Exodus and the Conquest in Chap. VII). Moab was likewise by-passed on its eastern border until the Arnon river was reached.

They arrived at the new Amorite kingdom of Sihon, stretching between the rivers Arnon, Yabbok and the Jordan. Sihon also refused them passage along the King's Highway, so the Israelites stormed the country, winning their first triumph with the conquest of Jahaz on the edge of the desert. A snatch of the poem celebrating their valour is preserved in Num. 21:27–30 and gives valuable hints of the forgotten history of national beginnings:

> "Therefore the ballad singers say,
> 'Come to Heshbon, let it be built,
>   let the city of Sihon be established.
> For fire went forth from Heshbon,
>   flame from the city of Sihon.
> It devoured Ar of Moab,
>   the lords of the heights of the Arnon.
> Woe to you, O Moab!
>   You are undone, O people of Chemosh!
> He has made his sons fugitives,
>   and his daughters captives
>   to an Amorite king, Sihon.
> So their posterity perished from
>   Heshbon, as far as Dibon,
> and we laid waste until fire
> spread to Medeba' ". (Num. 21:27–30)

Next on the list was Og, the celebrated "giant" king of Bashan, the lush country north of the Yabbok river. He was defeated at the Battle of Edrei. After this Israel was in possession of the territory from the River Arnon and including the land of Bashan east of the Jordan. The kingdoms of Edom and Moab had been left intact. This route was repeated with small variations in Deut. 2:1–8.

Wadi-el-Arish, about 25 miles from Kadesh-barnea, between Sinai and the edge of the promised land. Mount Hilal, seen in the background, is believed to be the site of Mt. Sinai by those favouring the theory of a northern route of the wanderings. See Ch. VII.

Valley of the Arabah, the last lap of the wanderings in the desert on the way to the Dead Sea and Moab. In the background the mountains of Edom, an area through which the Israelites had to pass.

There is evidence that a Hebrew group may have entered the country independently of, and before, the conquering progress of tribes led by Moses as in Num. 20. The Pentateuch gives the story of another route of march which the Israelites followed after they left Kadesh, to Mount Hor; they then deviated and marched right through the territories later known as Edom and Moab, down to the Jordan. Num. 33: 47–49 describes Zalmonah in the Arabah, on their route, the memory of which is preserved in Roman annals, and Punon, a mining town in the Arabah. Then they marched through Moab without giving battle and arrived at Dibon-Gad (modern Dibban) north of the river Arnon. Then they encamped before Jericho, at the Jordan. They had followed the regular 'King's Highway' without any opposition.

CONQUESTS EAST OF JORDAN IN THE LIGHT OF ARCHAEOLOGICAL EVIDENCE

Archaeology gives these two traditions new significance. The exploration of Transjordan by Nelson Glueck established that for some five or six hundred years previous to the 13th century B.C.E., the inhabitants of the territory, like the Hebrews, had lived a roving, nomadic existence. Then suddenly, towards the end of the 14th and early 13th centuries new towns

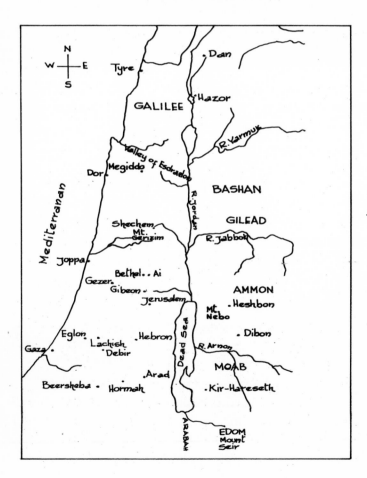

The conquest of Transjordan and Canaan— from the 14th to 12th centuries B.C.E.

and kingdoms sprang up all over central and southern Transjordan. New peoples were settling there. These were the Edomites in Mt. Seir, the Moabites and Amorites. When they first emerged into history these people were ruled by kings, as evidenced by Gen. 36: 31–39; Num. 20: 14 ; 22: 4. An Amorite state with its capital in Heshbon sprang into existence north of Moab, extending itself south of the river Arnon at the expense of the former King of Moab (21:26), before Israel arrived on the scene and conquered him in turn.

The account in Num. 33 therefore presupposes the conditions existing before the creation of these kingdoms, namely before the early 13th century.

Modern scholars recognize that the biblical traditions combine, in a single account, two-fold reminiscences of entries into the land from the wilderness.

The earlier account (Num. 33) would accord well with the group of clans known as the Joseph tribes (also called the Rachel tribes): Manasseh, Ephraim, and Benjamin among others, who were descended from Jacob and Rachel. According to this theory they crossed the Jordan, captured Jericho and settled in central Palestine, around Shechem. They brought with them Joseph's coffin and buried it in the plot of land which, tradition tells us, Jacob had bought from the people of Shechem.

Conditions in the 14th Century

Those who hold this theory believe that this first peaceful wave from Kadesh-barnea arrived in Palestine about the 14th century, namely during the el-Amarna period which is marked by the presence of Khapiru (equated with Hebrews) in central Palestine. The kingdoms of Edom and Moab had not yet been established.

The conditions of the Amarna age, marked by the intrigues of the governors of the Syrian and small Canaanite city-states between themselves or against Egypt, together with the incursion of Khapiru, have already been described. This forms the backdrop of the end of the patriarchial period, when the warlike Hebrew tribes appeared on the scene. Some had remained in Israel and some were coming out of Egypt, apparently in successive waves. Chaotic conditions worsened around the turn of the 13th century.

Egyptian influence in the Near East had undergone considerable decline after the death of Ikhnaton. This encouraged the Hittites to expand south and annex the Amurru states in Syria and invited the incursion of eastern nomads into Syria and Transjordan.

A SECOND WAVE OF CONQUEST IN THE 13TH CENTURY

The second wave described in Num. 21 happened, according to this theory, in the 13th century. The eastern detour around Edom and Moab accords well with the conditions, when the frontiers of Edom and Moab had been secured by a line of fortresses.

As pointed out by Prof. B. Mazar, the clash between Israel and the Amorites east of Jordan accords well with general historical conditions in the Near East. The Hittites had rivalled Egypt for control of central and southern Syria, known as Amurru, at the end of the 14th century and the beginning of the 13th.

The pharaohs of the 19th dynasty, Seti I and Rameses II, conducted several extensive

The Jordan above the fords which the Israelites crossed.

Aerial view of the mound of Jericho. Modern Jericho is in the centre. The Dead Sea and the Mountains of Moab can be seen in the distance.

The mound of Lachish in Judea. On the right is the city gate. On the terrace are the remains of an Israelite fortress and shrine. Lachish was rebuilt after the conquest.

The city gate of Lachish.

Rameses III attacks Syrians (left). The drawing (right) shows him in his chariot charging over bodies of Hittites. Relief of Medinet Habu.

military campaigns with a view to subjugating the Canaanite kings and strengthening Egyptian rule. Boasts of triumph are recorded in the stelae these pharaohs erected. Then came a serious clash between Egyptian and Hittite rulers. A great battle was fought at Kadesh (on the river Orontes in Syria) about 1280, which ended in a truce. But it was followed by a further expansion of Hittites and their Amorite vassals into the land of Api, which included Damascus and northern Transjordan.

B. Mazar connects this event with the biblical tradition quoted in the poem in Num. 21:27–30 about the foundation of Sihon's Amorite kingdom in Heshbon and his expansion south to Moab.

The capture by Amorites of the northern part of Transjordan was proof of serious changes which unsettled the balance of power east of Jordan. The appearance of Hebrews striking westwards is in an historic context. The background of unsettled political conditions permitted the Israel tribes settled on the eastern border of Transjordan to fight their way through and conquer the invading Amorite kingdoms of Gilead and Bashan.

This conquest associated Moses and the Leah tribes, namely those who are ascribed by the biblical genealogy as descendants of Jacob and his wife Leah. These included the tribes of Reuben and Gad, Judah and Simeon, Issachar and Zebulun. This implies that these tribes, some of whom had settled east of Jordan, crossed the Jordan from secure positions which, according to biblical tradition, had been conquered by Moses, and that they were later led by Joshua.

Such echoes are worthy of notice if only to trace the pre-literary stage of the Hebrews before they settled in Canaan. It seems that older folkloric material reflecting the love of peaceful landscapes underlay the episodes of settlement. This appears for instance in a reference to an ancient ballad native to the land, which may possibly be a fragment from a pre-literary document which was lost before the Bible was written:

> "Wherefore it is said in the Book of the Wars of the Lord,
> 'Waheb in Suphah,
> and the valleys of the Arnon,
> and the slope of the valleys
> that extends to the seat of Ar,
> and leans to the border of Moab'". (Num. 21:14–15)

> "Then Israel sang this song:
> 'Spring up, O well! — Sing to it! —
> the well which the princes dug,
> which the nobles of the people delved,
> with the sceptre and with their staves'". (Num. 21:17–18)

Beneath the pebbly bed of the wadis lie water holes, called wells in the poem, which the Beduins of today dig with their staves. This explains the choice of the tools in the ancient poem, echoing old ways of eastern countrymen.

Another memory of the earliest Mosaic period from the Hebrew tribal centre east of Jordan is preserved in other early epic material, such as the Balaam poems in Num. 23 – 24.

Balaam was a diviner summoned from Mesopotamia to pronounce a potent curse against the successful Israelites by the ruler of Moab who hoped that they would be halted by magic. This involved a special ritual, every act of divination following rigid rules of sacrifices on many hilltop altars. But favourable results were not obtained anywhere. The omen was always the same. Then Balaam gave up divination and began to utter prophecies blessing Israel:

> " 'How fair are your tents, O Jacob,
>   your encampments, O Israel!
> Like valleys that stretch afar,
>   like gardens beside a river,
> like aloes that the Lord has planted
>   like cedar trees beside the waters.
> Water shall flow from his buckets,
>   and his seed shall be in many waters,
> his king shall be higher than Agag,
>   and his kingdom shall be exalted'". (Num. 24:5–7)

The story had elements of popular humour and fancy, as, for example, the incident of the talking ass. But the main point of the story was that magic had no effect on the plans of God. The stories and poems seem to reflect the consternation occasioned by the Israelite victories. Balaam's legendary figure became a classic example of everything a man should not be.

Valley of Ajalon and Beth-Horon, scene of Joshua's second campaign.

A section of Canaanite Hazor at the time of Joshua's occupation.

THE DEATH OF MOSES

Tradition gives the period of wandering in the desert before the entrance to the promised land as a round number of forty years, but this is Hebrew idiom, which need not be taken as exact. In fact what it meant is a "generàtion" ("dor"). It indicates a lapse of time between that spent at the edge of the wilderness, and the more decisive events attributed to Moses and Joshua. Deuteronomy is cast in the form of three farewell addresses given by Moses in the plains of Moab before the Hebrews could cross the Jordan. Moses rehearsed the highlights of Israel's recent past, the Exodus, the making of the Covenant of Sinai, the wandering in the wilderness and the victories east of Jordan, and exhorted his people to remember with gratitude all that Yahweh had done, and to be faithful to the Covenant obligations.

The book of Deuteronomy ends with an impressive account of the death of Moses. He sang his swan song (Deut. 32), blessed the tribes (Deut. 33), then ascended to a high vantage point and looked forth over the Jordan Valley and Palestine across the Jordan:

> "And the Lord said to him, 'This is the land of which I swore to Abraham, to Isaac, and to Jacob, "I will give it to your descendants". I have to let you see it with your eyes, but you shall not go over there'. So Moses the servant of the Lord died there in the land of Moab, according to the word of the Lord, and he buried him in the valley, in the land of Moab opposite Bethpeor; but no man knows the place of his burial to this day".
> (Deut. 34:4–6)

The last symbol of Moses' extraordinary destiny was the tradition of his death on Pisgah, overlooking the promised land which, by the command of his God, he was not to enter. It is a moot point whether Pisgah refers to an actual spot—to a vantage point on Mt. Nebo with a panoramic and glorious view of the promised land, or whether it is merely Hebrew for "summit" or "portion". The mystery of the whereabouts of this place, and also of that where he was buried, increases the tragedy of his prohibition from entering the promised land itself.

DEUTERONOMY AND THE BOOK OF JOSHUA

In the Hebrew Bible, the Book of Deuteronomy ended with the *Law*. For continuity's sake, the story in the Pentateuch had to be sustained because it points forward to the possession of the land. But according to religious philosophy, the next biblical books, after the Law, were those of the "earlier prophets", who used historical tradition as the basis of their exhortation and teaching. But these are properly a source of history rather than the relation of history.

The story of conquest is resumed in the book of Joshua, where it is reshaped into epic form. But it bears also characteristic viewpoints of the writers of Deuteronomy and similar literary elements.

THE TRADITIONS OF THE BOOK OF JOSHUA

The three campaigns

The first section of the book of Joshua (1 to 12), the main account, represents the conquest as a concerted effort by a single army of all Israel in three swift campaigns, which were sudden, bloody and complete, lasting seven years in all. First a foothold was gained on the central ridge with the capture of Jericho and Ai; this was followed by a Judean and a Galilean campaign.

The first campaign

First came the marvellous crossing of the Jordan (Josh. 3–4) with the holy Ark. This entrenched them on the west side of the river, in Canaan proper. The first centre may have been at Gilgal. They laid siege to Jericho and at the sound of their trumpets, as tradition has it, the walls of the small city fell (Josh. 6.).

Then they moved several miles up into the hill country north of the fortress of Jerusalem and captured the city of Ai by means of a tactical ambush (Josh. 8).

The second campaign

In their second campaign they had to face a large coalition of local kings. That there were so many of these in so small a country was because they were rulers of little city-states, divided by the hills and valleys. One Canaanite group of four cities, the Gibeonites, realized that it could not stand against the Hebrew invaders, united as they were in a common effort. The Canaanite feudal kings had small armies and lacked the dynamic religious faith of the Hebrews who were bent on "holy war". By a ruse they extracted a treaty from Joshua (9:3–15). But even though the promise of protection was obtained through guile, the Hebrews, in accordance with the standards of the times, felt obliged to respect the covenant. When the Gibeonites, because of their defection to Israel, were threatened with reprisals from a coalition of five Amorite (Canaanite) kings, the Israelites moved swiftly to their defence in an all-night march from Gilgal in the Jordan Valley, took the enemy by surprise and defeated the kings of Jerusalem, Hebron, Jarmuth, Eglon and Lachish at the battle of the Beth-horon pass (Valley of Aijalon).

At this point the biblical text quotes some of its rare written sources, the anthology of Israelite poetry, the Book of Jashar, now lost — a fate that has also befallen other early sources named in the Old Testament:

> "Then spoke Joshua to the Lord in the day when the Lord gave the Amorites over to the men of Israel; and he said in the sight of Israel,
>   'Sun, stand thou still at Gibeon,
>   and thou Moon in the valley of Aijalon'.
> And the sun stood still, and the moon stayed,
> until the nation took vengeance on their enemies.
> Is this not written in the Book of Jashar? The sun stayed in the midst of heaven, and did not hasten to go down for about a whole day". (Josh. 10:12–13)

The original epic must have expressed the desire for nature's help in their surprise attack: namely that the rising sun should tarry over Gibeon on the eastern horizon and that the setting moon should not yet set in the western valley. But the prose chronicler must have interpreted the poetic apostrophe literally and, in his enthusiasm, believed that the sun actually stopped in its course. The next verses (16–27) describe how the fleeing kings hid in a cave, but were found and put to death.

The city that fell next was Lachish in the Shephela or foothills country of Judea. After capturing other towns in the plain and in the hills Joshua's traditions state that he circled southwest and took Hebron, then the east fortress at Debir (Kiriat Sepher).

The third campaign — Hazor

Finally, say the Joshua traditions, the Israelites under his leadership carried out a third successful campaign in the northern hill country of Galilee, above the valley of Esdraelon. A confederation of kings was defeated at the battle of the "waters of Merom". The Israelites destroyed and burnt Hazor, chief city of the region:

> "for Hazor formerly was the head of all those kingdoms. And they put to the sword all who were in it, utterly destroying them. There were none left that breathed, and he burned Hazor with fire. And all the cities of those kings, and all their kings, Joshua took, and smote them with the edge of the sword, utterly destroying them, as Moses the servant of the Lord had commanded". (11:10-12)

For some reason the Book of Joshua singled out Hazor as the only city out of quite a number captured in the north "that stood on their mounds". Archaeological evidence, mentioned later, bears on this point.

THE RENEWAL OF THE COVENANT OF SHECHEM

The tradition of Joshua ends with the impressive ceremony at Shechem where he had mustered the Tribal League:

> "Then Joshua gathered all the tribes of Israel to Shechem, and summoned the elders, the heads, the judges, and the officers of Israel; and they presented themselves before God. And Joshua said to all the people, 'Thus says the Lord, the God of Israel, "Your fathers lived of old beyond the Euphrates, Terah, the father of Abraham and of Nahor; and they served other gods" '. (Josh. 24:1–2)

He rehearsed Israel's sacred history, then challenged the people to decide either to serve Yahweh in sincerity or the tribal gods their fathers had served beyond the Euphrates and the gods of the Amorites (Canaanites). The people affirmed their decision to serve Yahweh and Joshua demanded that they put away the foreign gods. The ceremony concluded with the making of a covenant, the giving of law, and the erection of a memorial stone beneath a sacred tree. Shechem, lying in the valley between Mt. Gerizim and Mt. Ebal, was in fact the great centre of the Tribal League, and the place of gathering of tribes was at the shrine on Mt. Ebal which Joshua built above it:

> "Then Joshua built an altar in Mount Ebal to the Lord, the God of Israel, as Moses the servant of the Lord had commanded the people of Israel, as it is written in the book of the law of Moses, 'an altar of unhewn stones upon which no man has lifted an iron tool'; and they offered on it burnt offerings to the Lord, and sacrificed peace offerings. And there, in the presence of the people of Israel, he wrote upon the stones a copy of the law of Moses, which he had written. And all Israel, sojourner as well as homeborn, with their elders and officers and their judges,

stood on opposite sides of the ark before the Levitical priests who carried the ark of the covenant of the Lord, half of them in front of Mount Gerizim and half of them in front of Mount Ebal, as Moses the servant of the Lord had commanded at the first, that they should bless the people of Israel". (Josh. 8:30–33)

The tradition stresses that the shrine and its altar were made from unhewn stone; no iron was used, in conformity with an ancient interdiction. Such altars were found in many parts of Palestine before the central altar of Jerusalem was built from hewn stones.

Other ancient elements also stand out in this liturgy embedded in a later literary strata. The Levites, carrying the Ark, led a procession to a sanctuary at the sacred Oak of Moreh, then on to a spot in the valley between Mt. Gerizim and Mt. Ebal. There the tribes divided, half standing in front of Gerizim, half in front of Ebal, to hear the Law, and to receive the blessing and the curse, and the solemn renewal of the Covenant. The role of the Levites in the ceremony of blessing and cursing is stressed. It is suggested (Scandinavian School) that this covenant renewal ceremony was carried out annually at this shrine during the New Year Festival at harvest time. The Shechem liturgy is related to parallel liturgical patterns in Deuteronomy (11:26–32; 27:1–26). These sources throw much light on the earlier, more primitive stage in the development of religious thinking and ritual, before later conceptions transformed those elements that came to the Hebrews as a part of their common Semitic inheritance.

The record concludes that Joshua's conquest achieved a peace that lasted for a number of years, so that the tribes could parcel out the land and settle down to normal life.

COMPLEXITY OF THE CONQUEST

Though to possess the land the Hebrews had first to conquer it, it is generally accepted that the tale of Joshua's conquest is carried on a tide of religious enthusiasm, which makes the facts appear much simpler than they actually were. The picture of a unified invasion of Palestine is too neat, too simplified and too idealized. Even more than is the case with the invasions of east of Jordan, it is a unified interpolation made up out of separate traditions. The narrators fell into the error of consolidating the evidence and ended with an evidently exaggerated and even schematic account.

It has been maintained by A. Alt and the German school that Joshua was an Ephraimite tribal hero who was secondarily the leader of a united Israel. They held that there was no concerted invasion, but that the Israelite tribes occupied Palestine by a gradual, and for the most part, peaceful process of infiltration. But this view was later modified.

We have already seen that archaeological evidence is sometimes ambiguous on the problem. The impressive findings of violent irruption into the land, accompanied by destruction of many cities in the 13th century, and the appearance of Israelite occupation shortly after, must be regarded as an authentic reflection of historical events.

THE NARRATIVE OF JOSHUA VERSUS JUDGES

There was evidently much work to be done before the narrator could claim that the land had rest from war (11:23). A more complex picture appears when we compare this epic with statements found elsewhere in the Bible. This picture indicates obvious inner contradictions between such statements.

In several passages in Joshua (15:16–17) and in Judges there is a clear admission that the Israelites were unable to expel the natives from a number of places and the Book of Judges asks:

> " 'Who shall go up first for us against the Canaanites, to fight against them' "? (Judges 1:1)

This emerges in this miscellaneous chapter, partly describing events of the occupation and partly the disturbed period after Joshua, namely the period of Judges. It bears out the presumption that cities taken by Joshua may or may not have been destroyed and were re-occupied again and again during repeated struggles (in the 13th century and later). Every town so far excavated was destroyed at least once in that period.

The incompleteness of the conquest is in any case evident. Canaanite enclaves remained — such as Jerusalem, which was not taken until the time of David.

> "But the people of Benjamin did not drive out the Jebusites who dwelt in Jerusalem; so the Jebusites have dwelt with the people of Benjamin in Jerusalem to this day". (Judges 1:21)

Israel was also unable to occupy the Plain of Esdraelon which separated central Palestine from Galilee.

This does not exhaust the evidence, but enough has been said to indicate the complexity of the problem. The historicity of Joshua must not be under-estimated, but must be compared with another tradition in Judg. 1. This indicates a more involved and lengthy process of conquest and settlement, so that the probability must be considered that the conquests of Joshua were incomplete and represent a unified story of two or more waves of migration and conquest.

THE "HEREM"

There is a marked tendency by the chroniclers, sometimes obscuring the military actions, to describe the conquest as a "holy war" or as a religious war, and to regard the Canaanites as no more than foils to the people of God, to be slain wholesale at "the edge of the sword". The ban, i.e. consecration to Yahweh for destruction ("herem" in Hebrew), meaning the slaughter of captives and civilians and the burning of spoils, is typical of semi-nomadic people, particularly in times of holy war. But constant repetition in the account is misleading and it is doubtful whether it was carried out systematically. That it was ideologically acceptable is illustrated by the very interesting Moabite Stone from the 9th Century B.C.E. to be described in connection with Omri, which spoke of "devoting to Chemosh (the Moabite God) Israelites captured in battles" (See Ch. XIV).

But the Canaanites were not wiped out or driven out in mass at this (or any other) time. When the Israelites felt strong in the Judean hills they reduced the local population, as in Gibeon, to servitude as "gatherers of wood and drawers of water" (Josh. 9:21 ff.)

Other traditions in Judges list Canaanite cities (Hepher, Tirza and Shechem), with non-Hebrew populations as being absorbed into Israel and incorporated into the tribal structure

Bronze sword of Merneptah, found at Ugarit.

Statue of Merneptah (1232–1224 B.C.E.)

Stela of the Pharaoh Merneptah (Thebes 1224 B.C.E.) celebrating his victory over the Libyans and other enemies of Egypt. The last lines contain a direct reference to the "people" of Israel. The king is represented standing between the god Horus (right) and the goddess Mut (left) on either side of the god Amun, shown double beneath the winged sun-disc.

of Manasseh. According to the simple philosophy of history in the Bible, there was a purpose in sparing the Canaanites (See Ch. X. The Rule of "Judges").

Nor were most of the captured cities destroyed. According to the account, Joshua had warred against thirty-one kings in Palestine to destroy the power of the city-states. Despite the enthusiasm conveyed by the epic style, the books of Joshua and Judges reveal that the purpose of the Hebrews' invasion was not primarily loot and that the land was kept as productive as possible and new ground was broken.

There is some reason to believe that as the Hebrews gained a foothold in the central range, (Mt. Ephraim) or in Gilead, east of Jordan, these were not settled centres, but were sparsely populated. It is recorded that the tribe of Joseph, which was populous, asked for more land for themselves, and Joshua advised them to clear the forest:

"And Joshua said to them, 'If you are a numerous people, go up to the forest and there clear ground for yourselves in the land of the Perizzites and the Rephaim, since the hill country of Ephraim is too narrow for you'. The tribe of Joseph said, 'The hill country is not enough for us; yet all the Canaanites who dwell in the plain have chariots of iron, both those in Beth-shean and its villages and those in the Valley of Jezreel'". (Josh. 17:15-16)

From all this it seems obvious that the occupation of Canaan must be seen as successive conquests with settlement, and not one conquest alone, an impression strengthened by reading the other books of the Pentateuch, (Numbers and Deuteronomy), the book of Joshua and the beginning of Judges.

THE CONQUEST IN THE LIGHT OF ARCHAEOLOGICAL EVIDENCE

Apart from the narrative of the conquest itself, we must turn, for the data needed for historical perspective, to various sources of outside evidence. Most important is the fact that these give us chronological premises which enable the archaeologist and the historian, by fixing the time of the break in Canaanite culture, to estimate when the first Israelite occupation occurred:

1 — *Merneptah's boast*

The process of intermittent conquest and settlement was probably under way during an invasion of Palestine and Syria recorded by the victory report of Merneptah (1234–1220 B.C.E.), one of the last rulers of the great 19th Egyptian dynasty. Like his predecessors he campaigned in Africa and Palestine and fought an invasion of Libyans and the Peoples of the Sea. Among countries and peoples defeated, he lists the people of Israel. This is the earliest reference to Israel in a contemporaneous inscription.

Most significantly the end of Merneptah's report reads:

"Libya is ruined' Khatti (Hittite land) is pacified;
The Canaanite land is despoiled
Ashkelon is carried captive; Gezer is conquered;
Yanoam (in Galilee) is made as though it did not exist
The people of Israel is desolate, it has no offspring;
Khurru (Phoenicia or Palestine) has become a widow for Egypt"!
(Trans. by W. F. Albright).

The way Israel is mentioned in the Egyptian stela of Merneptah indicates that this was not yet a fully sedentary people, but sufficiently dangerous to be considered an enemy of Egypt. The significance of this is that by 1220 B.C.E. Israel, the people which was to give its name to the nation in Palestine, was already in its home, and had already struck roots in the country. The Egyptian boast of the destruction of Israel is a hackneyed exaggeration of a type that fills Near Eastern annals. The Bible does not mention this campaign, but a reminiscence of it may perhaps be preserved in the spring of Nephtoah or Me(r)neptah, (Josh. 15:9 and 18:15). In any case, a definite date in the early 13th century is given. Furthermore, biblical and external evidence points to a succession of waves of conquest which preceded, in part, Merneptah's campaign.

2 — The excavations of the Judean mounds

Excavations in mounds of Judean towns bear witness to the terrific destruction which must have taken place during the last quarter of the 13th century. Additional verification of this date is furnished by a piece of pottery which, found in Lachish, and reconstructed from fragments, was used by an Egyptian tax collector to record wheat deliveries. Specialists date it to the time of Merneptah and before the destruction of Lachish.

The excavations at Tel Beit-Mirsim, which is identified by W.F. Albright with Debir, south of Lachish, which he excavated, reveal that it was completely destroyed, the fortifications demolished and the town burned in a conflagration so fierce that the layer of ashes found there was in some places three feet thick. The manifold evidence of terrific destruction suffered by other cities such as Bethel, Lachish, Eglon, during the 13th century, suggests that a planned campaign such as that conveyed by Josh. 10 was carried out.

3 — The archaeological survey in Galilee

In a recent survey conducted by an Israel archaeologist, Y. Aharoni, a pottery workshop and new type of pottery was discovered in northern Galilee, which can be attributed only to Hebrew settlers of the 13th century. It differs from Canaanite pottery found at older levels. His survey proved the existence of a large number of Hebrew settlements dating from the middle of the 13th century onwards, in the territory of Naphtali (eastern Galilee) and particularly in wooded sections which had not been previously inhabited by Canaanites. These new settlements can be attributed only to Hebrews.

Actually, Hebrews were known in western Galilee even in the 14th century. In the opinion of the Israeli archaeologists, S.Yeivin and Y. Aharoni, the appearance of the name Asher in Egyptian documents of the time of Seti I in the late 14th or early 13th century implies the presence of Hebrew clans, later connected with the tribe of Asher. Scholars associate their presence with the inroads of Khapiru in the 14th century, and believe they arrived in a previous wave or that when the Israelites arrived there they absorbed kindred people already present in the land who had perhaps participated neither in Exodus nor in the conquest of Joshua.

Remains of this Canaanite city have recently been excavated by a team of Israeli archaeologists headed by Prof. Y. Yadin. The expedition carried on the excavation for five years. They discovered that this city, north of the Sea of Galilee, on the highway leading from Egypt through Palestine to Syria, had been the *largest city in Palestine* and that is why it was said "for Hazor formerly was the head of all those kingdoms". It covered some 200 acres and had an estimated population of 40,000.

In the El Amarna letters written to Pharaoh by Abdi-Tarshi, he is the only one who calls himself "King of Hazor" and not just "thy servant". Most other kings addressed Pharaoh thus, giving their names without mentioning the towns which they ruled.

But opinion is divided among the archaeologists as to the date of the destruction of Hazor. It is not certain whether it was destroyed by the Egyptians in the 14th Century, or by Joshua in the 13th. The biblical description may well be an authentic reflection of historical events, but recent discussion among Israel scholars tends to place the battle of the "waters of Merom", attributed to Joshua, at about the same time as the war with the Canaanites celebrated in the Song of Deborah in Judges 4 and 5. The Joshua tradition declares that it was utterly destroyed so that the story in Judges would contradict it, unless the two stories indicate events relating to the same period, before the Canaanites were eliminated as a dangerous factor to the Hebrew settlers.

Evidence of the excavations has made it plain that there was a break in the continuity of culture at certain sites, such as those we mentioned, in the 13th century. In the settlements built on their ruins a marked decline in the general level of culture is noted throughout central and southern Canaan between the late Bronze (Canaanite) Age and the early Iron (Hebrew) Age.

The new towns rebuilt on the ashes and ruins, as was the case at Bethel, Lachish and Eglon, were totally different from the former well-built Canaanite towns. While the latter were "Kingly Cities" fortified by thick walls, with acropolis and temple, those that took their place were poor occupations with thin walls, and it is assumed that they were built by Israelites who had been until then semi-nomads. It was very difficult to excavate them. New towns from this Israelite period appeared also at Beth-Shemesh and Shiloh in the 12th century.

THE EVIDENCE AUTHENTICATES SEVERAL PHASES OF THE CONQUEST OF JOSHUA

But archaeologists do not deny that the picture of a complete conquest of all of Palestine within Joshua's time is an exaggeration. Nor do they incline to the theory that the Hebrews took over the country by gradual assimilation of Canaanite culture, as was believed until recently.

UNSOLVED PROBLEMS — JERICHO

Some problems, impossible to reconcile with the Joshua traditions, defy solution. Such are those of Jericho, Hazor, and Shechem. The extensive excavations of Jericho by the late

Remains of the upper mound of Jericho which was destroyed before the time of Joshua.

Prof. J. Garstang and by Dr. K. Kenyon have been a source of much discussion. Surprisingly, nothing remains at the site which dates from between 1500 and 1200 B.C.E., and this would seem to place the end of the latest Canaanite occupation of that town at about the middle of the 14th century, and not at the time attributed to the beginning of Joshua's conquest. "It is a sad fact" Miss K. Kenyon writes, "that of the town walls of the late Bronze Age, within which period the attack by the Israelites must fall by any dating, not a trace remains..... as concerns the date of the destruction of Jericho by the Israelites, all that can be said is that the latest Bronze Age occupation should, in my view, be dated to the third quarter of the 14th century". It was a small place by then and unlike other Canaanite towns it did not have a double wall when it was destroyed. The story of the miraculous conquest by the sound of trumpets can hardly be pressed.

The main hall of the palace of Ai which lay in ruins a thousand years before Joshua's time.

The question of Ai is even more difficult, because the city was completely destroyed about a thousand years before Joshua's time, and had never been inhabited since then. This was shown by an expedition conducted in 1933 by Mme. Marquette Krause. The Book of Joshua says: "And Joshua burned Ai and made it for ever a heap of ruins ("tel" is the modern word), as it is to this day". There were many such mounds of ruins which had been accumulating for centuries by the time the narrator wrote of it: and he mistakenly attributed its destruction to Joshua.

If Ai is identified with the tel excavated in 1933, it could not have been taken by Joshua for that is known to have been destroyed many centuries before the conquest. The most plausible explanation is that Ai was confused with neighbouring Bethel which was destroyed in the latter half of the 13th century.

Bethel. The lowest level of this excavation shows the remains of an olive oil factory of Canaanite times. In the centre a squared pier from an Israelite house built above the lower level.

THE TRIBAL LEAGUE AT SHECHEM

One of the main outstanding problems of the conquest is the way in which the Hebrews settled in Shechem and central Palestine. Possibly future excavations may bring closer the solution of this question. For though the account of the conquest mentions Joshua's three campaigns of Ai, Judea and Galilee, we hear nothing of his actual conquest of central Palestine, with the mighty city of Shechem, a vital region where the important Joseph tribes, Ephraim and Manasseh, had settled. Yet Israel was certainly in possession of that area, which was the centre of the gathering of the tribal league.

Most scholars believe that the Israelites found kindred clans, with whom they were able to make a covenant, already in control of the district, and this is probably reflected in Josh. 24 as recorded above. These clans were "Hebrew", or probably related to the Khapiru of the Amarna period, or of a former period, who had not been in Egypt and did not take part in the Exodus. It has been suggested by some that they had been with the Hyksos in Egypt, or were part of that movement, and settled in central Palestine when the Semitic rulers were driven out of Egypt about 1550 B.C.E. It is tempting to associate the presence of pre-conquest Hebrews in Shechem with the story of Gen. 34 which described how the warlike clans of Simeon and Levi attacked and overcame Shechem in patriarchal times. Some have pointed out the relationship of this story with events described in the Amarna letters, which mention the Khapiru attack on Shechem and the rebellious attitude of the local people to Egyptian rule. It is possible therefore that during the sojourn in Egypt a mixed Hebrew-Canaanite group of clans had controlled Shechem, worshipping Baal-berith (Lord of the Covenant), and that they re-established the Covenant as related in Josh. 24. Otherwise we would be at loss to explain the tradition related there and the formation of the tribal league without the presence of its important kindred elements in central Palestine, before the conquest.

It is possible that this marked the amalgamation of the covenanters of Baal-berith, who had not been involved in the Covenant of Sinai, with the newcomers, who "cut" the new covenant in the name of Yahweh.

CONCLUSION

It is now generally admitted that not all the ancestors of the Hebrews who were eventually amalgamated after the conquest, took part in the descent into Egypt and the Exodus. But by the time the conquest traditions were compiled, the significance of Yahweh's intervention in the events of Exodus and Sinai was of such supreme importance that it was believed that the ancestors of all Hebrews took part in them, whereas they may have formed part of the history of the one group of tribes whose entry is attributed to the 13th century. The traditions of the tribes who had settled in Canaan, possibly in scattered groups, in the 14th century or who were there from pre-conquest times, were probably combined with and submerged in the dominating tradition of the invaders of Joshua's time, the bearers of the Exodus and Sinai tradition.

Waves of conquest in the light of evidence

In weighing the foregoing evidence there seems to be justification for a theory held by many modern scholars — W. F. Albright in the U.S.A., B. Mazar and S. Yeivin in Israel — who consider that the conquest of east of Jordan and Canaan was in two or more waves and was carried out by different groups of tribes, between the 14th and 12th centuries. These waves are respectively correlated with the migrations and conquests of the Rachel (Joseph) tribes on the one hand, and the Leah tribes on the other.

The Joseph tribes

The occupation of the Judean ridge of Gibeon and the alliance with its people is, properly speaking, the kernel of the conquest by the Joseph tribes under Joshua during the middle of the 13th century B.C.E. His role was prominent also in the establishment in central Palestine, in alliance with the pre-Joshua Hebrew elements, and in consolidating the tribal league there.

Biblical tradition accords the largest role to Joseph in Genesis and Exodus. The genealogical lists of the Bible relate the tribes of Benjamin, Ephraim and Manasseh (central Palestine) to him. One might speculate that the Rachel (Joseph) tribes had long been in Egypt, as in the story of Joseph and his brothers, and then were joined later by elements of the Leah clans. It is possible that elements later found in all twelve tribes were in Egypt, or boasted a pedigree reaching back to the central events of Exodus.

It is possible that all the Joseph, Rachel and Leah tribes were not in Egypt at the same time. We do not know which of the twelve tribes were in Egypt and participated in the Exodus. But we cannot speak of organized Hebrew tribes in Egypt, for the classical tribal system had not yet arisen. They were more a conglomeration of Hebrews and Semites from nearby countries ruled by Egypt.

The Leah tribes

Despite the tradition of the Book of Joshua, other evidence points to the occupation of other parts of lower Galilee, namely the territories of Issachar and Zebulun, early in the 13th century, by another wave of Leah tribes, not led by Joshua. Joshua had not occupied the valley of Esdraelon which separates central Palestine from Galilee. This may put the capture of Hazor towards the 12th century.

Judah and Simeon

The expansion of the tribes of Judah and Simeon, the most important element in the Leah tribes, began in the 3rd quarter of the 13th century. This is described particularly in Judges 1. According to this tradition their settlement in Canaan followed the death of Joshua. Judah and Simeon came through Transjordan and separated from their kindred, the Reuben and Gad clans which had settled there:

"The Lord said, 'Judah shall go up; behold, I have given the land into his hand'. And Judah said to Simeon his brother, 'Come up with me into the territory allotted to me, that we may fight against the Canaanites; and I likewise will go with you into the territory allotted to you'. So Simeon went with him. Then Judah went up and the Lord gave the Canaanites and the Perizzites into their hand; and they defeated ten thousand of them at Bezek". (Judges 1:2–4)

After capturing Bezek which commands the road from the Jordan Valley to central Palestine, these tribes penetrated inland. Some authorities relate Simeon and Levi's early capture of Shechem to this episode, but opinion is divided on this obscure point. The tribes wandered further south and captured Jerusalem (which their descendants did not hold) and other fortified Canaanite towns such as Debir (Kiryat Sepher), Lachish, Eglon and Jarmuth, leaving Gezer in Canaanite hands. The conquest of southern Palestine represents the conquest in the second campaign attributed secondarily to Joshua, but it happened at the end of the 13th century as proved by archaeological evidence.

"And the descendants of the Kenite, Moses' father-in-law, went up with the people of Judah from the city of palms into the wilderness of Judah, which lies in the Negeb near Arad; and they went and settled with the people. And Judah went with Simeon his brother, and they defeated the Canaanites who inhabited Zephath, and utterly destroyed it. So the name of the city was called Hormah. Judah also took Gaza with its territory, and Ashkelon with its territory, and Ekron with its territory". (Judges 1:16–18)

This source and others indicate that other non-Israelite elements such as Kenites and Calebites of the Negev amalgamated with Judah to conquer and settle towns of southern Palestine, among them Hebron. In the light of these sources it is wrong to attribute this conquest to Judah and Simeon but it must be seen as a lengthy process of conquest and settlement by various clans, who gradually evolved into the great tribe of Judah. Simeon apparently remained a nomadic tribe, south of Judah in the Negeb.

It is believed that Israelite elements were joined by others. These were converted to the Mosaic faith, or Yahwism, with a consequent filling of Israel's tribal structure. This is true of the events surrounding the occupation of Transjordan, of central Canaan and, somewhat later, of Judea.

This process of absorption went on for a time and assumed its normative form. The history of the people of Israel may be said to have begun from that time.

Fragments of Leviticus written on parchment in the ancient Hebrew script; found near the Dead Sea along with the other scrolls. This is one of the oldest known Hebrew documents recording a part of the Pentateuch. From left to right: 19:31–33; 20:20–23; 21:24–22,3; 22:4–5.

CHAPTER IX

THE LAWS OF EARLY ISRAEL

The last few chapters outlined basic elements of Israel's early faith and law which are germane to the Mosaic period: the Exodus, the Sinai Covenant, the experience of the wanderings, the Conquest, and the functioning of the Tribal League.

As we move from the earlier to the later Pentateuch, that is to say, in the second part of the book of Exodus, the books of Leviticus, Numbers and Deuteronomy, there is an increase in the legal data. This makes the Pentateuch a heterogeneous mass, in which haphazard elements abound. But the logic of the Hebrews made it reasonable to connect the expounding of the law with the desert experiences, even though from the point of view of the modern scholar it appears more relevant to the time when Israel had settled to a more sedentary form of life.

Individual items of tradition in the Pentateuch are older than the rest. Especially those dealing with law and history bear upon the religious and social life of earlier Israel.

EARLY COLLECTIVE LIFE AS ILLUSTRATED BY THE COVENANT

The Covenant, expressing Israel's primitive beliefs, was founded upon the ethic of her religious obligations towards Yahweh. The Tribal League, at the time of the occupation of Canaan, was the sacred institution based upon the faith of the Covenant, and expressing it. From this it would appear that a measure of homogeneity may have been achieved in the collective life of Israel by that time.

It has been clearly shown that the origin of the national unity of Israel, like its religion and law, was connected with the great crisis in experience of the entry into Canaan.

The faith of Israel at this time was not related to an abstract idea of God; it was founded upon her experiences in the past. But it must be equally understood that the laws of the Book of the Covenant are not a legal code in the ordinary sense, but are impregnated throughout by religious considerations. Not to realize this is to misunderstand the entire Old Testament.

THE OLDEST CODE

In very early times short lists of rules were arranged in series of fives and tens so that they could be easily memorized. These were absorbed into larger collections, as in their present form. The Decalogue and the Book of the Covenant, and fragments of legislation in Ex. 34, is the oldest Hebrew code known. Next in order of age, and closest to it, is the code in Deut. 12:26, while, latest of all, as most scholars think, come the laws of Leviticus and Numbers.

Comparison of the general features, the contents and style of these various codes of law, seems to prove that they are not the work of one person, nor even the product of one age. Some of the laws are suitable only to a sedentary people, and would have been meaningless to the semi-nomads under Moses. The probability is that the laws left by Moses were added to those made in the period of Judges, and all were gathered together into a code for the people in the latter period, and at the time of the early monarchy.

THE PENTATEUCH IS COMPOSITE

The differences in religious conception, style and vocabulary are plainly to be seen in the narrative and legal portions of the Pentateuch. It is obvious that whoever put the Pentateuch into its present form drew material from literary sources which had been composed by various schools at various times.

The stages of formation of these literary strata can be discerned; the outline betrays a living movement and spiritual development not attributable to one man or group of men, and suggesting stages ranging from the oral to the written versions of the Pentateuch.

The age of the Pentateuch and its legal data

How old are the narrative and legal data of the Pentateuch? The part with which we have been dealing originated in Palestine between the 12th and the 6th centuries B.C.E. It passed through the various stages of oral recitation, general literature, and finally canonical literature after the Exile. Much that we shall have to say about it would be valid also for the book of Joshua, the structure of which is connected with the Pentateuch. It is present-day usage among many scholars to add Joshua to the five books and to call the whole the Hexateuch (the six-fold book).

The orthodox approach

It is obvious that in the early days a religious movement was bound to centre round a personality uniting in himself qualities of priest, prophet and statesman. While many modern scholars agree that the Decalogue — apart from later expansions — can be traced to Moses, the orthodox school, with its rigid, all or nothing convictions, attributes all laws, every element of Israel's theology, and the whole of the Pentateuch to him. This lays too great a burden on credulity, and allows nothing for the modern spirit of critical appraisal.

PERSPECTIVES ON PENTATEUCHAL LITERATURE

It is necessary to approach with critical objectivity the earliest phase of the development in Israel's faith and law, and to evaluate in their true perspective the various elements (mainly of the Pentateuch) that go to make up early Hebrew life and religion.

Upon one point almost all shades of modern opinion are agreed: that the Exodus and the entry into Palestine was a turning point in the formation of the Hebrew religious system, as was the gradual transition from that of a nomadic-pastoral to a settled agricultural life in the midst of the highly developed Canaanite background. This transition took many generations, but the creation of law is a living growth rooted in social experience.

In the last century it has been conceded that almost all the documents from which the Pentateuch was compiled were produced later, namely in the time of Judges and the monarchy, many centuries after Moses. Four hypothetical documents compiled by "editors" were identified: the "Jahwist Codex" (J) which was composed about 850–900 B.C.E. in the Kingdom of Judah, owing its name to its use of the name Yahweh whereas the name Elohim (God in Hebrew) alone appears in another source; the Elohist Codex (E) composed about 750–770 in the Northern Kingdom; Deuteronomy (D) was composed about the time of King Josiah in 630; finally, the Priestly Codex (P) the heart of which is Leviticus. This dated mostly from after the Exile and was combined with the preceding material in the 5th century B.C.E.; the total of all these being the Pentateuch. These later "editors" of the sources of the Pentateuch faithfully transmitted many earlier traditions, but their own biases and theological concerns frequently appeared in the text as glosses, interpretations, or as part of the framework. The creator of the school which propounded this theory was Wellhausen.

They doubt that the Pentateuch in its later (the present) form, affords much reliable information regarding the actual beliefs of the Mosaic period, and believe that the religion of Israel was the end product of an evolutionary development from lower to higher forms.

They hold that the lofty monotheistic concept of God, the positive ethical elements in the biblical exposition of Mosaic religion, the notion of Covenant itself, were retrojections of a later and more sophisticated belief. This school assumed that Israel became united only with the rise of the monarchy and, since codes of law and the official cult are likely to develop only when a degree of external unity is achieved, then it was reasonable to assume that the laws and the cult reflected those later conditions.

The critical school concludes that there were only a few creative periods in the Bible's legal history, and those were marked by the great codifications of the Pentateuch at a much later period. Most scholars agree on the actuality of these "documents" as sources of the Pentateuch though they do not agree on what they include and exclude.

That theory robs the early religion of Israel of its historical content. It gives us no clue to appreciate which features, if any, are primitive, and which reflect beliefs and social laws of the time of the kings and prophets. The findings of archaeology, the methods of "form criticism" and the views of the Israel school of bible research have provided a third and more positive picture of Israel's early religion.

PENTATEUCHAL LAW AND FORM CRITICISM

In recent years the German and Scandinavian schools have followed new lines of research into the Old Testament by classifying such laws according to the varying individual literary form and content, and through these attempting to fix the settings in which they were formulated. This seems to give a clearer picture and yields better results. This changed outlook was brought about by the objective information given by archaeological research into the literature and religion of the people of the Near East, in particular Mesopotamia and Ugarit.

Comparison of Old Testament material with Near Eastern literary sources shows that a great part—that from which the Pentateuch was compiled—is more archaic than the Wellhausen school had assumed. The Scandinavian school (Engnell and others) have pointed out the inadequacy of the unaided hypothetical resource of literary criticism (source analysis), and have emphasized the importance of the workings of oral tradition, which must often have transmitted accounts long before they were reduced to writing. This resultant composition was thus made of different strata as well as compiled from different sources, according to Bentzen. Hence modern biblical criticism, though it has no system comparable with that of Graf-Wellhausen has modified the latter on many points: firstly in the matter of oral tradition, and secondly, the elements of the hypothetical system of sources have been modified.

The J source has been split into two. The new source so distinguished is called the Lay Codex (L) and has no priestly notions. Moreover, a common ground, called G. has been suggested by Noth for E and J sources. D and P have been assigned earlier dates.

THE "SACRED LAW RECITATIONS"

Recent studies are emphasizing the fact that a long oral tradition often preceded the written formulation of the laws. This must have been the case with the Decalogue. The school of literary criticism detects three redactions of this tradition. One is the traditional form (Ex. 20) which goes back to a very remote antiquity, and which is repeated with slight variations in Deut. 5:6–21.

The other is in Ex. 34 which this school attributes also to the old "Yahwist" source, and is entirely ritualistic in nature. The third form, of the same general character, appears in Ex. 21–23 (in the Covenant Code) and is attributed to an "Elohist" source. The differences in the literary styles of the Decalogue are explained by S. Mowinckel by the theory that originally there existed more than one formulation of the Commandments and that they varied in content from shrine to shrine; the two older decalogues were literary remnants of pronouncements made by the priests at local shrines. A specific series of religious requirements grouped together in that form represented a kind of "sacred law", recited by the priests at the entrance to the shrine before the start of cultic ritual, as a reminder to the participants of what constituted ritual purity. This theory has the merit of placing the laws in living

The jewelled breastplates worn by Hebrew priests (described in Ex. 28) were similar in form—though not in design—to those worn by Egyptian priests.

Offerings to the deity according to an ancient Egyptian ceremonial.

Egyptian offering table, limestone, dating from the late 3rd millenium.

relationship to the religious life of the people and in emphasizing social origin.

Among passages showing that the law was intended to be recited, especially at festivals, when the people were gathered together are the following:

"When all Israel comes to appear before the Lord your God at the place which he will choose, you shall read this law before all Israel in their hearing". (Deut. 31:11)

"According to the instructions which they give you, and according to the decision which they pronounce to you, you shall do; you shall not turn aside from the verdict which they declare to you, either to the right hand or to the left". (Deut. 17:11)

HOW OLD IS THE PRIESTLY CODE?

While we find a certain degree of unanimity among scholars about the early date of the Book of the Covenant, two schools of thought are sharply divided over the age of the Priestly Code, the major part of the Book of Leviticus.

The school of literary criticism maintains that the Priestly Codex is a priestly book in the true sense. With its schematic expose of laws governing sacrifice, priestly cleanliness and the Law of Holiness, it bears the stamp of later Judaism (after the fall of the Jewish State) or of a code written by the priests of Jerusalem in the 7th century B.C.E.

But J. Pedersen believes that underneath the schematism and sometimes hidden in it, there are laws which cannot have been framed suddenly after the downfall of the State or shortly before it, because they point to a real life and old rural customs. This is true of both cultic and social laws dealt with in Leviticus but is naturally more discernible in the latter.

Such legislation as recorded in Leviticus, stems from old accepted customs. But these customs were the same in the 11th (the first century after the occupation) as in the 6th century B.C.E. Even in the days of Judges (11th century) elders of clans adjudicated controversies in accordance with traditional procedure. In fact, it would be impossible to make a clear distinction between old and new, and still more to decide categorically that the legislation as a whole belongs only to a Code of the priests of Jerusalem.

The remote origin of the priestly code

O. Eissfeldt has identified within the Priestly Code various small corpora of law, each a distinct unit dealing with a single subject and formulated in a single style. He argued that they must be the literary crystallization of earlier stages of legislation and were independent entities at the time of legislation. It is true that the cultic regulations in their present form in Leviticus reflect the practice of the Temple in the days of the late monarchy; but the rituals they refer to were almost all old, and were drawn from the cult of earlier generations at the local shrines, before the cult was centralized in Jerusalem. These small groups of laws, in his opinion, went back perhaps even to a stage when they had been transmitted in the form of oral tradition. Thus the present comprehensive codes had been preceded by smaller collections of regulations dealing with particular subjects. He conceived Israel's law as a living, growing thing, developing in the hands of the elders, or the priests, either in the environment of actual practice at the courts "within the gates" where justice was rendered, or in the sanctuaries of the local shrines.

THE ANCIENT PRIESTLY CODE

Starting from different premises the Israel school, under Prof. Y. Kaufman, has reached similar conclusions, and regards the priestly writings as a gradual and continuous growth. In his monumental work on the history of Israel's religion Prof. Kaufman maintains that the priestly tradition is the oldest and most characteristic of Israel's religious history, and that the literature is the oldest stratum of the Pentateuch, antedating the "Deuteronomist" source, which the school of literary criticism had considered to be older. The ideological content, he avers, is quite independent of the teachings of the prophets, and reflects the period of the early monarchy and that just preceding it, rather than the post-exilic age (5th century B.C.E.). By that time the people of Israel were an ecclesiastical community, interested in the religious exercises of the Second Temple. This attitude was far different from that of the people at the time of the Conquest, the Judges and the monarchy, when the "congregation of Israel" was a camp of the hosts of Israel. The high priest stood beside, not in place of, the leader of the people, aiding him with advice from oracles at the "tent of meeting". Furthermore he

A fragment of Deut. 32 (the Song of Moses) from Qumran (Dead Sea).

maintains that the priestly literature was not the successor to previous religious writings, but a parallel and independent tradition, developing from beginnings which were actually older than those of the rest of the Pentateuch, and contemporaneous with the ritual of the local sanctuaries.

The early religious and legal system continued to evolve, and especially its many rituals and laws were essentially complete before the foundation of the monarchy.

The Book of Numbers features mainly dates, genealogies and lists of the "numbers of the Children of Israel" (1–4), whence its title. Nomadic life in the wilderness is not described. There are also threads of narrative, such as the date of the Exodus from Egypt in the opening verse; it then takes the story of wandering from Sinai to Paran (10–11) then to Kadesh, the holy spring. The latter part of Numbers (from 22 on) brings the Israelites out of the wilderness into the plains of Moab in Transjordan, and recounts the strange episode of Balaam, which scholars take to have a non-Israelite origin.

The Book of Deuteronomy is framed in the form of three addresses delivered by Moses to the Children of Israel in the plains of Moab, beyond the Jordan (4:1 to 4). The first covers 1:6 to 4. The second address forms the body of the book (4:4 to Ch. 28). The larger portion (12 to 28) is a revised and enlarged edition of the Book of the Covenant in Exodus 20 to 23:33, and kindred laws in Exodus. The third address is a concluding exhortation (29 to 30). Chapters 31 to 33 are additions, while 34 describes the death and burial of Moses.

Central among the statutes and judgements in the enlarged edition of the Book of the Covenant in Deuteronomy is that ordaining that the major cult and the centralization of worship must be "into the place where Yahweh shall cause his name to dwell". Many scholars take it for granted that the purport of the ordinance in Deuteronomy is centralization of worship in Jerusalem, although in their inchoate form the words may have indicated the central sanctuary of Shechem, which was the rallying point of the Tribal League at the early stages.

"But the holy things which are due from you, and your votive offerings, you shall take, and you shall go to the place which the Lord will choose". (Deut. 12:26)

HOW OLD IS DEUTERONOMY?

Biblical scholarship since the 19th century relates an important part of Deuteronomy to a creation of the time of the religious reform of King Josiah in 622 B.C.E., and to the fact that the Book of the Law (Deuteronomy) which was found by his priests in the foundations of the Temple, could not date from Mosaic days, but was much more recent. This hypothesis is built on the similarity between the provisions of reform attributed to Josiah by II Kings 23 and the injunctions of the Book of the Law. It is an accepted oriental custom to attribute one's writing to a revered ancient, so no dishonesty is implied in this hypothesis.

The interpretation of the demand for centralization (as in Deut. 12:26) serves many modern scholars with an explanation for the purport of a very meaningful section in the opening part of Moses' second address:

"The Lord our God made a covenant with us in Horeb. Not with our fathers did the Lord make this covenant, but with us, who are all of us here alive this day". (Deut. 5:2–3)

Despite the ancient accent of the language, a consensus of European schools of literary criticism insists that this formula was used by every generation of Israel in the ceremony of the renewal of the Covenant made at Horeb (Sinai), by which, the decisive moment of the past is made present. The later Hebrews attributed the formula of renewal of the Covenant to Moses. Thus the theme "not with our fathers did the Lord make the covenant, but *with us today*" refers to the *today* of the reform of King Josiah.

Later editors of the 7th century B.C.E. faithfully transmitted an earlier tradition, but their biases and concerns clearly appear in the text and make it contemporaneous with the needs of the religious reform of King Josiah.

The Scandinavian school believes, on the other hand, that the presence or absence of the demand for centralization of the worship in Deuteronomy, is no criterion for determining the age of the "Deuteronomic document" from which Moses' address is supposedly drawn. They do not agree that the *today* of Deuteronomy is the today of the Josianic reform. Many other scholars contend that the Book of Deuteronomy can be traced to a few centuries before Josiah's time. Its "discovery" then implies that he was the first king to listen to its prescriptions and make them national law, not that it was previously unknown. Similar views are shared by many scholars in Germany, England, and Israel. Though avowedly critical in their methods they date the document earlier than the Wellhausen school had done.

Prof. Y. Kaufman accepts many of the findings of the critical analysis and form criticism in a modified form. He recognizes among the earliest documents of the Pentateuch the Book of the Covenant, the Deuteronomic Code and the Priestly Code, and that the JE (Jahwist-Elohist) combined source dates from the periods of Judges and the early monarchy.

The Deuteronomic Code is not relevant to the issue of the central worship in Jerusalem and its composition antedates the Josian reform and may belong to the middle of the period of the monarchy or about the 9th or 8th century B.C.E. A.C. Welch holds that purity of worship is the prevailing aim of Deuteronomy and that "the place that Yahweh chooses to make his name dwell there" is not Jerusalem, but any and every sanctuary consecrated to Him and His worship. In his view Deuteronomy would be earlier than the period assigned by the critical school.

S. Yeivin attributes Deuteronomy to the early days of Solomon. Its form and contents in his opinion are more in harmony with the centralization of worship in the newly built Temple of Jerusalem and justify the prerogatives and duties of the new monarchy. Its setting also bears close relationship to the agricultural and economic state of the dynamic kingdom.

Prof. C. R. Cross observed that the tendency to date the source of the Pentateuch earlier than the critical school does, is influenced, consciously or unconsciously, by archaeology. Hence if archaeology can prove that the principle of sacrifice at a single sanctuary, outside Jerusalem, is earlier than the seventh century B.C.E., it may overthrow the critical position. That it has not done it so far is no indication that independent research, not necessarily influenced by critical dogmatism, cannot reach such conclusions.

Gunkel and Gressman believe that the books of the Pentateuch evolved gradually out of fragments, topographical lists, single stories and legends and of course legal corpora like the Decalogue and the Book of the Covenant of Exodus which were gathered into complex

Hammurabi, king of Babylon, receives from the sun-god, Shamash, the symbols of authority and the code.

A portrait of Hammurabi (1792–1750 BCE.) on a scene sculptured on top of a stela known as the "Hammurabi Code".

cycles. They had nevertheless reached a certain fixity in oral tradition even before being incorporated into written traditions by a succession of unknown authors and schools. But their genesis is far more remote than the hypothetical "documents" suggested by the orthodox critical school.

EARLY ISRAEL'S LAWS AND ORIENTAL LAW

By conceding that much of the basic legal material in the Pentateuch goes back to the earliest period modern biblical research has gained a firmer understanding of the legal institution of Israel at the time she was going through the process of settling in Canaan. Further light has also been shed by comparing early biblical with Oriental law.

The middle part of the stela of Hammurabi, showing the laws inscribed in cuneiform characters.

Intensive study during the past fifty years into the nature and purpose of Oriental law Codes of second millenium Mesopotamia reveals numerous similarities to Pentateuchal laws, mainly in form.

It is admitted today that Israelite law must to some degree depend directly or indirectly upon earlier codifications of case law of the end of the third millenium. We now have seven different codes or fragments, from seven nations of the ancient Near East. They are translated by various scholars in the "Ancient Near Eastern Texts" (Editor: J. Pritchard):

The Code of Ur-Nammu of Ur in Sumer about 2050 B.C.E.

The Code of Bilalama and Eshnunna (Accadian) about 1925 B.C.E.

The Code of Lipit-Ishtar of Isin (in Sumerian) about 1865 B.C.E.

The Code of Hammurabi about 1700 B.C.E.

The Hittite Code about 1450 B.C.E.

The Assyrian Code about 1350 B.C.E.

The Covenant Code about 1100-1000 B.C.E.

Three of these traditions of collected laws antedate the famous code of Hammurabi.

Hammurabi's was not a law code in the modern sense of the word. It may be described as a new formulation, reaching back to and resting upon a widespread ancient legal tradition of the codes of Ur-Nammu, Lipit-Ishtar and Eshnunna. The later codes or the Covenant Code (Ex. 21 to 23) are apparently formulations of the same ancient, or similar traditions.

The Hammurabi code cannot be regarded as new legislation intended to displace former legal procedures, but according to G.E. Mendenhall was an effort on the part of the early Babylonian state to provide administrators, officers, judges and kings with an official record of the legal tradition. It is likely that it served as a referee between various legal traditions current in different cities and provinces of Babylonia. It is of great interest for the light it sheds on the social organization of that time and particularly for its likenesses to the Covenant Code and other laws of the Pentateuch.

These conclusions may indicate that the early Hebrew tradition reaches back to the earliest period of her tribal life, and even to a time when Israel had no known contacts with Mesopotamia, as, for instance, before the late monarchy. As already mentioned, a population akin to the ancestors of the patriarchal Hebrews was actually in north western Mesopotamia, in Nuzu and Aram-Naharaim (Harran) in the first half of the second millenium B.C.E. and the patriarchal customary law bore a close affinity to theirs. But scholars are emphatic that though Pentateuchal law has parallels with the ancient Mesopotamian legal traditions, it had nothing in common with anything known in Canaan. It antedated Canaan. The Mesopotamian traditions, which bear a similarity to early Hebrew law, did not come via Canaan, even though they influenced Canaanite legislation.

Israelite laws may have been eventually adapted to conditions in Canaan, just as Hittite laws were linked to property transactions in the time of Abraham. Though we know the Hittite laws from the 14th century, their origins and influence in Palestine must lie centuries further back.

Hebrew religious and civil law was derived directly from divine revelation. Religious life, moral life, legal life were, one and all, prescriptions having their binding power from Yahweh alone, and operating for the purpose of ritual exactitude, righteousness and observance. This observance constituted holiness before the Lord. Israel's law was Covenant law and did not recognize any separation between the secular and the religious realms.

Although a similar outlook was present throughout the ancient Near East, among the Hebrews it was more accentuated. Hebrew law apparently developed independently, being bound up with the social and political conditions surrounding the Covenant itself and the Tribal League, the medium through which these traditions were expressed.

THE FORMS OF ANCIENT LAW AND COVENANT

Important studies by A. Alt and G.E. Mendenhall have brought to light important similarities between Pentateuchal legislation and other law codes and covenants or international treaties of western Asia during the 2nd millenium B.C.E. Laws of the Pentateuch fall into two main categories as regards form: The "devarim" or "words"—direct and absolute divine commands (Ex. 20—21)—and "mishpatim" or "judgements"—judicial decisions or common law. (Ex. 21-24). The Decalogue form belongs to the category termed apodictic (absolute) law ("thou shall/shalt not-".) These commandments are religious in nature and do not cover specific regulations dealing with practical eventualities. They are a distinctly Hebrew element in the prescriptions of the Covenant Code. In this sense the Decalogue, for the most part negatively stated, is not a law code, for it neither covers every possible contingency nor provides any legal sanctions—save the implicit wrath of God.

Another category, widely paralleled in other ancient codes, both as regards form and content (and not distinctly Israelite) is called conditional or case law ("if a man steals—then he shall" and so on.). They are "judgements" or "decisions" closely resembling the laws of the ancient world. This category was found in the famous code of Hammurabi of the 18th century B.C.E. and seven different codes (Sumerian, Babylonian, Assyrian, Hittite, etc.) or fragments from various nations of the ancient world, three of which antedate the Hammurabi code. They were presented as promulgated by kings, and had a thoroughly secular spirit and lacked the religious and humanitarian basic characteristic of later Hebrew law.

The difference between the two types of law may be seen by comparing the casuistry of the law about buying a Hebrew slave (Ex. 21:2-6) with the absolute command "Whoever curses his father or his mother shall be put to death" (21:17). It is thought that law of this type is the oldest element in the Book of the Covenant.

> "When you buy a Hebrew slave, he shall serve six years, and in the seventh he shall go out free, for nothing. If he comes in single, he shall go out single; if he comes in married, then his wife shall go out with him. If his master gives him a wife and she bears him sons or daughters, the wife and her children shall be her master's and he shall go out alone. But if the slave plainly says, 'I love my master, my wife, and my children; I will not go out free,' then his master shall bring him to God, and he shall bring him to the door or the doorpost; and his master shall bore his ear through with an awl; and he shall serve him for life". (Ex. 21: 2-6)

As a parallel to the Decalogue form in extra-biblical sources, for example, there is an international treaty between Mursilis, king of the Hittites, and Kupanta Kal, his vassal, which included the stipulation: "Thou shalt not desire any territory of the land of Hatti". This, as Prof. Mendenhall points out, is the precise mixture of case law and apodictic law, as

A wooden door of biblical times from Sur-Baher near Jerusalem.

that found in the so-called "Covenant Code" of Exodus 21–23. In Mendenhall's opinion "the Covenant of Sinai was the formal means by which the semi-nomadic clans, recently emerged from state slavery in Egypt, were bound together in a religious and political community". The text of that Covenant is the Decalogue.

This may answer the question of why the Decalogue consists only of absolute (apodictic) law, whereas the Covenant Code and other Pentateuchal laws, deriving from the same religious fount, are a mixture of apodictic and case law. Case law derived from the old social background of the Hebrews, even from the days of wandering. New instances of such law developed after the Covenant as need for them arose. We may then conclude that though Moses was not the author of all the laws of Pentateuch, as tradition had it, he must have been the prime agent in laying down the constitutive stipulations of the Covenant, and some of the legislation that stems from it, expressing its intent. So that the Covenant Code is based upon the morality and policy of the Decalogue, but is not a slavish copying of the Ten Commandments.

WHAT CHARACTERIZES THE LAWS OF THE COVENANT CODE?

The earlier legal community was a much smaller unit than the nation under the monarchy, the unit being the clan, the tribe or the village. Legal procedures were in the charge of the elders who carried out judgements at the city gate. It is this situation that is presupposed in the Covenant Code at this level of community life.

THE LAW OF RETALIATION AND ITS MITIGATION

Let us take the well known "lex talionis":

"If any harm follows, then you shall give life for life, eye for eye, tooth for tooth, hand for hand, foot for foot, burn for burn, wound for wound, stripe for stripe". (Ex. 21:23–25)

"When a man causes a disfigurement in his neighbour, as he has done it shall be done to him". (Lev. 24:19)

The Book of the Covenant explicitly formulates retaliation as the fundamental principle of penal law. But though this may be primitive, representing an early stage of the development of law, it is mitigated by the fact that responsibility is limited to the extent of injury done. The loss of an eye or a tooth does not grant the avenger the right to execute the offender, in contrast with primitive Semitic law illustrated in the Song of Lamech (Gen. 4:23-24). That law is mitigated by allowing the injured party the alternative to choose compensation as "vengeance". Hence the "eye for an eye" represents a statement of policy in the Covenant Code. In its laws, the Covenant may be regarded as a description of legal policy. On the other hand, the group, the family, and even the individual, was placed under the protection of the Covenant, namely under the direct protection of God. So God himself punished sin, even in the sinner's posterity, should he incur the enmity of God. This placed great responsibilities on the law for the protection of each member of the community, regardless of his status. As alternative application of the law of retaliation, penalties were inflicted for the crime of calumniating a young maiden.

In the Code of Hammurabi the law of retaliation appears also, applying to injuries inflicted by a man of the aristocracy, the seigneur, upon another member of the same class. The Ur-Nammu, Eshnunna and Hittite laws are similar in that they prescribe fines or damages to be paid to the injured person.

All the stipulations of the Decalogue are protected by the Covenant Code with a provision for legal sanctions.

Wherever a stipulation of the Decalogue is dealt with, the penalty — with two exceptions — is death. Those are unpremeditated murder, and theft.

The alternative to retaliation as compensation is explicitly excluded in the case of homicide, but involuntary homicides might profit from the right of sanctuary at an altar, in the precincts of sacred buildings, or in cities of refuge. In the case of wilful and treacherous killing, the man may be taken away from the protecting altar and executed (Ex. 21:12–14). The law lays down (Num. 35:22-25) that the avenger may not take the law in his own hands if the murderer has found sanctuary. The community must decide whether the killing was really murder or not. For instance, there is a case where the owner of a goring ox is guilty of negligence (Ex. 21:30).

Unlike the Code of Hammurabi, the law of retaliation did not apply to slaves, for whom penalties were lighter. The condition of slaves was better among the Hebrews than in neighbouring lands, the law in some cases protecting the slave against his master, who might be forced to set free a maltreated slave (Ex. 21:26). Slaves were not allowed to work on the Sabbath, and runaways had to be harboured and not returned to their masters.

THE RIGHTS OF THE INDIVIDUAL

Murder was crime; theft a civil offence, whereas the Code of Hammurabi demanded the death penalty for it. The death penalty was rare in the Pentateuch, and exacted only for the theft of persons (21:16). The Code named at least ten varieties of mutilation as punishment for various offences, such as the cutting of a doctor's hand for performing an unsuccessful operation, However, Hebrew law in general protected every member of the community, including the thief himself (Ex. 22:3). Deuteronomic Law differentiates motives for cases of murder and rape. It also placed individuals under God's protection, this being the concern of all covenants. Its disregard of status seems to be the source of the perpetual concern for individual justice characteristic of Hebrew law. The distinction between patricians and plebians in Mesopotamian society, was typical of social conditions much more highly developed than those of the Hebrews. The society reflected in the law of Hammurabi was divided in three classes: (a) an upper class, "awilum" whose members had the greatest responsibilities and rights; (b) an intermediate class "mushkerum"; (c) the slaves — "wardum". Society was carefully regulated and laws for all situations were worked out clearly and in detail. Practically no distinction existed between free citizens. The Hebrews all enjoyed the same rights after attaining majority, as fixed in Num. 1:3, at the age of twenty.

Legal procedure and sanctions

Contending parties presented themselves before the judges and pleaded their own cases. Where there was no plaintiff, there was no trial. The simple machinery of the law was set in motion only by request.

Slave-beating; from a tomb painting at Sakkarah, late 3rd millenium.

Wooden models of Egyptian slaves engaged in a bakery and brewery. In the back — corn grinders. Those squatting are sifting flour. The ovens and dummy jars are fermenting vats for beer. At right-hand, back view of the foreman.

A passage in Deuteronomy 25:2 shows that penalties had to be inflicted immediately after the passing of sentence, at the city-gate or the tribal court.

Corporal punishments, apart from those resulting from the application of the law of retaliation, included flogging, to which a limit was set of forty blows (Deut. 25:1–3).

The commonest form of capital punishment was death by stoning. In the nomadic period the condemned person was taken outside the city, and the first stones were cast by the witnesses. The punishment for the prostitution of a priest's daughter (Lev. 21:9) was to be burned alive. This crime meets with a like punishment in the Code of Hammurabi.

Imprisonment as a means for the defence of society was unknown in Hebrew law and is entirely absent from the judicial tradition of the ancient Near East.

The protection of property

Justice at the level of village judgements concentrated mainly on disputes between citizens concerning property damages.

The penalties attached to the violation of the rights of property are remarkably mild, especially as compared with the frequency of the death penalty for this class of crime in the Code of Hammurabi. Thieves were obliged to make restitution, often of more than the amount of the theft, or if unable to do so, were reduced to slavery like other insolvent debtors. Similar penalties were assigned for embezzlement.

Rights of "Gerim"

The foreigners ("gerim") like slaves, did not enjoy the same rights as free citizens. They were of two classes: those linked with the tribes, who had a claim to their protection, and those who had no such claim.

The reconciliation of man and beast fits into a pervasive aspect of biblical law. Domestic animals had to keep the Sabbath.

"But the seventh day is a sabbath to the Lord your God; in it you shall not do any work, you, or your son, or your daughter, your manservant, or your maidservant, or your cattle, or the sojourner who is within your gates". (Ex. 20:10)

Regard for the animal kingdom is illustrated in Deut. 22:1–4. This signifies reverence for motherhood of animals and limits the use of unprotected birds.

"If you chance to come upon a bird's nest in any tree or on the ground, with young ones or eggs and the mother sitting upon the young or upon the eggs, you shall not take the mother with the young; you shall let the mother go, but the young you may take to yourself; that it may go well with you, and that you may live long". (Deut. 22:6–7)

THE FAMILY

The father's authority was supreme in the family, which was the real nucleus of Hebrew social life. Polygamy was legalized; betrothal took place when the bridegroom paid the marriage price and so obtained authority over the bride. The status of woman, though she was held in considerable honour, was inferior in Israel than in Mesopotamia. Although her dowry remained hers after divorce, divorce itself was not hers by right. Even a wife's rights of inheritance were limited and conditional; sons divided inheritances but daughters could not, except if there were no sons.

The biblical law of divorce (Deut. 24:1) permits the man to put away his wife. But the Babylonian codes also allowed the wife to do so in certain circumstances.

Commercial law was of course much more limited and primitive than in Mesopotamia (or Canaan). Loans and credit were treated in a very elementary fashion. Usury was prohibited and loans on security were restricted to the mildest possible terms (Ex. 22:25–27). Every seven years not only were all Hebrew slaves freed but all debts remitted.

These few samples of biblical law illustrate our remarkably increased understanding of the earlier stage of the laws of Pentateuch, and of Near Eastern law in the second millenium B.C.E. Biblical law is no longer isolated and can be related to a more precise historical setting and thus less subject to theorizing.

Even where there is similarity of form and content between Israelite Law and other Near Eastern codes, there are yet great differences. Hebrew law is impregnated throughout by religious considerations which are lacking in Mesopotamian law, such as the detailed ritual laws which are included in the Covenant. It is characterized by a humane spirit, an emphasis upon ethics and a pervading religious fervour which makes it unique. "Thou shalt love thy neighbour as thyself" (Lev. 19:18) is expressive of inner religion among the ritual regulations. The meaning of this is extended to include the non-Israelite "ger" or sojourner. It rooted itself deeply in Jewish psychology and became the basic tenet of western civilization.

The laws protected not only the stranger but also the widow, the orphan, the poor and those obliged to borrow money:

> " You shall not wrong a stranger or oppress him, for you were strangers in the land of Egypt. You shall not afflict any widow or orphan. If you do afflict them, and they cry out to me, I will surely hear their cry; and my wrath will burn, and I will kill you with the sword, and your wives shall become widows and your children fatherless. 'If you lend money to any of my people with you who is poor, you shall not be to him as a creditor, and you shall not exact interest from him. If ever you take your neighbor's garment in pledge, you shall restore it to him before the sun goes down; for that is his only covering, it is his mantle for his body; in what else shall he sleep? And if he cries to me, I will hear, for I am compassionate' ". (Ex. 22:21–27)

The tithes collected by the sanctuary were retained for the poor and the strangers. They were "rates for the poor" — those under the protection of the community:

> " 'And the Levite, because he has no portion or inheritance with you, and the sojourner, the fatherless, and the widow, who are within your towns, shall come and eat and be filled; that the Lord your God may bless you in all the work of your hands that you do' ". (Deut. 14:29)

> " When you reap the harvest of your land, you shall not reap your field to its very border, neither shall you gather the gleanings after your harvest. And you shall not strip your vineyard bare, neither shall you gather the fallen grapes of your vineyard; you shall leave them for the poor and for the sojourner: I am the Lord your God' ". (Lev. 19:9–10)

> " 'When you reap your harvest in your field, and have forgotten a sheaf in the field, you shall not go back to get it; it shall be for the sojourner, the fatherless, and the widow; that the Lord your God may bless you in all the work of your hands. When you beat your olive trees, you shall not go over the boughs again; it shall be for the sojourner, the fatherless, and the widow. When you gather the grapes of your vineyard, you shall not glean it afterward; it shall be for the sojourner, the fatherless, and the widow. You shall remember that you were a slave in the land of Egypt; therefore I command you to do this' ". (Deut. 24:19–22)

The Code prods the conscience of the landowner by insisting on a provision for the poor:

> " 'All the firstling males that are born of your herd and flock you shall consecrate to the Lord your God; you shall do no work with the firstling of your herd, nor shear the firstling of your flock' ". (Deut. 15:19)

Justice

The perpetual concern for justice which pervades Israelite law, regards it not so much as a right in itself, but as a responsibility which confers rights on everybody, as well on a foreigner as on a citizen. This is epitomized in the famous saying which is a preamble to judicial procedure:

"Justice, and only justice, you shall follow, that you may live and inherit the land which the Lord your God gives you". (Deut. 16:20)

THE YEAR OF "RELEASE" AND EMANCIPATION OF SLAVES

Every seven years slaves and debtors were released from servitude and debts. The law warned against assuming that the needy would be cared for by somebody else. The command to release slaves after six years (in Ex. 21:2–4, the oldest code), repeats:

" 'You shall remember that you were a slave in the land of Egypt, and the Lord your God redeemed you; therefore I command you this today' ". (Deut. 15:15)

The emancipated slave was not to be cast penniless into the world, but had to be endowed. The owner, furthermore, was not to take this amiss, for he had received six years of service, and had himself been blessed by Yahweh.

JUBILEE THE YEAR OF "DEROR" (RELEASE)

The custom of "geulah", or redemption, protected poor men who had sold themselves to sojourners or strangers, or were defaulting debtors. They could be released if a kinsman paid the required sum, or through the operation of the Year of Jubilee. A debtor remained a "slave" only until then, when (in the 50th year) land also reverted to its original owner, whether, having been a slave, he redeemed it himself, or whether it was freed by a kinsman. The rights of an original owner according to this custom, were inalienable.

The principles underlying these customs were primitive, being based upon the fullest possible protection of the freedom of the family and its property, and the commonly owned land of clan or village. The Jubilee reflects the religious conception that the earth is God's and men are only its tenants:

"And you shall hallow the fiftieth year, and proclaim liberty throughout the land to all its inhabitants; it shall be a jubilee for you, when each of you shall return to his property and each of you shall return to his family". (Lev. 25:10)

"If a stranger or sojourner with you becomes rich, and your brother beside him becomes poor and sells himself to the stranger or sojourner with you, or to a member of the stranger's family, then after he is sold he may be redeemed; one of his brothers may redeem him, or his uncle, or his cousin may redeem him, or a near kinsman belonging to his family may redeem him; or if he grows rich he may redeem himself". (Lev. 25:47–49)

Then this law concludes significantly:

"And if he is not redeemed by these means, then he shall be released in the year of jubilee, he and his children with him. For to me the people of Israel are servants, they are my servants whom I brought forth out of the land of Egypt: I am the Lord your God". (Lev. 25:54–55)

This is a reiteration of an important social principle:

" 'And if your brother becomes poor beside you, and sells himself to you, you shall not make him serve as a slave: he shall be with you as a hired servant and as a sojourner. He shall serve with you until the year of the jubilee"; (Lev. 25:39–40)

D. Daube finds that the laws governing "redemption" stem from the most ancient social laws of the Hebrews. They confirm the Hebrews' outlook upon the Lord's relationship to the redemption of the entire people in Exodus.

As a Hebrew redeems his property it becomes his own again. So when the Lord redeemed the Hebrews, they reverted to being His own property. The Exodus from Egypt was a legal act of redemption and exercised a tremendous influence over the conventual relationship between the Hebrews and Yahweh.

The relationship of overlordship by the Lord who redeemed the slaves from Egypt, thereby regarding them as His own, coupled with the acceptance of this status by the Hebrews, is clearly emphasized in Exodus 6: 6–7:

> "Say therefore to the people of Israel, 'I am the Lord, and I will bring you out from under the burdens of the Egyptians, and I will deliver you from their bondage, and I will redeem you with an outstretched arm and with great acts of judgment, and I will take you for my people, and I will be your God; and you shall know that I am the Lord your God, who has brought you out from under the burdens of the Egyptians' ". (Exodus 6:6–7)

This is stressed in the meaningful words of the ancient epic (Ex. 15:16), describing the crossing of the sea.

> "till thy people, O Lord, pass by
> till the people pass by whom thou hast purchased". (Ex. 15:16)

The Hebrews, as the Lord's own, accepted his terms. This implied the keeping of the "ordinances" to which they agreed in the Covenant Ceremony described (cf. Ex. 21:1; 24:3).

THE MESOPOTAMIAN BACKGROUND OF "DEROR"

The law of Jubilee was called "deror" (release) in the above passage (Lev. 25:10) and modern investigation has uncovered its remote pre-Mosaic background. The word "deror" according to Prof. Julius Lewy, is derived from "duraru" and "Anduraru" meaning the release of debts or liberation of slaves as proclaimed by royal decree in Mesopotamia as early as the 3rd millenium B.C.E. Examples are known from the first dynasty of Babylon and even on the eve of Assyria's downfall. The biblical Jubilee regulation represents a measure of social legislation operating within a fixed framework of fifty years *without benefit of royal decree*. In Prof. Lewy's opinion: "Such a regulation, which offered the advantage of making the proclamation of release independent of an absolute ruler's arbitrariness was obviously imperative in states not headed by a monarch". He concludes: "The regulation, which defines the 'Jubilee Years' as the years of the releases to be proclaimed at fifty years' intervals, can be adduced as an additional piece of evidence which links the socio-economic measures advocated in Lev. 25:10–15 with Israel's pre-monarchic period...... The Amorites (of Mesopotamia) used an ancient calendar the fundamental principles of which were bound to lead to the creation of a time-unit of fifty years."

Portion of a modern scroll of the Hebrew Torah (Pentateuch) copied by hand on parchment.

CONCLUSION

This survey of early biblical law leads to certain interesting assumptions:

1) As opposed to the primitive aspect of "lex-talionis", of the remote Semitic background, Hebrew law appears from its earliest times to stand on a far higher ethical level and postulates moral human relationships which do not seem to be equalled in other Near Eastern legislations. The Covenant was more than an ancient law code. It was a religious and moral code as well.

2) Its care of the needy, the stranger and the slave places biblical law almost on the level of modern social altruism. This is not surprising as the latter evolved from a later refinement of biblical law.

3) The utopian character of certain laws derived from the development of ancient legislation: A striking example is the social corrective to the law of release of debts every seven years, (shemitta). To encourage the lending of money in later ages, Hillel the Elder legislated that the law court as trustee for the lender had the right to collect the debt at any given time so that the law of release could not cancel the obligation. According to this law called "prozbul" the lender declared in court that he authorized the judges to collect his loan whenever he chose.

4) This poses the decisive question of whether Israel continued to uphold the social ideals postulated in its ancient legislation and whether the laws later operated according to their early spirit. The answer lies in the later history of Israel. This is the subject of the second part of this book.

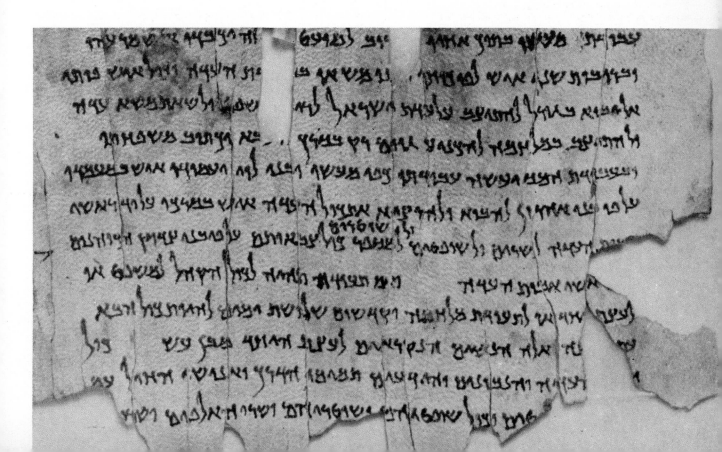

Syrian or Palestinian carrying a vase accompanied by a deer. Such were the people and their dress in Canaan in the days of Judges.

CHAPTER X

THE FIRST TWO CENTURIES IN CANAAN

I. THE PERIOD OF JUDGES

"And the tribe of Joseph spoke to Joshua, saying ,'Why have you given me but one lot and one portion as an inheritance, although I am a numerous people, since hitherto the Lord has blessed me?' And Joshua said to them, 'If you are a numerous people, go up to the forest and there clear ground for yourselves in the land of the Perizzites and the Rephaim, since the hill country of Ephraim is too narrow for you'. The tribe of Joseph said, 'The hill country is not enough for us; yet all the Canaanites who dwell in the plain have chariots of iron, both those in Beth-shean and its villages and those in the Valley of Jezreel'. Then Joshua said to the house of Joseph, to Ephraim and Manasseh, 'you are a numerous people, and have great power; you shall not have one lot only, but the hill country shall be yours for though it is forest, you shall clear it and possess it to its farthest borders; for you shall drive out the Canaanites, though they have chariots of iron, and though they are strong'. "(Josh. 17:14–18)

. . . .

"And the Lord was with Judah, and he took possession of the hill country, but he could not drive out the inhabitants of the plain, because they had chariots of iron". (Judg. 1:19)

. . . .

"Asher did not drive out the inhabitants of Acco, or the inhabitants of Sidon, or of Ahlab, or of Achzib, or of Helbah, or of Aphik, or of Rehob; but the Asherites dwelt among the Canaanites, the inhabitants of the land; for they did not drive them out. Naphtali did not drive out the inhabitants of Beth-shemesh, or the inhabitants of Beth-anath, but dwelt among the Canaanites, the inhabitants of the land; nevertheless the inhabitants of Beth-shemesh and of Beth-anath became subject to forced labor for them". (Judg. 1:31–33)

"Issachar is a strong ass,
    crouching between the sheepfolds;
he saw that a resting place was good,
    and that the land was pleasant;
so he bowed his shoulder to bear,
    and became a slave at forced labor". (Gen. 49:14–15)

THE PROCESS OF SETTLEMENT

These passages sum up some major problems facing the Hebrews in the process of settlement: their hunger for additional land, their weak position vis-a-vis the still unconquered Canaanites and the intermingling of tribal society with the old civilization of Canaan.

Though the Hebrew tribesmen held large areas in the mountains of Palestine, a range running through its centre from north to south, their holdings did not constitute a united territorial unit. They did not possess the coastal plain. There were also large fertile valleys which separated Palestine into isolated cantons, each apparently maintaining it own traditions and customs.

The period was that of settlement and adjustment from a semi-nomadic to a sedentary life of the clans on small farms. Additional land in Ephraim, the territory of the Josepn tribes, and adjacent territory, was secured for cultivation by clearing the forests and scrub. As the Israelites learned the techniques of building and water preservation they built new towns and villages where none had existed before. Between 1200 and 1000 B.C.E. the hill country became dotted with such settlements. Several have been excavated: Shiloh, Mitzpah, Bethel, Ai, Gibeah, Beth-Zur and Debir. They were cruder than the Canaanite towns; excavations show that they were poor and straggling with none of the refinements of Canaanite buildings.

One very positive evidence of material culture was the introduction of baked lime plaster for the lining of cisterns to store rain-water for the long dry season. This enabled the settlements in the mountain range to support a larger population. In fact clans began to move east, across Jordan, and clashes became frequent as pressure and encroachments multiplied. The introduction of camel-transport for long distance and inland transport throughout the Near East had its counterpart in the steady economic development that helped to anchor the Hebrews to the soil in spite of adverse political factors. There is evidence of the expansion of sea-borne transport in the north of the country in which members of certain Hebrew tribes seemed to have participated in peaceful co-operation with Canaanite natives:

"Gilead stayed beyond the Jordan;
    and Dan, why did he abide with the ships?
Asher sat still at the coast of the sea,
    settling down by his landings". (Judges 5:17)

THE CANAANITE ENCLAVES

But while adaptation continued on an economic and material level Israel was still a country of mixed political strengths and pressures. Their military situation was particularly weak. Fighting on foot with primitive weapons they could not face the horse-drawn chariotry of the Canaanite city-states in the coastal strip and the Valley of Esdraelon, which cuts across the central mountain range and separates central Palestine from Galilee. The Hebrews were less advanced technologically than the longer settled peoples of Canaan. Many who had not been displaced kept their independence in the large enclaves of Gezer, Jerusalem, and the strongholds of Megiddo, Taanach, Beth-Shean, as well as those of Hazor, Laish and others in Galilee. The Hebrews in Galilee were circumscribed in a belt closely surrounded by Canaanites.

Central Palestine and the tribes facing it east of the Jordan were completely isolated from Judea and southern Palestine and there was no communication between them. The territorial possessions of the northern and southern groups of Hebrews were at the mercy of any military power such as the Philistines, who aspired to control the land as Egypt had done. The Hebrew clans either settled and intermingled with the natives or were treated as vassals where they were weaker and helpless. This is strikingly borne out by the passage in Judg. 1:31-33 above. As a whole the city states and nations round about were highly organized, though seldom united to resist the Hebrews.

In contrast to the strongly organized political groups around her, Israel was at best a large tribal confederation held together by no central political figure or government, but by the religious bond of the Covenant. Otherwise the various tribes, jealous of their independence, were completely free of central authority.

THE OLDEST TRIBAL LEAGUE OF ISRAEL

According to the epic tradition, after the Canaanites had been subdued the land was apportioned among the twelve tribes. This is indicated in the remaining chapters of Joshua, which consist for the most part of lists of the tribal borders and towns, which received the land. Actually these are territorial lists belonging to a later stage, but were attributed to Joshua's time. But the pattern of twelve connected with the tribes was always adhered to in biblical history, and reveals the existence of a tribal league really in Israel's tradition. Its basis was a covenant community built around social laws and religious culture. The cultic centre was the seat of a genealogical tradition of ancestral tribes and hero epics. The function of the league was to determine religious and military obligations of the tribes. It decided the traditional form of the cult at the holy places. We have seen numerous examples of this in the stories of Genesis. It seems that Kadesh–barnea before the invasion of Canaan was the cult centre. The nucleus of the tribal league, which may have originated in Egypt, was perhaps the Rachel tribes (Joseph, Manasseh, Ephraim) and Benjamin, in central Palestine. It grew through a considerable accession of kindred clans and converts. After these groups thrust themselves into Palestine and were established there, older elements, already established, were drawn into their structure, as described in the Covenant renewal ceremony at Shechem (Ch. VIII).

The tribal league had its focal point at the shrine which housed the Ark of the Covenant. This was eventually located at Shiloh in the heart of the central mountain range through most of the first period. This form of tribal confederacy with its twelve-fold pattern was similar to the six or twelve tribe alliances known as the "Amphyctiony" of Greece and Italy slightly later. Hebrew tribal society was a patriarchal organization, without the social stratification and material wealth characterizing the feudal pattern of Canaan. Under these precarious circumstances the isolated tribes were in constant danger of attack from raiding parties and foreign "oppressors". In telling in fragmentary manner incidents of resistance to local enemies, the book of Judges occasionally reports the union of a few clans or tribes in a common cause. But the rally of the clans was usually in direct ratio to the proximity of the danger and local interests tended to take precedence over the common good.

THE RULE OF "JUDGES" AND THE FRAMEWORK OF THE BOOK

The main feature of the Book of Judges is the attempt to bind the originally separate narratives into the framework of the tribal league order, and its mode of operation in times of danger, under the temporary leadership of Judges. But it still conveys an impression of extreme disunity. The book is stamped with a simple philosophy of history in comparison with the theological stance of the Pentateuch and the Book of Joshua.

Palestine during the period of Judges and the settlement of the tribes. The Canaanite enclaves situated around fortified royal Canaanite cities are identified by (C).

A stereotyped framework characterizes the main part of the book. Each of the episodes is prefaced by the formula:

"And the people of Israel did what was evil in the sight of the Lord, forgetting the Lord their God, and serving the Baals and the Asheroth. Therefore the anger of the Lord was kindled against Israel, and he sold them into the hand of Cushan-rishathaim king of Mesopotamia; and the people of Israel served Cushan-rishathaim eight years. But when the people of Israel cried to the Lord, the Lord raised up a deliverer for the people of Israel, who delivered them, Othniel the son of Kenaz, Caleb's younger brother. The Spirit of the Lord came upon him, and he judged Israel; he went out to war, and the Lord gave Cushan-rishathaim king of Mesopotamia into his hand; and his hand prevailed over Cushan-rishathaim". (Judg. 3:7–10)

Following the story of the oppressing enemy and the judge, the statement is appended:

"So the land had rest forty years. Then Othniel the son of Kenaz died". (Judg. 3:11)

This explains God's purpose in sparing the Canaanites and other peoples for the purpose of keeping Israel strong by the constant necessity of fighting. The people, however, had turned to the gods of surrounding peoples. Therefore Yahweh's anger was kindled because they also intermarried with the natives and led their way of life: "And they took their daughters to themselves for wives, and their own daughters they gave to their sons; and they served their gods". So He delivered them into the power of their enemies and they could not possess the land. But when the enemy inflicted disaster on the clans the Hebrews were temporarily contrite. According to this theory of the later chroniclers, apostasy from Yahweh caused disaster, but change of heart and a return to Yahweh purged them of their apostasy, and led to deliverance from the oppressors under the leadership of a "saviour" or judge, then back to the orthodox worship of God under the Covenant. However, when the "judge" died, the people turned again to idolatry, and so the formula repeated itself many times.

This theme is formulated in the introduction and conclusion to the actual events recorded. But the substance of the stories and their actual contents contrast with the theological theory of the narrators. This is because the substance and the milieu are older than the framework. It is important to keep this in mind when reading the stories.

NATURE OF THE TRADITION

The opening chapter of Judges is different from the sweeping saga of Joshua. It shows the Conquest as a long-drawn-out process of both conquest and settlement, not brought about by campaigns but by individual tribes acting independently — which is borne out by modern research.

Following this introduction the narrative proper begins at 2:6. Dealing with the deeds of six "major" judges, and five "minor" ones, of whom little data is given, it continues thus to Judg. 12. Then follows the Samson saga (13 – 16), a narrative distinct from the rest, and a description of the migration of the Danite clans to northern Palestine (17 – 18); the book concludes with the gruesome story of the outrage of Gibeah (19 – 21).

Although these five sections run consecutively, they are not so in fact: many episodes of the judges and the oppressions were almost contemporary. The exploits of the judges named successively would yield a period of some 410 years, but the records themselves speak in favour of its being no more than two centuries, 1200 – 1020 B.C.E. In any case the contents of the book of Judges read more like fragments of tribal traditions than continuous history. The events recounted are mostly local episodes not affecting Israel as a whole, with the exception of the Battle of Kishon under Deborah. The stories rather deal with the deeds of individual local heroes, or small bands of what we would call partisans today, the struggle of the few against the many. At first handed down orally within the tribes themselves, they were later written and collected. As this must have happened many generations later, they received the impress of the views of later narrators.

SAVIOURS IN CRISIS

Without a foe the leadership was dormant. But in times of danger there arose a judge ("saviour" in Hebrew) who led a segment of the Hebrews into battle, a man upon whom the spirit of Yahweh rested. He was the recipient of divine power that suddenly seized him and made him irresistible, even impervious in battle. The special nature of the judge was that his gifts were spiritual. And six "saviour" judges seem to have had this in common. There was something about them, fanaticism, military prowess or some special gift which set them apart from ordinary men, a quality called "charismatic"; it proved to their fellows that they were men of Yahweh! In most cases the judges did not exercise judicial skill; neither was their authority permanent, absolute, nor hereditary. It was an authority which expressed perfectly the patriarchal tribal organization and the faith and constitution of early Israel. Once the "saviour" had accomplished his mission, he would disappear from the scene. Perhaps later chroniclers imagined this to be a pan-Israelite convention, whereas the ancient tradition emphasizes the isolated nature of the deeds of the charismatic judges. As to the other five "minor judges" (so-called to differentiate them from the mission of the major judges) it is assumed that they were charged with law and jurisdiction of all the tribes.

OTHNIEL, EHUD AND SHAMGAR

The first judge Othniel is said to have repelled the invasion of Cushan-rishathaim of Aram-Naharaim (Mesopotamia). It is not certain who the invader was: his name is manufactured (Cushan of double wickedness) and the lack of specific details has raised questions as to the historicity of this narrative. Many consider it legendary, though A. Malamat (Israel) equates him with a Semitic usurper who invaded Egypt early in the 12th century during the confusion attending the fall of the 19th dynasty. Othniel is said characteristically to have established peace for forty years.

Then Eglon, the king of Moab, in the area just opposite the Dead Sea, pushed across the Jordan and invaded Benjaminite territory in eastern Palestine.

"But when the people of Israel cried to the Lord, the Lord raised up for them a deliverer, Ehud, the son of Gera, the Benjaminite, a left-handed man. The people of Israel sent tribute by him to Eglon the king of Moab. And Ehud made for himself a sword with two edges, a cubit in length; and he girded it on his right thigh under his clothes. And he presented the tribute to Eglon the king of Moab". (Judg. 3:15–17)

The story of the single-handed saviour, Ehud, who came ostensibly to deliver "a secret errand" but actually to assassinate Eglon, is deftly related. The fate of the people hung on the bold terrorist's skill in executing the enemy and delivering the people. The story of the victory over Moab concludes by saying that he gave the land peace for "eighty" years.

The mention of Shamgar ben Anath seems to be a later insertion; it is even assumed that this was done to make up the number of judges to the classical twelve. He was not called a "judge" and was apparently not even an Israelite. The name is Hurrian and his reputed mother is Anath, the Canaanite warlike goddess-mother, appropriate for an epic hero in Canaan. He might have been a city king of Beth-Anath of Galilee who repulsed an onslaught of Philistines, of whom he slew "six hundred men with an oxgoad". He may have relieved both Canaanites and Hebrews from the menace.

A Handful Against a Multitude

The deeds of these three early judges apparently took place at the beginning of the 12th

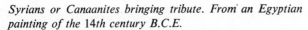

Syrians or Canaanites bringing tribute. From an Egyptian painting of the 14th century B.C.E.

Canaanite woman, dated 1350-1150. Carved on ivory, from Megiddo, a Canaanite town.

century, before Deborah. With more specific details, valuable insight can be gained into the background of these stories. Above all they vibrate intensely with real life and have precise geographical settings which made them of keen interest to Israel in recent years. There was a partisan-like character to the operations, as for instance the raids of Gideon, Jephtah and the first encounters with the Philistines. There would be no point in attempting to relate these stories to moral standards. They were a lusty young people of their time, afire with vigour and the joy of life. They were ruled by a fierce code and were struggling to survive. This is most apparent in the epics of Deborah, Gideon and even Samson.

THE EPIC OF DEBORAH

The wars of conquest of the north of Palestine were alternately attributed to Joshua (11) and, by the Book of Judges, to the "prophetess" Deborah and Barak. But they may have dealt with the same events, for the tribes had enemies in many quarters, the most formidable of whom was king Jabin, from the strongly fortified northern city of Hazor, the biggest and strongest Canaanite city of Galilee. A confederation of well-armed Canaanite city-kings had apparently subjugated the Hebrew tribes of Galilee. To cut off communications between them and those of the central mountain range, Jabin's general, Sisera, who could throw nine hundred iron chariots into the field, terrorized the northern tribes. A saviour arose in Deborah, a prophetess and a judge, who chose Barak ben Abinoam as her general. A prose account in Judg. 4 gives one account of the battle which is also celebrated in the Song of Deborah in Judg. 5. Among the finest songs of the world, it is considered one of the oldest extant monuments of Hebrew literature, for it seems to have been written by one who stood very near to the events described in vignettes which breathe the spirit of the action.

The condition to which the central tribes had been reduced by the Canaanite oppression is colourfully pictured and also their helplessness, for there were scarcely any weapons among them:

> "In the days of Shamgar, son of Anath,
>   in the days of Jael, caravans ceased
>   and travelers kept to the byways.
> The peasantry ceased in Israel, they ceased
>   until you arose, Deborah,
>   arose as a mother in Israel.
> When new gods were chosen,
>   then war was in the gates.
> Was shield or spear to be seen
>   among forty thousand in Israel?" (Judg. 5:6–8)

The God of Sinai is pictured as coming out of His holy mountain and using all of nature, especially the storm, to rout the enemies of His people. He emerged from Seir (Edom) amidst earthquakes and strode into Canaan at the head of His victorious army, to save His tribes. At this early stage of belief, Yahweh was conceived as a battle-god and poetic symbols concerning him were strongly anthropomorphic.

This theophany shows that the desert southland was the real home of Israel's God and the region of Edom and Seir, near Kadesh, the place of His origin. The Hebrews in the spirit

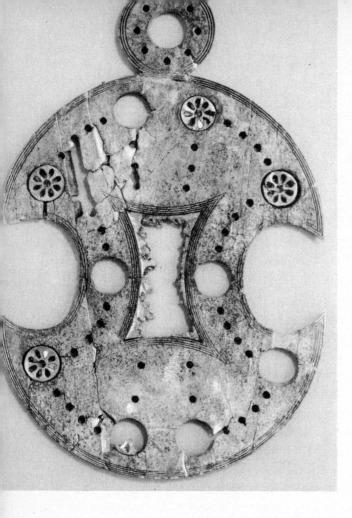

Megiddo was once the largest and strongest of the Canaanite cities of the Valley of Esdraelon, and was destroyed in the early part of the 12th century, before the battle immortalized by Deborah. In the treasure-room of its large temple-fortress, excavators found many gold, ivory and alabaster objects, which vividly illustrate the wealth and culture of the royal Canaanite cities. Ivory game-board and comb, figures of Canaanite workmanship were found there.

On an ivory plaque from Megiddo, the king is shown seated on his cherub-throne, drinking from a bowl. Before him a lady of the court, a musician playing a lyre, and captives. The king's throne is supported by winged sphynxes (cherubim), implying that he was enthroned on them. These ivories were mostly used for inlay on furniture, boxes and the cedar walls of drawing-rooms.

of the Covenant continued to look there, outside Canaan, for their standards and impetus. To them the event was overwhelming because of its religious meaning. Exactly as the con temporaries of the Exodus saw Yahweh in the miracles of the Reed Sea, and the cloudy pillar, so the tribes perceived His active presence in the cloudburst over the valley of Esdraelon. The guerilla fighters made up in ferocity and dedication what they lacked in weapons and manpower compared to the vastly superior troops of Sisera.

Not all the tribes responded to Deborah's call, but many of them mustered and are praised in the poem, while those that remained aloof are reviled. The town of Meroz is singled out for particular contempt in that its people did not participate. They did not act as "the people of Yahweh", the exclusive Lord of the tribal league. The Hebrew force under Barak, ten thousand strong, marched on to Mt. Tabor, at the edge of the valley of Esdraelon, apparently hiding on the fortified summit:

> "And I will draw out Sisera, the general of Jabin's army, to meet you by the river Kishon with his chariots and his troops; and I will give him into your hand' ". (Judg. 4:7)

The battle took place along the Kishon torrent which flows from Megiddo to the sea. It was an insignificant stream before it became a raging and overflowing torrent which, according to the poem, bogged and swept away the enemy's chariotry so that the Hebrews could slay the dismayed Canaanite army. As the poem tells, even the stars, Yahweh's heavenly host, joined in the battle.

A silver bowl of Phoenician design. Sisera drank milk from a "lordly bowl" which Yael offered him.

A woman looking out of a recessed window. This was known in ancient Palestine, according to the Talmud, as a "Tyrian (Phoenician-Canaanite) window". It stands over a little balcony, supported on small columns. From an ivory panel at Arslan-Tash, northern Syria.

A Canaanite god in bronze covered with gold leaf. Micah had made a similar graven image. A parallel story is recorded of Gideon.

"The kings came, they fought;
    then fought the kings of Canaan,
at Taanach, by the waters of Megiddo;
    they got no spoils of silver.
From heaven fought the stars,
    from their courses they fought against Sisera,
The torrent Kishon swept them away,
    the onrushing torrent, the torrent Kishon.
March on, my soul, with might!
"Then loud beat the horses' hoofs
    with the galloping, galloping of his steeds". (Judg. 5:19–22)

The glory of the victory went to a woman as Deborah prophesied. According to the prose account in Judg. 4, Sisera fled on foot to the tent of Yael, a Kenite nomad woman. He trustedher hospitality. But her hatred for the enemy of the people of the Covenant, (who were probably allied with her people) cancelled traditional usage. After Sisera drank from the "lordly bowl" which Yael offered him, she killed him with a tent peg while he slept. It was a grievous breach of oriental hospitality, but the end was held to justify the means. For sheer drama this, possibly the earliest complete Hebrew epic, has no peer in ancient literature. The poem ends on a note of pathos, Sisera's mother waited in vain for her son to return from Israel with spoils:

"Out of the window she peered,
    the mother of Sisera gazed through the lattice:
'Why is his chariot so long in coming?
    Why tarry the hoofbeats of his chariots?'
Her wisest ladies make answer,
    nay, she gives answer to herself,
'Are they not finding and dividing the spoil?—
    A maiden or two for every man;
spoil of dyed stuffs for Sisera,
    spoil of dyed stuffs embroidered,
    two pieces of dyed work embroidered
    for my neck as spoil?' " (Judg. 5:28–30)

GIDEON'S EXPLOITS

The career of Gideon seems to have been after the time of Deborah. In his days the valleys and even the highlands were subjected to oppressive raids by Midianites and their allies from the Syrian desert similar to the invasion of Canaan by the Israelites a few generations before. This story gives the earliest mention of domesticated camels from the Arabian and Syrian desert being used on so large a scale. It must have been terrifying for the Hebrews for they took refuge in inaccessible hideouts and —

...."made for themselves the dens which are in the mountains, and the caves, and the strongholds". (6:2)

Gideon was filled with zeal for Yahweh. The description of his destruction of an altar and the adjacent idol of the Canaanite mother-goddess Ashera, belonging to his father, is an interesting indication of the conflict between Yahweh and Baal among the clansmen of the hill country of Manasseh. Traces of older Canaanite paganism survived among the Hebrew clans or infiltrated the popular religion.

"Then Gideon built an altar there to the Lord, and called it, The Lord is peace. To this day it still stands at Ophrah, which belongs to the Abiezrites. That night the Lord said to him, 'Take your father's bull, the second bull seven years old, and pull down the altar of Baal which your father has, and cut down the Asherah that is beside it; and build an altar to the Lord your God on the top of the stronghold here, with stones laid in due order; then take the second bull, and offer it as a burnt offering with the wood of the Asherah which you shall cut down' ". (Judg. 6:24–26)

Gideon's memory was immortalized by such exploits as that which tells why he chose a corps of three hundred Yahweh worshippers to fight the Midianites:

"The Lord said to Gideon, 'The people with you are too many for me to give the Midianites into their hand, lest Israel vaunt themselves against me, saying, "My own hand has delivered me". Now therefore proclaim in the ears of the people, saying, "Whoever is fearful and trembling, let him return home". And Gideon tested them; twenty two thousand returned, and ten thousand remained. And the Lord said to Gideon, 'The people are still too many; take them down to the water and I will test them for you there; and he of whom I say to you, "This man shall go with you", shall go with you; and any of whom I say to you, "This man shall not go with you", shall not go' ". (Judg. 7:2–4)

"And the number of those that lapped, putting their hands to their mouths, was three hundred men; but all the rest of the people knelt down to drink water. And the Lord said to Gideon, 'With the three hundred men that lapped I will deliver you, and give the Midianites into your hand; and let all the others go every man to his home; So he took the jars of the people from their hands, and their trumpets; and he sent all the rest of Israel every man to his tent, but retained the three hundred men; and the camp of Midian was below him in the valley". (Judg. 7:6–8)

GIDEON'S NIGHT RAIDS

"And he divided the three hundred men into three companies, and put trumpets into the hands of all of them and empty jars, with torches inside the jars. And he said to them, 'Look at me, and do likewise; when I come

This scene, from a campaign of the Assyrian Ashurbanipal in which Arab camel riders were engaged, is reminiscent of the Midianites in Gideon's days.

The spring of Harod, scene of Gideon's exploits.

to the outskirts of the camp, do as I do. When I blow the trumpet, I and all who are with me, then blow the trumpets also on every side of all the camp, and shout, "For the Lord and for Gideon" '. So Gideon and the hundred men who were with him came to the outskirts of the camp at the beginning of the middle watch, when they had just set the watch; and they blew the trumpets and smashed the jars that were in their hands. And the three companies blew the trumpets and broke the jars, holding in their left hands the torches, and in their right hands the trumpets to blow; and they cried, 'A sword for the Lord and for Gideon!' They stood every man in his place round about the camp, and all the army ran; they cried out and fled". (Judg. 7:16–21)

The narrator of Judges recited grisly scenes to illustrate that the period was one of barbarism and crude disregard for life. In the process, he revealed other primitive traits of the tribesmen's faith and customs. Such was Gideon's dealings with the clans he mustered to fight the Midianites. According to routine procedure throughout the ancient Near East, the heads of two Midianite chiefs, Zeeb and Oreb, were cut off as trophies and evidence of the success of the tribe of Ephraim. Another way of counting the slain foe was by cutting off the palm of the victim's hand, as evidenced in Ugarit, Egypt and Mesopotamia.

As Gideon proceeded to Succoth, east of Jordan, against two other Midianite chiefs, Zebah and Zalmunna, he asked for supplies and help and was answered sarcastically:

"Are Zebah and Zalmunna in your hand, that we should give bread to your army?" (8:6)

Gideon saw the cogency of this argument, but he vowed to punish the people of Succoth with torture for their lack of co-operation and after capturing the two chiefs he carried out his threat.

His victories must have won him great authority. His people, sensing their vulnerability, wished to crown him as their king. Gideon refused with the standard formula, consistent with the formulation of Israelite theocracy:

"I will not rule over you, and my son will not rule over you; the Lord will rule over you". (8:23)

To record the number of enemy dead, the hands of the corpses were cut off and piled. In this scene a scribe is keeping the account. From a temple of Rameses II at Abydos.

Indeed, the idea of monarchy was anathema to true Israelites, for it was Yahweh, their overlord who saved them through his inspired representatives, rather than through hereditary kings. The Israelites were not inclined to imitate the city-state pattern of Canaan. But according to A. Lods and E. Nielsen this negation of royalty seems to be an insertion expressive of later views and Gideon was apparently crowned king. At Ophrah he erected an "ephod", which appears to be a statue or divination object, weighing 1700 shekels of jewelry donated by the victors:

"And they answered, 'We will willingly give them'. And they spread a garment, and every man cast in it the earrings of his spoil. And the weight of the golden earrings that he requested was one thousand seven hundred shekels of gold; beside the crescents and the pendants and the purple garments worn by the kings of Midian, and besides the collars that were about the necks of their camels. And Gideon made an ephod of it and put it in his city, in Ophrah; and all Israel played the harlot after it there: and it became a snare to Gideon and to his family". (Judg. 8:25–27)

The sequel is contained in Abimelech's story, where Gideon's offspring dispute whether to divide this embryo Israelite kingdom among them or whether one of them should inherit it whole.

ABIMELECH'S RISE AND FALL

After Gideon's refusal of the kingship, and probably in the last days of the tribal league, Abimelech, Gideon's son by a Shechemite concubine, set himself up as king in Shechem. He was able to muster the citizenry behind him because of his mother's connections, and, through treachery and the money given him by the priests from the treasury of the Baal-berith (Lord of the Covenant of Shechem), he hired rascals or mercenaries and forthwith liquidated all of his father's numerous progeny, except the youngest son, Jotham. Standing on Mt. Gerizim, Jotham told the famous fable of the trees, which seeking for a king to rule over them, asked the olive, the fig and the vine in turn, and finally had to settle for the thorn, which grows abundantly in the area:

> "But the fig tree said to them, 'Shall I leave my sweetness and my good fruit, and go to sway over the trees?' And the trees said to the vine, 'Come you, and reign over us.' But the vine said to them, 'Shall I leave my wine which cheers gods and men, and go to sway over the trees?' Then all the trees said to the bramble, 'Come you, and reign over us,' And the bramble said to the trees, 'If in good faith you are anointing me king over you, then come and take refuge in my shade; but if not, let fire come out of the bramble and devour the cedars of Lebanon' ". (9:11–15)

> "If you then have acted in good faith and honour with Jerubbaal and with his house this day, then rejoice in Abimelech, and let him also rejoice in you; but if not, let fire come out from Abimelech, and devour the citizens of Shechem, and Beth-millo; and let fire come out from the citizens of Shechem, and from Beth-millo, and devour Abimelech". (9:19–20)

The Shechem temple; view from the north-east.

The implication was that Abimelech's rule, like the thorn which destroys, would be a tinder-box for the fire of revolution. This criticism of the monarchy came ill from a king's son. Either the fable is an independent piece inserted later, or it may be an expression of the spirit of people still not far removed from the proud independence of nomads who brooked no rule over them. Abimelech ruled for three years, but the Shechemites rebelled on the occasion of a Canaanite grape-harvest festival which reflects the sensuousness of their ways (9:27). Shechem was burned by Abimelech. He was killed and the experiment in monarchy failed, but the event cast a fateful shadow of things to come. The days of the tribal league were coming to an end, for a central government was needed when the league broke down under the last oppression of the Philistines.

JEPHTAH

The Ammonites wanted to extend their holdings into the Israelites' portions east of Jordan. Jephtah, a freebooter, was chosen by the men of Gilead because of his ability, initiative and inspiration, not by virtue of his questionable birth. He denied the Ammonite chiefs' claims to Israel territory, which they made in the name of their national god, Chemosh:

"Will you not possess what Chemosh your god gives you to possess? And all that the Lord our God has dispossessed before us, we will possess". (Judg. 11:24)

His message is interesting as illustrating the religious views of the times. He did not deny that the Ammonites had Chemosh, just as Israel had Yahweh, but since the latter was the only God, their rights prevailed. At that stage Hebrew monotheism did not deny the existence of other national gods, as it did later.

Because of a hasty vow he had made to sacrifice the first person that would welcome him home, Jephtah was compelled to kill his own daughter. The story shows that human sacrifice, though rare, was still practised.

The Israelite tribal covenant could not apparently enforce the purity of Yahwism, nor persuade the tribes to act concertedly, nor prevent inter-tribal rivalry from flaring into civil war. Jephtah was insulted by the inimical tribe of Ephraim because of a feud with the men of Gilead. They warred on Ephraim which seemed to claim a hegemony over other tribes, and won. When the Ephraimites tried to get across the Jordan, the victorious Gileadites were in possession of all the fords:

"And the Gileadites took the fords of the Jordan against the Ephraimites. And when any of the fugitives of Ephraim said, 'Let me go over', the men of Gilead said to him, 'Are you an Ephraimite?' When he said, 'No', they said to him, 'Then say Shibboleth', and he said 'Sibboleth', for he could not pronounce it right; then they seized him and slew him at the fords of the Jordan. And there fell at that time forty-two thousand of the Ephraimites". (Judg, 12:5–6)

This is an interesting indication of dialectical differences between Israelies living in their isolated provinces, even at this early period.

Stela of Rameses II (13th century) found at Bethshean. In trying to re-establish the Asiatic empire of this forefathers, he rebuilt this town as a frontier post and guard of the Valley of Esdraelon which was one of the royal granaries. Rameses (right) raises his hand in a gesture of address. The god wears a crown with double plumes. At the bottom of the stela are name-rings of the foes of the Pharaoh, surmounted by the upper part of the body of bound captives.

Forces of Rameses III attack a Syrian town.

Prisoners of Rameses III: A Lybian, a Syrian, a Hittite, a Philistine, a Lybian. The later Philistines were called "Sea People". From Medinet Habu.

THE PHILISTINES

While the wars of conquest and clashes with the kings of Canaan and the neighbours of Israel were proceeding and the tribes were gradually taking possession of the lands, the third great enemy, destined to become the most serious of all, loomed more dangerous every year: the Philistines. For more than a hundred years, since the 13th century, Egyptian influence in Palestine had been waning. The pressure from the north had also decreased since the breaking up of the Hittite empire and its hold on Syrian provinces. This interregnum enabled Israel to establish itself firmly in the conquered Canaanite towns and newly developed territories. The restoration of Egyptian power in western Asia might have had serious consequences had it not been so brief.

The forces of Rameses III (left) engaged in a sea battle with the invading Sea People (with feathered helmets).

The Peoples of the Sea (Philistines) had proved a serious threat to Merneptah (C. 1220) and only by great energy and a fearful battle was he able to repel them. This horde from the Aegean or other islands invaded the coast from the west. This wave seems to have resulted from the break–up of the Mycenean confederacy when ancient Greece and the Aegean world in general was overwhelmed by the Dorians, just prior to, or during, the Trojan war. The people called Tjikar by the Egyptians' who in the Odyssey were called "Sikel" were perhaps from Sicily. Large groups such as Achaeans, Sardinians, Sicilians and Lycians seized coastal and island possessions and ranged the Mediterranean coasts. Lacking the strength to eject them, the Pharaoh seems to have made a virtue of necessity and invited the Sikel to settle as his nominal vassals. This was probably a generation or two after Israel's own arrival. But the aggressive and well armed Caphtorian (Philistine) ranks meant the subjugation of the Hebrews to them during the period of the Judges.

The Philistines now dominated the Palestinian sea-coast from an urban pentapolis which consisted of Gaza, Ashkelon, Ashdod, and of Ekron and Gath which they took over or built anew. Each town was ruled by a "seren" (tyrant, derived from the Greek tyrannos). They slowly assimilated the religion and customs of Canaan but proved even superior in material culture. The pentapolis was organized as a united military confederation. The Philistines en-

*The native hills of Samson. On the hill at the top right is the site of his home town, Zor'ah.
In the centre is the mound of Beth-Shemesh, another Israelite town dominated by the
Philistines.*

joyed a local monopoly of the manufacture of iron, the secret of which they had apparently
learned from the Hittites or Aegean kinsmen from the north. This gave them a tremendous
and dangerous advantage over the Hebrews. The Philistines dominated Judea, and border
incidents became inevitable. The friction did not come at once to open war.

SAMSON

At an early stage of Philistine expansion there are stories of Samson of fabulous strength,
which have become legendary, through engaging and bawdy pranks. The stories are typical of early Hebrew storytelling, with comparatively few definite occurrences, but with
colourful scenes of life on the Philistine-Judean border in the period of the early Judges.
He may be a prototype of heroic partisans who tried to resist the Philistines but fought a
losing battle. These stories gradually formed into a cycle and finally became attached to one
central figure. This material was then utilized for historical purposes, and religious touches
were added.

The Jordan at Dan, the extreme north of Palestine. Southern Hermon is seen in the background.

The historical element connects the cycle with the Philistine menace; a picture of social life and the meeting of two civilizations may be seen in what was originally no more than a village folk tale. It is possible that ancient Hebrew mythological elements became interwoven. A. Jeremias and other scholars have long ago pointed these out. The name of the hero: (Shimshon = "sun-man") expresses the idea of the lion as a solar symbol; the midsummer heat favours the work of the bees; Samson's seven locks of hair perhaps symbolize the sun's rays. After his ebullient exploits, Samson was enmeshed in the toils of Delilah, whose name is connected with the Hebrew word for night – "layla". Night spread a curtain over the sky as Delilah wove his seven locks (sun's rays) with a web. The power of the sun decreases as night overmasters his rays; as Delilah shaved his locks, she deprived him of strength. Then night reigned supreme, as Samson was blinded.

The "Sit-Shamsi" ceremony to the rising sun is a primitive Semitic cult. Notice the stepped ziggurat at both sides of the priests; the sacrificial offerings; the pillars (matzeboth) and the altar. Behind the priest is the water trough. One priest pours water on the other's hand in a rite of purification. From Susa, Media.

The blending of these elements into the classic story is a vivid example of how epic treatment evolves from folkloric material. Samson's story was not typical of the Book of Judges, but the dramatization and setting are the best example we have of primitive and genuine Judean lore.

DANITES AND THEIR SANCTUARY

Two episodes complete the Book of Judges: the story of how the sanctuary in Dan came to be founded, and the gruesome story of the Gibeah outrage. The story of Micah is better founded historically. He was a wealthy and influential Hebrew who made himself an idol with an "ephod", a cult object used for obtaining oracles, and "teraphim" (household gods), with a view to setting up a private chapel for himself:

> "So when he restored the money to his mother, his mother took two hundred pieces of silver, and gave it to the silversmith, who made it into a graven image and a molten image; and it was in the house of Micah. And the man Micah had a shrine, and he made an ephod and teraphim, and installed one of his sons, who became his priest. In those days there was no king in Israel; every man did what was right in his own eyes". (Judg. 17:4–6)

It does not seem to have been out of the ordinary, that, as the narrative implies, his own son served as priest, for in those days priests did not come only from the tribe of Levi.

Then clans of Danites, who had been living precariously on the Philistine border and were probably dislocated as a result of fresh onslaughts, began to look for new territory. They sent spies to the north to find a place where the native Canaanite people would not be able to resist them. On the way the spies met Micah's household, and he secured a favourable oracle for them. As they moved north, the Danites forced the priest to move with them, taking his master's cult objects with him, despite unavailing protests. Warriors needed a properly equipped priest to deliver oracles, deciding whether war should be launched and whether or not to take various tactical steps. They came suddenly upon the tranquil and unsuspecting Canaanite town of Laish, near the source of the Jordan and easily conquered it, changing its name to Dan, the northernmost town of Israel. Hence the saying "from Dan to Beersheba" to indicate the ultimate limits of Israel. The Danite cult became important after the northern kingdom of Israel had been established:

> "And the Danites set up the graven image for themselves; and Jonathan the son of Gershom, son of Moses, and his sons were priests to the tribe of the Danites until the day of the captivity of the land". (Judg. 18:30)

This is a most significant incident, for the unnamed Levite is now paralleled by "Jonathan the son of Gershom the son of Manasseh" and it gives a historical background to the origin of the Danite priesthood. In the Hebrew text the short name Moshe (Moses) is given, but it has an "n" suspended over the text making it Me(na)she, thereby seeking to hide the distasteful fact that this priest, practising a Canaanite rite, traced his descent from Moses.

AN INFAMY IN ISRAEL

The extraordinary narrative in Judg. 19–21 relates that a Levite's concubine who had tarried with him for the night in Gibeah, was abused to death by some Benjaminites. Incensed, the Levite dismembered her corpse into twelve pieces and sent them throughout "all the territory of Israel" (to each of the tribes of the League,) to rouse them to revenge:

"And all who saw it said, 'Such a thing has never happened or been seen from the day that the people of Israel came up out of the land of Egypt until this day; consider it, take counsel, and speak'. Then all the people of Israel came out, from Dan to Beersheba, including the land of Gilead, and the congregation assembled as one man to the Lord at Mizpah. And the chiefs of all the people, of all the tribes of Israel, presented themselves in the assembly of the people of God, four hundred thousand men on foot that drew the sword". (Judg.19:30 to 20:2)

The dissection of slaughtered animals and circulation of the pieces far and wide seemed to arouse people into concerted action. The shocking thing in this case was that a human being was treated in this way. The infamy was the greater since it was a transgression against tribal law which the Hebrews held in great respect. Many of the people of Gibeah had taken part in committing the infamy and the tribal league imposed sanctions and quoted the prescribed formula of prosecution: "and give sentence". But even though the tribes united against Benjamin and almost wiped them out, human consideration prevailed when the tribe was on the verge of extinction. To provide wives for the remaining Benjaminites, girls were secured from across the Jordan. In Jabesh-Gilead which was destroyed, according to another tradition, the men were instructed to capture the girls at the Shiloh shrine during a religious festival. This episode, the last in the Book of Judges, ends with the revealing refrain:

"In those days, there was no king in Israel. Everybody did what was right in his own eyes". (Judg. 21:25)

It seems probable that the narrative contains a historical kernel but the incident cannot have taken place during the period of Judges, but earlier. Jabesh-Gilead was already a flourishing town in the days of Saul.

SAMUEL — THE LAST JUDGE

It was customary for Israelites to make a pilgrimage each year to Shiloh to sacrifice to Yahweh. There Eli, the high priest was "minister to Yahweh" and the boy Samuel was serving under him. He had been dedicated to Yahweh before his birth by a Nazirite vow. But there was so much corruption in the household, particularly on the part of the two sons of the high priest, that reform was necessary.

The most severe crisis of Israel's history was at hand. The Philistines who had gradually occupied part of Judea and the South, had come into possession of Ephraim and Benjamin, where the Isrealites had felt safe in their mountains since Joshua's days. They had inflicted many losses on Israel and the battle was going against them. The elders suggested that the Ark of the Covenant be brought out to the battlefield, as had often been done in the past:

"And when the troops came to the camp, the elders of Israel said, 'Why has the Lord put us to rout today before the Philistines? Let us bring the ark of the covenant of the Lord here from Shiloh, that he may come among us and save us from the power of our enemies'. So the people sent to Shiloh, and brought from there the ark of the covenant of the Lord of hosts, who is enthroned on the cherubim; and the two sons of Eli, Hophni and Phinehas, were there with the ark of the covenant of God. When the ark of the covenant of the Lord came into the camp, all Israel gave a mighty shout, so that the earth resounded". (1 Sam. 4:3–5)

The Philistines realized that "the gods have come into the camp", but they braced themselves and decisively defeated Israel at Aphekah and the Ark was taken into Philistine territory as a trophy. Eli fainted, broke his neck and died. From a biblical viewpoint, God allowed his ark to fall into the hands of the Philistines because of the corruption of the Hebrew leaders and people. The Philistines invaded the hill country, destroyed Shiloh, the league's central shrine, and a number of other Israelite towns. They placed garrisons at strategic points, and to protect their monopoly of iron, deprived Israel of what metal industry she had, making her dependent on Philistine smiths for the manufacturing and repair of ploughs and tools. The tribal league, its forces scattered and disarmed, its central shrine destroyed and the priesthood dispersed, collapsed:

> "Then the Philistines took the ark of God and brought it into the house of Dagon and set it up beside Dagon. And when the people of Ashdod rose early the next day, behold, Dagon had fallen face downward on the ground before the ark of the Lord. So they took Dagon and put him back in his place. But when they rose early on the next morning, behold, Dagon had fallen face downward on the ground before the ark of the Lord, and the head of Dagon and both his hands were lying cut off upon the threshold; only the trunk of Dagon was left to him."
> (1 Sam 5:2-4)

This passage is a bit of secular folklore. The narrators, whose holiest possession was the Ark, relate with glee that the Ark was no blessing to the Philistines and that Dagon, their

Broken stela from Ugarit with a dedication to the god Dagon, a Canaanite and Philistine deity similar to the Baal.

Bronze tools and swords from Ugarit; 15th century.

The gods of Canaan and Syria were considered potent even in Egypt. Ramu, a sick Egyptian and his family are bringing offerings to Astarta. His deformity may have been due to infantile paralysis. Stela of the 18th century B.C.E.

god was humiliated. Eventually the Philistines returned the Ark to the Hebrews in their town of Beth-Shemesh.

HEBREW CULTIC USAGES.

To appreciate the nature of the struggle in the turbulent period of Judges it is necessary to know something of the religion of Canaan and the commingling of the two cultures, the Hebrew and the Canaanite, in the first centuries of Hebrew settlement

The faith of the semi-nomads was different, more austere and higher than that of the natives they conquered and lived amongst. But on the material level the Hebrews' culture was lower than that of the Canaanites or the Philistines. For many centuries Canaan had been under the civilizing influence of the great empires of Babylonia, Egypt and the other centres of influence of the ancient Near East. Nevertheless Israel was a religious society and early resisted the political organizations of the day, having her tribal organization by sacred covenant with Yahweh. The Bible stresses, and history does not disprove, that in the days following settlement, most of the tribes remembered their covenant and tried to adhere to its faith, especially in times of crisis, despite a tendency sometimes to retrogress and compromise with local customs.

The central religious institution was the tribal league focussed around the central sanc-

Altars of incense; incense stands with bowl; from the 11th cent., found at Megiddo.

tuary which changed according to events and geographic convenience. Shiloh seemed to be the main sanctuary, but others existed: Gilgal, Gibeon, Bethel, Shechem and presumably Beersheba for the southern tribes. Sacrifices were offered at the "bamah", located on a high hill or under trees. Among cult objects at the bamah there was the stone pillar (Matzebah) and the wooden pole (Asherah) as well as incense altars evidently placed at "high places" (See the stone altar at Ophrah, described in Gideon's story, Judg. 6:25). The clans met there on festal occasions, prayed, heard liturgical recitations, made vows, slaughtered and then ate sacrificial animals. These gatherings were at new moons, sabbaths and annual feasts, and, according to the cultic usages in vogue, in addition to the sacrifice of sheep, goats and large cattle, included offerings of grain, wine and oil, of flax and wool, figs and raisin cakes. Gifts were either made to the priests (Levites) who had charge of the "holy place" or "high place", or were consumed in picnic fashion by the worshippers:

"Now the sons of Eli were worthless men; they had no regard for the Lord. The custom of the priests with the people was that when any man offered sacrifice, the priest's servant would come, while the meat was boiling, with a three-pronged fork in his hand, and he would thrust it into the pan, or kettle, or cauldron, or pot; all that the fork brought up the priest would take for himself. So they did at Shiloh to all the Israelites who came there". (1 Sam. 2:12–14)

The Canaanite temple at Hazor.

"ZEBAH" — SACRIFICE

We have now a great deal of information about the cultic sacrificial usages of both Hebrews and Canaanites and others.

Central to the Israelite concept of worship was the offerings given to the deity. These were the product of the offerings of the flocks of the people. It seems that the Canaanite sacrificial ritual was even more elaborate than the Hebrew.

The dedicated altar for offerings may have been a large rock, with or without cupped grooves (to contain offerings of produce), a high pillar (matzebah) or a pile of earth over which were erected a heap of unhewn stones, as prescribed in Exod. 20: 24 – 26. This formed the platform over which sacrifices were offered. Sacrificial altars terminating in horns at the four corners have been discovered and are familiar in the biblical record:

"So Gideon went into his house and prepared a kid, and unleavened cakes from an ephah of flour; the meat he put in a basket, and the broth he put in a pot, and brought them to him under the oak and presented them. And the angel of God said to him, 'Take the meat and the unleavened cakes, and put them on this rock, and pour the broth over them.' And he did so. Then the angel of the Lord reached out the tip of the staff that was in his hand, and touched the meat and the unleavened cakes; and there sprang up fire from the rock and consumed the flesh and the unleavened cakes; and the angel of the Lord vanished from his sight". (Judg. 6:19–21).

The law insisted on the unblemished condition of sacrificial animals. A "zebah"(sacrifice) was one at which the flesh was eaten by the participants in the ritual act, after the blood

Cultic object, including a "matzebah" excavated in the temple of Hazor.

and the intestinal fat had been received by God. Blood was considered connected with the "nephesh" or life (Lev. 17: 11, 14; Deut. 12: 23). The prohibition against consuming intestinal fat may have had something of the same significance and it was burned. Yahweh as the "living God" was the giver of life and to Him life must return.

CANAANITE SACRIFICES AT LACHISH

Among the debris around the platform where sacrifices were offered at the Canaanite temple at Lachish (destroyed and burned by the Hebrews about 1220 B.C.E.), a large number of animal and bird bones were found during excavations. The animals were all young and all identifiable bones were of the upper part, or the right foreleg, which had been cooked by boiling. According to the cultic usage, in common with biblical law, the priest's portion, after boiling, was the right shoulder. It is presumed that the rest could be eaten by the participants outside or in another chamber of the sanctuary:

The debris of the temple-fortress at Lachish, showing an altar.

"And the right thigh you shall give to the priest as an offering from the sacrifice of your peace offerings; he among the sons of Aaron who offers the blood of the peace offerings and the fat shall have the right thigh for a portion". (Lev. 7:32–33)

Near the altar at Lachish the portions were found set aside for the priests by this law concerning "peace offerings". It seems that many of the rules of sacrifice were common to both Canaan and Israel. It is accepted that much of the sacrificial ritual in Leviticus was adopted either from Canaan or from old Semitic tradition. Canaanite tablets from Ugarit show that some at least of the offerings had the same names in Canaan as in Israel, such as "shelem" for peace offering and "asham" for trespass offering.

Common Cultic Usages

Asherah— The Israelites seem to have found and adopted in Canaan sacral objects and practices which had been unknown to them. Among them was the Canaanite "asherah", found near Hebrew sacrificial altars. This cultic object, standing erect, was made of wood and was placed near the altar. The asherah is known from Ugaritic literary texts as the symbol of the mother goddess or "El's" consort, chief of all the gods of Canaan and head of its divine family. The Bible record refers to the wooden asherah as a sacred cultic object. The Israelites did not seem loth even to adopt the Canaanite private cult of female figurines which have also been found in abundance in the remains of Israelite towns and villages from after the settlement. While no graven image of Yahweh was ever found in these settlements (the Canaanite cities possessed numerous figures of male deities, mostly identified with Baal), large numbers of female figurines, apparently representing the mother-goddess "Ashtoreth" (Astarta), were found in excavations of the period. They are taken to be amulets designed to help expectant mothers, or for the inducement of fertility. They are artistically crude, but they were not the goddesses of Canaan.

The Canaanite Fertility Cult

The Canaanites followed the widespread Near Eastern cults of the great divinity of fertility, Ashtoreth—the goddess-mother—and of a young god who represented vegetation which follows the rhythm of the Palestinian climate where a rainy season (November-March) alternates with a long, rainless summer (April-October). Some scholars (after Frazer) suggest that this cult was involved with the "sacral marriage" whose participants represented and dramatized the sacral union of the divinities and gave rise to ritual prostitution at the sanctuaries.

A Saturnalian spirit seized revellers at the harvest festivals, especially at "grape-gathering", as described in Judg. 9:27, 21:19-21. Canaanite religion was crude, vitalistic, with a strong allure for the simple folk on account of its orgiastic revelries and ritual prostitution. One purpose of this ritual was to induce fertility in the land through sympathetic magic:

> "And the people of Israel again did what was evil in the sight of the Lord, and served the Baals and the Ashtaroth, the gods of Syria, the gods of Sidon, the gods of Moab, the gods of the Ammonites, and the gods of the Philistines; and they forsook the Lord, and did not serve him". (Judg. 10: 6)

This specific geographic distribution of the divinities of the Canannite pantheon is also richly attested by archaeological discovery of the Canaanite Baals of Ugarit and other parts of Syria and Palestine. These, cast in bronze, or covered with gold and silver, were the "graven images" which were a blasphemy to pious Israelites.

We now infer from Canaanite texts dealing with the mythology of their gods, that the archaic beliefs in El and Ashtoreth, were linked at a later time with the cultic celebration of their son "Baal", (Lord). This divinity had multiple manifestations, ranging from the archaic "Baal of heaven", the thunder and rain-god, to the local Baals who were also the givers of life and fertility, as well as the sources of other material blessings. The god of Shechem was Baal-berith, as we know. The patron deity of Tyre was "Melkart", i.e. Melek-kert — the King of the City.

Baal's female consort or counterpart was Asherah, represented by a wooden object (a pole). At the same time, figurines and amulets of "Astarta" were cherished as stimulants by women. A sacrificial cult provided many types of offerings by which the unseen, but anthropomorphic powers, could be approached and won to man's favour.

The "Sit Shamsi" rite is a striking example of this Semitic cult on a "high place" (See colour illustration above

YAHWEH AND BAAL IN THE POPULAR RELIGION

It was perhaps natural that popular religion would, like the Canaanites, see the manifestations of Baal as the god of the land, the giver of rain and grain, new wine and oil. The mythological Ugarit epic dating from the Amarna age, of the resurrection of Baal, symbol-

The Phoenician (Canaanite) legend of Aleyn Baal; a cuneiform Ugaritic text.

Aleyn Baal is described as a warrior, holding a club in one hand; in the other the symbol of thunder. He wears the symbol of fertility on his head. Under his feet is the representation of waters on which he steps.

izing the revival of fertility, describes the drama in the following words:

> In a dream, O Kindly One, God of Mercy (?)
> In a vision, Creator of Creatures,
> The heavens rained oil,
> The dry valleys flowed with honey;
> So I know
> That Triumphant Baal lives,
> That the Prince, Lord of Earth, is Alive!

(Translated by W.F. Albright – Interpreter's Bible).

The same rites and customs were adopted by Hebrews and Canaanites in the worship of Yahweh and Baal. The name of the latter was often applied to Yahweh. There may have been a fusion of the concepts of Yahweh and Baal in the popular religion. It is possible that the concept of the desert deity, the jealous God, may have lost much of its earlier sternness, and though Yahweh nominally triumphed over Baal with Israel's settlement, His religion may actually have succumbed to Baal later to a large degree.

While the enlightened religious leadership of Israel might have held to the monotheist faith of Yahweh, the mass of the people were more imitative of the way of the "people of the land", adopting consciously or unconsciously, many of the ways of their neighbours.

We know little of the effect that the agricultural ethos of the sown land had over the religious conceptions of the semi-nomadic tribes who had come in very close contact with Canaanite civilization. The biblical narrators laid tremendous emphasis on the retrograde tendencies due to the corroding influence of the religion of the Canaanites and the absence of any outstanding religious leaders. That is why they relentlessly recited the score of turbulent scenes which point the moral and indicate the spurious religion from which it resulted. The religion of Yahweh did not become entirely submerged due to the small nucleus of worshippers which persisted despite adverse circumstances. In the opinion of W. F. Albright there existed "an unusually powerful centripetal force in the Mosaic tradition... the religion of Moses was a missionary faith with dynamic appeal to the nomadic and semi-nomadic tribes of that time". We get the impression that the form of religion was Yahweh-worship, but that it adopted also the Baal worship. A tension arose from this which was the perennial concern of the Bible narrators.

Israel's popular religion, like her material culture, was so similar to that of Canaan as

Figurines of a Canaanite mother-goddess. Hundreds of figurines and nude female figures were found in almost all excavations in Palestine. Canaanite (Middle Bronze) and Early Iron (Israelite) Age.

God with shield and weapon, from Megiddo.

to make it virtually impossible to distinguish the two, at least before the prophetic movement reversed the course back to Israel's ancient faith. It is certain that the Hebrews sought to adjust themselves, and that their tribal organization and mode of life, on many levels, became modified by the exigencies of sedentary life and by influences from without. The majority of Canaanites were farmers, but commercial enterprise, among others the dyeing industry, made possible the development of strong urban centres such as Gezer, Megiddo, Hazor, where Hebrews had become equally adept at these arts by the 10th century. These few examples of adaptation are impressive evidence of the great cultural and material debt of the Hebrews to the Canaanites.

The biblical tradition stresses that it was the manner of Canaan, its mode of life and beliefs, which seemed strange to the faithful Israelites whose thinking was conditioned by the severe demands of divine will. Biblical stories reflect a traditional prejudice about the licentiousness and predatory habits of the natives with women. The Israelites, in accordance with the strict discipline of patriarchal life, where clan life and taboos determined every detail of the behaviour, naturally considered the easy going ways of the Canaanites as "abominations". Indeed the enlightened Israelites may have struggled against Canaanite influence not because the two peoples were so different, but because they had so much in common. This made the allure of Canaanite religion more pervasive and insidious.

The two centuries between Moses and Samuel were times of severe testing and religious strain between the popular religion and the adherents of the pure faith. The tension was not clearly formulated but is glimpsed in matters of national interest and civic justice. Hebrews

A masculine deity.

God with feathered headdress.

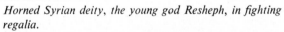

Horned Syrian deity, the young god Resheph, in fighting regalia.

The goddess Qadesh (Astarta) on a lion, flanked on the left by Min and by Resheph, god of war, on the right.

did not devote attention in those days to what we call theology or to the philosophical implications of faith. Faith was expressed in sacrificial offerings or in simple prayer. The written tradition of that period reflects little homogeneous belief—but the Israelites were becoming increasingly conscious of their peculiar religion which set them apart from the followers of the local Baals and divinities as well as of the increasing danger of the Philistine menace.

THE STORY OF RUTH AND BOAZ

The Book of Ruth, a winsome and warmhearted folk story casts a mellow concluding light on that troubled period. The tale is not primarily historical. The interest lies in its revelations of ancient Israelite customs. It comes after the Book of Judges in the old Greek and Latin Versions, as well as in the English Bible. In the Hebrew Scriptures it is in the third, latest and least venerated group of sacred books known as the "Ketubim" (Writings). Many scholars believe that the story was written and circulated in Nehemiah's day, the time of the return of the exiles, while others think it was written by a contemporary of David. That is because of the authentic milieu of the rural setting of the time of Judges, and because the descendants of Ruth are only given as far as the third generation, close to David's time. It has long been held that the story was told to show that Ruth, a Moabitess who settled in Bethlehem, was actually an ancestress of David who was born there.

A famine in Judah had driven Elimelech and his wife Naomi and two sons to emigrate from their native Bethlehem, to cross the Jordan and to sojourn in the land of Moab, rich in grain. Later, both sons, one of whom had been married to Ruth, died. Naomi returned to Bethlehem in Judah but her daughters-in-law insisted on following her despite her attempt to dissuade them:

> "But Ruth said, 'Entreat me not to leave you or to return from following you; for where you go I will go, and where you lodge will I lodge; your people shall be my people; and your God my God; where you die I will die, and there I will be buried, May the Lord do so to me and more also if even death parts me from you'. "(Ruth 1:16–17)

THE GLEANER IN THE FIELDS

Ruth was young and used to gruelling labour. She became a gleaner in the harvest fields, an old custom for the aid of the poor:

Gleaning in the fields of Bethlehem, the locale of Ruth's story.

Sickle.

"Now Naomi had a kinsman of her husband's, a man of wealth, of the family of Elimelech, whose name was Boaz. And Ruth the Moabitess said to Naomi, 'Let me go to the field, and glean among the ears of grain after him in whose sight I shall find favor'. And she said to her, 'Go my daughter,'. So she set forth and went and gleaned in the field after the reapers; and she happened to come to the part of the field belonging to Boaz, who was of the family of Elimelech". (Ruth 2:1–3)

Boaz's gracious attitude to the foreigner made it plain that he did not continue to regard her thus but as a kinswoman. Boaz was a "stalwart warrior", a term that characterized him as an upstanding landowner, well regarded by the town council and citizens, the prototype of the Israelite "big man" in the countryside, and the pillar of the Israelite rural class. He was occupied with his herds and crops, matter-of-fact, and little interested in racial prejudices relating to foreigners. He was just such an ancestor as David might have had, hearty, manly, mighty in toil and conscious of his obligations.

The practical Naomi devised a stratagem to stimulate Boaz to decision and action concerning his privileges and duties as a "go'el" (redeemer) of her late husband's house. According to this "levirate" marriage custom, a man was duty-bound to marry his brother's widow if the deceased had left no sons (as was the case) and thus to continue the family:

"Now is not Boaz our kinsman, with whose maidens you were? See, he is winnowing barley tonight at the threshing floor. Wash therefore and anoint yourself, and put on your best clothes and go down to the threshing floor; but do not make yourself known to the man until he has finished eating and drinking". Ruth 3:2–3)
....
So she went down to the threshing floor and did just as her mother-in-law had told her. And when Boaz had eaten and drunk, and his heart was merry, he went to lie down at the end of the heap of grain. Then she came softly, and uncovered his feet, and lay down". At midnight the man was startled, and turned over, and behold, a woman lay at his feet! He said, 'Who are you?' And she answered, 'I am Ruth, your maidservant; spread your skirt over your maidservant, for you are next of kin'. And he said, 'May you be blessed by the Lord, my daughter; you have made this last kindness greater than the first, in that you have not gone after young men, whether poor or rich. And now, my daughter, do not fear, I will do for you all that you ask, for all my fellow townsmen know that you are a woman of worth. And now it is true that I am a near kinsman, yet there is a kinsman nearer than I. Remain this night, and in the morning, if he will do the part of the next of kin for you; well, let him do it; but if he is not willing to do the part of the next of kin for you, then, as the Lord lives, I will do the the part of the next of kin for you. Lie down until the morning' ". (Ruth 3:6–13)

Ruth took a great risk, but her obedience to Naomi's counsel only enhances her more than filial submissiveness and shows the strength of her loyalty and dedication to the continuity of the family. It is Ruth's loyalty that must be stressed, not her sentimental affection for Naomi nor her love for Boaz. Among the pictures of ancient life is that of the farmer lying down to sleep at the end of the heap of grain, the revelry accompanying the harvest, and Ruth's appeal to Boaz to take over the Levirate responsibility (which most men are anxious to avoid).

The climax of the story is Ruth's marriage to her kinsman. Boaz submitted the whole matter to a council of the elders of the community and it is clear that there was no objection to the marriage of an Israelite to a foreigner, provided there were no barring circumstances. These marriages seemed to have been beneficial to the nation at large. Naomi's neighbours after the birth of Ruth's son did not hesitate to declare that her foreign-born daughter-in-law had been to her "better than seven sons". And Ruth's crowning honour is that she became the ancestress of David, founder of the united kingdom of Israel. This seems to be the real point of the story, to make which the tale is told.

Man playing a lyre, on a vase from Megiddo, dating about 1000 B.C.E.

CHAPTER XI

TRIBALISM AND NATIONHOOD

THE LAST JUDGE

"Then Samuel said, 'Gather all Israel at Mizpah, and I will pray to the Lord for you'. So they gathered at Mizpah, and drew water and poured it out before the Lord, and fasted on that day, and said there, 'We have sinned against the Lord'. And Samuel judged the people of Israel at Mizpah. Now when the Philistines heard that the people of Israel had gathered at Mizpah, the lords of the Philistines went up against Israel. And when the people of Israel heard of it they were afraid of the Philistines". (1 Sam 7:5-7)

The gathering of the Hebrews at the sanctuary of Mizpah in the highlands of Benjamin made the Philistines afraid that they would unite against them.

Symbolic of Philistine supremacy was the garrison stationed in the heart of the hill country at Gibeath-Elohim, and the Hebrew state of disarmament. Liberation from the Philistines is attributed to Samuel's initiative, though he is said to have accomplished it, not by military leadership, but by prayer and sacrificial rites. He could not have won sweeping victories "so that the Philistines were subdued and did not again enter the territory of Israel" (7:13). This tradition anticipates the liberation effected by Saul under Samuel's leadership.

Samuel was famous as a holy man and a giver of oracles. He seems to have succeeded the judges, and was probably concerned in the administration of covenant law among the clans. There being no longer a tribal centre, he moved in a regular circuit between certain important shrines, of Gilgal, Bethel and Mizpah, where he settled legal disputes and tried to keep alive the league's tradition and spirit. This is how the first book of Samuel pictures his career.

PHILISTINE RULE IN WESTERN PALESTINE

The end of the 11th to the middle of the 10th centuries B.C.E. was the heyday of Philistine military power over the coast, the south and the highland hinterland of western Palestine after the disaster of Aphek. They seem to have paralyzed the operation of the tribal league; but their strongest effect upon the development of the Israelites was the withholding from them of the use of iron for agricultural tools which came into common use only by the middle of the 10th century. Until the first kings broke the Philistine military power, the Philistines closely guarded the secrets of its production, and kept a "corner" on the iron market.

An interesting illustration of the stranglehold which the Philistines had over Israel (as Saul tried to turn the tide), is given below:

> "Now there was no smith to be found throughout all the land of Israel; for the Philistines said, 'Lest the Hebrews make themselves swords or spears'; but every one of the Israelites went down to the Philistines to sharpen his plowshare, his mattock, his axe, or his sickle; and the charge was a pim for the plowshares and for the mattock, and a third of a shekel for sharpening the axes and for setting the goads. So on the day of the battle there was neither sword nor spear found in the hand of any of the people with Saul and Jonathan; but Saul and Jonathan his son had them". (1 Sam 13:19–22.)

(The value of a "pim" is 2/3 of a shekel: 11.4 to 12 grams or 2/5 oz.).

The Hebrews had no central authority in Palestine. Canaan had only city kingdoms ruled by a military aristocracy which maintained itself by recruiting local draftees, and imposing heavy fines and forced labour on the people, whose land was confiscated for the benefit of the military caste.

The dilemma facing the Israelites was not that of strengthening the patriarchal tribal league which had become weak and anachronistic. Times had changed and the people craved for unity and a strong monarchic regime.

They had made peace with the native Canaanites: "There was peace also between Israel and the Amorites". (1 Sam 7:14)

The organization of open opposition to the Philistines and the creation of the necessary leadership was started off in the tribe of Benjamin, at Gibeath-Benjamin and Ramah. Its central figure was Saul.

THE BATTLE OF JABESH-GILEAD

The story of Saul's private anointment as "nagid" or leader is closely followed by that of the battle of Jabesh-Gilead which proved the real turning point in his career. This was his test of military leadership in the eyes of the people. But it did not yet involve the Philistine oppressors. The crisis arose when the Ammonites of east of Jordan attacked Jabesh-Gilead, whose inhabitants were kinsfolk of the tribe of Benjamin. Isolated from the tribes west of the Jordan, they wanted to negotiate a treaty, but the Ammonite king jeeringly demanded that the people of the town submit to the brutal humiliation of each having one eye struck out. This form of punishment is mentioned also in Ugarite literature.

When the news came to Benjamin, Saul was ploughing behind a yoke of oxen. Suddenly "the spirit of God came mightily upon Saul" in a manner reminiscent of the ancient charismatic Judges and impelled him to do an exceedingly significant thing:

"He took a yoke of oxen, and cut them in pieces and sent them throughout all the territory of Israel by the hand of messengers, saying, 'Whoever does not come out after Saul and Samuel so shall it be done to his oxen!' Then the dread of the Lord fell upon the people, and they came out as one man". (1 Sam 11:7)

The declaration of a crisis affecting all the people or a call to arms by this device was apparently an approved tradition. It is essentially the same as that of the Levite of Gibeah in cutting up his abused and murdered concubine. It was calculated to rouse the people to concerted action. Inspired by Saul's leadership the tribesmen gathered at Bezek, which was out of reach of Philistine garrisons and defeated the Ammonites at Jabesh-Gilead by an enveloping action from three directions. But Saul did not return home after this action as the judges of old had done. Still keeping a safe distance from the Philistine garrisons, he set out to organize the tribesmen near the sanctuary at Gilgal in the Jordan valley, east of Ephraim and Benjamin.

TIMES OF TRANSITION

"Then all the elders of Israel gathered together and came to Samuel at Ramah, and said to him, 'Behold you are old and your sons do not walk in your ways; now appoint for us a king to govern us like all the nations' ". (1 Sam 8:4–5)

This theme dominates the Books of Samuel and epitomizes the final conflict between Hebrews and Philistines for supremacy in Palestine. Saul's career, with its tragic finale, is the prelude to the Hebrew War of Liberation which took place barely two centuries after the settlement.

A change as radical as that from the rule of judges to that of kings could only be caused by major social and political factors. These are apparent in the two Books of Samuel, which consist of strands of stories from various sources: royal chronicles; individual stories; official records from the royal archives, which justify the Davidic dynasty, and finally epic stories and folklore.

As might be expected at such times of significant changes in Israel, differing views are reflected. There were those who conservatively desired to maintain the patriarchal leadership; and conversely the popular clamour for unity against the common danger under strong dynastic leadership.

FROM THE RULE OF JUDGES TO THE RULE OF KINGS

The account of Saul's election to kingship has come down to us in parallel narrations, giving an ambiguous account of Samuel's attitude and behaviour. He yielded with angry protests to the popular demand, as quoted in the opening passage of 1 Sam. 8.

The demand for a new type of leadership appears to have been spontaneous, and its popularity developed with success. In Israel, unlike the established civilizations of the Near East, kingship came late. The new type of leadership corresponded to that of Israel's strong neighbours and may have been looked upon as pagan because it attempted to "do as other peoples". By Samuel and many of his contemporaries this was interpreted as a rejection of Yahweh:

> "And the Lord said to Samuel, Hearken to the voice of the people in all that they say to you; for they have not rejected you, but they have rejected me from being king over them. According to all the deeds which they have done to me, from the day I brought them up out of Egypt even to this day, forsaking me and serving other gods, so they are also doing to you. Now then, hearken to their voice; only, you shall solemnly warn them, and show them the ways of the king who shall reign over them' ". (1 Sam 8:7–9)

Many scholars, who cannot harmonize the differing traditions about Samuel and Saul attribute Samuel's anti-monarchist stand to a later tradition, from the period of later kings, reflecting experience of the ways of Israelite kingship, its taxation and obligations. The date at which a biblical tradition is written does not necessarily indicate the date at which it originated, but the original tradition is still a reflection of what people felt and thought at the time the events took place. Samuel earnestly warned the people of what the change would entail. He feared where it would lead, yet acted under pressure.

"THE MANNER OF THE KING"

> "He said, 'These will be the ways of the king who will reign over you: he will take your sons and appoint them to his chariots and to be his horsemen, and to run before his chariots; and he will appoint for himself commanders of thousands and commanders of fifties, and some to plow his ground and to reap his harvest, and to make his implements of war and the equipment of his chariots. He will take your daughters to be perfumers and cooks and bakers. He will take the best of your fields and vineyards and olive orchards and give them to his servants. He will take the tenth of your grain and of your vineyards and give it to his officers and to his servants. He will take your menservants and maidservants, and the best of your cattle and your asses, and put them to his work. He will take the tenth of your flocks, and you shall be his slaves". (1 Sam 8:11–17)

Samuel's denunciation of kingship is interpreted by I. Mendelsohn on the basis of new data from Ugarit and Alalakh, a kingdom to the north of it, dating from the 18th to the 13th centuries B.C.E. This gives "an authentic description of the semi-feudal Canaanite society as it existed prior to and during the time of Samuel....." The author of the verses quoted above "could conceivably have been the prophet himself or the spokesman of the anti-monarchical movement of that period".

The Canaanite city state recruited its foot soldiers from the common people and its professional warriors from the ranks of the aristocracy, the "maryannu", who fought in horse-drawn chariots. For their services to the king the maryannu received crown lands, the income derived from the estates providing them with the means of maintaining themselves and their expensive war equipment. The king amassed his crown lands, consisting of fields, vineyards, orchards and olive yards, and such movable property on the land as sheep, oxen, asses and slaves, mainly by expropriation as a result of victorious wars, by confiscation from the people and by purchase.

The common people were also subject to the king's service, or corvée, for the construction of roads, the erection of fortresses, the building of temples and the tilling of crown lands. The Samuel text says that the king "will take your male slaves and female slaves . . . and put them to work". Mendelsohn concludes that Samuel's summary of "the manner of the King" is not "a rewriting of history" by a late opponent of kingship, but is an eloquent appeal to the people by a contemporary of Samuel, not to impose upon themselves an alien Canaanite way of life.

This theme is illustrated in Saul's characteristic utterance, many years later, on this very subject:

> "Now Saul heard that David was discovered, and the men who were with him. Saul was sitting at Gibeah, under the tamarisk tree on the height, with his spear in his hand, and all his servants were standing about him. And Saul said to his servants who stood about him, 'Hear now, you Benjaminites; will the son of Jesse give every one of you fields and vineyards, will he make you all commanders of thousands and commanders of hundreds". (1 Sam 22:6–7)

NATIONAL RESISTANCE AND THE "BANDS OF PROPHETS"

The Samuel story describes another dynamic factor that must have played a dominant role. Religious enthusiasts, "the sons of the prophets", entered the scene under the stress of the Philistine peril.

They were bands of devotees, distinguishable from other men by their hairy mantles, their tattoo marks or tonsures, who worked up an ecstatic frenzy by dancing, music and other means. Similar manifestations were known at the time throughout the Near East and even in Greece. In Palestine these bands would seem to have been the inspiration and backbone of the national resistance to the oppressor. In one of the stories of Saul's anointment, Samuel foresaw that his protégé would meet with such a band:

> "'After that you shall come to Gibeathelohim, where there is a garrison of the Philistines; and there, as you come to the city, you will meet a band of prophets coming down from the high place with harp, tambourine, flute, and lyre before them, prophesying. Then the spirit of the Lord will come mightily upon you, and you shall prophesy with them and be turned into another man. Now when these signs meet you, do whatever your hand finds to do, for God is with you. And you shall go down before me to Gilgal; and behold, I am coming to you to offer burnt offerings and to sacrifice peace offerings. Seven days you shall wait, until I come to you and show you what you shall do'. When he turned his back to leave Samuel, God gave him another heart; and all these signs came to pass that day. When they came to Gibeah, behold, a band of prophets met him; and the spirit of God came mightily upon him, and he prophesied among them". (1 Sam 10:5–10)

But those Saul met were not of the same type as the great prophets of the 8th century and after. The latter were more akin to Samuel, whom the narrator describes as ro'eh (seer). There may have been a resemblance between this type of a diviner prophet and his counterpart among West Semitic tribes to be described below.

The people who had seen Saul's ecstatic fit were surprised to see him in such a company. They asked ironically, "Is Saul also among the prophets?", which became proverbial. But that nondescript company had its merits. In a crude way it conveyed Yahwism at a popular level at a time when its original power was in danger of dissipation; they were the only supporters of Saul endowed with spiritual force to fight God's enemies.

EARLY PROPHECY IN THE ANCIENT NEAR EAST

Prophetic inspiration or divination was not uniquely Israelite, for the Bible itself tells of Balaam and the 450 prophets of Baal and the 400 prophets of Asherah in the story of Elijah. (1 Kings 18:19). Other evidence of non-Israelite prophecy comes from the archives of Mari in Mesopotamia where "a man of the god Dagan" delivered oracles to the king under divine directive.

A. Malamat points out that the biblical term "anoh" (to respond) is repeatedly used in the Mari archives to describe revelation by a divine messenger, called by the Accadian term "apilum" (a respondent). The apilum sometimes acted in groups, outside the official cult. Their domain seems to have been the "mashkanum" (biblical "mishkan") or tent shrine or tabernacle. The evidence suggests that the biblical institution had its antecedents among the West Semitic Amorites and Babylonians, namely from the original home of the first Hebrews, centuries earlier.

Another interesting parallel is the experience of an Egyptian, Wen Amun, who went to Byblos in Syria in the 12th century on a diplomatic and economic mission. Egyptian prestige collapsed and Wen Amun was snubbed and his mission seemed a failure, when a miracle intervened on his behalf. One of the pages at the temple had a prophetic seizure: "Bring up (the) god! Bring up the messenger who is carrying him. Amun is the one who sent him out!" The Prince of Byblos could not disobey the word of a god and received the emissary and allowed him to buy the cedar wood used for building the ceremonial boats of Amun-Re.

SAUL ANOINTED BY SAMUEL

One of the two narratives about Saul's accession to kingship is interesting as background material rather than as history.

The popular story goes that Saul, the son of Kish of Gibeath-Benjamin, "a handsome young man... from his shoulders upward he was taller than any of the people", set out in search of his father's asses. He had almost given up the search when, at the suggestion of his servant, he decided to obtain some advice from the "seer" Samuel in Ramah, in return for a fee. Ramah was about 5 kms. north of Gibeath-Benjamin:

> "(Formerly in Israel, when a man went to inquire of God, he said, 'Come, let us go to the seer'; for he who is now called a prophet was formerly called a seer.) And Saul said to his servant, 'Well said; come, let us go. So they went to the city where the man of God was". (1 Sam 9:9–10)

Samuel the "Seer" was not only a priest who officiated at the "high place"; his function was also to determine the will of Yahweh by oracle, or by revealing secrets. He was a renowned seer but a later writer thought him worthy to be called a prophet — "he who is now called a prophet was formerly called a seer". Samuel was the guiding spirit in Israel through the dark period of Philistine domination. His career is not only significant for his relentless fight against the Canaanite worship (as stressed by this tradition) but also for the transition from the old type of leadership to more stable government under a monarchy. This transition was fraught historically with tremendous crises.

Samuel secretly anointed Saul at Ramah, and he was later elected king by a drawing of lots at a gathering of the clans at Mizpah (9:17—25). As a military leader, Saul had the task of welding together disunited tribes, and then, unarmed, of organizing the defence of Gilgal and facing a well-armed foe. This folklore epic may be the account of a phase in Samuel and Saul's organization of an "underground". Saul was in fact elected king at

Gibeat Benjamin or Gibeat Shaul (modern Tel-el-Ful), three and a half miles north of Jerusalem. The site shown below was excavated by W. F. Albright.

Gilgal only after he had proved himself a successful leader.

The second story describing Saul's election to kingship — by public acclamation after his victory over the Ammonites — is generally accepted as more accurate historically:

"And on the morrow Saul put the people in three companies; and they came into the midst of the camp in the morning watch, and cut down the Ammonites until the heat of the day; and those who survived were scattered, so that no two of them were left together. Then the people said to Samuel, 'Who is it that said, "Shall Saul reign over us?" Bring the men, that we may put them to death'. But Saul said, 'Not a man shall be put to death this day, for today the Lord has wrought deliverance in Israel'. Then Samuel said to the people 'Come, let us go to Gilgal and there renew the kingdom'. So all the people went to Gilgal, and there they made Saul king before the Lord in Gilgal. There they sacrificed peace offerings before the Lord, and there Saul and all the men of Israel rejoiced greatly". (1 Sam 11:11-15)

No longer acting as a tribal league but as a people, Israel had again elected a leader; but this time he was crowned and founded a dynasty. It was politically an important change which altered the course of Israel's history.

SAUL'S UPRISING AGAINST THE PHILISTINES

Philistine oppression had become the dominant theme of the times. Action was needed and the people placed their hopes in the new king to fight "Yahweh's battle".

His entire army had originally consisted of some 3000 recruits divided in three camps at various distances from the Philistine headquarters in the hills of Benjamin:

The dress of Palestinians after the 14th century, as depicted by the Egyptians.

"And raiders came out of the camp of the Philistines in three companies; one company turned toward Ophrah, to the land of Shual, another company turned toward Beth-horon, and another company turned toward the border that looks down upon the valley of Zeboim toward the wilderness". (1 Sam 13:17–18)

At the sight of the Philistine "raiders" and armour, the discouraged handful deserted. Saul was left in command of a battalion of 600 men, the standard biblical army unit.

Jonathan, Saul's son, was in command near Michmash and Geba, and he boldly attacked a Philistine outpost almost single handed. The narrative breathes the intensity of the conviction that Yahweh himself was actively engaged in the conflict:

"In the pass, by which Jonathan sought to go over to the Philistine garrison, there was a rocky crag on the one side and a rocky crag on the other side; the name of the one was Bozez, and the name of the other Seneh. The one crag rose on the north in front of Michmash, and the other on the south in front of Geba. And Jonathan said to the young man who bore his armor, 'Come, let us go over to the garrison of these uncircumcised; it may be that the Lord will work for us; for nothing can hinder the Lord from saving by many or by few'. And his armorbearer said to him, 'Do all that your mind inclines to; behold, I am with you, as is your mind so is mine'". (1 Sam 14:4–7).

It appears that Saul pinned his hopes on the discomfiture of the "Hebrew" mercenaries in the Philistine garrison:

"Then Saul and all the people who were with him rallied and went into the battle; and behold, every man's sword was against his fellow, and there was very great confusion. Now the Hebrews who had been with the Philistines before that time and who had gone up with them into the camp, even they also turned to be with the Israelites who were with Saul and Jonathan. Likewise, when all the men of Israel who had hid themselves in the hill country of Ephraim heard that the Philistines were fleeing, they too followed hard after them in the battle". (1 Sam 14:20-22)

The term "Hebrews" here is apparently used to mean Khapiru, who betrayed their masters and joined the Israelites. Those who had deserted rallied to Saul. The Philistines set out in three sorties to prevent the escape of the guerillas east of the Jordan but they were beaten by Saul.

The daring exploit of Jonathan's little commando force between Michmash and Geba

Fighting and hunting weapons of the period.

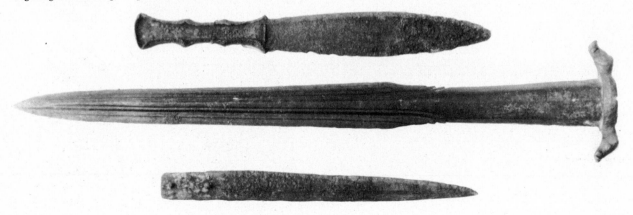

Michmash (modern Mukhmas) lying northwest of Gibeat Benjamin.

was the first real victory over the Philistines. It was followed by the capture of their stronghold in Gibeah, where Saul established his first royal town.

Saul's kingdom was at first very small. Excavations at Gibeah have confirmed the biblical picture of the rustic simplicity of his court. He was no wealthy or learned cosmopolitan statesman such as there might have been among his neighbours. He was a warrior and a "saviour". He continued the early tribal democracy, claiming authority among the tribes and their leading families because of the "spirit of God that was upon him". His kingdom was based on the national unity of tribes even though scattered among the territory of enemy peoples. His administration was composed mainly of members of his family, though some foreign chiefs joined his army. We know little of his taxation system at this stage nor many details of his reign (about 1020–1000 B.C.E.), except that "there was hard fighting against the Philistines all the days of Saul". The cited length - two years - of his reign is an error.

Geba in Benjamin (modern Jaba) standing on its "tel" (mound) facing Michmash.

He is described as a saviour in the campaign against the Amalekites to free the sheep herders of Judah and the allied Calebites, and against the Ammonites and other neighbours of Israel east of Jordan as far as the southern Negev. But the people and Saul transgressed the tradition of the "herem" (sacrificial ban) in their victory over Amalek:

> " 'But the people took of the spoil, sheep and oxen, the best of the things devoted to destruction to sacrifice to the Lord your God in Gilgal'. And Samuel said:
> 'Has the Lord as great delight in burnt offerings and sacrifices, as in obeying the voice of the Lord?
> Behold, to obey is better than sacrifice, and to hearken than the fat of rams.
> For rebellion is as the sin of divination, and stubbornness is as iniquity and idolatry.
> Because you have rejected the word of the Lord, he has also rejected you from being king' ". (1 Sam 15:21-23)

This was dearly paid for by Agag, the Amalekite chief. With fierce devotion, Samuel performed the sacrificial act:

> "And Samuel said, 'As your sword has made women childless, so shall your mother be childless among women'. And Samuel hewed Agag in pieces before the Lord in Gilgal". (1 Sam 15:33)

The incident of Saul's war against the Amalekites is further proof of his discomfiture before God. It belongs to an anti-Saul tradition quoted probably by a chronicler in David's time, to justify David's accession to Saul's throne.

DAVID AND SAUL

Saul faced odds that would have taxed the most balanced of minds. He was evidently very impetuous and excitable and of ungovernable temper. But with brilliant leadership he started resistance to the Philistine menace, welded the tribes into a new political pattern and organized the first permanent Israelite army which would serve as a check to the formidable enemy. But he was unable to cast off the yoke of the Philistines from the hill country or deal them a lasting blow. He became subject to acute mental depression and violent explosions of anger which were interpreted by the later narrators as possession by an "evil spirit" (which had invaded his personality), sent by God, or else as his unhappiness at being rejected by Samuel. He began to be haunted by the feeling that the "spirit of God" had left him, and that his popularity which had rested on the people's conviction that he was Yahweh's "designated", had slipped away.

David was a skilled musician, a likely young man for Saul to attach to his person. Thus it was that David, a shepherd from Bethlehem was brought to Saul's court, according to one tradition. One story — not considered historically true by some — tells that Samuel, under divine inspiration, anointed him as king in Saul's stead while he was still a shepherd in his father's home:

> "Then Samuel took the horn of oil, and anointed him in the midst of his brothers; and the Spirit of the Lord came mightily upon David from that day forward. And Samuel rose up, and went to Ramah. Now the Spirit of the Lord departed from Saul, and an evil spirit from the Lord tormented him". (1 Sam 16:13-14)

A musician playing the harp.

According to another tradition of David's youth, he came to the Israelite camp, in the Valley of Elah at a critical moment, when the Philistine Goliath challenged a Hebrew champion to single combat. The tale is reminiscent in some respects of the epic encounters of heroes in Homer's Iliad. Though unarmed and unable to carry the heavy coat of mail (which Israelite officers had by then come to wear, in imitation of the Philistines), David gallantly slew Goliath with his sling, in the style of athletic shepherds:

"And David put his hand in his bag and took out a stone, and slung it, and struck the Philistine on his forehead; the stone sank into his forehead, and he fell on his face to the ground". (1 Sam 17:49)

A Philistine defeat followed this exploit. It gained David tremendous fame which has come down in a popular song about him. When Saul returned from battle, the women met him with music and song, but his charming armour-bearer, David, received the greater praise:

"And the women sang to one another as they made merry,
    'Saul has slain his thousands,
    And David his ten thousands'.
And Saul was very angry, and this saying displeased him; he said 'They have ascribed to David ten thousands, and to me they have ascribed thousands; and what more can he have but the kingdom?' ". (1 Sam 18:7)

2 Sam 21:19 credits the feat to Elhanan Ben Yaari of Bethlehem. The author of the Books of Chronicles, which give a parallel account of David's career (beginning with Chr. 1, ch 10), had before him the Books of Samuel, but seeing the discrepancies, he tried to harmonize the two versions. It is possible that the deed of another lesser warrior was thus transferred to the great hero, David. It is believed that Ben Yaari is a corruption of Ben Ishai and Elhanan may have been the second name of David.

So David won fame and position. Saul made him a "captain over a thousand; and he went out and came before the people". He took a prominent part in Saul's wars with the Philistines, and won the undying friendship of Saul's son, Jonathan, whom "he loved as he loved his own

Sling stones from the Israelite period.

soul". He married Saul's daughter, Michal.

The dramatic irony of the fall of Saul and the rise of David is underscored at every turn by the Judean narrators. It seems that Saul fared somewhat harshly in the judgement of later chroniclers, who were disposed to emphasize everything unfavourable to him. David was attended by good fortune while Saul was driven into deeper frustration, and at times acted outside the bounds of rational behaviour:

> "And Saul eyed David from that day on. And on the morrow an evil spirit from God rushed upon Saul, and he raved within his house, while David was playing the lyre, as he did day by day. Saul had his spear in his hand; and Saul cast the spear, for he thought, 'I will pin David to the wall'. But David evaded him twice. Saul was afraid of David, because the Lord was with him but had departed from Saul". (1 Sam 18:9-12)

The demoniac darkness of Saul's condition took on the quality of unrelenting doom, and events moved with grim inevitability. Saul feared that the people regarded David as their national hero and that they would want to make him king.

WHY WERE GIBEON AND NOB DESTROYED?

During the reign of Saul the expansion of Israel in the hill country broadened the territorial and ethnic basis for the struggle against the Philistines. As Judah and its allied clans were gradually absorbed into the Israelite tribal area, the group of Canaanite towns, among them Gibeon and Jerusalem, became an enclave in this territory. The temptation to be rid of this awkward wedge of towns and communications between the northern and southern parts of the nascent kingdom was irresistible. The biblical source cites Saul as the exterminator of the Gibeonites. The reason appears in a parenthetical remark in 2 Sam 21:

> "Now the Gibeonites were not of the people of Israel, but of the remnant of the Amorites; although the people of Israel had sworn to spare them, Saul had sought to slay them in his zeal for the people of Israel and Judah". (2 Sam 21:2)

Saul's "zeal" is significant in this context, for it amplifies his devotion to the confederate tribes of Israel and Judah. Another parenthetical quotation concerning Beeroth nearby, illuminates the political status of the Gibeonites vis-a-vis their close neighbours, the Benjaminites:

"(For Be-eroth also is reckoned to Benjamin; the Be-erothites fled to Gittaim, and have been sojourners there to this day)". (2 Sam. 4:2–3)

Scholars connect the abolition of the Gibeonite confederation with the presence of the "bamah" or high place of Gibeon, as a central sanctuary. After his flight from Saul, David found refuge and help in Nob, where the high priest Ahimelech, descended from the ancient priestly house of Eli, was officiating, and the biblical source gives this as the reason why Saul exterminated the priests of Nob, which lies next to the bamah of Gibeon:

"Then the king said to Doeg, 'You turn and fall upon the priests', And Doeg the Edomite turned and fell upon the priests, and he killed on that day eighty-five persons who wore the linen ephod. And Nob, the city of the priests, he put to the sword; both men and women, children and sucklings, oxen, asses and sheep, he put to the sword". (1 Sam 22:18–19)

This does not seem to be the real cause of this sanguinary act. The priests were jealous of their power and ancient privilege of collecting the tithes at the central sanctuary. But it had become the king's right to levy all the taxes and this would have reduced the priests and Levites to a subordinate position in the king's administration. (That situation prevailed in David's days.) Blood existed between the house of Saul and the priests of Nob and Gibeon and it was resolved in a bloodbath.

But Saul could not yet utilize in full this increase of power, although it helped him in no small degree and increased the strength of the kingdom in the time of David.

Shepherds' fields at Bethlehem.

DAVID THE OUTLAW

Saul unwittingly gave David another means of increasing his ritual power. Of all the priests of Yahweh killed at Nob, only Abiathar, Ahimelech's son, escaped. He fled to David and brought the ephod. David retained him and sought from him the oracles of Yahweh, which he consulted at every turn. This gave divine respectability to the band of "outlaws" gathered around him in the years before Saul's death, indicating that those social and political malcontents were not as disreputable as appeared:

> "And every one who was in distress, and every one who was in debt, and every one who was discontented, gathered to him; and he became captain over them. And there were with him about four hundred men". (1 Sam 22:2)

David scored military successes in accordance with Abiathar's oracles; when he advised him to retreat, he obeyed. Oracles were used in the ancient Near East to determine tactics and strategy. Priests who understood warfare were assigned to regular army duty.

David managed for some time to maintain himself and his partisan band in the wilderness at the eastern edge of Judah by protecting the large flocks of sheep of the "great men" (25:2), herdsmen of Judah. He tried to strengthen his position by alliance with influential families in the region, and married twice, first Ahinoam, then Abigail the widowed wife of Nabal. This incident is illustrative of conditions in the days before David succeeded to the throne.

Nabal, a wealthy herdsman, gave a party and David sent ten men to convey good wishes and collect tribute to which he thought himself entitled as "protection money".

These chiefs were a force to be reckoned with and Nabal, a man of uncertain temper, resented the levy upon him and refused to pay. Abigail thought better of it, and went to David with gifts. Although furious at Nabal's cavalier treatment, David allowed himself to be appeased; he was much impressed by Abigail's beauty, and married her after Nabal's death. This gave him social status as a Calebite chief. With raids on the nomad tribes from the Negev, David also gained a reputation as a useful if irregular public protector in the southern region, which it was impossible for Saul to emulate.

David had several opportunities to kill Saul, who pursued him in his desert hideouts, and was completely in his power at Engedi and the wilderness of Ziph. David refrained from harming him, out of respect for Yahweh's anointed, but broadcast his magnanimity in sparing him, and gained a good deal by his generosity as he publicly belittled Saul and protested his own innocence:

> "And he said, 'Why does my lord pursue after his servant? For what have I done? What guilt is on my hands? Now therefore let my lord the king hear the words of his servant. If it is the Lord who has stirred you up against me, may he accept an offering; but if it is men, may they be cursed before the Lord, for they have driven me out this day that I should have no share in the heritage of the Lord, saying, "Go, serve other gods". Now therefore, let not my blood fall to the earth away from the presence of the Lord; for the king of Israel has come out to seek my life, like one who hunts a partridge in the mountains'". (1 Sam 26:18–20)

David was not bent on destroying Saul's line; in fact he vowed not to destroy his seed, a vow which he later kept.

The wilderness of Judah, overlooking the Dead Sea. The Mountains of Moab are seen across the lake.

DAVID — CHIEFTAIN OF ZIKLAG

David complained that Saul drove him and his "gedud" of six hundred men to seek protection with Achish, King of Gath, to whom he offered his services as a mercenary chief. This, he contended, would cut him off from the inheritance of Yahweh and force him to worship the Philistine gods. This reflects the idea held at that time that each god was a local deity and could be worshipped only on his own soil.

Achish accepted David as a vassal and gave him the town of Ziklag in the Negeb as a feudal holding. From this border of Judah, he was expected to make trouble for the neighbouring towns and villages. But he was careful only to raid the Amalekites and other nomads, sparing his kinsmen, the Jerahmeelites and the Kenite clans of the Negeb:

Engedi in the wilderness of Judah, where David fled from Saul.

"And David smote the land, and left neither man nor woman alive, but took away the sheep, the oxen, the asses, the camels, and the garments, and came back to Achish". (1 Sam 27:9)

By this, and also by a judicious distribution of booty to Achish, and to strategic towns and clans of Judea, he convinced his own people that he was still their loyal protector, friend and "saviour". Indeed, after Saul's death these clans with whom David had ingratiated himself were the first to crown him king.

Hormah, a city in southern Judah, whose chiefs shared in the booty sent by David. In the days of the wanderings in the Negev, the Israelites were repulsed at Hormah in an attempt to break through into southern Canaan (see chap. VII).

TRAGEDY AT GILBOA

The Philistines who could not maintain their power in the hills, pushed along the coast and into the valley of Esdraelon. They decided to attack the young kingdom of Israel from the northern edge of the hills of Ephraim. They arrayed for battle against Saul at the foot of Mt. Gilboa where they could deploy their chariotry and count on the help of the friendly Sea People and Canaanite city-kings of the valley:

"When Saul saw the army of the Philistines, he was afraid, and his heart trembled greatly. And when Saul inquired of the Lord, the Lord did not answer him, either by dreams, or by Urim, or by prophets". (1 Sam 28:5–6)

Samuel was dead and Saul was without inspiration. No poverty was greater than being forsaken by God, who refused to give His precious word. Saul turned in desperation to the supernatural powers which could be called forth by the witch of Endor, who surreptitiously engaged in the art of spiritualism which Saul himself had outlawed. Official religion opposed occult practices which were held to be evil. But the necromancer could perhaps surpass the oracles of any living prophet with those of the greatest prophets of the past. Appearing in disguise, Saul persuaded her to call up the spirit of Samuel, commonly believed to be living in Sheol, the underworld. The shade of Samuel, goes the story, was indignant that he who had not listened to him during life had disturbed his rest in Sheol. He pronounced the final curse of doom upon the pitiable royal hero:

"And Samuel said, 'Why then do you ask me, since the Lord has turned from you and become your enemy? The Lord has done to you as he spoke by me; for the Lord has torn the kingdom out of your hand, and given it to your neighbour, David. Because you did not obey the voice of the Lord, and did not carry out his fierce wrath against Amalek, therefore the Lord has done this thing to you this day". (1 Sam 28:16–18)

Defeat was a foregone conclusion and Saul was soon to enter Sheol, where the righteous Samuel and the erring Saul alike were believed to go after death.

Saul had to fight a major pitched battle against an army such as he had never faced. This time no guerilla tactics could help him, but there was no turning back. He bore himself with pride and dignity. The battle of Gilboa seemed lost before it began, for so it had been foretold by Samuel's shade. The outcome was total disaster. The Israelite forces were cut to pieces on the slopes of Mt. Gilboa. Severely wounded and unwilling to die at the hand of the enemy, Saul fell on his own sword. His three sons were killed. The crushing defeat eclipsed the great gains of his endless wars against the Philistines. The heads of Saul and Jonathan were cut off and their corpses hung on the walls of Beth-shean.

Saul's grateful allies from Jabesh-Gilead stole the bodies at night and gave them decent burial. The shock of the people at the loss of the great leader is expressed in the moving dirge, which David infused with deep love and respect for the fallen heroes. The poem bears evidence of having been composed on the occasion and this is quite probably a true "psalm of David". In fact this dirge, like the song of Miriam and the Song of Deborah, is one of the earliest masterpieces of Hebrew poetry which has been preserved. Part of it runs:

"Thy glory, O Israel, is slain upon thy high places!
How are the mighty fallen!

"Ye mountains of Gilboa,
    let there be no dew or rain upon you, nor upsurging of the deep!
For there the shield of the mighty was defiled,
    the shield of Saul, not anointed with oil.
. . . .
"Saul and Jonathan, beloved and lovely!
    In life and in death they were not divided;
they were swifter than eagles,
    they were stronger than . lions.
. . . .
"How are the mighty fallen,
    and the weapons of war perished! (2 Sam 1:19, 21, 23, 27)

Popular belief has it that there was a curse of drought and sterility on land where heroes were slain. Which explains the lament that no dew nor rain would vivify Gilboa. Similar words were used by the Ugarit Danael when he cursed the site where the hero Aqhat had been murdered.

David had been spared the dilemma of joining his Philistine allies in battle against Saul, for he was excused at the request of Achish's confederates, who did not trust his loyalty. It is presumed that he stayed with Achish only a few months.

Mount Gilboa, scene of Saul's defeat. View from the west.

The "tel" of Bethshean with the Canaanite city-fortress at the top. View from the modern town, lying below, which has preserved its name.

Left: *Ruins of the Canaanite temple of Bethshean and its sacrificial highplace. Right: City-gate of Bethshean.*

Harp of Asiatic origin, dating from the 14th century. David the 'sweet psalmist of Israel" or the Levite singers may have accompanied themselves on such an instrument.

CHAPTER XII

THE GOLDEN AGE

THE HOUSE OF DAVID

"After this David inquired of the Lord, 'Shall I go up into any of the cities of Judah?' And the Lord said to him, 'Go up'. David said, 'To which shall I go up?' And he said, 'To Hebron'. So David went up there, and his two wives also, Ahinoam of Jezreel, and Abigail the widow of Nabal of Carmel. And David brought up his men who were with him, every one with his household; and they dwelt in the towns of Hebron. And the men of Judah came, and there they anointed David king over the house of Judah". (2 Sam. 2: 1–3)

Having no king, the clans of Judah, as well as the Kenites and Jerahmeelites to whom David had proved himself a saviour, united under his leadership. At Saul's death David was no longer an outlaw leader, but a man whom the Judeans undoubtedly welcomed back in his tribal land because he was one of them, a strong, acknowledged leader, still closely associated with the Philistines. They had followed their advantage, after Gilboa, and virtually ruled large sections of western Palestine. David did not return to Bethlehem, his native town, to foment trouble among kinsmen, thus allaying the suspicions of the Philistine overlords. He was already a feudal lord with personal holdings and wealth in Judah, though a vassal of his foreign neighbours. He was crowned king at the tribal and ritual centre of Hebron. In acclaiming him, the people of Judah acted without reference to the northern tribes, or those east of Jordan. A state of Judah emerged as a separate political entity within Israel. This was effected apparently with the consent of the Philistines who followed a policy of "divide and rule" among the Israelites of Judah and the north.

DAVID AND ISHBAAL

David hoped to find supporters outside Judah and sent messengers to Jabesh-Gilead saying "for Saul your lord is dead, and the house of Judah has anointed me king over them". But he had misjudged his popularity with the people of the north. Unknown to David, Saul's general and kinsman, Abner, had taken Saul's only surviving son, Ishbaal, and crowned him king at Mahanaim in Gilead, out of reach of the Philistines. Kingship was hereditary in Israel from the very start, and Abner acted promptly, because his claim was valid and he could command the people's loyalty to the House of Saul, in keeping with ancient Near Eastern custom. Ishbaal was not crowned in Giveah of Benjamin, apparently from fear of the Philistines. His house considered David an usurper; customarily such a ruler would eliminate every surviving member of the former ruler's family, as potential pretenders to the crown. The biblical sources emphasize that David departed from this custom in not destroying the house of Saul. This situation explains the events during the years between the end of Saul's reign and David's rule over the whole country. But political rivalry between the two houses continued; the army of Judah was led by Joab, while that of the House of Saul was led by Abner.

THE MEETING AT THE POOL OF GIBEON

Internal and external social factors could not tolerate two ruling houses under such precarious conditions. The two kings may have kept the peace but their generals and officers kept things astir at meetings at the pool of Gibeon — neutral ground which belonged to neither of the two royal domains and was near the ancient "high place" where the clans gathered for festivals. The reason for these meetings is not explained in the biblical narrative, which perhaps took them for granted. Officially, they were tournaments between twelve young warriors from each side, in which the participants engaged in mortal combat. These seem to have been the wrestling bouts dear to the ancient Greeks and Near Easterners. Known as belt wrestling, the contestants tried to unbalance one another from under the hip, snatch the belt, then stab to death.

But these rough sports developed into a real fight between the troops of the opposing camps. Abner was pursued by a brother of Joab, who tried to take his belt as a trophy. He asked him to desist then killed him in self defence. This sealed Abner's fate.

"There was a long war between the house of Saul and the house of David; and David grew stronger and stronger, while the house of Saul became weaker and weaker". (2 Sam. 3: 1)

Contestants wrestling; on the left one contestant lifts his opponent's foot. From an ancient Mesopotamian plaque of the 3rd millenium.

Shortly afterwards Abner had a dispute with the House of Saul. He sought Rizpah, the King's widow, in marriage and was upbraided by Ishbaal, possibly because the request suggested designs on the throne. In righteous indignation Abner decided to transfer his allegiance to David and offered him a covenant with the promise of bringing all Israel over to him. David accepted his allegiance, demanding that Saul's daughter, Michal, whom he had married in his youth, be restored to him, apparently in order to improve the legitimacy of his kingship of all Israel. Abner fulfilled his part and proceeded to win the northern tribes over to David. But Joab resented the power Abner was gaining as kingmaker. Through treachery and under the pretext of avenging the blood feud originating at the pool of Gibeon, he got Abner aside and murdered him.

The partial breakdown of government, and also the rigid application of the relentless desert custom of "lex talionis", blood revenge, are to be seen in these stories. According to custom Joab was the first in line to avenge his brother's death. At Hebron, Abner was under the protection of David. But in spite of this, Joab sought an opportunity to meet Abner and kill him. David's grief, expressed in fasting and a dirge for his comrade in arms, greatly impressed Abner's men.

David in turn was then bound to kill Joab, but he did not do so — he had not the courage to slay his general. But when he was about to die, tradition relates, he charged Solomon to kill Joab and thus clear his house from guilt (1 Kings 2:28).

Soon afterwards, Ishbaal was murdered and his head brought by the assassins to David who, instead of rewarding the murderers, put them to death.

Egyptian wrestlers. From tomb painting of the 3rd millenium at Sakkarah.

The present village of Gibeon and the pool of Gibeon, where the wrestling contest took place, with circular stairway leading to the bottom.

This ended the ambiguous relationship between David and the northern people and the shadow of illegitimacy on David's occupation of the throne of Judah. The "elders of Israel" discovered that they were of the same flesh and blood as David, whom, even in Saul's time, Yahweh had ordained to be shepherd and prince of Israel:

> "Then all the tribes of Israel came to David at Hebron, and said, 'Behold, we are your bone and flesh. In time past, when Saul was king over us, it was you that led out and brought in Israel; and the Lord said to you, "You shall be shepherd of my people Israel, and you shall be prince over Israel"'". (2 Sam. 5: 1–2)

This is the terminology of the old theocratic ideal, known also in Sumer, where a king claimed only to be the shepherd who pastured God's human flock. A covenant was made between the king and the people. The king had to abide by this "berith" which was a sort of constitution. Its stipulations had been the condition for the anointment which conferred the kingship on him.

The new kingdom was a departure from the old order. A military chief, David had been crowned by acclamation and anointed at a shrine of ancient prestige. The Kingdom of Judah, which he already ruled, and the area claimed by Ishbaal in the north, were united in his person. This still left sectional jealousies which were never settled.

JERUSALEM, "THE CITY OF DAVID"

David recognized that it would be impracticable for the King of Israel and Judah to maintain his seat of authority from a point as far south as Hebron. His strength rested on the support of the Judeans and his nearness to Benjamin and Ephraim, north of Jerusalem. Through his marriage to Saul's daughter Michal, he had become the son-in-law of the King of Israel, which legitimized him in the eyes of the northern tribes. He had, moreover, tightened his relations with them and could also exert direct influence in Benjamin.

> "And David dwelt in the stronghold, and called it the city of David. And David built the city round about from the Millo inward. And David became greater and greater, for the Lord, the God of hosts, was with him". (2 Sam. 5: 9–10)

The significant words of the chronicler: "The Lord, the God of hosts, was with him" epitomizes David's rising prestige and power. He was not represented as the artisan of his own fate but as one who acted under the guidance and counsel of Yahweh. This idea is imbedded in the unfolding story of the succession of the kings of Israel.

David could now effect the territorial consolidation of the northern and southern tribal territories by integrating the Jerusalem enclave into the new state and by capturing the north-south highway of the mountain range. Jerusalem was also a crossroads with the main artery from southern Transjordan. After about eight years of rule in Hebron, David moved quickly against the Jebusites, Canaanite people inhabiting the mountain "fortress of Zion". This enclave, in the heart of the central mountain range, lay within the territory of Benjamin between Judah to the south and Israel to the north. He seized the town by surprise with his "gedud", or personal army of professional soldiers, without using the tribal levies, and then transferred his household and considerable retinue there. He named it the "City of David"

Site of the "City of David" or Zion — indicated by broken line — which stood on the rock spur south-east of the walled medieval Jerusalem, and below it. The Kidron Valley lies at the bottom, east of walled Jerusalem.

and regarded it, according to custom, as his own city-state. He and his considerable entourage were treated by the inhabitants as the legitimate heirs of the Jebusite city-kings by right of conquest. The natives were not slaughtered or displaced. In the terms of the day, Jerusalem was independent of the state of Israel or Judah. David designated it his capital city because the "City of David" was his own by right. Centrally located on neutral ground between the two sections of the state, and within the territory of none of the tribes, it afforded a political and geographical compromise. It was elevated to a status above tribal

Remains of an old fortification in Ophel.

North-east angle of a bastion of the Canaanite fort of Zion, called Ophel.

jealousy, another departure from the old order. A historical event of the first magnitude for Israel and the City of David took place, the significance of which was to impress itself upon the minds of future generations.

Zion of those days was not sprawled over its eastern and western hills. It had been a small Canaanite hilltop town as far back as 3000 B.C.E., lying on the southern spur of what was later the eastern ridge of the medieval walled city of Jerusalem. It was topped by the massive fortification of Millo, then dropped steeply to the valley of the Kidron and the Gihon spring which supplied the small population. This spur, called the hill of Ophel, is lower than the surrounding mountains but it is encased within deep valleys on either side, and the Jebusites felt safe behind their walls.

THE END OF THE PHILISTINE THREAT

The Philistines, who had apparently considered David as a vassal, had not interfered in the internal affairs of his kingdom. But the fusion of the two kingdoms, Israel and Judah, under a former vassal represented a threat to their supremacy. It is probable that they invaded the area of Jerusalem occupied by David after he had conquered Zion:

"When the Philistines heard that David had been anointed king over Israel, all the Philistines went up in search of David; but David heard of it and went down to the stronghold". (2 Sam. 5: 17)

The battle took place in the territorial enclave of Jerusalem, inhabited by Canaanites, which still separated the northern and southern sections of the hill country. The Philistines tried to drive a wedge between them by occupying the area, cutting off David from the northern tribes at this vulnerable point. David did not deploy the massed tribes against the Philistines but, with the help of his tough little army of mobile trained mercenaries, repulsed them at Baal-Perazim, by surprise guerilla tactics and by applying their own methods of warfare.

The Philistines attacked in force again later, when Jerusalem was definitely in David's possession. They realized that the moment of decision had come. Their army tried to enter Benjamin through Beth-Horon but was beaten and pursued west of Jerusalem, from Gibeon to Gezer in the coastal area. It seems that a year after this decisive victory, David brought the war into Philistine territory and again crushed their power near Gath, or Lachish. Our scanty sources do not give a detailed account of the end of Philistine domination over Palestine, apart from a few epic episodes and reports of the exploits of "the mighty men" of David (2 Sam 21:15–22). According to the biblical account, David could then move northward along the coast, the Plain of Sharon, from the river Yarkon to the Valley of Esdraelon which had been in Philistine power for two generations or more, and consolidate his rule in the tribal areas far removed from Zion. From the time the Philistines found their match in a determined and vigorous foe, they ceased to endanger the new state and seemed to lose their warlike character. They retired into their coastal plain of Philistia, where they remained as minor vassals of David. Contingents of professional soldiers, the Cherethites and Pelethites, subsequently appeared in David's service as his personal troops. By 996 B.C.E. David had occupied all western Palestine, barring the southern coastal strip south of the Yarkon (present-day Tel-Aviv). For the first time in its history, Israel had access to the eastern Mediterranean, and this was to have a tremendous impact on the course of its development and relationships with the wider horizons of the ancient world.

THE ARK IN ZION

David sought to link the new state to Israel's ancient order and sacred institutions of the past, thus identifying it as the patron and protector of the ancient ritual. When he had consolidated his position, he decided to enhance the prestige of his new capital by transforming it into a ritual and religious centre in addition to its status as the centre of administration.

The Ark of the Covenant is conceived as an old and simple box, arranged with poles so that it could be carried.

With great pains and enthusiasm, the people brought to the capital city the Ark of the Covenant which had lain neglected for more than a generation in Kiriath-Jearim:

> "And it was told King David, 'The Lord has blessed the household of Obed-edom and all that belongs to him, because of the ark of God'. So David went and brought up the ark of God from the house of Obed-edom to the city of David with rejoicing; and when those who bore the ark of the Lord had gone six paces, he sacrified an ox and a fatling. And David danced before the Lord with all his might; and David was girded with a linen ephod. So David and all the house of Israel brought up the ark of the Lord with shouting, and with the sound of the horn'. As the ark of the Lord came into the city of David, Michal the daughter of Saul looked out of the window, and saw King David leaping and dancing before the Lord; and she despised him in her heart. And they brought in the ark of the Lord, and set it in its place, inside the tent which David had pitched for it; and David offered burnt offerings and peace offerings before the Lord". (2 Sam. 6: 12–17)

According to biblical tradition David had intended to establish a permanent temple for Yahweh in Zion, but the memory of the archaic tent-tabernacle was still dear to the people, and they could not adjust themselves to the idea of transforming it.

The dream of building a temple arose late in David's life, but an oracle of the prophet Nathan advised him that this must wait for the peaceful reign of his son. Meanwhile God must dwell and move "in a tent and in a tabernacle" among his people. David's plan was postponed for a generation and the Ark was housed in a tent in the City of David until the reign of Solomon.

In any event, the ancient Hebrew sanctuary had now been placed in David's town. The priests who officiated were no longer independent sanctuary priests; though the latter lost none of their appeal. They were royal officials consecrated to the sanctuary at Zion. The tribes thereafter regarded the central sanctuary with the same religious fervour as they had had for their old sacral institutions. "Mount Zion", where the sanctuary was located became in time a consecrated expression in the religious thought of Israel.

DAVID AND JERUSALEM

There is a difference between the kingship of Saul, which developed out of the charismatic leadership of the period of Judges, and the kingship of David. The latter developed as a result of conquests and the adoption of new royal forms such as those of the neighbouring empires. These were expressed in political and religious symbols. A significant new symbolism which would affect Hebrew religious thinking and poetry was provided by David's conquest of Jebusite Zion. Like other empire builders, who usually came to terms with the principal god of newly acquired territory, so David did in Zion.

El-Elyon, known since Patriarchal days as the head of the Canaanite pantheon and god of Salem (Jerusalem), now blended with Yahweh. Gen. 14 endowed Melchizedek with the functions of high priest and king. An old tradition regarded the king of Zion as the heir of Melchizedek and his titles. David and his successors inherited these titles from the Jebusite rulers of Zion. We get a fairly clear picture of this from a number of Coronation oracles, liturgies and hymns which develop this theme. Psalm 110 in particular establishes the continuity between Melchizedek and the Davidic sacral institutions. It opens with an oracle apparently spoken by a temple prophet to the king on the occasion of the coronation ritual climaxing in the declaration of the king as the priest of Yahweh after the order of Melchizedek:

> "The Lord says to my lord:
>   'Sit at my right hand,
>   till I make your enemies your footstool'".
> The Lord sends forth from Zion your mighty scepter.
>   Rule in the midst of your foes!" (Ps. 110: 1–2).
> ....
> "Blessed is the man who makes the Lord his trust,
>   who does not turn to the proud,
>   to those who go astray after false gods!" (Ps. 40: 4).

CANAAN IN THE MELTING POT

What had happened to the enduring Canaanite civilization which had made up the bulk of the urban and rural population of Palestine? How did the older civilization assimilate into the new kingdom? Had it been wiped out in the process? Had the Israelites absorbed it or reconstructed it? They had apparently absorbed it.

This amalgamation was not accomplished without resistance. First there was the society of the Philistine overlords and their allies among the Canaanites, and, second, that of the Canaanite aristocracy and ruling classes. Until then the Israelite tribal areas had not been well defined, for they were separated by Canaanite-occupied towns and provinces in their midst. The steady liquidation of Canaanite power is referred to in the summary of Judg. 1: 27–35:

"When Israel grew strong, they put the Canaanites to forced labor, but did not utterly drive them out". (Judg. 1: 28)

David took severe measures to change Canaanite areas into Israelite territory. He captured Megiddo which was destroyed at the time. He displaced the Canaanites without destroying them, and put Hebrews in their place. The Canaanites became landless people with the status of "gerim" (sojourners). This system was pursued systematically by Solomon who changed all Canaanite settlements into pure Israelite territory. The frequent biblical references to sojourners during the early days of the monarchy is evidence of this change in the status of the population.

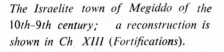
The Israelite town of Megiddo of the 10th–9th century; a reconstruction is shown in Ch XIII (Fortifications).

This transition, and the deep changes involved, are attested to by archaeological evidence. The sites at Megiddo or Beth-Shean, Tel-Qasile or Jaffa (the area of modern Tel-Aviv) show that the levels of habitation occupied by Canaanites until about the 10th century were destroyed. In their place, new Israelite towns arose, laid out differently, and bearing signs of a different civilization. There was a general increase in population, an improvement in building techniques, in pottery making, and in the standard of living.

Now that Israel had expanded to the borders of Phoenicia, after engulfing all previous Canaanite territory in Galilee, David worked out advantageous diplomatic and economic relations with the city of Tyre, the paramount city of Phoenicia, so that the two countries supplemented one another. Phoenicia was seafaring and rich in timber and the wares of the Orient; Israel rich in agriculture, human resources and able to protect the roads of commerce.

The roads of commerce and local industry which had hitherto been the monopoly of Canaanites and Philistines, came to represent the mainstay of Israelite prosperity and rapid growth. The iron tool and weapon industry which had been controlled by the Philistines now became common property. The cloth-dyeing industry and trade, previously Canaanite, was now part of the Israelite economy. That is the significance of statements in the First Book of Chronicles (which parallels Samuel and 1 Kings) on the period:

> "David also provided great stores of iron for nails for the doors of the gates and for clamps, as well as bronze in quantities beyond weighing, and cedar timbers without number; for the Sidonians and Tyrians brought great quantities of cedar to David". (1 Chr. 22: 3-4)

Tyre supplied the building materials and the skilled craftsmen for David's palace:

> "And Hiram king of Tyre sent messengers to David, and cedar trees, also masons and carpenters to build a house for him. And David perceived that the Lord had established him king over Israel, and that his kingdom was highly exalted for the sake of his people Israel". (1 Chr. 14: 1-2).

King David came into possession of vast estates and wealth throughout the land, as graphically described in Chronicles, which serves as an overall view of the Israelite agricultural economy in Palestine of the 10th century:

> "Over the king's treasuries was Azmaveth the son of Adiel; and over the treasuries in the country, in the cities, in the villages and in the towers, was Jonathan the son of Uzziah; and over those who did the work of the field tilling the soil was Ezri the son of Chelub; and over the vineyards was Shimei the Ramathite; and over the produce of the vineyards for the wine cellars was Zabdi the Shiphmite. Over the olive and sycamore trees in the Shephelah was Baal-hanan the Gederite; and over the stores of oil was Joash. Over the herds that pastured in Sharon was Shitrai the Sharonite; over the herds in the valleys was Shaphat the son of Adlai. Over the camels was Obil the Ishmaelite; and over the she-asses was Jehdeiah the Meronothite. Over the flocks was Jaziz the Hagrite. All these were stewards of King David's property". (1 Chr. 27:25–31)

David's greatest achievement was the creation of Israel as an integrated political entity out of a group of patriarchal tribes and allied clans. He incorporated them into a homogeneous people with social and legal standards and a religious personality as pronounced as his own. He did more, for after conquering by the sword all the autochtone races within Canaan and Transjordan and on their borders, he fused them into one nation, which assumed a political and geographical entity distinct from its neighbours and endowed with a civilization, social cast and administration which became known in history as Israel.

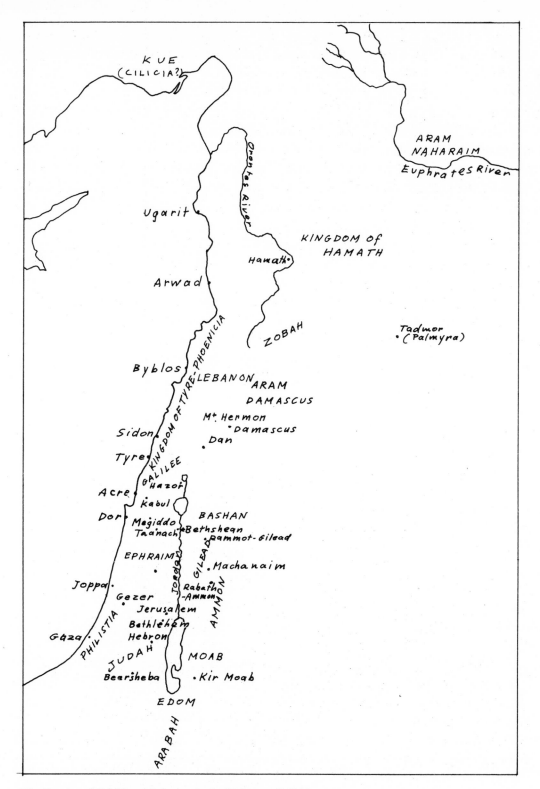

The Empire of David and Solomon in the 10th cent. B.C.E.

DAVID CARVES AN EMPIRE

The transmission of political rule throughout Palestine, and eventually in bordering lands in the dynamic days of David's Kingdom, is correctly estimated by A. Alt. The Philistines had considered themselves the heirs of Egyptian rule in Palestine. Their defeat implied the passage of the entire Egyptian province into the hands of Israel. The kingdom could develop apace, south, north and east, due to the continuing weakness of the Egyptian, Assyrian and Hittite kingdoms. The period 1200–900 B.C.E. has been described as the "Era of the Little Peoples". Among the smaller powers, David's state emerged as the dominant force. His chroniclers, after describing the final Philistine defeat, continue the narrative of his conquests outside the borders of Palestine, leaving aside for the time being the important internal events of his reign.

David's rule over the bordering territories was essential to his strategic and economic plans. The might of the new state can be gauged especially from his conquest of the east side of Jordan.

He established his rule in Gilead, Bashan and neighbouring territory, and then appointed a governor (Natziv) to each new province which he joined to the kingdom or conquered. These governorships were the administrative framework of his growing empire.

Expansion brought serious clashes with the Moabites and Ammonites on the southern Transjordanian border; it took many years to subdue them, mainly because their military alliance was helped by the expanding power of the Arameans from the north of Transjordan. When he had beaten the Moabites, David exterminated two-thirds of their army. Perhaps he exacted this terrible vengeance because the Moabites had killed his own family, when his mother and father had taken refuge in Moab when David had been a fugitive from Saul.

Moab became his vassal, thus ending for generations to come the incidents from which Israel had suffered from its Transjordanian neighbours.

THE CONFLICT OF ISRAEL AND ARAM

The expansion of the kingdom of Israel did not halt in northern Transjordan where it confronted the Aramean kingdoms of Aram-Zobah and its confederates, another political bloc much like David's own. The Aramean king, Hadadezer, was a contemporary of David. He extended his rule over vast territories in eastern Syria, his hegemony reaching to the eastern border of the kingdom of Ammon in southern Transjordan, and to the upper Euphrates in the north.

The occasion of war arose over the intervention of Hadadezer and his allies to relieve the Ammonites who had declared war upon David:

"And Hadadezer sent, and brought out the Syrians who were beyond the Euphrates; and they came to Helam, with Shobach the commander of the army of Hadadezer at their head. And when it was told David, he gathered all Israel together, and crossed the Jordan, and came to Helam. And the Syrians arrayed themselves against David, and fought with him. And the Syrians fled before Israel; and David slew of the Syrians the men of seven hundred chariots, and forty thousand horsemen, and wounded Shobach the commander of their army, so that he died there. And when all the kings who were servants of Hadadezer saw that they had been defeated by Israel, they made peace with Israel, and became subject to them. So the Syrians feared to help the Ammonites any more". (2 Sam. 10: 16–19)

Allowing that the figures quoted for the Aramean forces were exaggerated, they give a fair idea of what Aram-Zobah could put into the field, added to the levies of the other Aramean confederates in Syria. But this military might could not withstand the Israelites. According to the biblical record they were routed three times; once by Joab at Medaba, where they came to help the Ammonites (1 Chr. 19:6–15); a year later the theatre of war had expanded farther north. At Chelam in northern Transjordan, Hadadezer and his allies lost 700 chariots and 40,000 footmen; the third encounter took place near Hamat in central Syria when David took 1700 charioteers and 20,000 prisoners. This time Aram-Damascus, another powerful opponent, had come to Hadadezer's help, but to no avail. The Israelites had little use for field cavalry. So they castrated the horses, kept 100 for chariots, of which they had not yet learnt the use. David brought back great booty.

There were now no independent territories left between the kingdoms of Israel and Aram-Zobah, and the outcome of the conflicts was bound to lead directly to the political hegemony over the area between Mesopotamia and Egypt. In fact, the power of Aram-Zobah declined. But the rivalry between Arameans and Israelites persisted a long time after the great clash when the new Aramean state of Damascus assumed the hegemony. As a result, the kingdom of Israel began to be larger than any independent political bloc ever established within the borders of Syria and Palestine:

"And he ruled over all the kings from the Euphrates to the land of the Philistines and to the border of Egypt" (2 Chr. 9: 26)

"This unprecedented territorial expansion" says, A. Malamat, "may be explained by assuming that David's kingdom was based on comprehensive political organizations which had existed before and which, through David's victories over their rulers, passed into his hands with their complex systems intact. It is a fact that these extensive conquests in the north established David's kingdom as a political factor as far as the region of Aram-Naharaim and brought it within the sphere of traditional Assyrian influence"

An inscription of a later Assyrian king, Shalmaneser II, relates that during the reign of a king Ashurrabi II (1012–972), a contemporary of King David, the ambitious king of Aram, was a serious danger to Assyria. It is history's irony that David was the agent who unwittingly relieved Assyria by his war with the Arameans.

David's last conquest appears to have been of Edom and Amalek in the Negeb. Edom was important mainly for the copper deposits, mining and metal industry of the Arabah, between the Dead Sea and the Gulf of Akaba (Elath). David placed garrisons and governors in Edom and ruled it as a conquered province. Iron was gradually becoming more common at this early date in the Iron Age, but copper was still the metal chiefly in use. Moreover, control of Edom and the Arabah valley meant control of the "King's Highway," and the inland caravan routes from Egypt to Syria. It made possible the opening of Elath as a port on the Red Sea. It was Solomon who developed, to a degree unknown before, navigation and commerce with Arabia and East Africa.

Thus the Davidic Empire extended in the north as far as central Syria and northern Lebanon, and in the east to the Syrian desert, and included the international caravan routes.

In the south it bordered on the Red Sea, the Arabian desert and Sinai. It ruled over the conquered peoples of Moab, Ammon, and of the Aramean state of Zobah. Where its western borders met the Mediterranean it was the dominating force over Philistia and the Phoenician sea coast cities, with whom friendly relations existed. Probably David had no harbour on the Mediterranean; the seaport of Joppa belonged to the Philistines.

This period gave rise to the Pentateuchal formation of the ideal extent of the land reputedly promised to Abraham: "from the river of Egypt to the great river, the river Euphrates" (Gen. 15:18).

BATHSHEBA

"In the spring of the year, the time when kings go forth to battle, David sent Joab, and his servants with him, and all Israel; and they ravaged the Ammonites, and besieged Rabbah. But David remained at Jerusalem. It happened, late one afternoon, when David arose from his couch and was walking upon the roof of the king's house, that he saw from the roof a woman bathing; and the woman was very beautiful. And David sent and inquired about the woman. And one said, 'Is not this Bathsheba, the daughter of Eliam, the wife of Uriah the Hittite?' So David sent messengers, and took her; and she came to him, and he lay with her. (Now she was purifying herself from her uncleanness.) Then she returned to her house. And the woman conceived; and she sent and told David, 'I am with child' ". (2 Sam. 11: 1–5)

At no other time in Israelite history could a historian have caught this vernal splendour of a king going forth for a show of power. Hebrew history-writing in the epic manner came into its own in David's time for the sense of national greatness aroused pride in the story of the nation. This is evident in the brilliant historiography of the first kings, disappearing after the story of Solomon.

Though David was the greatest epic hero of biblical history and the model for kings of his line, no attempt was made by his narrator to exculpate him or cover the sin he committed in the case of Bathsheba. The history of the early monarchs is not primarily religious. Sending Uriah, Bathsheba's husband, his loyal mercenary officer, to be killed in battle so that he could have an affair with his wife, was the worst part of his crime. The child born of adultery died and though David married Bathsheba he was never forgiven, as shown by the words of Nathan the prophet:

"'Why have you despised the word of the Lord, to do what is evil in his sight? You have smitten Uriah the Hittite with the sword, and have taken his wife to be your wife, and have slain him with the sword of the Ammonites. Now therefore the sword shall never depart from your house, because you have despised me, and have taken the wife of Uriah the Hittite to be your wife' ". (2 Sam. 12: 9-10)

The Bathsheba scandal happened in the year of the Ammonite war. The storyteller had another splendid trail to follow in the personality of Joab. Before capturing Ammon, Joab sent word to his king to conquer the city himself at the head of his people, so he might deal the death blow and get the glory. David was crowned king of Ammon but dealt cruelly with its people so that they might never rise to defy him.

The story is told with great restraint. It is devoid of the uncompromising and fierce clarity of earlier periods. It obviously reflects David's unique personality, as told by those who well knew him to be a man who could live with himself, with his virtues and vices. He was jovial, hearty, manly, magnanimous, mighty in toil and in the pleasures of life and when necessary in war. In balancing the vicissitudes and triumphs of his existence they knew as he did that his success was due to only one cause. Yahweh was with him. No more needed to be said by his contemporaries. They, like him, were direct, primitive in their bravery and lust. David had given the same answer when he was upbraided for dancing before the ark almost indecently and indecorously:

> "And David said to Michal, 'It was before the Lord, who chose me above your father, and above all his house, to appoint me as prince over Israel, the people of the Lord — and I will make merry before the Lord". (2 Sam. 6: 21)

DAVID'S STATE

Jerusalem, now the metropolitan capital and heart of the empire, was also the head of the military organization. Of this the oldest and most important part was the "sarei hagibborim asher le-David" — David's council of companions-at-arms, which he had organized at Hebron and which directed the army and the country. David's personality and brilliant exploits have distracted attention from his administrative achievements, which are nowhere chronicled as such:

> "So David reigned over all Israel; and he administered justice and equity to all his people. And Joab the son of Zeruiah was over the army; and Jehoshaphat the son of Ahilud was recorder; and Zadok the son of Ahitub and Ahimelech the son of Abiathar were priests; and Shavsha was secretary; and Benaiah the son of Jehoiada was over the Cherethites and the Pelethites; and David's sons were the chief officials in the service of the king". (1 Chr. 18: 14–17)

His first cabinet, composed of "Servants of the King" after the Canaanite term, included Joab as commander of the local "tzava" (levies); the commander of the foreign mercenary troop, the Cherethites and Pelethites (mainly Cretans and Philistines), and men of Gath, which formed an essential part of the regular army; the royal herald ("mazkir") who broadcast the king's orders; the secretary of state ("sopher"); the two high priests, Zadok and Abiathar, and David's two sons. He also appointed other high officers and officials of the court and of the country in general, some of whom were able Canaanites; there were also governors of conquered provinces. Religious affairs were administered by two chief priests, and all the priests and Levites attending the sanctuaries were now servants of the crown. A second and later list included an officer of the corvée, who was presumably intended to supervise Canaanites and other foreigners working on forced labour on construction projects and royal estates.

This new composite state of Israel was a sweeping change from the old tribal patterns. Lacking native precedents, the bureaucracy was modelled on those of neighbouring countries, mainly Egypt, Canaan and Phoenicia. David was at its centre as absolute monarch. This development was natural, following David's adoption of the "manner of the king" (1 Sam. 8:11–17), the imposition of taxes, the rise of new social classes, and the organizing of the economy on national lines. Among the official institutions which David copied from his neighbours was the division of the functions of the "mazkir" and the "sopher". The adoption of the name Shavsha or Shisha for the king's secretary, is similar to "Se-a we-a," a western

Egyptian scribe writing on a partly opened roll of papyrus. From Sakkarah, 24th cent. B.C.E.

Semitic title for that functionary; it was later Hebraized to "Seraiah" the "sopher", (2 Sam. 8:16). Scribes and secretaries are mentioned in Egyptian records under their Canaanite equivalent, "t(u)-p(i)-(i)r" or "sopher".

Central in the administrative reorganization of the state was David's allocation of 48 priestly cities and towns, (intimately connected with the cities of refuge) containing sanctuaries, to which the unjustly accused might flee. This idea was common throughout the ancient Near East. David also resettled the Levites throughout his realm:

> "These are their dwelling places according to their settlements within their borders: to the sons of Aaron of the families of Kohathites, for theirs was the lot". (1 Chr. 6:54)

These cities are also listed, anachronistically, in Joshua 21. Their settlement with Levites would have been impossible before the time of Saul or David, for many of them were still Canaanite in Joshua's time, as confirmed in Judges 1; and many had not yet been founded. There must have been such cities before David, but he selected many more for their accessibility and to conform to an administrative plan. He also divided functions among the Levites, as servants of the crown, both for religious and administrative duties as officers, judges, officials of the sanctuaries, teachers, and tax collectors. Many Levite cities were in the territory of Benjamin, near Jerusalem, presumably on account of its proximity to the capital or for the supervision of the king's estates there:

Egyptian royal scribes.
From the New Kingdom.

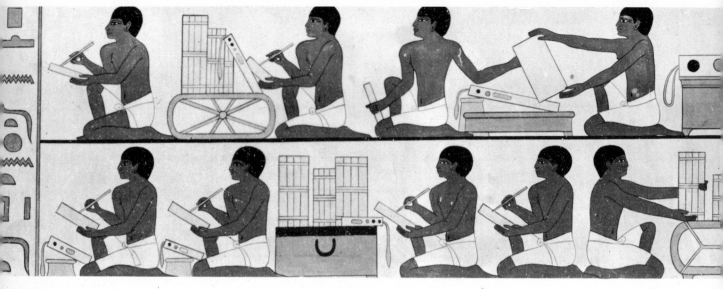

Scribes and their records. Their period preceded David by over a thousand years.

Restored writing equipment of an Egyptian scribe: writing reed attached to palette and water jar. (c. 1550–1350)

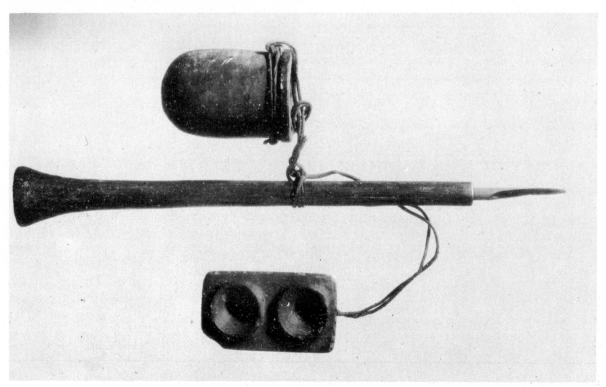

"Of the Izharites, Chananiah and his sons were appointed to outside duties for Israel, as officers and judges. Of the Hebronites, Hashabiah and his brethren, one thousand seven hundred men of ability, had the oversight of Israel westward of the Jordan for all the work of the Lord and for the service of the king". (1 Chr. 26: 29–30)

"King David appointed him and his brethren, two thousand seven hundred men of ability, heads of fathers' houses, to have the oversight of the Reubenites, the Gadites, and the half-tribe of the Manassites for everything pertaining to God and for the affairs of the king. (1 Chr. 26: 32)

A HOUSE FOR YAHWEH

It was at a later stage in his life, and certainly after he had gained authority in the Phoenician sphere that David was able to proceed with his plan for building a royal palace and the altar on Mt. Zion, above Ophel, which is west and within the walled enclosure shown in the illustration of the sloping Jebusite hillside site. His aim had been gradually to detach the people from the tribal separatism associated with worship at the ancient sanctuaries such as Shiloh and Bethel, and to gather them at festivals in the new sanctuary at Zion.

The real significance of David's career emerges from the Davidic Covenant described in the oracle of the prophet Nathan. In his "response" to David's expressed desire to build a "house for Yahweh" the word, "davar" of Yahweh is communicated by the oracle solemnly designating him King:

" 'Now therefore thus you shall say to my servant David, "Thus says the Lord of hosts, I took you from the pasture, from following the sheep, that you should be prince over my people Israel"'. (2 Sam. 7:8)

" 'When your days are fulfilled and you lie down with your fathers, I will raise up your son after you, who shall come forth from your body, and I will establish his kingdom. He shall build a house for my name, and I will establish the throne of his kingdom for ever. I will be his father, and he shall be my son. When he commits iniquity, I will chasten him with the rod of men, with the stripes of the sons of men; but I will not take my steadfast love from him, as I took it from Saul, whom I put away from before you. And your house and your kingdom shall be made sure for ever before me; your throne shall be established for ever'. In accordance with all these words, and in accordance with all this vision, Nathan spoke to David". (2 Sam. 7: 12–17)

The oath of Yahweh expressed a new and far-reaching development in the Covenant idea. At Sinai the Covenant was ratified between Yahweh and the Chosen people of Israel and its symbol was the "Kingdom under God", a theocracy peculiar to Israel, based on the Lord's declaration in Ex. 4:22 :"Israel is my first-born son". New trails led from the tribal league that had occupied Canaan to the charismatic kingship under Saul. From that had emerged David's empire, with Zion at its centre, backed by effective organization of the people as a nation. Though new forms had developed from the older ways, the symbols embodying social order persisted. A further symbol had to be evolved to the Covenant idea to include the new form of the monarchy. As the people at Sinai were the adopted sons of Yahweh, serving their redeemer (go'el) — so now the Davidic kings would be his adopted sons. The dynasty thus became the vehicle of the Covenant between Yahweh and Israel. The people would endure in their relationship with Yahweh through David's dynasty, to which the oracle promised perpetuity. Thus the destiny of Israel became inseparable from that of the Davidic dynasty.

This theme, and the theology of David's kingship, is echoed in some of the contemporaneous royal psalms. They express Yahweh's choice of Zion, the perpetuity of David's line, that the king was Yahweh's son, his first-born, his "anointed" and that, though kings might be chastened for their sins, yet the dynasty would never be cut off. As the king was established by Yahweh in Zion, no foe would prevail against him, and foreign nations would submit to his rule: he was elected as Yahweh's vice-regent and bound under the Covenant. He was to promote justice and would be punished if he broke his pledge:

"Thou hast said, ' I have made a
  covenant with my chosen one,
  I have sworn to David my servant' ": (Ps. 89: 3)
. . . .

"He shall cry to me, 'Thou art my Father,
  my God, and the Rock of my salvation'.
And I will make him the first-born,
  the highest of the kings of the earth". (Ps. 89: 26–27)
. . . .

" 'I have set my king on Zion, my holy hill'.
  I will tell of the decree of the Lord:
He said to me, 'You are my son,
  today I have begotten you.
Ask of me, and I will make the nations your heritage,
  and the ends of the earth your possession.
You shall break them with a rod of iron,
  and dash them in pieces like a potter's vessel'.
Now therefore, O kings, be wise;
  be warned, O rulers of the earth.
Serve the Lord with fear,
  with trembling kiss his feet,
Lest he be angry, and you perish in the way;
  for his wrath is quickly kindled.
Blessed are all who take refuge in him". (Ps. 2: 6–12)
. . . .

"May he have dominion from sea to sea,
  and from the River to the ends of the earth!
May his foes bow down before him,
  and his enemies lick the dust!
May the kings of Tarshish and of the isles render him tribute,
May the kings of Sheba and Seba bring gifts!
May all kings fall down before him,
  all nations serve him!" (Ps. 72: 8–11)
. . . .

"Who givest victory to kings,
  who rescues David his servant.
Rescue me from the cruel sword,
  and deliver me from the hand of aliens,
Whose mouths speak lies,
  and whose right hand is a right hand of falsehood". (Ps. 144:10–11)
. . . .

"Give the king thy justice, O God.
  and thy righteousness to the royal son!

May he judge thy people with righteousness,
    and thy poor with justice!
Let the mountains bear prosperity for the people,
    and the hills, in righteousness!
May he defend the cause of the poor of the people,
    give deliverance to the needy,
    and crush the oppressor!" (Ps. 72: 1–4)

WAS THE KINGSHIP DIVINE?

We gather from the biblical text that after the Philistine wars, David's victories, and the historic developments surrounding his enthronement as King in Zion under Yahweh, there emerged the notion of the chosen King who, in case of conflict, took precedence over all. These developments make it clear that David's kingship, laid on a broader foundation than Saul's, conveyed a new meaning to the minds of the people, i.e., all the confederate Hebrew tribes who recognized themselves as the Chosen People of Yahweh under His Berith (Covenant) with them.

Many in Israel had approached the problem of kingship with misgivings and it still remained a problem in more ways than one. M. Noth notes that the people did not view the institution of kingship, and more specifically the kingdoms of Judah and Israel, as elements in an unchanging order of things. In the concept of Near Eastern antiquity kingship had been instituted from times immemorial by the gods and its absolute nature derived from its divine origin.

The Near Eastern concepts connected the role of the king with that of mediator between god and man, which was expressed in cult and ritual. This pattern, though it varied with the land concerned, embraced the Egyptian and early Mesopotamian mythical representation of the birth of gods, the myth of creation, the ritual combat between gods and their enemies, their sacred marriage and the triumphal processions of the gods. Here the king played the part of the god, followed by a train of lesser gods or visiting deities. This ritual underlay new year festivals, coronation rituals and initiation ceremonies in the ancient Near East, with the king as the symbolic mediator between godly and social order.

The oracular words of Yahweh happen to be an Egyptian coronation formula, according to A. Alt. This does not mean that the king of Israel aspired to be Yahweh's mediator in the same sense as the pharaoh was the mediator of the gods for his people. But since Israel wanted a king "like other nations", kingship involved the use of current symbols. So Hebrew symbols and cult patterns, mostly shorn, however, of the myths of their neighbours, are to be found in the biblical literature of the time.

It would not be correct to assume that Israelite kingship was modelled on that of the Canaanites simply because there are parallel symbols in the Israelite and the Ugarite and other Near Eastern records. The Hebrew psalms may have contained and borrowed recognizable Canaanite material and expressions—due to the absorption of the Canaanites and the common background of the two groups; yet polytheistic and mythological elements had been trimmed away and the borrowings were harmonized with the faith of Israel. This helps to explain their metaphorical significance.

Some scholars have interpreted certain enthronement psalms—47, 93, 96, etc.—as meaning that Israel celebrated a New Year feast of Yahweh which was analogous to the Babylonian New Year ritual or a ritual pattern expressing the pagan theory of kingship, allegedly common to other Near Eastern neighbours. On the occasion of the New Year festival, the king was regarded as a divine or semi-divine being who, symbolizing the dying and rising god of fertility, ritually re-enacted the myths of creation, the combat with a dragon, the victory over chaos, the sacred marriage and the god's resumption of his throne. This symbolic cult-drama, the ancients believed, ensured the annual revival of nature. The well-being of the land and the kings's place on the throne were thereby secured for another year. Alternatively this type of theory assumes that the mythological allusions in the psalms are not a vestige of re-enactment of a ritual struggle with antiquity and mythical gods, but with Yahweh's (and Israel's) foes. Others, however, hold that Yahweh's alleged New Year feast was not one of his enthronement, but in celebration of His coming to Zion to take up His abode there, and of His promise to David that the rule of his line should be eternal.

Unlike its neighbours, Israel was not heir to the traditions of kingship, for that institution was *conditioned by a specific historic development*. But on the other hand its definition of kingship was not secular like that of the Canaanite city-kings. Kingship in Israel, as elsewhere, was a sacred institution, provided with cultic and theological legitimization:

> " 'Yea, does not my house stand so with God?
> For he has made with me an everlasting covenant,
>   ordered in all things and secure.
> For will he not cause to prosper
>   all my help and my desire?' " (2 Sam. 23:5)

In popular thought the designation of David and the presence of Yahweh in His Temple guaranteed the continuance of the state. To suggest that it could fall would be tantamount to attributing to Yahweh a breach of this Covenant.

The conception by which David's kingship was defined bears a certain resemblance to contemporary oriental principles but its form and purport were different. The king was not divine by nature, nor had he divine attributes. He was called in Psalms Yahweh's son, but only in the sense that he had been *chosen and adopted* as a son, and his choice as a ruler was legitimized accordingly. By the same token the successors of David's house were legitimized, which made the Covenant perpetual under Yahweh. M. Noth suggests that when David ascended the throne in the City of David, the liturgical formula was uttered which perpetuated the right of kingship by virtue of this adoption, as quoted in Psalm 2:6–9 above. As later prophets referred to this hallowed theme they enlarged the concept of Davidic kingship whereby the new dynasty had been promised perpetuity and included Yahweh's designation of the house of David as Israel's ruling house. Yahweh was with Israel when Israel was with David and his house. The Berith (Covenant) of Yahweh with Israel was at the same time a Berith with the house of David, and its kingship became perpetual.

An unbreakable bond has since been established in the thought of the people between three meaningful notions: David, the City of David and the Kingdom of David, or more specifically, the House of David, Mount Zion in Jerusalem and the People of Israel.

In time the symbolism created by the succession of Jerusalem became of even wider significance. The symbols of Hebrew kingship under God permeated the religious concepts of later Judaism. Mount Zion, a holy place for countless generations, assumed also a deeper significance of transcending holiness in the minds of worshippers.

THE LITERARY CHARACTER OF HEBREW HISTORY IN DAVID'S TIME

Side by side with David's victories, his tremendous political influence, and the economic and social revolution and prosperity in Palestine in the tenth century, there was the rise of a native literature. This reflected the sense of national greatness and the consciousness of historic significance stimulated by the monarchy. It is to be seen in the expansion of letters under the influence of the Levites and priests who represented the cultured class of the Israelites. The historiographic writing in biographies of David and Solomon was a prose expression of the same renaissance.

The age of David and Solomon in the 10th century was undoubtedly the first golden age of Hebrew literature. Though little of the original has been preserved unchanged, other writings of the time prove that the literary genius of Israel was already developed. The most important contemporary document is the court history of David quoted in Chapters 9-20 of the Second Book of Samuel, as well as the inauguration of Solomon's reign in 1 Kings 1-2.

In the historiographic field the Hebrew historians usually applied epic values to current events as their ancestors had in the Song of Moses, the Song of Miriam, and the Song of Deborah, or as the Canaanites applied epic values to their mythical legends of Anath, Aqhat and Danael in poetic forms and language akin to that of the ancient Hebrew.

With David the nation came of age. Genuine triumph made epic exaggeration less necessary. The annalistic records of the scribes brought real history to the fore.

In the composition of real, interpretative history, the ancient East has little to compare with the core of the Second Book of Samuel, or the Court History of David (2 Sam 9-20 and 1 King 1-2) for it is in the main straight, reliable narrative, presenting the facts without bias, a distinct achievement in this sense from the literary point of view. It is considered an eye-witness account of David as a real king of flesh and blood, describing and evaluating his personal history in relation to current events. The magnitude of the theme of Saul and David and the exalted mood which infuses it give it truly epic proportions. But David's historian has remarkable biographic objectivity and insight into the character of his hero. He transfers the human values inherent in the tragedy of David's family to the events at hand, as for example the story of Bathsheba, and the tragedy of Amnon and Absalom. Students of the Bible regard the story of Absalom's rebellion viewed as part of David's own life or as an episode in the history of his court as "the richest jewel in the antique historical writing in Israel" (Gunkel).

Among the historians and priests of Egypt and Babylon the official accounts of a reign were usually sheer bragging or deification. It needed the literary genius of Israel to create historiography in the 10th century B.C.E. by combining current events with epic traditions and finding a harmonious balance between the two. We find in David's narrative a combination of the spirit of earlier epic with later Israelite historiography. But post-Davidic history is virtually devoid of the old Canaanite epic current, however much the language continues to echo the epic style and expression. This accounts for the unique literary value of the Books of Samuel and Kings and the momentous contribution to civilization which this tiny nation brought at that stage of history. David's biographer was a man of genius, for without any previous model as guide he wrote a masterpiece, unsurpassed in historicity, insight, dramatic power and style. Actually Hebrew historiography antedated the fifth century Greek historians Herodotus and Thucydides by half a millenium. Now that we are acquainted with Ugarite and other Near Eastern forms of historiography, the origin of Hebrew historiography is no longer a mystery. It had its roots in the contemporary consciousness of historic significance.

TRAGEDY IN DAVID'S HOME

Effective in diplomacy though he was with outsiders, David was sentimental in his role as father to his many children, whom he spoilt. Their disobedience and misbehaviour, frankly related, is one of the most striking examples of narrative writing in Israel's history. To outline the drama — Chapters 2-20 of 2 Samuel give the whole story. It opens with Amnon, David's first-born, and his passion for his half sister Tamar, whom, although it was permissible, he was not allowed to marry. He seduced and then humiliated her. Later, her brother Absalom slew Amnon, then fled to his mother's father, the Aramean king of Geshur, with whom he stayed for several years. The story continues with the sorrow of David and the exile of the handsome favourite son. His father eventually forgave him on the intervention of Joab, his general. He brought forward a woman of Tekoa who pleaded that her son had killed his brother; now the family was going to kill the slayer and she would lose both her children. David decided that the slayer should not be touched. The woman then hinted that the same verdict should apply to David's own guilty son. (2 Sam. 14:5-17)

DAVID'S COURT

All this was at first a family affair but when Absalom returned he plunged into politics, played the demagogue and plotted to seize the throne. He went to Hebron ostensibly to pay some religious vows at the old family shrine but had himself anointed king there, then launched a full-fledged rebellion with the aid of malcontents and marched on Jerusalem with a considerable force. The drama then became of national importance. David, advanced in years and caught unawares, could not assemble loyal troops quickly enough to combat Absalom's forces, but his court, the ecclesiastical authorities and, above all, his foreign mercenaries, stayed with him, loyal "whether for death or for life". He fled to Transjordan where he could depend on better defence and plan a return. The scene now became crowded with actors. Each man had to make his choice and take up his position in relation to the King. The "wise" Ahitophel, Absalom's counsellor, was watched by Hushai, David's counsellor who, with the priests, acted as liaison and relayed messages to David.

Ahitophel advised Absalom to take over his father's harem, showing that he had succeeded him, then to gather in haste 12,000 troops and pursue his father before he could assemble forces against him. Hushai slily convinced Absalom that he should wait until he could gather an overwhelming force which David's generals and veteran troops could not resist. Disgraced, Ahitophel committed suicide. David was meanwhile kept informed of developments through the priests of the sanctuaries. Absalom finally moved to Transjordan with a motley force under Amassa, but the grim and determined Joab made short work of them. Absalom himself met an ignominious death at Joab's hands, when the prince's luxuriant hair caught in the branch of an oak tree as he swept on in flight. David's last wish was that his men should deal gently with Absalom. But the messenger who brought him the sad tidings disillusioned him.

It was again Joab's forcefulness that saved the day. His patience at last worn out, he reproached the aged king and forced him to refrain from further expressions of grief which were an offence to the morale of his victorious troops. Brought to his senses David again sat "in the gate" as ruler of his people.

One of the most touching incidents at the conclusion of the story is the attitude of Barzilai who had supported David in Gilead and whom the king invited to his court:

> "But Barzilai said to the king, 'How many years have I still to live, that I should go up with the king to Jerusalem? I am this day eighty years old; can I discern what is pleasant and what is not? Can your servant taste what he eats or what he drinks? Can I still listen to the voice of singing men and singing women? Why then should your servant be an added burden to my lord the king? Your servant will go a little way over the Jordan with the king. Why should the king recompense me with such a reward? Pray let your servant return, that I may die in my own city, near the grave of my father and my mother. But here is your servant Chimham; let him go over with my lord the king; and do for him whatever seems good to you' ". (2 Sam. 19:34–37)

The tribe of Judah came to the Jordan to welcome the king across. From all over Palestine people hastened to make peace with him and restore him to his throne. David responded with characteristic magnanimity.

But before David returned to Jerusalem another rebellion broke out, led by Sheba, an Ephraimite. It was caused by friction between the tribes in the north and Judah. David realized the fragility of the unity between the tribes connected with him, and saw in this rebellion an attempt to withdraw northern Israel from its union with Judah. It worried him even more than Absalom's treachery. He despatched Amassa, his new general to call out the levies of Judah, but he was apparently slow in fulfilling the task. Joab came out with his mercenaries. With his usual fierceness where honour was at stake he approached Amassa as if to kiss him, seized his beard and slew him. Pursuing Sheba, Joab finally cornered him in a small fortress. Throwing up earthworks against the wall, he would have captured the fort. But a woman there pointed out in characteristic style:

> "Then she said, 'They were wont to say in old time, "Let them but ask counsel at Abel"; and so they settled a matter. I am one of those who are peaceable and faithful in Israel; you seek to destroy a city, which is a mother in Israel; why will you swallow up the heritage of the Lord?' Joab answered, 'Far be it from me, far be it, that I should swallow up or destroy! That is not true. But a man of the hill country of Ephraim, called Sheba the son of Bichri, has lifted up his hand against King David; give up him alone, and I will withdraw from the city'. And the woman said to Joab, 'Behold, his head shall be thrown to you over the wall'. Then the woman went to all the people in her wisdom. And they cut off the head of Sheba the son of Bichri, and threw it out to Joab. So he blew the trumpet, and they dispersed from the city, every man to his home. And Joab returned to Jerusalem to the king". (2 Sam. 20: 18-22)

The formula "each man to his tent" harks back to nomadic days. Israelites no longer lived in tents, but the old phrase still lingered in the language.

"THERE IS BLOOD GUILT ON SAUL AND ON HIS HOUSE"

At the beginning of David's story — though the compiler placed it at the end — there is a wonderful picture of the life of the period. There was a severe famine, caused by a drought. The underlying leitmotif of the story is one of collective guilt, which makes it of great significance from the religious point of view of the narrator and his audience: The underlying feeling seems to have harked back to Israel's first contact and settlement with the Gibeonites (See Ch. VIII: Joshua's Second Campaign). Its memory lingered in the harsh events surrounding Saul's massacre of the people of Gibeon (See Ch. XI: Why Were Gibeon and Nob Destroyed?).

In the original version of the story of the Gibeonites, it was not emphasized that Joshua's treaty with them did not spare them from the "herem", or ban on conquered peoples. However later chroniclers made an issue by refusing to regard the Gibeonites as privileged citizens. They found in this point the motivation of Saul's antagonism towards them and the reason for their massacre. But the memory of the act (and possibly the massacre of the priests of Nob) rankled as an unsocial act, and a guilt-laden breaking of the covenant between the Gibeonites and the Israelites. Therefore the Gibeonites claimed revenge and justified their shedding the blood of Saul's offspring. The people interpreted the famine as God's punishment for the broken treaty: "there is blood guilt on Saul and on his house", they said. There is a story similar to this in the Hittite annals and in an Ugarite tale, in which a king's wrongdoing involved his realm in a famine.

The expiation demanded by the Gibeonites was the killing of the seven "sons". David acceded, but spared Mephibosheth, Jonathan's son, in pursuance of his promise not to wipe out Saul's line.

The story relates that God was satisfied with this pacification of the Gibeonites, and the famine ended. The seven executed sons were those of Rizpah and Michal, Saul's womenfolk.

"Then Rizpah the daughter of Aiah took sackcloth, and spread it for herself on the rock, from the beginning of harvest until rain fell upon them from the heavens; and she did not allow the birds of the air to come upon them by day, or the beasts of the field by night". (2 Sam 21:10)

There is a touching picture of the mother watching over the bodies of her sons so that they might have the burial without which there would be no rest for the dead.

A CENSUS AND ITS SEQUEL

One of David's important acts — reported with obvious theological bias by a chronicler who did not appreciate its political and economic necessity — was the taking of a census. This innovation was bitterly resented by the liberty-loving Israelites. It was considered a revolutionary and reprehensible act, a break with hallowed tradition or a lack of faith in divine protection. In that sense it was a sin which would be dearly paid for. Even Joab, it was pointed out, vainly sought to dissuade David from the undertaking. The army leaders made a circuit of the boundaries in connection with the project which is said to have been accomplished in nine and two-thirds months:

"They crossed the Jordan, and began from Aroer, and from the city that is in the middle of the valley, toward Gad and on to Jazer. Then they came to Gilead, and to Kadesh in the land of the Hittites, and they came to Dan, and from Dan they went around to Sidon, and came to the fortress of Tyre and to all the cities of the Hivites and Canaanites; and they went out to the Negeb of Judah at Beersheba. So when they had gone through all the land, they came to Jerusalem at the end of nine months and twenty days. And Joab gave the sum of the numbering of the people to the king: in Israel there were eight hundred thousand valiant men who drew the sword, and the men of Judah were five hundred thousand". (2 Sam. 24:5-9)

The purpose of the count was to estimate military potential, and for administrative reasons connected with the imposition of the corvée (forced labour). Northern Israel, the censors found, was the greater part of the united kingdom with twice the population of Judah. The former felt that they were imposed upon. The narrative explains that the taking of the census was followed by a pestilence which the Lord, allegedly, inflicted on David as a punishment. David realized hat he had incurred God's anger. He was offered a choice of three disasters — famine, defeat or a three-day pestilence. He chose the third. God was appeased by the erection of a new altar on the threshing floor of Araunah the Jebusite, north of the city wall and hill of Ophel, and by a sacrifice there of oxen. The altar, of course, stood on the exact spot where subsequently that of Solomon's Temple was erected. It is probable that the sacred use of this area may have been older than the writer thought. Holy places were usually holy since times immemorial. The tale brings out Israelite and western-Semitic features of thought and life. When a census was taken in Mari (for purposes similar to those of David), the gatherers took an oath before the gods and the king, and underwent rites of purification. It seems that census-taking might have been a "sin", which necessitated the propitiation of the gods, or "atonement".

THE SWEET PSALMIST OF ISRAEL

Unparalleled though it was in David's time, historiography is only one aspect of Israel's literary genius. Hebrew poetic form had already achieved great heights in the Psalms. The memory of David's own musical prowess and of the musical institutions which he founded was so strong in later generations that many of the Psalms were erroneously attributed to him. Undoubtedly many were in fact composed and written in his generation by Levites, priests, bards, teachers and musical guilds.

But we know from the Bible itself that David was a musician and that he wrote secular poetry. There is no reason to believe that he did not also write certain of the Psalms with whose composition he is credited. The titles of the Psalms themselves give clues to their authorship. Seventy of them are attributed to David, twelve to Asaph, nine to the sons of Korah, two to Solomon, and one each to Heman, Ethan and Moses. The Chronicler mentions repeatedly their names among the heads of the musical guilds:

"David and the chiefs of the service also set apart for the service certain of the sons of Asaph and of Heman, and of Jeduthun, who should prophesy with lyres, with harps, and with cymbals". (1 Chr. 25:1)

"All these were the sons of Heman the king's seer, according to the promise of God to exalt him; for God had given Heman fourteen sons and three daughters. They were all under the direction of their father in the music in the house of the Lord with cymbals, harps, and lyres for the service of the house of God. Asaph, Jeduthun, and Heman were under the order of the king. The number of them along with their brethren, who were trained in singing to the Lord, all who were skilful, was two hundred and eighty-eight. And they cast lots for their duties, small and great, teacher and pupil alike". (1 Chr. 25: 5-8)

Psalm 30 was used at the festival of the dedication of the Temple; Psalm 92 was a song for the Sabbath, Psalm 100 was a thanks offering. Others of them — 24, 48, 82, 94, 81, 93 — were connected with the days of the week. The description of the conditions leading to the composition of this collection of songs and liturgical music gives a picture of the times themselves

Study of their titles, and of the dates when they were read in Jewish worship leads to the conclusion that they were originally connected with sacrificial ceremonies; which argues in favour of the extreme antiquity of Hebrew psalmody.

It devolved upon the musical guilds and great poets to enhance the prestige of kingship, the broadening concepts of religion and the glory of Yahweh. Over them all towers the romantic figure of David, the immortal "Sweet Psalmist" of Israel. The poetic creation in a number of the psalms (many of those in the psalter reflect of course the concepts of later centuries) serves as a document illustrating the character of the national religion. The psalmist contrived to impress the people of Israel with God's great deed in choosing Zion and Jerusalem as His seat and His choice of His servant David from the sheepfold so that he "shall pasture my people Israel".

Psalm literature may be seen as part of the whole poetic creation that came from the soul of ancient Israel. The Song of Miriam and the Song of Deborah are much in the style

Silver pipes from Ur. "The people piped with pipes" when Żadok anointed Solomon. (I Kings 1:40)

Cymbals, castanets and percussion instrument from Phoenicia.

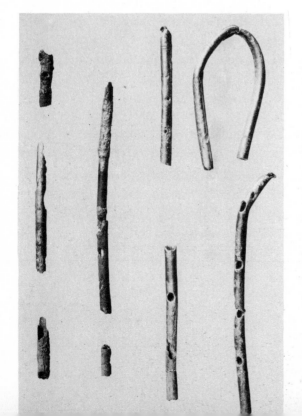
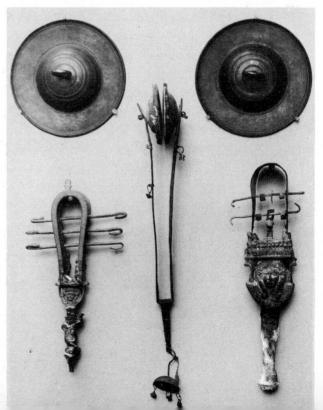

Musical instruments.

of Psalms. This suggests that psalmody in Israel has a long history reaching back before the Davidic era. One tradition regarded musical and orchestral guilds as pre-Israelite or Canaanite in origin. Though David was not the organizer of the first religious music in Israel, it is due to him that the musical guilds flourished and created much of Israel's unparalleled poetry and song. The Chronicler mentions repeatedly the names of Asaph, Heman and Ethan or Yeduthun among the heads of these guilds.

The suggestions of the Scandinavian school give useful new insights into the actual background of various types of psalms, and their use in cultic practices, and make them meaningful by descriptions of the situations for which they had been created. They stress the ritual

Dancing to music, according to an Egyptian tomb painting (23rd century B.C.E.). Male dancers perform with clasped hands. The female dancers hold their hands over their heads.

and cultic factor in the religion of the day, which the psalms expressed. The psalms were not just romantic poetry; in addition to their use at specific festivals, they were related to specific acts in the ritual of the sanctuary, or were composed by the priests for use by suppliants to suit individual needs of expression. Some psalms are described by this school as "instructions" pronounced by the priest before the worshipper at the entrance to the shrine:

"Lift up your heads, O gates!
  and be lifted up, O ancient doors!
  that the King of glory may come in.
Who is the King of glory?
  The Lord, strong and mighty,
  The Lord, mighty in battle!
Lift up your heads, O gates!
  and be lifted up, O ancient doors!
  that the King of glory may come in!
Who is this King of glory?
  The Lord of hosts,
  he is the King of glory!" (Ps. 24: 7-10)

"To thee, O Lord, I lift up my soul.
O my God, in thee I trust,
  let me not be put to shame;
  let not my enemies exult over me". (Ps. 25: 1-2)

Still others were responses spoken by prophets attached to shrines as cult officials, whose duty it was to communicate the divine answers to the prayers of the worshippers:

"God has spoken in his sanctuary:
  'With exultation I will divide up Shechem
  and portion out the Vale of Succoth.
Gilead is mine; Manasseh is mine;
  Ephraim is my helmet;
  Judah is my sceptre.
Moab is my washbasin;
  upon Edom I cast my shoe;
  over Philistia I shout in triumph' ". (Ps. 60: 6-8)

OTHER INTERESTING DATA IN 1 CHRONICLES

Following the war and internal trouble, quieter years ensued which enabled David to look again to the administration of the country and probably to its final division into twelve districts. A parallel source in 1 Chr. 22 relates in detail the organization of the "gerim" (the conquered peoples) into forced labour camps, each of which gave one month yearly, for the empire required taxation in labour as well as in kind to carry on public works. David also appointed a council of representatives from all the twelve tribes as well as the Levites. The narrative in 1 Chr. 23 to 26 stresses the extensive functions of the Levites appointed to religious duties and as musicians and singers, as well as their administrative functions. The administration of justice was the domain of the elders of the tribes with the king as final arbiter.

Alleged ancient burial crypts of kings at the southern end of David's City. Excavated by Warren and Weil, these rock tombs are believed to be the royal tombs from the 10th to the 7th centuries B.C.E. David may have been buried there.

Tripod metal stand of Phoenician design with decorative pomegranates, described in the account of cultic objects of the Temple; from Ugarit, 15th century. See description of the Temple of Solomon.

CHAPTER XIII

SOLOMON'S WEALTH AND POWER

ADONIJAH AND SOLOMON

David was seventy years old and his health was declining. But his despotic authority and military power were so great that none dared oppose the decisions he took from his sick bed. It is possible that he was unduly influenced in his senile condition. This is borne out by the sudden struggle concerning the succession which burst from the dark corners of the palace.

It was more or less a foregone conclusion that Adonijah was David's successor, for he was the eldest after Absalom. He was personable and popular as his older brother had been, and he equipped himself in princely style with fifty splendidly-attired horsemen and charioteers with whom he toured the land to impress the people. He enlisted the help of Joab, the veteran general and Abiathar the high priest, which would seem to have been a powerful combination. These leaders of the State meant to maintain policy on the lines of the past and to follow a strict system of primogeniture in the succession. But other opinions and interests preferred that the sovereign choose his successor. Bathsheba, one of the favourite wives, though not a queen, schemed to get the succession away from Adonijah and win it for her son, Shelomoh (Solomon). She enlisted the aid of a still more powerful combination, two younger, rising men, whose ambition was apparently to replace Joab and Abiathar: Benaiah, who commanded all the "mighty men whom David had" (the veteran knights) and the mercenaries; and Zadok the high priest, Abiathar's equal. She had on her side the prophet Nathan, subtle but deeply devout, whose influence on David was considerable:

"Adonijah sacrificed sheep, oxen and fatlings by the Serpent's Stone, which is beside Enrogel, and he invited all his brothers, the king's sons, and all the royal officials of Judah, but he did not invite Nathan the prophet or Benaiah or the mighty men or Solomon his brother". (1 Kings 1:9–10)

In not advising his father of the sacrificial gathering he had convoked — for such it was, held at a holy place — nor inviting his half-brother Solomon, the high priest Zadok, Benaiah, the prophet Nathan and other prominent men, Adonijah gave the impression that he had inaugurated a momentous political move. This impelled the court factions to take sides openly and Nathan and Bathsheba decided that the time had come to take matters in hand. She told David of the matter, and said that Adonijah was engaging in subversive activity aimed at seizing the throne that was destined for her son, and reminded him of his promise to put Solomon on the throne. Nathan went to the old king after her and the two convinced him that the time to crown his son Solomon was while he, David, was still alive. David determined to demonstrate that he was still king and could do as he pleased:

"King David said, 'Call to me Zadok the priest, Nathan the prophet, and Benaiah the son of Jehoiada'. So they came before the king. And the king said to them, 'Take with you the servants of your lord, and cause Solomon

A horned incense altar with curved projections at the corners. Adonijah seized the protecting horns of the altar. From Megiddo.

my son to ride on my own mule, and bring him down to Gihon; and let Zadok the priest and Nathan the prophet there anoint him king over Israel; then blow the trumpet, and say, "Long live King Solomon!" You shall then come up after him, and he shall come and sit upon my throne; for he shall be king in my stead; and I have appointed him to be ruler over Israel and over Judah". (1 K. 1:32–35)

The trumpet was blown and the royal retainers in the City of David joined in the jubilations as the new king returned to the palace and ascended the throne. Adonijah and his guests were not present at Solomon's regal procession. They were no sooner disillusioned than Adonijah fled to the sanctuary where those accused of a crime could seek asylum and could not be apprehended, and seized the projecting "horns" of the altar. He refused to leave this haven until he received Solomon's assurance that no harm would befall him (he was safe while David remained alive).

And so, as Solomon was proclaimed king in 963 B.C.E. political conditions in the kingdom were so acute that the narrative soberly emphasizes the drama of the opening phase of his career. Though the narrator did not know it, these were fateful moments fraught with consequences vital to the development of Jewish religion and history. Had Solomon not succeeded to the throne the form of worship at the Temple and the internal history of Israel before the Exile would have developed on other lines. Solomon's influence and the discipline of the Temple rites accounted in great part for the continued survival of post-Exilic Judaism and its underlying spiritual force.

"Then David slept with his fathers and was buried in the City of David". (1 K. 2:10)

No details are given of the death of Israel's greatest king, the founder of one of the most significant historical dynasties, which was to rule Judah for four centuries. There is considerable doubt about the location of his tomb. The traditions of the Crusaders and Mohammedans places it on the western edge of the walled city where pilgrims now flock. This does not minimize the credibility of the biblical tradition, as quoted, that he was buried in a crypt of the "City of David" near Ophel, on the southeastern edge of ancient Zion.

Solomon's claim to leadership was based solely on his birth and the political influence of his supporters. He was not as magnanimous and unafraid as David, for he proceeded in the manner of the ancient orient to make a reckoning with all rivals. Adonijah and Joab were slain, the latter at the altar where he took refuge. So was Shimei, the last survivor of the house of Saul:

"Then the king commanded Benaiah the son of Jehoiada; and he went out and struck him down, and he died". (1 K. 2:46)

"Solomon loved the Lord, walking in the statutes of David his father; only, he sacrificed and burnt incense at the high places. And the king went to Gibeon to sacrifice there, for that was the great high place; Solomon used to offer a thousand burnt offerings upon that altar". (1 K. 3:3–4)

Solomon's sacrifice, with great ceremonial, of a thousand burnt offerings at the ancient shrine of Gibeon, was an act of great importance for which there may also have been some legal reason. The chronicler apologized for Solomon by saying that at first he had to worship

The Temple from the Kidron Valley, as seen by an artist.

The Dome of the Rock standing over the sacred rock which bore the sacrificial altar of the Temple. It was built by Byzantine architects in the service of the Arabs.

in "high places" which meant any shrine built on a height, as no temple had yet been built. This is connected with Solomon's dream in which God promised him wisdom and admonished him to adhere to the good way of life.

A MAN OF PEACE AND AN ORGANIZER

The scarcity of political data in Solomon's reign is remarkable when compared to its abundance for the reigns of the two preceding kings. On the other hand, the chroniclers have given many details about the Temple, its form. execution, and the materials and dimensions specified, and also the palaces, which are an unusual feature of biblical writing (apart from the description of the Tabernacle in the Pentateuch). The way in which these descriptions are set forth is in itself indicative of a peculiar feature of Solomon's career; events seem to have occurred according to a pre-ordained plan whose source was not in political and other factors, but in the mind of Solomon alone, who was bent on consolidation, colonization, great construction projects, and fortification rather than on increasing the military power left to him by David.

After the beginning of his reign Solomon intended to shape it according to his own will and brilliant intelligence. David had carved out a great realm which still needed organization; but Solomon could develop his father's labour in peace. This is the key to Solomon's reign. The task before him was not to expand the great realm, but to maintain amicable relationships externally and with his vassals.

REORGANIZATION OF THE KINGDOM

"Solomon had twelve officers over all Israel, who provided food for the king and his household; each man had to make provision for one month in the year". (1 K. 4:7)

Then follows a list corresponding to the twelve administrative districts which had gradually been evolving since David's days, and were now established on an efficient administrative basis. It is significant that their listing begins with Ephraim (the heart of the country) and ends with the further side of the Jordan. This order corresponds roughly with David's gradual rounding up of the different parts of Palestine after he had become king. The administrative divisions show, where possible, consideration for the older tribal system but they included now the Canaanite city-states subjugated by David and Solomon which were incorporated into districts based on their territories and important towns. W.F. Albright estimates that many of these districts had populations of about 100,000. This arrangement made for smooth implementation of national policies, raising of revenue and levies in kind and of forced labour and the exploitation of manpower for the king's plans. The division into twelve had also a practical aim as well as the tribal and traditional appeal. Each district had to maintain the cost of government and the royal household for one month. This came to be a severe strain on many districts.

At the head of each district Solomon placed a "nitzav" (officer) as supervisor of the levies charges and conscription. A member of his cabinet "al hanitzavim" (over the officers) controlled the whole system. This was a new and radical departure from David's system and an indication of how the tribal structure, after the absorption of the Canaanite city-states, became part of the new administration.

THE EXPLOITATION OF MANPOWER

"All the people who were left of the Amorites, the Hittites, the Perizzites, the Hivites, and the Jebusites, who were not of the people of Israel—their descendants who were left after them in the land, whom the people of Israel were unable to destroy utterly—these Solomon made a forced levy of slaves, and so they are to this day. But of the people of Israel Solomon made no slaves; they were the soldiers, and his officers, his commanders, his captains, his chariot commanders and his horsemen". (1 K. 20–22)

Solomon was no empire builder like David. He craved peace, but he also carried a big stick. He consummated what David had begun by eliminating Canaanite enclaves. He completed the final subjugation of autochthone elements to the realm. He dispossessed the remaining Canaanite towns and estates, without exterminating them and reduced the inhabitants to the status of labourers. It is probable that the old Canaanite cities furnished most of the equipment for the expansion of armaments and fortifications. In an economic system dependent for productivity, industry and construction on human energy this was essential. The Canaanites were no longer sufficient for the rough work and Israelites were included in the system after the "manner of the king". The figure for the Israelites employed in manual labour is given at 30,000. Ten thousand of them worked each month; a man obliged to render such service would spend two months at home and one at forced labour. Adoniram was in charge of the vast system of the corvee.

The exploitation of manpower. From an Assyrian bas-relief.

SOLOMON'S EMPIRE

"Judah and Israel were as many as the sand by the sea; they ate and drank and were happy. Solomon ruled over all the kingdoms from the Euphrates to the land of the Philistines and to the border of Egypt; they brought tribute and served Solomon all the days of his life". (1 K. 4:20–21)

"And Judah and Israel dwelt in safety, from Dan even to Beersheba, every man under his vine and under his fig tree, all the days of Solomon". (1 K. 4:25)

This idealized picture alleges that Solomon was generally successful in holding David's empire together, although not in the sense that David had.

Solomon's sovereignty over Syria which the record claims, did not involve administrative and military control. However, the ruler of a kingdom comprising all Palestine, east and west of the Jordan, with Edom and Moab annexed, with Philistia as a vassal, was in a position to dominate southern Syria. Assyria and Egypt, immobilized by internal problems, could not assert themselves in Solomon's sphere, which extended from Typhsah on the Euphrates to Gaza.

The international caravan route ran from western Mesopotamia to Egypt's border. Solomon used the recently domesticated camel for long hauls over the inland desert routes, and probably controlled the traffic and levied toll on it. He tried to control the northerly route through Syria as he did that south of his realm.

During the first twenty years of Solomon's reign the essential structure of this vast realm apparently remained unimpaired. But as the warlike qualities of Israel relaxed after many years of peace, some of the subjugated provinces grew rebellious. Solomon also had trouble with Egypt, which he managed to settle; but worse was in store from the Arameans of Damascus.

SOLOMON, EGYPT AND HADAD

"But when Hadad heard in Egypt that David slept with his fathers and that Joab the commander of the army was dead, Hadad said to Pharaoh, 'Let me depart, that I may go to my own country.' But Pharaoh said to him, 'What have you lacked with me that you are now seeking to go to your own country?' And he said to him, 'Only let me go' ". (1 K. 11:21–22)

The Edomite prince had been a refugee at the court of the Pharaoh, Siamon, since the victory and massacre by Joab at the beginning of the 10th century; and he was waiting for the chance to regain his kingdom. He had married into Pharaoh's family and, apparently encouraged by the Egyptians, made himself king over an inaccessible mountain district of eastern Edom. This reverse probably happened in the latter half of Solomon's reign. In spite of it he apparently retained control of western Edom, the mines of the Arabah, and the port of Ezion-Gaber (Elath), on the Red Sea. Pharaoh too embarked on a campaign in the coastal Philistine district, occupied Gezer, killed the Canaanites and destroyed the town. But Egypt was no longer the force it had been and he proceeded no further and negotiated a peace with Solomon, even giving him his daughter—an action without parallel in Egyptian-Israelite history. Pharoah gave his new son-in-law Gezer as a wedding gift. These events show both Egypt's desire to regain influence in the area and also Solomon's ascendance, which Egypt was forced to recognize:

One of the earliest Hebrew inscriptions in existence is the "Gezer Calendar", listing agricultural months with the occupations appropriate to each. It begins with the month of ripening barley, in spring. Probably from the time when Gezer was incorporated into the realm. Many Palestinian towns had such local calendars before a uniform system was adopted.

"Solomon made a marriage alliance with Pharaoh king of Egypt; he took Pharaoh's daughter, and brought her into the city of David, until he had finished building his own house and the house of the Lord and the wall around Jerusalem". (1 K. 3:1).

"Solomon also made a house like this hall for Pharaoh's daughter whom he had taken in marriage ". (1 K. 7:8)

It is noteworthy that Pharaoh's daughter appears to have had a position of honour among Solomon's "one thousand wives" (an oriental way of indicating a very large number). His harem included many other princesses, but the chronicler carefully points out that a palace was built for her.

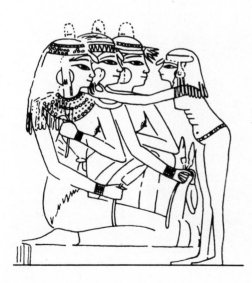

Egyptian ladies having their earrings arranged by a serving maid.

Modest in its proportions, the Temple was nevertheless exquisitely wrought in the finest traditions of Phoenician architecture. The site chosen by Solomon was the ancient holy place of Zion connected by tradition with the threshing floor of Araunah. Its natural rock altar had been holy, immemoriably. The exposed limestone ridge is venerated even today by Moslems who have built the "Dome of the Rock" directly over it.

The alleged ancient rock-altar of the Temple beneath the Moslem "Dome of the Rock" in Jerusalem.

A reconstruction of Solomon's Temple showing the huge ornamental cypress east door facing the rising sun and the two elaborately decorated bronze free-standing pillars, Jachin and Boaz. Ten steps led to the Temple. The high altar of sacrifice or burnt offering was in the courtyard in front of the Temple where the congregation worshipped. The priest ascended the ten steps, passed through the east door, entered the vestibule "Ulam" then entered through another cypress door into the main sanctuary, the "Hechal", a huge room, 60 ft long, 30 ft. wide and 45 ft. high, panelled with cedar and floored with cypress. Its flat roof was supported by huge cedar beams. The sanctuary was dimly lit by latticed windows on either side, just below the ceiling. This contained the sacred furniture; the seven-branch golden candlesticks, the table of shewbread, and a small cedar altar for incense situated in the centre and decorated with gold leaf. There were also lamps, cups, braziers, common to oriental sanctuaries.

The Israelite lay worshipper did not enter the Temple, but only penetrated as far as the area in front of it. There, he slaughtered his sacrificial animal and watched the priests put parts of it upon the altar. The courtyard contained the enormous Molten (Brazen) Sea "wrought like the brim of a cup, like the flower of a lily" which held 2000 measures (10,000 gallons) of water for sacrificial purposes, and ten smaller wheeled lavers for washing utensils. The priests themselves entered the Temple only to bring the daily supplies for the holy place.

They made an impressive procession, bringing replenishments for the table of shewbread, incense for the little gold altar and oil for the lamps. The Israelites observed the great national festivals in their homes or in the Temple courtyard.

A flight of stairs led to the "debir" — Holy of Holies, a raised cubic room 30 × 30 × 30 ft. entered by a small double door. Lined with cedar it had no windows, and was pitch dark. There stood two giant "cherubim" 15 feet high, made of olive wood decorated with gold leaf. The ark of the Covenant reposed beneath their outstretched wings. There the invisible and imageless Yahweh was believed to be enthroned, guarded by the two cherubim. Unlike all other temples of antiquity, in Solomon's there was no idol.

On the Day of Atonement (Yom Kippur) the High Priest ascended the stairs in the sight of all Israel, passed the hechal on his way to the debir and there made atonement for himself and all the people.

The Howland-Garber model (above) is a reconstruction of Solomon's Temple, derived from a comparative study of the biblical record and relevant archaeological discoveries. It was not large and ornate in the manner of other oriental temples, but was renowned for its dignified simplicity and the excellence of its craftsmanship. Previous models of reconstructions are now regarded as products of architectural and artistic imagination.

Jachin and Boaz, the two "pillars of brass" (copper alloy) flanking the porch entrance of the Temple, may have been associated with the Molten Sea, as symbols of Yahweh's lordship over the elements of the world.

Capital of a column found at Megiddo, and thought by the excavator to be a vessel for incense. The top of this column is similar to the floral type of the two freestanding pillars, Jachin and Boaz. They bring to mind the twin columns of gold and emerald of the temple of Tyre, described by Herodotus: "I visited the Temple and found it richly adorned with a number of offerings, among which were two pillars, one of pure gold, the other of emerald, shining with great brilliancy at night. In a conversation I had with the priests, I enquired how long their temple had been built... They said that the temple was built at the same time as the city was founded." It may have been in existence in Solomon's day.

The Molten Sea was a great bowl 15 ft. in diameter and 7 ft. high, with a capacity of about 300 barrels. It was made of cast copper alloy and weighed between 25 and 30 tons. It rested on twelve brazen bulls which appeared to support it. Its symbolism is obscure, but may have been related to the cosmic meaning of the subterranean fresh-water ocean inherent in the conception of the world of the ancients (see Ch. I). Notice the design of the bowl's brim "like the brim of a cup, like the flower of a lily". (I.K.7: 26).

Star of David, or six-pointed star, discovered at Megiddo, dating from Solomon's time.

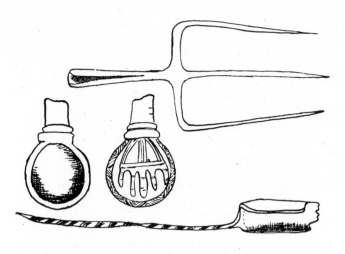

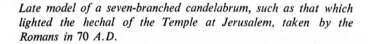

Utensils of Sacrifice: The precise significance of the reference to tongues, bowls, snuffers, basins, spoon and censers, (1 Kings 7: 49: 50), utensils presumably used in connection with sacrifices, is not known. A number of similar objects have been uncovered, as shown here.

A Megiddo metal stand or lampholder.

Late model of a seven-branched candelabrum, such as that which lighted the hechal of the Temple at Jerusalem, taken by the Romans in 70 A.D.

Ivory carving of cherubim, from Megiddo, of similar pattern to those in the Temple, dated 1350–1100 B.C.E.

Solomon was a cosmopolitan and attempted to place his country on the cultural map of his world. Phoenicia was his nearest and dynamic pattern. Solomon's Temple was naturally in keeping with the architectural style ot his times. It was built and equipped in the best Phoenician taste of the day. In the Holy of Holies was a vast screen formed by "Cherubim" They were of gilded olive wood, each ten cubits high and ten broad and:

"He put the cherubim in the innermost part of the house; and the wings of the cherubim were spread out so that a wing of one touched the one wall, and a wing of the other cherub touched the other wall; their other wings touched each other in the middle of the house. And he overlaid the cherubim with gold. He carved all the walls of the house round about with carved figures of cherubim and palm trees and open flowers, in the inner and outer rooms". (1 K. 6:27–29)

Similar temples have been unearthed at Tel Tainat in Syria and very recently at Hazor in Galilee. The archaeological discoveries at Ugarit, Arslan Tash, Tel Tainat in Syria, and Megiddo and Hazor in Palestine show great similarities of building techniques, art and decorative design, of temple, palace and urban architecture and planning. The three-fold division of the Temple into open vestibule, main sanctuary and inner holy chamber is common ancient Near Eastern practice.

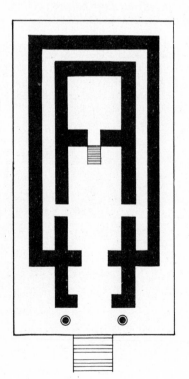

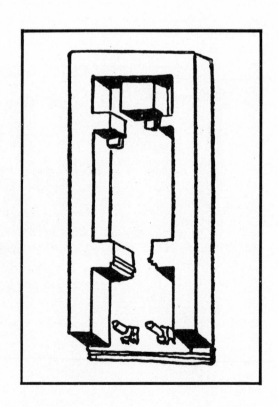

On the right:
A royal chapel built according to Phoenician design from the period of the Israelite Kingdom and excavated at Tel-Tainat in Syria, suggests the form of Solomon's Temple. 9th century B.C.E.

On the left:
Suggested plan of the Temple of Solomon based on the biblical description and upon details suggested by archaeological discoveries. The Temple was essentially a house of two halls arranged lengthwise, the vestibule and the sanctuary.

Ancient underground quarries in the northern part of Old Jerusalem, popularly designated "Solomon's Quarries", though they had in fact no connection with his undertakings. The great stone blocks used for Solomon's buildings were carefully shaped in the quarry so that they would fit exactly without trimming on the site. "There was neither hammer, nor axe, nor any tool of iron heard in the house while it was building" (1 K. 6: 7). No sound of song or other noise was heard within the Temple. It was a silent shrine.

THE SYMBOLISM OF THE SOLOMONIC TEMPLE

" 'But will God indeed dwell on the earth? Behold, heaven and the highest heaven cannot contain thee; how much less this house which I have built! Yet have regard to the prayer of thy servant and to his supplication, O Lord my God, hearkening to the cry and to the prayer which thy servant prays before thee this day; that thy eyes may be open night and day toward this house, the place of which thou hast said, "My name shall be there", that thou mayest hearken to the prayer which thy servant offers toward this place. And hearken thou to the supplication of thy servant and of thy people Israel, when they pray toward this place; Yea, hear thou in heaven thy dwelling place; and when thou hearest, forgive' ". (1 K. 8:27–30)

In this moving prayer Solomon went to the root of the problem of worship in the ancient world. Could the gods representing the sky, the sun, the moon, the storm, live in earthly houses? The polytheist temple was filled with statues and other man-made symbols of the gods to indicate their presence. The statue which represented the deity *was* the deity. He was present in it as he was in the expression of the powers in nature: the sun, the moon, the storm. The polytheist did not trouble himself with transcendence, a theologic notion of later times.

But the Israelite ritual was otherwise. Implicit in it is the belief that God cannot dwell on earth like humans nor can He be represented by a statue. Traditionally the house of Yahweh was a development of the old tent-sanctuary, where Yahweh's non-material presence was believed to be enthroned with the "cherubim" in the Holy of Holies, in the innermost dark room of the Temple. The Temple bore His name and was the focus of religious attention, and prayer and sacrifice.

THE HIGH PLACES AND THE TEMPLE

Many believe that the Jerusalem temple was not intended by Solomon (or many of his successors) to be the sole centre of worship. It did not replace the sanctuaries at Gibeon, Hebron, Bethel, nor was its erection accompanied by suppression of the Canaanite high places in the towns which were amalgamated into Israel's life. To most Israelites the building of the new sanctuary in Jerusalem did not imply that it had become the only one and so it did not require any revolution in their religious beliefs and practice. That was the situation at the time, and it has no connection with what happened in later times.

Solomon built several high places. Their existence around Jerusalem was necessary in the capital of a king who married princesses from foreign lands. Solomon's foreign policy was based on developing the country's potentialities by a programme of judicious alliances with neighbouring kingdoms, and many of these were sealed by marriage with noble brides, the most distinguished of whom was the Egyptian princess.

He had to grant his brides shrines and chapels in which they could worship their native gods. This courtesy was also required as an attraction to foreign traders who came to Jerusalem and sometimes stayed for months, or even longer.

The eo-existence of the high places and the Temple was not a religious contradiction, but was easily understood by everybody. The Temple had a dual purpose. It was a dynastic shrine, and its chief priest, a member of the king's cabinet, was his appointee. Sacrifice was another function of the Temple, though we know little of the differences of the ritual here from that at the altars of the high places. But Solomon was exalted, even above Saul and David, for his devotion to Yahweh and glorified for building the Temple by transposition of a later tradition.

THE DEDICATORY PRAYER

The significance of the Temple grew with time, for its full symbolism was probably not expressed by Solomon or his contemporaries. To his later chroniclers Solomon loomed correspondingly larger than reality as the great designer and builder and man of wisdom. Appreciation of the man who was credited with having created so splendid a place of worship, expressing so much holiness, is conveyed in the beautiful dedicatory ceremony and prayer attributed to Solomon:

> "Then Solomon assembled the elders of Israel and all the heads of the tribes, the leaders of the fathers' houses of the people of Israel, before King Solomon in Jerusalem, to bring up the ark of the covenant of the Lord out of the city of David, which is Zion. And all the men of Israel assembled to King Solomon at the feast in the month Ethanim, which is the seventh month. And all the elders of Israel came, and the priests took up the ark. And they brought up the ark of the Lord, the tent of meeting, and all the holy vessels that were in the tent; the priests and the Levites brought them up. And King Solomon and all the congregation of Israel, who had assembled before him, were with him before the ark, sacrificing so many sheep and oxen that they could not be counted or numbered. Then the priests brought the ark of the covenant of the Lord to its place, in the inner sanctuary of the house, in the most holy place, underneath the wings of the cherubim". (1 K. 8:1–6)

Thus was the dedication of the Temple and the moving of the Ark from Zion, the City of David, into the Holy of Holies. It was solemnly celebrated before the assembled elders of

Israel and the heads of the clans. God is said to have showed his acceptance of the Temple by permeating it in the form of a cloud called "The Glory of Yahweh" that filled the interior. In biblical terms this probably meant that a mist enveloped His divine presence.

"There was nothing in the ark except the two tables of stone which Moses put there at Horeb, where the Lord made a covenant with the people of Israel, when they came out of the land of Egypt". (1 K. 8:9)

Yahweh is designated as "He who thrones (or is enthroned) upon the cherubim". He may have been thought of as having been invisibly enthroned in the Holy of Holies upon the Ark, or perhaps above the cherubim who were guardians of the Temple, as they had been at the east of the Garden of Eden. They visually symbolized the dignity of the invisible God:

"Then Solomon said,
'The Lord has set the sun in the heavens.
But has said that he would dwell in thick darkness.
I have built thee an exalted house, a place for thee to dwell in for ever' ". (1 K. 8:12–13)

In the prayer of dedication is a poetic couplet which many scholars believe expressed the belief of the Temple builders in the importance of the dark Holy of Holies. But its real meaning must be sought in the symbols of the nature of the deity in the time itself, and not through later theological interpretations. Ancient Israelite belief in Yahweh retained his connection with storm clouds, the prohibition of images, His Covenant with the Chosen People. But other Canaanite concepts, and the rituals of the Canaanite high places had probably penetrated the symbolism and popular understanding of God:

" 'When thy people Israel are defeated before the enemy because they have sinned against thee, if they turn again to thee, and acknowledge thy name, and pray and make supplication to thee in this house... When heaven is shut up and there is no rain because they have sinned against thee, if they pray toward this place, and acknowledge thy name, and turn from their sin, when thou dost afflict them' ". (1 K. 8:33–35).
....

" 'If they sin against thee—for there is no man who does not sin—and thou art angry with them, and dost give them to an enemy, so that they are carried away captive to the land of the enemy, far off or near; yet if they lay it to heart in the land to which they have been carried captive, and repent, and make supplication to thee in the land of their captors, saying, " We have sinned, and have acted perversely and wickedly"; if they repent with all their mind and with all their heart in the land of their enemies, who carried them captive, and pray to thee toward their land, which thou gavest to their fathers, the city which thou has chosen, and the house which I have built for thy name' ". (1 K. 8:46–48)

In Solomon's dedicatory prayer and theophany divine sanction of the act is an integral part of justice. It is his will that justice should be done. By serving God and carrying out his commandments, drought could be avoided or ended, people saved from famine, pestilence, locusts and other calamities of nature and defeat could be averted. Moreover, God's rewarding of his people's devotion would prove to foreigners that he was really associated with his Temple.

"My name shall be there" was a compelling bond, for the "name" in antiquity was a presence and a reality. Indeed, how else could the service in the Temple be effective? Sinners or captives, his people would be rescued by turning to him and brought back to their homeland, the only place where they could possibly worship him. With Yahweh's presence ensured materially on that holy spot, his people could always find him there. True, the words of verses 28–29, put into Solomon's mouth, may denote a spiritual appreciation of God's nature that contradicted his material presence on earth. It is regarded as a later interpolation. But his "name" connected with the Temple, in any event, was a religious assurance consonant with the times.

> "So Solomon held the feast at that time, and all Israel with him, a great assembly, from the entrance of Hamath to the Brook of Egypt, before the Lord our God, seven days". (1 K. 8: 65)

This is the forerunner of the house-warming party of today. When Assur-Nusir-Pal II rebuilt Calah (879 B.C.E.) as the capital of Assyria, he gave a munificent feast to which he invited 69,574 guests "the happy peoples of all the lands together with the people of Kalhu (Calah) for ten days I feasted, wined, bathed and honoured them, and then sent them back to their homes in peace and joy".

ISRAEL AND ARABIA

The Israelite realm bestrode the great trade route from Egypt and Arabia to northern Syria and the Euphrates, which in itself was a great source of revenue to Solomon; and his monopoly of transport made him the greatest merchant and supplier of the kingdoms north of Palestine:

> "Now when the queen of Sheba heard of the fame of Solomon concerning the name of the Lord, she came to test him with hard questions. She came to Jerusalem with a very great retinue, with camels bearing spices, and very much gold, and precious stones; and when she came to Solomon, she told him all that was on her mind. And Solomon answered all her questions; there was nothing hidden from the king which he could not explain to her". (1 K. 10: 1–3)

The story confirms the existence of the great camel caravans which brought minerals and spices from the Sabean kingdom of South Arabia, a journey of several weeks. This trade was

Camel rider from Southern Arabia, with Sabaean inscription.

not new, as attested by the discovery of a clay stamp of about the 9th century, found at Bethel.

From Palestine the caravans travelled into Syria and Mesopotamia. Now, they used Palestine as the main trading post and clearing-house with the Near East. The Queen of Sheba's purpose when she "told him all that was on her mind" was to consolidate economic relations between the two regions, since Solomon's commercial organization influenced the southern sphere. Her visit was satisfactory for "King Solomon gave to the Queen of Sheba all that she desired". That queens ruled among ancient Arabs is also attested by a cuneiform record of Tiglathpileser III (735 B.C.E.) dealing with relations between Mesopotamia and Arabia.

"Now the weight of gold that came to Solomon in one year was six hundred and sixty-six talents of gold, besides that which came from the traders and from the traffic of the merchants, and from all the kings of Arabia and from the governors of the land". (1 K. 10 : 14–15)

It is no wonder that Solomon waxed so rich.

SOLOMON AND PHOENICIA

The king of Tyre, Hiram, (979–946 B.C.E.) was already at the helm of his state in David's time and still active in that of Solomon. The Syrians had rebuilt Tyre in the 12th century as their capital on the Syrian coast. Hiram had conquered the people of Kition (capital of Cyprus) thereby beginning the great Phoenician expansion and colonization which marked the following centuries.

By the end of the 10th century Phoenicia, with its seaports of Tyre, Sidon, Gebal, and its colonies along the Mediterranean shores and islands as distant as Sardinia (Tarshish), Spain and north Africa, had become the hub of the commerce of the world. The Phoenicians mined copper both in Sardinia and Cyprus and developed important textile industries, chiefly blue and crimson dyes, and initiated glass blowing and fine metal-working. Tyre and Sidon, states R.D. Barnett, now replaced Byblos (Gebal) as the Phoenicians' principal cities "although the memory of Byblos still survived through one of its main exports. Egyptian papyrus, traded through Byblos, became known to the early Greeks under the name of the city whence it was first obtained. In the form of *Biblos* the word came to mean a book, and through the Greeks to mean to us the Book *par excellence* — the Bible".

The Phoenicians (Canaanites), had a unique style of architecture. What they learned they did not imitate, but incorporated into their own. Everywhere they went they were evidently both teachers and learners in the arts. One great innovation of theirs was the stylizing by 1500 B.C.E. of the cumbrous picture script of the Egyptians (hieroglyphics) into signs with letter-values. Several attempts at an alphabet have been found in the area. Among these was the Hebrew script of Sinai, written in an early alphabet based on Egyptian hieroglyphics (Proto-Phoenician). It is known that the Phoenicians, who maintained close ties with the Aegean shores and the Greek mainland, disseminated this system there about 800 B.C.E. The Greek alphabet, borrowed from the Phoenicians, is the source of all Western alphabets. The Phoenicians were Solomon's tutors not only in building, decoration and in commercial development but also in the literary arts.

EGYPTIAN HIEROGLYPH	SINAI SCRIPT c. 1500 BC	REPRESENTS	S. ARABIAN c. 300 BC	PHOENICIAN c. 1300 BC	EARLY HEBREW c. 600 BC	GREEK c. 500 BC	ROMAN c. 100 AD	LATE HEBREW c. 100 AD	CONVENTIONAL NAME	PHONETIC VALUE
☿	♉	ox-head	Ħ	K	ⱪ	Ɐ A	A	א	'aleph	'
⌑	□	house	⊓	૬	૧	ⴷ B	B	ⴺ	bêth	b
⟩		throw-stick	⅂	⋏	⋏	1 Γ	C	ⵏ	gîmel	g
◖		door	⋈	◁	◭	◭ △	D	ⴳ	dāleth	d
𓀃	⚘	man with raised arms	Ψ	⋌	ⴺ	ⴺ E	E	ⴻ	hē	h
⟜		hand	℉	⟨	ⴑ	⟩ I	I	'	yōdh	y
	ⵡ	palm of hand	⊓	⋁	ⴼ	ⴽ K	K	ⴲ	kaph	k
∿∿	⋀	water	⧤	⋛	ⴻ	ᵚ M	M	ⵎ	mēm	m
⅂	⌐	snake	ⴽ	ⴑ	ⴹ	Y N	N	ⵏ	nûn	n
⟜	⬭	eye	o	O	0	⬚ O	O	ⵖ	'ayin	'
⌒	⌒	mouth	0	⌐	ⴑ	Γ Π	P	ⵏ	pē	p
ꝙ	Q	head	>	⋒	⋒	⋒ P	R	ⵔ	rēsh	r
ⵞⵞⵞ		papyrus clump	ⵛ	W	W	Ϛ Σ	S	ⵓⵍ	shîn	s
✝	X	cross	X	X	⋌	⟨ T	T	ⵞ	tāw	t
i	ii	iii	iv	v	vi	vii	viii	ix	x	xi

The Proto-Phoenician, Phoenician, early Hebrew, Greek and Roman alphabets developed from the picture-script of Egypt and Sinai, as shown in this table. The early Phoenician alphabet on column five, and early Hebrew on column six, are cursive forms of the hieroglyphic pictorial script.

Sphynx found at Serabit-el-Khadem in Sinai (15th century) inscribed in a Semitic dialect (Proto-Phoenician) in an early alphabet based on Egyptian picture-script. The inscription bears the name of the goddess Baalat.

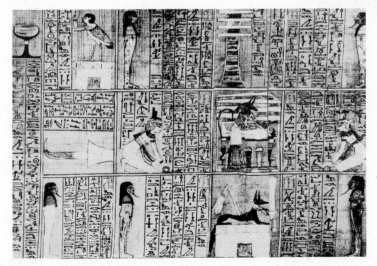

Egyptian papyrus was traded through Phoenician Byblos, a name which came to mean "book" (the Bible). Such material served for the drawing of this Egyptian document.

SOLOMON'S BUILDING

"And Hiram sent to Solomon, saying, 'I have heard the message which you have sent to me; I am ready to do all you desire in the matter of cedar and cypress timber". (1 K. 5: 8)

Solomon began his great construction works at the very beginning of his reign, first with the royal palace, then the Temple. He tripled the town's area by including in it the whole of Mount Zion and then fortified it in the style of the 10th century. His skilled labourers and architects were Sidonians and Tyrians (Phoenicians), for the Israelites had not yet acquired these arts. The lumber (cedar and pine) also came from the hinterland of Sidon and Tyre. He facilitated his construction programme by alliances, notably that with Hiram of Tyre. He paid Hiram with wheat and olive oil of which the Phoenicians, with no cultivable hinterland, were much in need. Solomon's labour battalions, ten thousand strong, felled and dragged the lumber to the sea. A very large force was quarrying, in the Jerusalem hills. Solomon's Temple and his palace were naturally built in accordance with the Phoenician architectural style.

"The king also made a great ivory throne, and overlaid it with the finest gold. The throne had six steps, and at the back of the throne was a calf's head, and on each side of the seat were arm rests and two lions standing beside the arm rests, while twelve lions stood there, one on each end of a step on the six steps. The like of it was never made in any kingdom. All King Solomon's drinking vessels were of gold, and all the vessels of the House of the Forest of Lebanon were of pure gold; none were of silver, it was not considered as anything in the days of Solomon." (1 K. 10: 18–21)

King Ahiram seated on a sphynx throne before a table of offerings, approached by attendants dressed in a long robe caught around the waist by a belt tied in front (Canaanite costume). On the lid of this sarcophagus of the king, a dedicatory inscription in Phoenician characters can be seen, which is the earliest known example of Phoenician inscriptions. (10th century B.C.E.) Solomon modelled his throne on that of the Phoenician court.

Two plenipotentiaries solemnly concluding an agreement; carved on a stela from Ugarit. The documents are placed on a high table between them.

Winged cherub from Arwad, an island port in Phoenicia, famed for its shipwrights' workshops.

The last existing remnant of the famous cedars of Lebanon.

Cedar logs from Lebanon carried by sea; on an Assyrian relief from Khorsabad.

Solomon also modelled his throne on that of Phoenician courts. There, the King sat on a throne flanked with cherubim in the form of female sphynxes (See illustration of King Ahiram enthroned). But we notice that Solomon, when designing his own throne of ivory, significantly caused it to be flanked with lions, not with cherubim, who were assigned to the Ark for the symbolic throne of Yahweh. This is the allusion which is applied to Him in Psalm 99:

"The Lord reigns; let the peoples tremble!
He sits enthroned upon the cherubim; let the earth quake". (Psalm 99: 1)

The famed cedars, cypress and pines of Lebanon were felled, brought to the coast, tied in rafts and floated down to Joppa or Tel-Qasile (an ancient harbour within the present area of Tel-Aviv), where the rafts were broken up and the trees hauled to Jerusalem.

JERUSALEM

"Solomon was building his own house thirteen years, and he finished his entire house. He built the House of the Forest of Lebanon; its length was a hundred cubits, and its breadth fifty cubits, and its height thirty cubits, and it was built upon three rows of cedar pillars, with cedar beams upon the pillars". (1 K. 7: 1–2)

The City of David was too small to contain Solomon's court, his official buildings and the people who flocked to Jerusalem. The city extended to the north of the Jebusite city wall. Contrary to the general impression, Solomon's building programme was not centred on the Temple which was only one item of it. His wealth was put to numerous building projects such as the lavish complex of structures on the acropolis of Jerusalem (Mount Zion) as well as military and industrial installations from Dan in the north to Elath on the Red Sea in the south.

The record tells us that the Temple took seven years to build, but that the king's palace on the acropolis took thirteen. He built the "House of the Forest of Lebanon" (so called because of the massive cedar pillars that supported it) which served as an armoury, a treasury, and a judgement hall, where affairs of state were transacted, and where the king's great ivory throne stood:

> "King Solomon made two hundred large shields of beaten gold; six hundred shekels of gold went into each shield. And he made three hundred shields of beaten gold; three minas of gold went into each shield; and the king put them in the House of the Forest of Lebanon". (1 K. 10: 16–17)
> . . . .
> "But Pharaoh's daughter went up from the city of David to her own house which Solomon had built for her; then he built the Millo". (1 K. 9: 24)

The Millo was a massive terrace-fortification between the old Jebusite wall and the new northern extension. Solomon then closed the wall that David had breached in capturing Jerusalem.

SOLOMON'S SHIPS IN DISTANT WATERS

> "King Solomon built a fleet of ships at Ezion-geber, which is near Eloth on the shore of the Red Sea, in the land of Edom. And Hiram sent with the fleet his servants, seamen who were familiar with the sea, together with the servants of Solomon; and they went to Ophir, and brought from there gold, to the amount of four hundred and twenty talents; and they brought it to King Solomon". (1 K. 9: 26–28)
> . . . .
> "Moreover the fleet of Hiram, which brought gold from Ophir, brought from Ophir a very great amount of almug wood and precious stones". (1 K. 10: 11)
> . . . .
> "For the king had a fleet of ships of Tarshish at sea with the fleet of Hiram. Once every three years the fleet of ships of Tarshish used to come bringing gold, silver, ivory, apes, and peacocks". (1 K. 10: 22)

Both Hiram and Solomon operated "ships of Tarshish" meaning a fleet of seagoing ships like those in which the Phoenicians transported smelted metal from Sardinia or Tartessus in Spain. In cooperation with Hiram, Solomon constructed a seaport and a fleet of

Ship of the Phoenician fleet, such as Solomon sent to distant waters. (Assyrian relief).

ships at Ezion-Gaber (Elath). These went to the distant ports which the Phoenicians had already been exploiting. The new maritime power began to exploit the commercial opportunities of the Mediterranean, mainly through Phoenician ports and probably through the Palestinian ports of Dor (south of Haifa) and Tel-Qasile. Also together with the Phoenicians, Solomon could trade in the Red Sea area and along the coasts of Arabia and Somaliland, where Ophir was probably located, and possibly the Indian Ocean. From there he brought gold, sandal-wood and many varieties of exotic products and artifacts.

A potsherd inscribed the "Gold of Ophir" was found at Tel-Qasile which shows that he carried on trade with distant places, by sea to points along the Mediterranean and southern warets (Red Sea coasts), and also by camel caravan.

THE SMELTING PLANTS AND METAL INDUSTRY

One of Solomon's most remarkable achievements—not mentioned in the biblical record—was his development of the copper-smelting plants in the Arabah, Edom and the southern Negev, mainly at Ezion, as attested by the excavations of Nelson Glueck in "Solomon's Mines".

Copper ore abounded in that region and in Sinai and mines have been found at many points throughout the region, where Solomon erected furnaces where the ore was first smelted. It was further refined into copper ingots, and then either shipped abroad, to be exchanged for foreign products, or used in the home manufacture of copper articles.

The smelting and refining plant of Ezion-Gaber, one of the largest so far known in the Orient, was situated in a narrow valley so that the strong north winds, which blow regularly, gave an excellent draught to operate the furnaces. The force of the wind, according to N. Glueck, made up for the poor heat from wood-fuel, the only supply there, and it was not even necessary to use bellows. Harnessed through a system of air-channels running

Copper slag heap in one of Solomon's mining camps at Wadi Meni'eh north of Ezion-Gaber.

through the holes of the smelters, the winds made the fire hot enough to refine the metal for working into ingots. The ore was put into crucibles in the smelter. The green copper stains on the walls of these buildings and the heaps of slag still show how and where the process was used. However, it is believed by others that the smelting was effected in a more primitive fashion with the use of bellows and that the winds were not the main source of draught.

Nelson Glueck visualizes the conditions existing there: "Thousands of labourers had to be assembled, housed, fed and protected at the chosen building site. As a matter of fact, most of them were probably slaves who had to be guarded and goaded to work. Skilled technicians of all kinds had to be recruited. Great caravans had to be collected to transport materials and food. An effective business organization had to be called into existence to regulate the profitable flow of raw materials and finished and semi-finished products. Ezion-Gaber represents one of his (Solomon's) greatest, if indeed up to the present time his least known, accomplishments".

Walled encampments found nearby ensured the peaceful progress of the operations and kept the forced labourers and slaves from running away.

Considering the experience of the Phoenicians in copper smelting and the knowledge of their guilds of metal workers of Phoenicia, it must be assumed that they helped in this work. A Phoenician craftsman, Hiram, (son of a Phoenician father and a Hebrew mother from Naphtali) is known to have organized Solomon's metal-furniture industry for Temple and home use. Archaeological evidence confirms that Solomon had casting done in the "Plain of Jordan" at Beth-Shean:

"In the plain of the Jordan the king cast them, in the clay ground between Succoth and Zarethan". (1 K. 7: 46)

THE NEW ISRAELITE URBAN CULTURE

The rapid integration of the Israelite and Canaanite elements of the population, the building of new towns and the growth of old cities and the multiplication of small holdings, were factors in the evolution from a tribal society with an elementary economic pattern into a more complex society engaged increasingly in commerce and industry as well as farming. The general raising of the living standard and the growth of a wealthy commercial class (of which Solomon, a superman of commerce and enterprise was typical) brought about very different conditions from those of the pastoral and agrarian society of the days of Judges, Saul and the Philistine domination. The state had become a dominant factor and the people were its subjects. Their productivity reached higher levels as security increased; where once they stored grain in pits inside the town walls, they now built storehouses. The iron-tipped plough was in general use. The wares of the entire civilized world became accessible and money was abundant, (though inevitably a rich class appeared) and class distinctions grew apace. With the increase of wealth in royal and official circles came increasing poverty amongst the masses. The population of Palestine was then about 750,000.

"Solomon also had forty thousand stalls of horses for his chariots, and twelve thousand horsemen. And those officers supplied provisions for King Solomon, and for all who came to King Solomon's table, each one in his month; they let nothing be lacking. Barley also and straw for the horses and swift steeds they brought to the place where it was required, each according to his charge". (1 K. 4: 26–28)

Though recorded at an early stage in his reign it is believed that Solomon only later realized the need to "modernize" his army and protect the frontier districts. He was probably influenced by the potential or actual threat of his powerful neighbours — Egypt and Aram. An achievement — unprecedented in Israel — was his development of a chariot army, which strengthened his forces comparably with those of other eastern rulers and the Arameans, his rivals. The use of horses was limited in David's time, and his victories had been gained by infantry. The horse was not extensively bred in Palestine, and it was too costly to buy them from outside. The military aristocracy or "Maryannu" of the Canaanite city-states had developed military chariotry, and as the states were absorbed into Israel, Solomon had probably adopted the chariot from them. In a few short years his fame was synonymous with his numerous horses and chariots. This cavalry and chariotry were maintained by the horsemen themselves as a "charge" upon them and was the discharge of their military service.

"And Solomon's import of horses was from Egypt and Kue, and the king's traders received them from Kue at a price. A chariot could be imported from Egypt for six hundred shekels of silver, and a horse for a hundred and fifty; and so through the king's traders they were exported to all the kings of the Hittites and the kings of Syria". (1 K. 10: 28–29)

"Horses from Kue"; an Anatolian horse, on a neo-Hittite stela from Mar'ash; 9th century.

Egyptian chariots; relief from Tel-el-Amarna, (14th century)

Kue or Cilicia in Anatolia was famed in ancient times for its horses (as Arabia and Syria became in modern times), as was Egypt for its fine chariots. In developing his army, Solomon gradually developed a monopoly of this foreign trade, augmenting his own and the national resources. This was done through the medium of "soharai hamelekh" as the royal merchants were known. Extensive stables for both cavalry and chariotry were needed. Many were discovered in the Chariot City at Megiddo in northern Palestine and were attributed to Solomon.

"And this is the account of the forced labor which King Solomon levied to build the house of the Lord and his own house and the Millo and the wall of Jerusalem and Hazor and Megiddo and Gezer... and all the store-cities that Solomon had, and the cities for his chariots, and the cities for his horsemen, and whatever Solomon desired to build in Jerusalem, in Lebanon, and in all the land of his dominion". (1 K. 9: 15, 19)

Fortifications

The work on the Jerusalem fortifications was only a part of Solomon's military undertakings. He also strengthened the defences of Hazor in the extreme north, of Megiddo in the Valley of Esdraelon, of Gezer in the plain of Shephela, of lower Beth-horon at the entrance of the hill country in the direction of Philistia and Egypt, of Baalath in Judah and of Tamar, on the road to the Dead Sea and the Arabah. Their walls were provided with massive gateways which served as forts and as housing for the guards of the gates. Identical gateways and buildings are now known at Megiddo, Hazor and Gezer.

Beth-Shemesh and Lachish were rebuilt as district centres for the receipt and storage of taxes paid in kind.

THE ARAMEANS REBEL

It appears that Solomon set out on his extensive reorganization of the army and the building of an elaborate line of fortifications during the second part of his reign, twenty years after he started building the Temple and royal palace. This may have coincided with the growing political tension because of foreign peril on the borders of Egypt, Edom and Aram.

The rebellion in Syria was of a more serious nature than that of Edom. An Aramean prince, Rezon, who had also taken refuge in Egypt in David's days, returned to Damascus and ruled over a new Aramean kingdom. This seriously damaged Solomon's control over

Ruins of the so-called Solomon's stables or "Chariot City" in the store-city of Megiddo. The pillars served as supports for the roofs and as hitching posts for the horses. Between them were stone mangers. Y. Yadin has proved recently that the "Chariot City" attributed to Solomon was in fact erected by Ahab, a later King of Israel.

Reconstruction of the stables which each held 24 horses. Two areas of similar buildings could accommodate 930 horses.

Reconstruction of the upper part of the mound of Megiddo attributed to the days of Solomon and the later kingdom. In the foreground is seen the Solomonic gateway consisting of an outer and inner gate at right angles to each other. In the back is the southern stable area and at its left the governor's palace set in a wall courtyard of its own. The round hole nearby is the grain pit. At the right of the stables is the wide water hole leading to the city's underground spring. At the left of the reconstructed model is seen the eastern stable area. The right side of the model shows the lower stratas of occupation by the Canaanites, before the days of David and Solomon.

his Aramean holdings. We do not know how Solomon reacted, unless this is connected with a certain military exploit reported of Solomon:

> "And Solomon went to Hamath-zobah, and took it. He built Tadmor in the wilderness and all the store-cities which he built in Hamath". (2 Chron. 8: 3–4)

The record implies that Rezon was never brought to terms. At the end of his reign Solomon had lost control of most of his Syrian possessions and the rich caravan route to the Euphrates. The clipping away of the vast domain left by David was explained by later historians as Yahweh's punishment for Solomon's senile defection.

ECONOMIC TENSION AND RELIGIOUS UNREST

In the second half of Solomon's reign tensions arose both without and within the kingdom. The tremendous expenses of the vast building programme, the fortifications, the reorganization of the army as well as the luxury of his court and extensive harem, must have taxed the kingdom's resources beyond Solomon's income, despite his fabulous attainments in the economic sphere:

> "At the end of twenty years, in which Solomon had built the two houses, the house of the Lord and the king's house, and Hiram king of Tyre had supplied Solomon with cedar and cypress timber and gold, as much as he desired, King Solomon gave to Hiram twenty cities in the land of Galilee. But when Hiram came from Tyre to see the cities which Solomon had given him, they did not please him. Therefore he said, 'What kind of cities are these which you have given me, my brother?' So they are called the land of Cabul to this day. Hiram had sent to the king one hundred and twenty talents of gold". (1 K. 9: 10–14)

It is assumed that the king took this means to reimburse Hiram, King of Tyre, for loans and building materials and that as collateral he had guaranteed stretches of Western Galilee near Phoenicia's southern borders. The loan was not redeemed and the towns of the territory of Cabul were ceded to Phoenicia.

Seeds of trouble

However the social and religious tensions were more serious, even though they were born out of the new order. All the splendours of the Solomonic period cannot efface certain disturbing facts that developed during its course.

The people, the "ten tribes", namely all of Israel to the north of Jerusalem, felt that they had to pay too heavily both in money and in forced labour for Solomon's glory and prosperity. They regarded the heavy hand of the crown as plain oppression. Dissatisfaction must have smouldered particularly in the "Tribe of Joseph" in Shechem (Ephraim), where the people felt abused by the Judean King. This was exploited by Jeroboam of Ephraim, the man of destiny. While Solomon was building the "millo" fortifications in Jerusalem, he had appointed Jeroboam as chief of the corvee, or labour conscription, in the "tribe of Joseph"; he was encouraged to plot against Solomon by the Ephraimite prophet Ahijah:

> "And this was the reason why he lifted up his hand against the king. Solomon built the Millo, and closed up the breach of the city of David his father". (1 K. 11: 27)

He and his followers raged against the tyranny of Solomon, regarding it as the embodiment of all that kingship ought not to be. They abominated the principles of dynastic succession of the house of David and the state as a divine institution.

The promotion of the "house of Joseph" to leadership was fertile ground for political ambition and religious opposition. It was the claims for the old rights of the ten or eleven tribes of the north against the one dominant centre of Judah, representing a smaller part of the population. The traditional separatism, inheritance of the tribal past, had not been eradicated by the monarchy.

> "And at that time, when Jeroboam went out of Jerusalem, the prophet Ahijah the Shilonite found him on the road. Now Ahijah had clad himself with a new garment; and the two of them were alone in the open country. Then Ahijah laid hold of the new garment that was on him, and tore it into twelve pieces. And he said to Jeroboam, 'Take for yourself ten pieces; for thus says the Lord, the God of Israel, 'Behold, I am about to tear the kingdom from the hand of Solomon, and will give you ten tribes (but he shall have one tribe, for the sake of my servant David and for the sake of Jerusalem, the city which I have chosen out of all the tribes of Israel'". (1 K. 11: 29–32)

The symbolic tearing of the garment into twelve pieces, giving ten to Jeroboam and reserving but two for the House of David was prophetic of trouble in the social and political sphere. Jeroboam was preparing for the moment of crisis for David's house. When in the 24th year of Solomon's reign his plotting became known, Jeroboam fled to Egypt where Shishak had become Pharaoh of the 22nd dynasty. The change of dynasty had brought a change of policy. This king lent a hand to all Solomon's enemies, within and without the house of David, so as to undermine the Israelite state and dominate it. Jeroboam was held in reserve by his new ally for future eventualities.

Added to all of these disturbing factors, Solomon had permitted a situation to arise that was bound to bring about serious religious tension.

> "Now King Solomon loved many foreign women: the daughter of Pharaoh, and Moabite, Ammonite, Edomite, Sidonian, and Hittite women". (1 K. 11: 1)
> "Then Solomon built a high place for Chemosh the abomination of Moab, and for Molech the abomination of the Ammonites, on the mountain east of Jerusalem. And so he did for all his foreign wives, who burned incense and sacrificed to their gods". (1 K. 11: 7–8)

The religious crisis was blamed on Solomon's foreign wives who wanted to worship their native deities, and for whom shrines were built on the Mt. of Olives east of Jerusalem. Solomon's sanctioning of many alien cults in Jerusalem side by side with the Temple, was the first stage in a long process of dilution and perversion of the traditional faith, and the amalgamation with it of incompatible foreign elements.

In the dispute the priests of the Temple were backed by the upholders of the old faith. They openly condemned Solomon's policy of tolerance and religious compromise which had been dictated by tactical and political considerations:

> "And the Lord was angry with Solomon, because his heart had turned away from the Lord, the God of Israel, who had appeared to him twice, and had commanded him concerning this thing, that he should not go after other gods; but he did not keep what the Lord commanded". (1 K. 11: 9–10)

This is the testimony of his opponents at the time and of later historians. It reflects the unease on the eve of the turning point in Israel's political and spiritual career.

THE SONG OF SONGS

The thrilling anticipation, the rapturous delights and the exquisite torments of shepherds and shepherdesses and rustic lovers is the theme of the Song of Songs. Its setting is the blossoming meadows and vineyards of Israel at the coming of spring. The literary splendour of the lyrics, both in the love poems and in the descriptions of nature is overpowering and instilled with a tenderness beyond anything in the poetic compositions of the Bible. Truly Oriental in its native and spontaneous freedom and imagery, it expresses throughout in its lovers' duets, in the song of bride and bridegroom at marriage ceremonies, a fundamental Hebraic feeling of the unalloyed wonder and the essential rightness of the "way of a man with a maid". Its audience was of course men and women in the villages and towns who loved life and its simple pleasures.

VARIOUS INTERPRETATIONS

Solomon himself was a patron of literature and the arts, and it is no accident that his name became intimately connected with the classic Hebrew Song of Songs, Proverbs and Ecclesiastes. But there is no reason to think that this book, any more than the other collections, goes back to the famous king.

These rural songs were circulated orally long before they were canonized. The composition found a place in the sacred canon Scriptures only through the allegorical interpretation of Rabbi Akibah (1st–2nd century A.D.) who detected a deeper meaning under the plain sense of the book. The lover and his beloved became identified with God and his beloved Israel, an interpretation adopted by the Christian Church. But it needs no apology for its secular character and the rabbis of the Talmud admitted that young people were not able to appreciate its hidden meaning and sang it "as a kind of secular song".

The work has been dramatized in different ways by interpreters, one theory basing it on the love of Solomon for the beautiful Abishag, who gave David warmth in his last days. But the collection of poems has no plot and no named characters, and there is no evidence that the Hebrews ever had a drama. It is regarded by many as an anthology of popular love songs dating from the earlier half of the third century. There are also various theories about the time of its composition in the present form, the process of its formation. What matters most is the *folkloric element* permeating it.

FAMILIAR ENVIRONMENT

A proper understanding of the lyrics must be sought in the actual familiar environment of bride and bridegroom in eternal Israel.

When applied to the work, form criticism reveals from twenty-five to thirty poems with the common theme of love. It is most significant that scholars and modern Israelis living in the environment itself, found striking parallels between the biblical songs and modern ones at Arab marriage festivals in Palestine and Syria, both in the expression of ideas and images and the grouping of words. The sensuous descriptions of physical beauty characteristic of the Song were present in the Arab compositions. This lends weight to the theory that the Song of Songs is an anthology of popular lyrics, spring and harvest songs, as well as sword dances, some of which had been sung at wedding ceremonies from time immemorial. They have in common many of the mores and literary forms prevalent in Semitic rustic society, which changed little until the last century. They provide the "situation in life" of many unforgettable lyrics of the Song. The correctness of this method of interpreting the book by reference to the familiar native environment is further confirmed by a comparison of Arab folklore poetry with ancient Egyptian and Assyrian love poems.

Here is a folk literature sprung from the peasant heart of Israel, redolent with the flavour of the native earth, intoxicating as the bloom of spring.

In keeping with the simple and broad interpretation of the biblical lyrics, opposite them we give well known traditional Palestinian and Syrian Arab lyrics which express similar ideas and figures of speech. The analogy is not drawn further.

A Serenade in the Springtime

"The voice of my beloved!
   Behold, he comes,
leaping upon the mountains,
    bounding over the hills". (Song 2:8)

"My beloved is like a gazelle,
    or a young stag.
Behold there he stands
    behind our wall,
gazing in at the windows
    looking through the lattice". (Song 2:9)
"for lo, the winter is past,
    the rain is over and gone". (Song 2:11)

"The flowers appear on the earth,
    the time of singing has come,
and the voice of the turtledove
    is heard in our land". (Song 2:12)

"The fig tree puts forth its figs,
    and the vines are in blossom;
    they give forth fragrance.
Arise, my love, my fair one,
    and come away.
O my dove, in the clefts of the rock,
    in the covert of the cliff,
let me see your face,
    let me hear your voice,
for your voice is sweet,
    and your face is comely". (Song 2:13–14)

Palestinian Arab Lyrics

"look, O my eyes my beloved is standing
outside, and his shock of hair is waving ...."

"The splendour has fled,
has passed away and gone!" (Beduin song)

"O my beloved, who are asleep;
the roses, in the flower-garden have budded".
. . . .
"I went up the hill in search of my bird".

"Cheer up, you, we have brought your dove,
. . . .
"We have brought your cousin,
we have brought your kinswoman".

At the harvesting of fruits

Song of Songs

"Let us go out early to the vineyards,
    and see whether the vines have budded,
whether the grape blossoms have opened

Palestinian Arab Lyrics

Gazelle. Egyptian ivory statuette of the 14th century. The base is painted to depict a desert crag, with desert flora.

"I compare you, my love, to a mare of Pharaoh's chariots" (1:9). *Egyptian painting of an Asiatic bringing a horse as a gift. (14th century).*

and the pomegranates are in bloom.
There I will give you my love". (Song 7:12)

"In the morning one plucks
the pomegranates of her breasts..

Love's irresistible power

The Song of Songs reaches its climax and deserves a place of honour among the best poetry of all times. Nowhere has this divine passion been more beautifully described than in the words with which a bride addresses her beloved as she enters his threshold:

"Set me as a seal upon your heart,
  as a seal upon your arm;
for love is strong as death,
  jealousy is cruel as the grave.
Its flashes are flashes of fire,
  a most vehement flame.
Many waters cannot quench love,
  neither can floods drown it.

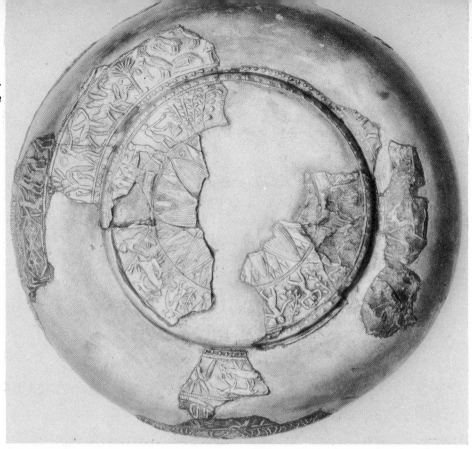

Harvesting of fruit. Egyptian metalwork of the 13th century

Women dance as they beat upon hand-drums. Men step in rhythm with upraised arms. Little girls clap castanets.

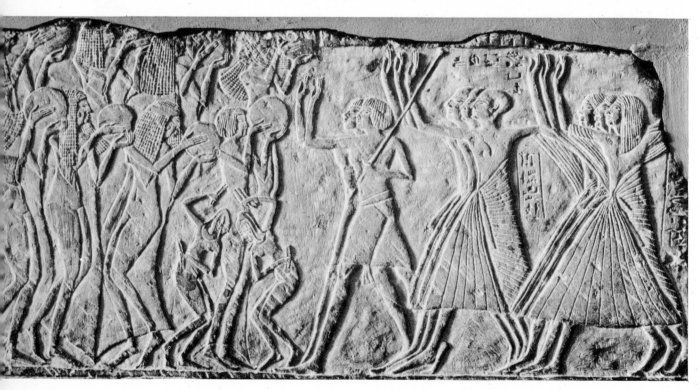

If a man offered for love
all the wealth of his house,
it would be utterly scorned". (8: 6–7)

The sword dances

One of the most significant parts of the final ceremony at Arab village weddings (at which ancient customs may have been preserved), is the sword dance, accompanied by fencing. In some parts of Palestine this was danced by the bridegroom; in some places the bride also took part. The primary purpose is to exhibit the physical prowess and endurance of the bridegroom or the bride. Several examples appear in the Song of Songs:

"Return, return, O Shulammite,
    return, return, that we may look upon you.
Why should you look upon the Shulammite,
    as upon a dance before two armies?" (6: 13)

(the alternative version of the last line: the camp of war dance).

A sword dance at wedding ceremonies

"My beloved is all radiant and ruddy,
    distinguished among ten thousand". (5:10)

"Your neck is like the tower of David,
    built for an arsenal,
whereon hang a thousand bucklers,
    all of them shields of warriors". (4:4)

"I only want a handsome
    man of good stature"
....
"As slim as a lance with a houri cheek".

"What a slim young man,
    (and his slimness suits him)".
....
"He has a mouth (like) a gold ring,
    set with pearls.........."

Dance songs

Such songs are recited at the popular festival gatherings of the peasants accompanying the "dabke" dance.

"For sweet is thy voice........"

"O you with the loosened braid,
Your speech is coquetry and prattle".

Songs at wedding ceremonies

"His eyes are like doves
    beside springs of water,
bathed in milk,
    fitly set". (5:12)

"His speech is most sweet,
    and he is altogether desirable.
This is my beloved and this is my friend,
    O daughters of Jerusalem". (5:16)

"Two doves went out
    strolling from this pool
    to that spring".

"You are all beauty,
You are beauty itself".

Girls dancing to music. Egyptian painting.

Love lyrics

"I say I will climb the palm tree
    and lay hold of its branches.
Oh, may your breasts be like clusters of the vine,
    and the scent of your breath like apples." (7:8)

"And your kisses like the best wine
    that goes down smoothly,
    gliding over lips and teeth". (7: 9)

"I am a rose of Sharon,
    a lily of the valleys". (2: 1)

"A fair one like a poplar tree... (from a Beduin "dabke")
    (A man of fine stature is likened to a palm tree).
"O mother look at his tall stature and
(so) the virgins have sung him".
. . . .
"O you have loaded the grapes (breasts), above
    the grapes there are apples (cheeks).
I stretched out my hands
    for the pomegranates
But their fair owner told me:
    It is forbidden".
. . . .
Her palate is crystal sugar.

A striking similarity is found in a Kurdish ditty from the Euphrates:

"O Addule, you come along there, all scented with roses and tulips".

"My beloved is mine and I am his,
    he pastures his flock among the lilies". (2:16)

"O, were I buried beneath them,
    Between jasmin and sweet basil".

"... the smell of thine ointments" Small stone cosmetic container from Megiddo.

"*From the top of Shenir and Hermon*" (S. 4: 8). Mount Hermon seen from the east.

*"Thy cheeks are comely with rows of jewels,
thy neck with chains of gold".* (S. 1: 10)

The mountains of spices

"Make haste, my beloved,
  and be like a gazelle
  or a young stag
  upon the mountains of spices". (8:14).

In modern Israel these lyrics have become popular again among the people, emphasis being placed on nature's beauty and the love theme. They are not an accompaniment of wedding ceremonies.

"I will climb the palm tree". (S. 7: 8)

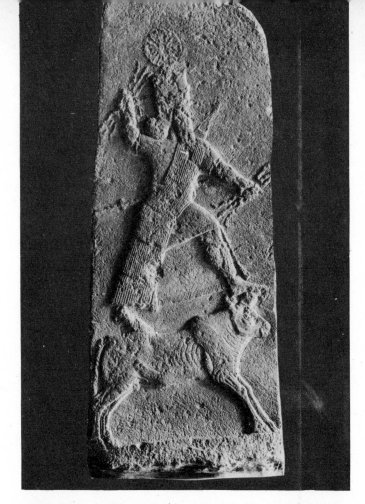

The storm-god Hadad, called Baal in Canaan, standing on a young bull, the symbol of fertility and power; from Arslan-Tash northern Syria, 8th century. This may be a representation of the contemporary cult of the golden "calves" (bulls) in Israel.

CHAPTER XIV

THE DIVIDED KINGDOM

THE BIBLICAL PERSPECTIVE

The editor of the Book of Kings began his work with the reign of Solomon. He recorded it in such a way that it would have a message for the people of his own time, that of the late monarchy. The sources from which he worked were the annals of "The Book of Acts of Solomon"; a biography of Solomon; and other material which originated in Judea and northern Israel. All of this he formed into a thesis meant to drive home certain great religious truths.

He saw in Solomon's reign an important step taken towards the religious ideals of the later monarchy, namely the suppression of the local sanctuaries and image-worship, and the centralization of sacrificial worship at Jerusalem. Recognizing the importance of the human values necessary for these advances, the editor emphasized that Solomon had always pursued wisdom which, together with his vision, his worldly knowledge and his gift for diplomacy had enabled him to administer the realm brilliantly, and to bring about its material development. But the seeds of spiritual retrogression had also been planted by Solomon's love of foreign wives, his toleration of their cults, and his ostentation. For this departure from wisdom, Solomon was punished through the instrumentality of his three enemies: Hadad the Edomite, Rezon the Aramean and Jeroboam the Ephraimite. The theme of reward and punishment for mistakes and sins committed applied not only to Solomon, who was a benefactor of religion, but also to the northern kingdom and even to the Judean state. The editors of Kings and Chronicles warned their readers emphatically that sin brings punishment and that rectitude and faith are eventually victorious. This view permeates the historiography of the period, brilliant as it was, and in advance of the times.

Patriotic members of the Judean kingdom and loyal subjects of the Davidic dynasty, the compilers viewed with obvious bias the events leading to the establishment of the northern Israel monarchy. To them the northern kingdom was spiritually moribund from the moment it rejected the Davidic dynasty and the official worship at the Temple. From that angle they had not the perspective of the modern historian, and could not see the complete picture of the great trends which would follow the united monarchy. The parallel story of the Book of II Chronicles does little to supplement the Book of Kings. We gain some knowledge of the religious and social developments of the period mainly from the writings of the great prophets of the eighth century, though they were also subjective in their views. Fortunately, archaeological discoveries and the inscriptions found in Assyria, Egypt, Phoenicia, eastern and western Palestine make it possible to reconstruct the overall picture on a more scientific basis in the spirit in which they were recorded.

They enable us to estimate the social, political and religious motives and movements which determined the lines upon which the national life progressed, both in Judea and in northern Israel, during the transition period after Solomon's death. Moreover, from the foreign inscriptions we can gauge the relationship of the Israelites to neighbouring nations. This is of paramount importance after the transition period and the dividing of the kingdom (described up to 1 K. 12). A characteristic feature of this historiography is that the story of each reign was fitted into a rigid framework of set literary formulas and conventional chronologies. But in the overall picture, we can, with outside contemporary evidence discern dynamic elements of life within this conventional literary construction.

REHOBOAM

"Rehoboam went to Shechem, for all Israel had come to Shechem to make him king. And when Jeroboam the son of Nebat heard of it (for he was still in Egypt, whither he had fled from King Solomon), then Jeroboam returned from Egypt. And they sent and called him; and Jeroboam and all the assembly of Israel came and said to Rehoboam, 'Your father made our yoke heavy. Now therefore lighten the hard service of your father and his heavy yoke upon us, and we will serve you'. He said to them, 'Depart for three days, then come again to me'. So the people went away". (1 K. 12: 1–5)

Rehoboam ascended his father's throne in Jerusalem by right of succession and without any discusion. But the matter was viewed differently by the northern Israelites. Rehoboam had to go north to Shechem, for an important part of the nation regarded the traditional shrine of Mount Gerizim as the true centre rather than Jerusalem. The elders of the tribes gathered there—and not in Jerusalem— to "make him king": namely to discuss with him under conditions suitable to themselves the matter of his succession. The feeling that there had to be a covenant between the ruler and the ruled persisted and a king, before being truly acclaimed, had either to prove himself by deed or to lay down a platform acceptable to the people. The elders of Israel had accepted David as Saul's successor under the convincing influence of Abner, and Solomon had followed David without discussion in the light of his father's tremendous prestige. In fact the elders had mixed feelings at least toward "the City of David" and its dynasty. They urged Rehoboam to reply mildly to the people:

"And they said to him, 'If you will be a servant to this people today and serve them, and speak good words to them when you answer them, then they will be your servants for ever' ". (1 K. 12: 7)

But Rehoboam turned to his young and arrogant entourage, failing to realize the gravity of the situation, and he insisted on maintaining, even more strictly than his father, the system of indentured labour:

"And the king answered the people harshly, and forsaking the counsel which the old men had given him, he spoke to them according to the counsel of the young men, saying, 'My father made your yoke heavy, but I will add to your yoke; my father chastised you with whips, but I will chastise you with scorpions . So the king did not hearken to the people; for it was a turn of affairs brought about by the Lord that he might fulfil his word, which the Lord spoke by Ahijah the Shilonite to Jeroboam the son of Nebat". (1 K. 12: 13-15)

The point of the narrator's story is that Yahweh, the master of history, had influenced Rehoboam to misjudge the situation because he wanted to bring about the revolutionary upheaval through Jeroboam's instrumentality, thus carrying out the destiny appointed for each of them. This is why the chronicler preceded the narration of the crucial events at Shechem by the story of how the prophet Ahijah had previously met with Jeroboam, rending his garment, and giving him ten pieces as a symbolic token of the rending of the kingdom and Jeroboam's future rule over ten of the tribes. Jeroboam, who had returned from exile in Egypt, took part in the negotiations (this is also testified by the parallel account in Chron. 10: 13). The dissatisfied northern tribes thereupon deserted Rehoboam:

"And when all Israel saw that the king did not
hearken to them, the people answered the king,
'What portion have we in David?
'We have no inheritance in the son of Jesse.
To your tents, O Israel!
Look now to your own house, David'.
So Israel departed to their tents". (1 K. 12: 16)

They summoned Jeroboam to a council to interrogate him and exact from him a new covenant. They then chose him for their first king (930 B.C.E.). Northern Israel, as a national entity, was never to rejoin the house of David, which continued to reign in Judah only.

"Then King Rehoboam sent Adoram, who was taskmaster over the forced labor, and all Israel stoned him to death with stones. And King Rehoboam made haste to mount his chariot, to flee to Jerusalem. So Israel has been in rebellion against the house of David to this day". (1 K. 12: 18-19)

Thus does the biblical editor express his verdict. His sympathies, as we know, are purely Judean and he must be read accordingly. The nation's chance of regaining the political strength which David had achieved for it, of remaining master of its own national destiny, was shattered for more than five centuries. It was only regained by the restoration of the remnants of both Judah and northern Israel.

THE NATURE OF THE SANCTUARIES OF BETHEL AND DAN

"And Jeroboam said in his heart, 'Now the kingdom will turn back to the house of David; if this people go up to offer sacrifices in the house of the Lord at Jerusalem, then the heart of this people will turn again to their lord, to Rehoboam king of Judah, and they will kill me and return to Rehoboam king of Judah'. So the king took counsel, and made two calves of gold. And he said to the people, 'You have gone up to Jerusalem long enough. Behold your gods, O Israel, who brought you up out of the land of Egypt'. And he set one in Bethel, and the other he put in Dan. And this thing became a sin, for the people went to the one at Bethel and to the other as far as Dan. He also made houses on high places, and appointed priests from among all the people, who were not of the Levites. And Jeroboam appointed a feast on the fifteenth day of the eighth month like the feast that was in Judah, and he offered sacrifices upon the altar; so he did in Bethel, sacrificing to the calves that he had made. And he placed in Bethel the priests of the high places that he had made. (1K . 12: 26-32)

The editor, who lived in the days of the later monarchy, paints Jeroboam as an irreligious and self-seeking usurper. He does so because, in his day, it was taken for granted that Jerusalem was the central sanctuary. But the concept of a central and single sanctuary arose only in the days of the late monarchy. Nonetheless he evaluated Judean kings according to their devotion to this sanctuary. The northern kings were bad "a priori" because they worshipped outside of the borders of Judah.

He describes the golden "calves" (a derogatory Hebrew expression for bulls), erected by Jeroboam at the northern sanctuaries as symbols of sheer idolatry. This is a moot point considering our new insight into those times.

From the point of view of the northerners, there is a kernel of historical fact underlying the partisan statements of the Bible. Jeroboam had to prevent his subjects from renewing their contacts with Judah, for Israelites continued to worship in the Temple which was considerably more impressive than any other shrine in the land. Furthermore, he gave his subjects exactly what their ancient traditions demanded: royal sanctuaries of their own, maintained at royal expense. To them, Solomon's Temple was a reminder of their forced and unwilling labour; its symbolism was evidence of Solomon's foreign proclivities beyond their rustic notions. On the other hand, Bethel had been holy since patriarchal times; its traditions and those of Jacob's altar had been preserved there. Holy places such as Bethel and Dan had been cultic centres to all worshippers of Yahweh, since the days of the patriarchs and the Judges and Jeroboam had no wish to flout their legitimacy. From political necessity, he acted as the national priest, strengthened the shrines and furthered the royal cult, just as David and Solomon had hallowed the royal cult of Zion. We know that the Judeans regarded them as tainted shrines and the religion practised there as the worst kind of apostasy. Is this the true verdict?

Jeroboam, himself a religious man, tried to counteract the political influence of the Temple by reviving earlier Israelite practices, prevailing since the days of the tribal league, where Yahweh was represented, according to F.W. Albright "as an invisible presence standing on a young bull". In the ancient cult and, probably, in the story of Aaron and the "golden calf" in the desert, the bull was the symbol whereby Yahweh was represented as the god of physical force (cf. Ex. 32:1–6). In the Holy of Holies of the Temple, Yahweh's invisible presence was seated on a throne borne by "cherubim" or semi-human and semi-animal symbols; (as illustrated by decorations of the period in the previous chapter). Scholars ask whether Jeroboam believed that the golden bull was actually a representation of Yahweh when he said: 'Behold thy God, O Israel, who brought you up out of the land of Egypt" or whether he believed he was invisibly riding or seated upon the back of a bull, according to a notion somewhat similar to Solomon's and apparently borrowed for his Temple. Israel's neighbours and the people who had assimilated into Israel were accustomed to represent Baal, the symbol of strength, as standing upon the back of animals or on thrones borne on animals. The archaeological evidence helps us to a clearer answer from contemporary and earlier parallels in the Near East illustrated below.

The answer seems to be somewhere between the two alternatives. The prophets and later writers accused Jeroboam of plain idolatry and bull worship because the representations of the deity at the sanctuaries of Bethel and Dan must have borne a resemblance to those of the Phoenician Baals. But their meaning for the worshippers of Yahweh may have been closer to the conception of the mysterious cherubim in Jerusalem, which they could not see or misconceive. They may have been worshipping Yahweh according to their lights. The objects worshipped were not intended as idols, but as symbols of Yahweh. In any case, the Baals of the Canaanites (and Phoenicians) were not local Baals but high gods of cosmic scope and cosmic function. We do not know how these Baals or the great storm god differed from the ancient beliefs of the Hebrews before the Israelite cult underwent, in the days of the Prophets, gradual spiritualization and demythologization. But it is not surprising that the cult of the principal deity of the Near East had been diffused in Israel in the earlier days of the amalgamation of the two races in Canaan.

In other words while the theology of the Temple was based on the principle of a covenant with the "anointed" king of David's house, the northern Israelites seem to have stressed the ancient covenant of Sinai. Jeroboam, as Joshua had done at the Shechem covenant, stressed again the age-old formula and reminder of the God of Sinai who brought his people "up out of the land of Egypt".

"For the Levites left their common lands and their holdings and came to Judah and Jerusalem, because Jeroboam and his sons cast them out from serving as priests of the Lord, and he appointed his own priests for the high places, and for the satyrs, and for the calves which he had made". (2 Chr. 11: 14–15)

This fact is pointed out as one of the sins of Jeroboam's regime. As he had sent away the Levites who had been public servants since David's time, both for cultic and administrative functions, he had then to augment the priests and public servants from among the laity.

Ritual was not yet restricted to the tribe of Levi. In the old days, the Levites seem to have formed guilds, similar to the musicians' guilds of Solomon's reign, and they qualified according to their proficiency in performing sacrificial rituals, providing oracles and teaching the Law of Yahweh. They were dedicated people who forsook home and parents to devote themselves to these services. When later they were given exclusive recognition in Israel and Judah, the hereditary and hallowed character of the priesthood became established. This situation is reflected in the portions of Deuteronomy which belong to the later monarchy (Deut. 33).

Jeroboam also changed the date of the harvest festival (Succoth) to a time when crops were actually gathered, roughly thirty days later than that observed in Judah. It seems obvious that posterity passed an adverse judgement upon a man who dared to withstand a king's tyranny and devoted his life to what, at the time, seemed best for his people.

Though Jeroboam stands condemned as an idol worshipper, the biblical record let slip an item which illustrates his deep religious sense in appealing to Ahijah, a true prophet of Yahweh:

> "At that time Abijah the son of Jeroboam fell sick. And Jeroboam said to his wife, 'Arise, and disguise yourself, that it be not known that you are the wife of Jeroboam, and go to Shiloh; behold, Ahijah the prophet is there, who said of me that I should be king over this people. Take with you ten loaves, some cakes, and a jar of honey, and go to him; he will tell you what shall happen to the child.' " (1 K. 14: 1–3)

The oracle was unfavourable and the boy died. Ahijah also predicted dreadful disasters for Israel because of Jeroboam's erection of the royal sanctuaries. That the Ark of the Covenant was the sole place of Yahweh's presence for all Israel, was apparently at the root of the pure tradition supported by the prophet. But the kings of the new Israel ignored this principle. In this sense even in their own times they represented, in the opinion of the Judean editors, a lower religious level than the kings of Judah. That, in any event, was the dominant feature of the internal policy of the kings of Israel vis a vis Judah.

By adopting an antagonistic stand towards the kings of Israel, late chroniclers could hardly give us a real history. Their characterizations of them are monotonously negative and they refer the reader for further details to "the memoirs of the Kings of Judah and Israel", since lost.

SHISHAK INVADES PALESTINE

Under Rehoboam, the kingdom of Judah retained only Judea and the territory of Benjamin immediately north of Jerusalem; of David's conquests only Edom remained. Israel had retained all the other eleven administrative districts organized by Solomon, namely the rich areas of Ephraim, Samaria, the coastland and the valleys, Galilee, the districts east of Jordan and the vassal lands of Moab and Ammon. The relations between the two kingdoms were unfriendly, with Judah trying to attract pilgrims to Jerusalem. Politically, both kingdoms were at a serious disadvantage, but Judah was the poorer of the two.

Golden bracelet, inlaid with precious stones, which belonged to Shoshenk.

In the fifth year of Rehoboam's reign both Judah and Israel were invaded by Shoshenk I, founder of the 22nd Egyptian dynasty, and a former ally of Jeroboam when he sought political exile in Egypt:

"In the fifth year of King Rehoboam, Shishak king of Egypt came up against Jerusalem". (1 K. 14: 25)

This tale and the parallel version in 2 Chr. 12:9 gives the impression of a swift raid. Rehoboam, we are told, bought him off with the palace treasures and even the golden shields of Solomon's bodyguard, thus saving Jerusalem from a siege. Fortunately we have a first-hand additional record of this event available—the inscription of Shoshenk in the temple of Karnak, where he lists the towns both in Judah and Israel, which he raided and destroyed. He started from Gezer, proceeded to Beth-horon and Gibeon, raided towns in Transjordan then recrossed the Jordan and continued his destructive raid through the fortified towns of Beth-shean, Megiddo in the Valley of Esdraelon and returned through the coastal plain to Egypt, destroying settlements in the Negeb on the way.

The raid weakened Judah and shattered its defences and was even more severely felt in Israel, most of whose fortified towns had been conquered. Rehoboam set out to fortify his borders:

"Rehoboam dwelt in Jerusalem, and he built cities for defense in Judah. He built Bethlehem. Etam. Tekoa". (2 Chr. 11: 5- 6).

"He made the fortresses strong, and put commanders in them, and stores of food, oil, and wine. And he put shields and spears in all the cities, and made them very strong. So he held Judah and and Benjamin". (2 Chr. 11: 11–12)

REHOBOAM'S EXPANSIONIST AMBITIONS

Rehoboam fortified the cities of the plain and the Judean hills that lay along the roads leading from the west and south to Jerusalem. One of these was Lachish, which was provided with a double wall and a strongly protected gateway. Such cities have been found to have a fortified citadel at the highest point on the mound, forming a defensive enclosure to which the people retreated in time of attack. The northern border remained unprotected, indicating Israel's weak position following the Egyptian raid. This reinforced Rehoboam's ambition to regain Israel territory close to Judah. Judah's influence in these areas grew as the king appointed his son Abijah (Abijam) over the borderland of Benjamin.

Rehoboam was succeeded in Judah by Abijah while Jeroboam continued to reign over Israel. The Judean king had strengthened the army and fortified the outlying towns and could now begin to encroach on neighbouring Israel territory. This led to war between the two. Israel was beaten and lost Bethel, Ephron and Jeshana, namely an important portion of southern Ephraim. Israel was also attacked from the west by the Philistines who occupied Gezer and Gibbethon. These defeats, plus a deterioration in the internal situation, gradually led to a revolutionary upheaval in Israel which brought Jeroboam's dynasty to an end. There followed two generations of sporadic warfare between the second-rate states, reaching no conclusion but further weakening both of them. Jeroboam was succeeded by Nadab and it is reported that he warred with the Philistines. They were no longer dangerous, but frontier fighting with them continued in Israel and Judah for a number of years. While besieging Gibbethon, near Gezer, Nadab was assassinated by Baasha, the commander of the troops, who usurped the throne, and then exterminated the entire house of Jeroboam.

From this point there is a sharp contrast between the continuity and stability of the royal lines of Israel and Judah. Judah continued under one line of kings, whereas in Israel extreme instability and a succession of bloody usurpations led to one dynasty after another. During the long reign of Asa in Judah six kings followed one another in Israel, and the throne changed hands three times in the first five years.

THE FORM AND THE SPIRIT OF THE BOOKS OF I KINGS AND II KINGS

The history of the monarchy both in Judah and in Israel is interpreted by the chronicler of the Book of Kings in the standard terms of the writer's fundamental religious conviction. Yahweh acts to bring His blessing to those who obey Him as prescribed by Deuteronomic law, and brings judgement upon those who flout His will, namely the hallowed ancient traditions. As with the stories of Judges, the historian followed an outline which varies only slightly in the case of each king of Judah or Israel. He begins with the opening of each reign, then synchronizes it with the corresponding king of Israel, or Judah, reigning at the time. He turns the spotlight alternately by cross-reference to the neighbouring king.

This is followed by the facts of his age, duration of reign and, in the case of Israel, the place of his capital. These data are based upon "the Book of the Chronicles of the Kings of Israel" or "the Book of the Chronicles of the Kings of Judah" (since lost), and the compiler refers his audience to these official records for further details. This form of annalistic composition is borrowed from the cuneiform source, the "Babylonian Chronicle" which relates the annals of the Kings of Babylon and Assyria simultaneously. The kings of Judah are evaluated by the compiler in comparison with "David his father". The Kings of Israel are in almost every case censured for the fact that "he did what was evil in the sight of Yahweh, and walked in the way of Jeroboam and his sin which he made Israel to sin"; that is, he instituted official worship at the shrines of Bethel and Dan, thus perpetuating Israelite cultic practices away from Jerusalem. The historian's purpose was to present the lessons of the past as a support for his own viewpoint and he cared little about the secular history of Israel, or even about the provincial cities of Judah. Here and there he gives valuable factual data, as in the case of Rehoboam's extensive fortification programme (2 Chr. 11: 5-12), but other information, for instance Shishak's extensive invasion, is omitted. His chief interest was the Jerusalem cult and priesthood.

The historian plainly tells his readers that if they are interested in other things, they may go to the royal archives: "Now the rest of the acts of — are they not written in the Book of the Chronicles of the Kings of Israel". No trace of these royal annals has been found and fragmentary quotation of their contents survives only in the historian's record in the biblical Books of Kings and Chronicles.

With this critical background, we can survey what happened in the two kingdoms, drawing from the sources mentioned and comparing them with the inscriptions, annals and facts known to archaeology from outside sources.

BAASHA'S DYNASTY AND ASA OF JUDAH

The founder of the second dynasty in Israel, Baasha, was not an Ephraimite, but a resident of Tirzah, north-east of Shechem, which had become the capital. He was not considered a usurper, for he had, like Jeroboam, prophetic designation, in the words of the prophet Hanani:

"Since I exalted you ······ and you have walked in the way of Jeroboam". (1K. 16:2)
....
"Now the rest of the acts of Zimri, and the conspiracy which he made, are they not written in the Book of the Chronicles of the Kings of Israel"? (1 K. 16: 20)

Baasha proceeded to fortify the city of Ramah on his southern border just north of the Judean border, as a defence against Judah and probably as a base for invasion. He blockaded traffic to and from Jerusalem, then gradually reconquered lost territory in Ephraim from the young King Asa of Judah (913–877), who had succeeded Abijah.

Asa of Judah

Judah at this time was enjoying economic well-being but there was also a growth of foreign religious cults. It is possible that since the days of Solomon, Judah had maintained commercial contact with the Tyrian kings, probably through the southern ports of Philistia. As in the past this was accompanied by the popularization of Phoenician cults, luxury and worldliness. Foreign influence must have been strongest among the aristocracy, led by the queen mother, Maacah. While her party was in power foreign pagan rites were free to flourish. These included the sacred prostitution of priests, known as "kedeshim" and priest-

A wall of the ruins of Samaria, the new capital of the Northern Kingdom, built by Omri.

esses, called "kedeshot" (already described), who were reputedly given to immoral practices, even in the Temple. But tension grew and a reaction set in.

Asa succeeded to the throne while still a child and the queen mother, Maacah, acted as regent during the first fifteen years of his reign and after that continued to influence affairs. But as Asa grew into manhood, he supported the priests and the bulk of the rustic people who held to the ancient traditions. He is especially praised for having deposed the queen mother because she had set up an "asherah", a wooden symbol, in honour of the Phoenician goddess Asherah (Astarta). Asa had the queen mother's idol chopped down and burned in the Kidron Valley, below the walls of Jerusalem. He suppressed pagan cults and enforced the traditional worship of Yahweh, first making a covenant to this effect with the assembled people of Jerusalem. His beneficial influence on internal conditions was felt for a long time. Trouble, however, was in store from Egypt and from Israel.

The account of the reign of Asa in 2 Chronicles 14, reports an invasion of Judah in his time by the Cushite Zerah who was helped by the governor of the Egyptian-held territory of Gerar, south of Gaza. Some authorities identify him with the Egyptian Pharaoh Osorkon. Zerah carried his raid as far as the frontier of Mareshah, where he was defeated by Asa, which ended Egyptian interference in Palestine for a century and a half. The Judean king then occupied Gerar. This reintegration of Israelite hegemony promoted the expansion of the Simeon shepherds' clans deep into the Negeb.

The King of Israel, Baasha, was unwilling to regard the frontier as fixed. At the end of his reign he began to fortify the northern approaches to Jerusalem and to threaten Judah's

Pharaoh Osorkon.

capital. Asa, in desperation, turned for help to the Aramean Ben-hadad I of Damascus and used whatever treasure was left in the Temple and palace to buy his aid:

> "Then Asa took all the silver and the gold that were left in the treasures of the house of the Lord and the treasures of the king's house, and gave them into the hands of his servants; and King Asa sent them to Ben-hadad the son of Tabrimmon, the son of Hezion, king of Syria, who dwelt in Damascus, saying, 'Let there be a league between me and you, as between my father and your father: behold, I am sending to you a present of silver and gold; go, break your league with Baasha king of Israel, that he may withdraw from me.' And Ben-hadad hearkened to King Asa, and sent the commanders of his armies against the cities of Israel, and conquered Ijon, Dan, Abel-beth-maacha, and all Chinneroth, with all the land of Naphtali". (1 K. 15: 18–20)

Asa could thus hold his northern towns and strengthen them, imposing total mobilization of the people to build fortifications:

> "Then King Asa made a proclamation to all Judah, none was exempt, and they carried away the stones of Ramah and its timber, with which Baasha had been building; and with them King Asa built Geba of Benjamin and Mizpah". (1 K. 15: 22)

Asa knew that the Arameans had a covenant with Baasha, and he urged them to break it. The Arameans agreed, and took the opportunity to invade Galilee in northern Israel. Asa's policy touched off Israelite-Aramean wars which were to continue for many years.

It encouraged the Arameans to invade northern Transjordan and stimulated rebellion of the vassal territories of Ammon and Moab. With his hands full in the north, Baasha had also to retreat from the fortification works he had started north of Jerusalem. Shortly after, he died and the situation in Israel deteriorated rapidly, His son and sucessor, Elah, while in the army, got drunk and was killed in a rebellion instituted by Zimri, commander of his chariotry. At that time the commander-in-chief of the forces, Omri, was in the field before Gibbethon

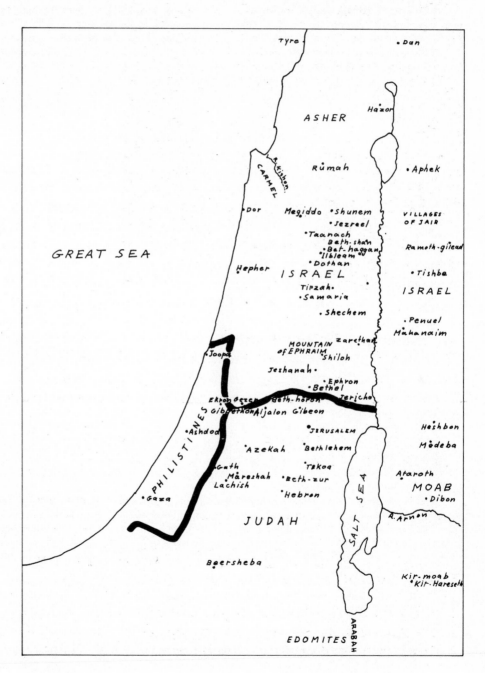

The kingdoms of Judah and Israel.

which the Philistines had attacked. He and the army refused to support Zimri, who realizing that he was lost, set fire to his palace in Tirzah and died in the flames after a reign of seven days. Omri claimed the throne, but the dynastic struggle continued for four years. Another usurper, Tibni, set himself up as ruler so that for some time Israel was divided between the two kings. In the end Omri prevailed and established a strong dynasty which brought back security and stability to Israel. He proved to be one of Israel's ablest kings and, moreover, he was regarded as the avenger of his former master, Elah, and not as a usurper like Zimri.

> "At that time Hanani the seer came to Asa king of Judah, and said to him, 'Because you relied on the king of Syria, and did not rely on the Lord your God, the army of the king of Syria has escaped you. Were not the Ethiopians and the Libyans a huge army with exceedingly many chariots and horsemen? Yet because you relied on the Lord, he gave them into your hand. For the eyes of the Lord run to and fro throughout the whole earth, to show his might in behalf of those whose heart is blameless toward him. You have done foolishly in this; for from now on you will have wars'. Then Asa was angry with the seer, and put him in the stocks, in prison, for he was in a rage with him because of this. And Asa inflicted cruelties upon some of the people at the same time". (2 Chr. 16: 7-10)

JEHOSHAPHAT AND HIS JUDICIAL REFORM

After a reign of thirty-nine years, Asa was succeeded by Jehoshaphat (871–849). In the main he followed his father's policy, purifying the worship at the high places and strengthening Judah. He reorganized the army with its "mighty men of valour", built well-manned fortresses, increased his cavalry and extended Judah's territory to the west (Philistia) and in the western Negeb to the south. He appointed a governor in Edom and revived copper mining in the Arabah and metal refining at Ezion-Gaber, for Judah still controlled the trade route leading south via Akaba. He also attempted to launch a fleet to trade in the Red Sea, but the ships were wrecked before they could sail from Ezion-Gaber.

His greatest achievement, however, was the reform of the territorial administration, carried on in the past mainly through the elders and heads of important families. He divided his kingdom into twelve administrative districts apparently under his own appointees, who supervised the collection of taxes, recruiting and all other matters, resulting in much greater efficiency. Some hold that this system goes back to David's time, but Jehoshaphat revived and improved it:

> "He appointed judges in the land in all the fortified cities of Judah, city by city, and said to the judges, 'Consider what you do, for you judge not for man but for the Lord; he is with you in giving judgment. Now then, let the fear of the Lord be upon you; take heed what you do, for there is no perversion of justice with the Lord our God, or partiality, or taking bribes'.
> Moreover in Jerusalem Jehoshaphat appointed certain Levites and priests and heads of families of Israel, to give judgment for the Lord and to decide disputed cases. They had their seat at Jerusalem. And he charged them: 'Thus you shall do in the fear of the Lord, in faithfulness, and with your whole heart: whenever a case comes to you from your brethren who live in their cities, concerning bloodshed, law or commandment, statutes or ordinances, then you shall instruct them, that they may not incur guilt before the Lord and wrath may not come upon you and your brethren. Thus you shall do, and you will not incur guilt. And behold, Amariah the chief priest is over you in all matters of the Lord; and Zebadiah the son of Ishmael, the governor of the house of Judah, in all the king's matters; and the Levites will serve you as officers. Deal courageously, and may the Lord be with the upright!' ". (2 Chr. 19: 5-11)

Jehoshaphat's reform of the administration of law and justice was especially significant.

On the basis of the ancient administration of customary law by village elders, he established a system whereby judges were appointed by the king in key cities—the walled provincial towns—with a high court of appeal in Jerusalem, headed by the chief priest for religious matters and a "nagid" or tribal elder of Judah for civil questions.

It appears that, since the religious reforms of Asa, the official book of laws, taught in the towns of Judah by the Levites (as officials of the crown), was the "book of the Law of Yahweh". This may have been an early compilation of Deuteronomy.

Following these internal reforms, instituted at the cost of no small effort and by heavy taxation of the population, Judah underwent a complete change in its foreign policy. She joined the political and economic alliance established between Israel and Tyre and the crown prince, Jehoram, married Athaliah, the daughter of Ahab, king of Israel. This new alliance, which brought the Judean kingdom into the orbit of Israel's political life, was a direct result of the phenomenal rise of Omri's new dynasty in Israel.

With the final suspension of the war with Israel, Judah entered a period of relative peace.

CHRONOLOGY OF THE DIVIDED KINGDOM

Chart I

B. C. E.	JUDAH	ISRAEL	MESOPOTAMIA	EGYPT	ARAM
1000	The house of David				
	Rehoboam (930–913)	Jeroboam (930–910)	Assyrian Decline	Shishak 22nd Dynasty c.935–915	Rezon
	Abijah (Abijam) (913–911)	Nadab (910–909)		Invasion of Palestine c.925	
900	Asa (911–871)	Baasha (909–886)			Tab-rimmon
		Elah (886–885)			
		Zimri (7 days)			
		The House of Omri			Ben-hadad
800	Jehoshaphat (871–849)	Omri (885–874)			

THE RISE OF THE HOUSE OF OMRI

"In the thirty-first year of Asa king of Judah, Omri began to reign over Israel, and reigned for twelve years; six years he reigned in Tirzah. He bought the hill of Samaria from Shemer for two talents of silver; and he fortified the hill. and called the name of the city which he built Samaria, after the name of Shemer, the owner of the hill". (1 K. 16: 23–24)

These two verses and the five that follow are all that the chronicler allowed Omri, the sixth king of Israel. But he rightly appreciated and therefore recorded the importance of Omri's founding of the new capital, Shomron (Samaria), the greatest of all the Israelite capitals.

This marked the re-emergence of the kingdom of Israel into the limelight of Near Eastern history (c. 880 B.C.E.) and into a position of leadership in the annals of Israel. Omri bought the mountain on which it stood for two (thousand) talents (approximatedly four thousand dollars), and Samaria became, like the City of Zion in the days of David, the private property and capital of the new king. It was beautifully situated some seven miles north-west of Shechem, the old capital, which, like Tirzah where he had spent his first six years, could not be easily defended. Samaria, on a tall hill in the midst of a fertile basin, was ideally defensible, surrounded by mountains to the east of Mount Ephraim, and at the head of the chief pass giving access to the cities in the valleys of Esdraelon and Jordan and to the Mediterranean coast. The key to the new king's foreign policy and the source of his fame was his alliance with the Phoenicians. Samaria became the new political, economic and cultural centre of northern Israel and maintained a dominant position long after the destruction of the state. Much later Isaiah spoke of it as the proud crown of the Ephraimites.

"Woe to the proud crown of
  the drunkards of Ephraim,
and to the fading flower of its
  glorious beauty,
which is on the head of the rich
  valley of those overcome with wine"! (Isaiah 28: 1)

The ruins left show that the city, begun by Omri and completed by Ahab, had fortifications unequalled in ancient Palestine for excellence of workmanship.

Ruins of Omri's palace in Samaria.

Omri's forceful and capable personality is clearly reflected in his plans and achievements. He was not only the great builder of Samaria, but also the organizer of a strong kingdom. He consolidated the authority and power of his government, re-established friendly relations with neighbouring nations following a score of years of unrest and restored Israel's economic prosperity. All this he achieved within a few years. Had the Judean compilers been writing a secular instead of a religious history of Israel's past and had they preserved narratives about Omri's achievements, comparable to those they preserved about David, they would have laid emphasis on the important features of Omri's role in internal and foreign affairs, detailed below.

The meagre seven verses devoted to his reign leave out data that did not serve their writer's purpose, but these verses when combined with other archaeological information, indicate that he was a king of great ability, especially notable for:

a) His statesmanlike alliance with Tyre.

b) His dynasty's wars with Syria; his concessions to Damascus. His conquest of Moab, which the Bible does not mention but which was recorded by Mesha, king of Moab, on the Moabite stone.

c) His widespread fame. Many Assyrian inscriptions allude later to Israel as "the Land of the house of Omri" or "bit Humri"—"the House of Omri" by the name of the founder of this great dynasty. Its Kings were styled "Mar Humri"—"son of Omri". Long after Jehu's revolution had established a new dynasty, the Assyrians still styled him by that name.

The compiler, however, points to a basic weakness of Omri's dynasty—namely its blindness to the religious and traditional feelings of its subjects, as expressed in the standard formula:

"Omri did what was evil in the sight of the Lord, and did more evil than all who were before him. For he walked in all the way of Jeroboam the son of Nebat, and in the sins which he made Israel to sin, provoking the Lord the God of Israel, to anger by their idols". (1 K. 16: 25–26)

The Alliance with Phoenicia

Omri's greatest achievement was an alliance of peace and friendship with Tyre, capital of the Eastern Mediterranean Canaanite (Phoenician), maritime, commercial power, which had then reached its zenith and was famed as the "merchant of the peoples". This alliance resulted not only from common political and economic interests, but mainly because of the expansion of Phoenician civilization and the growing settlement of Phoenician traders, sailors and craftsmen on the coasts of Palestine. At the same time the sea-borne trade in which the two peoples were closely engaged was also expanding. With so many shared interests it is not surprising that the Phoenician tradition was more strongly preserved in the Northern Kingdom.

The Rise of Aram

The Aramean kingdom of Damascus grew in power in inverse ratio to the weakening of Israelite influence after the days of Solomon. Intermittent warfare with Aram continued for over a century. It had already encroached on eastern Galilee and pressed Omri hard until he was obliged to make considerable concessions and to grant it special trading rights in Samaria:

> "And Ben-hadad said to him, 'The cities which my father took from your father I will restore; and you may establish bazaars for yourself in Damascus, as my father did in Samaria'. And Ahab said, 'I will let you go on these terms'. So he made a covenant with him and let him go". (1 K. 20: 34)

One may gather from this verse that Omri's clashes with Ben-hadad of Damascus were disastrous and that he had had to cede territory to Syria. It is probable that the Arameans continued to expand over certain parts of northern Palestine, south of Damascus, until the days of Ahab.

THE STONE OF MESHA, KING OF MOAB

A monument with one of the most interesting and important Canaanite inscriptions ever found was discovered through the efforts of Clermont-Ganneau in 1868 at Dibon, the capital of Moab, east of the Dead Sea. The Arab natives had broken this slab of black basalt

The Mesha Stone containing an account of the wars between the House of Omri and the Moabites.

into many pieces in order to discover the treasure which they believed must be hidden in it. The pieces were recovered and the stone put together in the Louvre Museum in Paris.

The text, 34 lines long, is written in the first person singular. It begins with a somewhat boastful recital by Mesha of his triumphs over the House of Omri, King of Israel. The monument tells us:

"As for Omri, King of Israel, he humbled Moab many years, for Chemosh (the Moabite God) was angry at his land. And his son (Ahab) followed him and he also said, 'I will humble Moab.' In my time he spoke thus, but I have triumphed over him and over his house, while Israel hath perished for ever."

Mesha further says that Israel had occupied Medeba, north of Dibon, throughout the time of Omri and "half the time of his son. forty years", meaning Omri's grandson as will become clearer from the chronicle of 2 Kings 3:4 ff. The Israelites had not only reconquered part of Moab's territory, but resettled it with followers of the neighbouring god, according to Mesha's record. Moab acknowledged Ahab's sovereignty over Gilead-Gad.

The sequel to Mesha's tale comes in his revolt against the house of Omri after the death of Ahab.

AHAB OF SAMARIA

Though Omri's reign merited only a few conventional verses, the reign of his successor, Ahab (874–852), was considered worthy of more ample treatment, in view of the great events, both internal and external, that then occurred:

"In the thirty-eighth year of Asa king of Judah, Ahab the son of Omri began to reign over Israel, and Ahab the son of Omri reigned over Israel in Samaria twenty-two years. And Ahab the son of Omri did evil in the sight of the Lord more than all that were before him. And as if it had been a light thing for him to walk in the sins of Jeroboam the son of Nebat, he took for wife Jezebel the daughter of Ethbaal king of the Sidonians, and went and served Baal, and worshiped him. He erected an altar for Baal in the house of Baal, which he built in Samaria. And Ahab made an Ashera. Ahab did more to provoke the Lord, the God of Israel, to anger than all the kings of Israel who were before him". (1 K. 16:29–33)

Certainly the editor condemns him even more severely than his predecessors, but he saw fit to combine the story of Ahab and Jezebel with the traditions of the prophets Elijah and Elisha for religious reasons. Ahab's reign served to introduce into the annals of the kings a new theme, that of the championship of the ancient cultic traditions by contemporary prophets.

Ahab's policy followed Omri's in maintaining good relations with his neighbours. He had inherited his expanded kingdom and sought by trade, conquest and alliance to secure a place in the developing constellation of ninth century powers. The house of Omri and Phoenicia had cemented their alliance by a marriage between Jezebel (pronounced Eezebel), daughter of King Ethbaal of Tyre, and the prince Ahab, while he was still acting governor during his father's lifetime. This followed the precedent of Solomon and the daughter of Pharaoh, though the editor is far more critical of the Israelite Ahab, than of Solomon the Judean. The Phoenician princess was followed by a large retinue of merchants, who came as part of the new commercial alliance. She was entitled to the courtesy of her own court and her own shrine, and the Phoenician retinue intended to continue their familiar way of life. Inevitably, this meant trouble.

The overall situation can be judged in the light of the sweeping social and political changes that moulded life in Palestine. The facts indicate the rise of Israel, with Judah in tow, to a higher level of material civilization, with all its attendant problems. The prosperity gained from the alliance with Tyre had given rise to a slow economic revolution in northern Palestine. Following that alliance, Ahab concluded a treaty with Judah, thus replacing the traditional enmity between the two kingdoms by military and commercial cooperation. The new relations were cemented by a marriage between Ahab's half-sister Athaliah, and Jehoram, son of Jehoshaphat, king of Judah. Thus the allied kings controlled the caravan trade route from Tyre to the Red Sea and Arabia, and their prosperity and power grew apace.

AHAB AND JEZEBEL

The new queen, Jezebel, was a woman of pronounced character, proud of her race and highly cultured; she was a priestess of Melkart-Baal in her own right. Capable and wilful, her considerable influence and impact became felt in every phase of the new cosmopolitan life of Samaria, in both religious and political affairs.

The name Eezebel (Isabelle in modern usage) is made up of Ee, an abbreviation of Ahi (my brother) or Abi (my father) and Zebul meaning prince or hierarchic chief, a name befitting the daughter of a Phoenician monarch. When she came to Ahab with her idols and train of priests, he erected a shrine to Melkart in the precincts of the palace, as well as a

Abdubast, a Phoenician king of the Hellenist period dedicates a votive shrine to Astarta. The manner was similar in Jezebel's time.

shrine to Asherah (Astarta goddess of fertility). He sacrificed to Baal in a temple which must have been very imposing judging from later descriptions:

> " 'Now therefore call to me all the prophets of Baal, all his worshipers and all his priests; let none be missing, for I have a great sacrifice to offer to Baal; whoever is missing shall not live'. But Jehu did it with cunning in order to destroy the worshipers of Baal". (2 K. 10: 19)

> "And Jehu sent throughout all Israel; and all the worshipers of Baal came, so that there was not a man left who did not come. And they entered the house of Baal, and the house of Baal was filled from one end to the other. He said to him who was in charge of the wardrobe, 'Bring out the vestments for all the worshipers of Baal'. So he brought out the vestments for them". (2 K. 10:21–22)

> " 'Now therefore send and gather all Israel to me at Mount Carmel, and the four hundred and fifty prophets of Baal and the four hundred prophets of Asherah, who eat at Jezebel's table' ". (2 K. 18:19)

> "He did what was evil in the sight of the Lord, though not like his father and mother, for he put away the pillar of Baal which his father had made". (2 K. 3:2)

Jezebel was no simple devotee. She appears to have been familiar with the secrets of the cult of Astarta (they are called in the Ugarite tablets "Athrat Z'rm", Astarta of the Tyrians):

> "And when Joram saw Jehu, he said 'Is it peace, Jehu?' He answered, 'What peace can there be, so long as the harlotries and the sorceries of your mother Jezebel are so many?' " (2 K. 9: 22)

A new cult had thus arisen in the capital in competition with the national cult of Yahweh. Not only was there a recrudescence of Canaanite Baalism, but a still more rapid fusion of the cult of Yahweh with Baalism was encouraged. The Phoenician deity the Israelites may have worshipped in Samaria did not seem to hold foreign attributes. He was the god of the earth, the bestower of her gifts; a universal god who could just as well be associated with the land of Israel as he could with the land of neighbouring Phoenicia. In the popular religion, Yahweh was the God of war and controller of nature, while the increase of animal and vegetable life was vested in the nature gods of fertility. The encouragement of Baalism is illustrated pointedly by the barbaric Canaanite custom of immolating children on the occasion of the foundation of new buildings as in Jericho which Ahab meant to restore:

> "In his days Hiel of Bethel built Jericho; he laid its foundation at the cost of Abiram his first-born, and set up its gates at the cost of his youngest son Segub, according to the word of the Lord, which he spoke by Joshua the son of Nun". (I K. 16: 34)

The reaction to this fusion of the old faith with Baalism came later under the prompting of new prophets, but dissatisfaction with the court's policy was rife in Ahab's lifetime, as can be seen from Elijah's clashes with the royal house.

Higher Levels of Civilization

Phoenician civilization with its accent on wealth, luxury and pomp influenced Ahab to aim at an autocratic, royal regime, accompanied by a growing bureaucracy and heavy taxation. This regime gave the upper hand to the rising wealthy class and aristocracy and encouraged the slow atrophy of ancient social patterns.

Thus the system of small peasant ownership by freemen achieved for the Israelites under Jeroboam began to give place to a pattern of large estates and practical serfdom, in which the poor found themselves at the mercy of wealthy landowners and merchants. Judging by its programme of building and fortifications, comparable in cost to that of Solomon, Ahab's era must have been one of the most prosperous in Israel's history. He engaged in building activity in Megiddo, in Hazor and elsewhere. Megiddo and its "City of Chariots" is now attributed to him and not to Solomon. This city was destroyed by Shishak's invasion and rebuilt by Ahab.

THE IVORY HOUSES

Evidence of the new trends, imitated from the neighbouring land, is seen in the style and technique of the extensive fortifications of Samaria and the imposing complex of palaces built by Ahab, with their ivory-inlaid furniture and other ivory luxury goods:

> "Now the rest of the acts of Ahab, and all that he did, and the ivory house which he built, and all the cities that he built, are they not written in the Book of the Chronicles of the Kings of Israel?" (I K. 22: 39)

A later prophet, the rustic Amos, scathingly denounced this luxury and the unseemly spectacles that took place in the palace. Ahab had built himself a "summer house" in Samaria and a "winter house" in Jezreel (the valley of Esdraelon, named after it). The first faced the summer breeze and the other faced south to give protection and catch the sun in winter. That type of palace soon became popular among the upper classes:

> " 'I will smite the winter house with the summer house;
> and the houses of ivory shall perish,
> and the great houses shall come to an end', says the Lord". (Amos 3: 15)

Ivory carving of a "cherub" from Ahab's palace in Samaria (left) and horned bull (right).

"Woe to those who are at ease in Zion,
  and to those who feel secure on the mountain of Samaria,
the notable men of the first of the nations,
  to whom the house of Israel come!
Pass over to Calneh, and see:
  and thence go to Hamath the great;
  then go down to Gath of the Philistines.
Are they better than these kingdoms?
  Or is their territory greater than your territory,
O you who put far away the evil day,
  and bring near the seat of violence?
Woe to those who lie upon beds of ivory,
  and stretch themselves upon their couches,
and eat lambs from the flock,
  and calves from the midst of the stall"; (Amos 6: 1-4)

Yet the compilers of Ahab's annals, and the Psalmists, must secretly have admired the style in fashion. Addressing "a song of love" to "the daughter of Tyre", the Psalmist sings:

"daughters of kings are among your ladies of honor;
  at your right hand stands the queen in gold of Ophir.
Hear, O daughter, consider, and incline your ear;
  forget your people and your father's house;
  and the king will desire your beauty.
Since he is your lord, bow to him;"
  the richest of the people with all kinds of wealth.

The bride of a king, from an ivory carving.

The princess is decked in her chamber with gold-woven robes;
  in many-colored robes she is led to the king,
  with her virgin companions, her escort, in her train.
With joy and gladness they are led along
  as they enter the palace of the king.
Instead of your fathers shall be your sons;
  you will make them princes in all the earth". (Psalm 45: 9-16)

Some damaged fragments of the ivories were found while excavating Samaria. The palaces were not built of ivory, but houses were adorned with inlaid panels and jewel boxes and other small objects of artistically carved ivory, such as the woman looking through the window, in the story of Sisera the Canaanite general. See illustrations.

ELIJAH — A TRIAL OF CREEDS

"Now Elijah the Tishbite, of Tishbe in Gilead, said to Ahab, 'As the Lord the God of Israel lives, before whom I stand, there shall be neither dew nor rain these years, except by my word'. And the word of the Lord came to him, 'Depart from here and turn eastward, and hide yourself by the brook Cherith, that is east of the Jordan'". (1 K. 17: 1–3)

"And now you say, 'Go, tell your lord, "Behold Elijah is here"; and he will kill me". (1 K. 18: 14)

Elijah stands out as a great and lonely figure. Coming from Tishbe on the eastern edge of Gilead, austere and ascetic, clad in the girdle or hair mantle of his calling, the prophet represented the most ancient faith of Yahweh of Sinai who brooked no rivals and was ever alert to declare a holy war upon pagan ways.

No mere Nazirite who shunned people and retired from life, a halo of legend enveloped his movements among his people. He found solace in the desert places, emerging in the thick of events as if by magic to do battle for Yahweh. When persecuted by his powerful enemies, he retired into the fastnesses of the wilderness, which had seen the origins of Israel's faith, as though to receive anew, through silent meditation, the spirit of the covenant which was being forgotten. Elijah thus became the embodiment of both the ancient faith and the spirit of rebellion against the attractive Phoenician urban civilization, which must have stirred a section of the Israelites. His works and actions, brooking no compromise, personified the ancient rustic manners, which were the complete negation of the temptations of Canaanite easy-going ways.

Elijah's tradition opens with the trial of creeds on Mt. Carmel. As the record stands, the Elijah stories are placed among the political history of Ahab's reign, to which they have little or no relation. Elijah held himself more or less aloof from practical politics and stuck to religion and morals in defence of Yahweh. His story is interrupted in 1 K. 20, to be taken up again at a later stage of Ahab's reign, the editor apparently contrasting the lives of the great prophet and the king in order to prove a religious lesson.

Following a severe drought lasting two years Elijah faced Ahab in the third with his conviction that the suffering had been brought about by his idolatry.

The drought had come about because Yahweh was offended. He alone could send rain or with-hold it. Only by eradicating idolatry would rain come and the nation be saved. He challenged the king to call for a test of God's trustworthiness as Lord of nature. The trial took place on an ancient altar of Yahweh on Mt. Carmel.

"And Elijah came near to all the people, and said, 'How long will you go limping with two different opinions? If the Lord is God, follow him; but if Baal, then follow him'. And the people did not answer him a word". (1 K. 18: 21)

This is a most revealing statement and an unconscious and objective evaluation of the religious crisis. That the masses held to the ancient beliefs is evident, but the allure of the Canaanite cult was equally powerful. So Elijah challenged the vacillating majority, who — as lazy-minded majorities will — went "limping with two different opinions", and demanded an end to compromise. He then proceeded to re-erect the ancient altar:

"Then Elijah said to the prophets of Baal, 'Choose for yourselves one bull and prepare it first, for you are many; and call on the name of your god, but put no fire to it'. And they took the bull which was given them, and they prepared it, and called on the name of Baal from morning until noon, saying, 'O Baal, answer us!' But there was no voice, and no one answered. And they limped about the altar which they had made. And at noon Elijah mocked them, saying, 'Cry aloud, for he is a god; either he is musing, or he has gone aside, or he is on a journey, or perhaps he is asleep and must be awakened'. And they cried aloud, and cut themselves after their custom with swords and lances, until the blood gushed out upon them. And as midday passed, they raved on until the time of the offering of the oblation, but there was no voice; no one answered, no one heeded". (1 K. 18: 25–29)

"And with the stones he built an altar in the name of the Lord. And he made a trench about the altar, as great as would contain two measures of seed. And he put the wood in order, and cut the bull in pieces and laid it on the wood. And he said, 'Fill four jars with water and pour it on the burnt offering, and on the wood'. And he said, 'Do it a second time'; and they did it a second time. And he said, 'Do it a third time'. and they did it a third time. And the water ran round about the altar, and filled the trench also with water.
And at the time of the offering of the oblation, Elijah the prophet came near and said, 'O Lord, God of Abraham, Isaac, and Israel, let it be known this day that thou art God in Israel, and that I am thy servant, and that I have done all these things at thy word. Answer me, O Lord, answer me, that this people may know that thou, O Lord, art God, and that thou hast turned their hearts back'. Then the fire of the Lord fell, and consumed the burnt offering, and the wood, and the stones, and the dust, and licked up the water that was in the trench. And when all the People saw it, they fell on their faces; and they said, 'The Lord, he is God; the Lord, he is God'. And Elijah said to them, 'Seize the prophets of Baal, let not one of them escape'. And they seized them; and Elijah brought them down to the brook Kishon, and killed them there". (1 K. 18: 32–40)

The story indicates that the altar of Yahweh was an apt symbol of His ancient worship and recognition of Him as sole God in the land, both as an earth deity and as a sky-god (the fire from heaven). The points in dispute between him and the priests and prophets of Baal were just these. They indicate Elijah's mockery of ineffective ritual, of the ceremonial and gods of his opponents and emphasize his position as herald of Yahweh, the giver of rain, functioning as a sky God.

There may also have been uncertainty in people's minds regarding their religion and the attributes of God. But in this episode of the trial of creeds, God's other transcendental attributes as the one universal god were still beyond the ken both of Elijah and of his opponents. The point of Elijah's story, of course, is the wonder of his legendary career, and the nature of his mission to the people at that early stage of prophecy in Israel. His message to the people is summed up in his words and ancient credo:

"He said, 'I have been very jealous for the Lord, the God of hosts; for the people of Israel have forsaken thy covenant, thrown down thy altars, and slain thy prophets with the sword; and I ,even I only, am left; and they seek my life ,to take it away' ". (1 K. 19: 10)

The theme of the story is Elijah's stand for the higher religion against Jezebel, who is described as the arch-enemy, with Ahab her weak companion. The defection of the priests of Baal was followed by severe reprisals from Jezebel, which drove Elijah to flee to the wilderness of Horeb (Sinai).

Ahab and his generation were apparently not imbued with the ancient traditions. Jezebel did not know, or ignored the covenant law. As long as Elijah's kind lived, there could be no reconciliation between the dynamic state and a large number of its citizens. Jezebel may not have set out deliberately to persecute Yahweh's devotees, but as she and her followers felt frustrated, she became enraged and resorted somewhat arrogantly to a policy of active suppression.

It is not easy to discern the historic kernel in Elijah's story, except for the association of his career with Ahab's. The story probably reflects a holy war between the devotees of Yahweh and those of Baal which took place on Mount Carmel with its altar situated on the border between Israel and Phoenicia. It may reflect some forgotten background to the relationship between the two peoples in this area.

Elijah was not of the type of ecstatic prophets like the "sons of the prophets" of Saul's day who went about in numbers. Here was an uncompromising prophet of more ample vision who challenged the absolute power of the king, threatening him with death from social and religious motives. It is due to his character and holiness that the Elijah legend, including his miraculous end, persisted through the ages:

> 'And as they still went on and talked, behold, a chariot of fire and horses of fire separated the two of them. And Elijah went up by a whirlwind into heaven. And Elisha saw it and he cried, 'My father, my father! The chariots of Israel and its horsemen!' And he saw him no more. Then he took hold of his own clothes and rent them in two pieces". (2 K. 2: 11–12)

According to this tradition, he did not die, but vanished mysteriously, the symbols of fiery Sinai still clinging to his memory.

Phoenician records of a later date, coming through a Greek source, relate that Solomon's contemporary, king Hiram, first instituted the ceremony of the awakening of the god Melkart-Baal in Phoenicia. The priests arose early and called on Melkart to awaken from his slumber. Some scholars see an echo of this ceremony in Elijah's taunt to the priests of Baal at the trial on Mt. Carmel (quoted above) that Baal may be asleep or absent on a journey. The ceremony may have been celebrated on Mt. Carmel.

Menander of Ephesus, a late Hellenistic historian, records that a famine of one whole year occurred in the reign of Ethbaal, Ahab's contemporary. He relates that many small farmers lost their lands. They had borrowed from the rich at usurious rates, mortgaging their lands, then forfeiting them. It is likely that similar conditions obtained in Israel, accounting for the dispossession of the poor and the rise of a rich and arrogant middle class.

AHAB'S RESISTANCE TO ARAM

Up to this point in the double story of Ahab and Elijah, Ahab's attitude, with his vacillating allegiance to Yahweh and his toleration of foreign cults, seems equivocal. Where the tale of Elijah's career is interrupted in K. 20, the compilers tell of Ahab's reign from an entirely different angle and Jezebel's compelling personality also seems to recede into the background.

The situation of Israel versus Aram had been an unhappy one since Omri's days. Matters came to a head when Ben-hadad II raided Israel again during a drought period and laid siege to Samaria. Ahab had hesitated about facing Aram in battle and had tried to pacify them with concessions; but now that they were bent on the subjugation of Israel, he decided, after due preparation, to fight it out. Fired by his new confidence, the people rose as one. In the thought of the writer, Ahab was so closely identified with the case of Yahweh, and Yahweh's people, that "a man of God" revealed to Ahab his enemy's plan of battle and he won a brilliant victory at Aphek, on the road to Damascus. The Israelities, in two divisions, which the writer neatly compares to two little flocks of goats, attacked and routed the Arameans.

On Ben-hadad's abject surrender, Ahab did not take his life but negotiated a peace on generous terms. He retrieved lost territory in northern Transjordan and established commercial agencies with traders' rights within the bazaars of Damascus, thus gaining an advantage in the profitable trade with the hinterland and the coast. Instead of reducing Syria to a vassaldom which would have exhausted her, he treated his neighbour (who was of comparable size and strength) mildly.

Ahab's statesmanship won him the reprobation of many people as shown in the opinion expressed by the writer. But he was still due to fight his last battle with Aram to recover the last stretch of Israel territory they held in Gilead. This Ben-hadad may be that very Bar-hadad who set up a stela to Melkart found in Aleppo. Its inscription reads:

An Aramean cavalryman of the 10th century. Stone bas-relief from Tel-Khalaf.

An Aramean prince (or a king?) on an ivory carving from Arslan-Tash.

"The stela which did set up Bar Hadad son of .... King of Aram to his Lord, to Melkart, which (stela) he did vow (to erect) to him (if he answered his prayer) and he hearkened to his voice".

NABOTH'S VINEYARD

The story of Naboth's vineyard illustrates a new trend in the days of Ahab's prosperity. This story brings Elijah back into Ahab's story, this time with the accent on the ethical values of Yahweh.

Naboth, a private citizen and freeholder, owned a vineyard, adjacent to the royal estate. The king requested him to exchange it, but Naboth resisted the king as of right. The king felt deeply frustrated for he could do nothing, according to tradition, against a man who refused to sell an inheritance handed down from his father. Jezebel reacted differently. According to her lights and background, kings had more rights and citizens fewer. She manufactured an accusation of blasphemy, alleging that Naboth had reviled the king, and had it attested by her henchmen, using the king's seal as a warrant for the justice of this trumped-up charge:

"So she wrote letters in Ahab's name and sealed them with his seal, and she sent the letters to the elders and the nobles who dwelt with Naboth in his city. And she wrote in the letters, 'Proclaim a fast, and set Naboth on high among the people; and set two base fellows opposite him, and let them bring a charge against him, saying, "You have cursed God and the king". Then take him out, and stone him to death'. And the men of his city, the elders and the nobles who dwelt in his city, did as Jezebel had sent word to them. As it was written in the letters which she had sent to them, they proclaimed a fast, and set Naboth on high among the people. And the two base fellows came in and sat opposite him; and the base fellows brought a charge against Naboth, in the presence of the people, saying, 'Naboth cursed God and the king'. So they took him outside the city, and stoned him to death with stones. Then they sent to Jezebel, saying, 'Naboth has been stoned; he is dead' ". (1 K. 21: 8–14)

Naboth was stoned to death by the multitude in accordance with a law whereby his property was also forfeited to the crown. Thereupon, the king took possession.

This story was remembered for a long time to come, longer than Ahab's varied career. It was not only a case of miscarriage of justice but it undermined the people's blind faith in the king's rule as the embodiment of the law of the land. The moral drawn is illustrated by Elijah's drastic condemnation and the king's deep repentance. The scene in which the prophet denounced the base cruelty and ruthless avarice of a despotic king is described in unforgettable terms:

" 'Arise, go down to meet Ahab king of Israel, who is in Samaria; behold, he is in the vineyard of Naboth, where he has gone to take possession. And you shall say to him, "Thus says the Lord, 'Have you killed, and also taken possession?' And you shall say to him, "Thus says the Lord: "In the place where dogs licked up the blood of Naboth shall dogs lick your own blood' " ". (1 K. 21: 18–19)

It is difficult to find in all literature a finer picture of the decisive conflict between opposed types of religion and social justice.

THE SHADOW OF ASSYRIA

Assyria appeared as a serious threat on the political horizon of the Near East in the 9th century, during the reign of Ashurnasirpal II (885-859). His formidable fighting machine began a systematic assault on the west and extended Assyrian power to Phoenicia who paid heavily in tribute. He kept clear of Damascus and Israelite territory. This king re-established the ancient Assyrian capital of Calah mentioned in Gen. 10 (Nimrud)

The Battle of Karkar

To the Judean editor of the Book of Kings, the wars of Ahab seem so unimportant that the great Battle of Karkar against Assyria is not even mentioned. But when the inscriptions of Shalmaneser III were deciphered in the middle of the 19th century it was realized that Ahab had participated with other allies in the battle. The account of his participation is of great value for the history of Israel during his reign, first because his was the second largest, although in a technical sense, the strongest force of all the alliance of the Syrian kings who fought Shalmaneser; secondly, because here we have the first certain date in the entire history of Israel that can be checked historically. The Assyrian dates being definite, this synchronism with the biblical story of Ahab is of vital importance for the chronology of Israel.

Finally this evidence of Ahab's wealth of chariots is proof of the strides he had made in strengthening his army, since the days when the Arameans had besieged him in Samaria. He had now risen to a position of great prominence, as witnessed by his chariot city at Megiddo.

Shalmaneser ended the era in which the small nations of Syria and Palestine had only each other to contend with. Since his accession, an annual campaign by the king or his commander-in-chief became a commonplace and a threat. The rulers now forgot their animosities and united against the common foe. Unlike his father Ashurnasirpal, Shalmaneser was ready to expand into Palestine. In the sixth year of his reign he left his capital of Nineveh on an expedition to the west. His march seems to have met no effective resistance until he came to the region of the kingdom of Hamath. Here he met a strong coalition of twelve kings. In June of 853 B.C.E. they did battle at Karkar on the river Orontes in Syria. The Assyrian scribe relates in the name of his king:

"I destroyed, tore down and burned down Karkara, his royal residence. He brought along to help him 1,200 chariots, 1,200 cavalrymen, 20,000 soldiers of Adad-idri (i.e. Ben-hadad) of Damascus, 700 chariots, 700 cavalrymen, 10,000 foot soldiers of Irhulem from Hamath, 2000 chariots, 10,000 foot soldiers of Ahab, the Israelite (list of allies follows including kings from Phoenicia, Cilicia in southeast Asia Minor, Ammon, camel riding Arabians)....... I slew 14,000 of their soldiers with the sword ..... The plain was too small to let all their souls descend into the nether world, the vast field gave out when it came to bury them. With their corpses I spanned the Orontes before there was a bridge."

(Translation from "Ancient Near Eastern Texts" J.B. Pritchard (ed.).

Despite his boastful claims, it appears from other records that the victory was far from decisive and that his advance was checked. Yet later in his reign, when he rewrote his "history", he claimed not 14,000 but 25,000 victims, which shows how little one can trust oriental statistics meant to glorify monarchs rather than to state sober facts.

King Ashurnasirpal II and his cupbearer. From an alabaster slab.

AHAB'S LAST BATTLE

According to an agreement with the Arameans after the battle of Karkar, they had to return to Israel Ramoth-Gilead, which occupied a strategic position on the north-south military and commercial highway running through Transjordan. Ben-hadad renegaded. As Ahab and Jehoshaphat, king of Judah, got together fraternally, the former suggested on the occasion of the latter's visit to Samaria, that they embark on a campaign together to win back Ramoth-Gilead. This time, as on former occasions, Ahab consulted the four hundred prophets that they "inquire first for the word of Yahweh". These prophets, appearing in droves, were apparently a variety of court flatterer and their oracle was whatever they judged would be agreeable to the king:

"Now the king of Israel and Jehoshaphat the king of Judah were sitting on their thrones, arrayed in their robes, at the threshing floor at the entrance of the gate of Samaria; and all the prophets were prophesying before them. And Zedekiah the son of Chenaanah made for himself horns of iron, and said, 'Thus says the Lord, "With these you shall push the Syrians until they are destroyed". 'And all the prophets prophesied so, and said, 'Go up to Ramoth -gilead and triumph; the Lord will give it into the hand of the king' . . . . And the messenger who went to summon Micaiah said to him, 'Behold, the words of the prophets with one accord are favorable to the king; let your word be like the word of one of them, and speak favorably' ". (1 K. 22: 10–13)

The prophets' ringleader, Zedekiah, had performed a symbolic action that was intended to dramatize the inevitable defeat of the Syrians.

Suspicious of the unanimous verdict king Jehoshaphat asked whether all the prophets had been heard. Ahab admitted reluctantly that there was one inspired man, Micaiah son of Imlah, who in the past had consistently prophesied evil of him. The religious interest of the

The prosperity of the time of Ahab is exemplified above all by the luxuriant use of ivory, as attested both in the Bible and in Palestinian and Syrian excavations. Ivory carving of a stag from Arslan-Tash. This style became prevalent at this time in Phoenicia and in Palestine.

The Cow and her Calf. A parallel is provided in Phoenician mythology: Anath is the cow and the calf, whom she tends, is her brother Baal. Ivory carving from Arslan-Tash.

Royal attendant carrying king's arms, on a bas-relief of Ashurnasirpal.

story (1 K 22) is centred in this lonely figure who hints at the different inspiration of false and true prophecy.

The prophet spoke in two oracles. In one he saw a vision of Israel in leaderless rout "scattered upon the mountains as sheep that have no shepherd"; a prediction of the failure of the expedition. The other oracle was a vision of Yahweh presiding over his heavenly court and commissioning "a lying spirit" to fill the prophets with a lying ecstasy because he wanted to ruin the House of Ahab. (The point had not yet been reached where such a stratagem by Yahweh would be unthinkable). Micaiah was sent to jail, pending the outcome, but he enunciated the test of prophecy by saying:

"And Micaiah said, 'If you return in peace, the Lord has not spoken by me'. And he said, 'Hear, all you peoples' !" (1 K. 22: 28)

He refused to compromise and found himself alienated from his fellow prophets. A schism in the prophetic orders had begun, which would never be healed.

The story goes on to relate how Micaiah's oracle was vindicated. The kings went forth to battle, described in vivid detail. Ahab was struck by a stray arrow. Knowing what would happen if this became known he ordered his men to hold him up in his chariot facing the enemy. He bled all day long, his blood staining the chariot throughout. At sundown, when the battle ended, he died, having literally bled to death:

"And about sunset a cry went through the army, 'Every man to his city, and every man to his country!' So the king died, and was brought to Samaria; and they buried the king in Samaria. And they washed the chariot by the pool of Samaria, and the dogs licked up his blood, and the harlots washed themselves in it, according to the word of the Lord which he had spoken". (1 K. 22: 36: 38)

Thus died one who, if greatness be measured by secular standards, was amongst Israel's greatest rulers, but the storyteller, who regarded him as an apostate, notes that the predictions of doom uttered against him by Elijah and Micaiah had come true.

The Shalmaneser Obelisk preserves for us the only contemporary representation of an Israelite figure known from the Bible: Jehu prostrating himself before the Assyrian king. **On** bottom panel are seen: Thirteen Israelites carrying "silver, gold, golden bowls, a golden case, golden tumblers, vessels, a block of tin, a royal staff for a king and wooden "puruhati" — fruit seen on a tray, as described on the inscription. They wear long garments covered with fringed cloaks, pointed soft caps and sandals with upturned toes.

CHAPTER XV

ISRAEL VERSUS ARAM AND ASSYRIA

AHAZIAH IN ISRAEL — JEHOSHAPHAT IN JUDAH

We hear nothing of what Ben-hadad did after the retreat of the joint Israelite and Judean forces from Ramoth-Gilead, and do not know whether he pierced deeper into Israelite territory. Jehoshaphat, king of Judah, had narrowly escaped death in the battle and thereafter acted more independently of Omri's house. Ahaziah, Ahab's son, succeeded his father in this hour of crisis (852–851). He was the eighth king. The fall of the strong Ahab left Israel exposed to outside danger, a fact of which vassals and enemies took immediate advantage. The first to rebel was Mesha, king of Moab, as attested in great detail in his stela. Ahaziah had no time to react for he died from the consequence of a fall "through the lattice in his upper chamber" (2 K. 1:2). Badly hurt, he sought the oracle of the Canaanite shrine of Baal-Zebub (or Baal-Zebul) in Ekron. He then died and was succeeded by his brother Jehoram (851–842).

A spring rain in the highlands of Edom.

In order to subdue Moab once more, Jehoram turned to Jehoshaphat, king of Judah, and obtained his help:

"And he went and sent word to Jehoshaphat king of Judah, 'The king of Moab has rebelled against me; will you go with me to battle against Moab?' And he said, 'I will go; I am as you are, my people as your people, my horses as your horses' ". (2 K. 3:7)

Together with the vassal king of Edom, they set out to attack Moab from the south, following a "circuitous march" by the "way of the wilderness of Edom", where the lack of water was a serious threat to their army.

At this point the prophet Elisha appeared in the ranks. Getting into the prophetic mood by listening to music, he prophesied rain and a successful campaign, then vanished as suddenly as he appeared. The correlation of the stories of the Moabite campaign and the appearance of Elisha was probably made to inculcate respect for the prophet and his office as herald of Yahweh as the only God of Israel, much in the manner of the accounts of the appearance of Elijah or Samuel, in previous narrations.

THE GREAT WRATH OF A GOD

Adopting a scorched earth policy, the three kings attacked the Moabite capital, Kir-hareseth (Kir-Moab). The Moabite king attemped a sortie which was repulsed. He then resorted to an extreme measure to obtain the favour of his god Chemosh:

"Then he took his eldest son who was to reign in his stead, and offered him for a burnt offering upon the wall. And there came great wrath upon Israel; and they withdrew from him and returned to their own land". (2 K. 3: 27)

The sequel to the great wrath that came upon Israel is stated cryptically. This is important not only historically, but also as a further indication of the Hebrew historian's idea of God. It appears, in his interpretation, that Chemosh, his pity aroused by the extreme sacrifice of King Mesha, turned his "great rage against Israel", from Moab to the people who had dared to enter his territory, the territory of the Moabite deity. In this conception, Chemosh holds in Moab the same position as Yahweh in Israel. Both deities are real, their power shown by the strength of their arm. The incident suggests that at that time Israel and Moab were on much the same level of cultural and religious development and that they shared similar concepts of divinity. Just as Yahweh had His land and His people, so Chemosh had his own land and people. The Hebrews may have been seized by a great religious or emotional unease at the sight of Mesha's human sacrifice. They retreated to their own country.

The Moabites not only recovered their land and repaired the damage of the invasion by the building programme outlined in Mesha's stela but, according to that inscription, also occupied other Israelite territory in southern Gilead. In the days of Omri and Ahab, says the inscription on Mesha's stela, Chemosh had been "angry with his servants" and had "afflicted Moab many years", which included the temporary success of Israel; but Chemosh was finally mollified by Mesha's supreme sacrifice and forgave Moab. So their god rescued his people from the hand of Yahweh and Yahweh's subjects. This indicates that rivalry between gods was seen as the source of warfare. Putting war on this religious plane justified its brutality, to which the Bible and other documents of the ancient Near East bear witness. From this point of view the Moabite reverses were clearly due to the anger of the national deity, just as similar events in Israel were ascribed to the wrath or favour of Yahweh. In Mesha's understanding, it was now the wrath of his god Chemosh that visited the Israelites and this may be the significance of his boastful inscription of his deliverance from Israelite rule.

JEHORAM—AHAZIAH

Israelite strength or weakness in Moab is the criterion for judging the strength of Judah in dominating Edom. When Judah, under Jehoshaphat was judged weak, Edom rebelled against Jerusalem. Edom, Moab and Ammon even attempted an invasion of southern Judah, which failed. This was attempted again after Jehoshaphat's death. In the days of his son Jehoram (849–843) Edom shook off Judah's rule and proclaimed itself an independent kingdom.

"In his days Edom revolted from the rule of Judah, and set up a king of their own. Then Jehoram passed over with his commanders and all his chariots, and he rose by night and smote the Edomites who had surrounded him and his chariot commanders. So Edom revolted from the rule of Judah to this day. At that time Libnah also revolted from his rule, because he had forsaken the Lord, the God of his fathers". (2 Chr. 21: 8–10)

The closest relations had been established between Jehoram of Judah and his namesake in Israel. Athaliah, half-sister of Ahab, married Judah's Jehoram. (See Ahab of Samaria in Ch. XIV). Israel was the leader and influenced Judah not only in its foreign policy, but in its religious course. This included the erection of a shrine to Baal which embittered the relations of king and people. Jehoram was a tyrant, his oppression springing apparently from weakness rather than strength. He had started his rule by a bloody family feud:

"Jehoshaphat slept with his fathers, and was buried with his fathers in the city of David; and Jehoram his son reigned in his stead. He had brothers, the sons of Jehoshaphat: Azariah, Jehiel, Zechariah, Azariah, Michael, and Shephatiah; all these were the sons of Jehoshaphat king of Judah. Their father gave them great gifts, of silver, gold, and valuable possessions, together with fortified cities in Judah; but he gave the kingdom to Jehoram, because he was the first-born. When Jehoram had ascended the throne of his father and was established, he slew all his brothers with the sword, and also some of the princes of Judah". (2 Chr. 21: 1–4)

Worse was to come. Jehoram of Judah apparently lost his chariot army in the battle which Syria, Israel and Judah fought against Shalmaneser in 845. Meanwhile, Judah's southern neighbours, the Edomites and Arabs, and the Philistines to the west, invaded the country. The king's sons tried to stem the tide but met with disaster and, except Ahaziah, were all carried off by the victors. When Jehoram returned from Karkar he found Judah a shambles.

JEHORAM, ELISHA AND ARAM

The deterioration of Judah's strength continued in the reign of Ahaziah (843–842) the son of Jehoram and the Israelite princess Athaliah. He joined forces with Jehoram of Israel in 842 to defend Ramoth-Gilead which was menaced by the Aramean usurper Hazael. A former general of Ben-hadad II, Hazael is called the "son of a nobody" by the Assyrians to whom he had eventually to pay tribute (an inscription in Aramaic script of the 9th century was found in Assyria. It is carved on an ivory object and states that it was made "for our Lord Hazael").

The fact that the prophet Elisha was contemporary with Jehoram, king of Israel, and the wars of Aram and Israel, provide a connecting link in Elisha's many–sided mission.

It is stated that Elisha was instrumental in Hazael's usurpation and had predicted it. This was intended as a support for the view that Elisha, as Elijah's successor, was to continue his mission and become God's tool in punishing the house of Omri which had been contaminated by Jezebel and the Baals and, through Athaliah, had also polluted the Davidic house.

One story about Elisha tells how Naaman, a captain of the Aramean army, came to the prophet seeking a cure for leprosy. (2 K. 5: 1–9). He obtained a cure by bathing nine times in the river Jordan and as a result, embraced Elisha's religion. He took back home with him two mule loads of Israel soil, so that he might worship in Damascus on Yahweh's earth, an action which reflects the belief that a national god was to be worshipped on his own soil. Naaman is apparently regarded as an instrument of Yahweh's plan to grant salvation to Aram. More important is a narrative taking Elisha to Damascus:

"Now Elisha came to Damascus. Ben-hadad the king of Syria was sick; and when it was told him, 'The man of God has come here', the king said to Hazael, "Take a present with you and go to meet the man of God, and inquire of the Lord through him, saying, "Shall I recover from this sickness?" ' So Hazael went to meet him, and took a present with him, all kinds of goods of Damascus, forty camel loads. When he came and stood before him, he said, 'Your son Ben-hadad king of Syria has sent me to you, saying, "Shall I recover from this sickness?" ' And Elisha said to him, 'Go, say to him, "You shall certainly recover"; but the Lord has shown me that he shall certainly die.' And he fixed his gaze and stared at him, until he was ashamed. And the man of God wept. And Hazael said, 'Why does my lord weep?' He answered, 'Because I know the evil that you will do to the people of Israel; you will set on fire their fortresses, and you will slay their young men with the sword, and dash in pieces their little ones, and rip up their women with child". And Hazael said, 'What is your servant, who is but a dog, that he should do this great thing?' Elisha answered, 'The Lord has shown me that you are to be king over Syria'. Then he departed from Elisha, and came to his master, who said to him, 'What did Elisha say to you?' And he answered, 'He told me that you would certainly recover". But on the morrow he took the coverlet and dipped it in water and spread it over his face, till he died. And Hazael became king in his stead". (2 K. 8: 7–15)

This story does not mention his anointing Hazael, king of Damascus, but it suggests that, the idea of bringing about Ben-hadad's death was initiated by the prophet. By some people this is seen as indicating a broadening of prophecy to take in international horizons. This is an advance over the older view which made Yahweh an exclusively national god, and may constitute a step in the process whereby Yahweh developed into the God of world history. But it is still a far cry from the writing (classic) prophets, i.e. those who composed special books to record their message.

ELISHA

The continuing tradition of Elijah and Elisha finds expression in the sequel to Elijah's miraculous end:

"Then he took the mantle of Elijah that had fallen from him, and struck the water, saying, Where is the Lord, the God of Elijah?' And when he had struck the water, the water was parted to the one side and to the other; and Elisha went over. Now when the sons of the prophets who were at Jericho saw him over against them, they said, 'The spirit of Elijah rests on Elisha'. And they came to meet him, and bowed to the ground before him". (2 K. 2:14–15)

Elisha's background is rural northern Galilee, and his life is closely connected with the village and city life of his day. He led no hermit's life, like Elijah, and was more elastic in his approach to the people and their rulers. We have seen that this mundane tradition connects him closely with the political developments of his day. However, his real importance lies in his leadership of the prophetic guilds and sectarian elements who stayed on the periphery of social and political life until suddenly inspired to take a leading role in events.

The characteristic feature of Elisha's story is that through him and other devotees of Yahweh, the troubles of Jehoram's reign—the Moabite rebellion, Israel's losses to the Arameans, the siege of Samaria and the years of drought—became linked in the popular mind with his view of them as sanctions from Yahweh for the idolatrous cults which had persisted in the kingdom.

THE RECHABITES

Although the biblical record does not connect Elisha with the Rechabites, there is good reason to believe that they were closely associated with Jehu. They may have been related to the prophetic guilds which are mentioned frequently in the stories of Elijah and Elisha. Their role in this dynastic revolution was more political:

"And when he departed from there he met Jehonadab the son of Rechab coming to meet him; and he greeted him, and said to him, 'Is your heart true to my heart as mine is to yours?' And Jehonadab answered, 'It is'. Jehu said, 'If it is ,give me your hand.' So he gave him his hand. And Jehu took him up with him into the chariot. And he said,

'Come with me, and see my zeal for the Lord'. So he had him ride in his chariot. And when he came to Samaria, he slew all that remained to Ahab in Samaria, till he had wiped them out, according to the word of the Lord which he spoke to Elijah". (2 K. 10: 15–17)

The Rechabites were a puritanical sect headed by Jonadab, son of Rechab. They were fanatically loyal to the ancient, austere and simple life of the desert, whose ideal was the Covenant religion of Sinai. They shunned intoxicating liquors, did not shave, lived in tents instead of houses, did not engage in agriculture and were strict devotees of Yahweh.

Aside from their part in the story of Jehu, the Rechabites are also significant as the kernel of that sect of which Jeremiah speaks in the 7th century. The sect may also have been the fore-runners of the Qumran (Dead Sea Scrolls) sect who lived in the desert near the Dead Sea and are thought to have played a part later, in the genesis of early Christianity.

JEHU

It is clear that Elisha played a leading role in the events leading up to Jehu's rebellion against the house of Ahab.

Jehoram had been wounded in battle and went to Jezreel, the winter palace, to recuperate. There, Ahaziah, the king of Judah, went to visit and consult him. Elisha chose this moment to act. He aroused Jehu to start a political and religious revolution in Israel out of the crisis that was brewing at Ramoth-Gilead. The narrative develops swiftly and dramatically:

"Then Elisha the prophet called one of the sons of the prophets and said to him, 'Gird up your loins, and take this flask of oil in your hand, and go to Ramoth-gilead. And when you arrive, look there for Jehu the son of Jehoshaphat, son of Nimshi; and go in and bid him rise from among his fellows, and lead him to an inner chamber. Then take the flask of oil, and pour it on his head, and say, "Thus says the Lord, I anoint you king over Israel." Then open the door and flee; do not tarry". (2 K. 9: 1–3)

"So he arose, and went into the house; and the young man poured the oil on his head saying to him, 'Thus says the Lord the God of Israel, I anoint you king over the people of the Lord, over Israel. And you shall strike down the house of Ahab your master, that I may avenge on Jezebel the blood of my servant the prophet, and the blood of all the servants of the Lord. For the whole house of Ahab shall perish; and I will cut off from Ahab every male, bond or free in Israel. And I will make the house of Ahab like the house of Jeroboam the son of Nebat, and like the house of Baasha the son of Ahijah. And the dogs shall eat Jezebel in the territory of Jezreel, and none shall bury her'. Then he opened the door, and fled. When Jehu came out to the servants of his master, they said to him, 'Is all well? Why did this mad fellow come to you?' And he said to them, 'You know the fellow and his talk.' And they said, 'That is not true; tell us now' And he said, 'Thus and so he spoke to me, saying, "Thus says the Lord, I anoint you king over Israel'". Then in haste every man of them took his garment, and put it under him on the bare steps, and they blew the trumpet, and proclaimed, "Jehu is king". (2 K. 9: 6–13)

Whatever the origin of the rebellion, Jehu, now a ruler backed by the army, acted with lightning speed, to a crafty and carefully worked-out plan. He had all the exits of Ramoth-Gilead guarded, so that no advance news could be sent to court and started off by chariot for Jezreel. The historians now had a rare occasion to recount the stages of the coming revolution with realistic vigour. Jehu's coming, announced by the watchmen on the tower, aroused great excitement and expectation. There followed a crisp and tragic interchange between the two rivals:

Joram said, 'Make ready'. And they made ready his chariot. Then Joram king of Israel and Ahaziah king of Judah set out, each in his chariot, and went to meet Jehu, and met him at the property of Naboth the Jezreelite. And when Joram saw Jehu, he said, 'Is it peace, Jehu?' He answered, "What peace can there be, so long as the harlotries and the sorceries of your mother Jezebel are so many?' Then Joram reined about and fled, saying to Ahaziah, 'Treachery, O Ahaziah!' And Jehu drew his bow with his full strength, and shot Joram between the shoulders, so that the arrow pierced his heart, and he sank in his chariot. Jehu said to Bidkar his aid, 'Take him up, and cast him on the plot of ground belonging to Naboth the Jezreelite; for remember, when you and I rode side by side behind Ahab his father, how the Lord uttered this oracle against him. As surely as I saw yesterday the blood of Naboth and the blood of his sons — says the Lord — I will requite you on this plot of ground". (2 K. 9: 21–26)

It is significant that Jehoram's death occurred on the site of Naboth's vineyard, thus pointing the moral of retribution.

Then Jehu had the visiting king of Judah killed as well. He went on to Jezreel which put up no resistance. When he entered the courtyard of the palace, Jezebel, after "painting her face", repairing her headdress and attiring herself to receive her enemy, looked down from a window (this is reminiscent of an ivory carving suggestive of Sisera's mother as illustrated in Ch. X). She treated him in a spirit worthy of a princess, and taunted him as another Zimri, meaning the usurper and assassin who had killed the last of Baasha's house (cf. 1K. 16: 9f):

"And as Jehu entered the gate, she said, 'Is it peace, you Zimri, murderer of your master?". (2 K. 9: 31)

Arrogant and born to the purple, she would not flinch nor miss her chance of humiliating Jehu, an upstart, and, to her, no better than an assassin. At his command his henchmen threw Jezebel out of the window. She was trampled under the hoofs of the spirited horses. There was little left of her but those remains Jehu had buried:

"Then he went in and ate and drank; and he said, 'See now to this cursed woman, and bury her; for she is a king's daughter." But when they went to bury her, they found no more of her than the skull and the feet and the palms of her hands. When they came back and told him, he said, 'This is the word of the Lord, which he spoke by his servant Elijah the Tishbite, 'In the territory of Jezreel the dogs shall eat the flesh of Jezebel". (2 K. 9: 34–36)

Two riders on a dashing chariot. The background is reminiscent of Jehu's lightning attack on Jezreel. From an Assyrian bas-relief.

Jehu had now to capture Samaria, the main capital, where all the enemies of Yahweh were expected to resist, while he was still heading a small force, and the army remained at Ramoth-Gilead. But the chiefs and notables of the city, in response to ambiguous letters from Jehu, gave him immediate proof of servile submission. They sent him the heads of the seventy sons of Ahab in baskets. These Jehu set up at the gate of Jezreel, probably in pyramidal heaps after the manner illustrated on Assyrian monuments. Jehu proceeded to wipe out the entire House of Ahab and all the people connected with the government, including priests. He also got hold of a party of Ahaziah's kin from Judah and slew them in cold blood. The narrator of 2 K. 10, relating one of the most stirring and cruel episodes of the Bible, was not shocked at this. To him everyone connected with Ahab, with the episode of Naboth and with Jezebel, was under a divine curse. There could be no peace in Israel until Naboth was at long last avenged and the matter considered closed.

Surprisingly, Elisha is not mentioned in connection with Jehu's further massacre of Baal's priests. The plan may have matured before Jehu's religious leanings were broadcast.

Pretending to arrange a festival in honour of Baal, he summoned his worshippers, eighty in number; then officiated as high priest of Baal. He stationed eighty well-armed guards at the exits, and they slew the assembly in cold blood. The shrine was destroyed and left as a dung heap. Israel was on the way to being purged of Baalism. The alliance with Tyre was broken and Yahweh's faith was triumphant. But the shrines of Bethel and Dan were still maintained by Jehu and he stands condemned for the same reason as Jeroboam:

"But Jehu did not turn aside from the sins of Jeroboam the son of Nebat, which he made Israel to sin, the golden calves that were in Bethel, and in Dan. And the Lord said to Jehu, 'Because you have done well in carrying out what is right in my eyes, and have done to the house of Ahab according to all that was in my heart, your sons of the fourth generation shall sit on the throne of Israel.' But Jehu was not careful to walk in the law of the Lord the God of Israel with all his heart; he did not turn from the sins of Jeroboam, which he made Israel to sin". (2 K. 10: 29–31)

It is possible that the landowners were of the same mind, for the new regime abolished the exactions introduced by Ahab under the influence of Jezebel and the Phoenicians. The old ideal still persisted that every Israelite sat "under his own vine and fig tree". But it seems that this ideal was a distant memory.

It is apparent from the story of Elisha that despite the growth of commerce and industry poverty increased. The common people frequently fell into debt and if they were not able to repay on time, they and their families were seized and enslaved. Their children were taken away by their creditors or they were obliged to sell them:

"Now the wife of one of the sons of the prophets cried to Elisha, 'Your servant my husband is dead; and you know that your servant feared the Lord, but the creditor has come to take my two children to be his slaves'. And Elisha said to her, 'What shall I do for you? Tell me; what have you in the house?' And she said, 'Your maidservant has nothing in the house, except a jar of oil'. Then he said, 'Go outside, borrow vessels of all your neighbors, empty vessels and not too few. Then go in, and shut the door upon yourself and your sons, and pour into all these vessels, and when one is full, set it aside." So she went from him and shut the door upon herself and her sons; and as she poured they brought the vessels to her. When the vessels were full, she said to her son, 'Bring me another vessel'. And he said to her, 'There is not another.' Then the oil stopped flowing. She came and told the man of God, and he said, 'Go, sell the oil and pay your debts, and you and your sons can live on the rest". (2 K. 4: 1–7)

The social changes and the manner in which the ancient legal traditions were treated will be dealt with below, in connection with the prophet Amos.

A CONTEMPORARY REPRESENTATION OF AN ISRAELITE KING

As we examine the biblical narrative in the light of contemporary history, we can gauge the impact of Jehu's internal revolution against current events. His purge may have halted the growing amalgamation of Israel with the sophisticated, material and pagan environment represented by Phoenician civilization. But he also annulled or at least paralyzed the structure of political and economic alliances by which his predecessors, the house of Omri, had brought Israel to a position of strength. Now, isolated, her prestige and economic prospects were weakened overnight and she was faced with greater external difficulties than ever before. The temporary military alliance made between Israel and Aram in face of the Assyrian threat had broken up. Jehu was hard pressed by the raids of Hazael of Damascus and found himself unable to defend his borders. He was probably financially too weak to face war with the Syrians. Relief came indirectly from Assyria in the first year of the reign of Shalmaneser III (841–814). At that time he attacked and defeated Syria (Aram), establishing control over it. These may have been the reasons that urged Jehu to forestall Assyrian invasion, do humble homage to Shalmaneser and pay him tribute.

Though the fact is not included in the biblical record, there is an important reference in the Inscription of Shalmaneser on his monument recounting his Syrian War in 841. Shalmaneser tells of tribute taken from the Tyrians, Sidonians and "Yaua son of Humri", i.e. Jehu, son of Omri. "Bit Humri", the "house of Omri" was the official name of the Assyrians for Israel, even though Jehu had usurped Omri's throne (See: The rise of the House of Omri in Ch. XIV.). This Assyrian memorial is particularly interesting as it is the only contemporary representation of any Israelite king. In any event this expedition of Shalmaneser into Syria and Palestine, and a subsequent one in 838 into Syria, saved Israel for the moment from Aram. Fortunately for Israel the Assyrians had not yet come to stay.

ARAM'S HOUR OF TRIUMPH

Though Shalmaneser had raged through Syria, defeated Hazael and invaded the territory to the south of Damascus, he was unable to make Hazael capitulate. In his later years, Shalmaneser was occupied with campaigns north and east of Mesopotamia. When Syria had recovered from the Assyrian raids, Hazael stepped up his campaigns in Israel, now isolated from Judah. Jehu managed to keep the territory of Israel intact almost to the end of his reign. The details of these wars with Damascus are unknown to us, but their results are given:

"In those days the Lord began to cut off parts of Israel. Hazael defeated them throughout the territory of Israel: from the Jordan eastward, all the land of Gilead, the Gadites, and the Reubenites, and the Manassites, from Aroer, which is by the valley of the Arnon, that is Gilead and Bashan". (2 K. 10: 32–33)

Close view of Jehu of Israel shown prostrating himself before Shalmaneser III, in the presence of an officer and attendant.

Close view of the bottom panel showing Israelites carrying tribute.

Shalmaneser III standing before the emblems of his gods. Inscribed on the face of the monument is an account of the battle of Karkar and the defeat of the Syrian alliance in which Ahab, King of Israel, was beaten.

The Aramean Domination

Aram was making a bid for the domination of all Palestine. It appears that Jehu was killed in one of the campaigns. His son Jehoahaz (815–799) was only able to hold on to the Samarian countryside and became a vassal of Aram. In Judah, the situation was equally precarious. The whole of Jehoash's reign (837–798) lay in the shadow of Aramean invasion. He bought Judah's security with all the money and valuables he could get out of the Temple and palace but, in 814, he too accepted vassaldom to Damascus. The latter days of Hazael and Ben-hadad III of Aram saw the political fortunes of the two kingdoms reach their lowest ebb.

> "For there was not left Jehoahaz an army of more than fifty horsemen and ten chariots and ten thousand footmen; for the king of Syria had destroyed them and made them like the dust at threshing". (2 K. 13: 7)

The report that the king of Damascus left Jehoahaz of Israel only 50 cavalry, 10 chariots and 10,000 infantry may be an authentic statement taken from the peace treaty with Aram. It appears that other stories, which do not name the Israelite king, also reflect Jehoahaz's humiliation:

Above: Shalmaneser III's campaign in north Syria showing impaled inhabitants of a Syrian town. Below: Tribute from his conquest of Tyre, Phoenicia. Captives from Hazazu on lower register. These scenes were hammered and engraved on bronze bands attached to the gates of his palace.

Above: Shalmaneser's assault on Hamath (upper register) and the escorting of female captives (lower register). Below: Chariots and cavalry (upper register) and the slaughter of the men of Hazazu (lower register).

"Afterward Ben-hadad king of Syria mustered his entire army, and went up, and besieged Samaria. And there was a great famine in Samaria, as they besieged it ,until an ass's head was sold for eighty shekels of silver, and the fourth part of a kab of dove's dung for five shekels of silver. Now as the king of Israel was passing by upon the wall, a woman cried out to him, saying, 'Help, my lord, O king!' And he said, 'If the Lord will not help you, whence shall I help you?' From the threshing floor, or from the wine press?' And the king asked her, 'What is your trouble?' She answered, 'This woman said to me, "Give your son, that we may eat him today, and we will eat my son tomorrow"'". (2 K. 6: 24–28)

ATHALIAH IN JUDAH

"Now when Athaliah the mother of Ahaziah saw that her son was dead, she arose and destroyed all the royal family. But Jehosheba, the daughter of king Joram, sister of Ahaziah, took Joash the son of Ahaziah, and stole him away from among the king's sons who were about to be slain, and she put him and his nurse in a bedchamber. Thus she hid him from Athaliah, so that he was not slain; and he remained with her six years, hid in the house of the Lord, while Athaliah reigned over the land". (2 K. 11: 1–3)

Following the murder of Ahaziah of Judah by Jehu, all ties with Israel were broken off. In Jerusalem, the queen mother seized power. She belonged to the dynasty and court of Omri and showed it in her actions. She encouraged the worship of Baal and ruled tyrannically with the support of mercenary troops. She knew that should a new king be chosen following the death of her son (Ahaziah) she would no longer have any role to play in Jerusalem. So she killed off all the House of David, although one grandchild, Jehoash, escaped and was hidden in the Temple precincts. Athaliah held power as queen for five years (842–837), but she faced powerful opposition in Judah. The high priest, Jehoiadah, backed by the people, finally headed a religious and political revolution which ended her regime.

On a prearranged Saturday, the Carite mercenaries (from Asia Minor) killed the queen. The Baal of the Temple was destroyed and the boy Jehoash was anointed king in the Temple.

The young king Jehoash (837-798) repaired and purified the Temple. The high priest carried out important reforms. An incident of Temple policy reflects the general depletion of the House of David and the poverty of the time:

"Then Jehoiada the priest took a chest, and bored a hole in the lid of it, and set it beside the altar on the right side as one entered the house of the Lord; and the priests who guarded the threshold put in it all the money that was brought into the house of the Lord. And whenever they saw that there was much money in the chest, the king's secretary and the high priest came up and they counted and tied up in bags the money that was found in the house of the Lord. Then they would give the money that was weighed out into the hands of the workmen who had the oversight of the house of the Lord; and they paid it out to the carpenters and the builders who worked upon the house of the Lord", (2 K. 12: 9–11)

The king was no longer able to pay for the maintenance of the court-Temple which had always been considered the dynasty's property but which had fallen into disrepair. A modest change in the Temple collections held undreamed of possibilities. Public participation in the cost of maintaining the Temple, meant that it would gradually become more and more the people's property until, with the fall of the dynasty, they would become its sole heir.

THE KING AND THE HIGH PRIEST

Other very interesting features bearing on the relationship between the king and the priesthood, omitted from the Book of Kings, are more explicit in 2 Chr. 24. The Chronicler, following a different tradition from the editor of the Book of Kings, declared that the monarchy was saved by the priesthood when Athaliah was killed, and that the king's godliness resulted from Jehoiadah's guardianship and influence which lasted throughout his life. The priests claimed great rights as a consequence and the priesthood gained a greater ascendancy than before in state religious affairs. But a reaction followed the religious reform and after Jehoiadah's death, Jehoash rebelled against overmuch priestly domination. He fell under the influence of the nobility, which opposed the priests and allowed pagan ways to creep back into the cult. When Zechariah, Jehoiadah's son rebuked him for it, and tried to re-assert his ascendancy, the king put him to death. Retribution followed ,whether due to the dislike of the people or military failure. The Arameans invaded Judah and the king was assassinated.

ADADNIRARI III OF ASSYRIA

The Aramean domination over Palestine continued until the beginning of the eighth century, when Assyria again intervened:

> "Then Jehoahaz besought the Lord, and the Lord hearkened to him; for he saw the oppression of Israel, how the king of Syria oppressed them. (Therefore the Lord gave Israel a savior, so that they escaped from the hand of the Syrians; and the people of Israel dwelt in their homes as formerly". (2 K. 13: 4–5)

After half a century of weakness the ending of the ascendancy of Damascus and improved fortunes in Palestine were attributed to a new "saviour" of Israel. This time it was the energetic Assyrian king, Adadnirari II who galvanized Assyria into becoming once more a dominant factor in Near Eastern affairs. The main adversary was, of course, Damascus. After capturing Mari, the Assyrians defeated Ben-hadad III on the southern coast of Palestine (805 B.C.E.). Thus Israel was freed of the Syrian yoke. The king, Jehoahaz, the son of Jehu, widened his rule over a larger area of Ephraim and reorganized the finances of the small kingdom. He was succeeded by his son, Jehoash, who slowly regained Israel's lost cities in Palestine and Transjordan.

The improving situation brought about by Adadnirari's emergence on the international scene is apparently reflected, in Prof. Y. Kaufman's opinion, in the opening verses of Amos:

> "Thus says the Lord:
> 'For three transgressions of Damascus and for four, I will not revoke the punishment;
>   because they have threshed Gilead with threshing sledges of iron.
> So I will send a fire upon the house of Hazael,
>   and it shall devour the strongholds of Ben-hadad.
> I will break the bar of Damascus, and cut off the inhabitants from the Valley of Aven,
>   and him that holds the scepter from Beth-eden;
>   and the people of Syria shall go into exile to Kir says the Lord". (Amos 1: 3–5)

Although the tide of Israel's fortune had at last begun to turn, improvements were not quick enough for the prophets, who now supported the king. The delay was attributed by Elisha, the foremost of the prophets, to the king's lack of confidence in Yahweh and indecision of character. This underlies a charming story of sympathetic magic which the king performed with arrows at Elisha's death bed:

"And Elisha said to him, 'Take a bow and arrows'; so he took a bow and arrows. Then he said to the king of Israel, 'Draw the bow'; and he drew it. And Elisha laid his hands upon the king's hands. And he said, 'Open the window eastward; and he opened it. Then Elisha said, 'Shoot'; and he shot. And he said, 'The Lord's arrow of victory, the victory over Syria! For you shall fight the Syrians in Aphek until you have made an end of them'. And he said, 'Take the arrows'; and he took them'. And he said to the king of Israel,'Strike the ground with them'; and he struck three times, and stopped. Then the man of God was angry with him, and said, 'You should have struck five or six times; then you would have struck down Syria until you made an end of it, but now you will strike down Syria only three times' ". (2 K.13: 15–19)

This scene, emphasizing the prophet's function, serves as an introduction to the report of the actual victory over the Syrians.

Amaziah and Jehoash

It is related that Amaziah, the king of Judah, decisively beat the Edomites, south of Judah and thus regained the southern trade route. At the conclusion of this story, an interesting parable of Syro-Phoenician origin is introduced to illustrate the bitter relations between the kings of Judah and Israel:

"Then Amaziah sent messengers to Jehoash the son of Jehoahaz, son of Jehu, king of Israel, saying, 'Come, let us look one another in the face'. And Jehoash king of Israel sent word to Amaziah king of Judah, 'A thistle on Lebanon sent to a cedar on Lebanon, saying, 'Give your daughter to my son for a wife'; and a wild beast of Lebanon passed by and trampled down the thistle. You have indeed smitten Edom, and your heart has lifted you up. Be content with your glory, and stay home; for why should you provoke trouble so that you fall, you and Judah with you?' But Amaziah would not listen. So Jehoash king of Israel went up, and he and Amaziah king of Judah faced one another in battle at Beth-shemesh, which belongs to Judah". (2 K. 14: 8–11)

There seems to be no clear motivation for this continuing quarrel between the two kings. However, as a result, Amaziah was attacked and only released by Jehoash, king of Israel, after buying him off with all the available treasure of the Temple.

THE AGE OF JEROBOAM II AND UZZIAH

During the reigns of the sons of the two rival kings, Israel and Judah enjoyed a remarkable recovery. These sister states could now reap to the full the benefits of their deliverance from Aram. Jeroboam II (784–744) not only restored David's frontier with Syria, but proved himself one of the greatest military figures of Israel, as the editor of the Book of Kings grudgingly admits, even calling him a "saviour" of Israel:

"And he did what was evil in the sight of the Lord; he did not depart from all the sins of Jeroboam the son of Nebat, which he made Israel to sin. He restored the border of Israel from the entrance of Hamath as far as the sea of the Arabah, according to the word of the Lord, the God of Israel, which he spoke by his servant Jonah the son of Amit--tai, the prophet, who was from Gath-hepher. For the Lord saw that the affliction of Israel was very bitter, for there was none left, bond or free, and there was none to help Israel. But the Lord had not said that he would blot out the name of Israel from under heaven, so he saved them by the hand of Jeroboam the son of Joash. Now the rest of the acts of Jeroboam, and all that he did, and his might, how he fought and how he recovered for Israel Damascus and Hamath, which had belonged to Judah, are they not written in the Book of the Chronicles of the Kings of Israel?". (2 K. 14: 24–28)

It was now Aram's turn to be conquered by Jeroboam II after he had reoccupied the northern part of Transjordan and added to his territory in every direction. The Moabites and Ammonites were ejected from Israelite territory and held severely in check.

The sister kingdoms controlled in area and in economic potential almost the full sweep of Solomon's empire. They had again a surplus of agricultural produce to exchange for foreign goods. The major trade routes between Egypt, Arabia, the Phoenician coast and Syria once more passed through Israelite held territory, and the free interchange of goods plus tolls from the caravans, poured wealth into Judah and Israel.

UZZIAH

Though a blanket of silence covers the reign of Uzziah of Judah (784–742), Jeroboam's young contemporary, in the Book of Kings, we know from 2 Chronicles 26 that he took an equal share in the economic and political developments taking place throughout Palestine:

> "He went out and made war against the Philistines, and broke down the wall of Gath and the wall of Jabneh and the wall of Ashdod and he built cities in the territory of Ashdod and elsewhere among the Philistines. God helped him against the Philistines, and against the Arabs that dwelt in Gurbaal and against the Meunites. The Ammonites paid tribute to Uzziah, and his fame spread even to the border of Egypt, for he became very strong. Moreover Uzziah built towers in Jerusalem at the Corner Gate and at the Valley Gate and at the Angle, and fortified them. And he built towers in the wilderness, and hewed out many cisterns, for he had large herds, both in the Shephelah and in the plain, and he had farmers and vinedressers in the hills and in the fertile lands, for he loved the soil". (2 Chr. 26: 6–10)

He repaired the defences of Jerusalem, reorganized and refitted the army, bringing into use novel siege engines (see illustration of Assyrian campaigns, below). He made war against his neighbours and extended his realm over the entire Negeb, including Edom. He opened up the port and refineries at Ezion-Gaber under their new name of Elath, a fact which has been verified; and, consolidating Judah's position on the Philistine coast, secured the southern and Mediterranean trade routes.

Uzziah appears in the annals of Tiglatpileser III of Assyria as Azriyau of Yaudi, (or Azariah of Judah) who paid his tribute. He seems to have been important enough to be listed prominently in the coalition of states in Western Asia who attempted to resist

One of the towers built by the Judean kings in the wilderness of Judah to protect the approaches to the Arabah and Edom (in the period between Solomon and Uzziah).

Epitaph to King Uzziah on a tomb to which his remains had apparently been removed in the post-exilic period.

An attendant leading camels. Israelite caravans traded through many countries in the days of Uzziah.

Tiglatpileser's first campaign. The Assyrian annals do not imply that Uzziah took part in any Syrian and Palestinian resistance, but if such a campaign did take place, it failed to halt the Assyrian advance. In the years between 743 and 738, most of the states paid tribute to Assyria.

Uzziah presumably died in 742 B.C.E., before Tiglatpileser's reprisals reached Judah, and his son, Jotham, did not join the Syro-Ephraimite coalition against Assyria.

Thus from the story in Chronicles and the evidence of Assyrian documents, a new picture of Judah's power and the history of the time emerges, different from that given by the biblical narrative alone.

'But when he was strong he grew proud, to his destruction. For he was false to the Lord his God, and entered the temple of the Lord to burn incense on the altar of incense. But Azariah the priest went in after him, with eighty priests of the Lord who were men of valor; and they withstood King Uzziah, and said to him, 'It is not for you, Uzziah, to burn incense to the Lord, but for the priests the sons of Aaron, who are consecrated to burn incense. Go out of the sanctuary; for you have done wrong, and it will bring you no honor from the Lord God'. Then Uzziah was angry. Now he had a censer in his hand to burn incense, and when he became angry with the priests leprosy broke out on his forehead, in the presence of the priests in the house of the Lord, by the altar of incense". (2 Chr. 26: 16--19)

The story of Uzziah's priestly act at the altar of incense is introduced by the chronicler as the explanation for his tragic disease. It is notable that, as late as the 8th century B.C.E., the reigning monarch still claimed the right and duty of acting as head priest in the Temple — a privilege first claimed by Solomon, although disputed by the priesthood.

When Uzziah was stricken, and retired to a house of lepers, his son, Jotham, acted as viceroy and co-regent. He inherited a wide and strong kingdom and gained a sweeping victory over the Ammonites. This fact, preserved in Chronicles, indicates that Jeroboam's rule did not reach as far as southern Transjordan.

Political and economic recovery in Palestine, however, was only one side of national life. It is evident from the writings of the contemporary prophets Amos, Micah and Hosea, and from archaeological sources, that economic prosperity brought in its train great social changes.

There was a deepening of the gulf between the privileged class of traders and land-owners and the toiling vassals, whose marginal economic status has been throughout the ages a permanent feature of Near Eastern life. The contemporary prophets constantly bewailed social injustice and the tyranny of the king and ministers, based apparently on the concentration of great properties in the hands of the crown and the landed aristocracy. Large numbers of working people were again being reduced to virtual serfdom because of their dependence on an influential and domineering ruling class.

It is believed by many scholars that the social changes derived from the contradiction between the customs, simple economy and morality of early Israel under the old Covenant Code, (see Ch. IX on the Laws of the Pentateuch), and the new legal system of the monarchy. Under the old code, all loans, whether for cultivation or other purposes, were made against the sole security of property. No other security or pledge was considered in those days and it was forbidden for an Israelite to be a "creditor" to the person of one of his fellows. But with the weakening of the old social structure, a new doctrine arose whereby the person of the debtor could be security for a loan.

The same situation existed in Judah, where the "great men" of the land ruled in unfettered liberty. At the same time, under the impact of Aramean and Assyrian rites, the popular religion, during the eighth century B.C.E., again reflected foreign influence.

Thus the small farmer or artisan, living on the edge of poverty, was at the mercy of the money lender and at any calamity — a crop failure or drought — liable to foreclosure, eviction or bond service, possibly without legal recourse or any right of appeal.

AMOS — THE HERDSMAN OF TEKOA

Such conditions are reflected in the writings of Amos and other contemporary prophets.

" 'I gave you cleanness of teeth in all your cities,
    and lack of bread in all your places,
      yet you did not return to me, says the Lord.
'And I also withheld the rain trom you when there were yet three months to the harvest;
I would send rain upon one city, and send no rain upon another city;
    one field would be rained upon, and the field on which it did not rain withered;
So two or three cities wandered to one city
    to drink water, and were not satisfied;
yet you did not return to me,' says the Lord.
'I smote you with blight and mildew;
    I laid waste your gardens and your vineyards;
    your fig trees and your olive trees the locust devoured;
yet you did not return to me, says the Lord". (Amos 4: 6–9)

"Thus says the Lord:
    'For three transgressions of Israel, and for four, I will not revoke the punishment;

because they sell the righteous for silver, and the needy for a pair of shoes—
   they that trample the head of the poor into the dust of the earth,
      and turn aside the way of the afflicted;
   a man and his father go in to the same maiden, so that my holy name is profaned;
they lay themselves down beside every altar upon garments taken in pledge:
   and in the house of their God they drink the wine of those who have been fined' ". (Amos 2: 6–8)

The prophets make no condemnation of the stratification of Israelite society, but they rebuke the injustice and extortion inflicted by the ruling classes. Their message is essentially an indictment of Israel for breach of the traditional Covenant, for the prophets preserved some memory of the old tradition. They were not so naive as to believe that the literal application of such a law would be adequate for their own times, but they protested violently against the way the legal doctrine, developed since the days of the early monarchy, was practised. The older legal code had tried to protect both creditor and debtor. But with the new commercial economy of the monarchy, this became inadequate. As the laws were not reformed the poor suffered.

This is the background to the prophet's social message. What is most important to remember is that Amos established a great precedent: His work was put in a book. Prophetic reform in Israel proper, as recorded in the prophetic books of the period, unlike Judah, stopped short of demanding the removal of the golden calves from the local shrines. Therein lies a difference between the writing (or classic) prophets and those, like Elijah and Elisha in Ahab and Jehu's time or the earlier prophetic orders ("Bene-hanneviim") called the ecstatic prophets.

Prophet and King

Amos, a Judean herdsman from Tekoa, was a new kind of religious leader. He appeared on the scene in the middle of the eighth century and with him there emerged into history a creative individuality in spiritual life, previously unknown anywhere in the world. True, he was wary of cities and their ways. The sight of material prosperity was anathema to a soul formed in the rustic simplicity of the land. Samaria especially aroused his denunciation and disgust:

"Woe to those who are at ease in Zion, and to those who feel secure on the mountain of Samaria, the notable men
of the first of the nations, to whom the house of Israel come!" (Amos 6: 1)

The beautiful ivories, the luxurious summer and winter palaces dating from the days of Ahab and Jezebel or of Jeroboam II, the teeming marketplaces and luxurious women of Samaria, whom he addressed as "Kine of Bashan", were loathsome to him. He proclaimed that Yahweh too loathed this spectacle:

"The Lord God has sworn by himself (says the Lord, the God of hosts):
'I abhor the pride of Jacob, and hate his strongholds; and I will deliver up the city and all that is in it (Amos 6: 8).

When he appeared at the high place of Bethel with his message, he was expelled by the high priest, Amaziah:

"Then Amaziah the priest of Bethel sent to Jeroboam king of Israel, saying, 'Amos has conspired against you in the midst of the house of Israel; the land is not able to bear all his words. For thus Amos has said,

> "Jeroboam shall die by the sword,
>   and Israel must go into exile
>   away from his land' ".

And Amaziah said to Amos, 'O seer, go, flee away to the land of Judah, and eat bread there, and prophesy there; but never again prophesy at Bethel, for it is the king's sanctuary, and it is a temple of the kingdom'.

Then Amos answered Amaziah, 'I am no prophet, nor a prophet's son; but I am a herdsman, and a dresser of sycamore trees, and the Lord took me from following the flock, and the Lord said to me, "Go prophesy to my people Israel".

> "Now therefore hear the word of the Lord.
> You say, "Do not prophesy against Israel,
>   and do not preach against the house of Isaac'.
> Therefore thus says the Lord:
> "Your wife shall be a harlot in the city,
>   and your sons and your daughters shall fall by the sword,
>   and your land shall be parceled out by line;
>   you yourself shall die in an unclean land,
>   and Israel shall surely go into exile away from its land' ". (Amos 7: 10–17)

The message of Amos

Animated by the strongest democratic sympathies, Amos was convinced that luxury and greed, injustice and hard dealing with the poor were hateful in Yahweh's sight; for these things religious enthusiasm or the high places would never atone. Moreover, Amos realized that under such conditions the prosperity and existence of the newly expanded kingdom of Israel would be undermined both outside and within.

> " 'Therefore thus I will do to you, O Israel;
>   because I will do this to you,
>   prepare to meet your God, O Israel!'
> For lo, he who forms the mountains,
> and creates the wind,
>   and declares to man what is his thought;
> who makes the morning darkness,
>   and treads on the heights of the earth—
> the Lord, the God of hosts, is his name!" (Amos 4: 12–13)

Yahweh's wrath was demonstrated by the catastrophies that befell the land: locusts, famines and other natural ills. Their sufferings made the people turn to Canaanite fertility rites, thus intensifying their religious fanaticism. This did not satisfy the great prophets.

The woes that beset Israel had aroused a new concept in the minds of the people and in the prophecy of the time: the Day of Yahweh:

> "Woe to you who desire the day of the Lord!
>   Why would you have the day of the Lord?
> It is darkness, and not light". (Amos 5: 18)

Among the people there may have been a belief that Yahweh would always intervene, as he had in the past, and fulfil his promises to their ancestors. But in the mind of Amos, this day would be the terrible day of reckoning when Yahweh would mete out punishment to the wicked and inaugurate a godly era.

The religious and moral truths which Amos expressed were not matters of abstract thought. They dealt concretely with the practical concerns of the Israel of his own age and her past and future history.

Amos's basic principles, according to J. Kaufman, were, first, that social righteousness was the source and guarantee of Israel's existence as a people. Should the people transgress the covenant law, they would be dispossessed of their land. This is in essence the tremendous ethical and spiritual concept which Amos brought for the first time into human thought.

Secondly, his most revolutionary innovation was that worship and sacrifice, however elaborate, are an insult to God when discharged as a mere cultic duty by those who do not conform to His ethical demands.

Amos was not concerned with the establishment of a central cult in Jerusalem or elsewhere in Israel. Nor does he stress current idolatry as one of his grievances against the Bethel shrine. No doubt the people recited in the religious ceremonies and reaffirmed periodically the gracious act of Yahweh and His Covenant with them. But it appears from Amos's message that they took this as sufficient to ensure His protection for all time whereas the obligations imposed by the Covenant had largely been forgotten. It was one thing to meet these obligations on the cultic level through elaborate ritual and lavish support of the shrines. But it was another matter when it came to translating them into every-day life.

The prevailing legal system, harsh as it was, was made harder by the greed of the wealthy who took advantage of the undefended position of the poor in order to enlarge their own holdings. They must have resorted to sharp practices and legal dodges to achieve their ends. Amos describes the merchants sitting around waiting for the end of the Sabbath and New Moon when they could again resume their trade:

"Hear this, you who trample upon the needy,
  and bring the poor of the land to an end,
saying, 'When will the new moon be over,
  that we may sell grain?
And the sabbath,
  that we may offer wheat for sale,
that we may make the ephah small and the shekel great,
  and deal deceitfully with false balances,
that we may buy the poor for silver
  and the needy for a pair of sandals,
  and sell the refuse of the wheat?' " (Amos 8: 4–6)

That meant to make small measure (ephah) and sell short, while overcharging the customer, who paid with weighted silver (shekels).

Amos's attitude towards what Yahweh wanted of men was summed up thus:

"I hate, I despise your feasts,
  and I take no delight in your
    solemn assemblies.
Even though you offer me your
  burnt offerings and cereal offerings,
  I will not accept them,
and the peace offerings of your fatted beasts
  I will not look upon.
Take away from me the noise of your songs;
  to the melody of your harps I will not listen.
But let justice roll down like waters,
  and righteousness like an ever-flowing stream' ". (Amos 5: 21–24)

"Justice" and "righteousness" had a parallel meaning, the first conveying a Hebrew prophetic meaning, unlike its significance today. It meant that specific justice protecting the poor and down-trodden who, in any conflict with the rich, were legally and morally in the right.

He rose above the narrow idea that Yahweh could only be interested in his Chosen People, and proclaimed that He was equally concerned for all mankind:

" 'Are you not like the Ethiopians to me,   and the Philistines from Caphtor
   O people of Israel?' says the Lord.   and the Syrians from Kir?' " (Amos 9: 7)
  'Did I not bring up Israel from the land of Egypt,

As Lord of history he helped these other nations long ago, caring no less for Ethiopians than for Israel. When prophesying to and against Israel, Amos would start with a survey of the surrounding world, mentioning the misdeeds of the individual kingdoms as the reason for the punishment that was to befall them.

As to Israel, Yahweh who was everywhere present was a merciful, but righteous God. His favours could be secured only by a life of righteousness.

Amos declared that things had gone so far that Israel must be destroyed with other nations. Only a small remnant would be saved so that those devoted to Yahweh would not disappear from the earth. Israel's faith must continue, but it was to be an ethical, not a cultic religion.

"I will restore the fortunes of my people Israel,   I will plant them upon their land,
  and they shall rebuild the ruined   and they shall never again be plucked up
    cities and inhabit them;   out of the land which I have given them,'
they shall plant vineyards and drink their wine,   says the Lord your God". (Amos 9: 14–15)
  and they shall make gardens and eat their fruit.

With these immortal words his book ends, on an undying message of hope.

THE REVIVAL OF ASSYRIA UNDER TIGLATPILESER III

Amos's realization that the proud days of prosperity would not last had been only too accurate. The decline came rapidly after the usurper Tiglatpileser III (744–727 B.C.E.) captured the Assyrian throne and began to set up the great world empire of Assyria. From the beginning he threatened the free states of Syria and Palestine. His policy of the ruthless expansion of Assyrian rule over the Near East took two forms; first, the elimination of the conquered kingdoms and their incorporation into his empire as permanent Assyrian provinces.

Secondly, the mass deportation of the conquered peoples and their transplantation in distant provinces. This was not simply a matter of exiling one people but of putting other exiles from distant areas into the evacuated land, thus preventing any continuity between the old population and the new.

The rulers in western Asia were certainly unprepared to meet this new onslaught. The brief revived glory of Israel under Jeroboam II was shattered after his death by internal revolution and unrestrained political anarchy. Within ten years Israel had five kings, three of them seizing the throne by violence. Jeroboam's successor, Zechariah (748) was assassinated by Shallum who was in turn killed immediately by Menahem of Tirzah. The house of Jehu thus came to a sorry end.

The pitiful picture of a country submerged in civil war and unspeakable atrocity is vividly described by the contemporary prophet Hosea and the compiler of the Book of Kings:

"At that time Menahem sacked Tappuah and all who were in it and its territory from Tirzah on; because they did not open it to him, therefore he sacked it, and he ripped up all the women in it who were with child. (2 K. 15: 16)

"Pul the king of Assyria came against the land; and Menahem gave Pul a thousand talents of silver, that he might help him to confirm his hold of the royal power. Menahem exacted the money from Israel, that is from all the wealthy men, fifty shekels of silver from every man, to give to the king of Assyria. So the king of Assyria turned back, and did not stay there in the land". (2 K. 15:19-20)

The Assyrian campaigns took place in 743 and 738. In his own inscriptions in Nimrud the king mentions "Minahim of the city of Samarina" (Samaria) among the western kings whose tribute he received, together with Rezin of Damascus, the king of Tyre, Byblos etc. The annals also refer, as we saw, to the tribute paid by Uzziah of Judah.

CHRONOLOGY OF THE DIVIDED KINGDOM

CHART II

B.C.E.	ASSYRIA	JUDAH	ISRAEL	ARAM
900	Ashurnasirpal (883-858)	Jehoshaphat (871–849)	Ahab (874–852) Ahaziah (852–851)	Ben-hadad II
	Shalmaneser III (858-824)	Jehoram (?49–843) Ahaziah (843–842) Athaliah (842–837)	Joram (Jehoram) (851–842) The House of Jehu Jehu (842–815)	Hazael
800	Adad-nirari III	Jehoash (837–798) Amaziah (798–785)	Jehoahaz (815–799) Jehoash (799–784)	Ben-hadad III
750		Uzziah (784–743) Jotham (759–743) (co-regent with Uzziah in his late years)	Jeroboam II (784–743)	

THE ASSYRIAN CONQUEST OF ISRAEL

The crucial years in the history of Palestine and the Near East, however, were those between 735 and 732 B.C.E.

Menahem's son, Pekahiah, who succeeded him, reigned only two years (736–735), then was murdered by Pekah and a group of Gileadites.

Faced with the threat of national extinction, the Near Eastern states, from Babylonia to Egypt continued with their plan of organizing a solid league against the crushing might of Tiglatpileser III. The prime movers of this league were Rezin, king of Damascus and Pekah, king of Israel (734–732), who was Aram's vassal. They tried to compel Ahaz (son of Jotham) king of Judah (743–727) to join this desperate resistance. But Ahaz refused, fearing that he would be crushed by the Assyrian might. Instead he despatched an embassy with tribute to Tiglatpileser:

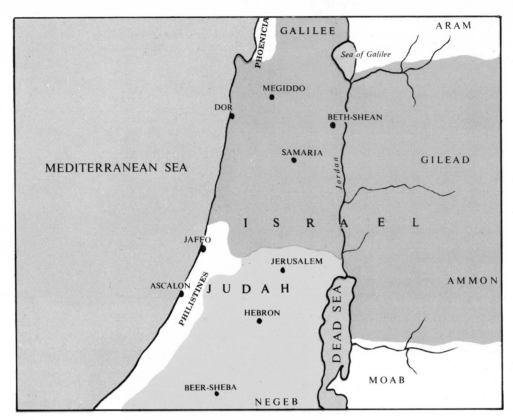

Israel and Judah in the 8th century, during the Assyrian conquest.

The Assyrian empire in the 8th century extended from east of the Tigris to the borders of Egypt and the west of Asia Minor.

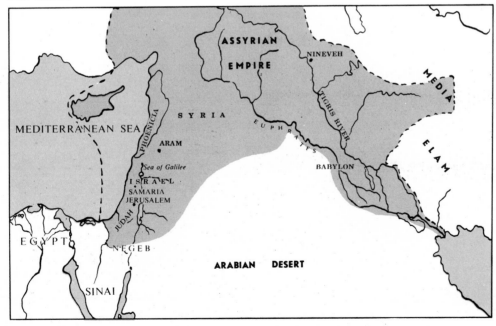

"So Ahaz sent messengers to Tiglath-pileser king of Assyria saying 'I am your servant and your son. Come up, and rescue me from the hand of the king of Syria and from the hand of the king of Israel, who are attacking me'. Ahaz also took the silver and gold that was found in the house of the Lord and in the treasures of the king's house and sent a present to the king of Assyria". (2 K 16:7–8)

This is confirmed by the inscription of Tiglatpileser, found at Nimrud, recording his conquests and his building operations. Among the tributary kings, Ahaz, king of Judah, is mentioned in the inventory of Tiglatpileser's booty which includes the following:

"I received the tribute of Sanipu of Bit-Ammon, Salamanu of Moab — Mittini of Ashkelon, Jehoahaz (Ahaz) of Judah, Kaushmalaku of Edom, Hanno of Gaza consisting of, gold silver tin, iron, antimony, linen garments with multi-coloured trimmings, garments of their native industries being made of dark purple wool . . . all kinds of costly objects be they products of the sea or of the continent, the choice products of their regions, the treasures of their kings, horses, mules trained for the yoke" . . . (Translation from Ancient Near Eastern Texts J. B. Pritchard (Ed.)

AHAZ AND ISAIAH

The consternation and heart searching in court and among the peoples finds an echo in the famous encounter between the young king Ahaz and Isaiah — the most "classic" of all prophets, alert to all that went on, but viewing events and their implications according to a perspective all his own:

"And the Lord said to Isaiah 'Go forth to meet Ahaz, you and Shearjashub your son, at the end of the conduit of the upper pool on the highway to the Fuller's Field, and say to him, "Take heed, be quiet, do not fear, and do not let your heart be faint because of these two smoldering stumps of firebrands, at the fierce anger of Rezin and Syria and the son of Remaliah" '. (Is. 7:3–4)

"For the head of Syria is Damascus,
    and the head of Damascus is Rezin.
    (Within sixty-five years Ephraim will be broken to pieces so that it will no longer be a people.)

The storming of a fortress, with the poignant scenes recorded in the Bible, here reproduced by an Assyrian artist in stone. On the right Assyrian archers, protected by a shield. A battering siege engine propelled from the inside, moves forward to attack the corner of a tower. Above it three citizens are impaled on stakes. The Assyrians exercized terror by such atrocities. On the left the attackers are attempting to scale the walls of the fort. On the ground lie the bodies of those who succumbed. The defenders on the walls are seen extending their hands in a gesture of surrender.

And the head of Ephraim is Samaria,
and the head of Samaria is the son of Remaliah.
If you will not believe,
surely you shall not be established". (Is. 7:8–9)

According to the partial version in Isaiah, it was planned by Rezin, the Aramean king, to depose Ahaz and crown the "son of Tabel", apparently a prince of Judah, whose maternal home and extensive holdings were in the land of Tabel, in Transjordan.

Aware of the fact that the king had decided to appeal to Tiglatpileser for help Isaiah warned him against the "two smouldering stumps" (Rezin and Pekah), assuring him that the confederates would never be allowed to carry out their purpose against Judah, and did not represent serious danger. In the eyes of the prophet the real danger lay in Ahaz's own cowardice and in his hasty readiness to capitulate to the Assyrian king instead of trusting in Yahweh's promises. He affirmed a cardinal principle: "If ye will not believe, surely ye shall not be established"; then as the king wavered, the prophet suggested that he choose an omen to verify the prophecy. But the king answered sceptically, with pious cant, that he did not wish to try Yahweh's patience.

From a political and military angle, the situation may not have appeared to the king in the comforting light in which Isaiah saw it as he portrayed it in the symbolic figures of the time before the assembled courtiers, the House of David:

" 'Ask a sign of the Lord your God; let it be deep as Sheol or high as heaven'. But Ahaz said, 'I will not ask, and I will not put the Lord to the test'. And he said, 'Hear then, O house of David! Is it too little for you to weary men, that you weary my God also? Therefore the Lord himself will give you a sign. Behold, a young woman shall conceive and bear a son, and shall call his name Immanuel. He shall eat curds and honey when he knows how to refuse the evil and choose the good. For before the child knows how to refuse the evil and choose the good, the land before whose two kings you are in dread will be deserted' ". (Is. 7:11–16)

The prophet here confronted the king with an omen that would prove that Yahweh was with him. A child was just, or about to be conceived; his name would be Immanuel (God with us): and before that child was old enough to understand anything, Aram and Israel would be desolated. "The passage is immensely difficult to interpret" states Professor R.W. Rogers, "and no absolute certainty or generally accepted explanation has even yet been secured".

Isaiah's device of giving symbolic names to children was practised by prophets of the time. When confronting the king, the prophet had come with his child, who bore a symbolic name: "Shear-yashuv" (a remnant will return).

Unable to gain support in the court circles, Isaiah appealed directly to the people and published in writing a message and motto on a large scroll, duly attested by sworn witnesses: "Maher-shalal-hash-baz" (the spoil hastens, the plunder comes quickly), as a reminder to the people of his prophecy that the Aramean-Ephraimite threat would soon be broken, and that they must resist the idea of foreign assistance from Assyria. To strengthen his plea, he called his own son, born then, by this name. His advice scorned by "this people", he withdrew among an inner circle of disciples (Limudim) to whom he handed a record of what he had said as a witness for the future:

"For the Lord spoke thus to me with his strong hand upon me, and warned me not to walk in the way of this people, saying: 'Do not call conspiracy all that this people call conspiracy, and do not fear what they fear, nor

Assyrian cavalryman pursuing Arabians. Slab from the palace of Tiglatpileser in Nimrud.

be in dread. But the Lord of hosts, him you shall regard as holy; let him be your fear and let him be your dread' ''. (Is. 8:11–13)

"Bind up the testimony, seal the teaching among my disciples. I will wait for the Lord, who is hiding his face from the house of Jacob, and I will hope in him. Behold, I and the children whom the Lord has given me are signs and portents in Israel from the Lord of hosts, who dwells on Mount Zion. And when they say to you, 'Consult the mediums and the wizards who chirp and mutter', should not a people consult their God? Should they consult the dead on behalf of the living?" (Is. 8:16–19)

CAPITULATION

As the siege of Jerusalem proceeded Ahaz, in desperate straits, resorted like the Moabite king Mesha before him, to the sacrifice of his son to propitiate his god:

"He even burned his son as an offering, according to the abominable practices of the nations whom the Lord drove out before the people of Israel. And he sacrificed and burned incense on the high places, ... and under every green tree". (2 K. 16:3-4)

Rezin had meanwhile helped Edom, south of Judah, to regain freedom and to capture Elath on the Red Sea. Other allies attacked Judah from the west. In his extremity Ahaz appealed for help to Tiglatpileser and accepted vassaldom. As the Assyrian emperor came down the coast, to meet all challengers in Palestine, the kings of Damascus and Israel must have withdrawn from Judah. But their punishment at the hands of Tiglatpileser was devastating.

In two campaigns in 733 and 732 B.C.E., Tiglatpileser finally delivered the death blow to the Arameans of Damascus. Its fate and that of its people, who were deported, is described:

"And the king of Assyria hearkened to him; the king of Assyria marched up against Damascus, and took it, carrying its people captive to Kir, and he killed Rezin". (2 K 16:9)

The biblical narrative has little to say about Pekah's disastrous participation in the struggle with Assyria:

Tiglatpileser III receiving the submission of a conquered foe.

"In the days of Pekah king of Israel Tiglath-pileser king of Assyria came and captured Ijon, Abel-beth-maacah, Janoah, Kedesh, Hazor, Gilead, and Galilee, all the land of Naphtali; and he carried the people captive to Assyria. Then Hoshea the son of Elah made a conspiracy against the son of Remaliah, and struck him down, and slew him, and reigned in his stead, in the twentieth year of Jotham the son of Uzziah". (2 K. 15:29-30)

It seems that Tiglatpileser annexed the greater part of Israel's Kingdom, in the north and and in Jordan, except for Mount Ephraim (Samaria) which remained a little state. He divided the territory conquered from Israel into three Assyrian provinces: Megiddo (Galilee and the valley of Esdraelon) Dor (a maritime port and the centre of the province of Sharon) and Gilead in Transjordan. Mass deportations of Israelites to distant Assyrian possessions followed and they were replaced eventually by other foreign deportees. Meanwhile, the last king of Israel, Hoshea, killed Pekah and was appointed by Tiglatpileser his vassal king of Samaria. The parallel version from Tiglatpileser's inscriptions from Nimrud is given below:

'They overthrew their king Pekah and I placed Hoshea as king over them, I received from them 10 talents of gold, 1000 talents of silver as their tribute and brought them to Assyria".

(a talent of silver was worth about two thousand dollars and a talent of gold about fifteen times as much.)

"When King Ahaz went to Damascus to meet Tiglath-pileser king of Assyria, he saw the altar that was at Damascus. And King Ahaz sent to Urijah the priest a model of the altar, and its pattern exact in all its details". (2 K.16:10)

Ahaz, by capitulating to Assyria as a vassal bound by a treaty (he went to Damascus to pay homage to the conqueror), had meanwhile saved Judah from Israel's fate, but he may have returned to Jerusalem a disillusioned man, possibly doubting the efficacy of Yahweh's help. It is recorded that he had accepted Assyria's pagan ways. This became evident from a serious religious crisis that was developing with the priesthood and the faithful of Yahweh.

THE PROPHET HOSEA

Thus does the history of the times appear to the Hebrew annalist or to the ambitious conqueror. We even saw how it appeared to a broad mind with world-wide horizons, like the prophet Amos. How did it strike a sensitive soul such as the prophet Hosea, a true northerner of Ephraim, in those days of anarchy? His whole love was for his country and his personality was expressed through his intimate personal relation to God. With the instinct for

Above: Assyrian soldiers lead away the inhabitants and sheep of a captured town, probably the biblical Ashtaroth east of the lake of Galilee. The inhabitants of the eastern part of Israel were deported in 732, ten years before those of Samaria in 722 B.C.E. Below: Tiglatpileser (called Pul in the biblical account) standing in his chariot with a driver and third man (cf. 2K 25: 19). Relief carving from Nimrud.

Evacuation and capture of a Syrian town in Tiglatpileser's campaigns. Assyrian scribes take account of the spoil. Flock of sheep and goats with drover on the right.

Dor, a maritime port since the days of the monarchy. It became the centre of one of the Israelite provinces incorporated in the Assyrian imperial administration.

dramatic symbolism characteristic of Hebrew prophecy, Hosea developed the theme of his own tragic personal life as a spring of his prophetic activity. His undying love for his unfaithful wife, Gomer, inspired him to seek her out and to reclaim her. Interestingly enough, he pictured his people's betrayal of God in terms of marital infidelity:

"For their mother has played the harlot;
she that conceived them has acted shamefully.

For she said, 'I will go after my lovers,
who give me my bread and my water,
my wool and my flax, my oil and my drink' ". (Hosea 2:5)

The declaration about the wife is the formula of divorce for an unfaithful wife in terms of the daily life of those days. Did not Yahweh feel toward Israel as Hosea felt towards his wife? Was not Yahweh's love for his bride, Israel, both a condemnation and her ultimate ground of hope? Hosea's contribution is the enrichment of the old idea of a close marriage between God and his people with a profound moral content.

The primary evils in Israel's relation to Yahweh were not the external acts of worship. Hosea in fact had very little to say in favour of current cultic practices, then in an immoral and degenerate state:

"I have spurned your calf, O Samaria.
My anger burns against them.
How long will it be
till they are pure in Israel?

The calf of Samaria
shall be broken to pieces". (Hosea 8:5–6)

Of course he poured scorn upon the Baal festivals and the practices of temple prostitution. But the worst form of moral apostasy in his view was that the name Baal, meaning lord or master, was applied to Yahweh as a matter of course, and the Baal or master worshipped on and around the altars was Yahweh:

"And in that day, says the Lord, you will call me, 'My husband,' and no longer will you call me, 'My Baal'. For I will remove the names of the Baals from her mouth, and they shall be mentioned by name no more". (Hosea 2:16–17)

Yet this worship, in his mind, was utterly alien to Yahweh. It belonged to a religion of nature which is at odds with the religion of the "spirit", imbued with righteousness and justice:

"And I will betroth you to me for ever; I will betroth you to me in righteousness and in justice, in steadfast love, and in mercy". (Hosea 2:19)

However, Hosea was definite in his confidence of the outcome, which would be the victory of Yahweh's persistent love, in a new and spiritual betrothal:

"Come, let us return to the Lord;
for he has torn, that he may heal us;
he has stricken, and he will bind us up". (Hosea 6:1)

This would be followed by a deeper repentance, when Israel would ask for the removal of its sinful spirit and repudiate its wordly confidence in the instruments of war and would have no more to do with the idols its hands had fashioned.

"Return, O Israel, to the Lord your God,
    for you have stumbled because of your iniquity.
Take with you words
    and return to the Lord:
say to him,
    'Take away all iniquity;
accept that which is good
and we will render
    the fruit of our lips.
Assyria shall not save us,
    we will not ride upon horses;
and we will say no more, "Our God",
    to the works of our hands.
In thee the orphan finds mercy' ". (Hosea 14:1 3)

Hosea believed therefore in a God of Covenanted love as well as of righteous judgement like Amos, but he was something more, for he penetrated to the need for a changed national life.

The Assyrians destroyed every town and kingdom that resisted them or refused to pay tribute, then deported their populations and replaced them by other captives.

Defendants of Lachish fight from a tower as fugitives carry their goods from the doomed town. Three figures (lower right) are impaled. This relief belongs to the series of Sennacherib's siege of the town, from the monuments of Nineveh at the British Museum.

CHAPTER XVI

JUDAH ALONE

THE END OF ISRAEL

Tiglatpileser's death in 727/6 encouraged a new rebellion, fomented by Egypt. King Hoshea, (732–724) who had started out as a vassal, turned against his Assyrian overlord and found allies among the Phoenicians. When Shalmaneser V arrived in Palestine, Hoshea surrendered and paid tribute, but he continued plotting with Egypt and finally was carried off in chains. The resistance did not end there. Samaria and the Phoenician cities carried it on while awaiting outside help. The cities were besieged and three years later, in 722 B.C.E. or shortly before, Samaria fell. The inhabitants were subsequently exiled to Assyria and Media, east of Babylonia:

"In the fourth year of King Hezekiah, which was the seventh year of Hoshea son of Elah, king of Israel, Shalmaneser king of Assyria came up against Samaria and besieged it and at the end of three years he took it. In the sixth year of Hezekiah, which was the ninth year of Hoshea king of Israel, Samaria was taken". (2K. 18:9–10)

As the biblical record stands, Samaria fell in the days of Shalmaneser V, who is mentioned by name. No Assyrian inscription, giving a detailed account of the event, has as yet been found, but it was assumed, on the evidence of the Khorsabad stone inscription of Sargon II (722–705), that it was he who had captured the city. This is tantamount to saying that the Assyrian monument corrected the biblical narrative, dating the event to 721, a conclusion widely accepted for many years. H. Tadmor of the Hebrew University, in dealing with the events of Sargon's reign, based on all available records, has shown conclusively that the clay prism and the Annals, which are more trustworthy, run the dating of this event one year earlier (722) than may be gathered from the famous stone inscription of Khorsabad. These records came from the earlier years of Sargon and are closer to the events described, whereas the Khorsabad stone monument commemorated the king's fifteen year career and bore an edited and revised version, designed to make the permanent official account glorify the name of the reigning king. They are less trustworthy than the earlier records. Therefore we are forced to the conclusion that the capture of the Israelite capital must be credited to Shalmaneser in the last year of his reign, and not to Sargon II.

Sargon II faced a domestic crisis in the first year of his reign (721), so he did not go out to war. He made up for it in the following year (720) by campaigning against an uprising of the kings of Syria, led by Yaubidi of Hamath. He inflicted heavy losses on an Egyptian army commanded by Sib'u on the Egyptian border and then came and reconquered Samaria. He deported the Israelites and rebuilt Samaria as the stronghold of a newly settled Assyrian province. H. Tadmor concludes: "All the references to the conquest of Samaria in Sargon's inscriptions thus refer to the events of 720. However the organization of the new province took some time; four years later Sargon settled Arabian tribes in Samaria......" This is stated in Sargon's inscription on a clay prism found in Nimrud.

Sargon gave the number of the Israelites he deported as 27,290 and 200 chariots. According to the biblical record he settled them in Halah, in the valley and in the cities of the Medes, east of Babylonia, namely in the far corners of the Assyrian empire.

THE AFTERMATH OF EXILE

"And the king of Assyria brought people from Babylon, Cuthah, Avva, Hamath, and Sephar-vaim, and placed them in the cities of Samaria instead of the people of Israel; and they took possession of Samaria, and dwelt in its cities. And at the beginning of their dwelling there, they did not fear the Lord; therefore the Lord sent lions among them, which killed some of them. So the king of Assyria was told, 'The nations which you have carried away and placed in the cities of Samaria do not know the law of the god of the land; therefore he has sent lions among them, and behold, they are killing them, because they do not know the law of the god of the land'. Then the king of Assyria commanded 'Send there one of the priests whom you carried away thence; and let him go and dwell there, and teach them the law of the god of the land' ". (2K. 17:24–27)

Sargon does not mention the colonization of the cities of Israel with Arabs, but he was not disposed to leave these cities desolate and colonization with aliens from many provinces

Sargon (left) in conference with his commander-in-chief. Palace of Khorsabad.

of the empire was customary. In any case, the deportations of Israelites carried out wholesale did not completely depopulate the country. Thousands who fled returned when the fighting was over.

The Kingdom of Israel never revived, despite desperate attempts by the survivors to reconstruct their land by joining uprisings of little states against Assyria from 720 up to the days of Esarhaddon and Ashurbanipal. During all this time Assyrian kings continued their policy of shuttling conquered rebel populations back and forth.

THE BOND WITH JUDAH

Many of the aliens intermarried with surviving Israelites and adopted their ways and religion though they also preserved much of their own customs and faith. But a fixed core of tradition oriented the remnant of the Israelites, left in the Assyrian province of Israel, to the kingdom of Judah. This was then ruled by king Hezekiah (727-698), mentioned in the biblical record in exceedingly favourable terms because he was a great religious reformer.

He put an end to the high places, the Asherah and pagan monuments. He went so far as to destroy an ancient bronze serpent called Nehushtan that had been used as a cult object since the earliest days of the desert:

This ivory carving with a lotus motif, illustrates a phase in the development of art throughout the ancient Near East. The man is represented holding a lotus tree and raising the other arm in a gesture of salute (Nimrud 8th century). Phoenician craftsmen incorporated also lotus-headed capitals into pillars. From pre-historic times the lotus has been more influential in art than any other flower. The Egyptian stylized lotus motif appears to be ancestor of the Greek Ionic.

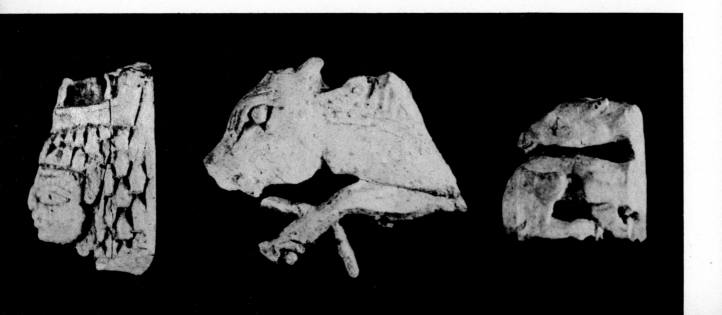

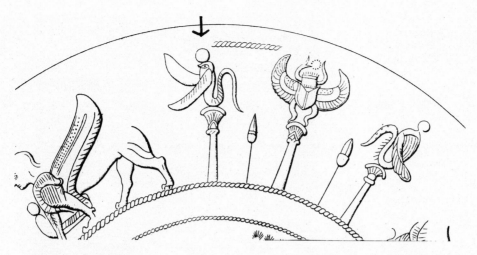

A serpent on a standard drawn on a bowl from Nimrud. It calls to mind the heathen symbol removed by Hezekiah.

"He removed the high places, and broke the pillars, and cut down the Asherah. And he broke in pieces the bronze serpent that Moses had made, for until those days the people of Israel had burned incense to it; it was called Nehushtan". (2 K. 18:4)

In the course of time the bond between the broken remnants and Jerusalem became stronger. Judah as "the remnant of Israel" became the living link with Israelites left in the captured kingdom and probably with those scattered over the length and breadth of ancient Asia. The ten tribes were therefore not lost irretrievably. Their remnant survived till after the Exile.

HEZEKIAH, KING OF JUDAH

The Temple of Jerusalem was restored again after Hezekiah's reforms as the spiritual centre for all the faithful of Yahweh. King Hezekiah took steps to reunite Judah and the north religiously as a preparation for political reunion:

"So they decreed to make a proclamation throughout all Israel, from Beer-sheba to Dan, that the people should come and keep the passover to the Lord the God of Israel, at Jerusalem; for they had not kept it in great numbers as prescribed. So couriers went throughout all Israel and Judah with letters from the king and his princes, as the king had commanded, saying, 'O people of Israel, return to the Lord, the God of Abraham, Isaac, and Israel, that he may turn again to the remnant of you who have escaped from the hand of the kings of Assyria' ". (2 Chr. 30:5–6)

....

"Now when all this was finished, all Israel who were present went out to the cities of Judah and broke in pieces the pillars and hewed down the Asherim and broke down the high places and the altars throughout all Judah and Benjamin, and in Ephraim and Manasseh, until they had destroyed them all. Then all the people of Israel returned to their cities, every man to his possession". (2 Chr. 31:1)

In this atmosphere of cultic reform, led energetically by Hezekiah, the great prophets of the faith began dreaming of a redemption of Israel and Judah as a united kingdom under a "saviour" king from the House of David. Hezekiah's influence made itself felt among the survivors in Galilee in the north, though separatism and opposition to Jerusalem still lingered on in the province of Samaria. His actual dominion covered southern Ephraim up to the

Assyrians at war; soldiers swimming across a river supported by air-filled water skins.

Philistine coast of the west, the whole south of Judah and the Negev where he organized a census.

The importance of Judah as a rallying centre increased when Philistia finally fell to Sargon II and became another Assyrian province (711). Judah was the only state left intact by the ravaging Assyrians and though she was its tributary, she was able to reinforce her status. Failing in his political objective of a united Palestine under his rule Hezekiah became the head of a coalition of small states which planned to revolt against Assyria with the promise of Egyptian and Babylonian backing. This was the political atmosphere of Palestine as the news came of Sargon's death in battle. It is expressed beautifully by the prophet Isaiah, Sargon's great contemporary:

"You will take up this taunt against the king of Babylon:
How the oppressor has ceased,
the insolent fury ceased!
The Lord has broken the staff of the wicked,
the scepter of rulers,
that smote the peoples in wrath
with unceasing blows,
that ruled the nations in anger
with unrelenting persecution.
The whole earth is at rest and quiet;
they break forth into singing.
The cypresses rejoice at you,
the cedars of Lebanon, saying,

'Since you were laid low,
no hewer comes up against us'.
Sheol beneath is stirred up
to meet you when you come,
it rouses the shades to greet you,
all who were leaders of the earth;
it raises from their thrones
all who were kings of the nations.
All of them will speak
and say to you:
'You too have become as weak as we!
You have become like us!' ". (Is. 14:4–10)

. . . .

"Those who see you will stare at you,
and ponder over you:
'Is this the man who made the earth tremble,
who shook kingdoms,
who made the world like a desert
and overthrew its cities,
who did not let his prisoners go home?'

All the kings of the nations lie in glory,
each in his own tomb;
but you are cast out, away from your sepulchre,
like a loathed untimely birth,
clothed with the slain, those pierced by the sword,
who go down to the stones of the Pit,
like a dead body trodden under foot". (Is. 14:16–19)

HEZEKIAH AND ISAIAH

When Sennacherib (705–681) came to the Assyrian throne, Hezekiah thought the moment propitious. He accepted the proposals of Egyptian and Babylonian embassies. In Babylonia the Chaldean Merodach-baladan (Marduk-aplu-iddina II) had seized the ancient throne of Babylon and sought allies against Assyria. Hezekiah withheld tribute from Sennacherib:

"At that time Merodach-baladan the son of Baladan, king of Babylon, sent envoys with letters and a present to Hezekiah; for he heard that Hezekiah had been sick'. And Hezekiah welcomed them, and he showed them all his treasure house, the silver, the gold, the spices, the precious oil, his armory, all that was found in his storehouses; there was nothing in his house or in all his realm that Hezekiah did not show them" (2 K. 20:12–13)

....

"Then Isaiah said to Hezekiah, 'Hear the word of the Lord: Behold, the days are coming, when all that is in your house, and that which your fathers have stored up till this day, shall be carried to Babylon; nothing shall be left, says the Lord. And some of your own sons, who are born to you, shall be taken away; and they shall be eunuchs in the palace of the king of Babylon'. Then said Hezekiah to Isaiah, 'The word of the Lord which you have spoken is good'. For he thought, 'Why not, if there will be peace and security in my days?'" (2 K. 20:16–19)

Hezekiah, a great religious reformer, was profoundly influenced by Isaiah and Micah, but only on a religious level. One of the distinctive contributions of Isaiah to Hebrew history was his insistence on the subordination of political Israel to religious Israel. He challenged the people and the king to have faith in Yahweh rather than in military alliances. But Hezekiah, a full-blooded nationalist in an era of deadly hatred of Assyria, did not heed Isaiah's warning in matters of foreign policy.

As revolt spread throughout Palestine, Syria, Phoenicia and Philistia, the coalition took form. Hezekiah sent envoys to Egypt to negotiate a treaty, in spite of the earnest warnings of Isaiah who branded the whole plan as folly and rebellion against the designs of Yahweh. It seems that Padi, king of Ekron, who had remained loyal to Assyria, was handed over by his subjects to Hezekiah who held him prisoner in Jerusalem in order to whip him into line. This is attested by Sennacherib:

"The officials, the patricians and the common people of Ekron—who had thrown Padi, their king, into fetters because he was loyal to his solemn oath sworn by the god Ashur, and had handed him over to Hezekiah, the Jew—and he (Hezekiah) held him in prison, unlawfully, as if he (Padi) be an enemy—had become afraid and had called for help upon the kings of Egypt and the bowmen, the chariot corps and the cavalry of the king of Ethiopia, an army beyond counting—and they actually had come to their assistance".

He then busied himself with his defences.

THE POOL OF SILOAM

The Books of Kings, Chronicles and Isaiah portray Hezekiah in a different light from their view of Ahaz.

Isaiah approached his young king with a message of reassurance as he was inspecting the water supply of Jerusalem. This could be a vulnerable spot in the defences of the town and the installation of a new reservoir was required to ensure water for the people in case of siege. The king's concern was to get water from the spring of Gihon situated outside the eastern wall of the City of David and bring it within the fortifications. Such a plan would help Jerusalem to withstand siege:

Inscriptions in the wall of the Siloam tunnel dating from Hezekiah's time. It describes how the cutting was effected by crews working from opposite sides of the hill. This explains why it was not cut in a straight line.

The Siloam receiving-pool where water was gathered.

The exit of the Siloam tunnel.

"This same Hezekiah closed the upper outlet of the waters of Gihon and directed them down to the west side of the city of David. And Hezekiah prospered in all his works". (2 Chr. 32:30)

" 'Because this people have refused the waters of Shiloah that flow gently, and melt in fear before Rezin and the son of Remaliah....." (Is. 8:6)

Though conduits had been constructed in the rock before, Hezekiah's teams hewed through the rock with bronze tools and cut a new conduit. This engineering feat is commemorated by the ancient Hebrew inscription of Siloam at the western exit of the tunnel where there was a reservoir to store water for the city.

HEZEKIAH AND SENNACHERIB

After Sennacherib had defeated Merodach-baladan in Babylonia in 703, he was free to strike westwards. First, he punished Sidon and Tyre which he devastated, replacing their rulers by governors of his own choosing. From then on Sidon and Tyre ceased to be the "merchant of nations" and were replaced in commercial importance by their own colonies in the Mediterranean, such as Carthage, and by the Greeks.

The other Phoenician states capitulated and hastened to Sennacherib with tribute. So did Judah's neighbours, except Ashkelon and Ekron. An Egyptian army sent to relieve the allies was defeated at Eltekeh near Ekron. Sennacherib wiped out all opposition, executing and deporting the offenders.

Having subdued Hezekiah's allies, Sennacherib determined to destroy Judah. He devastated the cities of the coast and the fortified towns of Judah, including Lachish, laid waste the countryside, then laid siege to Jerusalem (701 B.C.E.). This is when Hezekiah proposed to pay tribute to save the town. A most elaborate description in stone of the Assyrian

Soldiers taking terror-stricken captives across a stream; fragment of a battle scene from a wall panel of the palace of Sennacherib.

siege of Lachish has been preserved on the reliefs in the palace at Nineveh as reproduced in detail below.

The biblical record deals with the campaign as a whole, without going into detail, except for the last stage of the siege of Jerusalem. The picture is considerably enriched by the account in Sennacherib's annals recorded on the clay prism, and it will be interesting to quote them in juxtaposition as they seem to fit and complement one another:

SENNACHERIB'S ANNAL

"In the fourteenth year of King Hezekiah Sennacherib king of Assyria came up against all the fortified cities of Judah and took them". (2 K. 18:13)

As to Hezekiah, the Jew, he did not submit to my yoke, I laid siege to 46 of his strong cities, walled forts and to the countless small villages in their vicinity, and conquered them by means of well-stamped earth-ramps, and battering rams brought thus near to the walls combined with the attack by foot soldiers, using mines, breeches as well as sapper work. I drove out of them 200,150 people, young and old, male and female, horses, mules, donkeys, camels, big and small cattle beyond counting, and I considered them booty. Himself I made a prisoner in Jerusalem, his royal residence, like a bird in a cage. I surrounded him with earthwork in order to molest those who were leaving the city's gate. His towns which I had plundered, I took away from his country and gave them over to Mitinti, king of Ashdod, Padi, king of Ekron, and Sillibel, king of Gaza. Thus I reduced his country but I still increased the tribute ... to be delivered annually.

"And Hezekiah king of Judah sent to the king of Assyria at Lachish, saying 'I have done wrong; withdraw from me; whatever you impose on me I will bear'. And the king of Assyria required of Hezekiah king of Judah three hundred talents of gold. And Hezekiah gave him all the silver that was found in the house of the Lord, and in the treasuries of king's house. At that time Hezekiah stripped the gold from the doors of the temple of the Lord, and from the doorposts which Hezekiah king of Judah had overlaid and gave it to the king of Assyria". (2 K. 18:14–16)

Hezekiah himself, whom the terror-inspiring splendour of my lordship had overwhelmed and whose irregular and elite troops which he had brought into Jerusalem, his royal residence, in order to strengthen it, had deserted him, did send me, later to Nineveh, my lordly city, together with 30 talents of gold, 800 talents of silver, precious stones, antimony, large cuts of red stone, couches inlaid with ivory, nimedu-chairs inlaid with ivory, elephant-hides, ebony-wood, box-wood and all kinds of valuable treasures, his own daughters, concubines, male and female musicians. In order to deliver the tribute and to do obeisance as a slave he sent his personal messenger.

(Translation from J. B. Pritchard (Ed), Ancient Near Eastern Texts)

ISAIAH AND THE SIEGE OF JERUSALEM

Three sources converge on this dramatic event and its unexpected ending: 2 Kings 18 and 19, Isaiah 36–37 and, indirectly, Sennacherib's annals, all bringing us into intimate contact with the situation and the underlying spiritual problems. While the siege of Lachish was in progress, Sennacherib sent an army to Jerusalem led by a Rabshakeh (a title meaning chief deputy), who demanded abdication in a shrewd propaganda speech, followed by a parley over the walls of Jerusalem:

"Then the Rabshakeh stood and called out in a loud voice in the language of Judah: 'Hear the word of the great king, the king of Assyria! Thus says the king: "Do not let Hezekiah deceive you, for he will not be able to deliver

Assyrians storming the walls and city gate. Judean captives led from Lachish.

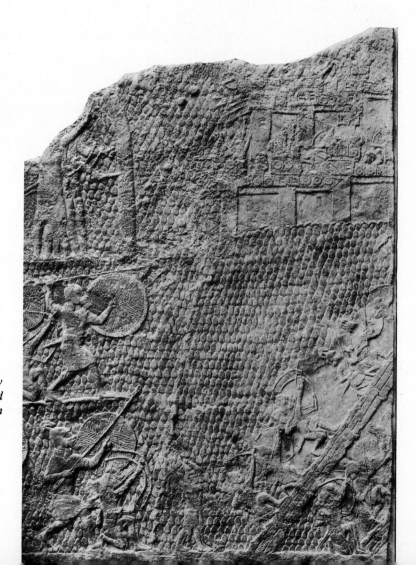

Sennacherib's attack on Lachish by siege engines pushed up an incline and protected by archers who shot from behind a shield.

419

A reconstruction of Lachish. The summit of the mound was surrounded by a wall and along the slope was a second wide wall.

Olive stones from the main gate of Lachish. This suggests that the battle took place in the autumn of the year when fresh olives are in season.

The columns from the prism of Sennacherib describing his military campaigns against Judah in 701 B.C.E.

Prisoners and spoil from Lachish.

421

Sennacherib on his throne, receiving the submission of the inhabitants of Lachish who kneel before him, and the booty taken. An inscription before him reads: "Sennacherib, king of the world, king of Assyria, sat upon a nimedu-throne and passed in review the booty taken from La-ki-su".

Camp and cavalry of Sennacherib before Lachish. A strong wall surrounded the camp. Relief of Sennacherib, from his palace at Nineveh.

you out of my hand. Do not let Hezekiah make you to rely on the Lord by saying, The Lord will surely deliver us, and this city will not be given into the hand of the king of Assyria'. Do not listen to Hezekiah; for thus says the king of Assyria: "Make your peace with me and come out to me; then every one of you will eat of his own vine, and every one of his own fig tree, and every one of you will drink the water of his own cistern; until I come and take you away to a land like your own land, a land of grain and wine, a land of bread and vineyards, a land of olive trees and honey, that you may live and not die. And do not listen to Hezekiah when he misleads you by saying, the Lord will deliver us. Has any of the gods of the nations ever delivered his land out of the hand of the king of Assyria? Where are the gods of Hamath and Arpad? Where are the gods of Sepharvaim, Hena, and Ivvah? Have they delivered Samaria out of my hand? Who among all the gods of the countries have delivered their countries out of my hand, that the Lord should deliver Jerusalem out of my hand!?"' But the people were silent and answered him not a word, for the king's command was, "Do not answer him"' ". (2 K. 18:28–36)

..}..

"Behold, you are relying now on Egypt, that broken reed of a staff, which will pierce the hand of any man who leans on it. Such is Pharaoh king of Egypt to all who rely on him. But if you say to me, 'We rely on the Lord our God', is it not he whose high places and altars Hezekiah has removed, saying to Judah and to Jerusalem, 'You shall worship before this altar in Jerusalem?' " (2 K. 18:21–22)

In the face of the arrogant Assyrian's threats that he would imprison Hezekiah in a besieged Jerusalem like a bird in a cage, Isaiah changed his reasoning. Earlier, he had proclaimed that the Assyrian was the rod of Yahweh's anger, who in turn would punish him:

"Ah, Assyria, the rod of my anger,
    the staff of my fury!
Against a godless nation I send him,
    and against the people of my wrath I command him,
to take spoil and seize plunder,
    and to tread them down like the mire of the streets.
But he does not so intend,
    and his mind does not so think;
but it is in his mind to destroy,
    and to cut off nations not a few;

for he says:
    'Are not my commanders all kings?,
Is not Calno like Carchemish?
    Is not Hamath like Arpad?
    Is not Samaria like Damascus?
As my hand has reached to the kingdoms of the idols
    whose graven images were greater
        than those of Jerusalem and Samaria..
shall I not do to Jerusalem and her idols
    as I have done to Samaria and her images?"

When the Lord has finished all his work on Mount Zion and on Jerusalem he will punish the arrogant boasting of the king of Assyria and his haughty pride". (Is. 10:5–12)

The terrible havoc wrought by the invader is the sign of God's judgement upon "a godless nation", the people of his choice:

"Shall the ax vaunt itself over him who hews with it.
    or the saw magnify itself against him who wields it?
As if a rod should wield him who lifts it,
    or as if a staff should lift him who is not wood!" (Is. 10:15)

It follows therefore:

"The Lord of hosts has sworn:
   'As I have planned,
     so shall it be,
and as I have purposed,
   so shall it stand,

that I will break the Assyrian in my land,
    and upon my mountains trample him under foot;
and his yoke shall depart from them,
    and his burden from their shoulder' ". (Is. 14:24–25)

That is why the man of faith should submit, not to the Assyrian yoke but to the yoke of Yahweh's sovereignty, and wait patiently for the time when he will humble the aggressor. It was out of this conviction that Isaiah had advised Hezekiah to shun political alliances and revolution against Assyria, choosing instead a neutral policy.

Now Isaiah, backed by the intransigent elements in Jerusalem, counselled against capitulation. Whatever was in his mind in earlier situations, Isaiah declared that Assyria was an instrument which Yahweh wielded to try his people. But now Isaiah affirmed that he would lay it aside when he had finished his "strange work" in Jerusalem. In Isaiah's religious perspective—and Isaiah was not a practical politician in our sense—whereas God gave Assyria power, so he could check it to take it away when he chose to do so.

Isaiah's stand during the invasion and his message as a whole turn out to be religiously consistent. Considering the existing situation, Isaiah became convinced that behind and within Yahweh's judgement was a purpose to deliver Jerusalem and prove his saving power:

" 'And the Assyrian shall fall by a sword,
 not of man;
and a sword, not of man, shall devour him;
and he shall flee from the sword,
 and his young men shall be put to forced labour.

, His rock shall pass away in terror,
 and his officers desert the standard in panic',
says the Lord, whose fire is in Zion,
 and whose furnace is in Jerusalem". (Is. 31:8–9)

So Hezekiah would not be caught in Jerusalem "as a bird in a cage" as Sennacherib boasted, but:

"Like birds hovering, so the Lord of hosts will protect Jerusalem;
 he will protect it and deliver it,
 he will spare and rescue it". (Is. 31:5)

THE DELIVERANCE OF JERUSALEM

Thus strong in his faith, Hezekiah gained the upper hand over the doubters, and Sennacherib's threats and psychological warfare were ignored:

"Then Isaiah the son of Amoz sent to Hezekiah, saying, 'Thus says the Lord, the God of Israel: Because you have prayed to me concerning Sennacherib king of Assyria, this is the word that the Lord has spoken concerning him:

"She despises you she scorns you —
 the virgin daughter of Zion;
she wags her head behind you —
 the daughter of Jerusalem.

'Whom have you mocked and reviled?
 Against whom have you raised your voice
and haughtily lifted your eyes?
 Against the Holy One of Israel!' " (Is. 37:21–23)

. . . .

" 'Have you not heard
 that I determined it long ago?
I planned from days of old
 what now I bring to pass,
that you shall make fortified cities
 crash into heaps of ruins,
while their inhabitants shorn of strength,
are dismayed and confounded,
and have become like plants of the field
 and like tender grass,

like grass on the housetops,
 blighted before it is grown.
I know your sitting down
 and your going out and coming in,
 and your raging against me.
Because you have raged against me
 and your arrogance has come to my ears,
I will put my hook in your nose
 and my bit in your mouth,
and I will turn you back on the way
 by which you came' ". (Is. 37:26–29)

"And the angel of the Lord went forth, and slew a hundred and eighty-five thousand in the camp of the Assyrians; and when men arose early in the morning, behold, these were all dead bodies. Then Sennacherib king of Assyria departed, and went home and dwelt at Nineveh. And as he was worshipping in the house of Nisroch his god, Adrammelech and Sharezer, his sons, slew him with the sword, and escaped into the land of Ararat. And Esarhaddon his son reigned in his stead". (Is. 37:36–38)

Whatever the explanation of Sennacherib's sudden withdrawal, the event made a deep impression upon the memory of the people. It was seen as the greatest miracle performed by God for his city, Jerusalem. These feelings contributed in no small degree to the later belief in Jerusalem's immunity from destruction:

"For he says:
'By the strength of my hand I have done it,
    and by my wisdom, for I have understanding;
I have removed the boundaries of peoples,
    and have plundered their treasures;
like a bull I have brought down
    those who sat on thrones.

My hand has found like a nest
    the wealth of the peoples;
and as men gather eggs that have been forsaken
    so I have gathered all the earth;
and there was none that moved a wing,
    or opened the mouth, or chirped' ". (Is. 10:13–14)

Both this account, a parallel account in 2 Kings 19 and the annals of Sennacherib, agree that Jerusalem was not captured; but the reasons given are somewhat at odds. For reasons unknown, the siege was lifted suddenly and the Assyrians withdrew from Jerusalem. One biblical account states that 185,000 Assyrians were slain in a single night "by the angel of Yahweh'. This tradition has the support of Herodotus, the Greek historian who tells of an epidemic of mice that ate the quivers of the Assyrians. Some surmise that they were stricken with bubonic plague which forced the army to return home:

' "Behold, I will put a spirit in him, so that he shall hear a rumor and return to his own land; and I will cause him to fall by the sword in his own land' ". (2 K. 19:7)

Difficulties at home are hinted at by the Assyrian record. This may have prompted Sennacherib to settle for what he could. But politically he had reduced Jerusalem and its surrounding territory to an isolated district and had given away most of Judah's territory to loyal kings in the plain of Philistia, besides exacting a tribute which left Jerusalem impoverished, and carrying off the bulk of Judah's population. When Hezekiah died shortly after, his son Manasseh gave up rebellion, which had cost Judah so heavily.

THE TOMB OF A ROYAL STEWARD

As a corollary to this dramatic tale it is interesting to mention a detail made vivid by archaeology. In the story of the siege, an incident is related about Shebna the scribe, who is also referred to as the "man over the house" and who drew Isaiah's scorn.

"And when they called for the king, there came out to them Eliakim the son of Hilkiah, who was over the household, and Shebnah the secretary, and Joah the son of Asaph, the recorder". (2 K. 18:18)
. . . .

"The Lord of hosts has revealed himself in my ears:
'Surely this iniquity will not be forgiven you till you die',
Thus says the Lord God of hosts, 'Come, go to this steward, to Shebna, who is over the household, and say to him:
... you who hew a tomb on the height, and carve a habitation for yourself on the rock?". (Is. 22:14–16)

This tomb may have survived and may be identified with a rock-cut tomb with a Hebrew inscription found at the foot of the ancient wall of Jerusalem in Siloam. If it is not the actual tomb of Shebna (or Shebnaiah) it is the tomb of another royal steward and helps to make vivid Isaiah's oracle over Shebna.

This inscription reminiscent of Shebna's (or Shebnaiah's) title "over the house" was recently deciphered by Professor H. Avigad of the Hebrew University and reads:

'This is the sepulchre of . . . . iah (Shebnaiah?) who is over the house. There is no silver and no gold here, but only (his bones) and the bones of his handmaiden with him. Cursed is the man who will open this (sepulchre)

CHART III

B.C.E.	MESOPOTAMIA	JUDAH	ISRAEL	EGYPT
750	Tiglatpileser III (745–727)	Ahaz (743–727)	Zechariah (744)	
			Menahem (744–735)	
			Pekahiah (735–734)	
			Pekah (734–732)	
	Shalmaneser V (736–722)		Hoshea (732–724)	
			The Exile of Israel (722–720)	
700	Sargon II (721–705)	Hezekiah (727–698)		
	Sennacherib (704–681)	Manasseh (697–643)		
	Esarhaddon (680–669)	Ammon (642–640)		Psametik I (c. 665)
	Ashurbanipal (668–630)	Josiah (639–609)		Frees Egypt from
	Ashuruballit II (612–609)	Jehoahaz (609)		Assyria
		Jehoiakim (609–598)		Neco 609
		Jehoiachin		Campaign on the
		597 (3 months)		Euphrates
600	Babylon			
	Nebuchadrezzar II (604–562)	Zedekiah (597–586)		

A MANUSCRIPT OF ISAIAH AND "THE DIAL OF AHAZ"

The Miracle of a Shadow

Y. Yadin has found a slightly different reading of verse 8 in Isaiah 38 in a Scroll from the Dead Sea and this has contributed to his suggested solution of one of the unsolved prob-

Inscription on the rock-cut tomb at Siloam in ancient Hebrew characters.

lems of the Old Testament. In an episode describing Hezekiah's illness and his encounter with Isaiah, the prophet foresees his recovery and gives him a "sign" as proof. This is related in two versions, one in 2 Kings, the other in Isaiah.

"And Hezekiah said to Isaiah, 'What shall be the sign that the Lord will heal me, and that I shall go to the house of the Lord on the third day?' And Isaiah said, 'This is the sign to you from the Lord, that the Lord will do the thing that he has promised: shall the shadow go forward ten steps, or go back ten steps?' And Hezekiah answered, 'It is an easy thing for the shadow to lengthen ten steps; rather let the shadow go back ten steps.' And Isaiah the prophet cried to the Lord; and he brought the shadow back ten steps, by which the sun had declined on the dial of Ahaz". (2 K. 20: 8–11)

Isaiah 38: 7–8 (according to the Manuscript from the Dead Sea scroll):

7. " 'This is the sign to you from the Lord, that the Lord will do this thing that he has promised:

8. Behold, I will make the shadow cast by the declining sun on the *stairs* (*to*) *the roof* (*of the house*) *of Ahaz* turn back ten steps.' So the sun turned back on the dial the ten steps by which it had declined". (Is. 38: 7–8)

The idea behind the discussion of the "sign" is that accelerating the process of nature is easy compared with reversing it, but it was one calculated to encourage Hezekiah. The reversal of the shadow on the steps of the "dial of Ahaz" portended divine intervention on behalf of the people's head against Assyria (just as another miracle had, according to the current tradition, annihilated Sennacherib's army before Jerusalem). The miracle of the "dial of Ahaz" was the miracle of a shadow, not of a long day numbering more hours than the normal.

The construction of this contrivance was recently suggested by Y. Yadin to be two rows of steps in the house of king Ahaz (Isaiah's contemporary), leading to the roof. One row of steps faced east, another west. A contiguous low wall apparently faced each row of steps, as is often found in such constructions in oriental architecture. As the sun rose over its top it cast the shadow of the wall on the top step, then travelled downwards, thus indicating the passing of time, till noon. No shadow was cast at noon when the sun was overhead. As it moved westwards, the shadow of the western wall cast a shadow on the contiguous steps and it moved *upwards* until sunset.

ISAIAH OF JERUSALEM

In the time of the classical prophets many religious historical conceptions which had previously only existed in outline, began to assume more precise formulation. From this point of view it is important to understand what faith and history meant to Isaiah.

To Isaiah faith demanded a complete and firm commitment of one's whole being to God in the confidence that He is the true king, and this demand he hammered home in his encounters with Ahaz. His view was a development of the beliefs which had formed the basis of the Mosaic Covenant, and which regarded God as the source of order in man, society and history. On this foundation, Moses had established a system of government which placed supreme authority in the hands of Yahweh. The community of Israel was thus seen as representing God's new dispensation for the world, in which they existed as a nation under His command, destined to become the seed of a world-wide kingdom of

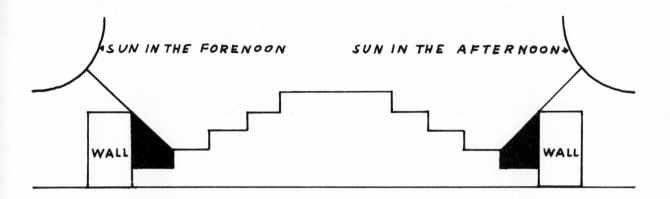

God. This attitude, Martin Buber has termed *Israel's theopolitical constitution* and it is fundamental to Isaiah's message.

THE PROPHET'S OUTLOOK ON THE COURSE OF HISTORY

Whether he preached on purity of worship or on collective conduct, Isaiah never failed to emphasize the retribution that would follow if his words were disregarded. Thus he framed all his prophecies in the dual symbolism of punishment and salvation.

Classical prophecy becomes nonsense if it is understood merely as the factual prediction of future events and its appeal to the conscience of the people ignored. The prophets were not in fact concerned with the future as such. Their province was the existing order and contemporary events, seen in the light of their view of the divine plan. The people had to be made to submit to the divine will through a change of heart. The prophet's audience fully understood this symbolism even if they chose to reject or misconstrue its meaning.

Three Phases in the Drama of God's Judgement

It seems possible that the experience of living through Jerusalem's deliverance from the besieging Assyrians had merged three separate oracles in Isaiah's Messianic vision. Professor Y. Kaufman sees this prophecy as a drama of Yahweh's intervention and judgement, played in three acts on the stage of world history.

In the first act, Assyria is visualized by Isaiah as the instrument of God's anger. No nation would be permitted to escape destruction at their hands and they would dominate the world: hence the futility of military alliance against Assyria. (See above, Isaiah and the Siege of Jerusalem).

The day of judgement follows in the second act:

"Therefore thus says the Lord, the Lord of hosts: 'O my people, who dwell in Zion, be not afraid of the Assyrians when they smite with the rod and lift up their staff against you as the Egyptians did. For in a very little while my indignation will come to an end, and my anger will be directed to their destruction. And the Lord of hosts will wield against them a scourge, as when he smote Midian at the rock of Oreb; and his rod will be over the sea, he will lift it as he did in Egypt. And in that day his burden will depart from your shoulder, and his yoke will be destroyed from your neck' ". (Is. 10:24–27)

> This is the purpose that is purposed
> concerning the whole earth;
> and this is the hand that is stretched out
> over all the nations.
>
> For the Lord of hosts has purposed,
> and who will annul it?
> His hand is stretched out,
> and who will turn it back?". (Is. 14:26-27)

In the day of judgement the destroyer would be condemned for he had raised his hand against Jerusalem. In that day, he would himself fall on the hills of Israel.

THE NEW KINGDOM OF THE HOUSE OF DAVID

Then follows the closing act of the divine drama, in one of Isaiah's most sublime oracles:

> "There shall come forth a shoot
> from the stump of Jesse,
> and a branch shall grow out of his roots.
> And the Spirit of the Lord shall rest upon him,
> the spirit of wisdom and understanding,
> the spirit of counsel and might,
> the spirit of knowledge and the fear of the Lord.
> And his delight shall be in the fear of the Lord.
>
> He shall not judge by what his eyes see,
> or decide by what his ears hear;
> but with righteousness he shall judge the poor,
> and decide with equity for the meek of the earth;
> and he shall smite the earth with the rod of his mouth,
> and with the breath of his lips he shall slay the wicked.
> Righteousness shall be the girdle of his waist,
> and faithfulness the girdle of his loins". (Is. 11:1–5)

It is interesting to note the symbols that characterize Isaiah's speech. For example, when he says that faithfulness will be the "girdle on the loins of the Messiah" he is borrowing an ancient image of combat that goes back to the heroic age of Near Eastern antiquity.

This longing for the coming of a better king is illustrated by the many Messianic oracles of Isaiah and his contemporary, Micah. They dream of a new branch of the house of David who, endowed with divine grace would initiate the reign of peace and justice and make the dynastic promises come true. The "saviour" (Messiah), shall come forth from the house of Jesse (David) as a branch bearing fruit. He will sit on the throne of David and the spirit and glory of Yahweh will descend upon him. With these endowments he will judge as no earthly king has ever judged. He shall be enthroned upon Mount Zion as Yahweh's unmistakable viceroy upon earth.

This picture of an ideal royal figure, wonderful in his power and far surpassing Hezekiah and all former kings in wisdom, was not intended as an accurate description of an historical figure. It is little wonder that the defenders of the Jewish faith have never been able to produce a real man who measured up to this image. The early Christians took this prophecy and many other references in the prophetic books as the prediction of their revelation of Christ. This portion of the doctrine of Isaiah has had the greatest significance for Christianity and has exercised great influence upon its development. However, this is a topic outside the scope of this book.

Isaiah's vision goes much further than an actual David. The ideal king will judge not by what he sees and hears, but by true justice and with fairness to the poor and the humble. The glory of Yahweh will transform the whole world into a kingdom without end, where all fear shall have been banished and peace and love shall reign upon earth:

"The wolf shall dwell with the lamb,
   and the leopard shall lie down with the kid
and the calf and the lion and the fatling together,
   and a little child shall lead them.
The cow and the bear shall feed;
   their young shall lie down together;
   and the lion shall eat straw like the ox.

The sucking child shall play over
   the hole of the asp,
   and the weaned child shall put
     his hand on the adder's den.
They shall not hurt or destroy
   in all my holy mountain;
for the earth shall be full of the
   knowledge of the Lord as the waters cover the sea.

In that day the root of Jesse shall stand as an ensign to the peoples; him shall the nations seek, and his dwellings shall be glorious". (Is. 11: 6-10)

This picture of the "kabod" (grace) of Yahweh pervading the structure of the world and bringing tranquility even to the animal kingdom is reminiscent of the belief in an initially blessed state in the Garden of Eden. There will be no more pain or destruction on God's mountain, for the earth shall be filled with the knowledge of Yahweh as the waters cover the sea.

IN THE END OF DAYS — CONCEPT OF UNIVERSAL PEACE

The symbols of the drama are resumed in Isaiah 2:2-4 in order to widen the picture of the transfigured Israel into a vision of universal peace that will replace the world empires.

"It shall come to pass in the latter days
   that the mountain of the house of
     the Lord
   shall be established as the highest
     of the mountains,
   and shall be raised above the hills;
and all the nations shall flow to it,
and all the nations shall come, and say:
'Come let us go up to the mountain of
     the Lord,
   to the house of the God of Jacob;

that he may teach us his ways
   and that we may walk in his paths'.
For out of Zion shall go forth the law,
   and the word of the Lord from Jerusalem.
He shall Judge between the nations,
   and shall decide for many peoples;
and they shall beat their swords into plowshares,
   and their spears into pruning hooks;
nation shall not lift up sword against nation,
   neither shall they learn war any more". (Is. 2: 2-4)

The spirit of god shall transfigure human nature, so that history and the order of society shall reflect Yahweh's glory.

"And the haughtiness of man shall be humbled
   and the pride of men shall be brought low;

and the Lord alone will be exalted in
   that day". (Is. 2: 17)

Side by side with this vision of ultimate bliss, Isaiah foresaw an end to idolatry and the turning of the heathen to Zion, thus emphasizing the idea of the universal God. This broad concept which appears for the first time in classical prophecy, was first stated by Isaiah. In his view, Israel's history was an integral part of the wider movement of world history in which Israel's destiny took the central role. This was how he viewed the relationship between developments in Assyria and Israel.

Whereas in remote antiquity the history of nations was seen as episodic and purpose-less, Isaiah in his vision of the end of days gave history a new coherence as the working out of God's purpose for the world. In the same way, once idolatry had been rejected, all peoples would share in the revelation and grace of God which had so far been vouchsafed only to Israel.

Isaiah's message was that it was not Yahweh's purpose to destroy Jerusalem. Instead, Yahweh intended to vindicate himself by crushing Assyria, thus sparing Jerusalem and Judah, and then building a new Jerusalem on the foundation of a "righteous remnant":

" 'Therefore thus says the Lord concerning the king of Assyria: He shall not come into this city, or shoot an arrow there, or come before it with a shield, or cast up a siege-mound against it. By the way that he came, by the same he shall return, and he shall not come into this city, says the Lord. For I will defend this city to save it, for my own sake and for the sake of my servant David' ". (Is. 37: 33–35)

"Therefore thus says the Lord God,   a stone, a tested stone,
'Behold, I am laying in Zion for a   a precious cornerstone, of a sure foundation:
    foundation   "He who believes will not be in haste." ' ". (Is. 28: 16)

CENTRAL THEMES IN THE BOOK OF ISAIAH

The essential elements that constitute the prophet's central theme may then be found in his appeal for faith in the holiness of Yahweh, king of the world and king of Israel, allied to his concept of the holiness of the Temple and the sacredness of the king.

The Prophet's Vision of the "Holy"

Isaiah raised the idea of God to a new and more exalted level by his definition of "holiness" in ethical terms. The concept of the "holy" or transcendent God is set forth in the glowing chapter which describes Isaiah's call to the office of prophet when, in a mystic trance, he saw Yahweh, the God of Israel. It has justly been observed that this vision should have been placed at the very beginning of the book of Isaiah, for it marked the turning point in his life:

"In the year that King Uzziah died I saw the Lord sitting upon a throne, high and lifted up; and his train filled the temple. Above him stood the seraphim; each had six wings: with two he covered his face; and with two he covered his feet, and with two he flew. And one called to another and said:
        'Holy, holy, holy is the Lord of hosts:
        the whole earth is full of his glory'.
And the foundations of the thresholds shook at the voice of him who called, and the house was filled with smoke". (Is. 6: 1–4)

It seems as real as though Isaiah's human eye had seen Yahweh on his throne. God revealed himself to Isaiah's inner spirit, but in recounting his experience, Isaiah had to use words that would be intelligible to his audience, which meant figures of speech and symbols drawn from the physical senses. His actual description of the event is in prose, but the speeches are in verse. There is a similar accent here to the concepts and background of the Temple Psalms:

"The Lord reigns; let the earth rejoice;   His lightnings lighten the world;
  let the many coastlands be glad!   the earth sees and trembles.
Clouds and thick darkness are round about him;   The mountains melt like wax before the Lord,
  righteousness and justice are the   before the Lord of all the earth.
    foundation of his throne.   The heavens proclaim his righteousness;
Fire goes before him,   and all the peoples behold his glory". (Psalm 97: 1 6)
  and burns up his adversaries round about.

"The voice of the Lord is powerful,
   the voice of the Lord is full of majesty.
The voice of the Lord breaks the cedars,
   the Lord breaks the cedars of Lebanon.
He makes Lebanon to skip like a calf,
   and Sirion like a young wild ox.

The voice of the Lord flashes forth flames of fire.
The voice of the Lord shakes the wilderness.
   the Lord shakes the wilderness of Kadesh.
. . . .
The voice of the Lord makes the oaks to whirl,
   and strips the forests bare;
and in his temple all cry, 'Glory!' ". (Ps. 29:4–9)

Yahweh's "train" of seraphim "filled the Temple", as did the smoke. He was "Holy, Holy, Holy". This repetition has come in Isaiah to have a moral meaning which it did not have in earlier times. To Isaiah's inner eye, Yahweh is the Holy One of Israel, unapproachable in holiness. By comparison Isaiah feels himself a man of sin.

The Holiness of the Temple

Isaiah's vision of the holiness of the Temple is a reiteration of the concepts already current in David's and Solomon's time and immortalized in folk traditions and in the Psalms, the liturgy of the Temple. W.F. Albright explains the concept of Yahweh's enthronement there "as the sole ruler of the entire cosmos; heaven, earth and underworld were all subject to him; all functions of all pagan deities were gathered into his hands. The Temple further symbolized the permanence of the Davidic dynasty, which was expected to stand as long as the two cosmic pillars Jachin and Boaz" (See Ch. XIII on the Temple).

Cherubim had a divine connotation in Phoenicia. This symbolism is present in Isaiah's vision.

Like Amos, Hosea and the earlier prophets, Isaiah was a "man of God", wholly dedicated to God. The prophetic vocation was founded on the charismatic grace of God, which came to them spontaneously, often when they neither expected nor wanted it. The compulsive nature of this religious vocation does not mean that they were in conflict with the priesthood. The prophets were often united in guilds and formed part of the personnel of a sanctuary.

Isaiah's oracles followed the two main lines of Amos's and Hosea's teaching: i.e. insistence on pure monotheism, rejecting any compromise with alien, or idolatrous, worship; and exhortation to moral righteousness. Like the earlier prophets, Isaiah hankered after the ancient simple life. In all their preaching there is the appeal to sentiments typical of a pastoral folk possessing a simpler and grander religious ideal than the beliefs of more sophisticated urban dwellers. But for Isaiah and his "remnant" of followers, the concept of God had moved forward and developed to a stage beyond the older ideal.

Unlike his predecessors, Isaiah was a city prophet. A native of Jerusalem, of good family and in close touch with the king and court, he had a considerable following in the heart of the Israelite community. From this came his political influence. It may also help to explain his messianic vision.

The Sanctity of the King

In Isaiah's doctrine, God's power was too vast for His purpose to be frustrated simply by the disobedience of the nation, or the king. Admittedly, King Ahaz had betrayed Isaiah's dynastic ideal of Yahweh's promises to the house of David, but he nonetheless continued to summon the nation to trust in him. In Israel, as in all ancient society, blessing and strength went out to the people through the person of their king. The soul of the nation was centred in the king, the "shield" of his people. The king was the "mashiah" (Messiah or anointed) of Yahweh. He was the channel of the divine spirit and consequently superintended the organization of the cults. But Isaiah proclaimed that God was supreme. The king must accept His word, as given by His prophet.

Thus the prophet reaffirmed David's theology, adding to it the element of submission to Yahweh and acceptance of the obligations of the Covenant. His broader message is only to be understood in the light of these concepts:

"The Lord will bring upon you and upon your people and upon your father's house such days as have not come since the day that Ephraim departed from Judah - the king of Assyria". (Is· 7: 17)

To Isaiah, the nation was in distress not because the promises to David were not true, but because they had not been believed. Hence the combination of foreboding and assurance in Isaiah's prophecy. They are not inconsistent.

In the meantime, Isaiah and his "children", his disciples, would wait for God's "Kabod" (glory):

"I will wait for the Lord, who is hiding his face from the house of Jacob, and I will hope in him. Behold, I and the children whom the Lord has given me are signs and portents in Israel from the Lord of hosts, who dwells on Mount Zion". (Is. 8: 17–18)

This message is meant for the remnant of the disciples who would have to await the outcome of the "child that will rule over them"

A LIFE OF STRUGGLE

We may now attempt to outline the main periods of Isaiah's career.

The first period covers his vision and initiation as a prophet at the beginning of the reign of King Ahaz ,who turned a deaf ear to Isaiah's message. Then comes the period of the Aram-Ephraim invasion. It is assumed that Isaiah tried to prevent the misuse of his words and oracles and entrusted his prophecies to a circle of "limmudim" (disciples and followers). We can well imagine the impact of his amazing eloquence on the spiritual life of his time. His words unquestionably contributed largely to the subsequent religious reforms and initiated the greater spiritualization of religion in the centuries that followed.

He decided to keep a record of his efforts to save the people from their folly:

> "And now, go, write it before them on a tablet,　　　　that it may be for the time to come
> and inscribe it in a book,　　　　　　　　　　　　　as a witness for ever". (Is. 30:8)

The third period comes some thirty years later, during the Assyrian invasion and the deliverance of Jerusalem, at which time Isaiah found in the new king, Hezekiah, a deeply religious personality.

In the fifty years during which his figure towered over the contemporary scene, Isaiah symbolized the spiritual crisis of his time. He guided his people through a testing time of tragedy and crisis and, in his relentless search for purity of worship and righteousness of conduct, he created a spiritual doctrine whose impact on future generations was unaffected by the tragic fate of the nation

ELEMENTS OF THE BOOK OF ISAIAH

The life and mission of Isaiah of Jerusalem is related in Isaiah 1–39. In addition, the book contains many prophecies which cannot have been written by him. The prophecies of Isaiah 40–66 all belong to another age and an entirely different environment, as will be explained in Chapters XIX and XX of this book.

There are other elements of especial beauty which are echoed elsewhere in the scriptures. Among them is the picture of the "doomed nation which is to be exterminated as a terebinth":

> "And though a tenth remain in it,　　　　whose stump remains standing
> it will be burned again,　　　　　　　　when it is felled.
> like a terebinth or an oak,　　　　　　　The holy seed is its stump". (Is. 6: 13)

The parable of the vineyard ,written in an attractive, musical verse, is full of native Israel imagery:

> "Let me sing for my beloved　　　　　　　and planted it with choice vines;
> a love song concerning his vineyard:　　he built a watchtower in the midst of it,
> My beloved had a vineyard　　　　　　　and hewed out a wine vat in it;
> on a very fertile hill.　　　　　　　　　and he looked for it to yield grapes,
> He digged it and cleared it of stones,　　but it yielded wild grapes". (Is. 5: 1–2)

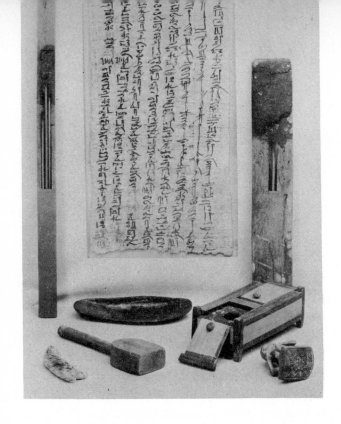

The scribe's equipment: Palette (left) and writing utensils (right); wood inkwell (under palette); seal (right-hand corner).

MICAH

The Fall of Zion Through Social Injustice

"Can I forget the treasures of wickedness in
  the house of the wicked,
and the scant measure that is accursed?
Shall I acquit the man with wicked scales
  and with a bag of deceitful weights?

Your rich men are full of violence;
  your inhabitants speak lies,
and their tongue is deceitful in
    their mouth". (Micah 6: 10–12)

In Micah, a contemporary of Isaiah, we find a simple and forceful summary of the demand for social justice voiced by Amos. His appeal is for a steadfast love binding men in covenant with Yahweh and with one another. This is repeated in Hosea and also in Isaiah's exhortation to the quiet deep faith of the "humble walk" with Yahweh.

"For the son treats the father with contempt,
  the daughter rises up against her mother,
the daughter-in-law against her mother-in-law;
  a man's enemies are the men of his own house.
But as for me, I will look to the Lord,
  I will wait for the God of my salvation;

my God will hear me.
Rejoice not over me, O my enemy;
  when I fall, I shall rise;
when I sit in darkness,
  the Lord will be a light to me". (Micah 7: 6–9)

Like Isaiah, Micah also insisted on the holiness of Yahweh and foresaw the universality and righteousness of divine government of the world. He, too, proclaimed the righteous God who deals with all nations, Israel included, on the basis of ethical principles.

The prophet's function, as Micah saw it, was not to predict the future, but to stir the popular conscience by confronting it with the ethical demands of Yahweh. Yahweh, he preached, asked only justice, uprightness and humility. These were the essentials and other manifestations of religious feeling merely trappings.

Unlike Isaiah, Micah did not believe that Jerusalem would remain inviolable because it was holy. On the contrary, he made a *revolutionary departure* in prophecy by attributing Zion's fall to the universal corruption of society.

"Hear this, you heads of the house of Jacob
   and rulers of the house of Israel,
who abhor justice
   and pervert all equity,
who build Zion with blood
   and Jerusalem with wrong.
Its heads give judgment for a bribe,
   its priests teach for hire,
   its prophets divine for money;

yet they lean upon the Lord and say,
   'Is not the Lord in the midst of us?
   No evil shall come upon us'.
Therefore because of you
   Zion shall be plowed as a field;
Jerusalem shall become a heap of ruins,
   and the mountain of the house a
      wooded height". (Micah 3: 9–12)

He rejected outright the confidence, supported by popular belief, and expressed in the Psalms, that Yahweh had chosen Zion as his eternal dwelling place. Like Isaiah, he maintained that this was not an unconditional promise but was one side of a covenant .The possibility of the withdrawal of God's favour was inherent in the ancient covenant.

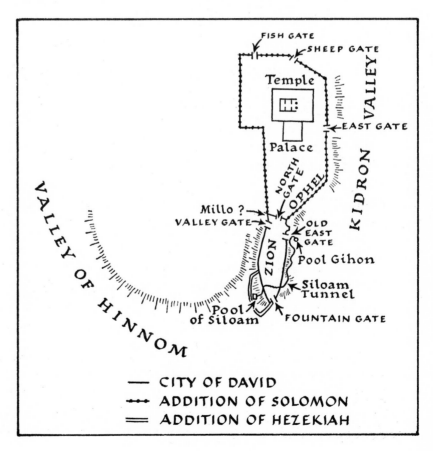

Jerusalem in the days of Kings.

Micah was long remembered for this condemnation of Jerusalem. It was quoted a century later by Jeremiah when his life was threatened because he had made a similar prediction about Jerusalem and its Temple:

" 'Micah of Moresheth prophesied in the days of Hezekiah king of Judah, and said to all the people of Judah: 'Thus says the Lord of hosts,

> Zion shall be plowed as a field;
> Jerusalem shall become a heap of ruins,
> and the mountain of the house a wooded height'.

Did Hezekiah king of Judah and all Judah put him to death? Did he not fear the Lord and entreat the favor of the Lord, and did not the Lord repent of the evil which he had pronounced against them? But we are about to bring great evil upon ourselves' ". (Jeremiah 26: 18–19)

The hope inherent in the Davidic dynasty and its covenant is still retained but with a difference. Jerusalem will fall, but Judah will be delivered by the grace of God and will be ruled by a prince and saviour descended "from of old, from ancient days", i.e. from the lineage of David, and he will usher in the age of peace.

The God whom Micah worships is no petty national deity, committed unconditionally to the support of his own city and people. If sufficiently provoked by their sin, he is prepared to hurl them to destruction.

Unlike the aristocratic Isaiah, Micah was a rustic prophet, in close touch and sympathy with the peasant class. He spoke for the poor farmers in his native hills to the south of Jerusalem, who suffered at the hands of exacting landlords. He even saw the social order as a civil war conducted by the upper class against the poor:

> "But you rise against my people as an enemy;
>   you strip the robe from the peaceful,
> from those who pass by trustingly
>   with no thought of war.
> The women of my people you drive out
>   from their pleasant houses;
> from their young children you take away
>   my glory for ever". (Micah 2: 8–9)

He insisted that cities were the source of these social vices and that the corruption of Israel had spread into Judah:

> "For this I will lament and wail;
>   I will go stripped and naked;
> I will make lamentation like the jackals,
>   and mourning like the ostriches.
> For her wound is incurable;
>   and it has come to Judah,
> it has reached to the gate of my people,
>   to Jerusalem." (Micah 1: 8–9)

Episode from the siege of a city by the Assyrians. From Nimrud.

Assyrian cavalry in the mountains. Alabaster slab from a wall.

Assyrian soldiers leading away prisoners of war and transporting women in a cart. Relief from the palace of Ashurbanipal at Nineveh.

CHAPTER XVII

THE VOICE OF ISRAEL'S CONSCIENCE

MANASSEH IN THE DAYS OF ASSYRIAN VASSALDOM

Manasseh, who followed Hezekiah, ruled for many years (697–643) as a vassal of Esar-haddon and Ashurbanipal. During the first years of his reign the legacy of destruction and foreign oppression left him by his father lay heavily on the amputated kingdom of Judah. Accordingly, under Manasseh, there was a reaction against the continuation of political re-sistance as well as the spirit of prophecy. As a vassal within the new world empire of Assyria he was discreet enough to stage no revolt, to pay his tribute on time and to keep out of trouble. But what loomed largest to the recorders of the Book of Kings was his thorough-going reaction away from his father's religious reform towards a degree of foreign cultism unheard of even in the days of his grandfather Ahaz. The Baal and Astarta cults on the high-places were restored and accompanied by male and female sacred prostitution at the shrines of "kedeshim" and "kedeshot", which was widely practised in the surrounding countries. Subservience to Assyria meant the invasion of the country by the astrological and divinatory rites of the conquerors as well as the revival of indigenous Canaanite cults:

"For he rebuilt the high places which Hezekiah his father had destroyed; and he erected altars for Baal, and made an Asherah, as Ahab king of Israel had done, and worshiped all the host of heaven, and served them. And he built altars in the house of the Lord, of which the Lord had said, 'In Jerusalem will I put my name'. And he built altars for all the host of heaven in the two courts of the house of the Lord. And he burned his son as an offering, and prac-ticed soothsaying and augury, and dealt with mediums and with wizards. He did much evil in the sight of the Lord, provoking him to anger". (2K. 21: 3–6)

" 'I will stretch out my hand against Judah,
  and against all the inhabitants of Jerusalem;
and I will cut off from this place the remnant of Baal
  and the name of the idolatrous priests;
those who bow down on the roofs
  to the host of the heavens;
those who bow down and swear to the Lord
  and yet swear by Milcom' ". (Zephaniah 1: 4–5)

" 'Did you bring to me sacrifices and offerings the forty years in the wilderness, O house of Israel? You shall take
up Sakkuth your king, and Kaiwan your star-god, your images, which you made for yourselves' ". (Amos 5: 25–26)

Assyria forced its own forms of worship on the peoples it conquered, and probably under this pressure, Manasseh allowed star and planetary worship and the cult of Moloch, an Ammonite deity, whose worship had close associations with astral divination.

Its ritual was characterized by the sacrifice of the first-born in which parents compelled their children to pass through or into a furnace of fire. Manasseh apparently sacrificed his own first-born, which to biblical tradition is not piety but the shedding of innocent blood:

"They served their idols,
  which became a snare to them.
They sacrificed their sons
  and their daughters to the demons". (Psalm 106: 36–37)

The political terrorism by which Manasseh held power, or perhaps a new fashion he may have set, is tersely summarized:

"Moreover Manasseh shed very much innocent blood, till he had filled Jerusalem from one end to another, besides
the sin which he made Judah to sin so that they did what was evil in the sight of the Lord". (2 K. 21: 16)

Hezekiah's reform had been cancelled completely. The voice of prophecy was silenced and it appears that those who protested were dealt with severely. Manasseh is branded as the worst king ever to sit on David's throne. It is thought that Manasseh could hold the throne as long as he did due to his loyalty to Assyria, both politically and culturally.

In this outburst of pagan cultism, altars were even erected within the Temple of Jerusalem. We may take this to mean that Manasseh and the common people had not entirely abandoned Yahweh as their national God, but that they were encouraged to think of foreign gods as members of Yahweh's heavenly host, who were associated with him in both the heavenly and earthly temples. Contrary to the ancient tradition that Yahweh permitted the worship of none but himself, he may have been regarded as the chief of a group of astral and other gods who had a particular appeal at the shrines.

It is assumed that the king gained the support of the people in the towns outside Jerusalem, especially the provincial priests, whose allegiance to their own shrines ran counter to the central shrine of Jerusalem. In addition, the tradespeople who wanted tranquillity and prosperity above everything were prepared to adapt themselves to the new political climate. An important element, "the people of the land", exercised a potent influence in public affairs.

They represented at that time the influential people in Judah, the landed class and the rural priesthood. Their leaders in Jerusalem who tended to come to the fore whenever they sensed a threat to the succession of the Davidic dynasty, made their first appearance in the latter days of Queen Athaliah. It was the "people of the land" who crowned young Josiah after the death of his father and Amon as well as Jehoahaz, thereby demonstrating their desire to maintain the traditional sacred kingship with the existing status quo. The conservatism of the people was thus in line with the interests of the large landowners, the bulwark of Judah's monarchy.

ASTRAL CULTS AND MAGIC

Throughout the Assyrian empire great importance was given to astral worship, for the Mesopotamians were the most star conscious people of ancient history. In addition, Assyrians and Arameans were enslaved to evil spirits and practised magic rites, divination, necromancy and every variety of demon-energized occultism.

Manasseh is said to have practised augury and used enchantments, and dealt with them that had familiar spirits (divining demons) and with wizards who were possessed of occult knowledge because they were under the control of a divining demon, as held in Assyrian demonology. Mesopotamia is our richest source for the study of early magic and divination tablets giving incantations, augural prognostications and rituals of exorcism have been found there in abundance.

Presentation by king Nabupaliddina (third figure wearing conical headdress) to the enthroned Sun god Shamash sitting in his shrine. Within the shrine are the emblems of the moon crescent (Sinn), the sun-disc Shamash and the eight-pointed star (Ishtar). Below the entire scene are wavy lines, a representation of the heavenly scene (Apsu). From a memorial tablet of endowment of the shrine at Sippar in Babylonia.

The goddess Nana, under the same symbols, Sinn, Shamash and Ishtar, receives the Babylonian king Meli-Shipak and his daughter. From a Babylonian boundary-stone (Kuduru) of the 13th century B.C.E.

Inscribed bronze statue of the demon Pazuzu

Symbols of the deities of the Babylonian pantheon inscribed on a boundary-stone of the 12th century B.C.E.

A Babylonian magic device was the inspection of the liver of an animal, correlating human destinies and the formation of the liver. Clay models like this were made of important omens for study and reference.

A prism of the Assyrian king reads: "*I assembled the kings of Syria and of the other side of the river. Balu᾽ King of Tyre, Menasseh, King of Judah (Menasi King of Yaudi), Kaushgbari King of Edom (Amor).*"

THE ASSYRIAN TREATMENT

Manasseh was humbled at one time by Esarhaddon, who lists him among those subject nations from whom he had commandeered labour to rebuild the great Front Palace at Nineveh.

It would appear that once during his long reign, and probably during the political upheavals that occurred in the time of Ashurbanipal, Manasseh became involved in one of the uprisings against Assyria. This accords well with the biblical record:

"Therefore the Lord brought upon them the commanders of the army of the king of Assyria, who took Manasseh with hooks and bound him with fetters of bronze and brought him to Babylon". (2 Chr. 33: 11)

We also have a realistic representation of the ignominious treatment accorded to rebellious vassals in an Assyrian sculpture which may reveal the occasion of Manasseh's trip to Assyria. This is described by Isaiah and also vividly remembered later by the prophet Ezekiel:

"Because you have raged against me
  and your arrogance has come to my ears,
I will put my hook in your nose
  and my bit in your mouth,
and I will turn you back on the way
  by which you came". (Is. 37: 29)

A vassal of Assyria, portrayed as held by a hook through his lips, the attached string being held in the hands of the conqueror. From a panel at the top of a broken obelisk of the 10th century, at Nineveh.

THE LAST GREAT KING OF ASSYRIA

Manasseh may have had to participate, along with other vassals of Esarhaddon, in the campaign against Egypt, a tremendous event of the time. The Babylonian scribes record several attempts, during one of which Esarhaddon was killed and was succeeded by Ashurbanipal who continued the operation and conquered Thebes in 667 B.C.E. The impression that the fall of that great city made on the world still rings through the Ode of Nahum on the fall of "the harlot", Assyria, and her victim, Egypt:

> "Are you better than Thebes
>   that sat by the Nile,
> with water around her,
>   her rampart a sea,
>   and water her wall?
> Ethiopia was her strength,
>   Egypt too, and that without limit;
>   Put and the Libyans were her helpers.

> Yet she was carried away,
>   she went into captivity;
> her little ones were dashed in pieces
>   at the head of every street;
> for her honored men lots were cast,
>   and all her great men were
> bound in chains". (Nahum 3: 8–10)

With Ashurbanipal Assyrian civilization reached its apex. The art in this period was enriched by contacts with Egypt and the west. Greater compositions, especially in relief, were now attempted than ever before. These reliefs, set on different horizontal lines, convey a feeling of depth unequalled in earlier Assyrian reliefs. When they do not hark back to a stereotyped tradition, the animals of this period are particularly fine. The hunting scenes, depicting pain of wounded animals, and the battle scenes are among the finest representations in world art, comparing favourably with such representations in Egypt at their best. It is interesting to note that this high point in the arts, civilization and commerce came just before Assyria's downfall. Assyria's successors in Mesopotamia inherited this civilization.

Nahum's verses recall Egypt's "great men". When this wooden statue of an Egyptian noble was excavated, the Arab workmen dubbed him "sheikh-el-balad" the headman of the village, for which he was the prototype.

Winged bull adorning Assyrian palaces.

Ashurbanipal carrying a basket for rebuilding the Esagila temple in Babylon.

Ashurbanipal offering a libation after the hunt, doing homage to his god "before whom he went", over the bodies of slain lions. Hunting was a part of royalty's obligations, not a mere sport.

Ashurbanipal's annals state that twenty-two vassal kings were made to join him in the campaign, among them Minishi of Yaudi (Manasseh of Judah). But this fact is either suppressed or forgotten by the chronicler of the Books of Kings.

ASSYRIA TOTTERS

The Assyrian empire, held together by force and a well organized administration had become unwieldy. Though it had no actual rival world power, it disintegrated under the pressure of conquered peoples within the empire and outside. Ashurbanipal's older brother, Shamash-shumukin, who governed the Chaldeans of lower Babylonia, rebelled in 652 with the support of Elam and Iranian highlanders to the east. The Semitic tribes of the Syrian and Arabian deserts began pressing hard on the periphery of the empire, while at the other end of the realm, Psammetic I gradually regained control of Egypt, then withheld tribute and proclaimed his independence (c. 655). Lydia in Asia Minor rebelled as well. After a bitter struggle which shook the empire to its foundations (652–648), Ashurbanipal mastered the situation though he could not reconquer Egypt. But he deported the defeated Elamites and Babylonians to Samaria and settled them there, which is evidenced much later by Ezra:

Ashurbanipal was the last great king of Assyria. In this scene, he reclining and his queen seated on the throne, are feasting in their garden and "toasting" a recent victory. The defeated victim's head may still be seen hanging from the tree facing the harpist.

mite prisoners partake of a meal beside a heavily loaded wagon.   Assyrians in camp near a fortified town.

Siege of an Egyptian city by Ashurbanipal, and shackled prisoners taken by the army. Relief from the King's palace at Nineveh.

"Then wrote Rehum the commander, Shimshai the scribe, and the rest of their associates, the judges, the governors, the officials, the Persians, the men of Erech, the Babylonians, the men of Susa, that is, the Elamites, and the rest of the nations whom the great and noble Osnappar deported and settled in the cities of Samaria and in the rest of the province Beyond the River". (Ezra 4: 9–10). — (Osnappar is Ashurbanipal)

As foreign domination relaxed about the middle of his reign, Manasseh took advantage of the troubled times to fortify Jerusalem and reinforce his garrisons in the fortified towns of Judah which had been destroyed by Sennacherib. The Chronicler also attributes to him a change of heart as well as independence of spirit:

"Afterwards he built an outer wall to the city of David west of Gihon, in the valley, to the entrance by the Fish Gate, and carried it round Ophel, and raised it to a very great height; he also put commanders of the army in all the fortified cities in Judah. And he took away the foreign gods and the idol from the house of the Lord, and all the altars that he had built on the mountain of the house of the Lord and in Jerusalem, and he threw them outside of the city. He also restored the altar of the Lord and offered upon it sacrifices of peace offerings and of thanksgiving; and he commanded Judah to serve the Lord the God of Israel". (2 Chr. 33: 14–16)

The brief reign of his successor, Amon (642–640) made no impact on the situation in Judah. Amon was assassinated by conspirators. However, the "people of the land" took control of the situation, slew the conspirators and enthroned his son Josiah, then a boy eight years old (640–609).

JOSIAH'S GREAT REFORM

The time was ripe for Judah to awake from its state of inertia. The young king was influenced by priests and others loyal to Yahweh and his impact was to be felt on all the subsequent history of Israel:

"For in the eighth year of his reign, while he was yet a boy, he began to seek the God of David his father; and in the twelfth year he began to purge Judah and Jerusalem of the high places, the Asherim, and the graven and the molten images. And they broke down the altars of the Baals in his presence; and he hewed down the incense altars which stood above them; and he broke in pieces the Asherim and the graven and the molten images, and he made dust of them and strewed it over the graves of those who had sacrificed to them. He also burned the bones of the priests on their altars, and purged Judah and Jerusalem. And in the cities of Manasseh, Ephraim, and Simeon, and as far as Naphtali, in their ruins round about, he broke down the altars, and beat the Asherim and the images into powder, and hewed down all the incense altars throughout all the land of Israel". (2 Chr. 34: 3–7)

While engaged on this sweeping reform, Josiah revived the anti-Assyrian policies of Hezekiah, and at the death of Ashurbanipal in 627 he annexed the Assyrian provinces of Samaria, Galilee and Gilead. His aspirations to restore the united kingdom of David and Solomon, were intensified by the shifting international political situation. The Assyrian empire had finally split in two when in 626 B.C.E. Babylon broke away and the new Babylonian kingdom of the Chaldeans was founded by Nabopolassar, a princeling from southern Mesopotamia. This foreshadowed a spate of national independence movements throughout the Assyrian Empire and in the coming struggle for control of the Near East, Palestine was the strongest independent state between Assyria, Babylonia, Media and Egypt. Thus, the anti-Assyrian policy and religious reforms of Hezekiah and Josiah ultimately enabled Judah to survive Assyria.

Josiah's stiffening attitude towards Assyria was accompanied by a movement of religious reform which was strengthened by the wave of nationalism. Stimulated by the teachings of the contemporary prophets, Jeremiah and Zephaniah, this movement had wide popular support and must have been growing for quite a few years. In many respects, it reflected the attempt of Yahweh's adherents to rescue the state and its people from their headlong rush to destruction. The issue as they saw it was the life or extinction of Judah: to obey Yahweh would ensure life and security as promised by the Book of the Law; to forsake Him meant utter disaster. The progress of this movement culminated in the dramatic series of events in the Temple and capital recorded in the stirring tale of 2 Chr. 34 and 2K. 22–23, which should be read in the context of the political situation of the time.

AN ANCIENT SCROLL IS RE-DISCOVERED

In the course of repairs and purification of the Temple, a remarkable discovery was made. This was in the 18th year of Josiah's reign (621 B.C.E.). Josiah's secretary came to the Temple to supervise the payment of the workers' wages and was informed that an ancient scroll had been discovered. This was the "book of the law". In the opinion of modern scholars it was the archaic form or the nucleus of the Book of Deuteronomy, though the traditional view is that it was the entire Pentateuch; but ancient scrolls were much shorter than the length of all the five books. (See Chap IX: How Old is Deuteronomy). The matter was immediately brought to Josiah's attention:

"And when the king heard the words of the book of the law, he rent his clothes. And the king commanded Hilkiah the priest, and Ahikam the son of Shaphan, and Achbor the son of Micaiah, and Shaphan the secretary, and Asaiah the king's servant, saying, 'Go, inquire of the Lord for me, and for the people, and for all Judah, concerning the words of this book that has been found; for great is the wrath of the Lord that is kindled against us, because our fathers have not obeyed the words of this book, to do according to all that is written concerning us' ". (2 K. 22: 11–13)

In great consternation over the neglect which such holy writing had suffered, and fearful because its commandments had not been followed, the king urged the High Priest to verify its authenticity and authorship. This was done by consulting the prophetess Huldah. Her reply cut deep into the people's conscience:

" 'Thus says the Lord, Behold, I will bring evil upon this place and upon its inhabitants, all the words of the book which the king of Judah has read. Because they have forsaken me and have burned incense to other gods, that they might provoke me to anger with all the work of their hands, therefore my wrath will be kindled against this place, and it will not be quenched. But as to the king of Judah, who sent you to inquire of the Lord, thus shall you say to him, Thus says the Lord, the God of Israel: Regarding the words which you have heard, because your heart was penitent, and you humbled yourself before the Lord, when you heard how I spoke against this place, and against its inhabitants, that they should become a desolation and a curse, and you have rent your clothes and wept before me, I also have heard you, says the Lord. Therefore, behold, I will gather you to your fathers, and you shall be gathered to your grave in peace, and your eyes shall not see all the evil which I will bring upon this place'. And they brought back word to the king". (2 K. 22: 16–20)

The wrath of God had been incurred and punishment would follow in accordance with the curse laid upon the nation when it disobeyed Yahweh's commandments:

" 'Behold, I set before you this day a blessing and a curse: the blessing, if you obey the commandments of the Lord your God, which I command you this day, and the curse, if you do not obey the commandments of the Lord your God, but turn aside from the way which I command you this day, to go after other gods which you have not known' ". (Deut. 11: 26–28)

" 'But if you will not obey the voice of the Lord your God or be careful to do all his commandments and his statutes which I command you this day, then all these curses shall come upon you and overtake you. Cursed shall you be in the city, and cursed shall you be in the field. Cursed shall be your basket and your kneading-trough. Cursed shall be the fruit of your body, and the fruit of your ground, the increase of your cattle, and the young of your flock. Cursed shall you be when you come in, and cursed shall you be when you go out' ". (Deut. 28: 15–19)

The prophetess made a favourable prognosis for Josiah's own reign, but ultimate wrath for previous disobedience was to bring destruction thereafter.

"Then the king sent and gathered together all the elders of Judah and Jerusalem. And the king went up to the house of the Lord, with all the men of Judah and the inhabitants of Jerusalem and the priests and the Levites, all the people both great and small; and he read in their hearing all the words of the book of the covenant which had been found in the house of the Lord. And the king stood in his place and made a covenant before the Lord, to walk after the Lord and to keep his commandments and his testimonies and his statutes, with all his heart and all his soul, to perform the words of the covenant that were written in this book. Then he made all who were present in Jerusalem and in Benjamin stand to it. And the inhabitants of Jerusalem did according to the covenant of God, the God of their fathers. And Josiah took away all the abominations from all the territory that belonged to the people of Israel, and made all who were in Israel serve the Lord their God. All his days they did not turn away from following the Lord the God of their fathers". (2 Chr. 34: 29–33)

This story of the rediscovery of the Mosaic Torah and the subsequent delivery of the Law, calls to mind the ancient Covenant convocations "before God" at Shechem, when the "book of the Torah of God" was read to the people (See Ch.VIII: The Renewal of the Covenant); and the original Covenant ceremony described in Ex. 24: 3–8, when Moses read "the Book of the Covenant", (See Ch. VII: The Covenant Ceremony).

It may also be noted that in this upsurge of nationalist and religious feeling Josiah convoked the Jerusalemites, the provincial Judeans and "the people of the land", who played a prominent role in public affairs. Added to them were the priests and prophets who were in the leadership of the religious reform and nationalist movements throughout Palestine.

The nucleus of the book of Deuteronomy did not, of course, explicitly designate Jerusalem as the central sanctuary, for the scroll and its composition had a long history and may well have dated from the days following the Conquest and the period of Judges. The original writers may well have meant the city of Shechem as the seat of the central shrine; this was the scene of the Covenant renewal under Joshua, and the city chosen by Jeroboam I as his first capital. Nevertheless, for the purpose of their reform, Josiah's generation identified the central sanctuary with Jerusalem.

Throughout the ancient Near East, it must be remembered, law codes were not followed literally and in practice were often disregarded. Judges and kings were guided by traditional custom, public opinion and common sense. Some of them may have referred to written codes, but the people at large were apparently ignorant of their content and spirit. Possibly, divine guidance had been sought both by the people of Judah and their kings from oracles or through the priests. Now, with this second giving of the law, the ancient Mosaic teaching could speak directly to the people and while the Covenant had barely survived in an oral tradition, there was now a favourable atmosphere for it to become generally known among the people. Into the ferment of insecurity and anxiety aroused by the doom-laden predictions of the prophets, the discovery of the ancient scroll burst like a thunderclap.

There was probably nothing new in the laws which it laid down, but they appeared as revered ancient traditions which had been forgotten. The reform movement, which had begun with Josiah's succession, had laid the foundation for a new appreciation of the older Mosaic Covenant to be superimposed on popular religion and the national covenant of David. The document imposed many forgotten obligations on the nation but the fact that it was regarded as divinely inspired and contained "the blessings and the curses" lent it the necessary authority.

The significance of this return to the ancient code is that for the first time in the history of Israel (and of the world) a written document was actually adopted as the permanent law-code of the nation. By it, Yahweh, king and people were bound for all time. High places, provincial priesthood and foreign worship, whether Canaanite, Phoenician or Assyrian, were finally rejected. This change was to have far-reaching consequences as will be related in the subsequent chapters.

THE CENTRAL SANCTUARY

Josiah had only to destroy the one remaining sanctuary at Bethel, in order to leave the Temple in Jerusalem the sole centre for sacrifice and pilgrimage. This he did. The Chronicler notes with pride how the people flocked again to Jerusalem to celebrate the Passover, a practice which had apparently fallen into disuse. Now, in accordance with the Law, a great Passover, such as had not been celebrated since the days of Judges, was celebrated under the king's orders. Combining nationalism with the drive for purity of worship, it was seen as a symbol of the restoration of a united Israel under a descendant of David, and thus appealed to every Jew who recalled the glory of the past. Since the miraculous deliverance of Jerusalem from Sennacherib's army in 701, the people and most of the prophets had felt confident that Zion would be spared and would be granted a happy future. This led to the proud certainty that God was on the side of the people, expressed in the motto "being in Zion". It grew with time and seemed to be one point on which priesthood and prophets could agree. Their agreement contributed to the success of Josiah's reform and to a revived sense of spiritual security.

Since the priests officiating in Jerusalem were also declared the only legitimate priests, the reform secured the backing of an official body whose own interests made it enlist the support of all its members. It made one sanctuary and one priesthood essential for true worship, since Yahweh could only be worshipped where his altar stood and this may have restricted the number of people who could reach Him. Only by a pilgrimage to the Temple in Jerusalem could men enter into full relation with Yahweh. The method in which the ritual was performed by the priests and the ceremonial law became of primary importance. The attention of priests and people was directed to exact observance according to the law as prescribed by the Book of Deuteronomy. Although important in breaking the pagan tradition of Manasseh's reign, the reform was in principle a return to the ancient mode which had long been outstripped by the more ethical thought of Israel under the influence of its prophets.

CHAPTER XVIII

THE DOOM OF THE NATION

I. UPHEAVAL IN THE NEAR EAST

The beginning of the collapse of the Assyrian empire came with the invasion of barbaric hordes from the north. These people, known to Greek historians as Cimmerians and Scythians, broke through the Caspian Gates, smashed the political barriers set up by the Assyrians and made their way into the Near East. Some scholars speculate whether a memory of their invasion of Syria may not be reflected in the prophecies of Zephaniah and some of the oracles of Jeremiah concerning the "people from the North". The invaders were not the type to establish a stable empire, but Herodotus tells us that they ruled over western Asia for twenty-eight years "during which time their insolence and oppression spread on every side". It must have been widely realized that Assyria's power over the west of Asia was at an end.

THE FALL OF ASSYRIA

The dynamic Ashurbanipal ruled Assyria until 633 B.C.E. His successors were short-lived and unable to prevent former vassals from breaking away from the tottering empire.

A Babylonian text, the "Chronicle of the Fall of Nineveh", describes the campaigns of Nabopolassar, the founder of the Babylonian empire (626–609 B.C.E.) who gradually changed the course of Mesopotamian and world history, together with the Medes, who appear on the scene for the first time. Striking for independence, Nabopolassar defeated the Assyrians outside Babylon in October 626. The following month he was acclaimed king in Babylon. He then invaded Assyrian-held territory on the Euphrates.

This change in the Near-Eastern balance of power aroused Egypt's interest. As a check to the anti-Assyrian alliance, Egypt allied itself to Assyria and sent an army to Mesopotamia, which arrived in 616, in time to check Nabopolassar even as a buffer state against the new alliances in Mesopotamia. He had attacked the ancient Assyrian capital of Ashur, but was repulsed. An indecisive battle developed between his Babylonian forces and the allied Assyrian and Egyptian army. However, the Medes under Kyaxares were now ready to take up the attack against Assyria. They descended from the north, stormed Ashur and took the city (614 B.C.E.). Nabopolassar had set out to join in the battle, but he arrived too late. Instead, he concluded a formal treaty with Kyaxares on the ruins of Ashur and each then returned to his homeland.

Two years later, Nineveh itself fell to a combined assault of the Medes and Chaldeans and was totally devastated. No quarter was given to the defenders and all, including the king, were massacred. The anticipated fall of this city, which had dominated the world for centuries, is vividly described in the third chapter of the book of the prophet Nahum. The event itself must have resounded throughout the ancient world.

The masters of siege operations (whose exploits are illustrated above) had themselves been mastered. Fragments of the Assyrian army and ruling class fled to Harran, in western Mesopotamia (whence had once come the first Hebrews in the days of Abraham and Jacob), and there established themselves under Ashur-uballit II.

HOPE AND DISILLUSIONMENT IN JUDAH

While the Assyrian empire disintegrated after the fall of Nineveh, her former vassals were consolidating their freedom. Surprisingly, Egypt did not attack Assyria, her old enemy, but prepared to meet the rising power of the Medo-Babylonian alliance which set out to take over the Assyrian empire.

Josiah, though still a vassal of Assyria, had been active politically along with his religious reform, in anticipation of the final overthrow of Assyrian authority. He had already taken control of the province of Samaria, formerly occupied by Assyria, and held Megiddo as well. His plans were to regain complete independence, but the day of small independent states in western Asia was over and with Assyria no longer a rival, the Egyptian Pharaoh, Neco II, intended to regain control of Palestine and Syria. However, the Judahites still pinned their hopes on divine protection of Zion, a popular theme strongly emphasized by priests and prophets. Moreover, there may have been a long-standing tradition of friendship between Judah and the Babylonians, apparently dating back 100 years to the days of Merodach-Baladan, the pioneer of Babylonian independence, and his encounters with Hezekiah in their schemes against the Assyrian conqueror of that day. In any event, the international balance of power had shifted in the last generation and new alignments were being sought by the independent states of the Near East. It would appear that Josiah, in support of his Babylonian ally Nabopolassar, planned to intercept and pin down the Egyptian forces on their way to Mesopotamia for their rendez-vous with the Assyrian army. This would leave the Babylonians to dispose of the Assyrians. It is not known to what extent Josiah's intervention at Megiddo in 609 diverted or delayed the main Egyptian forces of Neco.

THE BIBLICAL RECORD AND THE BABYLONIAN CHRONICLE

At this point it becomes important to reconstruct events by comparing the parallel record of the Bible with a collection of Babylonian tablets preserved in the British Museum, known as the "Babylonian Chronicle" which record events between the crucial years 626–556 B.C.E:

> "In his days Pharaoh Neco king of Egypt went up to the king of Assyria to the river Euphrates. King Josiah went to meet him; and Pharaoh Neco slew him at Megiddo, when he saw him. And his servants carried him dead in a chariot from Megiddo, and brought him to Jerusalem, and buried him in his own tomb. And the people of the land took Jehoahaz the son of Josiah, and anointed him, and made him king in his father's stead". (2K 23:29–30)

Although the account in Kings implies that Neco's intentions toward the Assyrian king were hostile and that he had urgent business with him on the Euphrates, the Babylonian Chronicle gives a clearer picture, from which it appears that Neco was hostile to the Babylonians. In the Revised Standard Version the corrected verse 29 records that Neco was going, not against the Assyrian king, but up to meet him and come to his aid at Harran near the Euphrates.

> "After all this, when Josiah had prepared the temple, Neco king of Egypt went up to fight at Carchemish on the Euphrates and Josiah went out against him. But he sent envoys to him, saying, 'What have we to do with each other, king of Judah? I am not coming against you this day, but against the house with which I am at war; and God has commanded me to make haste. Cease opposing God, who is with me, lest he destroy you'. Nevertheless Josiah would not turn away from him but disguised himself in order to fight with him. He did not listen to the words of Neco from the mouth of God, but joined battle in the plain of Megiddo. And the archers shot King Josiah; and the king said to his servants, 'Take me away, for I am badly wounded'. So his servants took him out of the chariot and carried him in his second chariot and brought him to Jerusalem. And he died, and was buried in the tombs of his fathers. All Judah and Jerusalem mourned for Josiah". (2 Chr 35:20–24)

The haste of the Egyptian to be on his way to Harran, or Carchemish on the Euphrates is stressed in the 2 Chronicles version. Perhaps all Josiah wanted was to confer with Neco, but the latter had no patience with the Israelite king. It is also interesting to note that the account in Chronicles represents Neco as speaking the word of God and blames the virtuous king Josiah for failing to "listen to the words of Neco from the mouth of God" and then joining battle with him.

Archaeological evidence indicates that Megiddo was besieged and destroyed in the summer of 609 and that Josiah was killed in this suicidal attempt to delay the Egyptian forces by forcing them to deploy for siege. He was brought back to Jerusalem in his chariot amid great lamentation and his son Jehoahaz was crowned in his stead.

"Jeremiah also uttered a lament for Josiah; and all the singing men and singing women have spoken of Josiah in their laments to this day. They made these an ordinance in Israel; behold, they are written in the Laments". (2 Chr. 35:25)

Ironically, he had only helped to save Nabopolassar and his crown prince Nebuchadrezzar, who would later destroy Jerusalem. Though Josiah's later years witnessed Assyria's downfall, this event was not calculated to help Judah or its neighbouring countries, for rival powers were gathering to divide the body of the fallen giant.

JEHOIAKIM AND NECO

"The people of the land took Jehoahaz the son of Josiah and made him king in his father's stead in Jerusalem. Jehoahaz was twenty-three years old when he began to reign; and he reigned three months in Jerusalem. Then the king of Egypt deposed him in Jerusalem and laid upon the land a tribute of a hundred talents of silver and a talent of gold. And the king of Egypt made Eliakim his brother king over Judah and Jerusalem, and changed his name to Jehoiakim; but Neco took Jehoahaz his brother and carried him to Egypt". (2 Chr. 36:1–4)

Pharaoh Neco's assault on Harran failed. Mesopotamia was left firmly in the hands of the Babylonians. But during the years before 605 B.C.E. the Egyptians consolidated their position west of the Euphrates and took control of Syria and Palestine. Neco summoned Jehoahaz to Riblah, in central Syria, deposed him and deported him to Egypt, then placed his brother Jehoiakim on the throne, Jehoiakim served him for three years.

THE NEO-BABYLONIAN EMPIRE

The Egyptians extended their control as far as the upper Euphrates and established a bridgehead at Carchemish. There in 605 B.C.E. the prince Nebuchadrezzar struck a sudden blow and sent the Egyptians fleeing in utter defeat. Thus Egypt was expelled from western Asia and this change in the delicate balance of power put Judah in imminent danger:

"Concerning the army of Pharaoh Neco, king of Egypt, which was by the river Euphrates at Carchemish and which Nebuchadrezzar king of Babylon defeated in the fourth year of Jehoiakim the son of Josiah, king of Judah:". (Jer. 46:2)

When his father Nabopolassar died in the same year, Nebuchadrezzar returned to Babylon in haste and "seized the hands of the god Marduk and his son Nebo" at the New Year Festival, i.e., he was crowned king of the neo-Babylonian empire which seemed outwardly as strong as the preceding Assyrian. Early the following year he took heavy tribute of the Khatti territory (Syria). As a result of Nebuchadrezzar's victory over Neco, Jehoiakim transferred his allegiance to Babylon:

"In his days Nebuchadnezzar king of Babylon came up, and Jehoiakim became his servant three years; then he turned and rebelled against him". (2 K 24:1)

Egypt contented itself with fomenting disaffection and revolt against the new overlord among the border states. Egged on by the influential pro-Egyptian party at court and by the nationalist zeal of the people — but against strong opposition from Jeremiah who insisted on submission to Babylon — the king gradually drifted into open rebellion:

The "roaring lion", a painting on a ceramic that decorated "Procession Street" in Babylon.

Megiddo, the city where Josiah was defeated and killed, is a symbol of disaster for armies which assemble there. The name Har-Megiddo was rendered as Armageddon — in Hebrew 'the mountain of Megiddo'. cf. Zechariah 12: 11.

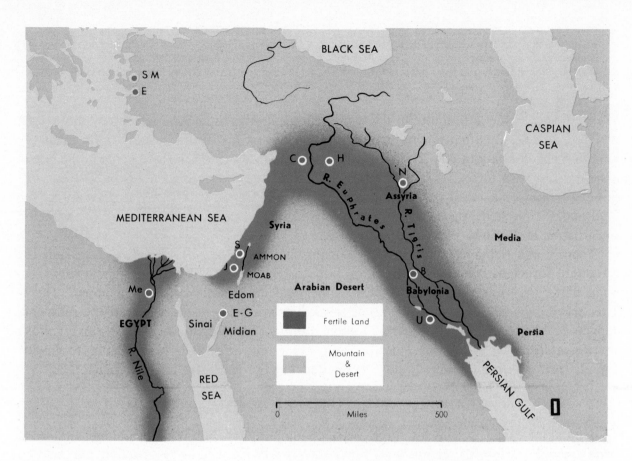

Key: *Assyria; C – Carchemish; H – Harran; N̲ – Nineveh. The Assyrian empire was centred upon Nineveh,
on the Tigris. Babylonia: B – Babylon; U – Ur. The Babylonian empire centred upon Babylon, on the Euphrates.
Palestine: S – Samaria: J – Jerusalem; E-G – Ezion-Gaber. Egypt: M – Memphis. Asia Minor: Sm – Smyrna;
E – Ephesus.*

The Euphrates at Carchemish.

"Then the word of the Lord came to Jeremiah the prophet: 'Thus says the Lord, God of Israel: Thus shall you say to the king of Judah who sent you to me to inquire of me, "Behold, Pharaoh's army which came to help you is about to return to Egypt, to its own land. And the Chaldeans shall come back and fight against this city; they shall take it and burn it with fire. Thus says the Lord, Do not deceive yourselves, saying 'The Chaldeans will surely stay away from us,' for they will not stay away" ' ". (Jer. 37:6–9)

We read a pathetic footnote to the history of these days in an Aramaic letter (discovered in Egypt in 1942), written to the Egyptian king Neco by his former vassal Adon, probably king of Ashkelon, about 604. He frantically begged him to send reinforcements immediately if he did not wish to see his loyal supporters in the area, bordering on Egypt, fall into the power of Babylonia. "But if the king of Babylon takes it, he will set up a governor in the land and...." No help was sent, and the Babylonian Chronicle records the fall of Ashkelon towards the end of 604.

Then in 601 Nebuchadrezzar marched against Egypt. A fierce battle took place near the Egyptian border with heavy casualties on both sides. The Babylonian Chronicle says: "In open battle they smote the breast of each other and inflicted havoc on each other". Thereafter the Babylonian king returned home immediately and spent the whole of the following year assembling horses and chariots in great number. The Egyptians made no overt move to re-establish their hold over Palestine and Syria but, with Babylon's failure to invade Egypt, their prestige recovered and they incited the border states against Babylon.

JERUSALEM IS CAPTURED — THE FIRST DEPORTATION OF JUDAH

Jehoiakim ended in 600 his three years' submission to Babylon and Judah enjoyed a brief freedom. However, Nebuchadrezzar countered his rebellion by enlisting the help of Judah's neighbours:

"And the Lord sent against him bands of the Chaldeans, and bands of the Syrians, and bands of the Moabites, and bands of the Ammonites, and sent them against Judah to destroy it, according to the word of the Lord which he spoke by his servants the prophets. Surely this came upon Judah at the command of the Lord, to remove them out of his sight, for the sins of Manasseh, according to all that he had done, and also for the innocent blood that he had shed; for he filled Jerusalem with innocent blood, and the Lord would not pardon". (2K. 24:2–4)

These measures must have proved insufficient, for in December 598 Nebuchadrezzar led the main Babylonian force against Judah. The siege and capture of Jerusalem are described in the Babylonian Chronicle:

"...the king of Akkad mustered his troops, marched to the Hatti land (Syria), and encamped against the city of Judah (Jerusalem) and on the second day of the month of Adar (March 597) he seized the city and captured the king. He appointed there a king of his own choice (heart), received its heavy tribute and sent them to Babylon".

"Against him came up Nebuchadnezzar king of Babylon, and bound him in fetters to take him to Babylon. Nebuchadnezzar also carried part of the vessels of the house of the Lord to Babylon and put them in his palace in Babylon". (2 Chr. 36:6–7)

Jehoiakim died in the same year, apparently before or during the siege.

Despite the ambiguity of the Biblical record, it seems more likely that the king whom Nebuchadrezzar appointed instead of Jehoiakim was not his son Jehoiachin, but Zedekiah,

Jehoiachin's uncle, known for his moderation and neutrality concerning Babylon (597–587 B.C.E.). It seems that the captive Jehoiachin was considered by his people to be the real king "de jure" although Zedekiah, appointed by a stranger, was the king "de facto". The captive king, it is recorded, "went forth" with his wife and courtiers, in unconditional surrender and this gained him honourable captivity according to usage. A surprising relic of his domicile in Babylon has survived in Babylonian tablets recording the payment between 595–570 of rations of oil, barley, etc. to the captives and others, including Jehoiachin and his five sons. He was apparently free to move about until the next rebellion in Judah. The sequel is told in the closing verses of Jeremiah:

> "And in the thirty-seventh year of the captivity of Jehoiachin king of Judah, in the twelfth month, on the twenty-fifth day of the month Evil-merodach king of Babylon, in the year that he became king, lifted up the head of Jehoiachin king of Judah and brought him out of prison; and he spoke kindly to him, and gave him a seat above the seats of the kings who were with him in Babylon. So Jehoiachin put off his prison garments. And every day of his life he dined regularly at the king's table; as for his allowance, a regular allowance was given him by the king according to his daily need, until the day of his death as long as he lived". (Jer. 52:31–34)

It is possible that the new Babylonian empire was less stable and weaker than the Assyrian. Nebuchadrezzar had often to parade his army through Syria to intimidate his subject nations. News of a local insurrection in Babylon — quickly suppressed —reached Jerusalem in 595 and added to the vassal state's false hopes of the empire's early collapse. The extent of anti Babylonian activity throughout the empire must have given rise to the hopes of independence and restoration in Judah which occur repeatedly in the biblical records of the period.

Within a year, when foreign envoys came to persuade Zedekiah to join the anti-Babylonian movement, the prophet Hananiah openly challenged Jeremiah in the Temple. He declared that God had broken the yoke of Babylon so that within two more years the Temple treasures and all the exiles would be returned, and Jehoiachin would be restored as king of Judah. This is vividly reported by Jeremiah who, according to prophetic custom, made a sign of a wooden yoke, which he put on his neck to dramatize his prophecy that it was Yahweh's will that the nations and Judah should submit to Babylon.

II. THE FINAL DISASTER

This incident is an indication of the formidable odds that Jeremiah and his younger contemporary, Ezekiel, faced in trying to persuade the people to keep the covenant of peace with the king of Babylon. No doubt they appreciated the military and political considerations involved, but their writings especially emphasized moral and religious — or as we would say today — ideological concepts in urging their policy on the people and the kings of Judah (see below). They saw in Nebuchadrezzar the chosen instrument of Yahweh through whom the divine purpose for Israel and the world was to be accomplished and they held fast to their position despite rumours about Babylonian difficulties and in the teeth of a militant nationalism.

"What concerned the prophets was the necessity of understanding the ultimate meaning of events, the meaning that gave significance not only to progress toward personal values, but also to suffering and even catastrophe" (H.H.Hahn). The real achievement of the prophets was in breaking completely with the world's way of thinking and creating a new "philosophy of history" to serve as the basis for belief and practice. "The deeper substance of their teaching was to be grasped, not by reading them in the light of conditions in present-day society — but by closer attention to their own interpretation of history, as expressed in their writings".

NEBUCHADREZZAR — THE GREAT BUILDER

In his inscriptions, Nebuchadrezzar stresses his constructive work and boasts very little of his conquests. Thus the exile of craftsmen from Judah fitted into Nebuchadrezzar's policy of transporting talent from conquered areas to aid in the vast building programme going ahead in his capital. He beautified and fortified Babylon, then the metropolis and commercial capital of the ancient world, and built new canals around it. Trade prospered throughout the empire, from east Arabia to the borders of Egypt. Armenian merchants came down the rivers from the north; ships from the Persian Gulf carried wares between Mesopotamia and the coasts of Arabia.

When any of the nomadic Arabs grew restive he knew how to quell them. But Media and Egypt were a much greater threat to Babylon; Nebuchadrezzar took measures to fortify the city against them and make it almost impregnable. Egypt, under Psametic II, was

Psametic II, contemporary of Nebuchadrezzar and Jeremiah.

The large clay barrel cylinder of Nebuchadrezzar, commemorating his construction work and restoration of temples.

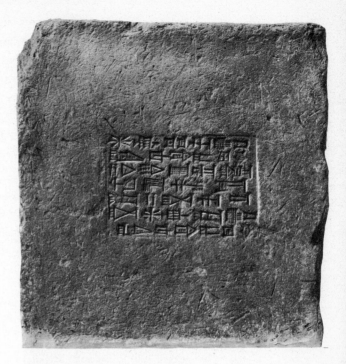

Reconstruction of Babylon and the Ishtar Gate. The wide Procession Street was built to celebrate the coronation of Nebuchadrezzar. Behind it are the ruins of the palace of his father. Everything in Babylon was built with brick and black cement, as the tower of Babel.

Brick inscribed with the name and titles of Nebuchadrezzar II.

the main troublemaker because it could not quietly accept the loss of the Palestinian and Syrian trade.

THE SIEGE AND TRAGEDY OF JERUSALEM

It appears that on several occasions the king was advised by Jeremiah and the anti-Egyptian party, who believed that the best hopes for the nation lay in passive surrender to Babylonia in order to save the country from destruction. Through a renewal of religious reform as in the days of Josiah, it was hoped to gain the favour of Yahweh, and this was coupled with social reforms such as the liberation of slaves, which may have been a means of improving the military situation. The slave owners, however, reintroduced slavery as soon as Babylonian pressure relaxed temporarily as a result of Egyptian intervention to help Judah.

Zedekiah had the right intentions but he was not the man to take charge of such a desperate situation. That he was a tool of others rather than a prime mover in the rebellion is shown by the fact that in the end his life, like Jeremiah's, was spared by the Babylonians.

The voice of moderation and conscience was drowned. The craving for independence and for the return of the exiles, including the legal king Jehoiachin, grew every year, stimulated by agitation in Babylonia, instigated by the court of Pharaoh Psametic II and his successor Hophra. Jeremiah intimates that after Jehoiachin's deportation the nobles left with Zedekiah were people of limited vision, unfit for counsel or leadership. The uprising in Judah was closely connected with rebellion in Phoenicia and the kingdoms east of Jordan. Ambassadors from these countries met in Jerusalem in the fourth year of Zedekiah's reign to discuss plans for revolt. This led to Jeremiah's clash with Hananiah and the incident of the yoke. The plot came to nothing at the time and Zedekiah sent envoys to Babylonia to affirm his loyalty (probably 594). But this was only a temporary postponement. The pro-Egyptian party apparently persuaded the king to renounce his allegiance to Nebuchadrezzar in 588.

To counter the conspiracy in Syria and Palestine, Nebuchadrezzar sent an army against Egypt and its allies. On his way south he laid siege to Tyre — a siege which lasted for thirteen years. He established his military headquarters at Riblah in central Syria, and before deciding whether to attack Ammon or Judah first, he consulted the auguries, as described vividly by Ezekiel:

> "For the king of Babylon stands at the parting of the way, at the head of the two ways, to use divination; he shakes the arrows, he consults the teraphim, he looks at the liver. Into his right hand comes the lot for Jerusalem, to open the mouth with a cry, to lift up the voice with shouting, to set battering rams against the gates, to cast up mounds, to build siege towers. But to them it will seem like a false divination; they have sworn solemn oaths; but he brings their guilt to remembrance, that they may be captured". (Ez. 21:21–23)

As the Babylonian troops invaded Judah in 588, false hopes were aroused in Jerusalem by news that Hophra had sent an army to help his allies and that Nebuchadrezzar had moved to southern Philistia to ward it off. Whether the Egyptians actually dared face their powerful enemy is not known but they retreated. The Babylonian army laid waste the Judean countryside, destroying town after town, subjugating the population and capturing the last fortified towns outside Jerusalem.

WE ARE WATCHING FOR THE SIGNALS OF LACHISH

Jeremiah refers to the conquest of Lachish and Azekah:

> "When the army of the king of Babylon was fighting against Jerusalem and against all the cities of Judah that were left, Lachish and Azekah, for these were the only fortified cities of Judah that remained." (Jer 34:7)

A new glimpse of the operations there was provided by eighteen pieces of pottery — ostraca — inscribed in the ancient Hebrew script, dating from the days just before Lachish and Azekah were attacked (587) or from the period of their siege, while they stood isolated. The sherds (deciphered by H. Tur-Sinai) were found in the debris of a guard-room of the bastion of the outer city wall where messages were received by the officer in charge. These short missives show how a network of communications existed between Jerusalem and the outlying garrisons in the fortresses of Lachish and Azekah, and how messages were passed between the garrison commander and his subordinates:

The reverse of Lachish letter IV, says that the fire signals of Azekah can no longer be seen:

"May Yahweh cause my lord to hear this very day tidings of good! And now according to everything that my lord

The Lachish Ostraca (letters).

The reverse of Lachish letter IV says that the fire signals of Azekah can no longer be seen.

hath written, so hath thy servant done; I have written on the door according to all that my lord hath written to me. And with respect to what my lord hath written about the matter of Beth-haraphid, there is no one there. And as for Semachiah, Shemaiah hath taken him and hath brought him up to the city. And as for thy servant, I am not sending anyone thither today, but I will send tomorrow morning. And let my lord know that we are watching for the signals of Lachish, according to all the indications which my lord hath given, for we cannot see Azekah''.

(Ancient Near Eastern Texts, J. B. Pritchard, Ed)

Azekah, one of Judah's last outposts, mentioned in the Lachish letters and by Jeremiah.

465

The sixth letter from Lachish complains that "the words of the prince are not good but to weaken our hands and to slacken the hands of the men who are informed about them". This was the very crime with which Jeremiah was charged in Jerusalem when the nobles demanded his death (See below: Jeremiah and His Contemporaries).

Even if these survivals do not give a detailed parallel to the biblical record, they illustrate the spreading of rumours (both optimistic and pessimistic), the pathetic hope of help from Egypt, charges of treason, defences and counter-charges — all the signs of stress and approaching doom.

The principals named in this correspondence — Yoash, Hoshaiah, Tobiah, servant of the king — cannot be identified with the persons mentioned in the Bible as the defenders of Judah at the time of its destruction. But this dossier of a military commander in forlorn Lachish gives us an insight, lacking in the official annals of the period, and has added a new chapter to the books of Kings and Jeremiah.

THE FALL OF JERUSALEM

"And in the ninth year of his reign, in the tenth month, on the tenth day of the month, Nebuchadnezzar king of Babylon came with all his army against Jerusalem, and laid siege to it; and they built siegeworks against it round about. So the city was besieged till the eleventh year of King Zedekiah. On the ninth day of the fourth month the famine was so severe in the city that there was no food for the people of the land". (2 K. 25: 1–3)

The siege began in January. Jerusalem held out heroically. Wishing to surrender, Zedekiah sent for Jeremiah from the guardroom where he had been imprisoned since the clamour of the pro-Egyptian courtiers. The land was parched, the food reserves were running out and the water supply was low in the cisterns where water was collected during the rainy season.

" 'Therefore, thus says the Lord: You have not obeyed me by proclaiming liberty, every one to his brother and to his neighbor; behold, I proclaim to you liberty to the sword, to pestilence, and to famine, says the Lord. I will make you a horror to all the kingdoms of the earth. And the men who transgressed my covenant and did not keep the terms of the covenant which they made before me, I will make like the calf which they cut in two and passed between its parts—the princes of Judah, the princes of Jerusalem, the eunuchs, the priests, and all the people of the land who passed between the parts of the calf; and I will give them into the hand of their enemies and into the hand of those who seek their lives. Their dead bodies shall be food for the birds of the air and the beasts of the earth. And Zedekiah king of Judah, and his princes I will give into the hand of their enemies and into the hand of those who seek their lives, into the hand of the army of the king of Babylon which has withdrawn from you. Behold, I will command, says the Lord, and will bring them back to this city; and they will fight against it, and take it, and burn it with fire. I will make the cities of Judah a desolation without inhabitant' ". (Jer. 34: 17–22)

Nevertheless, Zedekiah feared to surrender. In July 586 B.C.E. as food supplies came to an end, the Babylonians breached the walls on the north side of the city and poured in:

"On the ninth day of the fourth month the famine was so severe in the city, that there was no food for the people of the land. Then a breach was made in the city; and all the men of war fled and went out from the city by night by the way of a gate between the two walls, by the king's garden, while the Chaldeans were round about the city. And they went in the direction of the Arabah. But the army of the Chaldeans pursued the king, and overtook Zedekiah in the plains of Jericho; and all his army was scattered from him". (Jer. 52: 6–8)

The Babylonian staff headed by Nergal-sharezer "came and sat in the middle gate", probably at the northern end of Jerusalem to accept the surrender.

Taking the opposite direction through the south-eastern gate, at the lower base of the City of David, the fleeing king and soldiers turned left into the Kidron valley, breaking through the besieging force at this point. They then reached the "King's Garden" situated near the pool of Siloam and, hastening through this area, poured into the arid valley which led east towards the Jordan, hoping to reach temporary safety across the Jordan or in the Arabah. But they were overtaken near Jericho and brought before Nebuchadrezzar at his headquarters at Riblah:

> "Then they captured the king, and brought him up to the king of Babylon at Riblah, who passed sentence upon him. They slew the sons of Zedekiah before his eyes, and put out the eyes of Zedekiah, and bound him in fetters, and took him to Babylon." (2 K. 25: 6-7)

The lane leading down from the lower gate of Jerusalem to the Kidron Valley. See colour picture of the Temple area and the valley below in Ch. XIII.

The seizure of the fleeing king is most poignantly described in these verses of Lamentations:

> "Our pursuers were swifter
>   than the vultures in the heavens;
> they chased us on the mountains,
>   they lay in wait for us in the wilderness.
>
> The breath of our nostrils, the Lord's anointed.
>   was taken in their pits,
> he of whom we said, 'Under his shadow
>   we shall live among the nations'". (Lam. 4:19-20)

The victorious Chaldeans had to await orders as to the next step; these were brought by Nebuzaradan:

> "In the fifth month, on the seventh day of the month—which was the nineteenth year of King Nebuchadnezzar, king of Babylon — Nebuzaradan, the captain of the bodyguard, a servant of the king of Babylon, came to Jerusalem. And he burned the house of the Lord, and the king's house and all the houses of Jerusalem; every great house he burned down. And all the army of the Chaldeans, who were with the captain of the guard, broke down the walls around Jerusalem. And the rest of the people who were left in the city and the deserters who had deserted to the king of Babylon, together with the rest of the multitude, Nebuzaradan the captain of the guard carried into exile. But the captain of the guard left some of the poorest of the land to be vinedressers and plowmen.
> And the pillars of bronze that were in the house of the Lord, and the stands and the bronze sea that were in the house

of the Lord, the Chaldeans broke in pieces, and carried the bronze to Babylon. And they took away the pots, and the shovels, and the snuffers, and the dishes for incense and all the vessels of bronze used in the temple service, the fire-pans also, and the bowls. What was of gold the captain of the guard took away as gold and what was of silver, as silver". (2 K. 25: 8–15)

The Temple and palaces of Jerusalem and all large buildings were pillaged and set on fire and the walls of the city levelled to the ground. Certain of the military, priestly and civil officers, and leading citizens were taken to Nebuchadrezzar's headquarters:

"Therefore he brought up against them the king of the Chaldeans, who slew their young men with the sword in the house of their sanctuary, and had no compassion on young man or virgin, old man or aged; he gave them all into his hand. And all the vessels of the house of God, great and small, and the treasures of the house of the Lord, and the treasures of the king and of his princes, all these he brought to Babylon. And they burned the house of God, and broke down the wall of Jerusalem, and burned all its palaces with fire, and destroyed all its precious vessels. He took into exile in Babylon those who had escaped from the sword, and they became servants to him and to his sons until the establishment of the kingdom of Persia". (2 Chr. 36: 17–20)

A further group of the population was deported to Babylon where many leaders of Judah, including the prophet Ezekiel, awaited them. Thousands fled to other countries, including Egypt. The state of Judah had ended leaving behind only clusters of peasants clinging to their soil, the vinedressers and farmers who were allowed to remain. Jeremiah, who was among the prisoners of war, was treated leniently and was given his freedom as well as an opportunity to join the exiles in Babylon.

EPILOGUE

Although he believed that the future lay with the exiles, he decided to stay with the broken remnant, and end his days in Judea. He cast in his lot with those who gathered in the provincial seat of Mizpah, a short distance from the ruins of Jerusalem. It is notable that, when the Babylonian army was pounding at the walls of Jerusalem and Jeremiah was imprisoned, he carried out a transaction whereby he acquired a field belonging to his cousin in his native village, thus redeeming family land from total loss. The invitation to acquire land was an omen that the people would still have a future in Israel:

" 'For thus says the Lord of hosts, the God of Israel: houses and fields and vineyards shall again be bought to this land' ". (Jer. 32: 15)

It seems that the repeated removal of the aristocracy and landed gentry had brought about a change in the social system. The poor people left behind were able to buy the abandoned land and other possessions of the exiles cheaply. The Babylonian administration might have helped them to acquire such land in order to gain support among those who benefitted from these economic and social changes. But the outsiders forgot to reckon with an abiding factor — the Judeans' trust in Yahweh.

In a letter sent to the exiles in Babylon, Jeremiah called on them to promise, in this spirit, to till the land, develop farms and start life anew, always trusting in Yahweh. Now he widened the promise to include other exiles who would be brought to repentance by the destruction of Judah:

" 'For thus says the Lord: Just as I have brought all this great evil upon this people, so I will bring upon them all the good that I promise them. Fields shall be bought in this land which you are saying, It is a desolation, without man or beast; it is given into the hands of the Chaldeans. Fields shall be bought for money, and deeds shall be signed and sealed and witnessed, in the land of Benjamin, in the places about Jerusalem, and in the cities of Judah, in the cities of the hill country, in the cities of the Shephelah, and in the cities of the Negeb; for I will restore their fortunes, says the Lord' ". (Jer. 32: 42–44)

The Jews now in Babylon represented the cream of Judah's political, priestly and intellectual leadership (hence their deportation). The prophet's message, looking beyond the present disaster, was most significant for it gave them a lifeline as a guide throughout the exile in Babylon.

WITH THE REMNANT LEFT IN JUDAH

After the debacle of 587, the Babylonians organized Judah into the provincial system of the empire. The officials were Babylonians, but Nebuchadrezzar appointed as governor Gedaliah ben Ahikam, a high officer of Zedekiah, who must have been, like Jeremiah, of the party that had opposed rebellion. His provincial seat was in Mizpah, for Jerusalem was uninhabitable. As groups of officers and warriors began to appear there, Gedaliah tried to conciliate them, solemnly telling them not to fear Chaldean reprisals but to settle down on their land. Refugees who had fled to neighbouring lands such as Moab, Ammon and Edom, started to come back. This remnant was considered incapable of making trouble, and Gedaliah proceeded with the consolidation of the administration and economy of Judah, trying to restore it to some semblance of normalcy.

But agitation against Babylon never ceased so long as Tyre could withstand the siege and while the Egyptians kept on whipping up opposition to Babylon among the peoples of Palestine, the Judeans in particular.

"Ishmael the son of Nethaniah and the ten men with him rose up and struck down Gedaliah the son of Ahikam, son of Shaphan, with the sword, and killed him, whom the king of Babylon had appointed governor in the land". (Jer. 41: 2)

Shortly afterwards Ishmael ben Nathaniah, a man of royal blood, was incited by the Ammonite king, Baalis, to kill Gedaliah and his Babylonian officers quite unexpectedly. Gedaliah's assassination was followed by a reign of terror by Ishmael and his confederates. They went so far as to kill a group of Israelites en route to the ruined Temple. Local reaction set in quickly. Johanan and other officers, living in outlying districts, drove Ishmael out of Mizpah and pursued him and his followers as they retreated eastwards. Ishmael took refuge in Ammon:

The Mizpah emigrants now deserted Ishmael and placed themselves under the protection of Johanan and his fellow-officers. But knowing that the murder of a Babylon-appointed governor with his officials would be mercilessly punished, they abandoned the Mizpah neighbourhood, taking the refugees under their wing. To escape Chaldean vengeance they determined to go to Egypt where a community had arisen in past generations. Although Jeremiah advised that the people should stay on, the new leaders, taking command of the situation, compelled him and his secretary Baruch to go with them. They settled among the Jewish communities of Migdol and Tahpanes just within the frontier in Noph (Memphis) and as far as the land of Pathros in southern Egypt. An utterance of Jeremiah concerning the Jewish refugees in Egypt impressively concludes the career of the aged prophet:

"Behold, I am watching over them for evil and not for good; all the men of Judah who are in the land of Egypt shall be consumed by the sword and by famine, until there is an end of them. And those who escape the sword shall return from the land of Egypt to the land of Judah, few in number; and all the remnant of Judah, who came to the land of Egypt to live, shall know whose word will stand, mine or theirs. This shall be the sign to you, says the Lord, that I will punish you in this place, in order that you may know that my words will surely stand against you for evil: Thus says the Lord, Behold I will give Pharaoh Hophra king of Egypt into the hand of his enemies and into the hand of those who seek his life, as I gave Zedekiah king of Judah into the hand of Nebuchadrezzar king of Babylon, who was his enemy and sought his life' ". (Jer. 44: 27–30)

This last prophecy apparently reflects current events in Egypt. In 570, Pharaoh Hophrah (Apries) was defeated by the Greek colony of Libya in north Africa, and then faced a mutiny in his army led by one Amasis. Hophrah lost his life and Amasis made himself king as described by Jeremiah. This is an early example of Greek emergence in this part of the Mediterranean. Within two and a half centuries they were destined to terminate Near East antiquity. Meanwhile, taking advantage of the resulting confusion, Nebuchadrezzar invaded Egypt as a warning against further meddling in western Asiatic affairs. Thereafter as long as the Babylonian empire survived, it maintained friendly relations with Egypt.

A third deportation in 582 B.C.E. is mentioned by Jeremiah and may represent belated Babylonian reprisals against Palestinian agitation:

"In the twenty-third year of Nebuchadrezzar, Nebuzaradan the captain of the guard carried away captive of the Jews seven hundred and forty-five persons; all the persons were four thousand and six hundred". (Jer. 52: 30)

It is known, however, that in one of the Babylonian expeditions against rebels in the area Ashdod was reduced to a Babylonian province. Tyre was also eventually captured and destroyed. The provincial administration in Judah lost its identity and was apparently abolished and its territory incorporated into the northern province of Samaria. The towns of Judah lay solitary and depopulated, but small pockets of rural population remained, together with towns in Samaria and the Negeb which had escaped destruction. Numbers of dispossessed people had taken refuge in the neighbouring provinces of Galilee, Samaria and Ashdod or in vassal lands such as Edom and Ammon. There they mingled with the native Israelites and kept alive the national traditions and faith of Israel until the eventual return of exiles from Babylon brought the new restoration. (See. ch. XX).

ABYSMAL SORROW

Of the former population of Judah, estimated at about a quarter of a million, a few sparse thousands were left. The pent-up emotion of the people at their miserable and precarious state and their sufferings during the debacle found expression in the poems of Lamentations which are sung on the annual fast day of the ninth of Ab, in remembrance of the fall of Jerusalem. They are striking for their bitter realism.

"My eyes are spent with weeping;
  my soul is in tumult;
my heart is poured out in grief
  because of the destruction of the
    daughter of my people,
because infants and babes faint
in the streets of the city.

They cry to their mothers,
  'Where is bread and wine?'
as they faint like wounded men
  in the streets of the city,
as their life is poured out
  on their mothers' bosom". (Lam. 2:11-12)

- -

"Young men are compelled to grind at the mill;
  and boys stagger under loads of wood.
The old men have quit the city gate,
  the young men their music.
The joy of our hearts has ceased;
  our dancing has been turned to mourning.

The crown has fallen from our head;
  woe to us, for we have sinned!
For this our heart has become sick,
  for these things our eyes have grown dim,
for Mount Zion which lies desolate;
  jackals prowl over it". (Lam. 5: 13-18)

The crux of the lament is the conflict between historical faith and stark reality. This was the greatest catastrophe that had ever befallen Israel in its own land. The impregnable and inviolable temple had been sacked and desecrated before their eyes. At one stroke, Israel's national existence had been extinguished. Jerusalem had been humiliated and with it all the institutions in which Judah's corporate life had expressed itself. Most of all there arose the anguish of disappointed hopes and a deep sense of having been deserted by men and God. To the orientals a god and his people are indissolubly cemented. The destruction of Yahweh's Temple and of his people, proved the "downfall of the God"; where is their god, they would ask?

". . . the Lord has brought to an end in Zion
  appointed feast and sabbath,
and in his fierce indignation has spurned
  king and priest". (Lam. 2: 6)

"My soul is bereft of peace,
  I have forgotten what happiness is;
so I say, 'Gone is my glory,
  and my expectation from the Lord' ". (Lam. 3: 17-18)

- -

"Restore us to thyself, O Lord, that
  we may be restored!
  Renew our days as of old!
Or hast thou utterly rejected us?
  Art thou exceedingly angry with us?". (Lam. 5: 21-22)

"The Lord is good to those who wait for him,
  to the soul that seeks him.
It is good that one should wait quietly
  for the salvation of the Lord.
It is good for a man that he bear
  the yoke in his youth". (Lam. 3: 25-27)

This expresses several of the dominant convictions of Judaism, which was to arise rejuvenated from the ashes of past experience and prophetic teaching: responsibility for sin, the disciplinary value of sufferings, the abiding justice and love of Yahweh and the inscrutability of his ways; the unconquerable trust of Israel's faith and the necessity for patience.

III. JEREMIAH — THE PROPHET OF YAHWEH'S JUDGEMENT

The Wrath of God

The belief in divine blessing (reward) and judgement (punishment) had been fundamental to Israel's faith from the very beginning. The revival of this doctrine through Josiah's reformation had affected the people in different ways. To most the renewal of the Mosaic

Covenant meant the divine promise of tangible blessings, such as security in the land, abundant crops, regular rainfall, long life or, in the recurrent Deuteronomic phrase "in order that your days may be long upon the land which Yahweh your Lord gives you" or "in order that it may be well with you".

There were other flaws in the people's understanding and application of the Decalogue and the Law in Josiah's time which conflicted with their spiritual demands. Civil and criminal, ritual and constitutional offences; abuses of power, station and wealth; hardness of heart and indifference to the misery of fellow men were all classified as violations of the fundamental command to listen to the voice of Yahweh. Moreover, the people at large, as also the court, were convinced that cultic worship at Jerusalem and the discharge of the responsibilities of the priesthood and kingship were sufficient fulfilment of the Law's commands proclaimed anew in Josiah's time.

That Jeremiah's work was deeply influenced by the newly discovered scroll can be seen from the fact that it is quoted almost two hundred times in the prophet's oracles.

It was inevitable that conflict would arise between the court and influential sectors of the people who considered their conduct constitutional under Covenant Law and Decalogue, and those, like Jeremiah, who condemned any conduct at variance with his own and who pitted his interpretation and prophetic authority against government and popular opinion on questions which brooked of no compromise. In his address at the Temple he threatened it and the people with destruction if they did not mend their ways. He did not maintain that cultic ritual itself was objectionable to God, only that it was so if the people came to worship but continued sinning as they did.

Here, indeed, was a formidable conflict. It is no accident that a prophet of this type saw life and religion in a different light from his contemporaries thereby dissociating himself from the ideas of his day and causing the deep tragedy of his lonely life. The living example of such tension in the last days of Judah was the life experience and problems raised by Jeremiah.

He was a member of a priestly family of Anathoth, a village in Benjamin. This was also the home of the high priest Abiathar, (a descendant of Eli of Shiloh) who had been expelled from Jerusalem by Solomon for complicity in Adonijah's attempt to seize the crown (see Ch. 13). Jeremiah was raised in the great traditions of Israel running back to the days of the sanctuary of Shiloh. He may have absorbed the spirit of opposition to Jerusalem. In the early days of his mission, Jeremiah sought inspiration in the nearby solitary gorge of Perath (13: 1 ff. which has been wrongly translated as the Euphrates). Dressed in the linen loin cloth of the hermit, he experienced the inner struggle recorded in the opening chapter of his book.

The Lonely Sorrow of a Prophet

Jeremiah had only to spend four years in Jerusalem to be sure of his total opposition to the priesthood, the pious followers of the Law, and optimistic prophets who trusted blindly in the mottoes of the day. Jeremiah saw things from a different angle. It is true that he did not preclude repentance from Manasseh's treachery, nor did he minimize the holiness of Zion — the seat of Yahweh, — but he did not believe his own generation worthy of forgiveness.

No former prophet had been so outspoken against the people's sins and complacency. He spared neither Jerusalem nor the house of David nor the Temple, but attacked all moral, social and religious evils with a new degree of passion. This left him in lonely sorrow.

Evidently Jeremiah supported Josiah's reform for a time, in keeping with his concern for the Mosaic tradition. But he must have turned against it later. He took no part in the rejoicing over the renewed Passover celebrations which brought pilgrims in their thousands to Zion. Centralizing worship in Jerusalem gave the people a false confidence that Yahweh was in their midst. But the Law written in a book was no substitute for Yahweh's law upon the heart.

> "How can you say, 'We are wise,   The wise men shall be put to shame,
> and the law of the Lord is with us'?   they shall be dismayed and taken;
> But, behold, the false pen of the scribes   lo, they have rejected the word of the Lord,
> has made it into a lie.   and what wisdom is in them?" (Jer. 8: 8–9)

The "wise", according to J. Lindblom and Rudolph were people who had devoted themselves as instructors of the people in questions pertaining to the law and the applications of its rules in practical life; and it seems as though the emergence of this class coincided with the appearance of the old scroll of the Law and Josiah's reform. The prophets upbraided them for falsifying, in these written laws, the older oral tradition focussed in the Decalogue, and for having rejected Yahweh's word, namely the words of the prophets.

For since the days of Moses the unforgivable sin of Manasseh had corrupted all the people of Judah and Jerusalem. The kings of Judah were not to be trusted if a ruler like Manasseh followed Hezekiah and reversed all that stood for the fear of God. Jeremiah was convinced that through such anomaly the existing state had failed in its obligations and could not be trusted to maintain its promise.

> And I will make you to this people
> a fortified wall of bronze;
> they will fight against you,
> but they shall not prevail over you,
> for I am with you
> to save you and deliver you,
> says the Lord". (Jer. 15: 20)

Divine compulsion kept him to his task. He was hated, jeered at and ostracized for his outspoken and drastic condemnation of State and Temple. But he felt as a "fenced brazen wall" facing an unfriendly world. Though his was the authentic voice of Yahweh's ancient faith, it came out of season to the doomed nation.

An Inward Relation to God

Jeremiah's special contribution to religion is the development of a direct personal fellowship with God, through external misfortunes and sorrows. Hence his book is not concerned with religious teachings so much as a religious personality of outstanding devotion to a cause. His ideal, of inward relationship with God, is contrasted with dependence of the Temple and its worship and conformity to an external written law:

" 'Do not trust in these deceptive words: "This is the temple of the Lord, the temple of the Lord, the temple of the Lord'. "For if you truly amend your ways and your doings, if you truly execute justice one with another, if you do not oppress the alien, the fatherless or the widow, or shed innocent blood in this place, and if you do not go after other gods to your own hurt, then I will let you dwell in this place, in the land that I gave of old to your fathers for ever". (Jer. 7: 4–7)

JEREMIAH AND HIS CONTEMPORARIES

From the moment he denied the need for a Temple worship devoid of spiritual meaning, the priests rejected him. It took longer for the laymen to recognize what was involved. But when the people who were straining every nerve to defend the state, discovered that Jeremiah counted national life quite secondary, they regarded him as a blasphemer and traitor and more than once sought to destroy and silence him.

Thereafter, in the reign of Jehoiakim, when the leaders of the people and the Court determined to rebel against Babylon, the prophet regarded the new world-power as the instrument God had chosen for the destruction of the city. The people should accept the yoke of Babylon to atone for the sin of Manasseh and Judah.

From that time, throughout the reign of Zedekiah, he never wavered in his conviction that Nebuchadrezzar would overrun Judah and destroy its capital. It was the divine will that this should be so.

In the Shadow of World Catastrophe

Jeremiah's inner conflict raged in the shadow of international upheaval. Not long before, Assyria under Ashurbanipal had ruled the world, yet by the time of Jeremiah's call to prophecy, Babylon reigned supreme. Little wonder that Jeremiah saw in Babylon God's chosen instrument for the execution of His purpose for the world. Jeremiah's views may justly be seen in the light of the great international events which changed the political and military scene in Syria and Palestine during the fourth year of Jehoiakim's reign. Nebuchadrezzar had driven Egypt out of the territory and conquered all of Syria. Jeremiah regarded Jehoiakim's rebellion against Babylon as a reckless step. The course of events may explain the prophet's new outlook on the role of Babylon in international events and Yahweh's guidance of world history.

SEVENTY YEARS — VISION OF THE FUTURE FOR ISRAEL AND THE WORLD

" 'For thus says the Lord: When seventy years are completed for Babylon, I will visit you, and I will fulfil to you my promise and bring you back to this place. For I know the plans I have for you, says the Lord, plans for welfare, and not for evil, to give you a future and a hope. Then you will call upon me and come and pray to me, and I will hear you. You will seek me and find me; when you seek me with all your heart, I will be found by you, says the Lord, and I will restore your fortunes and gather you from all the nations and all the places where I have driven you, says the Lord, and I will bring you back to the place from which I sent you into exile' ". (Jer. 29: 10–14)

Jeremiah's morbid concern with Babylon was a part of his over-all religious-historical vision. The idolatrous nations of the world, equally created by God, would accept submission to Babylon. Even the beast of the field would submit and none should escape. Israel would be subjected and sent into an exile which would last seventy years. "Seventy years" is apparently a standard appointed time for punishment in ancient literature. It was used by Isaiah in an oracle concerning the restoration of Tyre.

This pattern of punishment, followed by restoration, was found by D.D. Luckenbill in an inscription of the Assyrian king Esarhaddon, the son of Sennacherib who destroyed Babylon. The inscription states that the gods had decreed a period of seventy years devastation for her, but out of pity they relented and shortened the period to eleven years, (this being the actual period during which it lay in ruins before Esarhaddon rebuilt it). Jeremiah's choice of seventy years therefore may follow an accepted tradition and he used it in contrast to the sanguine prediction of another prophet, Hananiah, who gave two years as the period of the exile. At the end of seventy years, proclaimed Jeremiah, the final world war would break out and put an end to imperial Babylon. In the meantime Israel should humbly accept the yoke, for at the end of this time it would return to God, repentant and purified in heart. In this lay Israel's ultimate salvation.

This is a further example of the dialectics of classical prophecy in which predictions of punishment and salvation are held out side by side in support of the appeal to return to God: Jeremiah's dialectic pivots on two seemingly contradictory arguments: Manasseh's sin lay heavy on the people. The only remedy, as a result, was total destruction. Full repentance, however, could save the people but destruction and doom were near at hand.

Jeremiah was not interested in politics. He did not offer the people a choice between a pro-Egyptian or pro-Babylonian policy. Rather, he viewed the crisis as God's intervention to destroy and then rebuild His world. This message was either too subtle or too unwelcome to the people of Judah. His revelation could be ignored and the chosen people behaved as though they did not want to be chosen at the price of ceasing to be a people like others, with an army and a sense of national pride. In his view, crisis and catastrophe had to come, curses heavy with doom had to be heaped upon a people who did not repent. These threats are in the true tradition of the curses invoked in Deuteronomy if the law were to be broken. For Yahweh is a jealous God who will not tolerate the worship of other gods. He will become a consuming fire to those who are unfaithful to the covenant. This is the burden of Chapter 28 of Deuteronomy.

The language of execration in the Bible is not native, but may have been derived from ancient Semitic custom based on a belief in the magic efficacy of curses. Many curses originating in Egypt, have been found inscribed on figurines, aimed at the enemies of Egypt. The figurines were then broken as a means of making the written curse effective upon the enemy.

THE KING BURNS THE SCROLL

In the fifth year of Jehoiakim's reign, the prophet, who did not dare come near the Temple for fear of being killed, sent his secretary Baruch, on a day of ritual fasting, with a scroll on which he had written in ink the words of Yahweh:

"And Jeremiah ordered Baruch, saying, 'I am debarred from going to the house of the Lord; so you are to go, and on a fast day in the hearing of all the people in the Lord's house you shall read the words of the Lord from the scroll which you have written at my dictation. You shall read them also in the hearing of all the men of Judah who come out of their cities. It may be that their supplication will come before the Lord, and that every one will turn from his evil way, for great is the anger and wrath that the Lord has pronounced against this people' " (Jer. 36: 5–7)

The scroll reached Jehoiakim as he sat near a burning brazier, for it was a wintry day. Whenever three or four columns had been read by an attendant, the king would cut them with his penknife and drop them on the brazier until the whole scroll was consumed:

"So they went into the court of the king, having put the scroll in the chamber of Elishama the secretary; and they reported all the words to the king. Then the king sent Jehudi to get the scroll, and he took it from the chamber of Elishama the secretary; and Jehudi read it to the king and all the princes who stood beside the king. It was the ninth month, and the king was sitting in the winter house and there was a fire burning in the brazier before him. As Jehudi read three or four columns, the king would cut them off with a penknife and throw them into the fire in the brazier, until the entire scroll was consumed in the fire that was in the brazier. Yet neither the king, nor any of his servants who heard all these words, was afraid, nor did they rend their garments". (Jer. 36: 20–24)

But these prophecies were rewritten and reworked in the light of events that were fresh in Jeremiah's mind. Some scholars also believe that parts of the book of Jeremiah were rewritten by his secretary, Baruch, or other editors during this active literary period.

IV. THE HISTORICAL AND UNIVERSAL ELEMENTS OF PROPHETIC THOUGHT

A New Covenant

Jeremiah preached a new covenant that would transfigure the world and society. This new covenant would spring from individual internal motives but would be thoroughly communal and national. He looked forward to a time when all would share his prophetic consciousness.

" 'Behold, the days are coming, says the Lord, when I will make a new covenant with the house of Israel and the house of Judah, not like the covenant which I made with their fathers when I took them by the hand to bring them out of the land of Egypt, my covenant which they broke, though I was their husband, says the Lord. But this is the covenant which I will make with the house of Israel after those days, says the Lord: I will put my law within them, and I will write it upon their hearts; and I will be their God, and they shall be my people. And no longer shall each man teach his neighbor and each his brother, saying, "Know the Lord," for they shall all know me from the least of them to the greatest, says the Lord; for I will forgive their iniquity, and I will remember their sin no more' ". (Jer. 31: 31–34)

This thought became the basis for the distinction between the Mosaic Covenant and the Covenant of the Christian Gospel. From it is derived the division of the Bible into the Old Testament and the New Testament (testamentum — covenant) or Christian Scripture.

The Composition of the Book of Jeremiah

To the casual reader everything in the book seems disjointed without regard for the sequence of events or any connection between the dominant ideas. The alternation of crisp poetry and passionate prose is also distracting. There are frequent repetitions of the same theme — another idiosyncrasy of Jeremiah's numerous oracles. According to Y. Kaufman it may be possible to discern three major strands in the book: Chapters 1–19 written before 605 and the appearance of Babylon on the scene. Then Chapters 20–41, where the Babylon theme dominates. Much of the second part was written in the latter days of King Jehoiakim and during the reign of King Zedekiah. The historical and biographical narratives span Chapters 26–45 and, thanks to the wealth of such material, his history is better known than that of any other prophet.

The closing section of the book, however, seems to be contained in Ch. 25 with the sublime oracle foretelling confusion and mutual destruction for the nations.

> "Thus the Lord, the God of Israel, said to me: 'Take from my hand this cup of the wine of wrath, and make all the nations to whom I send you drink it. They shall drink and stagger and be crazed because of the sword which I am sending among them'. So I took the cup from the Lord's hand, and made all the nations to whom the Lord sent me drink it: Jerusalem and the cities of Judah, its kings and princes, to make them a desolation and a waste, a hissing and a curse, as at this day; Pharaoh king of Egypt, his servants, his princes, all his people". (Jer. 25: 15–19)

It is now recognized that an appreciable amount of heterogeneity in the literary form of the prophetic writings, in Isaiah as in Jeremiah, is not incompatible with their conceptual unity. Northern research has attempted to identify a specific literary type. Certain prophetic compositions, complex in form, but unified in thought, were literary unities. This approach to the interpretation of prophetic literature represents a healthy reaction against the former fragmentation of the prophetic books into small literary units.

The Septuagint (Greek) translation inserted the foreign oracles, originally given in Ch. 46–51, after 25: 13, which seems more logical.

ZEPHANIA

Just as Jeremiah had done in his early days, so did his contemporary, the prophet Zephania, prophesy against all the nations round about, including Assyria, the most oppressive and hated of all:

> "The great day of the Lord is near,
>   near and hastening fast;
> the sound of the day of the Lord is bitter,
>   the mighty man cries aloud there". (Zeph. 1: 14)

He also stressed the Day of Yahweh since he believed that the civilization of his day was intolerably corrupt, Judah included. Therefore God would sweep away the existing order:

> "Yea, at that time I will change the
>   speech of the peoples
> to a pure speech,
>   that all of them may call on the name of the Lord
> and serve him with one accord.
>   From beyond the rivers of Ethiopia
> my suppliants, the daughter of my dispersed ones,
>   shall bring my offering". (Zeph. 3: 9–10)

Since the one God is Yahweh, the Judean ideal would be extended to all mankind. This closely resembled the teaching of the earlier prophets. Yahweh is the God of the universe, a God of righteousness and holiness. In the higher strata of prophecy, universality was apparently triumphing over narrow nationalism. After the destruction of the old order, the survivors would have a happy future "in Zion", and these would be the poor and humble who had trusted in God. The people who would be left in the world would live a life of simplicity and harmlessness as in the golden age of innocence long ago.

THE PROPHET HABAKKUK

Was Yahweh Just and All-sufficient?

Habakkuk, who was teaching in Jehoiakim's days, also lived in the shadow of the crucial years that changed the history of western Asia. Babylon had assumed world power by the overthrow of Assyria, the defeat of Egypt in 604–5 B.C.E. and by conquering all the territories formerly held in subjection by the Assyrian empire. Following the tradition of Isaiah and Jeremiah, Habakkuk regarded the invaders as the instruments of Yahweh's discipline.

Entrance to the palace of Nebuchadrezzar in Babylon

What, in fact has happened? inquired Habakkuk. The prophet complained of the injustice and brutality within Judah and asked how long this was to continue. Moreover, God had promised (through his prophets) that Assyria's yoke would be broken after many days, and in fact it had fallen. Why did God now raise another cruel host — the Chaldeans — to rule the world? Where was the just and sovereign rule of the God of history?

"For lo, I am rousing the Chaldeans,
    that bitter and hasty nation,
who march through the breadth of the earth,
    to seize habitations not their own.

Look among the nations, and see;
    wonder and be astounded.
For I am doing a work in your days
    that you would not believe if told". (Hab. 1: 5–6)

When the Babylonian invasion struck in 604–601 it seems that some voices arose to question whether Yahweh was just or did possess all-sufficient and sovereign power to protect his people. The literature of the period exhibits a strong preoccupation with the problem, and this represents the major theme of Habakkuk.

Jeremiah asked the same question and answered it: God had raised Babylon to rule the nation for an appointed time of seventy years only. Habakkuk answered differently:

"And the Lord answered me:
'Write the vision;
    make it plain upon tablets,
    so he may run who reads it.

For still the vision awaits its time;
    it hastens to the end — it will not lie.
If it seem slow, wait for it;
    it will surely come, it will not delay". (Hab. 2: 1–3)

He did not specify the appointed time would come when world would be rid of Babylon. But this is followed by a list of woes that await her through God's mighty intervention and judgement on Babylon. Woe to the oppressor, woe upon his lust for land, upon the cities he has built and woe upon his unholy banquets and his idols:

What profit is an idol
    when its maker has shaped it,
    a metal image, a teacher of lies?

For the workman trusts in his own
    creation". (Hab. 2:18)

RELIGION DENATIONALIZED AND UNIVERSAL

Thus before its collapse Jeremiah and his contemporaries handed the people the truth by which their souls might live. Though the Temple and the state of Judah must perish, true religion could and should continue among the humble worshippers of Yahweh cast away as exiles in Babylon.

Finally, according to Y. Kaufman, it was Jeremiah and Habakkuk, who originated the great debate against the idolatry of the nations. From this developed the belief that Israel's special mission was war on heathen worship. It had no reason to exist and Israel must end it, for all humanity was one and must acknowledge one God. This aspiration was carried forward in the message of Second Isaiah. These ideas were to be crystallized in the post-exilic literature dealing with "the end of days", in Daniel and in the literature of the Apocrypha. And so, though the nation did not accept Jeremiah's teaching in its full scope at the time, his words were remembered in the following century, after the Exile.

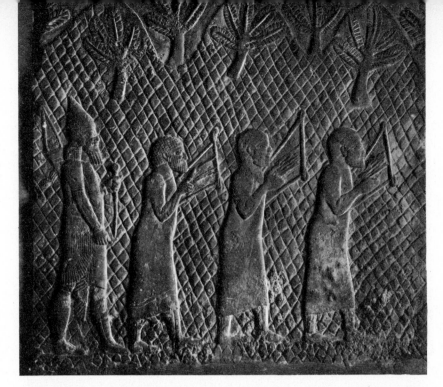

Barefoot lyrists conducted by a soldier over a wooded mountain. Note the similarity between the men wearing caps, and those depicted in the siege of Lachish in Chap. XVI.

CHAPTER XIX

THE DAWN OF A NEW ERA IN EXILE

THE EXILE IN BABYLONIA

"The Spirit lifted me up and took me away, and I went in bitterness in the heat of my spirit, the hand of the Lord being strong upon me; and I came to the exiles at Tel-abib, who dwelt by the river Chebar. And I sat there overwhelmed among them seven days". (Ezekiel 3: 14–15)

All direct knowledge about the areas of Babylonia to which the exiles were taken and about actual events there has been lost. We have some clues as to where some of the captives lived from places mentioned long afterwards in the book of Ezra as the points of origin of the group that returned from the captivity to Judah. In addition, of course, there is Ezekiel's classic reference to Tel-Abib (3: 15). The name of this settlement is probably the Hebrew form for the Babylonian Til-abubi — a term used for any long uninhabited mound. It has given its name to modern Tel Aviv in the new Israel. We hear also of Tel-Melach, Tel-Harsah, Cherub, Addan etc., (Ezra 2: 59). The Babylonian business documents of the firm of Murashu Sons in the Babylonian city of Nippur refer to a canal Kabaru, near that city in central Mesopotamia identical with the river Chebar in Ezekiel:

"In the thirtieth year, in the fourth month, on the fifth day of the month, as I was among the exiles by the river Chebar, the heavens were opened, and I saw visions of God. On the fifth day of the month (it was the fifth year of the exile of king Jehoiachin), the word of the Lord came to Ezekiel the priest, the son of Buzi, in the land of the Chaldeans by the river Chebar; and the hand of the Lord was upon him there". (Ezek. 1: 1–3)

We know from Jeremiah's reference and from the Babylonian Greek historian Berossus, that the exiles settled mainly as farmers, keeping their social organization much as it had been in Judah:

"Build houses and live in them; plant gardens and eat their produce. Take wives and have sons and daughters; take wives for your sons, and give your daughters in marriage, that they may bear sons and daughters; multiply there, and do not decrease. But seek the welfare of the city where I have sent you into exile, and pray to the Lord on its behalf, for in its welfare you will find your welfare". (Jer. 29: 5–7)

There is some confusion about the total number of people taken into captivity but it is clear that the Exile did not involve the wholesale movement of the Judean population to Babylonia. Nebuchadrezzar did not practise the exchange of entire populations which marked Assyria's colonization and which had brought foreign peoples to Israel. The handful left in Judah, however, was crippled by the deportation of their leaders and skilled workers and by the infiltration of neighbouring Edomites around Hebron.

The artisans among the exiles were mobilized by Nebuchadrezzar for his extensive building programme in the city of Babylon, side by side with exiles from the Phoenician cities of Tyre, Byblos and Arwad. In the course of time they adapted themselves to the conditions in the cities and some became traders. According to the records of the Murashu family of the 5th century B.C.E. they must have expanded and prospered. The impact of their new environment is also reflected in their adoption of the Babylonian calendar system and

In Babylonian times the unit of money was a mina, worth 60 shekels. This one-mina weight of Nebuchadrezzar II (left) weighs 978 gms. The bronze lion weight (right), with an Aramean inscription, weighs 2 minas.

month names. The hold of their national language faded and they adopted Aramaic, the lingua-franca of the Near East. Like the other subject national groups, they had no political power but organized themselves into religious or ethnic communities. Exile, service in Babylonian projects and their isolation must also have resulted in intermarriage. However the people identified themselves by their ancestral name. They called themselves after Judah (Yehuda or Yehudi for Judean). The name Jews was derived in Hellenistic circles from Judeans. No specific reference to Jews or Judaism is, however, found in the Old Testament.

ADJUSTMENT

Their most serious problem was in religious adjustment. Their whole faith had centred in Palestine, the ancestral belief in Yahweh, and the Temple in Jerusalem, the place where He caused His "name" to dwell. The danger was that in time this old faith, torn from its moorings, would become submerged in the far superior Babylonian environment. Babylonia was the scene of thriving agriculture, highly developed industry, marvellous architecture and a cultic magnificence far more elaborate than the modest way of life that the exiles had known in Judah. Just as after settling in Canaan, they had faced the problem of coming into close contact with the higher Phoenician civilization in the days of Solomon, Omri, Ahab, Athaliah and Manasseh, now even the most devout Jews raised this question in despair. The mood is reflected in Psalm 137:

"By the waters of Babylon,
   there we sat down and wept,
   when we remembered Zion.
On the willows there
   we hung our lyres.
For there our captors
   required of us songs,
and our tormentors, mirth saying,
   'Sing us one of the songs of Zion!'

How shall we sing the Lord's song
   in a foreign land?
If I forget you, O Jerusalem,
   let my right hand wither!
Let my tongue cleave to the roof
   of my mouth,
   if I do not remember you,
if I do not set Jerusalem
   above my highest joy!" (Ps. 137: 1–6)

Jeremiah was right

In Jeremiah's letters to the deportees from Israel and Judah he insisted that even in a faraway land, where there was no Temple of Yahweh, men could have access to God through prayer.

The great prophets, as we know, had paved the way for the new expression of Israel's faith by insisting that God was not bound to the Temple of Jerusalem. Down to the Exile, the rank and file of Judeans had adhered to their localized religion and the priestly view which maintained the exclusive legitimacy of the Temple cult. Would the historic cultic religion cease because sacrifice was legitimate only in Jerusalem? The Exile and the prophetic teaching forced upon the Jews a belief in the *universality* of Yahweh, who would follow them wherever they might wander. This teaching stood the exiles in good stead for they realized that they could turn to God anywhere, thus maintaining the link with their past in the confidence that He would be near, and that He would be their sanctuary even in a foreign land:

"Therefore say, 'Thus says the Lord God: Though I removed them far off among the nations, and though I scattered them among the countries, yet I have been a sanctuary to them for a while in the countries where they have gone' ". (Ezek.11: 16)

A New Chapter in the History of Israel's Faith

The faith in Yahweh was strengthened by the Exile and accompanying misfortunes because the prophets had predicted them and put forward valid solutions. This renewed belief found expression in many of the prayers (now found in the book of Psalms) which were composed during the Exile by unknown individuals, priests and prophets who, like Jeremiah, cried to Yahweh:

"Out of the depths I cry to thee, O Lord!
  Lord hear my voice!
Let thy ears be attentive
  to the voice of my supplications!

If thou O Lord shouldst mark iniquities,
  Lord, who could stand?
But there is forgiveness with thee,
  that thou mayest be feared". (Ps. 130: 1–4)

During this period the Jews undoubtedly met in small groups, after the manner of the elders who consulted Ezekiel, the prophet of the Exile in his house, to be instructed in their traditions and to worship informally:

"In the seventh year, in the fifth month, on the tenth day of the month, certain of the elders of Israel came to inquire of the Lord, and sat before me. And the word of the Lord came to me: 'son of man, speak to the elders of Israel, and say to them, Thus says the Lord God, Is it to inquire of me that you come? As I live, says the Lord God, I will not be inquired of by you. Will you judge them, son of man, will you judge them? Then let them know the abominations of their fathers' ". (Ezek. 20: 1–4)

EZEKIEL

Jeremiah's teaching was reinforced in faraway Babylonia by that of his younger contemporary, Ezekiel. He also proclaimed that Judah's downfall was the righteous judgement of Yahweh. Ezekiel, a priest of the Temple, was carried away in the first deportation of 597, and continued to preach among the exiles for over twenty years, or for some fifteen years after the fall of Jerusalem. Until that event his had been a message of unalterable condemnation:

"And you shall speak my words to them, whether they hear or refuse to hear; for they are a rebellious house. 'But you, son of man, hear what I say to you; be not rebellious like that rebellious house; open your mouth, and eat what I give you'. And when I looked, behold, a hand was stretched out to me, and lo, a written scroll was in it". (Ezek. 2: 7–9)

Ezekiel rejected the nationalistic faith in the everlasting stability of the Temple and Jerusalem as sternly as did Jeremiah. Believing that Yahweh had decreed the destruction of the city, he compared the prophets who gave hopeful oracles to fools who whitewash over a bulging, decaying wall. He did not, as we shall see, surrender the traditional faith in God's covenant with David's dynasty, but he removed it from dependence on the existing state. In visions he looked to a future when Yahweh's presence, as it were, would rise from His throne in the Temple, emerge from the shrine, hover over it and depart:

"And the cherubim mounted up. These were the living creatures that I saw by the river Chebar. And when the cherubim went, the wheels went beside them; and when the cherubim lifted up their wings to mount up from the earth, the wheels did not turn from beside them. When they stood still, these stood still, and when they mounted up, these mounted up with them; for the spirit of the living creatures was in them. Then the glory of the Lord went forth from the threshold of the house, and stood over the cherubim. And the cherubim lifted up their wings and mounted up from the earth in my sight as they went forth with the wheels beside them; and they stood at the door of the east gate of the house of the Lord; and the glory of the God of Israel was over them". (Ezek. 10: 15–19)

Yahweh had withdrawn his choice of Zion and no longer resided exclusively in His house. The national disaster, in Ezekiel's view, was Yahweh's own doing and His judgement on the nation's sin was the vindication of himself as sovereign God:

"For thus says the Lord God: How much more when I send upon Jerusalem my four sore acts of judgment, sword, famine, evil beasts, and pestilence, to cut off from it man and beast! Yet if there should be left in it any survivors to lead out sons and daughters, when they come forth to you, and you see their ways and their doings, you will be consoled for the evil that I have brought upon Jerusalem, for all that I have brought upon it. They will console you, when you see their ways and their doings; and you shall know that I have not done without cause all that I have done in it, says the Lord God' ". (Ezek. 14: 21–23)

While Jeremiah and Hosea idealized the ancient Israel of the desert period as a faithful and pure community, Ezekiel characterized Jerusalem as the mixed offspring of sinful ancestors, stating that the Hebrews came from a variety of stocks. He did, in fact, contribute a semblance of historical analysis of Israel's early ancestry and customs by drawing on tradition not found elsewhere in the Bible:

"And say, Thus says the Lord God to Jerusalem: Your origin and your birth are of the land of the Canaanites; your father was an Amorite, and your mother a Hittite. And as for your birth, on the day you were born your navel string was not cut, nor were you washed with water to cleanse you, nor rubbed with salt, nor swathed with bands". (Ezek. 16: 3–4)

INDIVIDUALIZED DIVINE JUSTICE

This sense of corporate guilt had created a fatalistic attitude. People would say, "what is the use, God is against us". But the prophet insisted that the individual Jew should not be condemned because he was the descendant of guilty ancestors. Each individual had his own standing before God and could be redeemed from his sinful past:

" 'What do you mean by repeating this proverb concerning the land of Israel, "The fathers have eaten sour grapes, and the children's teeth are set on edge"? As I live, says the Lord God, this proverb shall no more be used by you in Israel. Behold, all souls are mine; the soul of the father as well as the soul of the son is mine: the soul that sins shall die' ". (Ezek. 18: 2–4)

"Yet the house of Israel says, 'The way of the Lord is not just'. O house of Israel, are my ways not just? Is it not your ways that are not just? Therefore I will judge you, O house of Israel, every one according to his ways, says the Lord God. Repent and turn from all your transgressions, lest iniquity be your ruin. Cast away from you all the transgressions which you have committed against me, and get yourselves a new heart and a new spirit! Why will you die, O house of Israel? For I have no pleasure in the death of anyone, says the Lord God; so turn, and live' ". (Ezek. 18: 29: 32)

It was in this sphere that Ezekiel made his great contribution to the development of religious thought. Earlier prophecy dealt with Israel as a collective unit. It was destroyed because of its social and religious wickedness. This gave rise to a feeling of corporate guilt. Now the aftermath of destruction raised the question of the future. A new and ideal state could only be created by reformed individuals and the merciful Yahweh would gladly forgive them if they repented. By individualizing divine justice, Ezekiel explained that each generation, each individual, had his fair chance before the bar of God's judgement.

Profanation of Holiness

Thoughout its history, claimed Ezekiel, Israel's crime had been the profanation of the holiness of God. The central theme of his conception was the idea of God as spiritual, powerful and, above all, holy. To punish the profanation of his holiness, God had been compelled to destroy the state. To the oriental mind a god and his people were inseparably connected. The destruction of a people and its temple would prove the impotence of its god. To Ezekiel, such an aspersion was intolerable and profaned God's holy name. So he proclaimed that it was not because of Israel's virtue that Yahweh was about to act, but only because other nations had inferred from Jerusalem's fall that He was powerless to save the city. Therefore Yahweh would vindicate His holiness (His "name", meaning His personality). The nations would know that Yahweh was God when He restored His helpless people:

> "'For thus says the Lord God; Behold, I, I myself will search for my sheep, and will seek them out. As a shepherd seeks out his flock when some of his sheep have been scattered abroad, so will I seek out my sheep; and I will rescue them from all places where they have been scattered on a day of clouds and thick darkness. And I will bring them out from the peoples, and gather them from the countries, and will bring them into their own land; and I will feed them on the mountains of Israel, by the fountains, and in all the inhabited places of the country". (Ezek: 34:11–13)

Thus he rebuked the taunts of Israel's enemies that her God had failed in his purposes.

Ezekiel was a strange figure among the prophets. Stern and harsh, rigidly self-controlled, one suspects profound, repressed emotions concealing passionate thought. In moments of ecstasy he would deliver his message through allegory and symbolic acts that to us seem strange. But such actions attributable to prophets and priests in Semitic thought convey more than literary symbols. They are "sympathetic magic", tending to produce the results of which they are symbolic.

One of Ezekiel's most tender touches was his grief over his wife. She was taken from him shortly before Jerusalem fell. He refrained from any outward sign of grief, taking her death instead as an omen of a disaster too deep for tears:

> "And the people said to me, 'Will you not tell us what these things mean for us, that you are acting thus?' Then I said to them, 'The word of the Lord came to me: "Say to the house of Israel, Thus says the Lord God: Behold, I will profane my sanctuary, the pride of your power, the delight of your eyes, and the desire of your soul; and your sons and your daughters whom you left behind shall fall by the sword. And you shall do as I have done; you shall not cover your lips, nor eat the bread of mourners. Your turbans shall be on your heads and your shoes on your feet; you shall not mourn or weep, but you shall pine away in your iniquities and groan to one another. Thus shall Ezekiel be to you a sign; according to all that he has done you shall do. When this comes, then you will know that I am the Lord God' "'". (Ezek. 24: 19–24)

In the inaugural vision of Ezekiel he describes winged figures that swell out of the cloud and two-faced cherubim, one of a man, the other of a lion. These must not be interpreted literally; they are images borrowed from Assyrian symbolism as depicted on this relief of a winged figure from Nimrud, on the left, and the colossal Assyrian winged bulls or lions with human head which adorned their temples and palaces, on the right.

The accompaniments of death in antiquity were unrestrained weeping, wailing and physical torments, such as tearing the hair, lacerating the flesh and beating the breast. The women did most of the wailing, the men rent their clothes and wept. Tear bottles were also used to collect the tears. (See picture of women mourners at end of Ch. V)

ISRAEL'S RESURRECTION

As long as Jerusalem was still standing, however, the exiles refused to believe that the nation would fall. They believed the prophet was uttering visions about the far distant future and not about their own times:

"'Son of man, what is this proverb that you have about the land of Israel, saying, "The days grow long, and every vision comes to naught'"?'". (Ezek. 12: 22)

"'Son of man, behold, they of the house of Israel say, "The vision that he sees is for many days hence, and he prophesies of times far off".'". (Ezek. 12: 27)

But the fall of Jerusalem established his reputation. The news came that Jerusalem was besieged (586) and finally a fugitive brought word that the city had fallen:

"In the twelfth year of our exile, in the tenth month, on the fifth day of the month, a man who had escaped from Jerusalem came to me and said, 'The city has fallen'". (Ez. 33: 21)

Until that day nationalist feeling had been strong and he, like Jeremiah, had believed his task to be to shatter illusions. After 586, when people were reduced to despair and remorse, his message changed to bring comfort and hope, and a deeper meaning to God's purpose. God was sovereign over man's false hopes and false despair, but He gave the unexpected new beginning. This is strikingly illustrated in his vision of resurrection, when Yahweh would breathe his spirit into the bones of the defunct nation. Ezekiel saw himself standing in the valley of dry bones. He gives both question and answer:

"And he said to me, 'Son of man, can these bones live?' And I answered, 'O Lord God, thou knowest.' Again he said to me, 'Prophesy to these bones, and say to them, O dry bones, hear the word of the Lord. Thus says the Lord God to these bones: Behold, I will cause breath to enter you, and you shall live. And I will lay sinews upon you, and will cause flesh to come upon you, and cover you with skin, and put breath in you, and you shall live; and you shall know that I am the Lord'. So I prophesied as I was commanded and as I prophesied, there was a noise, and behold, a rattling; and the bones came together, bone to its bone. And as I looked, there were sinews on them, and flesh had come upon them, and skin had covered them; but there was no breath in them. Then he said to me, 'Prophesy to the breath, prophesy, son of man, and say to the breath, Thus says the Lord God; Come from the four winds, O breath, and breathe upon these slain, that they may live'. So I prophesied as he commanded me, and the breath came into them, and they lived, and stood upon their feet, an exceedingly great host. Then he said to me, 'Son of man, these bones are the whole house of Israel. Behold, they say "Our bones are dried up, and our hope is lost; we are clean cut off" ' ". (Ezek. 37: 3–11)

Like Jeremiah Ezekiel regarded the Exile as an interim period beyond which lay God's future. The old national hope was thus retained, but projected into the future and made wholly dependent upon a new act of divine salvation. The nucleus of the restored people was to come from among the exiles, whom Ezekiel saw as the true heirs of the promise.

The Architect of Restoration

In the nation's extremity, the prophet did not only look back at past woes. He became the architect of Zion's restoration. Chapters 40 to 48 of his book represent a detailed blueprint for the new Jerusalem. He mapped out the construction of the Second Temple and the regulations for its priesthood. This was to be limited to descendants of Zadok:

"They shall not come near to me, to serve me as priest, nor come near any of my sacred things and the things that are most sacred; but they shall bear their shame, because of the abominations which they have committed. Yet I will appoint them to keep charge of the temple, to do all its service and all that is to be done in it. 'But the Levitical priests, the sons of Zadok, who kept the charge of my sanctuary when the people of Israel went astray from me, shall come near to me to minister to me; and they shall attend on me to offer me the fat and the blood, says the Lord God". (Ez. 44: 13–15)

This view was further developed by other members of the priestly dynasty of Zadok who were carried into exile. Different priestly families, such as those associated with the shrines outside Jerusalem, were to remain in the ranks of the Levites and serve the priests.

Ezekiel laid great stress on Temple rituals and the laws of purity and sanctity, particularly the purity of the priests concerned with sacred duties. The provisions in these chapters were intended for a regenerated people giving proper expression to its devotion to Yahweh.

Ezekiel, no less than his forebears, explained Israel's tragedy in advance, in terms of faith and divine judgement. By so doing the ancient faith was preserved, even though its national institutions had been swept away. The catastrophe drove many to heart-searching and penitence, and encouraged the formation of a new social and communal attitude, which would survive the wreckage of the old national-cultic community to which every Israelite automatically belonged. If Israel was to survive as a people, a new attitude based on individual decision and worship would have to replace the old corporate traditions.

SECOND ISAIAH

Many have wondered how it was that Israel was not absorbed into the life of the Babylonian empire along with the other small nations, and maintained her identity as a special religious group. What part could Yahweh, patron deity of the Temple of Jerusalem, be expected to play now that His people had been uprooted? How could they worship Him when the Temple had crumbled in ashes? Such questions were implicit in the religious situation of the exiles and their adjustment to their new environment as a community. This problem and its implications are the burden of Chapters 40–66 of Isaiah.

Thus, the climax of Old Testament prophecy is contained in the work of the anonymous prophet who penned the exhilarating poetry of Isaiah 40-66. His conception of divine control over history, of the virtue of righteous suffering, of the spiritual essence and universality of God, are stated with a literary magnificence equalled by few of the pages of the Bible and are without parallel in the entire literature of the ancient oriental world.

One of the indisputable conclusions of modern biblical science is that Chapters 40-66 of the book of Isaiah were not written by the prophet Isaiah of Jerusalem in whose book they now appear. This is borne out by their Hebrew style and language, by their ideas, which are more uniform and vast in their conception, by their theological content and by their historical background. Each prophet faced an entirely different situation and presented a different message to meet it. Isaiah of Jerusalem preached mainly of doom, with a morally conditional message about the "remnant". In Second Isaiah, (also termed Deutero-Isaiah), the new age of redemption was at hand as the experience of the anonymous prophet matured. He is assumed to have lived during the decade just before the collapse of Babylon and the appearance of Cyrus on the Near Eastern scene. The keynote of his message is that punishment, indispensable before and during the Exile, is now over. Nevertheless, as no temples for Jewish services existed in Babylonia, Ezekiel and Second Isaiah made great efforts to keep faith alive and to call the exiles back to religious thought and meditation.

Martin Buber assumes the prophet to have been a member of a circle deriving from the"Limmudim" or disciples of Isaiah of Jerusalem who were entrusted with the secret of salvation. This interpretation stresses the new prophet's place in the Isianic tradition and explains that the writings of Isaiah of Jerusalem and Second Isaiah were not assembled in one book by accident. Together they seem to represent the body of traditions preserved by these "limmudim" for a century and a half, in which the original idea of salvation reaches its climax in the magnificent concepts of Second Isaiah (See Ch. XVI "A Life of Struggle").

The "Redeemer"

"Comfort, comfort my people
    says your God.
Speak tenderly to Jerusalem,
    and cry to her

that her warfare is ended,
    that her iniquity is pardoned,
that she has received from the Lord's hand
    double for all her sins". (Is. 40: 1–2)

Liberation was assured the exiles because Israel's God was both Creator and Redeemer, Lord of the world and of men.

" 'And the glory of the Lord shall be revealed.
    and all flesh shall see it together,
    for the mouth of the Lord has spoken' " (Is. 40:5)

"Have you not known? Have you not heard?
The Lord is the everlasting God,
    the Creator of the ends of the earth.
He does not faint or grow weary,
    his understanding is unsearchable". (Is. 40: 25–28)

Though much of this was implicit in the first Isaiah, the second rose to great heights of eloquence in portraying God as the universal creator, the omnipresent ruler, bringing encouragement for the exiles:

Break forth together into singing,
    you waste places of Jerusalem;
for the Lord has comforted his people,
    he has redeemed Jerusalem.
The Lord has bared his holy arm
    before the eyes of all the nations;
and all the ends of the earth shall see
    the salvation of our God.

Depart, depart, go out thence,
    touch no unclean thing;
go out from the midst of her, purify yourselves,
    you who bear the vessels of the Lord.
For you shall not go out in haste,
    and you shall not go in flight,
for the Lord will go before you,
    and the God of Israel will be your rear guard". (Is. 52: 10–12)

Yahweh would personally lead his flock to Zion, and establish his rule over a new, redeemed, charismatic Israel.

The vision of Second Isaiah borrows an ancient Mesopotamian image of humbled people trodden in the dust under the king's foot. This is indicated on the base of the statue of Ur-Ningirsu from the late third millenium. Isaiah said: "....and you have made your back like the ground, and like the street for them to pass over".

The opening oracle of consolation of Second Isaiah also marks a new stage in the history of prophecy. In the first Isaiah we had the conception of the "messianic king", in the Second there is the "suffering servant". The first insisted on the remnant who should return and this idea is faintly present in the Second Isaiah. But here there is a break with the classic form of the great prophets with their stress on the dual symbolism of punishment and salvation, hinging on the appeal of return. The new form, however, retained one of the alternatives of this symbolism: the suffering of Israel, namely the suffering servant — which remains one of the major concepts of the new prophecy. Hence *suffering* and *salvation* are both present, but they have changed their character. They are no longer alternatives. For the problem of the people's conduct and its punishment now lay in the past. Israel had been punished and forgiven. The prophet was no longer concerned with conduct gauged by the ancient standards of the harsh Sinaitic legislation. His appeal was now for the acceptance of Yahweh as Redeemer. The salvation announced by Second Isaiah was not expressed as a slow divine drama transfiguring the history of Israel but as the spontaneous revelation of Yahweh the Redeemer.

The word "redeemer" in the English text corresponds to the Hebrew word "go'el". This concept had a wide range of meaning. "Go'el" is a term belonging to Hebrew family law. It denoted the male relative who was bound to act as champion for his family, upholding the rights of its other members. He acted as protector and avenger and represented the family in questions of ownership of land. It was a concept rooted in the people's own experience. Thus Yahweh is shown as "redeemer" appearing in the role of the champion of his people. He would act to glorify His "name" through a redeemed Israel, not out of vanity, but because Yahweh was faithful to his charge as the "redeemer" or champion of Israel. Since, however, His success depended upon a human response, Second Isaiah appealed to the people not to reject the message of salvation:

> " 'I, I am He
> who blots out your transgressions
> for my own sake,
> and I will not remember your sins' ". (Is. 43: 25)

A UNIVERSAL GOD VERSUS THE IDOLS

We have already seen that it was Jeremiah and Habakkuk who initiated the idea that Israel's aim should be to disown and fight idolatry so that all nations would realize that humanity is one, worshipping the one God. This forms a militant background to Second Isaiah's prophecy, and represents one of the major themes of the book:

> "Have you not known? Have you not heard?
>   Has it not been told you from the beginning?
>   Have you not understood from the foundations of the earth?
> It is he who sits above the circle of the earth,
>   and its inhabitants are like grasshoppers,
> who stretches out the heavens like a curtain,
>   and spreads them like a tent to dwell in;
> who brings princes to nought;
>   and makes the rulers of the earth as nothing.
> Scarcely are they planted, scarcely sown,
>   scarcely has their stem taken root in the earth,
> when he blows upon them, and they wither,
>   and the tempest carries them off like stubble".
> (Is. 40: 21–24)

The opening oracle of Second Isaiah refers to the heathen surroundings of the Jews in Babylonia. Everywhere about them were imposing temples or splendid ritual processions each with its statue or image representing a presiding deity–Marduk, Nabu, Shamash, Ishtar. To the prophet all these images were the work of men's hands valuable only as the raw material of his sublime rhetoric and invective against heathenism. There was no comparison between stone or wooden images, and Yahweh. This was the crux of his judgement of mighty Babylon and her religio-cultural challenge to the Jews of his time. To face this challenge Second Isaiah restated the Israelite conception of God, opening vistas unimagined by any previous prophet.

His obvious conclusion was sounded like a clarion call to the nations:

> " 'Turn to me and be saved
> all the ends of the earth'.
> For I am God, and there is no other". (Is. 45: 22)

There could be no other allegiance, neither for Israel nor for other nations. If the nations refused to worship Yahweh, they would have no gods to worship because their gods simply did not exist.

With Second Isaiah the Judaism of the Exile was finally formulated as an explicit monotheism. The principle of Yahweh's power over all nations had been propounded from the time of Moses. But the novelty of Second Isaiah lay in the fact that he stood on the ruins of the old world, scanned the horizons and found that the God of his puny people was the Lord who encompassed the world with his fullness, determined the destinies of nations, gave breath to all men, and was the ultimate source of all power. Second Isaiah daringly glimpsed the day when all the peoples of the earth would share his faith.

"Set Forth Your Case"

Such was the answer to the challenge of Babylon. In the antagonism between the two faiths and peoples, the Jews had found their champion to oppose Babylon's culture and Babylon's gods. As if in a court of law, God appears against the gods of all other peoples, with Israel as his witness and defender. The arguments presented are supposed to prove God's triumph. God challenges any other people to show that their gods had been able to predict or bring about the rise of Cyrus, Babylon's great rival. But they were idols. They could not justify their power:

> "But when I look there is no one;   Behold, they are all a delusion;
>   among these there is no counselor   their works are nothing;
>   who, when I ask, gives an answer.   their molten images are empty wind". (Is. 41: 28–29)

There is no substitute, as stressed elsewhere, for reading the literature itself, or still better, for reading these poems aloud, thus absorbing with ear and mind the artistic blend of motif and metre. These poems will be seen to be an elaboration of his opening and major theme: Yahweh's imminent coming to inaugurate his kingdom, and his sweeping message of hope. Many have compared this poetic cycle to a musical fugue which introduces a major theme and subjects it to complex contrapuntal development. We can call attention to only a few of the major themes in these poems and evaluate them.

The metaphorical use of the course of a lawsuit proceedings in ancient Israel where the adversary is hailed before the court to uphold the rights of the poor, is applied in a most developed, perfected form. It may have resulted from the way in which he fulfilled his prophetic mission in discussion and dispute. This literary skill projects the two distinguishable subjects of his leading theme: the superiority and incomparableness of Yahweh, the Creator, the ruler and director of world-history, as against all other gods, and the fair and just and righteous way in which He had treated his wayward people in punishment, forbearance and redemptive loyalty.

THE POEMS OF THE SUFFERING SERVANT

The dramatic representation of the preceding scenes in Is. 41, seems to be amplified in the visions of the "Suffering Servant", and may provide a clue to their understanding, according to the views recently put forward by Yehezkel Kaufman. The alternation of speech and rhetoric in the poems is not made clear by any "casting directions", there is no dramatis personae as it were, but the style is suggestive to those versed in the Hebrew prophetic idiom. Collective Israel, humble, suffering and faithful, is God's witness and His "servant". Due to limitation of space, the reader is advised to read the full text of these visions.

In the first of Second Isaiah's visions on this theme, the servant appears in the presence of God and the prophet. The opening speech is God's:

"Behold my servant, whom I uphold,
  my chosen, in whom my soul delights;
I have put my spirit upon him,
  he will bring forth justice to the nations.
He will not cry or lift up his voice,
  or make it heard in the street;
a bruised reed he will not break,
  and a dimly burning wick he will not quench;
  he will faithfully bring forth justice.
He will not fail or be discouraged
  till he has established justice in the earth;
  and the coastlands wait for his law". (Is. 42: 1–4)

In the following verses 42: 6–9, the prophet speaks for God and completes the thought. In future, Israel will be appointed to a new mission as "the light of the nations".

In a second vision, 49:1–14, the servant and the prophet appear together. The servant's words set the scene of antagonism between Israel and the nations. They express both Israel's agony and her hope. This is followed by Israel's commission, viewed by the servant (49:6–7), which the prophet explains. A third vision, 50: 4–9 expresses the servant's endowment.

In a fourth sublime vision, the servant, described as the "suffering servant", appears under the protective arm of God:

"Behold, my servant shall prosper,
  he shall be exalted and lifted up,
  and shall be very high.
As many were astonished at him —
  his appearance was so marred,
  beyond human semblance,
and his form beyond that of the sons of men —
so shall he startle many nations;
  kings shall shut their mouths because of him;
for that which has not been told them they shall see,
  and that which they have not heard they shall
    understand" (Is. 52: 13–15)

Whereupon, the common people of all nations who have witnessed God's protection of his servant, pour out in chorus the confession which only the humble and contrite can utter. The vision closes with God's answer (53:11–12).

Numerous books have been written on the significance of the "suffering servant" and interpretations vary. Some regard him as a mythological figure; others as the prophet himself or some other suffering personage of his time: others regard it as a prophecy of the coming of Christ. The last and most significant is the collective theory. The decisive criterion of this theory, in which the suffering servant represents Israel, is that the interpretation of the servant includes the historical grandeur and richness of the people's age-long history. The prophet's real intention and symbolism in the figure of the servant will probably always remain in dispute on theological grounds. But it is clear that Second Isaiah intended his visions to be a summons to the Israel of his time and to succeeding generations.

Interpretation of the Bible depends on a study of its text in the context of history. The servant in peoples' minds may be a figure that fluctuates between individual and group, future ideal and present appeal. Second Isaiah's symbols must be read in terms of the writer's evolving experience in the 6th century B.C.E. His message was the revelation of God in terms of the needs of his own day and the days immediately at hand. This theme eschews visions of a distant future. The classical prophets had predicted the future but they were concerned with events near at hand, with the very existence of Israel.

EXILIC EXISTENCE AND DIVINE GOVERNMENT OF THE WORLD

Exile was often hailed by the prophets as a necessary instrument of divine government of the world. Some hold that this view derived from the fact that only in dispersal could the Jews act as "the light of the nations". Such an interpretation gains cogency from an attempt to take into account the varying philosophies of history held by the different writers of the Old Testament. This allows for the significance which the ancient heritage had for these biblical writers who were concerned both to interpret and shape that heritage.

Modern scholars refer to this philosophy of history as "historical monotheism". Y. Kaufman and S.W. Baron maintain that its achievement dates from the very beginnings of Israel's religious history in the Mosaic formulation. W.F. Albright believes also that the general possibility of Mosaic monotheism can be granted. Others hold that it was rather the gradual achievement of Israel's thinkers, and represents a long process of pondering the meaning of history while it was actually being lived. H.H. Hahn comments correctly that "it is this philosophy of history, implicit in the biblical writings, which gives them their meaning and provides the key to an interpretation of the Old Testament which has not only a basis in scientific method, but substance as an exposition of the supreme attempt of the mind of man to understand his place in the world and in history".

A GREAT LITERARY AND RELIGIOUS UPSURGE

The period of the Exile was remarkable both as a demonstration of the people's ability to retain its religious and social traditions in a foreign environment, and also for the preservation of literary treasures of the past. In the first place, there is the ardent, though utopian, programme envisaged by such prophets as Ezekiel and Second Isaiah, proclaiming the new Jerusalem and the reconstituted state. The eyes of the exiles evidently turned faithfully to that dream for it was powerful in shaping their future. The records and literary traditions of the past were jealously preserved and, in the view of many scholars, great literary activity was carried on in collecting, expanding and codifying. This ultimately produced the prophetic books and the bulk of the Holiness and Priestly Code in the book of Leviticus, reflecting the practice of the Jerusalem Temple. It is also probable that certain other parts of the books of the Pentateuch were amplified and codified as a means of ensuring their preservation. An awakened recollection of Yahweh's past deeds now brought home to the emerging new community both emotional and ideological aspects which their ancestors had accepted as a matter of custom and precedent. The new community, shorn of its focal centre and the visible symbols of its faith, must have idealized cultic practices, ancient institutions and the traditions pertaining to them. Strict observance of the Sabbath, of circumcision and other aspects of the national cult, became increasingly the mark of a loyal and devout Jew. The people now *lived* the traditional past more intensively and consciously, and naturally regarded their present state as an interim period at whose end would come national restoration.

On a material level life in Babylon had opened up many opportunities that would never have been available in less prosperous Judah. Many Jews became tradesmen and some grew rich. The outstanding example is the considerable documentation concerning contacts maintained by Jewish people in many parts of the country with the Babylonian house of Murashu and Sons which prospered particularly in the 5th century B.C.E. Its owners, who were not Jews, were bankers, real estate operators and traders on an imperial scale, with headquarters at Nippur, in lower Mesopotamia. They had a network of agencies extending from the north of Babylonia to the "Countries of the Sea". Some 730 tablets preserved from their archives help us to reconstruct the daily routine of one of the most ancient banks in the world and highlight the social and legal background of a rural society in which the Jews took an active part. Many of these Jews would never return to Palestine but would form one of the important nuclei of the emerging "diaspora" of permanent Jewish communities scattered throughout the Near East and the eastern Mediterranean.

Phalanxes of sculptured figures of alternating Median and Persian guards, and Elamite archers, adorn the eastern stairway of the Apadana at Persepolis, or Hall of the Throne.

CHAPTER XX

RETURN AND RESTORATION

THE LAST DAYS OF THE BABYLONIAN EMPIRE

The Babylonian empire, created by Nebuchadrezzar and his father, was extremely un-stable. Nebuchadrezzar himself was able to hold the empire intact and even to enlarge it. But he had a most dangerous rival in Cyaxares, king of Media, who in the past had been Babylon's ally in destroying Assyria. Babylonia had absorbed the erstwhile Assyrian empire and territories to the west and south west, while the Median king extended his rule over the area north of Babylonian territory through Armenia and Asia Minor,. But the neo-Babylonian empire was short-lived indeed. With Nebuchadrezzar's death in 562, 25 years after the fall of Jerusalem, Babylonian power declined rapidly. The throne changed hands three times within seven years. Amel-Marduk, mentioned in the Bible as Evil-Merodach released Yehoiachin from prison. This raised great hopes among the Jews of Babylon. He was succeeded by his brother-in-law, Nergal-shar-usur, then by a son of the latter, Laba-shi-Marduk, a minor who was speedily removed by Nabu-naid (Nabonidus), the son of the high priestess of Sinn in Harran, who usurped the throne and reigned from 556 B.C.E. He was the last Babylonian king.

SECOND ISAIAH HAILS CYRUS

"Who stirred up one from the east whom
  victory meets at every step?
He gives up nations before him,
  so that he tramples kings under foot;
he makes them like dust with his sword,

like driven stubble with his bow".
....
"The coastlands have seen and are afraid,
  the ends of the earth tremble;
  they have drawn near and come". (Is. 41: 2, 5)

Elamite archer of the Persian guard, with curled hair and beard, holding light spear in both hands; on coloured tiles from the palace of Artaxerxes II (known from the annals of Ezra). The strong leadership and phenomenal success which the Iranians enjoyed in the Near East was due partly to the use of archers, whose hail of arrows was irresistible. Iranian infantrymen carried lances and daggers with which to engage the enemy at close range, while the cavalry, skilled by the long attachment of the Aryans to the warhorse, supplied mobility where it was needed.

This vivid description of "one whom victory meets at every step" refers to the far-flung victories of Cyrus, ranging from Media in the east of Mesopotamia, to as far west as the Aegean Sea and its Isles. On historical grounds, it predicates that the Persian conqueror was already a prominent political figure.

The fall of Babylon (in 539 B.C.) had not yet taken place, though many observers were expecting it momently. This poem, therefore, bears a historic connotation in the context of the stirring events of the years 546 to 539, which cover Cyrus' victorious campaign. Addressed to the Judean exiles in Babylon, it belongs to the cycle of Second Isaiah.

He affirmed emphatically that it was Yahweh who had "stirred up" the victor from the east. Moreover, the event was part of his universal plan and was announced ahead of time; for Yahweh directs the course of history, which he has always oriented according to a vast plan, though its leading figures are not aware of its workings. The prophet foresaw the doom of Babylon and declared that the rising victor would be God's instrument in bringing it about:

> "I stirred up one from the north, and he has come,
>   from the rising of the sun, and he shall call on my name:
> he shall trample on rulers as on mortar,
>   as the potter treads clay". (Is. 41: 25)

In the prophetic vision, God had challenged the nations to his tribunal, pronounced the worthlessness of their idols, then declared His choice:

> "...calling a bird of prey from the east,
>   the man of my counsel from a far country,
> I have spoken, and I will bring it to pass;
>   I have purposed, and I will do it". (Is. 46: 11)

Many people throughout the neo-Babylonian Empire were observing the course of events at that time. The Jewish exiles, too, were watching the happenings with bated breath. The hope of these Jews for a return to Zion burned intensely. They felt that the time for miracles was at hand, and that even empires would fall. Second Isaiah's message of pardon, deliverance, restoration and grace set their hearts beating with faith and hope. In one of the greatest poems of this cycle, he exulted over the impending fall of Babylon. Ecstatically, he envisaged the restoration, and sang of Cyrus as the deliverer whom Yahweh would raise up.

Second Isaiah affirmed that Cyrus, although he would not realize it himself, would be the agent by whose hand Yahweh would redeem his people:

"Thus says the Lord to his anointed, to Cyrus,
  whose right hand I have grasped,
to subdue nations before him
  and ungird the loins of kings,
to open doors before him

that gates may not be closed:
'I will go before you
  and level the mountains
I will break in pieces the doors of bronze
  and cut asunder the bars of iron, (Is. 45: 1–2)

....

"I have aroused him in righteousness,
  and I will make straight all his ways;
he shall build my city

and set my exiles free,
not for price or reward.
  says the Lord of hosts' ". (Is. 45: 13)

THE DECLARATION OF CYRUS AND THE RISE OF EMPIRE

While the Hebrew prophet saw the great conqueror anointed by Yahweh for the particular purpose of releasing the Jewish captives and restoring them to their homeland, Cyrus himself claimed to be sent by the god Marduk. His own account of his Babylonian triumph is recorded in the famous "Cyrus Cylinder" — an inscription written on a clay barrel in the Babylonian language (now in the British Museum). Thereon, the Persian conqueror claimed to be chosen by the god Marduk to end the reign of terror that had prevailed under the "evil Nabuna'id" (Nabonidus), the last king of Babylon. According to the usual pattern in Mesopotamia, the account is couched in an apparently propagandist spirit; it was

The inscription recorded on a clay barrel relates the amazing story of the conquests of Cyrus, who plainly regarded himself as a man of destiny. He boasted of his efforts to obtain peace in Babylonia; he claimed to have abolished forced labour, to have improved housing conditions, and to have enjoyed the affection of the people. The account ends by referring to the fame of his name and his renown throughout the world, due to his power and benevolence. It is explicitly stated that he returned their sacred images to the peoples from whom they had been taken, and rebuilt their sanctuaries; that he gathered together foreign exiles from the various parts of his realm and returned them to their former homes.

inspired by the priests of Mesopotamia in the city of Babylon, whose power and influence had been diminished by Nabonidus:

(From Cyrus' inscription)

"He (Marduk) scanned and looked (through) all the countries, looking for a righteous ruler willing to lead him (i.e. Marduk) (in the annual procession). (Then) he pronounced the name of Cyrus, king of Anshan, declared him to become the ruler of all the world ..... He made him set out on the road to Babylon, going at his side like a real friend. His widespread troops — their number, like that of the water of a river, could not be established — strolled along, their weapons packed away. Without any battle, he made him enter his town Babylon, sparing Babylon any calamity. He delivered into his (Cyrus') hands Nabonidus, the king who did not worship him (i.e. Marduk)".

This view of Cyrus' divine mission is vividly illustrated by the parallel prophetic message of the great contemporary Hebrew poet. There are striking affinities between the language of the Cyrus Cylinder and Isaiah — so much so, indeed, that some scholars have conjectured that Second Isaiah must have been acquainted with the Babylonian document.

THE PHENOMENAL CAREER OF CYRUS

The empire of the Medes which had enjoyed ascendancy in the plateau of Iran had expanded north of Nabonidus' realm and was now ruled by Astyages, son of Cyaxares. Revolt broke out about 550 B.C.E. led by Cyrus the Persian, vassal king of Anshan in southern Iran. Nabonidus, rejoicing over the turn of events, must have supported Cyrus at first, but he miscalculated. By then Cyrus had dethroned Astyages in his capital Ecbatana and taken over the vast Median empire. He then launched upon a series of brilliant campaigns which struck terror far and wide (witness the impact on Second Isaiah!). Within a few years he took over the politically chaotic coastal countries of Greek Asia Minor, and defeated the proverbially wealthy Croesus, king of Lydia. In 539 to 538 he moved south against Babylon. By that time serious Babylonian resistance had come to an end, and Cyrus conquered its capital without shooting a single arrow.

Cyrus' subsequent propaganda accused Nabonidus, not only of neglecting Marduk — considered the supreme deity governing the world and all its happenings — but also of having offended the entire pantheon, by exiling the various gods to Babylon — apparently to keep them at his side. According to his own version of the matter (given in a recently discovered inscription) Nabonidus believed fanatically in the omnipotence of the moon god, Sinn. He thereby aroused the opposition of the priests of Marduk; and finally he left Babylon, accusing its people of deceitfulness:

"The sons of Babylon, Borsippa, Nippur, Ur, Erech, Larsa, priests and people of the capital of Accad (Babylon) ... forgot their duty; whenever they talked, it was treason, and not loyalty; like a dog they devoured one another ...., but I hid myself afar from my city of Babylon. On the road to Teima, Dedan, Fadak, Khaibar, Yadih, and as far as Yathrib (now Medina); for ten years I went away from them".

Cyrus told his pagan subjects later that Marduk had summoned him to restore the gods (taken by Nabonidus to Babylon) to their rightful shrines. This was a significant policy. It explains also Cyrus' restoration of the God of the Jews to Zion. The fact remains that in a few years Cyrus had wrought a vast historical and political transformation. A great empire, stretching from present-day Pakistan to the Balkans, fell into his hands.

As it happens, neither the biblical references to the fall of Babylon, nor accounts handed down in Greek sources really give the full story of the initial downfall of the great Babylonian empire under the attack of Cyrus, nor the historical and political background of the event. The fifth chapter of the enigmatic book of Daniel gives a strange and haunting reminder of the overnight character of the collapse of Belshazzar, who is referred to as "King of the Babylonian kingdom".

The Ghostly Hand: It is related how, in a wild orgy at the king's palace in Babylon, this "king", who had refused to take warning from the fate of his "father", Nebuchadrezzar, made sacrilegious use of the sacred vessels from the temple of Jerusalem. Suddenly the festivities were interrupted by a miraculous and ghostly hand, that wrote on the wall a mysterious message:

"Immediately the fingers of a man's hand appeared and wrote on the plaster of the wall of the king's palace, opposite the lampstand; and the king saw the hand as it wrote". (Daniel 5: 5)

"And this is the writing that was inscribed: MENE, MENE, TEKEL, and PARSIN. This is the interpretation of the matter: MENE, God has numbered the days of your kingdom and brought it to an end; TEKEL, you have been weighed in the balances and found wanting; PERES, your kingdom is divided and given to the Medes and Persians'". (Daniel 5: 25–28)

The end of this most dramatic story is related as follows:

"That very night Belshazzar the Chaldean king was slain, And Darius the Mede received the kingdom being about sixty-two years old". (Daniel 5: 30–31)

In order to keep the biblical text in focus, insofar as it reflects general historical events, we quote the book of Daniel, though it is now generally believed to have been written during the Greek period; it is the latest book of the Old Testament and belongs to the class of biblical literature known as apocalyptic (see last chapter). As Daniel is widely read as a biblical book, few people realize that Belshazzar was not actually the king when Babylon fell; that the spectacular writing on the wall, and the great hush that fell on the scene of merriment in the doomed palace have symbolical meaning but, in fact, no actual reality, and do not tell of an event which really occurred, even though the background is faithful to the Babylonian locale. The words probably expressed some popular judgement on political happenings in symbols which would be recognized immediately by the audience.

The "writing on the wall" — and now, so long afterwards, we can only guess at its significance — was in the Aramaic language, and may have looked something like this inscription.

Who Was Belshazzar?

Belshazzar was "son of the king" according to Babylonian texts, though not the son of Nebuchadrezzar, but of Nabuna'id (Nabonidus). Since he had handled the affairs of the government as co-regent for ten years (during the absence of his father in Teima, south east of Edom in northern Arabia), it is natural that he would be remembered as the "king of Babylon". Moreover, the mention of Darius "the Mede" as conqueror of Babylon seems to be a mis-statement. Contemporary records which give detailed accounts of the events, demonstrate that the Neo-Babylonian empire was overthrown by Cyrus, and that the first king by the name of Darius came not before but after him.

Darius, as he appears in the book of Daniel, is really a figure of fiction rather than history. It is not difficult to see how, in this tale, Cyrus, who took Babylon in 539, came to be confused with Darius "the Mede", who recaptured it in 520 B.C.E., following serious insurrections in the Persian empire.

Sometimes statements that seem to be proved errors in the Bible are later upheld by supporting evidence. This is the case with the statement in the Daniel story that Belshazzar was the last king of Babylon, which was held, for a very long time, as strong evidence against he accuracy of the biblical account. The solution of this seeming discrepancy became obvious when evidence was found indicating not only Belshazzar's association with Nabonidus on the throne, but also demonstrating that during the last part of his reign Nabonidus had spent ten years in the Arabian desert — as we know now from the stele deciphered by Gadd — wishing, it would seem, to create an international empire of the Middle East. He left the administration of his government to his son who was thus in effect the ruler of Babylon. But little did he know from which direction the blow would strike, nor could he suspect the strange turn that events would take in the unpredictable game of politics.

CYRUS' EDICT OF LIBERATION

This information enables us to place the Judean return from the Babylonian exile in its proper context. And it is against this background that we should read the account of the edict of liberation that Cyrus proclaimed to the Jewish exiles in the first year after Babylon's fall — 539 B.C.E. The edict is preserved in two versions. One of them, in Hebrew, appears in the four opening verses of the book of Ezra. The first seven chapters of the book relate the events of the restoration between 539 and 516 B.C.E. The other chapters of the book are the actual memoirs of Ezra's experience, dating more than sixty years after the building of the Second Temple:

> "In the first year of Cyrus king of Persia, that the word of the Lord by the mouth of Jeremiah might be accomplished the Lord stirred up the spirit of Cyrus king of Persia so that he made a proclamation throughout all his kingdom and also put it in writing:
> 'Thus says Cyrus king of Persia: The Lord, the God of heaven, has given me all the kingdoms of the earth, and he has charged me to build him a house at Jerusalem, which is in Judah". (Ezra 1:1–2)

The proclamation reproduced here was apparently announced verbally. Now turning to his Jewish listeners, the royal herald declared:

" 'Whoever is among you of all his people, may his God be with him, and let him go up to Jerusalem, which is in Judah, and rebuild the house of the Lord, the God of Israel — he is the God who is in Jerusalem; and let each survivor, in whatever place he sojourns, be assisted by the men of his place with silver and gold, with goods and with beasts, besides freewill offerings for the house of God which is in Jerusalem' ". (Ezra 1: 3–4)

The other version of the same edict is written in the same book in Aramaic. It was apparently couched in the terms of a memorandum of the chancellory, recording an oral decision of the king or of a high official, and was intended to initiate administrative action. Aramaic, which was still the lingua franca of the Middle East, was used by the Persian administration as its official language. This version reads:

"In the first year of Cyrus the king, Cyrus the king issued a decree: Concerning the house of God at Jerusalem, let the house be rebuilt, the place where sacrifices are offered and burnt offerings are brought; its height shall be sixty cubits and its breadth sixty cubits, with three courses of great stones and one course of timber; let the cost be paid from the royal treasury. And also let the gold and silver vessels of the house of God, which Nebuchadnezzar took out of the temple that is in Jerusalem and brought to Babylon, be restored and brought back to the temple which is in Jerusalem, each to its place; you shall put them in the house of God' ". (Ezra 6: 3–5)

The two versions together show well the shrewd diplomacy of the conqueror who ended the Jewish exile, and ardently represented himself to other peoples as their deliverer, and the servant and champion of their respective gods.

THE FIRST ATTEMPT AT RESTORATION

The annalistic portion of Ezra now proceeds:

"Then rose up the heads of the fathers' houses of Judah and Benjamin, and the priests and the Levites, everyone whose spirit God had stirred to go up to rebuild the house of the Lord which is in Jerusalem; and all who were about them aided them with vessels of silver, with gold, with goods with beasts and with costly wares besides all that was freely offered. Cyrus the king also brought out the vessels of the house of the Lord which Nebuchadnezzar had carried away from Jerusalem and placed in the house of his gods. Cyrus king of Persia brought these out in charge of Mithredath the treasurer who counted them out to Shesh-bazzar the prince of Judah". (Ezra 1: 5–8)

It is surmised that the first attempts of the exiles to return were modest in scope, and also were fraught with tremendous difficulties. To lead the entire Jewish return from exile, Cyrus chose a man named Sheshbazzar, Prince of Judah, as governor of Judah. Admittedly, Sheshbazzar made no great mark on his age — he was overshadowed by other leaders — but his appointment was, none the less, significant, for he was the son of Jehoiachin, the exiled king of Judah, whom many Jews and Persians regarded as the legitimate though deported king of Judah; so that in effect Cyrus was handing over the leadership of the Jews to a prince of the Davidic line. The presaged restoration was at hand.

Little is known about the number of pioneers who set their faces towards the homeland. There was certainly no mass exodus from Babylonia. It is generally believed, according to Ezra, that:

"The whole assembly together was forty-two thousand three hundred and sixty, besides their menservants and maidservants of whom there were seven thousand three hundred and thirty-seven; and they had two hundred male and female singers. Their horses were seven hundred and thirty-six, their mules were two hundred and forty-five, their camels were four hundred and thirty-five, and their asses were six thousand seven hundred and twenty". (Ezra 2: 64–67)

However, it has also been suggested that the list quoted above (repeated with variations in Nehemiah 7), putting their number at about 50,000, is excessive for Sheshbazzar's party. It is best taken as including those who came during a long period, and is an expanded census list from the time of Nehemiah, several generations later; or, it might be an account of the communities supporting the Jewish Temple, and enumerating the men in outlying places. The number of returnees, in any case, was certainly smaller than those given above in Ezra 2, and the emigration and restoration took place over a period of several generations until the times of Ezra and Nehemiah.

UNIVERSAL RELIGIONS IN THE EAST

In contrast to other oriental conquerors, especially the Assyrians with their "scorched earth" tactics of destruction and the wholesale deportation of entire peoples, Cyrus was depicted as benevolent and humane. He has been called by early Greek historians, one of the most enlightened and tolerant rulers in human history. This may have been because he understood the futility of trying to crush and lash people of diverse backgrounds and national traditions into subservience. He also apparently knew the limitations of power, and may have realized that an emperor who receives the loyalty of his people also enjoys increased honour and power.

Some of Cyrus' qualities, so unusual for his age, may have been due to his religious background. The Persians worshipped Ahuramazda, the good god. In the sixth century B.C.E. all great national gods throughout the Near East tended to be identified with the divine World Ruler. Ahuramazdaism was geared to tolerance, for it made a place for "foreign" gods, as helpers of Ahuramazda. Evidently Persian policy was not alone in allowing observance of other religious customs, and even, to a limited degree, in permitting the nations to be left in peace. Cyrus was, in fact, the first "liberator" — the converse of a conqueror — one who tried to restore national and religious status to conquered peoples.

In the days of the Achaemenid kings, the Persian religion had lost some of the purity of Zoroaster's teaching of a single divine being. The Ahuramazdaism of later days was essentially a dualist religion. Its basic tenet was that the good god Ahuramazda was now battling — and in the end of days would conquer — the evil deity Ahriman. According to an ancient legend, when Ahuramazda, who is described as an invisible god, had created the world, Ahriman swept into it like a fly, and thus infected it. Since then evil, like vermin, had bred on earth and in men's hearts. The present conflict between good and evil, which would be resolved at the end of time, would result in a victory for good, and of the "good of life, of purity and of truth", which would endure for all eternity. This Zoroastrian religion, to which Cyrus adhered, was a religion of a new type, the kind to which Judaism also belongs.

There was a widespread religious awakening during the middle centuries of the first millenium B.C.E. Great religious figures ranged between the Far East and Iran. To them must be added the religious awakening which lay behind the writings of Second Isaiah. The age of the exile and the reconstruction of Israel was one of unrest and change. Nevertheless,

A Persian king, as depicted on an ancient Greek vase. Note, at the top, the Athenian owl, emblem of Athens.

Ahuramazda, the Persian god, was a celestial being, and is portrayed with the winged sun disc in the heavens. He was the acknowledged creator of heaven and earth.

the awakening of Judaism in Babylonia was not influenced by these other trends. In communicating with the Persians, the Jews emphasized the universality of God to distinguish Him from the god of the peoples, as in the decree of Cyrus, quoted above, qualifying him a "God of heaven" (Ez. 1: 2).

As Near Eastern antiquity passed, two historical trends converged: the rise of religions of the type described above, and the rise of the great Persian Achaemenid empire, which ruled the east from India down to the southern Egyptian frontier of Ethiopia, an empire that would endure for two hundred years, until the rise of Alexander the Great. Its policies provide the background of the Jewish community in Babylon and in Israel, which slowly came back to being during the sixth and following centuries.

Neither Cyrus nor those who followed him relaxed their power. The Persian army had proved itself to be a puissant fighting force; and the Persian government soon developed a system of rapid communication, using fast chariots, which linked the various countries. This made it possible to supervise and control the far-flung empire which was also divided into provinces, or "satrapies" — making for still more efficient direction — by Darius, who succeeded Cyrus.

Cedars of Lebanon

"Then arose Jeshua, the son of Jozadak, with his fellow priests, and Zerubbabel, the son of Shealtiel with his kinsmen, and they built the altar of the God of Israel, to offer burnt offerings upon it, as it is written in the law of Moses the man of God. They set the altar in its place, for fear was upon them because of the peoples of the lands, and they offered burnt offerings upon it to the Lord, burnt offerings morning and evening". (Ezra 3: 2–3)

....

"From the first day of the seventh month they began to offer burnt offerings to the Lord. But the foundation of the temple of the Lord was not yet laid. So they gave money to the masons and the carpenters, and food, drink, and oil to the Sidonians and the Tyrians to bring cedar trees from Lebanon to the sea, to Joppa, according to the grant which they had from Cyrus king of Persia". (Ezra 3: 6–7)

Before actual work on the Temple was begun, one of the first acts of the community was the rebuilding of the altar for burnt offerings; as we have read above, this part of the ancient worship at least was resumed as early as the seventh month in the first year of the return, according to Ezra's account. The sixth verse indicates that the altar was constructed in less than a day, of unhewn field stones, in accordance with the earliest prescriptions for altars as recorded in the law of Moses (Ex. 20: 25 and Deut. 27: 6). The cedar trees from Lebanon were ordered from the Phoenicians to be floated by sea to Palestine. They were landed at Tel-Qasile, now within the boundaries of Tel Aviv, and transported overland to Jerusalem, as in the days of Solomon (See illustrations in Ch. XIII).

"When the Lord restored the fortunes of Zion
  we were like those who dream.
Then our mouth was filled with laughter,
  and our tongue with shouts of joy;
then they said among the nations,
  'The Lord has done great things for them.'
The Lord had done great things for us;
  we are glad.

Restore our fortunes, O Lord,
  like the water-courses in the Negeb!
May those who sow in tears
  reap with shouts of joy!
He that goes forth weeping,
  bearing the seed for sowing,
shall come home with shouts of joy,
  bringing his sheaves with him". (Psalm 126: 1–6)

The date of this psalm would fit in the troubled period soon after 537 or in the later time of Ezra and Nehemiah.

ZERUBBABEL

The curtain that shrouds the first years of the restoration of the exiled Jewish community— following an interruption in the rebuilding of the Temple — is briefly lifted in the second year of Darius the Great (about 520 B.C.E.). This is thanks to the annals of Ezra, namely chapters 4: 24 to 5: 2, and the books of Haggai and Zechariah (1 to 8), which both provide the chronology and give further insight into the history of the Jews at this period. It seems likely that Zerubbabel was appointed governor by Darius. Probably, after seizing the throne Darius filled all the governorships of his provinces with men sworn to him. Zerubbabel was a scion of the house of David, and in the eyes of the Judeans he was the heir apparent to the vacant throne. Many other Jews returned to Palestine with Zerubbabel, hoping to attain important posts if the monarchy should be restored. When some of the prominent heads of families came to the site of the Temple and saw the remains of the havoc wrought, more than half a century before, by Nebuchadrezzar's army, they contributed generously to the funds needed to carry out the work:

"Some of the heads of families, when they came to the house of the Lord which is in Jerusalem, made freewill offerings for the house of God, to erect it on its site; according to their ability they gave to the treasury of the work sixty-one thousand darics of gold, five thousand minas of silver, and one hundred priests' garments". (Ezra 2: 68–69)

As a sequel to this story Ezra relates how Haggai and Zechariah encouraged the people:

"Now the prophets, Haggai and Zechariah the son of Iddo, prophesied to the Jews who were in Judah and Jerusalem, in the name of the God of Israel who was over them. Then Zerubbabel the son of Shealtiel and Jeshua the son of Jozadak arose and began to rebuild the house of God which is in Jerusalem; and with them were the prophets of God, helping them". (Ezra 5: 1–2)

DARIUS THE GREAT

Although the biblical narrative is obscure and ambiguous about events before 520 B.C.E., we know that Cyrus, who reigned until 529, was succeeded by Cambyses. During the reign of the latter the Persian empire was rocked by many revolts. He, in turn, was succeeded by Darius I. Rarely has any king faced such a herculean task as did Darius in reaffirming the power of the Achaemenid dynasty of Persia. But he celebrated his triumph, and gave a detailed account of the events in the large, autobiographical inscriptions carved high up on the face of a mountain on the Rock of Behistan, on the road from Baghdad to Hamadan. The inscription is in three languages: Old Persian, Elamite, and Babylonian. By deciphering the Persian, which is closely related to Sanscrit, and the sacred books of the Zoroastrian Parsees in India, scholars of the fifties and sixties of the last century were able to decipher the other two. The transcribing of the Babylonian version, in particular, was of great help in the subsequent deciphering of the Babylonian literature of early Mesopotamia, the first known literature of the world (See Chapters I-II).

THE VISIONS OF HAGGAI AND ZECHARIAH

While the Judeans took no part in the revolts, many of them must have regarded them as a portent of the coming disintegration of the new World Empire that was to be replaced by the glorious restoration of the messianic Judean kingdom. This kingdom would be the centre of world affairs, the one to which all the nations of the earth would submit; and her people would be the one people that all the others would flock to join. These hopes and expectations, and the manner in which the new Judeans and their leaders faced both the

Darius I — "The Great" — on his throne, receiving foreign dignitary. Behind him stands the Crown Prince Xerxes (Biblical Ahasuerus). Relief from a portico in the treasury of the Persian government at Persepolis, Iran. The style of the relief shows a touch of Greek influence; and this may be due to an authentic Greek contribution to the Achaemenid plastic arts.

Remains of the Audience Hall, the Apadana, at Persepolis, begun by Darius. Thirteen of the seventy-two columns that once supported the roof of the spacious hall still stand.

intrigues of their neighbours and the shifting international situation of the years around 520 B.C.E., find interesting echoes in the books of the late prophets, Haggai and Zechariah. Both these prophets were probably awaiting the messianic coming of the Kingdom of God, praying that the heathen Achaemenid empire would disintegrate, and that Zerubbabel would be reinstated on the Davidic throne. Haggai's first oracle exhorted the people to restore their temple and their capital city, despite the opinion of the pessimists, that "the time has not yet come":

> " 'Thus says the Lord of hosts: Consider how you have fared. Go up to the hills and bring wood and build the house, that I may take pleasure in it and that I may appear in my glory, says the Lord. You have looked for much, and, lo, it came to little; and when you brought it home I blew it away. Why? says the Lord of hosts. Because of my house that lies in ruins, while you busy yourselves each with his own house. Therefore the heavens above you have withheld the dew, and the earth has withheld its produce. And I have called for a drought upon the land and the hills, upon the grain, the new wine, the oil, upon what the ground brings forth, upon men and cattle, and upon all their labors' ". (Haggai 1: 7–11)

Such was the pathetic picture of the situation, and such the morale of the returned exiles in Jerusalem; and the prophet plainly encountered considerable difficulty in arousing the people to take up the long overdue rebuilding of their temple. In his second oracle, speaking in the name of God, the prophet induced Zerubbabel to take the lead, and work began at the end of 520 B.C.E., building operations going ahead in spite of the havoc wrought by drought and the resulting famine:

> " 'Speak now to Zerubbabel the son of Shealtiel, governor of Judah, and to Joshua the son of Jehozadak, the high priest, and all the remnant of the people, and say, Who is left among you that saw this house in its former glory?

Persian Empire, about 500 B.C.E.

How do you see it now? Is it not in your sight as nothing? Yet now take courage, O Zerubbabel, says the Lord; take courage, O Joshua, son of Jehozadak, the high priest; take courage, all you people of the land, says the Lord; work, for I am with you, says the Lord of hosts' ". (Haggai 2: 2–4)

The work was eventually completed in the year 515 B.C.E., in the early spring. It was a very modest temple, far smaller than Solomon's. Haggai explicitly states that it was in depressing contrast to its former glory. This throws some light on the actual scale of the rebuilding of Jerusalem as a whole. It proved to be the turning point in its history and the inauguration of the era of the "Second Temple".

Zechariah's prophecies, contemporaneous with Haggai's, also reflected the troubled situation of the times. They dealt with the triumph of Darius over his foes; but also with the hopes which were nurtured for the restoration of the Davidic throne. He spoke on behalf of a God of infinite power and compassion, whose purpose was to bring healing and restoration to the returned remnant in the situation which confronted them. His message was conveyed almost entirely by means of vision and symbol:

"And the Lord said to Satan, 'The Lord rebuke you, O Satan,! The Lord who has chosen Jerusalem rebuke you! Is not this a brand plucked from the fire?' ". (Zechariah 3:2)

The new community was indeed a brand badly burned, but plucked from a fire that would otherwise have completely destroyed it.

In a vision of the New Jerusalem, Zechariah gathered the elders, and the High Priest and the Prince of Judah, and said to them:

" 'Thus says the Lord of hosts, "Behold, the man whose name is the Branch: for he shall grow up in his place, and he shall build the temple of the Lord. It is he who shall build the temple of the Lord, and shall bear royal honor, and shall sit and rule upon his throne. And there shall be a priest by his throne, and peaceful understanding shall be between them both' " ". (Zechariah 6: 12–13)

"The Branch" is a symbolic term for the descendant of David's dynasty.

It is held by many that the Haggai and Zechariah prophecies belong to a period following the uprising in the Persian empire.

THE END OF A DREAM

In any event the visionary dreams did not come true. Whether Zerubbabel was removed from office or not, considering the ambiguous stand of the Jews in those troubled years of the empire, and the hopes they nurtured of the restoration of the Davidic throne, we do not know from the biblical record. One thing stands out clearly: Zerubbabel disappears from history and the reason is unknown; the hopes of the Judeans in the restoration of an independent state were dashed and they had to resign themselves instead to remaining a province of the Persian empire. From that time onwards the new Judean province was, in the main, ruled by the High Priest as virtual leader of the community. Political matters were also regulated by a governor appointed by the Persian court. This was the end of

Darius, carved at the entrance of his palace at Persepolis.

Palace of Darius in Persepolis. General view.

One of the gigantic capitals that surmounted the forest of columns supporting the cedar roof rafters of the Apadana or Hall of the Throne of the palace of Artaxerxes II in Susa. The palaces of Susa and Persepolis followed a similar pattern.

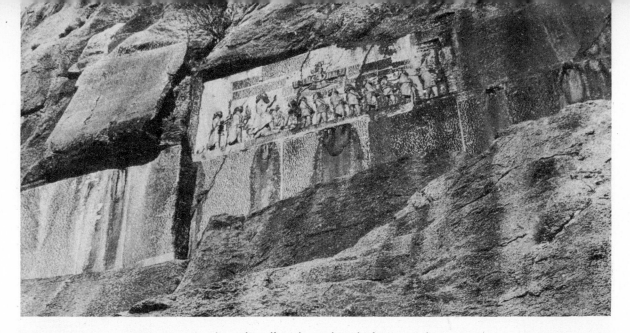

This carved inscription high above the plain, that all might read, is the longest and most important Achaemenid inscription known, and commemorates the victory of Darius, called the Great, over rebels who seized the Persian throne. Darius I, followed by two soldiers, left, places his foot on the prostrate rebel chief, Guamata, behind whom are standing nine other bound captives, their necks tied together with a rope. The victor points with one hand to the winged disc, symbol of the Zoroastrian god, Ahuramazda, which is much like the symbol of the old chief god of Assyria. The king, with a motion of his hand, dismisses any suggestion of mercy for these prisoners.

Davidic aspirations and the beginning of the rule of High Priests which lasted until the days of the Hasmonean princes.

Meanwhile important events had taken place on the international scene; and all of Palestine, Syria, and finally Egypt were brought back again into the Persian sphere. The Judeans gradually began to cooperate with the Persians. In the end, whatever illusions of glory they may have cherished, were dispelled when Darius was victorious in 519 B.C.E. and every spark of rebellion was extinguished. The Gentile World Empire was more firmly established than ever and commonsense showed that Judah, far from being the centre of the world, would have to remain a little province in a great gentile world where the empire provided good external conditions, and the basis for trade and public security. But such blessings were small consolation for a frustrated people whose dreams of their own Messianic world had apparently vanished into thin air. Darius upheld his predecessor's policy of allowing the Jews to maintain their own commonwealth and their temple. Judah remained a small province within the fifth Persian satrapy, one of many small states within a large mosaic. It is unlikely that the Judeans would have maintained their identity for many generations but for the eventual reforms introduced by Ezra and Nehemiah.

The Satrap Steps in

As related by Ezra, complaints were eventually lodged against the Temple project by the satrap Tattenai the governor of the "province Beyond the River" and other officials in the days of Darius, and they summoned the Jews before them:

" 'Who gave you a decree to build this house, and to finish this structure?' "

They also asked them this:

" 'What are the names of the men who are building this building?' But the eye of God was upon the elders of the Jews, and they did not stop them till a report should reach Darius and then answer be returned by letter concerning it". (Ezra 5: 3–5)

It is assumed that the satrap of the "province Beyond the River" (apparently the Persian governor of the Syro-Palestine satrapy beyond the Euphrates) wanted to obtain the names of the men engaged in the building project, or perhaps the groups under the command of the local governor who were willing to support the rebuilding of the Temple. Such a list, called the "golah" (returned captives) list, is seemingly indicated in Ezra 2 and Nehemiah 7, and is in the nature of an account of the communities supporting the Jewish Temple. It itemized the number of men at various outlying places in Judah and even further north, where communities were being established again. The letter of Tattenai to Darius related the story of the Jewish attempts at rebuilding from the beginning:

" 'Then this Sheshbazzar came and laid the foundations of the house of God which is in Jerusalem; and from that time till now it has been in building, and it is not yet finished. Therefore, if it seem good to the king, let search be made in the royal archives there in Babylon, to see whether a decree was issued by Cyrus for the rebuilding of this house of God in Jerusalem. And let the king send us his pleasure in this matter' ". (Ezra 5: 16–17)

The Archives of Ecbatana Vindicate the Jewish Claim

Tattenai suggested a verification of this with the aid of the archives of Babylon. A memorandum, as described above, was thereupon found, not in Babylon, but in Ecbatana, the summer capital of Cyrus in Media. The document found in Ecbatana (see the Aramaic version quoted above of Cyrus' Edict, (Ezra 6: 3–5) vindicated the Jewish claims. The whole matter was accordingly cleared up, and Darius ordered that the Jews be permitted to continue their activity unmolested; and he further ordered a gift of animals, incense, salt, wine and wheat to be given to the Hebrew priests for sacrifice. Even more, he decreed that they were to receive a subsidy from the taxes of the province "Beyond the River" and that sacrifices were to be brought there daily at government expense on behalf of the life of the king and his children:

"Let the work on this house of God alone; let the governor of the Jews and the elders of the Jews rebuild this house of God on its site. Moreover I make a decree regarding what you shall do for these elders of the Jews for the rebuilding of this house of God; the cost is to be paid to these men in full and without delay from the royal revenue, the tribute of the province from Beyond the River. And whatever is needed — young bulls, rams, or sheep for burnt offerings to the God of heaven, wheat, salt, wine, or oil, as the priests at Jerusalem require — let that be given to them day by day without fail". (Ezra 6: 7–9)
....

"And this house was finished on the third day of the month of Adar, in the sixth year of the reign of Darius the king" (Ezra 6: 15)

See Map of Judah in the time of Ezra and Nehemiah in the following chapter. (Boundaries of the Fifth Persian Satrapy)

Columns and monuments of the palace of Persepolis.

Persian drinking horn of bronze and silver (sixth century B.C.E.) from the Oxus Treasure. The vessels of silver and plate used in Susa the Capital were regal in the true sense of the word.

By the 4th century B.C.E. the community in Judah, in the rest of Palestine and in Babylon was not the main body of Jewry. The Diaspora (i.e. dispersal of the Jews beyond the limits of Palestine) was ever widening. From Babylonia Jews spread to Susa in Media and westward to the provinces of the Persian empire.

"In the days of Ahasuerus, the Ahasuerus who reigned from India to Ethiopia over one hundred and twenty-seven provinces, in those days when King Ahasuerus sat on his royal throne in Susa the capital, in the third year of his reign he gave a banquet for all his princes and servants, the army chiefs of Persia and Media and the nobles and governors of the provinces being before him, while he showed the riches of his royal glory and the splendor and pomp of his majesty for many days, a hundred and eighty days". (Esther 1: 1–4)

Jewish tradition, since late in the Persian period, or Hellenistic times, has celebrated the light-hearted festival of Purim, at which is recapitulated the immensely popular and glamorous tale of Esther, allegedly queen of Ahasuerus, or Xerxes. The book of Esther places Susa — or Shushan — the winter capital of Persia, in the mind's eye, as one of earth's

Air view of the mound of ancient Susa.

memorable cities of all time. The scene is laid in the third year of the reign of Xerxes (485–465 B.C.). The story purports to reflect a phase from the history of the Jewish Dispersion in Persia, relating intrigues in the court and metropolis of Susa, which had far-reaching repercussions throughout the empire of Xerxes. Although contemporary research has not gone towards proving the historicity of the story, the Book of Esther is a valuable mirror of the Achaemenid court and times. It supplies ample illustrative evidence which points to its genuineness; such as the author's evidently first-hand knowledge of the material background of the royal palaces and customs of the times. In fact there is no event in this story whose structural surroundings can be so accurately checked against actual excavations. It is clear that the writer was especially familiar with the construction of Susa, the scene of Esther's story, the rows of columns with animal heads at their tops, the rich decoration of the walls, with coloured enamel tiles portraying weird animals.

Though little is known of Susa, the winter capital of the kings of Persia, it is assumed that the court bore many similarities, both structurally and decoratively, to the palace of Persepolis described above.

As told in the following chapter of her story, Esther was not made queen until Ahasuerus had been in the throne for seven years. The story describes the pomp, wealth and luxury of their banquets:

> "Drinks were served in golden goblets, goblets of different kinds, and the royal wine was lavished according to the bounty of the king". (Esther 1: 7)

The storyteller was familiar with the administration of the Persian Kingdom, and with the customs of the Court. He knew of the seven nobles who enjoyed the intimacy and confidence of the king:

> "The men next to him being Carshena, Shethar, Admatha, Tarshish, Meres, Marsena, and Memucan, the seven princes of Persia and Media, who saw the king's face, and sat first in the kingdom.... ". (Esther 1: 14)

On the deposition of Queen Vashti, Esther, not known to be a Jewess and kin of Mordechai — was chosen from among all the beautiful women of the kingdom to become queen. To please their lord, the women of the harem not only perfumed their bodies, but also donned rich raiment:

> "And let the king appoint officers in all the provinces of his kingdom to gather all the beautiful young virgins to the harem in Susa the capital, under custody of Hegai the king's eunuch who is in charge of the women; let their ointments be given them". (Esther 2: 3)

> "And the maiden pleased him and won his favor; and he quickly provided her with her ointments and her portion of food, and with seven chosen maids from the king's palace, and advanced her and her maids to the best place in the harem". (Esther 2: 9)

> "Now when the turn came for each maiden to go in to King Ahasuerus, after being twelve months under the regulations for the women, since this was the regular period of their beautifying, six months with oil of myrrh and six months with spices and ointments for women — ". (Esther 2: 12)

The enigmatic quality of the story and its composite origin is further enhanced by the

Harem of King Xerxes at Persepolis, with eastern and southern facades of main wing, as restored. The foundations and inscriptions from the building of the harem, discovered in 1931, reveal that Darius chose Xerxes as his successor, and stepped down from the throne in his favour. The ancient treasury appears in the foreground.

influence of ancient mores that have persisted in the Near East almost to this day. In times of stress, or in order to avoid personal danger, Orientals belonging to particular sects pose without qualm as members of another religion. Mores permit such dissimulation, subject to unmasking, and so it was in the times of Esther. She hid her Jewish affiliations in that same spirit:

> "Esther had not made known her people or kindred, for Mordecai had charged her not to make it known". (Esther 2: 10)

The new favourite used her charms upon the king in order to frustrate the plot of Haman, who had determined to exterminate all the Jews of the empire upon a certain, single day, the thirteenth day of Adar:

> "In the first month, which is the month of Nisan, in the twelfth year of King Ahasuerus, they cast Pur, that is the lot, before Haman day after day; and they cast it month after month till the twelfth month, which is the month of Adar". (Esther 3: 7)

Especially illuminated by the discoveries at Susa is Haman's method for fixing upon the date of the destruction of the Jews by casting dice. Rectangular prisms were uncovered in Susa on which were engraved the numbers one, two, five, and six. So that the explanation, "they cast Pur, that is the lot", means that they cast lots amongst them.

The story several times mentions the royal ring with which the king's orders were sealed. It was handed to Haman; later to Mordechai, then to other officials:

> '... and the king took off his signet ring, which he had taken from Haman, and gave it to Mordecai. And Esther set Mordecai over the house of Haman". (Esther 8: 2)

The seal was hollow, and was pressed into the soft clay of the written tablet. This mechanical procedure was a substitute for a signature, and this function was delegated to his first minister by the king.

Finally the king ordered the execution of Haman and elevated Mordechai to the rank of vizier. The latter then sent out a new royal decree which counteracted Haman's previous (though irrevocable) decree. The storyteller knows that the Law of the Medes and the Persians is immutable:

"And you may write as you please with regard to the Jews, in the name of the king, and seal it with the king's ring; for an edict written in the name of the king and sealed with the king's ring cannot be revoked". (Esther 8:8)

As the story reaches a climax, the tables are turned on the enemies of the Jews; and the native Iranians had good cause to fear them, and even to pretend to be Jews themselves:

"And in every province and in every city, wherever the king's command and his edict came, there was gladness and joy among the Jews, a feast and a holiday. And many from the peoples of the country declared themselves Jews for the fear of the Jews had fallen upon them". (Esther 8:17)

Chapters 47:1 7—49:8 from the Scroll of Isaiah found near the Dead Sea

Striking representation of a Syrian or Palestinian of the 5th century B.C.E. From a relief of Persepolis.

CHAPTER XXI

EMERGING JUDAISM

Very little is known of the fortunes of the new Jewish community of Judah during 70 years following the completion of the Temple in 515 B.C.E., that is, the period between Zerubbabel and Ezra-Nehemiah. The rallying effect of the Temple had assured the community's survival but it could not be re-established in the old manner of the Jewish nation, with its kings and prophets. These were now only glorious memories. The new Judah formed a small province within the vast Persian empire, with a form of worship and rights of internal autonomy guaranteed by royal decree. The total population was only a fraction of what it had once been. But numerous towns were now inhabited. In addition many towns north and west of Judah were also settled with Jews. The land was not thickly populated and Jerusalem itself had very few inhabitants as the walls and houses of the city still lay in ruins.

Internal legislation was entrusted to a succession of high priests who, realistically, tried o harmonize the different elements old, and new, that made up the population of Judah and the adjoining provinces. These included the region east of the Jordan, where Jews had lived since olden times and where they had again migrated after the destruction of the state. They consisted of the "people of the land", the descendants of those "poor of the land" left after the destruction and the families of the exiles who had returned from Babylon. In addition there were influential neighbours to the north and east of Jerusalem who considered themselves Israelites and were accepted as such by the leading families of Jerusalem and by the high priests. We gather from the memoirs of Ezra and Nehemiah that the heads of these border provinces were men like Sanballat, governor of the province of Samaria, whose family was later allied by marriage to the high priests of Jerusalem. Another Israelite of ancient lineage was Tobiah, governor of Ammon, east of Jordan. With these two were associated Geshem, designated "the Arab", who governed the province of Northern Arabia which included Edom and the territory south of Judah.

Intermarriage and fraternization between these communities had been going on for a long time. It is apparent that as in pre-Exilic days popular religion and social mores had also been affected by the old customs of the country. It is difficult to judge from the biblical record whether the exiles transplanted from Babylon and their immediate descendants developed a somewhat defensive attitude towards fellow-Israelites living to the north, south and east of them, or whether they regarded them as less faithful to the law of Moses. These became, however, the great burning issues of life in Palestine after the appearance of Ezra and Nehemiah on the scene.

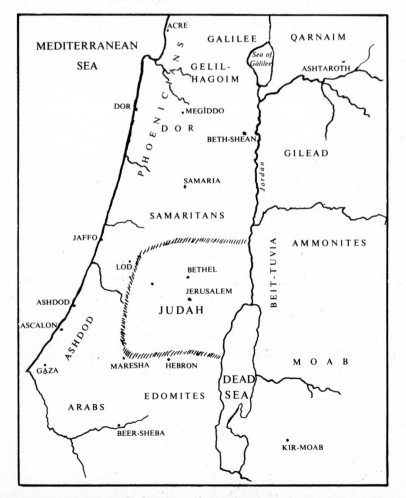

The Province of Judah between the 5th and 4th centuries B.C.E. It was surrounded by the other Palestinian provinces of the Fifth Persian Satrapy. But it appears that the Jews colonized also southern Judea and the northern Negeb around Beersheba and that this area was annexed by the province of Judah under Nehemiah.

The reasons for this may be sought in the state of the community's morals and its religious and moral laxity. There is evidence for this in the later Nehemiah memoirs and in the words of the contemporary prophet Malachi, who deplored the curse of drought and locusts lying upon the land. The last of the prophets, Malachi also disputed with his contemporaries for the blight on their hearts and on their faith. According to him the priests saw nothing wrong in offering sick and injured animals, for sacrifice. Then follows his great utterance which stamps him as a prophet indeed:

"Will man rob God? Yet you are robbing me. But you say, 'How are we robbing thee?' In your tithes and offerings. You are cursed with a curse, for you are robbing me; the whole nation of you. Bring the full tithes into the storehouse, that there may be food in my house; and thereby put me to the test, says the Lord of hosts, if I will not open the windows of heaven for you and pour down for you an overflowing blessing". (Mal. 3: 8–10)

On a social level, employers cheated their workmen over wages, and poor people who had mortgaged their land in time of drought, then found themselves foreclosed and reduced to servitude, together with their children:

" 'Then I will draw near to you for judgment; I will be a swift witness against the sorcerers, against the adulterers, against those who swear falsely, against those who oppress the hireling in his wages, the widow and the orphan, against those who thrust aside the sojourner, and do not fear me, says the Lord of hosts' ". (Mal. 3: 5)

Further Encroachments

Complications arose from friction with provincial officials or from the growing hostility of the "people of the land" by which is probably meant the natives of Palestine, to other people who had encroached upon Judean soil from the surrounding districts and partially filled the vacuum left by Jewish exiles. The country south of Jerusalem had been taken over by the Edomites, pushed from their homeland by Arab pressure. Likewise the Moabites, Ammonites, "Ashdodites" from Philistia laid claims or harassed the newcomers. The Samaritans living to the north of Jerusalem, turned out in time to be particularly troublesome. We are told by Ezra that they accused the Jews of sedition in the reign of Xerxes, possibly around 486/5:

"Then the people of the land discouraged the people of Judah, and made them afraid to build, and hired counselors against them to frustrate their prupose, all the days of Cyrus king of Persia, even until the reign of Darius king of Persia. And in the reign of Ahasuerus, in the beginning of his reign, they wrote an accusation against the inhabitants of Judah and Jerusalem". (Ezra 4: 4-6)

Though the Temple was rebuilt, the city was still desolate. Intrigues and complaints against Jerusalem were carried on for a long time by officials of the Persian king. They wrote letters to the court warning against the efforts of the Jews, described as dangerous rebels, to rebuild their town. Rebuilding a town and its walls was a natural security measure, but it could be interpreted by enemies as a move towards political independence. The king was convinced and wrote back to his representatives authorizing them to prevent the rebuilding of the walls by force so as to keep Judah permanently defenceless:

" 'Therefore make a decree that these men be made to cease, and that this city be not rebuilt, until a decree is made by me. And take care not to be slack in this matter; why should damage grow to the hurt of the king?' Then, when the copy of King Artaxerxes' letter was read before Rehum and Shimshai the scribe and their associates, they went in haste to the Jews at Jerusalem and by force and power made them cease". (Ezra 4: 21–23)

One such accusation made during the reign of Darius had proved futile. The second time the effects were disastrous. The walls were pulled down and the fortified gates burnt. This indicates, moreover, that the Judeans were not much in favour with the court at the time. It is tempting to link this turn of events with the ambitions of a Persian general, Megabyzus. He had fought the Egyptians and the Greeks of Cyprus with the help of the Phoenician fleet and he may have been supported by local Palestinian levies. This may have encouraged the Jews to fortify Jerusalem. Eventually, Megabyzus revolted against his king, Artaxerxes I, but later made his peace. It is likely that the accusations of the provincial governors against Judah occurred at this time.

THE FORMATIVE PERIOD OF JUDAISM

Nevertheless, there are indications in the biblical record that a resurgence of interest in the fate of Judah made itself felt in Babylon and Persia in the days of Artaxerxes I. Highly placed Jews desired to join the Judeans. Their arrival brought not only material help but also the broader and deeper outlook on Jewish life which had been cultivated in the Exile, with the appreciation of the Torah and the message of the prophets.

During the Exile a great change had come about in the religion of Israel. A higher, more spiritual stage of religion was reached under the influence of the prophets, whose message had been vindicated. While this process was going on, the question arose: how may the lapses of the past be avoided in the future? One answer was to insist upon obedience to the precise rules and regulations of the Torah. The Law of Moses, or Torah, had been expanded from its original nucleus (namely parts of Exodus, Leviticus, Deuteronomy) to form the five books of the Pentateuch.

The Passing of Prophecy

The new spiritual climate was marked by an absence of the prophetic spirit. Gone were the days when the prophets as his chosen, inspired messengers, proclaimed the word of Yahweh to an awed population. Ezekiel, with his message of redemption to the exiles seemed to mark the end of the great prophetic movement. Malachi marked its end in Palestine.

Actually, after him, Jewish tradition ceases to speak of prophecy. Oracular prophecy came to an end, and, at the same time, people ceased to make use of the "Urim and Thummim", oracular objects which had been the stock in trade of popular augury. There may remain a mystery in the fact that the belief in oracles ceased in Israel at about this time, whereas it was to survive in Delphi for several centuries.

In the opinion of Y. Kaufman, prophetic activity had shown signs of faltering for a century previous to Ezra's reforming activities. This check to prophecy was a natural result of the downfall of the nation with its implied withdrawal of God's favour, which had been the inspiration of the prophets. The house of David had not been restored and it seemed that God's wrath against his people persisted. The spirit of prophecy had always surged forward at times of national crisis and found expression in divine revelation and the ancient Messianic hope. Now, however, there was no new crisis which demanded a renewed soul-searching and the spiritual and literary activity of prophecy fell into abeyance.

It can be said that at that time two simultaneous processes were going on. Original prophecy faltered, but the observance of the ancient law advanced. Exaltation of the Torah did not, however, exclude reverence for the former prophets, as some have believed. The prophetic writings were preserved in the canon of the Old Testament with no less devotion than the Torah.

The last stirrings of Israelite prophecy were muted into a new type of vision about the end of the world. Thus the fate of prophecy became involved with the hope of redemption by a Messiah. With Second Isaiah in Babylon and Malachi in Judah, there was a brief revival. Thereafter it flickered out to reappear only in the idiom of Messianic hopes which centered around the house of David. A movement of this kind appears to have developed around Zerubbabel (cf. Ch. XX). This same urge towards a heavensent saviour found new expression in the last vision of Malachi:

" 'Behold, I will send you Elijah the prophet before the great and terrible day of the Lord comes. And he will turn the hearts of fathers to their children and the hearts of children to their fathers, lest I come and smite the land with a curse' ". (Mal. 4: 5-6)

This is the first reference of Elijah who had left the world about four hundred years before. He is recast now in the new role of an angel of peace sent from heaven to continue his role of God's messenger and appear at the end of the days. It seems likely that this new inspiration left its impact of visions of the end of days that appear in later generations.

Preserving the Traditions of the Past

Although there was no longer any dynamic urge of prophecy, a need to preserve the traditions of the past arose in exile and in Palestine. The people ordered their lives according to the Book of the Law and its commandments and this provided a new framework for communal life. Thousands among the exiles had returned to Judah, out of a deep religious and patriotic urge, to rebuild the Temple and to renew its ritual. Those who remained behind made communal worship their link with the past. Prayer came to replace the old Temple ritual. Exaltation of the Law, its reading and the singing of psalms became prominent as a substitute and reminder of the Temple service.

In view of the Law's ban on local cults and shrines, the synagogue inevitably developed into the rallying point for worship and learning. These assemblies expanded and multiplied and it is inconceivable that the dispersed Jews (termed the Diaspora) could have survived without these centres of communal worship and learning under their Levites and priests.

The Torah (Book of the Law) had acquired sacred status. All vestiges of paganism had disappeared. Indeed, the writings of the time reflect Jewish propaganda against heathen forms of worship. New criteria and a new ideal had been given them: boundless faith in the living God, the God of Israel and His age-old message, as laid down for eternity in the Torah. From this they now sought guidance and consolation. Their entire intellectual and theological thinking would be conditioned by the urge to preserve this treasure of the past, and above all, to bring its meaning to the people.

THE SOFERIM (SCRIBES)

It was at this time, during the third quarter of the 5th century, that two personalities appeared in Babylonia and initiated a thoroughgoing reorganization of the life of the Jewish community in Judah. They were Ezra, who reformed its inner and spiritual life, and Nehemiah, who gave it political status and administrative reform. Although scholars continue to disagree over the relationship between the careers of these two great men, it seems that they lived roughly about the same time.

To Ezra and Nehemiah reports of prevailing conditions came from Judah. The intelligence was distressing and men of their calibre were naturally moved to offer help or instruction to the Judeans in their plight. The opportunity came first to Ezra.

The role of the scribe ("sofer") in Jewish life in Exile was apparently at its height in the 5th century. With the end of the prophetic age Jewish law and the Torah needed interpreters to bring the meaning to the people. The "soferim" pored over the sacred scrolls, compared contrasting laws and adapted them to new uses by applying them to contemporary life. Ezra, who was a priest and a "scribe", became the great exemplar of this new class of scholars and interpreters of all the social and religious implications of the law of the Torah. The soferim corresponded in some respects to the priests of earlier days, but in other ways they were so different that they are justly placed in a separate category. They represented the transition from the pre-Exilic and prophetic order to the new post-Exilic order which transformed the Torah into a living, sacred guide to the way of life of the people at large.

"The Scribe for the Law of the God of Heaven"

It was apparently Artaxerxes' desire to stabilize the situation in Palestine and to ensure internal tranquility there, that caused him to adopt plans drawn up by Ezra and submitted through influential Jewish circles. Ezra was especially commissioned by royal decree that granted him extensive powers to apply religious law and to set up an administrative system, with powers of enforcement among Jews living throughout the satrapy of Abar-Nahara, "Beyond the River", namely Syria and Palestine. His official title upon his appointment by Artaxerxes was "The Scribe (royal secretary) for the Law of the God of Heaven", meaning the God of Israel.

The post of royal scribe had developed into a very important element in the administration of public affairs in the Persian empire. Sometimes governors of districts and ministers of state were royal Mesopotamian scribes. The cast pride of the scribes was unmatched in antiquity and they were a highly respected element in the Persian hierarchy.

EZRA'S MISSION

The debate as to how far Ezra and Nehemiah were contemporaries continues, and the sequence and chronology of these two leaders is still hotly contested. Our view that Ezra

A scribe holding pen-case and bound wooden tablets standing before the Aramean king Bar-rekub of Sam'al (northeastern Syria) in the 7th century B.C.E. Ezekiel refers to him as a man "clothed with linen, with a writer's inkhorn by his side". Ezra may outwardly have belonged to this scholarly class, but his work in compiling the Law put him in a class apart, as explained in the text.

came first is not prompted by traditional belief alone, it is also supported by a closer affinity it finds between the events and the literary sources. Moreover, Nehemiah seems to have completed the task which Ezra initiated but could not have finalized without Nehemiah's aid.

The first part of the book of Ezra records events of some seventy years previously. Then, in chapter 7, the narrative changes to first person. The chroniclers, who wrote down the book covered the seventy years' transition from historic narrative to Ezra's memoris by the scant few words, "now after these things" They then followed with his mission:

> " 'I make a decree that any one of the people of Israel or their priests or Levites in my kingdom, who freely offers to go to Jerusalem, may go with you'. (Ezra 7: 13)

> " 'And you, Ezra, according to the wisdom of your God which is in your hand, appoint magistrates and judges who may judge all the people in the province Beyond the River, all such as knows the law of your God; and those who do not know them, you shall teach. Whoever will not obey the law of your God and the law of the king, let judgment be strictly executed upon him, whether for death or for banishment or for confiscation of his goods or for imprisonment" (Ezra 7: 25–26)

> " 'And I, Artaxerxes the king, make a decree to all the treasurers in the province Beyond the River: Whatever Ezra the priest, the scribe of the law of the God of heaven, requires of you, be it done with all diligence, up to a hundred talents of silver, a hundred measures of wheat, a hundred baths of wine, a hundred baths of oil, and salt without prescribing how much' ". (Ezra 7: 21–22)

Ezra came to Judah with about 1760 compatriots who had decided to cast in their lot with this second attempt at restoration. With him he brought the scroll of the Torah which he was commissioned to impart to the people. These were pious enough but badly off. He undoubtedly hoped to intensify religious zeal and devotion, enrich the forms of worship and quicken spiritual life. The coming of this great man and his company must have been met by great enthusiasm. He probably waited for a suitable occasion to inaugurate his teaching and thus delayed carrying out the larger purpose of his mission. Nevertheless he immediately engaged in social and religious reforms. The wealthier class were concerned with worldly affairs and were on intimate terms with non-Jews. Ezra decided first on a reform that meant putting away foreign wives and children, but the uproar over these mixed marriages involved him in great difficulties. He decided to take drastic action, choosing first the way of moral persuasion. He wept and rebuked the sin of the congregation until people, conscience stricken, acknowledged their fault, asked for a new covenant and agreed to divorce their foreign wives:

> "And Shecaniah the son of Jehiel, of the sons of Elam, addressed Ezra: 'We have broken faith with our God and have married foreign women from the peoples of the lands, but even now there is hope for Israel in spite of this. Therefore let us make a covenant with our God to put away all these wives and their children, according to the counsel of my lord and of those who tremble at the commandment of our God; and let it be done according to the law. Arise, for it is your task, and we are with you; be strong and do it.' Then Ezra arose and made the leading priests and Levites and all Israel take oath that they would do as had been said. So they took the oath". (Ezra 10: 2–3)

Ezra continued meanwhile his fasting and prayer in the chamber of a priest. Thus the way was prepared for his task of introducing the Torah and its code of laws which he had brought from Babylon.

The Book of Ezra breaks off at the point where he mentions a list of those who had taken foreign wives. His name appears again, in the third person, in the Book of Nehemiah, where he is described in a new capacity, and at the climax of his career which came, apparently, a few weeks after the last events recorded in the Book of Ezra.

THE COVENANT

Nehemiah's narrative relates first how Ezra had won over the people, their princes, priests and leaders. They ordered all the people to present themselves in Jerusalem in three days' time. There they received Ezra's rebuke docilely. All mixed marriages were dissolved. Then the people gathered for a solemn confession of sin, after which they engaged in a covenant to live according to the Torah.

This story in the Book of Nehemiah describes how the Torah was read to the people with full pomp and dignified ceremonial, how Ezra expounded and enforced the injunctions of the Torah (the Law of Moses) and how the covenant was sealed:

> "Because of all this we make a firm covenant and write it, and our princes, our Levites, and our priests set their seal to it". (Nehemiah 9: 38)
> ....
> "The rest of the people, the priests, the Levites, the gatekeepers, the singers, the temple servants, and all who have separated themselves form the peoples of the lands to the law of God, their wives, their sons, their daughters, all who have knowledge and understanding, join with their brethren their nobles, and enter into a curse and an oath to walk in God's law which was given by Moses the servant of God, and to observe and do all the commandments of the Lord our Lord and his ordinances and his statutes". (Nehemiah 10: 28–29)

In accordance with the spirit of the Torah and with the points under discussion at the time, the people bound themselves specifically not to enter into mixed marriages, to refrain from work on the Sabbath, and to let the land lie fallow in the sabbatical year, with its remission of debt — a boon for the poor debtor class — as commanded by the ancient code (see Ch. IX)

These decisions, adopted c. 445 B.C.E., and based on a fuller knowledge of the Torah, now became the constitution for the community. This gave the Jews a status as a legal community permitting them to regulate internal affairs in accordance with their own law although politically they were subject to Persia. Henceforth, the distinguishing mark of a Jew would not be political identity but adherence to the Torah, even if he lived outside Palestine and did not participate in the Temple cult. After the Exile, Jewish nationality became identified with ethnic solidarity — common descent, destiny, religion and culture — rather than territorial status.

NEHEMIAH'S MISSION TO ISRAEL

"Now I was cupbearer to the king. In the month of Nisan, in the twentieth year of King Artaxerxes, when wine was before him, I took up the wine and gave it to the king. Now I had not been sad in his presence. And the king said to me, 'Why is your face sad, seeing you are not sick? This is nothing else but sadness of the heart.' Then I was very much afraid. I said to the king, 'Let the king live for ever! Why should not my face be sad, when the city, the place of my fathers' sepulchres, lies waste, and its gates have been destroyed by fire?' Then the king said to me, 'For what do you make request?' So I prayed to the God of heaven". (Nehemiah 2: 1–4)

The direct and energetic manner in which Nehemiah starts his memoirs offers a clue to his later career. He refers to himself without pretension although he occupied the important and trusted post of cupbearer to the king. He had a deep love for the home of his ancestors and he was deeply stirred by the information he had received from some Palestinian Jews about the sad state of Jerusalem's defences. He therefore felt impelled to go to Judah in order to help his brethren (445 B.C.E.). Deftly he made his request to the king: to be allowed to rebuild the city of his forefathers. The king granted him leave and he was appointed lay governor. When he arrived, he was struck by the dilapidated state of the walls and gates of the city. The dispirited people completed a sad picture. The walls had been pulled down as a result of the intrigues of Rehum and Shimshai. As a statesman and a man of action he set about reversing the action previously taken by the king at their instigation to stop the building activities in Jerusalem (cf. Ezra 4: 21–23 above). He therefore summoned the leaders and inspired them with enthusiasm for the task of reconstruction. The neighbouring governors and their people were perturbed by fear of Jewish pressure and expansion beyond the precincts of the Judean province. In an attempt to prevent the restoration, the neighbouring provincial officials Sanballat, Tobiah and Geshem tried intrigue which failed, and then ridicule. They even incited an attack upon the builders of Jerusalem:

"....who were building on the wall. Those who carried burdens were laden in such a way that each with one hand labored on the work and with the other held his weapon. And each of the builders had his sword girded at his side while he built. The man who sounded the trumpet was beside me. And I said to the nobles and to the officials and to the rest of the people, 'The work is great and widely spread, and we are separated on the wall, far from one another. In the place where you hear the sound of the trumpet, rally to us there. Our God will fight for us' ". (Nehemiah 4: 17–20)

All the machinations, including an attempt to capture Nehemiah, were foiled and the wall, whose reconstruction had been begun earlier, was completed in fifty two days. All Jerusalem and the other towns in Judah were roused to action. Priests and Levites, goldsmiths and perfumers, even high officials, joined the people in hard manual labour.

His next step was to increase the population of Jerusalem. It had been the holy town and it was inhabited by leading families and the priests and Levites officiating at the Temple.

After fortifying it and making it secure, Nehemiah gradually changed it into the effective centre of the resurgent province of Judah. He took measures to compel the leaders and a fixed percentage of the rest of the people to settle in Jerusalem, even casting lots among them to decide who should do so.

At about the same time as rebuilding Jerusalem's fortifications, Nehemiah enforced the release of the poor people who had become enslaved to the land gentry, in the customary oriental fashion. Disastrous years of drought, heavy taxation and other calamities had brought in their wake the foreclosing of mortgages and enslavement of the distraught borrowers and their families. He went further:

> "'Return to them this very day their fields, their vineyards, their olive orchards, and their houses, and the hundredth of money, grain, wine, and oil which you have been exacting of them'. Then they said, 'We will restore these and require nothing from them. We will do as you say''. And I called the priests and took an oath of them to do as they had promised". (Nehemiah 5: 11–12)

Social and economic reforms went ahead with the reorganization of communal religious affairs. He made sure that the priests and Levites received their share of the offerings, as prescribed by the Torah, and in particular, that the tithes were collected. These were brought to the treasuries and properly administered and distributed. Like intermarriage, trading on the Sabbath was banned. He divided the work of the priests and Levites in suitable rotation to prevent confusion and neglect and made sure that the wood fuel for holo-austs would be made ready at the right times. The ground was prepared for a new mode of life in Judah and it is believed that all this activity preceded the great assembly and covenant, whose purpose was to solemnize and confirm these thoroughgoing reforms.

Nehemiah's Second Term

With his first term of office completed, Nehemiah left for Persia to give an account of his stewardship. There he persuaded the king to re-appoint him. But on his return he found his old enemies in power in the Temple. The laws of the Sabbath had been violated, the Levites were neglecting their service and mixed marriages had begun again. Nehemiah banished from Jerusalem a grandson of the high priest Eliashib, who had married the daughter of Sanballat, the governor of Samaria.

Left: A coin of 4th century Judah. Above the figure is what scholars once read as Yhu ("Yahu" for Yahweh). The letters are now read Yahud or Judah. Before the Persian period, sums of money were weighed on scales. The Persians adopted the Greek invention of the coinage. During the second half of the 5th century coins with Hebrew letters appeared in Judah. Right: Seal impression on jar handle of the same period inscribed YHD, Judah.

He then set about re-establishing the reforms he had introduced for the collection and supervision of the tithes, and appointed honest treasurers and administrators. A new spirit-ual and intellectual resurgence now followed in the wake of the great changes. It may be safely assumed that the vigorous national and religious reawakening among the congrega-tion of Israel in Judah and the newcomers were assured for a long time. Proof of more stabilized conditions may be seen in the preservation of Israel's spiritual treasures of the past and in new literary creations. The most notable of these is the work of the Chronic-lers who wrote the historiographic work, the Book of Chronicles, and the books of Ezra and Nehemiah which form its natural sequel.

The Congregation of Israel

Under the impact of Ezra and Nehemiah the "Congregation of Israel" had moved a long way from life under the monarchy. Whereas in the old days the high priest stood beside the kingly leader of the people, he had now taken his place and had assumed not only spi-ritual but in many respects, temporal power. The high priests belonged to the house of Zadok. Their influence made itself felt both in the province of Judah and in the various countries where Jews were dispersed. They were allowed to mint their own coinage.

Religious and civil affairs generally were regulated by the "Great Synagogue", an assembly of ecclesiastical and lay leaders, presided over by the high priest in Jerusalem. The origin of the institution of the Great Synagogue is attributed by tradition to Ezra, though it evolved for many generations before it assumed the functions and responsibilities for which it became known in the later days of the Second Temple.

THE SAMARITAN PROBLEM

The policies introduced by Ezra and Nehemiah in Palestine soon brought to the fore the irreconcilable factors in the relationship between the Jews and the Samaritans.

Peoples from Mesopotamia who had been deported to Samaria by the Assyrians in the early part of the 8th century B.C.E., added to the remnants of the native Palestinian popu-tion, made up for the strong Samaritan community ruled by Sanballat in the days of Ezra and Nehemiah. Under native influence the new settlers had turned to the authentic, local religion of Israel, the "law of the god of the land". But the Judeans and the strictly orthodox element, represented chiefly by the Babylonian Jews, regarded them as interlopers, both racially and ritually. The Jews' feeling of exclusiveness may have been rooted in the relig-ious awakening that took place during the Exile, and the belief that they were the "prophetic remnant", which would usher in the Messianic age. Whether it was large or small, such a remnant had to be pure and it had to consist of the select few among the Chosen People who had remained true to Yahweh in both race and faith. It was this exclusiveness — intensified by the exile in Babylon — which prevented the returning Jews, particularly in the days of Ezra and Nehemiah, from admitting the Samaritans into the fold. However, the presence of this foreign element in Israel caused a great deal of embarrassment, and created a special problem. In pre-Exilic times, the ancient mores had permitted the acceptance and naturali-zation of foreign "gerim" into the community of Israel — either as individuals or clans —

even though they did not enjoy the same social status as the natives. But with the fall of the state this custom had lapsed. The returning Judeans, imbued with new theological concepts, were not ready to accept the "Judaized" Samaritans as co-religionists, who could share in the Messianic ideals. In the later days of the Maccabean resurgence a new policy of religious proselytizing and the wholesale conversion of peoples was to be accepted; but the time was not yet ripe for this.

The Samaritans, on the other hand, regarded themselves as the proud descendants of the northern Israelites, accepting the Pentateuch as the Law of Moses. They could hardly acquiesce in the notion, classically expressed by Ezra and Nehemiah, that the true Israel consisted of *the restored remnant of Judah*. These strict Jews, rejecting the Samaritans as heterodox, did not welcome them into the Temple community. The fact that they were such close neighbours, sharing essentially the same faith, ancient law and ritual, was not sufficient to bridge the emotional gap which separated the two communities. The hand which the Samaritans had once offered in friendship was soon clenched, and an age-old enmity hardened and flourished. Thus, Jewish tradition has conferred orthodoxy on Judaism while making heretics of the Samaritans.

Some time after the reorganization of the Jewish community under Ezra and Nehemiah, the Samaritans built their own temple on Mt. Gerizim. Josephus says that this was done by Sanballat, governor of Samaria, after his son-in-law had been banished from Jerusalem.

As always in Israel's history and as in the days of Rehoboam and Jeroboam (see Chapter XIV) religious and political separation went hand in hand. The political separation of Judah and Samaria, which followed the work of Ezra, was therefore inevitable.

THE JEWS OF THE DISPERSION IN THE 5TH AND 4TH CENTURIES

The authors of the Book of Chronicles, who apparently also compiled the books of Ezra and Nehemiah, recorded the names of high priests down to the end of the 5th century and

Samaritan scroll of the Law. Its writing preserves the archaic Hebrew characters. The present-day descendants of the Samaritans have preserved a simple form of worship reminiscent of pre-Exilic times. They claim to observe only the teaching of the Pentateuch and recognize no other book as sacred. The Samaritans are the only Jewish sect to have preserved the custom of sacrifice of lambs.

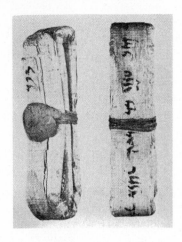

An unopened papyrus roll with seal and string from Elephantine. The endorsement around the roll reads: "Document about a house which Anani ben Azariah the Servitor wrote to Yehoyishma his daughter".

Papyrus No. 13 (Kraeling) written by Sherve bar Zekeriah to a man named Yislah in Elephantine.

also the descendants of David to about the same time (1 Chr. 3: 17–24). Shortly after the reforms of Ezra and Nehemiah, Artaxerxes I died (424). We do not know when Nehemiah's second term of office ended, but by 411, a Persian named Bagoas occupied his position. We *now reach the point where the history recorded in the Old Testament ends.* It is followed by a period of almost total obscurity in Jewish history. But the last quarter of the fifth century was illuminated by the existence of a Jewish colony at Elephantine (Yeb) as evidenced by its texts which represent an interesting archaeological mystery story.

The Jewish Colony of Elephantine

In 1893 A.D. an American scholar, C.E. Wilbour, who spent his summers cruising on the southern Nile, bought a quantity of papyri from some Arab women on the island of Elephantine on the upper Nile. There were nine intact rolls with the seals and strings still about them and many other broken papyri. Wilbour died without having divulged his discovery. The papyri had all been put in a trunk and stored.

The trunk was eventually bequeathed to the Brooklyn Museum after the death of Mr. Wilbour's daughter. The writing was identified as Aramaic by Prof. E. Kraeling. On being deciphered the rolls supplemented the important information gathered by A.H. Sayce and A.E. Cowley in their original finds early in the century. They shed a most interesting light on the popular religion of Jews outside Palestine as well as the historic background of the post-Exilic period in Jewish history, and the overthrow of Persian domination over Egypt towards the end of the 5th Century B.C.E. Most of the documents in these finds are of a private, business and legal nature, illustrating daily life there, but some are official communications with the Persian court and Persian governors in Palestine. They demonstrate the official interest which the Persian court took in regulating the religious affairs of its subject peoples (as evidenced in the books of Ezra and Nehemiah). One document, for example, the "Passover Papyrus", sent in the name of the Great King to the Persian governor of Egypt, Orsames, authorizes the Jewish colony to celebrate the feast of Passover at the appropriate season, in 419 B.C.E. This is confirmed by another letter from a Jewish official in Egypt, Hananiah, to the Jews of Yeb, enjoining them to conform to the precise regulations fixed by Jewish law. He seemed to have occupied in Egypt a post similar to Ezra's in Palestine as the King's commissioner for Jewish affairs.

THE TEMPLE OF YEB (ELEPHANTINE)

A fortress named Yeb was garrisoned in the 5th century by a colony of Jews who had erected a Temple (egora) there, dedicated to the god Yahu (Yahweh), with an altar for blood sacrifice. Second Isaiah already knew of the colony of exiles from the land of Sinim (nearby modern Assuan), and they may have been recruited from Jewish elements who came to Egypt after the fall of Jerusalem in 586 or, possibly, this Jewish garrison was founded under the Pharaoh Hophra (Jer. 44: 30). In any event, they were absorbed by an Aramaic speaking environment in the days of the Persian empire. The founding of a Yahu Temple may have been permitted by order of the government, and the Egyptian priests told to regard Yahu as a visiting god, paying homage to Khnub or Khnum, the ram-headed god of Elephantine. The Jews, on the other hand, possibly considered this temple a refuge for their god, who had departed from Jerusalem. When they took service with the Persian conquerors of Egypt in 525 their status may have changed in Egyptian eyes and in time they may have desired to get rid of them. In a letter sent by the Jews of Elephantine to Bagoas, the Persian governor of Yehud (Judah) in 407, they reveal that the temple of Yahu was destroyed by the Egyptians in 410 B.C. The Jews fasted and mourned for three years and sent letters to many influential people. The one sent to the Persian satrap in Egypt, Orsames, went unheeded for he was absent. They also wrote to Jochanan, the high priest in Jerusalem, but received no reply. But the appeal to Samaria was answered by Delaiah, Sanballat's son, and Bagoas, who advised that a petition be addressed directly to the satrap Orsames. Most scholars are now of the opinion that the Jews of Elephantine worshipped Yahu only, according to the Jerusalem cult of the 6th century and not a mixture of Yahwism and paganism.

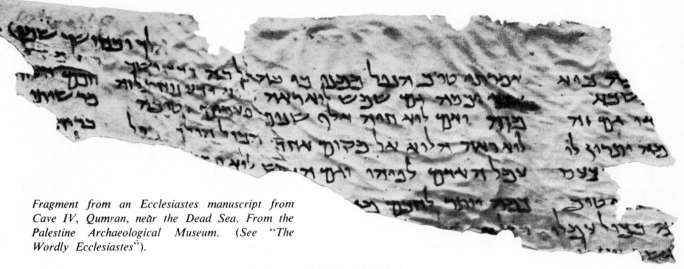

Fragment from an Ecclesiastes manuscript from Cave IV, Qumran, near the Dead Sea. From the Palestine Archaeological Museum. (See "The Wordly Ecclesiastes").

C H A P T E R   X X I I

JEWISH WISDOM LITERATURE

The biblical books we have so far introduced to the reader deal directly with the historical and religious traditions of the Hebrews.

The third part of the Hebrew canon of the Old Testament is termed "Writings" (Hagiographa) and it follows the Pentateuch and the historical books, which include the prophets. This last section opens with Psalms and is followed by Proverbs, Job, The Song of Songs, Ruth, Lamentations, Ecclesiastes, Esther, Daniel, Ezra, Nehemiah and Chronicles. In the Christian canon, no such three-partite division of the Bible appears. Moreover, the books of Ezra, Nehemiah and Chronicles precede there the wisdom and poetical books and the prophets come after them.

Some of the biblical books appearing in the last part of the Scriptures, however, are of an international rather than an exclusively Hebraic character. They are concerned with spiritual concepts of universal applicability. This is particularly true of the Wisdom Literature. In this appears proverbs and allegories; particularly in the anthology of Proverbs, which was devoted to teachings, especially for the youth. Its main theme is what will make men good and, consequently, happy. On the other hand, there is also the group of speculative thinkers, typified by complete books such as Job and Ecclesiastes, who probed deeper and more sensitively into fundamental issues. While they used the same ideological weapons, their solutions were far less orthodox.

THE BOOK OF PROVERBS

Circles of "the wise"

These tenets were developed in circles of "the wise", professionals whose teachings were considered sufficiently important to be classed with the priests and the prophets, though this literature developed on totally independent lines from the former.

Their aim was to induce certain principles or modes of behaviour by means of colourful parables drawn from everyday life. This produced a style rich in allegory and metaphor. This type of rhetoric, full of repetition and metaphysical dialogue can also be found in the prophetic writings, but they served a different purpose, as we shall see.

The maxims and reflections of the Book of Proverbs recall similar products of the literature of neighbouring peoples. Their contents are often poetic in character, poetry being the usual oriental form for this type of didactic literature, and consist of a balance or rhyming of the thought. Frequently, the second line of a couplet will repeat the thought of the first, varying the words used to express it:

"Wisdom cries aloud in the street;
  in the markets she raises her voice". (Prov. 1: 20)

"A wise son makes a glad father,
  but a foolish son is a sorrow to his mother". (Prov. 10: 1)

Or the second couplet extends the thought of the first by concluding the idea:

"But these men lie in wait for their own blood,
  they set an ambush for their own lives". (Prov. 1: 18)

"Like a gold ring in a swine's snout
  is a beautiful woman without discretion" (Prov. 11: 22)

This repetition in the second couplet, is believed to stem from the form of early Hebrew song. As the first line stated a thought, the second line served as a refrain which would be sung in unison by singer and audience together. The Hebrew poets were little concerned with a careful metre such as distinguishes classical Greek poetry. The natural stress of the voice provided a rhythm which satisfied the Hebrews, and therefore this poetry suffers little in the process of translation.

Major Themes

The book is an anthology of collections of different origin. They include both secular and religious schools of thought. God, of course, is the source of all things, directing every move of man. The theology of the secular school is akin to that of Job, Ecclesiastes and Psalm 104.

vases and kohl tubes of Egyptian make (12th century).

The book opens with a section attributed to Solomon. The first nine chapters form a prologue, with a dominant theme of the value of wisdom. This means moral conduct as well as knowledge. It begins therefore with the wise man's programme of religious education. The clauses of this programme are: to know wisdom and understand; to discern the words of understanding; to receive instruction in wise dealing, in righteousness, judgement and equity, to allow young and old to have a part in the programme, to appreciate the literary forms of proverbs and their significance.

The proverbs show a positive, healthy view towards wordly affairs, suggesting that the good life can be won through diligence, sobriety, and prudence. The marks of the good life are success, well-being, and a long fruitful life.

The Hebrew sayings resemble prudent advice given in Egypt, Babylonia and elsewhere according to the dictates of common sense. Many of them deal with ordinary situations which can hinder man from attaining a full life. Success is difficult to define but the proverbs emphasize the virtues of diligence and hard work. Generosity, good-will, and unselfishness are also qualities that make for success:

"One man pretends to be rich, yet has nothing;
  another pretends to be poor, yet has great wealth.
The ransom of a man's life is his wealth,
but a poor man has no means of redemption.
The light of the righteous rejoices,
  but the lamp of the wicked will be put out". (Prov. 13:7-9)

A Patrician Outlook

Other proverbs briefly extoll the virtues of moderation and restraint from such things as drunkenness (23:20–21), unwise business dealings (11:1–5) relations with harlots or liaisons outside marriage (7:5–10). The women against whom the warning is issued are not the street-walkers but kept women, often married, living luxuriously:

Lamp with its open bowl with 7 places for the wicks. It shows a rare development from the earlier and common dish-type (the slipper type of earthenware lamp).

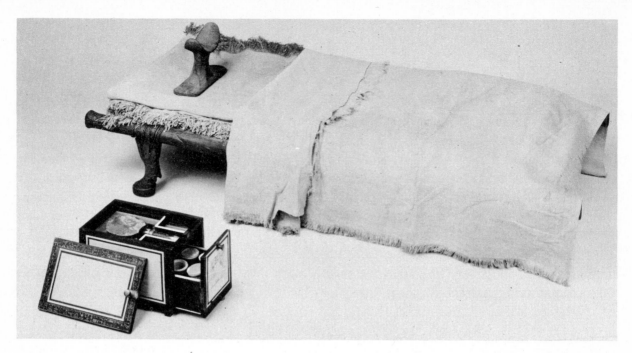

Bed, head rest, linen sheets and toilet chest for which Egypt was famous. From the time of the 11th and 12th dynasties.

"I have decked my couch with coverings,
  coloured spreads of Egyptian linen;
I have perfumed my bed with myrrh, aloes, and cinnamon.

Come, let us take our fill of love till morning;
  let us delight ourselves with love".(Prov .7: 16-18)

R. Gordis, following L. Finkelstein maintains that this utilitarian Hebrew wisdom literature was mainly the product of the Jewish upper classes who were conservative in outlook and fundamentally content with the status quo. The same conservatism can be found among the more unconventional wisdom teachers and is noticeable, besides Proverbs, in Ecclesiastes and Job. The high value which the wisdom teachers placed on economic prosperity does not imply low moral standards. Instead material success is uniformly regarded as a reward for moral conduct while poverty was considered an evil. This collection of upper-class moral teachings, however, has been subjected to revision by more plebian writers.

It is generally recognized that "wisdom" (hokhma) was taught in special schools for young men. The only ones who would be able to afford to go to school in olden times, were the sons of the wealthy. The poor lacked both the leisure and the means to give their sons higher education. There may be a parallel with the Hebrew schools of "hokhma" taken from another great culture, the Periclean age of Greece, (5th century) and its schools of sophists.

The religious sections of Proverbs show, however, the influence of the higher social ideals reached in the days of the classical prophets. The wisdom tradition was well adapted to Israel's faith. The "fear of Yahweh" and "the knowledge of God" being synonymous, they shared a conception with which the prophets would have agreed. Many things in life are more precious than riches, such as religious experience, or love.

Describing an abstract concept like wisdom, in personal terms, is not merely a literary form. It represents an interesting development in Hebrew widsom traditions.

The sages of old believed that the wisdom is not only human understanding but also the divine purpose by which men and the world are directed and according to which man should order his life. Further, wisdom is regarded as an entity (hence the personal metaphor) who was present with Yahweh at the time of the Creation:

"The Lord created me at the beginning of his work, the first of his acts of old. Ages ago I was set up, at the first, before the beginning of the earth. When there were no depths I was brought forth, when there were no spings abounding with water". (Prov. 8: 22–24)

W.F. Albright has pointed out that Chapters 8 and 9 of Proverbs are full of Canaanite words and expressions. The verses quoted are full of references to Canaanite myths, e.g. "El created me at the beginning of his dominion". In the Baal epic of Ugarit we read about El who is wise above all Gods, "A life of good fortune is thy command". The biblical verses reflect older Canannite mythological imagery. El. brought forth wisdom even before he had conquered the primordial dragon Tehom and established his home. In verse 8: 24 above, we have a direct allusion to the Phoenician myth in the Baal epic, in which El is said to dwell "at the sources of the Two Rivers in the midst of the fountains of the Two Deeps".

In addition, there are isolated Canaanite parallelisms throughout the book of Proverbs, though we have no space even to mention a fraction.

All the Wisdom of Egypt

Modern scholarship calls attention to the affinity between Proverbs 22: 17 — 24: 22 and the instruction of Amen-em-ope "the true silent one in Abydos", who also taught a commonsense view of life. The wise man said to his son: "Give your ears, hear what is said — at a time when there is whirlwind of words, they will be a mooring stake for your tongue".

King Solomon's annalist describes the great wisdom of the king as excelling "all the wisdom of Egypt". Many writings of this kind bear witness to Egypt's reputation for this type of literature. Some at least of her wisdom was known and appreciated in ancient Israel. The giving of instructions was a well-documented practice of Egyptian sages throughout many centuries.

The earliest wise sayings written by the Egyptian scribes in papyri are those bearing the name of Ptah-hotep, the vizier of a king of the Fifth Dynasty (late third millenium). Having reached the ideal age of one hundred and ten (Joseph, also a vizier of an Egyptian Pharaoh is said to have died at this same age), he handed down to his son what wisdom he had learned in deeds and in speech. This document, like many of the biblical proverbs, is a guide for success. So are the maxims of Amen-em-ope dating from about the 12th century B.C.E.

A Cosmopolitan Culture

Many similar proverbs are to be found among different ancient peoples for they arose from a common cultural background and it is not easy to determine their first origin. The wisdom literature of the Bible contains a high proportion of material which originated from outside Israel. At the same time it is full of original Israelite religious and moral concepts which were foreign to the other peoples of the ancient Near East. But this does not alter the fact that proverbs and wisdom literature have a much more cosmopolitan character and, of all the Bible, come closer to similar contemporary writings.

Certain terms in Proverbs which have long been misunderstood by translators have been clarified by recent Ugarite and Assyrian discoveries. For instance:

"It is better to live in a corner of the housetop than in a house shared with a contentious woman" (Prov. 21: 9)

The rendering "community house" for "beth-haber" in the Hebrew is inexact. The Hebrew term meant in fact a brewery, or the ancient equivalent of an ale house and the verse may better be rendered:

Dwelling in a roof corner is better than a quarrelsome woman and a public house.

COMPOSITION OF THE BOOK

Of the first 22 chapters, most scholars regard 10 to 22 as the oldest portion of the book of Proverbs. They are made up of largely disconnected aphorisms and appear to belong to the Solomonic tradition.

The authorship of the book was ascribed to Solomon because of the original impulse which he gave to wisdom literature and letters in general. Hence the mass of such literature which appeared later was attributed to him, just as the Psalms were largely attributed to David and the Pentateuch to Moses.

Proverbs 25: 1 ff. introduce more so-called Solomonic wisdom, but now the contents are said to have been transmitted by "the men of Hezekiah, king of Judah", among the circle of "the wise" of a later time.

Many scholars believe that other sections are not even Israelite as for instance:

"The words of Agur son of Jakeh of Massa.
The man says to Ithiel, to Ithiel and Ucal". (Prov. 30: 1)
"The words of Lemuel, king of Massa, which his mother taught him:" (Prov. 31: 1)

Such captions as "the words of Agur" in the first passage, or "the words of Lemuel, king of Massa" are ascribed to personages not directly associated with the Hebrew people. It is likely that such stories circulated orally for many generations before they were written down. The compilers of Proverbs took such stories and the meditations that they occasioned, and placed them within the framework of the book because they paralleled the Hebrew themes. This literary form seems to appear also in the compositions of Job and Ecclesiastes.

The last wisdom collection in Proverbs is followed by the famous alphabetic poem on the good house wife, too well known to be quoted (31: 10–31). This poem is an anonymous composition from the words of King Lemuel and may be considered a closing section of the book. The nagging-wife theme is also fairly frequent (27: 15–16).

One can regard the whole anthology as a complex tradition, extending throughout almost the whole of the Old Testament period.

When was Proverbs composed?

The popular Solomonic tradition started among circles of scribes and its earliest expression comes from the early monarchy:

"And the Lord gave Solomon wisdom, as he promised him; and there was peace between Hiram and Solomon; and the two of them made a treaty". (1 K. 5: 12)

In view of the fact that the maxims of Amen-em-ope may be dated around the 12th century and since many of the Canaanite items in Proverbs are even more remote and have their closest extra-biblical analogies as early as in the days of the Patriarchs, (the Bronze Age), one is tempted to agree with W. Baumgartner in regarding a Solomonic nucleus as probable, even though much of the material may not have been used in the present book of Proverbs. The tradition that Proverbs goes back to Solomon or his court would be incomprehensible otherwise. Even so, we can discount the extravagance of the writer's description of his wisdom and munificence.

It would be most unreasonable to assume that wisdom literature appeared any later in Palestine or Syria than in any other area of antiquity. They might be expected to share in the general cultures of the area which are known to us (as related in Chapters XIII to XVIII of this book). "We should expect influences from Egypt and Mesopotamia to be represented in all periods and in all important literary categories" (W.F. Albright). This scholar is of the opinion that there is no need to date any of the contents of Proverbs later than the sixth century B.C.E. or to assume that the book contains any post-Exilic material. The final editing of it, however, may be as late as the fifth or fourth century. This contradicts any myth which has arisen that the "wise men" of Israel flourished in the Persian or early Hellenistic period about the fifth-third centuries B.C.E.

JOB

A Spoken Drama Framed in Great Poetry

The anonymous author of Job can claim a rare and outstanding achievement, unique in the literature of antiquity and infinitely more engaging than anything else written in the ancient Near East. It is neither epic, drama, lyric nor didactic poetry; yet it embraces something of each of these in its argument and spoken drama, framed in great poetry. It is also considered as the peak of genuine Israelite, individual religious consciousness.

Job, a righteous man, is bewildered by his suffering. The point at issue is one that has tantalized wise men of all ages: Why do the innocent suffer? In telling its story the Book of Job discusses the question at the deepest levels of reflection and conscience.

The only way to understand Job is in realizing that it has three sharply defined divisions: a prose prologue, a prose epilogue and between these the drama in poetry, constructed as a debate in three rounds.

The prose prologue forms Chapters 1–2 and the prose epilogue section 42: 7–17 and this framework provides interesting clues to the story The poem, begins with the hero's curse of the day of his birth and his great lament.

There is a first cycle of speeches by Job's friends, with Job's answers to each (chaps. 4–14); a second cycle of speeches, with Job's answers, follows in chapters 25–21, and a third cycle in chapters 22–28. Job's summary, argument and defence cover chapters 29–31, and the intervening Elihu speeches chapters 32–37. The debate is wound up by Yahweh's first speech from the whirlwind followed by Job's submission, his second speech and Job's repentance (ch. 38–42: 6).

It is misleading to think of Job as a historic figure and to theorize about the time and place in which he lived. These are minor questions in the interpretation of the poem. A more fruitful line of research lies in determining the nature and components of this most important and complex work, and in deducing from its elements what they represented in the literature of the time. Then one can appreciate what each debater has to say at each stage of the discussion and what contribution he makes to the general subject, and what, in each case, Job says in reply. Finally one can gather what God says and appreciate the significance and meaning of the book.

Job in the Prologue

The issue is first introduced in the prose prologue, where Job is described as a prominent nomad chief, of blameless character. He displays a righteousness and faith unaffected by circumstance. Because Satan insinuates that Job's relation to God is not unqualified fidelity, but is designed to obtain the blessings of health, reputation, family and long life, he is put to the divine chastisement. He is completely submissive and, despite his vast misfortunes does not "sin with his lips". This prose narrative has a quality reminiscent of the pariarchal legends in Genesis or the simple folk tales of Semitic heroes.

Job of the Poetic Dialogue

It is generally agreed that the author of the poetic sections did not compose the story which appears in the prologue and epilogue. In the poems Job is a·different person altogether. He lives a settled existence, admits to some measure of sin, and Satan and the notion of suffering as a test do not appear. Instead of acquiescing, Job, as he lies stretched on his dunghill, rebels and rails defiantly. Job's lament begins with the moving poetry of his curse on the day of his birth:

"Let the stars of its dawn be dark;
   let it hope for light, but have none,
   nor see the eyelids of the morning;
because it did not shut the doors of my mother's womb,
   nor hide trouble from my eyes.
'Why did I not die at birth,
   come forth from the womb and expire?' ". (Job 3: 9–11)

He maintains his integrity and demands to meet God in fair debate in order to vindicate himself:

"I hold fast my righteousness, and will not let it go;
   my heart does not reproach me for any of my days
                                    (Job 27: 6)"
"Surely I would carry it on my shoulder;
   I would bind it on me as a crown;
I would give him an account of all my steps;
   like a prince I would approach him". (Job 31: 36-37)

The poetical dialogue not only shows psychological and intellectual insight. It gives a vivid picture of a divine-human encounter; of a man of outstanding intellect who doubts, rebels and shouts defiance at God. The poem sustains this tension throughout the three cycles of speeches and into the Yahweh whirlwind speech, undiminished.

The features that make the poem so appealing and distinctive are that men are represented not just talking about religion but testing the strength and relevance of moral and religious conviction at their highest theories about reward and punishment. This had been done before him, as we know from early Babylonian literature. His purpose was to present to his audience a concept of man vis-a-vis God that deserves to be heard in its own right. Accordingly, the critical problems that arise are: How were the prose and poetry portions brought together? What was the purpose and literary origin of the poetic dialogue?

From the prose narrative of the prologue, relating Job's background, we pass to the dialogue and the poetry. At once there is a change in the use of the divine names. The name Yahweh is never used outside the prose sections, save in the dramatic verses connecting the sections of the composition. Instead the non-national names El, Eloah and particularly Shaddai known in a wide Semitic sphere and similar to the names given by the patriarchs to the deity, previous to Mosaic times, are used (See chapters II and VI of this book). In His whirlwind speech to Job the name of God is changed to Yahweh. The lapse of time between the composition of the poetic dialogue and the archaic prose framework of Job's story, would also account for the fact that in the more ancient poem Job questions God's justice. He rails bitterly against Shaddai's injustice to himself and expresses doubts about the divinity's effective rule over the earth, the heavens, the sun, the moon or the stars, or even over the cherubim and the heavenly host:

" 'How you have helped him who has no power!
How you have saved the arm that has no strength!
How you have counseled him who has no wisdom,
 and plentifully declared sound knowledge!' ".
                                                  (Job 26: 2–3)

"By his power he stilled the sea;
 by his understanding he smote Rahab.
By his wind the heavens were made fair;
 his hand pierced the fleeing serpent
Lo, these are but the outskirts of his ways;
 and how small a whisper do we hear of him!
But the thunder of his power who can understand?' ".
                                                  (Job 26: 12–14)

The Poetic Dialogue

Undeserved suffering is the point at which the author takes up the story. The hero is a man whose scale of values and estimate of the divinity's ways have undergone a tremendous shock. It is worth pointing out that several phases of the book and its character can best be understood in relation to the Hebrew mentality. Some relevant aspects are the notion of retribution and the concept of the after-life. One accepted principle of Hebrew wisdom — and this is the underlying argument of his companions — was that God rewards the just and punishes the wicked in this life. But Job's anxiety is caused by the apparent wantonness of his suffering which is more terrible than the torment of physical pain. It can be assuaged only by death. Job's death-wish, springs from his sense of the emptiness of life when he is estranged from a meaningful relation to God. The common conception of the after-life was of Sheol, the underworld where all the dead, without distinction, assembled to endure a shadowy sort of existence, cut off from all earthly contact.

Thus the idea of retribution in the after-life was not part of Job's faith. The traditional explanation of suffering was that it was a punishment for sin. Job's protest springs from his inner conviction of his own innocence and from a refusal to accept the wisdom expressed by his comforters, that he was being punished because of his sin. He contends that this belief does not stand the test of experience, which shows that often it is the innocent who suffer while the wicked prosper.

Eliphaz tries to comfort Job by suggesting that the fault lies in Job himself. All men have sinned; therefore he should confess his sin rather than protest to God. Since the fault lies within him, as this friend and Zophar argue, the remedy is also within his power:

" 'If iniquity is in your hand, put it far away,
  and let not wickedness dwell in your tents.
Surely then you will lift up your face
  without blemish;
you will be secure, and will not fear' ". (Job 11: 14–15)

" 'Agree with God, and be at peace;
  thereby good will come to you.
Receive instruction from his mouth,
  and lay up his words in your heart' ".
                 (Job 22: 21–22)

Job stubbornly insists on his innocence. In the third cycle of speeches, the friends become more vehement in their accusations. They openly accuse him of adding presumption to his previous sin. Attempting to defend the majesty of God, they use every available argument to demonstrate that God is just in his dealings according to the orthodox formula of reward and punishment. They accuse Job of pride, charging him with rejecting the finite limits of mankind. If he were really honest, they argued, he would have to admit that God had punished him more lightly than he actually deserved. Again and again they entreat him to abandon his arrogant insistence on his own righteousness and to make supplication to God.

Sincere though they are in their stand and in their eloquent expression of faith, they cling desperately to their orthodoxy. But Job is forced to arguments that conflict with the traditional beliefs — but these are pitilessly reiterated as the dialogue proceeds. We become aware at such moments of the supreme art of the poem. If it is not dramatic in that there is an entire absence of action, yet the anonymous poet has set out sharply the triple conflict — the

Behemoth from an Egyptian painting.

conflict between Job and his friends, between the more benignant and the more cruel forms of their orthodoxy, and between the rapid shifting of Job's emotions and the steady advance to a transcendant conception of the divinity of which they could understand and know nothing.

The Voice of Yahweh from the Whirlwind

When Yahweh finally answers Job, He does not do so in response to Job's plea for vindication, or to endorse Job's innocence. His speech, instead, forms a series of ironical questions that make Job's assumptions irrelevant. The effect is to remind Job — and all men — that he is a creature whose limited standards are inadequate for judging the Creator. It comes in the form of a rebuke, reminding him that the religious obligation of the creature is to acknowledge and glorify his Creator. His answer is to remind Job of the power and might of God. He draws pictures of nature in poetry of unsurpassed beauty and bids Job behold the perfection of His work. The references to animals may seem to come rather as an anticlimax and some scholars think this section may be a later addition. As its tone is unquestionably Egyptian it is possible that it may come from some source of Egyptian wisdom literature.

" 'Who has let the wild ass go free?
Who has loosed the bonds of the swift ass,
to whom I have given the steppe for his home,
  and the saltland for his dwelling place' ". (Job 39: 5–6)

" 'Behold, Behemoth,
  which I made as I made you;
  he eats grass like an ox' ".
  (Job 40: 15)

This argument is placed in Job's own mouth:

" 'But ask the beasts, and they will reach you;
  the birds of the air, and they will tell you;
or the plants of the earth, and they will teach you;
  and the fish of the sea will declare to you'". (Job 12: 7–8)

As his final word, Job retracts his rash charges:

" 'Who is this that hides counsel without knowledge?'
Therefore I have uttered what I did not understand,
  things too wonderful for me, which I did not know.
'Hear, and I will speak;
  I will question you, and you declare to me.'
I had heard of thee by the hearing of the ear,
  but now my eye sees thee;
therefore I despise myself,
  and repent in dust and ashes' ". (Job 42: 3–6)

The prose epilogue which follows takes it for granted that Job submits in all humility and admits his error. Whereupon God graciously gives His blessing.

"And the Lord restored the fortunes of Job, when he had prayed for his friends; and the Lord gave Job twice as much as he had before". (Job 42: 10)

The Prose Epilogue

In the prose epilogue Yahweh praises Job for the manner in which he answered Him. Evidently the original prose story ended on that note. But it goes further, for it reproves Job's three companions for being false friends:

"After the Lord had spoken these words to Job, the Lord said to Eliphaz the Temanite: 'My wrath is kindled against you and against your two friends; for you have not spoken of me what is right, as my servant Job has'". (Job 42: 7)

By implication this is one of the most important conclusions and is a justification of Job's passionate revolt and philosophic doubts. Bildad and his friends are apparently reproved for representing a traditional and exploded view of suffering, or, as complacent advisers, they never rose above matter of fact and utilitarian praise of God's judgement. It is this view of suffering that the book rejects. Their arguments were too obvious and had not been tested by the strain of real suffering, the mental pain of which begets doubts. Nevertheless no one can read the book sympathetically without feeling the impact of the clash between Job's questioning mind on the one hand, and his deep faith on the other. The obstacles to trust in God are ruthlessly represented and the final triumph of his faith is as convincing as the hero's most savage protests. Even though nature and experience both cry out against his creed, justice and goodness are vindicated and the religious purpose of the sublime poem is a clear proclamation of "faith in spite of".

What then is one intended to say to the book's central question, "What will the good man do when put to the test?" One may perhaps regard these dialogues as an interlude, and, as Job did not really renounce Yahweh, find the answer in the fact that, purified by his sufferings, Job will be restored to his erstwhile prosperity.

While the book has no systematic conclusion by implication it declares that there is no necessary connection between suffering and sin. By the same token, it is not to be thought that goodness will be requited materially. The reward for righteousness is an inner satisfaction of one's conscience and the certainty of God's approval rather than outward prosperity, health or the approval of friends.

Hebrew Poetry and the Traditions of Semitic Antiquity

N. H. Tur-Sinai (Torczyner) developed the theory that the prologue and epilogue were traditional material — a familiar tale about Job. The anonymous poet took this as his starting point and went on to develop his own interpretation and analysis of the great sufferer.

Job was not a Hebrew from any familiar sphere of biblical history in Palestine. He may have been a hero of Semitic antiquity, a "great man" from the desert bordering east Jordan, according to one theory. Or the Job legend may have originated in Edomite territory round Teman, according to another:

"There was a man in the land of Uz, whose name was Job; and that man was blameless and upright, one who feared God, and turned away from evil". (Job 1: 1)

....

"Now when Job's three friends heard of all this evil that had come upon him, they came each from his own place, Eliphaz the Temanite, Bildad the Shuhite, and Zophar the Naamathite. They made an appointment together to come to condole with him and comfort him". (Job 2: 11)

It has been suggested that Job's companions, Eliphaz, Bildad and Zophar are only different forms of the Edomite list of kings named in Gen. 36. It is known that ancient poets used to appropriate old stories as a framework within which they wove songs or speeches recited as folk poetry. The ancient story may have been the starting point for many popular poetic meditations. Their highlights remained the climactic points of the saga which the audience would remember.

This literary form of poetry within narrative framework has many parallels in the literary traditions of the ancient Near East. The literary framework of many stories of the Old Testament also suggested the narrative history of a people interwoven with folk poetry. Job would be one of the sublime examples of this literary tradition.

Related Themes in Mesopotamian Literature

The theme of the suffering of the righteous man is a very old one. The question why he is tried by suffering and the problem of evil have a long history. It finds earlier parallels, centuries before Job, in Mesopotamian literature and appears again and again, first in Sumerian tales and among the Babylonians and Assyrians. A righteous sufferer recites his misfortunes and the treatment received from his god. Some of his complaints recall Job. The hero protests his innocence and insists that the will of the god was beyond human understanding. Finally he is restored to fortune by Marduk and prosperity returns. The teachers and sages of Mesopotamia believed that man's misfortunes were the result of his sins and his deeds. But there the resemblance ceases: the Babylonian sufferer is outwardly far more orthodox than Job, and is convinced that he must have transgressed unintentionally, a frequent motif in Babylonian psalms, and he never suggests that heaven is unjust to him. Furthermore, the Babylonian poem is an unrelieved monologue and not a dialogue.

The Historical Background of the Story of Job

Whether the Job prose legend was in oral or written form when the anonymous poet received it is uncertain. Scholars are divided as regards its literary source and the facts are still obscure. In order to solve the riddle of the legendary kernel of the Job's narrative — as distinct from its poetic contents — N. H. Tur-Sinai even went so far as to suggest that the work was originally an Aramaic composition which was translated into Hebrew during the period of the Exile.

B. Mazar has pointed out the close affinity between the historical background of the narrative proper and the background of the patriarchal period, chiefly the Bene-Qedem, semi-nomadic tribes who lived mainly by grazing (See Chapter IV). Uz, Buz and Kesed, three people mentioned in Job appear in fact in the genealogical list of Gen. 22: 20–24 among the sons of Nahor, namely the tribes or people belonging to the tribal clans of Bene-Nahor who ranged from the western banks of the Euphrates around the towns of Nahor (Nahuri) and Harran, to the Syrian desert. The "sons" of Nahor and the "sons" of Abraham were related clans which traced their descent to common ancestors of the Euphrates region. The life of the patriarchal period is reflected in Job in much the same manner as in Genesis, particularly in reference to the Bene-Qedem, the original home of Job and his friends. B. Mazar concludes that the story of Job may run parallel to the stories and legends of Genesis. Such old traditions must have been known in ancient Israel.

W.F. Albright is of the opinion that the date of the hero himself should be pushed back into the first half of the second millenium i.e., to the patriarchal period. On the other hand, he points out that further knowledge of Ugarit and Phoenician sources will clear up many problems concerning the use of words in Job. Much of the book's imagery clearly derives from lost Phoenician sources of the Iron Age, (the period of the monarchy in the Bible); for instance the reference to the "sons of God" (mythical figures, of whom one is Satan) and the "sons of Resheph", may be proofs of the remote origin of the prose narrative of Job (in the prologue). The remote antiquity of the narrative is indicated by archaic traits such as characterize the stories of Genesis. As regards the literary composition of Job, it remains highly probable that its author "lived in the cosmopolitan atmosphere of the sixth or fifth century B.C. and he was certainly conversant with a wide range of lost pagan North-west Semitic literature, although Hebrew was still his literary language".

THE WORLDLY "ECCLESIASTES"

The wisdom literature is closed by the poem of Kohelet (Ecclesiastes), meaning the "master" of an assembly, discussing the vanity of things and the pointlessness of the endless round of affairs. It was customary to consider it a composition of late Persian or Hellenistic period, showing traces of such influence. Recent research has suggested, however, a revision of this view. H.L. Ginsberg, on the one hand suggests an Aramaic provenance of the original before its adaptation to the Hebrew. A more tempting view, on the other hand, is that suggested by M.J. Dahood to the effect that the composition of the book bears the earmarks of Phoenician linguistic influence. In any event, no other book is so closely related, both in form and content to the literature of Phoenicia and perhaps Persia and has such striking affinities with Egyptian, Babylonian, Greek and other literary remains:

"Vanity of vanities, says the Preacher,
  vanity of vanities! All is vanity
What does man gain by all the toil
  at which he toils under the sun?

A generation goes, and a generation comes,
  but the earth remains for ever.
The sun rises and the sun goes down
  and hastens to the place where it rises". (Eccles. 1: 2–5)

"All things are full of weariness;
  a man cannot utter it;
the eye is not satisfied with seeing,
  nor the ear filled with hearing.

What has been is what will be,
and what has been done is what will be done;
and there is nothing new under the sun". (Eccles. 1; 8–9)

This book is no mere collection of unrelated precepts. One principal idea dominates the whole, and the book appears to be the work of a single writer developing the one theme. However, on closer inspection, it becomes clear that, as in Job, the narrative part comes from a folk tale. The author seems to have taken a well-known story and used it as a framework for his philosophical meditations. As a result, prose and poetry combine in a coherent argument.

The author catalogues his changing moods of pessimism, pleasure-loving, sophism and faith. He explores every field of knowledge, and then draws his conclusions from this experience.

He makes four different quests for the real profit in life. The first is the quest for practical wisdom (1:12–18). The second is the quest for pleasure (2:1–11). This he interprets not in a vulgar way, but in the manner of Solomon building palaces for his enjoyment and surrounding himself with all the luxury that great wealth could buy. Koheleth's third quest

The Egyptian "blind harper" is represented at the formal funeral sacrifice of the courtier Patenemheb, depicted in his mortuary chapel. Dating from the Amarna period.

is for labour and riches (2:18—6:12). But Koheleth is convinced that there can be no net gain. All things move in a circle accomplishing nothing. There is nothing new under the sun, and death ends all. His fourth quest is for fame (7:1:11:8):

"Cast your bread upon the waters,
   for you will find it after many days.

Give a portion to seven, or even to eight,
   for you know not what evil may happen on earth".
                                    (Eccles. 11: 1–2)

Nevertheless, after a long life of struggle and doubt he has been given a new revelation. Here comes the climax of the book. He knows of course that "the dust returns to the earth". But there was more: "and the spirit returns to God who gave it" (Eccles. 12:7). This does not mean that he gains individual immortality; merely that the body is re-absorbed into the earth and the spirit into God. He wails: "vanity of vanities, all is vanity", as all material achievements in themselves, with the final disappearance of the individual, are meaningless and disappointing

Koheleth's recurring motifs bring to mind another masterpiece from Egyptian literature, the song of the "harper":

Those who build houses, their dwelling place is no more
What has befallen them?
I have heard the words of
    Ii-em-hotep and Hordedef,
With whose discourses men speak so much.
What are their places now?
Their walls are broken apart, and their places are not –
    As though they had never been!

There is none who comes back from over there,
That he may tell their state,
That he may tell their needs,
That he may still our hearts,
Until we too may travel to the place where they
    have gone
Let thy desire flourish,
    In order to let thy heart forget the beatifications
    for thee

The song ends with a refrain:

Make holiday, and weary not therein!
    Behold, it is not given to a man to
    take his property with him,

Behold, there is not one who departs
    who comes back again!

(According to Ancient Near Eastern Texts; J. B. Pritchard (Ed.)

The Wisdom of Babylon

The words of Ecclesiastes are also reminiscent of a Babylonian satiric speculation about life's values. This ends as a dialogue between a master and his servant. The master makes a proposal for a certain course of action and the servant obliges with an appropriate proverb which supports the master's suggestion. Whereupon, the master suggests the opposite course, to which the servant has ready at hand an equally good supporting saying. For instance, the part of the dialogue on the subject of public service, says:

"Servant, obey me.
Yes my lord, yes.
I will do something helpful for my country".
Do it, my lord, do it.
The man who does something helpful
for his country, — his helpful deed
is placed in the bowl of Marduk.

No, servant, I will not do something
helpful for my country.
Do it not, my lord, do it not.
Climb the mounds of ancient ruins and
walk about: look at the skulls of late and
early men; who among them is an evildoer,
who a public benefactor"

....

On suicide and murder:

"Servant, obey me.
Yes, my lord, yes.
Now, what is good? To break my neck, your neck.
throw both into the river — that is good.
Who is tall enough to ascend to heaven?
Who is broad enough to embrace the earth?

No, servant, I shall kill you and send you
ahead of me.
Then would my lord wish to live even three
days after me?"

(According to Ancient Near Eastern Texts; J. B. Pritchard (Ed.)

Epilogue

The epilogue of the book, 12: 9–14 is regarded as an editorial postscript, for now the recital changes to the third person and commends the author's literary ability and wisdom. This "orthodox" conclusion was apparently added by editors who were trying to make sure that the book would be included in the scriptures. But it contradicts the genuine spirit and central theme of Ecclesiastes.

"My son, beware of anything beyond these.
Of making many books there is no end,
and much study is a weariness of the flesh.
The end of the matter; all has been heard.

Fear God, and keep his commandments;
for this is the whole duty of man.
For God will bring every
deed into judgment, with every secret
thing, whether good or evil". (Eccles. 12: 12–14)

CONCLUSION
Wisdom Writers of Near Eastern Antiquity

Israel emerged from a Northwest Semitic background, which included the peoples of Syria (Phoenicia), Canaan, East of Jordan, Edom and North Arabia. The peoples of this area shared a common material culture and we know that their languages had much in common. This being so, one would expect to find a close relationship in all aspects of culture, with the exception of the Israelite religion. It would therefore be strange if Hebrew and Canaanite learned circles in Palestine and Phoenicia did not share an appreciation of didactic wisdom literature, such as is found throughout the area.

From ancient times, the "wise" learned men of the area had cultivated a special kind of literature which had many characteristics in common. In form, it produced the "proverb" and the contents were uniformly moralistic and didactic. It aims at teaching a practical philosophy of life, which inevitably had a religious basis. In Near Eastern antiquity, true wisdom is the "fear of God", but on this basis a system of morality and virtue is put forward which has a generally international character. The term "wisdom" included not only moral and religious rules, but also the whole body of knowledge of the ancient oriental world.

"The Wise" and the Prophet

In Israel, this form of writing developed independently of the literature of the law or of prophecy, although it shows a parallel development. In spite of its remote international origins, the literature was adapted to the national religion of Israel and was deeply influenced by its spirit. Here and there, as in the Psalms, the two streams converged. Elsewhere this literature retained its archaic formulas expressing general truths or specific ideas which were characteristic not only of Israel itself but of the whole ancient milieu.

Although the class of teachers known as "the wise" are not often mentioned, they certainly existed during the time the great prophets were active. Traces of their teachings are to be found in the prophetic writings. The prophets must have known the "wisdom" writings of foreign pagan peoples, for they speak about it in traditional terms, as demonstrated recently by J. Lindblom.

However there is a great difference between "the wise" and the prophets. When "wisdom" seemed to be opposed to divine inspiration, then it became an object of scorn and derision to the prophets. Wisdom is concerned with material well-being, success and happiness, whereas the whole preaching of the prophets centred around the relation between God and man: sin and doom, repentance, forgiveness and salvation were the subjects of the prophets. In the wisdom literature, there is no place for concepts such as God's direction of history, social justice or the union of national loyalty and international peace. (See Chapters XVII-XIX). There is no sense of dissatisfaction with the existing world because of a vision of its potentialities, there is no idea of freedom as an inalienable human right.

Wisdom literature is, therefore, separate from prophetic writings and is not influenced by them. It developed from the "wisdom writers" of a wider, more ancient lineage and is independent of prophetic thought. Also, it is older than prophecy, even though its written formulation came much later.

A mythical beast painted on enamel tiles in the palace of Susa. The visions of the beast in Daniel are strongly influenced in their imagery by figures of Babylonian myth. (See below "The Book of Daniel's Visions").

CHAPTER XXIII

THE END OF THE OLD TESTAMENT

I. DANIEL — APOCALYPTIC WRITINGS BEYOND THE AGE OF PROPHECY

The book of Daniel is unmistakably the apocalyptic book of the Old Testament. Similar traits have frequently been noticed in Isaiah and Ezekiel among the great classic prophets, and Zechariah, Joel and Jonah among the minor prophets; but the apocalyptic book of Daniel marks the final mutation from prophetic literature to this form, towards the third and second centuries B.C.E. A score or more other apocalypses are known in extra-biblical literature of the time but they were not included in the canon of the Old Testament. They consist of the Apocryphal or Pseudepigraphic writings of the Hellenistic period of Jewish literature. The Book of Revelations to John in the New Testament is also a fair example of this new form. The apocalyptic writings are included only in the Roman Catholic and Eastern Orthodox Old Testament, but not in the Protestant bible.

This novel form of revelation is a later outgrowth of the pre-Exilic prophetic teaching about the future, including God's relation to man within history. It represents the "eschatological" aspect of theology which dealt with final things or with events such as we encountered in the post-Exilic prophets, Second Isaiah, Ezekiel and Malachi. Their predictions did not carry them beyond the Persian period. Beyond that a new cycle of apocalyptic prophecy begins.

The authors of this new school believed that the events of their day were moving to the climax of history's ultimate struggle which would establish the victory of God over evil and the vindication of the elect. Events of world history reflected a movement towards the Final Judgement, and a new dawn. It was usually claimed that these obscure books had been written by an ancient sage and 'hidden' or stored up to await publication at the end of history. The reason for placing them in the mouths of prophets long dead is that the age of prophecy had ended at about the time of Malachi. As they also foretold the future, they became characterized by this device or pseudonymity. Favourite eras for securing pseudonyms were the primeval period (Adam, Enoch, Noah, Abraham) or the era of Restoration (under the pseudonyms of Baruch, Ezra, Daniel).

Their visions are expressed in a bizarre form in which objects of nature serve as vehicles for the divine message. Nations and historical individuals appear as mysterious beasts. Among the common symbols are animals in place of world empires, the horn as a powerful individual leader, and the sea as the realm of evil. These symbols were obviously influenced by the later period of Mesopotamian mythology. The writers sought to calculate the exact time of the impending end of the world by manipulating numbers. World history was divided into separate phases, generally dominated by the world empires of the day, each successive phase degenerating, thus bringing closer the divinely appointed end. This is the characteristic sign of apocalypse.

A tendency developed to attribute evil to the temptation of man by an angelic being, Satan. Allied with him, hosts of fallen angels participated in a cosmic struggle between light and darkness. Patron angels determined the destinies of individual nations. Names and distinctions in rank were given to the angels, and in many apocalypses the writer provided an interpreting angel to expound his cryptic symbolism.

The writings leave no doubt, however, that God is in control and that in the new world and age beyond history he would save his own and consign these evil spirits to eternal punishment. The classical prophets' vision of the Day of Yahweh and the future hope of Israel appeared there in a new dimension. Circles with strong eschatological leanings were fascinated by the attempt to prove the heavenly secrets, while recognizing that the ways of God were past finding out. This questioning about ultimate problems was often expressed in wild, extravagant, and largely profitless, speculation. This proved to be especially popular in periods of crisis, for though the speculations were concerned with the future, they were seen as a return to a halcyon period in the past. It must be recognized, however, that an incipient philosophy of history lay close to the surface of apocalyptic literature. A striking example is the Book of Daniel.

WHY WAS THE BOOK OF DANIEL WRITTEN?

The majority of scholars agree that, though this book was composed during the period of the desecration of the Temple and the persecutions of Antiochus Epiphanes, about 168/6 B.C.E., much of the material, particularly the first six chapters, is quite a bit older than the historic period with which it is concerned. Its narrative is symbolic of the first attempt to destroy a nation's religion and literature by persecution, and of the sublime faith with which the worshippers of Yahweh met such a crisis. Daniel is a tract for the times but like other apocalyptic books is primarily didactic. It is made up of two distinct elements. Its authors are many and with the open intention of arousing patriotic sentiments in the face of disasters, they seek to impress upon their readers great religious truths in order to sustain their faith in God and in the ultimate triumph of His Kingdom.

The fact that the faith of the Jewish community was kept alive through a time of deep distress was due to the combined effects of the Maccabean revolution and the reading of this book. Its original authors and later compilers chose this literary form as one wholly appropriate in its cultural setting to such times of crisis. They aimed at keeping their fellow Jews loyal to the traditions of their fathers, even at the price of martyrdom. They believed that within a few years the trouble would be over. The Greek-Syrian tyrant (though he was referred to only by implication and not by name) would be dead and deliverance would come. To express this hope and make the appeal for steadfastness, they made use of the venerable figure of Daniel, a Jew of the last days of the Babylonian exile. This is the main clue to the division of the book into two parts, so different in content and thought.

The Narratives and Visions are Distinct Entities

The first half of the book, chaps. 1–6, contains narratives about Daniel and his three friends in the Babylonian exile, related in the third person. The second section, chaps. 7–12, is devoted to visions, and is described by Daniel, speaking in the first person. The book of Daniel is not a book of prophecy proper, for Daniel had no mission to the people, as had the prophets and he did not perform miracles as they did to prove their prophecy true. His story was set in an aura of miracles and bizarre happenings which he was asked to interpret. Thus he was no prophet but a sage, speaking his mission in his own name. At the time the book was prepared, the stories about him were projected into the past. But this happened when prophecy had already ended. The narrative part of Daniel forms the dividing line between the end of prophecy and the apocalyptic literature. No prophetic works exist between the prophecy of Malachi and the apocalyptic writings of Daniel. Moreover, the first half of the book of Daniel does not refer to a period of national persecution, in contrast to the second half which is permeated by the sense of the cruelties of Greek suppression.

THE DANIEL NARRATIVES

In these narratives the courage, wisdom and loyalty of Daniel and his fellow martyrs are displayed, and the place of importance to which he was promoted as chief of the wise men of Babylon is emphasized. At the time of the Babylonian empire a number of youths were selected from among the leading families of the subject nations and trained to become members of the guild of wise men, soothsayers and interpreters of mysteries. The later literature of the Bible uses the word "Chaldeans" to describe this body of magicians, astrologers and diviners who were consulted when necessary by the king and people, to interpret dreams and other omens and give auguries, incantations, and so forth. At the end of three years' training Daniel and his three friends (whose Hebrew names are replaced by Babylonian names) were presented to the king along with other graduates.

A magical incantation bowl written in Aramaic. Such bowls were intended and written specifically to help women in childbirth, the sick and the troubled.

The Dream

With this story the Aramaic section of the book begins with the words "in the Syrian (Aramaic) language". Aramaic was a Semitic language akin to Hebrew. This was the lingua franca of Babylon and Persia and was the ordinary tongue of Palestine from the fourth or third century B.C.E. It was, of course, used for the older material in the book which originated from a Babylonian story, translated later into Hebrew. In the story, the royal diviners had been summoned to interpret a dream of Nebuchadrezzar, but they were helpless. Then Daniel, the master of the magicians, came forward and declared that it was beyond the powers of any man to interpret the dream:

"'But there is a God in heaven who reveals mysteries, and he has made known to King Nebuchadnezzar what will be in the latter days. Your dream and the visions of your head as you lay in bed are these'" (Daniel 2: 28)

....

"'You saw, O king, and behold, a great image. This image, mighty and of exceeding brightness, stood before you, and its appearance was frightening. The head of this image was of fine gold, its breast and arms of silver, its belly and thighs of bronze, its legs of iron, its feet partly of iron and partly of clay. As you looked, a stone was cut out by no human hand, and it smote the image on its feet of iron and clay, and broke them in pieces; then the iron, the clay, the bronze, the silver, and the gold, all together were broken in pieces, and became like the chaff of the summer threshing floors; and the wind carried them away, so that not a trace of them could be found. But the stone that struck the image became a great mountain and filled the whole earth'". (Daniel 2: 31–35)

The diminishing value of the materials of the statue is a token of the growing evil in world affairs. No better image could be found of an empire which was superficially strong and brilliant but had no real foundation. The statue was made of iron and clay (which, as

Daniel stressed, could not mix) and stood on feet of clay! A stone, dislodged from a neighbouring mountain struck the image on its feet and ground it into dust, which was blown away. The stone then became a mighty rock filling the whole earth.

As Daniel interpreted the dream, Nebuchadrezzar represented the statue's head of gold. Three kingdoms would follow in order of declining merit, presumably the Median, the Persian and the Macedonian or Greek empires. Under the rule of Alexander the Great, this last kingdom would be formidable and oppressive, but of unreliable strength and, like the legs of the image, it would be divided. This apparently referred to the two states nearest to Palestine, the Seleucid in Syria and the Ptolemaic in Egypt, that succeeded the disintegration of Alexander's empire. But the time would come when the God of the Jews, the universal God, would establish his own kingdom (represented by the stone) which would supersede and destroy all world empires and would endure forever. It would not rest on military strength but on divine power. According to the legend, the Babylonian Nebuchadrezzar and then the Persian Darius, confessed that God was supreme among all gods. As the author lived long after, he had his record of the succession of the kings woefully mixed. As we saw in Chap. XX the Persian period and the post–Exilic period in Palestine were a virtual dark age in Jewish history. All ancient records of the period, biblical, and extra-biblical, including the history of Josephus, suffer from confusion.

Other types of trials in the narrative, are lessons of fidelity and courage. The three companions in the fiery furnace are brought to punishment because they refused to worship the king's idols. In Daniel 6 the legendary element is heightened by the flickering flames which consume the attendants who cast the young men into the furnace. The false accusers of Daniel, who had caused him to be thrown in the lion's den, are voraciously devoured in mid-air by the lions that had been docile towards Daniel.

Scholars of the past did not abandon the literal interpretation of the stories of Daniel until historical research proved that their theme was not the few individuals who were cast into the fiery furnace and the den of lions, but a nation.

The narratives in Daniel 1–6 proclaim the transience of kingdoms and the frailty of monarchs, witness the proud Nebuchadrezzar turned by insanity into an animal eating grass (Dan. 4); and the story of Belshazzar (Dan. 5) who saw the handwriting of God's judgement on the wall of his palace (cf. Chapter XX).

PRAYER OF NABONIDUS

A document from the caves of Qumran, identified by J.T. Milik in 1956, is closely related in language, style and genre to the cycle of tales collected and edited in the Daniel narrative. It may throw light on the oral and possibly literary sources behind the fixed edition of the Old Testament book of Daniel. The fragments read: "The words of the prayer which Nabonidus, king of Assyria and Babylon, the great King, prayed ...". The prayer relates how the king came down with a "dread disease by the decree of the Most High .... set apart from men" for a seven-year period in the Arabian oasis of Teima. A Jewish diviner, presumably Daniel (the broken texts do not give a name), intervenes and speaks of the king's worship of "gods of gold, bronze, iron, wood, stone, silver". Compare this to Daniel's text.

"They drank wine, and praised the gods of gold and silver, bronze, iron, wood and stone". (Dan. 5: 4)

It is also strongly reminiscent of Daniel's story of Nebuchadrezzar (Daniel 4) being driven from men for seven years, during which he learns:

"At the end of the days I, Nebuchadnezzar, lifted my eyes to heaven, and my reason returned to me, and I blessed the Most High, and praised and honored him who lives for ever;
    for his domination is an ever lasting dominion,
    and his kingdom endures from generation to generation." (Daniel 4: 34)

It is believed that the new document preserves a more primitive form of the tale. It will be remembered that in Daniel's story of Belshazzar's feast, his father is given as Nebuchadrezzar in place of Nabonidus. The latter is said to have given up his throne for seven years. whereas Nebuchadrezzar kept his. This suggests that in an older stage of the tradition the text included stories of Nebuchadrezzar, Nabonidus and Belshazzar. The change of name from Nabonidus to Nebuchadrezzar in Dan. 4 probably reflects a shift from a lesser name to a greater in the course of the legend's oral transmission.

Judaism versus Idolatry

The narratives in Daniel 1–6, according to Yehezkel Kaufman, are obviously a literary creation of the Exilic period. They mark not only the disappearance of the last vestige of pagan cults from among the Israelites, but also the culmination of the great prophetic drive against idolatry among other nations — a drive which seems to have borne fruit. The supremacy of the Jewish faith is the theme of the Daniel narratives; in post-Exilic Judaism, monotheism triumphed completely. The Daniel theme of God's control of world empires serves therefore to unite the legends of Daniel 1–6 to the visions which follow it but in a different historical context.

THE BOOK OF DANIEL'S VISIONS

The second part of the book (7–12), contains five visions witnessed and described by Daniel. The theme of the dream about the statue recurs several times. The vision of the Four Beasts and the Son of Man in Daniel 7 is the most significant for later apocalyptic development. There is really no break in continuity between Jewish and Christian apocalyptic literature, but certain special historic circumstances brought about an increased emphasis upon particular elements of the pattern (This phase is outside the scope of the present work).

The four beasts referred to in Daniel's three visions (7–8) are world powers, the Babylonian, the Median, the Persian and the Macedonian or Greek. They are described in terms which leave no doubt as to their model, namely the "little horn", Antiochus Epiphanes, the last of fourteen horns representing kings and pretenders to the dynasty of Alexander. God, in the majestic scene of judgement, is described as "the ancient of days". At His command the "beast" is slain and the eternal Kingdom delivered to "one like a son of man". This figure is interpreted as the loyal and vindicated "saints of the Most High".

This was the occasion of Daniel's removal from the lions' den. Though there does not seem to be an historical basis for this incident it seems that the religious particularism of Jews in Babylon and their contention with the heathen had caused at times friction which may have resulted in reprisals against militant opponents to the official religion at court. The ideological motivations behind this antagonism between the Jewish faith and heathenism, so brilliantly expounded by second Isaiah, have been explained in Chapter XIX. Another example of a background flare-up of anti-Jewish feeling in the Persian empire is the setting of the story of Esther and Mordechai (Chapter XX). Some similar situation or an intrigue in the guild of wise men or soothsayers close to the royal court, may account for the treatment accorded to Daniel and to his companions.

The vision of the angel and the Resurrection in Daniel 11–12 has as its purpose the foretelling of future history down to the end of time. Careful interpretation will discover in the account of alliances, wars and assassinations a faint outline of the familiar history of the period from Alexander to Antiochus, whose "abomination that makes desolate", perpetrated against the Temple, is grimly described. The sequence of events is far more accurate in the second part of Daniel than in the first. Antiochus's victories are recounted and a summary comment tersely delivered. The events related at the end of the vision are quite different from the closing events of Antiochus's reign and we have no record of them. The king died not in Palestine but in Persia.

II. HOW OUR BIBLE CAME TO US

During the latter days of the Persian empire and the Hellenistic/Hasmonean period, namely the 2nd century B.C.E., the literature of the Old Testament was virtually brought into the form in which we have it today. This was two centuries after the idea of a Canon of Hebrew sacred literature had first come into being.

Final Transmission of the Torah

It is assumed that the Pentateuch, virtually in its present form, was finished by the time of Ezra. Most scholars are of the opinion that when he returned to Judah to reform the Jewish community, he brought with him an edition of the Pentateuch, probably incomplete, which had been prepared by the exiled priests and "soferim".

On the trustworthy authority of the priestly Chroniclers (4th century B.C.E.) it was Ezra who promulgated the "Book of the Law" at the great assembly recorded in Nehemiah 8–10. In any case, the age which immediately followed Ezra and Nehemiah saw the full recognition of the first part of the Hebrew Canon, namely of the Torah (Pentateuch). That, of course, does not mean that the books themselves were not of much earlier date. (We have discussed this in Chapter IX). The various strata in the book of Deuteronomy and other books of the Pentateuch are variously assigned by scholars to dates between 950 and 750 B.C.E. The priestly book (Leviticus) included an ancient nucleus, and its final compilation is attributed to the early post-Exilic period, contemporary with, or just before, the time of Ezra. There is still great divergence in the views of the scholars, as we have seen, and none can claim decisive authority.

The Torah alone was the first canonical Scripture. Then came "Prophets", namely the books from Joshua to Kings, followed by Isaiah and other prophets ("Nebi'im"), and the Writings ("Kethubim" or Hagiographa).

It is also apparent that by the 4th century the canon of the Prophets and the books of Psalms and Job had virtually reached their final form. Previously the sayings of the prophets of the 8th and 7th centuries B.C.E. had been passed on orally or in written form by their disciples, as we learn from Isaiah 8:16 and 30:8. Jeremiah 36 tells us how the scribe Baruch wrote down what the prophet dictated (See Chapter XVIII). After the scroll was destroyed by the king, Jeremiah dictated the text anew to Baruch with certain additions. In any case a later editor compiled Jeremiah. The Minor Prophets were compiled somewhat later than the Major Prophets and were treated as a *single work*. This is the main reason for the fact that the Hebrew Canon comprises 24 books, while the Christian Bible numbers 36.

The third group in the Hebrew Canon, "Writings", comprises the poetical books, Psalms, Proverbs, Job; the five scrolls ("megilloth"), Songs of Songs, Ruth, Lamentations, Ecclesiastes, Esther; the remaining books, Daniel, Ezra and Nehemiah (the two latter form one book) and Chronicles. The last two books were the work of the Chroniclers.

Chronologically, with the work of the Chroniclers in the early 4th century, the whole collection of historical material in the books of Chronicles, Ezra and Nehemiah was completed. The contents of the book of Proverbs date from pre-Exilic days though their final edition belongs to the fifth or fourth century B.C.E. The only books left to account for by the time of Alexander the Great were Esther, the Song of Songs, and, of course, Daniel.

THE MASSORETH

The text of these scrolls was not completely stabilized, even at that time. The way of passing on the text was still fluid. Moreover differing traditions still persisted. The authoritative Hebrew Massoretic, or traditional, text, and its pronunciation was established and fixed in the first century A.D. The rabbis thereby sealed off any variants, one of which was the Samaritan text of the Pentateuch, which remained their exclusive and sacred possession (See Chapter XXI on the Samaritan Problem). However, the Scrolls existed in their archaic form in the two preceding centuries and were probably already considered as belonging to a special canonical collection.

What is meant by the canonical collection is the bringing together by the rabbis, after the destruction of the Second Temple in Roman times, of several books (written on scrolls) regarded as equal in value and authority. The canon was a controlling principle which made sure that the text and the books themselves would be carefully preserved. The task was entrusted to able and conscientious scholars who preserved the best readings. Before this was done the text and selection of books were full of variations. But an accepted version had to be established, for the priesthood, and later the Sanhedrin, could not maintain their authority if different schools had their own text and listing of the Scriptures. Those with whom the decision rested for selecting these books for the canon believed that they heard the revelation of the divine will in them. The nation was so far developed as to accept not only that such revelation through human literature was possible, but that it could be authoritative!

The archaic text of the Hebrew Bible, existing in the third century B.C.E., was translated into Greek during the third and second centuries in Alexandria, then the intellectual centre of the ancient world.

WHICH IS THE CORRECT TEXT?

For about nine centuries after its canonization, the Massoretic text was preserved by scribes and had to be relied upon as the authoritative text. It was written down in the 7th century A.D. with a system of vowels which followed the tradition of pronunciation established in the first century A.D. We have no actual written evidence of the scribes' work until the 10th century Hebrew edition of the Old Testament, known as the Ben Asher Manuscript. Between this and the original authoritative text there is a gap of nine centuries. In other words, the only evidence of the archaic Hebrew scrolls, dating from the period of the Second Temple, was the complete Hebrew Old Testament in this medieval Hebrew edition, although smaller portions and scraps of books had been discovered long before, as for example, the 4th century A.D. Codex Vaticanus and Codex Sinaiticus.

In order to get behind the standardized Hebrew text for the purpose of comparing obscure texts or making corrections, scholars went to the early Greek translation (Septuagint). There are, however, many variations between the Greek translation and the present Hebrew text. The difficulty of deciding such questions led modern scholars to rely more and more on the Hebrew text and to make fewer alterations on the basis of the earliest Greek translation. With the help of added collateral knowledge acquired from the study of associated ancient Semitic languages (the Accadian, Assyrian, Arabic, Aramaic), by the deciphering of inscriptions, especially Canaanite inscriptions from Ugarit and Phoenicia, considerable new light has been thrown on the biblical narrative, its form of expression and the mentality of the Hebrews and other ancients.

III. SIGNIFICANCE OF THE DEAD SEA SCROLLS

Above all, we were, until recently, in the dark about the processes of transmission of the Scrolls of the Bible between Old Testament times and the fixing of the Massoretic text.

However, the position has changed since the phenomenal discovery of the Dead Sea scrolls in the caves of Qumran, beginning in 1947 and continuing since then in the same area. The story is well known and does not need repetition. The biblical scrolls from Qumran are of the greatest importance for Old Testament studies. This is equally true of the complete scroll of Isaiah from Cave I, and the hundred odd incomplete scrolls of Old Testament books found in Cave IV, such as the commentary on Habakkuk, or the remarkable manuscript of Samuel found in Cave IV.

The surprising fact is that these fragments show little significant variation from the accepted *Hebrew* text. They give proof of the antiquity of the textual tradition which has survived in the traditional Hebrew Bible (Massoretic text). A number of the fragments illustrate variant textual traditions of the type we quoted in the text of Isaiah (38:7–8) over the "Dial of Ahaz" (cf. Chapter XVI). Another example may serve to illustrate how many of

Fragment of Isaiah manuscript discovered near the Dead Sea. Except for the Book of Isaiah, there is no complete scroll of a biblical work among the 2,000 year-old manuscripts recently discovered, nearly every other book of the Old Testaments being represented only by fragments. The discovery of these manuscripts, which date from within 300, or even 100, years of their actual composition, was something for which no one had dared to hope in the field of Bible study.

the books are compilations: a commentary on Habakkuk found in Qumran stops at the end of the second chapter. The present book consists of three chapters, the third being a psalm which was apparently added to the original book.

The Hebrew texts are also strikingly similar to the Septuagint, which proves that this translation rested on a valid Hebrew text (Massoreth) which was actually known in the second century B.C.E.

But all this does not minimize the fact that the task of the textual critic of the Bible is not an easy one. Insofar as textual criticism is concerned it is not too much to say that the Qumran scrolls have revolutionized the science of Old Testament textual criticism and begun a new period in the study of the text. They assist scholars (a) in reconstructing the history of the Old Testament through its stages of transmission; (b) in the critical evaluation of readings of the Septuagint; (c) in the study of present Hebrew Massoretic texts compared with the most ancient texts found in these scrolls.

It is not too much to hope that the new finds will help to establish a genuine text of the Old Testament before the first century B.C.E., and that we shall make progress towards a still more intelligible Old Testament.

Another vital aspect — which we mention in passing as it is outside our present framework, namely the Qumran scrolls — is that the caves contained a large number of apocalyptic, non-biblical manuscripts, written by the Essene sectarians who lived in the settlement of Qumran near the famous caves. The Essenes were the carriers, and to no small extent the producers, of the later apocalyptic tradition. The study of these non-biblical manuscripts points to the relation of primitive Christianity and its writings to the Jewish background. Modern scholars have emphasized the apocalyptic milieu common to the sectarians of Qumran and the early Church.

IV. AS WE CLOSE THE OLD TESTAMENT

With the book of Daniel the Old Testament comes to a close. History, pregnant with dramatic events, moved on; but this phase of the story of Israel and of Palestine lies beyond the province of our discussion.

At the beginning we explained briefly the main features of apocalyptic thought of which Daniel is a canonical example. The main motive of the apocalyptic movement has been described as a late Jewish attempt to revive the Old Testament doctrines of history so vividly illustrated by the biblical writers' form of narration of Israel's own historic data, as well as the prophetic understanding of world history. In a world containing such a rich variety of ideas, many of Iranian, Hellenistic and Oriental origin, the circles close to the apocalyptic writers aimed at recapturing the old prophetic conception of the history of salvation. This resulted in the creation of a new theology of history obsessed with "last things", with death, the last Judgement and the end of the world. The concept of world history received its final shape in apocalyptic literature, i.e., in Daniel and in the Apocrypha, or inter-testamental books. The broad image of the single Kingdom became crystallized in Daniel. A symbol had been created by which the four heathen empires of the world would be transformed into one, the Kingdom of God. This belief maintained that idolatry had been a sin from its inception and that people upholding it were being punished.

THE OLD TESTAMENT'S VIEW OF WORLD HISTORY

Of course, biblical Israel and her prophets and their universal creed were unique in the ancient Near East. It would not be fair not to recognize that their pride and exclusiveness, and possibly a sense of intolerance to the heathen, arose from a passionate concern for the ideal of "the holy people" and from the conviction that Israel could never fulfil herself if she mixed with other nations. A more tolerant spirit could not have kept the faith alive.

The biblical concept of one God is a human responsibility and consequently an obligation upon all nations. That is why it is incumbent upon them all, according to this concept, to be like "Israel" in spirit and to accept the faith of Israel. The heathen peoples were doomed. This was the foundation of Israel's quarrel with the heathen. There was no room for two different world concepts. Gradually it came to be believed that through adopting Israelite beliefs and practice, all mankind might enjoy the fruits of God's bounty which He had promised to His own people, Israel, through His prophets.

It is evident, in the light of this ideology, that classical prophecy marked a stage in the development of world civilization and also the transition between the beliefs of antiquity and apocalyptic literature. Within the prophetic movement we have already noted the line of evolution that runs from Elijah to Isaiah and Zephaniah; from the latter to Habakkuk, Jeremiah and Second Isaiah. This development reflected the material conditions of the time. The contrast between Israel's actual political conditions and status, in post-Exilic times, and its vast and grandiose aspirations based on its beliefs, constituted the central religious problem of Israel. This lasted from the first search for a solution in Isaiah's time, to the period of the attempts at an apocalyptic solution.

As their estimate of the power and moral character of their God developed, so the idea that Israel was His peculiar people expanded until it produced a world view according to which their God was the omnipotent ruler of the universe, and his people, Israel, the centre of world history.

ACKNOWLEGEMENTS FOR ILLUSTRATIONS

(Identified by page numbers)

Alinari-Giraudon, Paris: 289; Alinari-Viollet, Paris: 439 top; Anderson-Giraudon, Paris: 315 left bottom; Ashmolean Museum, Oxford: 26;

Archives Photographiques, Paris: 20, 27 left, 33 bot., 47, 53 le 55, 63, 65, 84 bot., 94, 204, 214, 223, 238 le, 245, 246, 249 t. le & r, bot. le, 250 r, 330, 344, 350, 354, 462 r;

B. V. Berry, Ames, Iowa: 512; Bildarchiv Marburg: 106 mid. & bot, 128 t.r, 228, 338 bot, 369 le, 440, 449 top le & r, 523;

British Museum, London: 5, 7, 17 le, 18 bot, 24 bot, 29 top le, 33 t, 34 bot, 35 t, 38, 39 t, 41 le, t & mid, 43 bot, 44, 45 t. r, 46 t & bot, 48, 75, 77, 78, 93 t, 101, 104, 108 t, 109, 112 t, 113, 114 t. le, the three at bot, 114, 116, 117 t, 123, 129, 133, 142, 144, 160, 161 m, 195 t. r, 207, 226, 249 bot r, 264, 274 t, 300 bot. le, 311 bot, 319 t & b, 322 t & m, 326, 342, 375, 376, 382, 385 t & b, 386, 387 t & b, 388 t & b, 393 r, 401, 403, 404, 405, 406 t, 408, 409, 411, 412, 413, 414, 419 t & b, 420 le. b & r. 421 b, 422, 423, 427, 442, 443 t. r & b, 444, 445, 447 t & b, 448 t & b, 449 b, 454, 463 r., 465 t, 480, 481 le & r, 486 r, 7, 527, 533, 551;

Brooklyn Museum: 99, 529 le; Museum of Etruscan Antiquities, Florence: 122; Giraudon, Paris: 127 t. le & r, 133 b, 95 t. le, 201, 320, 323, 324 t. r, 360, 362, 416 t, 446, 489, 508; Albert Guillot, Paris: 34 m. r, 84 t, 251, 278 le & r, 303, 309, 12, 417 r, 442, 443 t. le, 459 b, 467;

Hebrew University, Jerusalem: 516, 557; Musee de l'Homme, Paris: 164, 510; Prof. James L. Kelso, Theological Seminary, Pittsburgh: 58 bot, 187 bot; Prof. Kathleen Kenyon, London: 77; Laboratorio Terra Santa, Jerusalem (A. Guillot): 416;

Louvre Museum, Paris: 1, 9, 10 le, 21, 27 le, 27 b. r (by R. David), 41 b. r, 200 le & r, 235, 304, 372 t & b, 446 le, 496, 540, 548;

Matson Photo Service, Los Angeles: 34 t, 43 t, 89, 90, 158, 167, 172 b, 176 t, 186, 250 le, 258 t, 261 t & b, 265, 267, 277, 275 t, 317, 341 b, 358;

Metropolitan Museum of Art, New York: 39 b, 73, 74, 76, 97, 100, 103 t & b, 108, 117 m & b, 124 t & b, 125, 138, 161 t & b, 182 b, 195 b, 206, 208, 214, 220 le, 274 b, 290 t, 301 t & b, 325, 336, 338 t, 372, 374, 417, 436, 439, 532, 534; Ruth Michaelson, Tel Aviv: 172, 243, 314, 377, 458 bot.

Ny Carlsberg Glyptotek, Copenhagen: 239, 459 b.; Orient Press Photo, Tel Aviv: 96, 281, 332; Oriental Institute, University of Chicago: 10 r, 24 t, 85, 105, 174 t, 222 t, 224, 231 t. r & b. r, 232, 233, 240, 248 le & r, 252, 305, 315 b. r, 341 t, 463 le, 505, 506, 509 t, 513, 515, 517;

Palestine Archaeological Museum, Jerusalem: 18 t., 364 le; Photo Boitier-Realites, Paris: 70, 71 (L. L. Roux); Beno Rotenberg, Tel Aviv: 131 t & b, 153, 156, 169 t & b, 173, 227, 234 t & b, 268 b, 270, 327, 392, 406 b, 465 b.; Staatliche Museum, Berlin: 50, 112 b, 116, 128 b.

Prof. Lawrence E. Toombs, Drew University, Madison, N.J.: 76 t, 78, 79; University Museum, Philadelphia: 42, 43 t. le, 45 bot., 231 le, 301 bot r, 462; Photo Viollet, Paris: 128 t. le, 130, 135, 147, 148, 149, 162, 288, 343, 478, 495. Prof. G. Ernest Wright, Harvard University: 191, 313, 529 r.

Prof. Y. Yadin, the James A. de Rothschild Expedition at Hazor: 55, 83 t, 176 bot, 241, 242;

DRAWINGS, AFTER: F. S. Bodenheimer, 166; Gressman, 259; S. H. Hooke, 4 le; E. Kraeling, 499; Meissner, 4; P. Montet, 140; A. Parrot, 19Y. Yadin, 429.

CORRIGENDA

p. 31, 28*th line, and p.*67, 31*st line:* "hubbum" *should read* "hubburu".

p. 44, 26*th line: Sumerian should read Babylonian.*

Illustrations and text printed by
E. Lewin-Epstein Ltd, Bat-Yam
Type set on Monotype by the
Jerusalem Academic Press Ltd.
Layout and jacket:
Paul Kor,
Tel-Aviv